KEY:

ROUTES OF THE VOYAGEURS

FUR TRADING ROUTES

Map reproduction from the 1780's

A SPECIAL TRIBUTE .....

Is due to Vincent Brass and Aluminum Co., now known as Vincent Metals, and its employees. The diligent and loyal service of the men and women of Vincent generated the very substantial funds for the cartographic work that comprise this atlas. Without that assistance, it is unlikely this atlas would have ever been completed.

For additional copies of the Atlas, visit your favorite bookstore.
Or write St. Thomas Academy, P.O. Box 22207, Robbinsdale, MN 55422.

The Vincent
ATLAS OF
MINNESOTA

ACKNOWLEDGEMENTS

Saint Thomas Academy is most grateful for the professional skills of the map-making staff of R.R. Donnelley & Sons Company at Lancaster, Pa. and for the untiring direction of Barbara Petchenik of Donnelley's; for the staff of Dorn Communications, who helped organize much of the information herein; for city map spreads of Michael C. Berg and Associates, Inc.; for the efforts of Nancy Ognanovich in presenting the History of Minnesota; and for the cooperation of the Minnesota Historical Society and the Minnesota Departments of Tourism and Natural Resources for their assistance in this project.

Last, but not least, a vote of thanks is due the stockholders of National Distillers & Chemical Corp., owners of Vincent Brass and Aluminum Co. when the maps were prepared, for devoting funds to defray the substantial costs involved in the production of the maps.

ISBN 0-9615710-0-4
First Printing

Published in the United States in 1985 by Saint Thomas Academy, St. Paul, Minnesota 55120.

Printed in United States of America.

Minnesota at a Glance

Facing the Facts

STATE FLOWER: Pink and White Showy Lady's Slipper
STATE BIRD: Loon
STATE TREE: Red or Norway Pine
STATE FISH: Walleye
STATE GEMSTONE: Lake Superior Agate
STATE GRAIN: Wild Rice
STATE MOTTO: L'Etoile Du Nord (Star of the North)
ADMITTED TO STATEHOOD: May 11, 1858 — 32nd state
POPULATION: (1983 est.) 4,144,000
METRO POPULATION (by county):

Anoka —	196,000
Carver —	37,000
Dakota —	194,000
Hennepin —	941,000
Ramsey —	460,000
Scott —	44,000
Washington —	14,000
Total 7 counties —	1,986,000

CITIES OF 25,000 OR MORE: 17
CAPITOL: St. Paul
NUMBER OF COUNTIES: 87
AREA: 184,068 square miles — twelfth largest state
NUMBER OF LAKES (over 10 acres): 11,842
TOTAL WATER AREA: 4,780 square miles
HIGHEST ELEVATION: 2,301 feet, Eagle Mountain
LOWEST ELEVATION: Lake Superior, 602 feet
AVERAGE ANNUAL PRECIPITATION: 26 inches
AVERAGE ANNUAL SNOWFALL: 46 inches
NUMBER OF STATE SENATORS: 67
NUMBER OF STATE REPRESENTATIVES: 134
NUMBER OF CONGRESSIONAL REPRESENTATIVES: 8
AVERAGE MEAN ALTITUDE: 1,200 feet

DEDICATION

Saint Thomas Academy has sponsored the publication of the Vincent Atlas of Minnesota in celebration of its one hundredth year in providing Christian education and leadership training of the highest order of excellence to boys of middle school and high school age from its superb campus in Mendota Heights. Academy graduates have an enviable record of success in the professions, the military, and in community leadership, not only in Minnesota, but across the Nation. The Atlas is dedicated to them, and to the faculty that served so well to instill in them the virtues of Duty, Honor, Country.

The Atlas was originally conceived to honor the entrepeneurs, engineers, and employees engaged in Minnesota metalworking, whose loyal patronage made it possible for ''Vincent Brass'' to celebrate its 50th Anniversary in 1986. Therefore, the Atlas is also a memorial to them, to Bob Vincent, its founder, and to his faith in Minnesota Industry, and to the sacrifices of Mary Vincent, wife to Bob's son, Paul who spent too much time in the business.

TABLE OF CONTENTS

III. The Maps

THE LAND OF LAKES

As they headed west from Lake Superior into what would later become Minnesota, early explorers and traders found a land rich with promise. A magnificent pine forest stretched as far as the eye could see. Water highways were gateways to America's greatest river, the Mississippi, and the American West beyond. Along the maze of streams and rivers, the early explorers collected the valuable furs of the beaver and other native animals and listened to Indian tales of the sleeping giant "Mesabi" and submerged iron deposits. To the south, they found a forest of maples, oaks and other hardwoods and a fertile prairie crossed by plentiful rivers and streams.

The configuration of the land as the Indians and explorers first saw it was the result of ancient geologic forces. More than 400 million years earlier, the area lay submerged beneath a tropical sea that covered the heart of North America. Before these waters receded, outpourings of lava and sediments of sand and mud were deposited on the sea bottom, forming the bedrock of the area. In the north, silica and iron oxides precipitated from the seawater to create layers of iron-rich deposits on top of the lava flows. Subsequent lava flows compacted the deposits to create a massive iron formation.

The surface of the land was carved by glaciers. Millions of years after the tropical sea receded, a succession of great ice sheets moved down over the northern part of the continent, extending to the Ohio River Valley and covering most of Minnesota. Enormous ice masses developed during a long cold period, and snow accumulated to a depth of thousands of feet.

As they spread southward, a series of glaciers carried rocks and boulders, scooped out hollows that filled with water and became lakes, and deposited finely ground rocks that would become fertile soils. While piling larger rocks into mounds and hills, the glaciers also swept away thick crusts of rock in the Iron Range country, leaving iron-rich deposits close to the surface. When the ice masses melted, the debris, or "drift," was strewn all over the land, in some cases forming high, hilly configurations. The sandy loam soil of much of the drift had high fertility, excellent for supporting cereal crops.

Another souvenir of the glaciers was a web of rivers and thousands of lakes that has profoundly influenced Minnesota's history and development. Glaciers retreating toward the North Pole created the Great Lakes. Geologists believe that when Lake Superior was formed more than 10,000 years ago, it was much larger and much deeper than it is now. But gradually, the lake began to rise, the land around the lake eroded, and the winding channels of the St. Louis River at the western end began to fill with sediment. Yet Lake Superior still remains the world's largest freshwater lake, covering more than 30,000 square miles. At its largest dimensions, Lake Superior is 351 miles long and 160 miles wide. One of the finest natural harbors in the world was created when a long sandbar formed at the western tip of the lake. Now the site of Duluth, its connection to the Atlantic via the St. Lawrence Seaway and the Great Lakes makes it the furthest inland port in the world. The lake has been vital to the movement of wheat, lumber and iron ore to eastern markets and beyond.

In contrast, Lake Agassiz, also left by the receding ice of the later glacial period, once covered the Red River Valley of Minnesota, North Dakota and Manitoba but is now extinct. The area of Lake Agassiz was greater than that of all the Great Lakes combined. But as the glacier retreated, the lake waters drained northward, with Red Lake the most extensive remains of the giant body of water. The flat and fertile Red River Valley is the ancient bed of the extinct lake.

Most of the other large lakes lie in the forested northern region of the state. Formed by glacial basins scoured in solid rock, they are generally deep, with rugged and rocky pine-covered shores. The lakes of the south, mostly occupying glacial moraines, are generally broader and more shallow. In all, more than 11,000 lakes were created, and these, along with numerous rivers and streams, give Minnesota more inland water than any other state. Minnesota boasts one square mile of water for every 20 square miles of land.

Three of the state boundaries are largely marked by waterways: the northern boundary by the Rainy and Pigeon rivers and the chain of border lakes; the eastern boundary by the St. Louis, St. Croix and Mississippi rivers; and the western boundary by the Red River.

The rivers were used as transport routes by the first Indian tribes in the area, eventually by the French explorers and French fur traders who opened the interior, and by the logging companies of later years. The sources of three of North America's great water systems are found in the state. From one watershed in northeastern Minnesota, the waters flow south by way of the Mississippi River into the Gulf of Mexico and north by way of the Red River to streams that empty into Hudson Bay. From another watershed in the northeast, waters flow east through the Great Lakes and the St. Lawrence River into the Atlantic ocean.

The largest of these three great river systems, and the largest river on the North American continent, is, of course, the mighty Mississippi. The Mississippi flows from its small beginnings in Lake Itasca southward through the state, taking in the waters of the Willow, Crow Wing, Prairie, Platte, Elk and Rum rivers before reaching the Falls of St. Anthony, the site of Minneapolis. For many years, the falls were the practical head of navigation in the state, and it was here that the United States government later established an outpost at Fort Snelling.

The largest of the Mississippi's tributaries within the state, the Minnesota River, originates in Big Stone Lake on the western border and flows across the state to join the Mississippi at Fort Snelling. From there, the Mississippi gathers the waters of another half dozen rivers before it leaves the state on its 2,300-mile journey to the Gulf of Mexico. When combined with its greatest tributary, the Missouri River, it makes up the third largest river system in the world after the Nile and the Amazon. Drawing from 31 states and two Canadian provinces, the Mississippi drains more than 1,125,940 square miles of the mid-continental U.S.

The early explorers found the quiet grandeur of the forests a sharp contrast to the awesome power of Minnesota's rivers. Towering trees grew on 70 percent of the state's land. At one time, a dense coniferous forest, made up mainly of white, Norway and jack pine, covered most of the northern part of the state. The "Big Woods," a region of broad-leaved hardwood trees 100 miles long and 40 miles wide, extended from the edge of the coniferous forest to the Minnesota River. In the south, the rolling prairie was interspersed with groves of oak and other deciduous trees.

The first French explorers found the beaver busily working along the many streams. The presence of the beaver, fox, wolf, marten, otter, muskrat, bobcat, raccoon and other fur-bearing animals prompted the French to push expeditions into the forests to tap the wealth of furs. Also prevalent were coyotes, black bears, lynx and various rodents. Deer, moose, elk and birds – duck, quail, sharp-tailed grouse and the ring-necked pheasant – were among the wild game of the forest and prairie. And the gopher could be found everywhere, giving rise to the nickname "Gopher State," later given to Minnesota.

Nature richly endowed Minnesota. Astride the great water highways of the mid-continent, the state served a vast region stretching eastward through the Great Lakes to the St. Lawrence River and on to the Atlantic Ocean, northward to Canada, westward through the Mississippi River system to the Rocky Mountains, and south to the Gulf of Mexico. The lines of travel converge d at the western tip of Lake Superior and at the Falls of St. Anthony on the Upper Mississippi. Within a few decades after the first settlements, these locations would become commercial and industrial centers for products that would find markets throughout the world.

THE FIRST MINNESOTANS: INDIANS, EXPLORERS AND TRADERS

Early Inhabitants

The earliest known inhabitants of the forests and prairies were not lumbermen and farmers but Indians, the descendants of Asiatic peoples who crossed into North America before the dawn of history. Archeologists believe that Indian ancestors were certainly in Minnesota during late glacial times, and, by the arrival of the white man in the seventeenth century, they had occupied the region for at least 10,000 years.

The state's earliest inhabitants survived for centuries on the plentiful game and fish, wild rice, fruits, berries and nuts. The great forest was quiet and nearly uninhabited then. The Indians lived along the streams, cutting only a few trees for fires and to build canoes and wigwams. Eventually they learned to grind stones and shape them to their use. They mined red stone or catlinite from quarries in southwestern Minnesota and carved it into pipes.

When the first white explorers and traders came to the region in the seventeenth century, the Sioux, or Dakota tribe, occupied most of the land. The Sioux were an organization of seven allied tribes that dominated the central plains as far west as the Missouri River. Of these tribes, four were found primarily in Minnesota. The Minnesota Sioux, "the people of the spirit or holy lake," were headquartered at Lake Mille Lacs.

By the middle of the seventeenth century, the Sioux had been driven from much of their land by the Chippewa, or Ojibway, a nation of the Algonquian stock. The Chippewa, who had been forced from their own home land along the St. Lawrence Valley by the Iroquois, initially found respite near Sault Ste. Marie at the eastern end of Lake Superior. But in their search for additional territory, they pushed west into the lands controlled by the Sioux. The Sioux, armed with primitive clubs, arrows and spears, were no match for the Chippewa, who in their travels had acquired firearms and other tools of the white men. During the 1740s the Sioux were gradually driven out of their northern villages, including their headquarters at Lake Mille Lacs. From then on, the Chippewa lived in the forests of the north while the Sioux inhabited the hills and valleys of the south and west. The peace was frequently broken as one side would make raids on the other.

The question of who were the first Europeans to have contact with the Indians remains a subject of controversy. An inscribed stone found near Kensington in the central part of the state bears writing in runic characters, and the date 1362, telling of a journey of exploration by 22 Norwegians and eight Goths. Though the "Kensington Runestone," as it came to be known, has had its defenders, most scholars doubt that it is an authentic record of a Scandinavian journey into Minnesota.

French Exploration

It was the French who first made claim on Minnesota as they pushed westward into the heart of North America by way of the Great Lakes. Searching for an inland sea leading to the Pacific, the French had reached the waters of Lake Superior before the Mayflower landed at Plymouth Rock in 1620. During the first half of the seventeenth century, the French continued to explore the Great Lakes, tapping the wealth of furs in the region. In the second half of the century, they pushed into the Mississippi Valley, established a thriving fur trade, sent missionaries out to christianize the Indians, and mapped the wilderness.

During the 1650s the Minnesota region was penetrated by two adventurers sent out by the governors of New France in Quebec, Canada. In the course of several expeditions, Pierre Radisson and his brother-in-law the Sieur des Groseilliers explored the southern shores of Lake Superior, collected highly prized furs, and were treated as visiting royalty by the Indians. When the profits from their voyages were confiscated by the French upon their return, they turned to the English for sponsorship of future expeditions. Their success at fur trading led to the founding of the Hudson's Bay Company by the English in 1670.

The explorations of Radisson and Groseilliers also added much to the geographical knowledge of the region. Similarly, Father Claude Allouez, a Jesuit missionary who built a station on Madeline Island, explored the western and northern shores of the lake, producing a detailed map of Lake Superior in 1670.

In 1663 Louis XIV set out to strengthen New France by making it a royal province and building its population and military resources. His representatives in the area sought to take possession of interior America for the glory of the king. Their aspirations running high, the French made a formal claim on the vast region around 1670. Although wars in Europe prevented them from gaining control over the area, explorations and fur trading continued.

In 1672 France commissioned Louis Jolliet to find the Mississippi River. Jolliet had hunted for copper in the Lake Superior country and knew the Great Lakes region from first-hand experience. Jolliet discovered a route from Green Bay, via the Fox and Wisconsin rivers, to the Mississippi, thereby opening another gateway to Minnesota. In doing so, the French proved the truth of the many rumors of a great river beyond the Great Lakes in the West. Jolliet traveled downstream as far as the Arkansas River but turned back before reaching the Gulf of Mexico. It was Rene Robert Cavelier, Sieur de la Salle, who planted the staff of Louis XIV at the river's mouth in 1682.

Jolliet's discovery gave impetus to the westward advance of the French during the 1670s and 1680s. So did the explorers' continuing fascination with Lake Superior, which was mapped again and again. Daniel Greysolon, Sieur du Lhut, set out for the western shore of Superior in 1679. He held council with the Sioux and Chippewa not far from Duluth, the city that now honors him with its name, and then pushed southward to Lake Mille Lacs, becoming the first white man to enter the Sioux village there. The following year he traveled down the lake shore to the Bois Brule River, up the Brule to the portage at the St. Croix, and then canoed to the junction of the St. Croix and the Mississippi. This trip revealed yet another route to the interior of Minnesota. While at the Mississippi, he rescued three Frenchmen, including Father Louis Hennepin, who were being held by the Sioux.

Hennepin had been sent into the region by La Salle to make the first exploration of the upper Mississippi. Before his rescue by Duluth, he had discovered and named the Falls of St. Anthony. Returning to France in 1682, he found his account of his voyage, the first book about the region, had been published and was being read with great interest by Europeans.

Over the next several years, Duluth made additional journeys into Minnesota. He built posts in the St. Croix region and on the North Shore of Lake Superior. In 1688, he journeyed to Minnesota and beyond to challenge the British in the Hudson Bay area.

In the final decades of the seventeenth century, explorers and traders filled out the map and expanded their knowledge of the area. Nicolas Perrot, named commandant of the West, established posts on the Upper Mississippi and claimed the Sioux country for Louis XIV at a ceremony at Fort St. Antoine in 1689. In 1695, Pierre Le Sueur, a long-time trader on the Mississippi, established a post on the river at Isle Pelee, or Prairie Island, between present-day Hastings and Red Wing. Five years later he ascended the Minnesota River to the mouth of the Blue Earth River, near present-day Mankato, and built Fort L'Huiller. Piece by piece, the stage was being set for colonization of the Upper Mississippi by the French.

Events in Europe, however, diverted French attention away from the region during the next several years. Count Frontenac, the energetic governor of New France who had encouraged excursions and trade in the region, died in 1698. Louis XIV became embroiled in warfare. All French garrisons in the northwest were withdrawn. Twenty-five years passed before another French expedition reached the region. Most of the forts and missions built by these later French parties were short-lived, with the exception of Fort St. Charles, established at Lake of the Woods in 1732. It was occupied for 20 years, longer than any other French establishment in the territory.

Established by Pierre Gaultier de Varennes, Sieur de la Verendrye, Fort St. Charles served as an important base for westward exploration and pioneered a chain of forts built beyond Lake of the Woods in Canada. The desire for beaver skins and the spirit of adventure drew many Frenchmen far into the interior. The frontier pushed past Fort St. Charles to posts at Lake Winnipeg, the Assiniboine River, and the Saskatchewan country. But important posts were retained in Minnesota. In the 1750s, the major French posts were La Jonquiere on Lake Pepin; Duquesne near the present site of Brainerd; and Vaudreuil in Iowa, opposite the point where the Wisconsin joins the Mississippi. Other posts were on the St. Croix River and at or near the junction of the Mississippi and Minnesota rivers.

Most French officers were called away from the frontier during the first half of the eighteenth century to fight in a series of French and British colonial wars and their counterparts in Europe. In the Treaty of Paris (1763), the French ceded to England all of their possessions east of the Mississippi, except the site of New Orleans. This marked the end of a prolonged struggle in both the old and new worlds for domination of the North American continent. Although the French never achieved their dream of finding a route to the Pacific, they opened the gateways to the American West and primed the Great Lakes region for settlement and development. The French influence lingered in the fur trade, with the French-trained voyageurs filling the ranks of the British and American fur companies. French remained the essential language of the trade, and French names were evident throughout the land. The French legacy is still seen on place names in Minnesota; and the state's official seal designates it as ''L'Etoile du Nord'' (The Star of the North).

British Domination

Like the French before them, the British who explored Minnesota had goals of developing commercial routes and trading with the Indians. A year before the French had officially ceded their claim to the region, British soldiers had planted the British flag at Grand Portage. Soon Grand Portage became the headquarters for fur trade in the region, and it eventually became the most important fur trading post in the world. Situated in a large bay on Lake Superior, Grand Portage was the head of a 2000-mile canoe route into the Canadian interior. The British used it for many years as a rendezvous site and Indians customarily awaited traders there. Eventually, independent traders began to build houses surrounded by stockades and Grand Portage became a virtual village in the wilderness. By the 1790s the North West Company had erected a huge stockade enclosing 16 buildings, including a great meeting hall. A small military fort occupied by a dozen British soldiers was also located here — the only military force to operate in Minnesota during the Revolutionary War.

As many as 500 people came and went from Grand Portage during the season, bearing packs of furs that were shipped to Montreal and then to the fur market in London. They traded for rum, guns, powder, ammunition, blankets, cloth, tobacco, kettles, axes, and beads that were sent out on large canoes and other vessels from Montreal. By 1778, the trade at Grand Portage was calculated at 40,000 pounds.

But the British were interested in more than furs. Like the French, they sought the Northwest Passage, a route to the Pacific. Major Robert Rogers, superintendent of Indian affairs for the British in the Northwest, who was headquartered at Mackinac, had ambitious ideas for a new empire.

Rogers' heroic deeds as a frontier ranger during the French and Indian Wars had made him famous throughout the colonies and in Great Britain. While stationed at Detroit he heard the tales of French voyageurs and the Indians about the vast interior territory and a series of interlocking waterways. Rumors flew about the existence of a connecting strait between Hudson Bay and the Pacific. While headquartered at Mackinac, Rogers sent an expedition to find the elusive passage.

The expedition included a Connecticut Yankee named Jonathan Carver who was to serve as both the map-maker and peacemaker with the Indians. Carver left Mackinac with some traders in the fall of 1766 on a journey that took him across Wisconsin from Green Bay to Prairie du Chien. From there they paddled upstream and spent the winter among the Sioux on the Minnesota River. He saw the Falls of St. Anthony and discovered the cave at St. Paul that bears his name. That spring he held council at the cave with the Sioux, winning both their friendship and a trade agreement for the British. Then Carver set out to find the western sea, traveling north toward Lake Superior. The journey ran aground, however, when the party found that Rogers had failed to send their supplies to Grand Portage, and they were forced to return to Mackinac.

Carver traveled to Great Britain where he spent years trying to persuade the government to reward him for his expedition. His account of his journeys, *Travels Through the Interior Parts of North America in the Years 1766, 1767, and 1768* was published in 1778 and, as the first book in English about the upper Mississippi, was widely read among the British. It later appeared in other editions and was translated into many languages.

For the most part, Carver's account was a ghost-written, sensationalized account of his New World adventures. Packed with tales of terrifying monsters and other imaginary events, the book nevertheless intrigued legions of readers. His descriptions were often vivid. The River St. Pierre, he said, was surrounded by ''eminences, from which you have views that cannot be exceeded even by the most beautiful of those I have already described; amidst these are delightful groves, and such amazing quantities of maples, that they would produce sugar sufficient for any number of inhabitants.''

Carver was not content simply to describe the natural wonders he had seen. He reported Indian accounts and his own speculations on western geography. He said he had information that the sources of the Mississippi and Missouri rivers lay within a mile of each other. He offered a simple solution to the enigma of the Mississippi's origin. He believed that Lake Pepin, in southern Minnesota, should be the river's source because above that point none of the tributaries was large enough, in his opinion, to be called a true river.

Although Carver's story was devoured by readers, the publisher reaped the profits, and Carver died from malnutrition, a pauper. And the British, although they dotted the region with trading posts and encouraged exploration, never adopted Carver's scheme to colonize the heart of America.

But the fur trade flourished under the British. Small partnerships were common until the increasing competition encouraged larger organizations. Eventually, an alignment of partnerships, the North West Company, was formed in Montreal in 1779. From then on, the fur trade was monopolized by businessmen instead of the government as it had been under the French. The magnates of the business, ''the Gentlemen of the North West Company,'' met at their headquarters, Grand Portage, to assign tasks and to consider the policies and problems of a thriving business, international in scope. Furs from the north country were auctioned every year not only in London but also in Leipzig, Germany. Many of these furs were bought by Russians, transported by caravan across Siberia and later sold in China. Each year the British fur trade handled well over $1 million in pelts.

Although Britain and the colonists were soon at war, at Grand Portage people were concerned only with furs and the exploitation of the wilderness. The furs and pelts of beavers, black bears, grizzlies, wolves, foxes, raccoons, otters, martens, minks, wolverines, moose, and muskrats continued to be shipped in record quantities to Grand Portage.

The growth of the North West Company in the 1790s was not without competition. Greater freedom in the fur trade was encouraged when the British no longer required traders to be licensed by the government. Groups of traders and small partnerships operated among the Sioux and Chippewa throughout the region. The North West Company's most serious competition came from the Hudson's Bay Company. The older company was moving posts further south, some close to or in the Minnesota country, to facilitate trade with the Indians. This competition resulted in bloodshed after the Earl of Selkirk obtained a large grant of land from the Hudson's Bay Company in 1811 for a colonization plan that threatened the North West Company's fur domain.

The boundary drawn between the United States and Canada at the end of the Revolutionary War was unclear in the Lake Superior region, and officials of the North West Company feared that the Grand Portage post was actually situated on American soil and would consequently be subject to American customs. After the British had vacated their posts at Detroit and Mackinac in 1796, Grand Portage seemed unprotected. It was abandoned in 1803, and a new base of operations for the North West Company, Fort William, was built at the mouth of the Kaministikwia River on Lake Superior. The company's uneasiness was justified, for in 1803 the United States bought the Territory of Louisiana from Napoleon Bonaparte.

The abandonment of Grand Portage was a sign of Britain's recognition of the United States' intent to assert herself in the unsettled regions beyond the 13 colonies. Once the capital of an western industrial empire, Grand Portage became a quiet little village. The wilderness regime of the North West Company also came to an end when in 1821 it merged with the Hudson's Bay Company — two years after the American flag was raised over a military fort at the junction of the Minnesota and Mississippi rivers.

AMERICANS ON THE FRONTIER

With the purchase of the vast Louisiana Territory, which included western Minnesota, America formally announced its intentions to develop the West. Almost immediately, President Thomas Jefferson commissioned Lieutenant Zebulon Pike to explore the Upper Mississippi River Valley. Pike, an obscure army supply officer, headed upriver from St. Louis in 1805 on the first American military expedition into Minnesota territory. Befriended by various British fur traders along the way, in early fall he camped at an island at the mouth of the Minnesota River. On what is still known today as Pike Island, the Stars and Stripes was raised for the first time on Minnesota soil.

By holding council with the Sioux, Pike achieved one of the missions of his expedition. The Sioux agreed to give up a tract of land at the junction of the Mississippi and Minnesota rivers upon which, in 1819, the U.S. would build Fort Snelling. Pike's ceremonies with the Sioux concluded with gifts, apportionments of rum and the promise of $2,000 or its equivalent in merchandise.

After this accomplishment, Pike and his expedition headed upstream to the North West Company fur posts at Sandy and Leech lakes. Pike found that although the move of the North West Company's headquarters to Fort Williams had been closely timed to the American acquisition of Louisiana territory, many British posts were still operating throughout Minnesota. Although he was cordially greeted and treated to roast beaver, Pike shot down the British flag flying over the camp and had his men hoist the American flag in its place.

Pike declared Leech Lake the main source of the Mississippi but, venturing further north, decided Cass Lake might be the river's "upper source." Since Cass Lake is only a few miles from the river's true source, Lake Itasca, Pike wasn't very far off. He returned to St. Louis in the spring of 1806 with the land agreement with the Sioux in hand.

The United States was slow to take advantage of Pike's accomplishments. No forts were built nor settlement attempted. By and large, the North West Company continued its domination of the Minnesota fur trade. During the war of 1812, the capture of American posts at Mackinac, Fort Dearborn and Detroit fueled British hopes that the new boundary arrangements would create a neutral Indian domain and prevent disruption of their fur trade. Their hopes were dashed when the British desire for peace let to a final treaty which did not disturb the sovereignty of the United States over the Indian tribes and territory of the Upper Mississippi.

In the year before the 1812 war, Lord Selkirk, a Scottish nobleman, had established an agricultural colony in the Red River Valley near present-day Winnipeg. The presence of this colony so close to American soil, and the disappointing performance of the American military during the war, led the United States government to hasten its own occupation of the region.

In 1815 the Sioux signed a treaty accepting the sovereignty of the United States. The following year Congress passed a law prohibiting all but Americans from trading with the Indians on American soil and also established the first three of a contemplated chain of forts on the frontier — Fort Armstrong at Rock Island, Ill., Fort Howard at Green Bay, Wis., and Fort Crawford at Prairie du Chien, Wis.

Finally the path was clear for American military occupation and trade in the Minnesota region. After the war forced the British to withdraw, the American Fur Company quickly moved in to reestablish their old trading territory. This enterprise was organized in 1808 by John Jacob Astor, a primary supporter of the law excluding aliens from the fur trade. He bought out the remaining interest in the South West Company and brought many former posts of both the North West and the South West companies under his control. He also urged the government to provide official military protection to the fur traders.

American fur trading interests played a significant role in the formation of frontier defense policy after the War of 1812. As the chain of forts went up along the Great Lakes, plans were initiated to defend the area to the north and west. A military expedition led by Major Stephen Long, an experienced topographical engineer, surveyed the region in 1817. Instructed to determine the most suitable site for a military post, Long chose the bluff overlooking the confluence of the Mississippi and Minnesota rivers.

The site, on "a high point of land, elevated about 120 feet above the water, and fronting immediately on the Mississippi," was that acquired some 14 years earlier by Lieutenant Pike. John C. Calhoun, then U.S. Secretary of War, agreed on the site selection and announced that a fort would be built there "for the protection of our trade and the preservation of the frontiers."

In the summer of 1819 a detachment of troops commanded by Colonel Henry Leavenworth traveled up the Mississippi River to establish the post. The soldiers constructed flimsy winter quarters on the south side of the

Minnesota River near the present site of Mendota. After a miserable winter when scurvy took the lives of at least 40 soldiers, plans were made for a permanent fort some distance north. The design and building of the fort was orchestrated by Colonel Josiah Snelling, who replaced Leavenworth that summer. Snelling selected the final site of the fort at the crest of the bluff above the river junction.

Building the fort was laborious and time-consuming. The soldiers had to travel upriver to the forests of the Rum River region to cut pine logs, then send them down to the Falls of St. Anthony where they built Minnesota's first sawmill. Limestone was quarried from the nearby bluffs and used to construct the post's walls, buildings and blockhouses.

The fort was near completion by the summer of 1824. Built in a diamond shape, it was completely enclosed by 10-foot stone walls. Hexagonal and round towers made of limestone overlooked the prairie and the Minnesota River valley. Both had loopholes for musketry, and at the other corners, pentagonal towers held a battery and lookout. Within the enclosure were officers' quarters, barracks, a commandant's house, shop, hospital, parade grounds, a guardhouse, commissary and quartermaster's store, magazine, a well and a schoolhouse. Inspecting it in 1824, General Winfield Scott was so impressed he recommended to the War Department that the post be renamed Fort Snelling. Fort Snelling dominated the wilderness like a medieval fortress, a symbol of American strength and permanence where only temporary fur-trading outposts had been before. For the next 30 years it stood as the northernmost military post of the Mississippi Valley. More than an isle of safety and military dominance in the region, Fort Snelling became a strategic center around which settlement grew. In time, the two largest Minnesota cities developed only a short distance above and below the fort. Fort Snelling was long the focus for Indians, traders, explorers, missionaries, settlers and travelers who came to the region. It mediated relations among these disparate groups and facilitated their travel and commerce. It also became a community of people whose own lives and activities influenced the developing culture of the state.

Major Lawrence Taliaferro, one of the first to arrive at Fort Snelling, was charged with keeping peace between the Chippewa and Sioux. Although their rivalry led to open warfare on several occasions, Taliaferro, the post's Indian agent for 20 years, had a good measure of success. In addition to delivering speeches on the virtues of peace and the good intentions of the Americans, he confiscated British flags, medals and other symbols of Indian allegiance to the British and accompanied a party of Sioux and Chippewa to Washington in 1824 to meet with President John Quincy Adams. The next year he managed to bring 385 Chippewa and Sioux to a large conference at Prairie du Chien to work out peace guarantees for the Northwest. At the conference, a boundary line between the Sioux and Chippewa was agreed to, but the line, running southeasterly from the Red River to the Chippewa River near present-day Eau Claire, did not stop marauding excursions entirely.

In 1830 another council produced an agreement giving a tract of land on Lake Pepin to traders who had intermarried with the Sioux. In 1837 two land-cession treaties were negotiated, opening the lands between the Mississippi and the St. Croix to white settlement. In return for annuities, allocations for medical aid and instruction in farming, the area was gradually opened for occupation by farmers and lumbermen.

The Army's work with the Indians was supplemented by that of the missionaries who followed them into Minnesota country. The first was Father Severe Dumoulin, a Catholic priest who began working among the Chippewa at Pembina in 1818. Among the best remembered of the missionaries, the brothers Gideon and Samuel Pond, spent their entire careers among the Minnesota tribes. Missionaries devised alphabets for the Indian languages and translated their spoken languages to writing.

Meanwhile, Taliaferro pursued his own plan for civilizing the Indians. He encouraged them to learn farming and established a method to have them vaccinated for smallpox. His most troubling concern was the use of liquor by fur traders to win favor with the Indians. Having witnessed the murder and warfare that often resulted from the Indian's use of whisky, he had traders' boats searched and liquor confiscated. But although federal law did prohibit the introduction of ''ardent spirits'' into the Indian country, whisky was never driven from the region. During 1839, Taliaferro's last year as agent at the post, the worst intertribal fighting in two decades erupted. In 1840, when there were numerous attacks and killings between the Sioux and Chippewa, a discouraged Taliaferro left the frontier outpost.

The fur trade in the area had long been monopolized by the American Fur Company which controlled more than 40 posts throughout the Minnesota region alone. In 1834, Henry Hastings Sibley, who was to become the regional lord of the company, oversaw a business worth more than $60,000. Muskrats were the most frequently traded skins, and the pelts of otters, beaver, buffalo, deer, mink, and marten were also an important part of the trade. Although this trade was impressive, the American Fur Company was declining. Shaken by the Panic of 1837 and changing tastes in fashion from beaver to silk, the company went into bankruptcy in 1842. Furs would be an important part of Minnesota commerce for some time to come, but enterprises such as farming and lumbering would soon eclipse it.

Although the region was opened up and surveyed by the Army and other explorers, the Indians still held title to most of it. After Fort Snelling had been established, many squatters took over the land around the post. As the federal government negotiated treaties with the Indians and obtained title to lands along the Mississippi and St. Croix rivers, these settlers were forced to leave the fort. Most had moved across the river by 1840, where they created a new settlement called Pig's Eye. Here, late in 1841, Father Lucien Galtier built a log chapel dedicated to Saint Paul. From the chapel, Minnesota's capital city received its name. A far cry from the urban development of today, St. Paul began as a quiet village of just 250 to 300 people living in a few dozen buildings.

The travels of a number of explorers, cartographers and Army officers did much to enlarge the knowledge of the area guarded by Fort Snelling. Lewis Cass, governor of Michigan Territory, searched for the Mississippi's source in 1820, and Major Stephen Long explored the Red River Valley in 1823. Giacomo Beltrami, an Italian who also wanted to discover the river's source, accompanied Long but narrowly missed his target. It was Henry Rowe Schoolcraft, with the assistance of a large exploring party, who discovered the source in 1832 and named the lake "Itasca," a combination of the two Latin words veritas, truth and caput, head.

Schoolcraft recorded the historic moment in his journal for July 13, 1832:

> Every step we made . . . seemed to increase the ardor with which we were carried
> forward. The desire of reaching the actual source of a stream which LaSalle had reached
> the mouth of, a century and a half before, was perhaps predominant; and we followed
> our guide down the sides of the last elevation, with the expectation of momentarily
> reaching the goal of our journey. What had been long sought, at last appeared suddenly.
> On turning out of a thicket, into a small weedy opening, the cheering sight of a
> transparent body of water burst upon our view. It was Lake Itasca — the source of the
> Mississippi.

Explorers after Schoolcraft mapped and observed the lakes and ponds of the headwaters region, claiming they had found other sources. But Lake Itasca has stood the test of time and remains, poets and explorers aside, the acknowledged source of America's greatest river.

Meanwhile, lumbermen were moving into the region, looking with covetous eyes at the stands of white pine along the St. Croix and Rum Rivers. Others speculated on the agricultural potential of the prairie. When Wisconsin was admitted to the Union in 1848, the territory west of the St. Croix was left without organized government and bore the generic name "Indian country." Early settlers pressed for the organization of this region as Minnesota Territory. Led by Henry Sibley, a group from the region successfully took their cause to Washington, where in January of 1849, a bill was introduced for the organization of Minnesota Territory.

Legally certified in March of 1849, the new territory included all of what is now Minnesota and portions of present-day North and South Dakota. St. Paul became the territorial capital, and Alexander Ramsey was appointed governor.

Representatives and councilors for the territorial legislature were elected and the first meeting was held in 1849. Among the tasks of the new leaders was to create a code of laws for a wilderness that would soon be dotted with thousands of settlers. They also needed to raise money to provide essential services, build schools and create a county organization.

For Governor Ramsey, a young Pennsylvanian, an initial high-priority task was to acquire "Suland," lands held by the Sioux that could support a large agricultural population. Farmers, speculators, townsite promoters, fur traders, and the federal government all clamored for its cession, but the Sioux were not brought to the bargaining table until 1851.

Although the Sioux chiefs were reluctant to give up their lands, they felt they had no choice but to negotiate. It was better, they believed, to negotiate for adequate compensation and reservations than to fight the whites who outnumbered them. Two important treaties were negotiated at Traverse des Sioux and Mendota in the summer of 1851 and ratified in 1852. Under their terms, the Sioux agreed to give up their claim to the lands west of the Mississippi as far as the Big Sioux River, most of southern Minnesota. The Indians were promised cash payments, annuities and a reservation on the upper Minnesota River.

Settlers immediately began to push into the Minnesota Valley, and speculators began laying out towns. Meanwhile, the lands of the Chippewa in northern Minnesota also were being negotiated away. In 1854 a treaty of cession was negotiated with the Chippewa living near Lake Superior, and, in 1855, with those living around the headwaters of the Mississippi. The last remaining Chippewa lands, in the Red River Valley, were ceded in 1863. The Chippewa also received reservations on which to live.

Within a few short years, more than 80 percent of the future state had been given up by the Sioux and Chippewa. Only the northwest and a north central area were controlled by the Indians. Meanwhile, settlement was eagerly encouraged. Pamphlets describing the area's attractions were printed in several languages, and such settlements as the German town of New Ulm and Swedish communities in Chisago County were created. Despite European immigration, most of the settlers were Americans. Many residents of New England, New York, Pennsylvania, Ohio, Indiana and other Midwestern states settled on the Minnesota frontier.

Steamboats plied the Mississippi and Minnesota rivers throughout the 1850s, some even reaching points north of St. Cloud. The number of steamboats in use on the Mississippi south of St. Anthony and St. Paul increased from five in 1850 to 62 in 1858. In the heyday of the river steamer, towns grew up in areas where boats could easily land. Where rivers and streams were frozen over during the winter, settlers built roads over which stagecoaches and freight sleighs could travel to future sites of inland communities.

The first people to settle in the region quickly cleared a few acres of land and planted crops to supply them with the bare necessities of life. Usually starting with a few potatoes, turnips, cabbages, corn, and other vegetables, they also would raise grain if seeds were available. This subsistence agriculture was inadequate for supplying the rapidly growing population. Most flour and other foodstuffs were sent upriver from St. Louis.

As farmers were able to clear more land, they increased the acreage devoted to field crops. Mills built along every stream that could furnish water power soon were grinding corn meal and flour. Wheat became "king" in Minnesota. A reporter visiting Hastings in 1859 commented that there was "wheat everywhere; wheat on the levee; wagon loads of wheat pouring down to the levee; wheat in the streets; wheat in the sidewalks; warehouses of wheat; men talking of wheat, and, verily, wheat was the one idea of Hastings the afternoon we arrived there." In 1858 wheat was shipped commercially from the state for the first time, and, just a year later, wheat exports exceeded furs in market value.

Newly arrived Yankee businessmen measured the territory's riches in terms of pine forests. After the fur trade, lumbering was Minnesota's earliest industry. Logging operations began even while the lands still belonged to the Sioux and Chippewa. Moving up the St. Croix and Rum Rivers, lumberjack crews turned trees into logs. The logs were gathered into great rafts and floated down the river to sawmills along the Mississippi. There they were processed into lumber to serve the building booms for the farms and cities on the unforested northwestern prairie.

Thousands of pine logs began to travel down the two rivers, and the area of cut-over lands grew larger. Although the first commercial sawmill was at Marine-on-St. Croix, the lumber industry soon was centered at the head of steam navigation on the Mississippi, the great falls of St. Anthony. St. Anthony became a critical location for water power and access to the Mississippi and the markets beyond. The same strategic advantages would enable St. Anthony (later known as Minneapolis) to grow into a great flour-milling and railroad center.

The territory's dramatic population growth after the approval of the Sioux treaties reflected the influx of settlers, farmers and lumbermen. In 1855, the territorial population had been estimated at 40,000. A year later, the estimate was 100,000, and an official census in 1857 showed more than 150,000 inhabitants. In response to the tremendous population changes, territorial officers began a statehood drive in 1854.

Congress, however, was not inclined to pass an enabling act for statehood. The issue wasn't a cause for debate in the House of Representatives, although many Southerners voted against it. When introduced in the Senate, however, it created a storm of controversy with southerners viewing it as an attempt to upset the delicate regional balance in the Senate. But, despite arguments that statehood was premature and the population sparse, the Minnesota Enabling Act passed in February, 1857.

Statehood itself was elusive. Back in Minnesota Territory, two delegates from each district had to be elected to draw up a constitution. This election was hotly contested, with slavery the dividing issue. Even when the constitutional convention was convened, progress was hindered by the emergence of two rival groups, one Democratic and the other Republican. Each drew up its own constitution and refused to meet with each other. Since neither group would sign a document drawn up by a neutral committee, Minnesota ended up with two slightly different but equally authentic constitutions.

Minnesota voters accepted the constitution and elected state officers, members of the judiciary and representatives to Congress. The legislature elected two senators to represent Minnesota in Washington: Henry Rice, a fur trader and St. Paul businessman, and General James Shields. In May of 1858, the president signed the bill that admitted Minnesota to the Union.

YEARS AT WAR

When Minnesota was admitted to the Union, the state's new Republican party was so strong it had displaced the Whigs and threatened the rule of the Democrats. Rallying behind the cause of antislavery, the party was led by Alexander Ramsey, who was elected governor in 1859.

By chance, Governor Ramsey was in Washington in 1861 when word was received that Fort Sumter had fallen. He immediately offered 1,000 Minnesota men for the Union forces. Thus, the second youngest state in the nation became the first to volunteer soldiers to fight for the Union in the Civil War. The First Regiment of Minnesota Volunteer Infantry was quickly organized, and, after a few weeks training at Fort Snelling, joined Union forces at the Battle of Bull Run. Later it played a key role in saving the Union army from defeat at Gettysburg. More than 25,000 — out of a state population of 172,000 — ultimately served in the Union army.

Minnesota was only two years old when the Civil War started. A year later, the state was plunged into a violent war with the Sioux. In August, 1862, four Sioux massacred five white settlers at a frontier cabin near Acton in Meeker County. Hearing of the incident, outlying Sioux bands, angry because of mistreatment and broken promises by the whites, gathered under Little Crow and attacked isolated farms, settlements and Fort Ridgeley. It was the bloodiest such outbreak in the state's history.

Although drained of its fighting men by the Civil War, the state quickly trained available men and sent them out to trouble spots under the leadership of Henry Sibley. After two assaults on Fort Ridgely and two on New Ulm were repulsed, the tide began to turn in favor of the state. After several skirmishes with the Indians, Sibley arrived at Fort Ridgely 10 days after the war had started. Within two weeks he had routed the Sioux at a decisive battle at Wood Lake and the hostilities ended for the time being.

More than 2,000 Sioux surrendered or were captured by Sibley's forces. Others fled to the Dakota prairies. Another 269 Sioux prisoners were turned over to Sibley at Camp Release in September. After military trials, 307 Sioux were condemned to death, but the executions were deferred pending review by President Lincoln. Although some were, in fact, guilty of atrocities, others were victims of circumstances over which they had little control. Episcopal Bishop Henry B. Whipple convinced Lincoln to free all but 38 of the condemned, who were hanged at Mankato in December 1862.

During the following year Sibley pursued the hostile Sioux to the Missouri country. This campaign, and that a year later led by General Alfred Sully, led to a series of clashes that continued into the late 1870s. Although the Sioux were driven from Minnesota, the warfare continued in other areas on the frontier.

The after-effects of the Sioux Uprising, as it became known, kept the northwestern frontier of Minnesota in turmoil during the Civil War. The widely scattered actions of the Sioux resulted in the deaths of at least 500 whites, most of them civilians. The homes of many settlers had been destroyed, and for a time, the uprising caused people to leave the state.

The Chippewa did not join the Sioux in the war and remained in Minnesota. In 1863 the federal government negotiated with them to cede the Red River Valley, a vast area of fertile land appropriate for settlement. Although the Chippewa were reluctant to lose the land, they eventually were won over with cash, annuities and the distribution of food and goods.

SETTLING A NEW LAND

Despite the negative impact of the Sioux uprising on the state's population growth, by 1870, eastern and southern Minnesota were well-settled. Hutchinson, Glencoe and Litchfield were growing in the western part of the state while on the Minnesota River, New Ulm was rebuilt. Along the Mississippi River north of St. Anthony, settlement had passed St. Cloud and reached Little Falls. Sauk Centre and Alexandria were growing settlements in the valley of the Sauk River. A few settlers could be found in the Red River Valley and at Duluth. The emerging pattern of settlement and, subsequently industry and manufacturing, was linked to the state's navigable waterways. But when the streams and rivers froze over in the winter, Minnesota was isolated. The situation prompted efforts to lay the track for a railroad system to assist commerce and encourage settlement.

By 1861, the St. Paul and Pacific had built about 1,500 feet of track between its steamboat wharf and the company roundhouse. It was a cause for celebration when the company offered service on its expanded line from St. Paul to St. Anthony the following year. After that, there was no stopping the railroads. By 1865 railroads operated on 210 miles of track. An all-rail link with Chicago was completed two years later. By 1872, 15 companies had built almost 2,000 miles of track within the state. Most of the lines linked settlements; others, such as the Northern Pacific and the St. Paul and Pacific, reached into the wilderness. Towns grew along the railroad lines, as they once had grown along the rivers.

In 1864 the Northern Pacific Railroad was chartered by Congress and given vast land grants to build a railroad from Lake Superior to the Pacific. By late 1871 the road from Duluth to Moorhead had been completed. But the Panic of 1873, which devastated the industry, virtually stopped railroad expansion in Minnesota and the northern tier of states. Little progress was made from 1873 to 1877, as railroad building continued to be plagued by panic and foreclosures.

James J. Hill, a St. Paul businessman and agent for the St. Paul and Pacific Railroad, became an owner of the railway during this period, helping to reorganize it, and renaming it the St. Paul, Minneapolis, and Milwaukee Railroad Company. Hill, who had come to St. Paul as an 18-year-old in 1856, soon earned a reputation as the "Empire Builder." Under Hill's skillful management, the company struck numerous deals enabling it to buy up land and push the railroad across Dakota to Great Falls, Mont., by 1887. By 1893, the Great Northern, as it was later known, reached Seattle, 1,816 miles from St. Paul.

Thousands of workmen, the bulk of them immigrants, were hired to build the railroads. Some railroad companies even undertook programs of colonization, dispatching agents to the East and to Europe and building immigration-receiving houses for temporary accommodations. Many Scandinavians new to Minnesota found their first jobs as workmen on the Northern Pacific and other railroads. The railroads also sold them land, eased their transport, and helped keep them in touch with the world they had left behind.

The railroads had an additional impact on settlement. Many sold land at generous prices through their land offices to encourage settlement and create freight and passenger business. Railroad company agents were even sent abroad to induce immigrants to settle along their lines.

The state board of immigration, established in 1867, also sent agents to New York and abroad to encourage immigration to Minnesota. Private individuals and clergymen played a role in settlement, with people such as Bishop John Ireland facilitating the settlement of Irish Catholics in Minnesota. Yankee, German, Norwegian, Swedish, Irish, Czech, Welsh and other settlements expanded with the influx of the foreign-born. According to the 1880 census, Germans made up the largest single immigrant group, with 66,592 settlers. Of the 107,768 Scandinavians, 62,521 were Norwegian, 39,176 were Swedish, and 6,071 Danish. English-speaking immigrants totaled 38,504. By 1880 Minnesota's population had increased to 780,773, approximately 30 percent foreign-born.

FROM WHEAT TO FLOUR

Most of the immigrants started their new life as wheat farmers. In 1880, nearly every Minnesota farmer planted wheat. The State Agricultural Society warned that continuous wheat-cropping year after year in the same field would exhaust the soil. Few heeded the warnings. In 1880, wheat production rose to 34 million bushels. Ten years later production would reach 95 million bushels.

By the 1870s, the reliance on one-crop farming had begun to take its toll. During the Civil War the average yield of wheat to the acre was 22 bushels. By the late 1870s, however, an acre of land was yielding little more than 11 bushels. Eventually some farmers began to diversify, raising cattle and hogs and making butter and cheese. But most were afraid to stop growing wheat because they could rely on a large, reliable market. The land continued to wear out and crops grew thinner. The same wheat seed, used year after year, became weak and susceptible to disease.

The post-Civil War development of Minnesota agriculture also was hurt by repeated grasshopper plagues and a wheat stem rust disease epidemic. Beginning in 1873, hordes of grasshoppers settled on farms in southwestern Minnesota, eating everything green in sight. Wheat yielded less than six bushels per acre that year and many families lost everything. The next spring, eggs laid the year before hatched, and grasshoppers spread east and north, infesting 23 counties.

Minnesota's state government used many measures to try and rid the state of the grasshopper plague. The legislature voted $5,000 for relief and lent farmers $75,000 for the purchase of seed grain. But four years after the first grasshoppers arrived, virtually no progress had been made against them. Fortunately, nature intervened, and, to the relief of the farmers, the grasshoppers grew wings in the summer of 1877 and left the state.

No sooner had the grasshopper plague ended than Minnesota farmers were faced with an even more devastating enemy. Rust, a parasite that grows on barberry bushes and other host plants, was carried by wind to nearby wheat fields, leaving withered stalks and wheat kernels. The rust epidemic of 1878 ruined many farmers. Other epidemics broke out in 1904 and 1916, and the attempt to eradicate the rust menace continued for decades.

Fewer farmers planted wheat as a result of those agricultural catastrophes. Those that did diversified. In the 1880s, dairy products became the state's leading agricultural product. With the growth of dairying came an increased emphasis on beef cattle and hogs. Forage crops, such as oats and corn, became popular feed crops.

Early flour mills at the Falls of St. Anthony had been built by lumbermen who needed flour to feed their lumberjacks. But as more wheat was raised, some farsighted lumbermen saw that flour milling would one day be more profitable than lumbering. The area around the falls soon became a busy industrial district, dominated by by the flour and lumber mills. By 1880, Minneapolis' milling capacity was the largest in the United States. Ten years later, it was the largest milling center in the world.

The mills spawned other enterprises. Waterwheels, milling equipment and flour barrels were built in the area. Businesses involved in the transportation and sale of wheat flourished. Products made from wheat were marketed by other companies. Attracted by the industrial development, hundreds of bankers, doctors, lawyers, teachers, merchants, millwrights and others settled near the falls.

In the 1850s and the early 1860s most of Minnesota's wheat had to be shipped east by water. Farmers were forced to sell their wheat before the rivers and lakes froze, and millers often had no wheat to grind when the demand for flour was the greatest. The railroads solved some of these problems. They shortened the farmer's trip to market and opened up new areas for settlement. Grain elevators built along the tracks stored grain. After storage in a county elevator, grain would be shipped by rail to Minneapolis or Duluth to be stored in huge ''terminal'' elevators for shipment to mills in the East or Europe.

But the railroads that eased some farmers' problems, created others. The railroad companies charged high freight rates and inspectors at the elevators often graded the wheat too low, cheating farmers out of 10 to 20 cents a bushel. Freight rates often took one-third of the price a farmer was paid for a bushel of wheat.

The farmers' anger at these prices led to the formation of an organization called the Grange to fight the railroad companies. The Grange argued that railroads, like public highways, should be regulated by the state government. The state responded in 1871 by setting up an office of railroad commissioner and establishing maximum fares and rates. In 1874 the legislature established a board of railroad commissioners who had the power to establish a rate schedule. These ''Granger Acts'' were precedent-setting in establishing principles of public regulation of common carriers.

RICHES FROM THE ROCKS

In 1865 the state geologist reported finding iron ore and a quartz rock supposedly containing gold near Lake Vermilion. Hordes of prospectors soon were making their way through the wilderness to Vermilion to search for gold. Scientists soon followed. Little gold was ever found, but one of the prospectors, George Stuntz, collected some iron ore specimens and persuaded Charlemagne Tower, a wealthy easterner, to pay for an expedition through the region. Accompanied by a geologist, Stuntz found samples of low-grade ore on the Mesabi and samples of high-grade ore on the Vermilion range. The finds persuaded Tower to buy up land on the Vermilion Range, leaving the ores of the Mesabi undiscovered for another 15 years.

Tower and other speculators were able to buy land cheaply on the Vermilion Range. But the task of mining and transporting the ore to the steel mills of Pennsylvania required tremendous amounts of money. Tower spent more than $2 million building a railroad from Soudan to Two Harbors on Lake Superior. But three years later, Tower sold his land, mines, railroads and docks for more than $7 million to buyers like John D. Rockefeller, who was also to play a large role in the development of the Mesabi range.

Through the 1860s and 1870s, several members of the well-known Merritt family had been consumed with searching the hills of the Mesabi for ore. Using the money they made at lumbering, they surveyed the area, eventually outlining what appeared to be the rims of basins of underground ore. By 1890 Leonidas Merritt had traveled every foot of the Mesabi, noting that in the softer spots of the ground there were deep ruts. In the summer of 1890, the Merritts dug into one of these spots under the pine trees and found deep red deposits of ore

— 64 percent iron. The first body of soft ore discovered on the Mesabi Range, the Merritts' discovery would become the Mountain Iron mine.

Geologists doubted the find, particularly since it was so close to the surface. The Merritts kept digging, however, and discovered more ore basins. They began to buy and lease the land, eventually bringing in steam shovels to clear the land and mine the ore. They built a railroad spur from the mines to a nearby railroad, and soon the ore was being shipped to the port at Duluth. Then, via the Great Lakes, the ore was sent to the mills in Ohio and Pennsylvania where it was manufactured into steel for bridges, railroad rails, ploughs and all the other needs of a country in the midst of an industrial revolution. By then no one doubted the Merritts' discovery, and they received several offers for their holdings. Knowing America needed their iron, but not realizing how much it would take to mine and ship it, they refused the fortunes offered them.

The opening of the Mesabi required more money than the Merritts could raise alone. They were lured into borrowing from John D. Rockefeller and other eastern tycoons and lost everything to their creditors in the depression of 1893. In four years they made and lost millions.

For several years thereafter, the Mesabi was dominated by several Eastern steel companies. Competition was intense. In 1901 they formed a more profitable alliance, the United States Steel Corporation. This huge organization then controlled most of the ore produced on the Vermilion Range and three-fourths of that produced on the Mesabi.

While the mining continued unabated on the Mesabi and Vermilion ranges, mining officials began to explore a new range - the Cuyuna in Crow Wing and Aitkin counties. Cuyler Adams, a resident, had criss-crossed the area for four years searching for ore. Even after the mining company officials had given up, Adams continued his search. As he drilled in the ground one day, he found high grade ore on the site that would become the Kennedy Mine. Explorers and prospectors poured into the area. By 1908, ore was being mined on the Cuyuna Range although a railway didn't reach the Kennedy Mine until 1911. The Cuyuna never became as well-known as the Mesabi, which, by virtue of its larger, more shallow deposits, could be more easily mined.

For Duluth-Superior, the pay-off from mining was not from smelting the ore but from shipping it to mills in Cleveland and Pittsburgh. Duluth became a funnel for iron ore leaving the region. The first ore from the Mesabi had been shipped to Allouez Bay in Superior, Wis., but after the Merritts built their railroad and dock at Duluth, it became the hub of the shipping industry for not only ore, but also timber and grain.

By 1900, new gravity-fed timber and steel ore docks had been built, and 6,000,000 tons of ore were being shipped out of the port each year. To accommodate the needs of the iron ore industry, harbor facilities kept expanding. By 1916, the port was handling 38,000,000 tons annually. During the years of World War I the demand for ore was so great that on one day, more than 200,000 tons were loaded from the Duluth, Missabe, and Northern Railroad docks alone.

Duluth, the emporium of a vast mining and lumbering region, was transformed from a small, isolated frontier town to a minor metropolis. Established in the 1850s, it initially grew slowly. Its population in 1880 was just 3,000, but with the rapid development of the iron ore industry, 10 years later Duluth boasted 33,000 inhabitants, and by 1920, its population reached 98,000. With 49 miles of waterfront, the Duluth port had plenty of space to build storage, processing and docking facilities. The iron ore shipping industry outranked all others in total tonnage, but the shipping of grain and timber to Eastern markets was a major activity as well.

Lumber from thousands of white pines also was shipped west from Duluth to the sites where the Northern Pacific Railroad was laying ties for a route to the coast.

On the Mesabi, the forests were cut over or burned, towns sprang up along the lines of iron deposits, and gaping chasms appeared in the ground as mining got underway. By the turn of the century, the Mesabi was the nation's greatest source of iron, requiring thousands of workers to man trains, ships, trucks and shovels and to mine the ore. They came from all over the world — Cornishmen, Swedes, Norwegians, Irish, Finns, French-Canadians, Germans, and, toward the end of the century, Poles, Slovenes, Ukranians, Romanians, Italians and others. As time went on, southeastern Europeans tended to replace the Scandinavians in the mines. By 1900, half of the Mesabi population was foreign-born.

DIVERSITY IN ECONOMIC DEVELOPMENT

By 1900 Minnesota had developed into a rich, agricultural state with several well-established industries. The lumber industry peaked in 1899 when Minnesota's production of more than two billion board feet made it the third-ranking lumber state. But as the lumbering frontier moved further north toward the Canadian border, production levels began to decline.

Everyone had expected the huge forests to last for years to come, but by 1920, the great pines were gone and the last big mill closed its doors. In less than a century, the state's most abundant resource had virtually disappeared. Lumbermen turned their attention to trees they had once considered useless - aspen, spruce, jack pine, balsam and others. They became the basis for Minnesota's modern paper and wood pulp industries.

Similarly, everyone thought there was enough iron ore to last hundreds of years. No one anticipated two world wars and the unprecedented growth of the steel industry. The Mesabi provided most of the iron needed to win the wars and fortify the economic foundation of the United States. During World War I, iron ore production reached nearly 90,000,000 tons, an achievement of critical importance in meeting the needs of the nation at war. World War II placed even heavier demands on the Mesabi — 338,000,000 tons were mined for the war effort. Although the production of ore continued well into the 1950s, depletion of the high-grade ore would eventually force the industry to look for ways to use the low grade ores, or taconite, that remained.

Minneapolis became the undisputed metropolitan center of the growing state. Flour milling, railroads and lumbering all contributed to a population increase from nearly 47,000 in 1880 to more than triple that during the next decade. By 1900, the combined population of Minneapolis and St. Paul topped a quarter of a million. The development of new equipment and processes revolutionized flour milling and consequently encouraged the agricultural development of the state. The milling industry spawned many companies that would later dominate Minnesota business, including General Mills, Pillsbury, Cargill, International Multifoods, and the Peavey Company.

In 1900 extractive industries such as lumber, flour milling and iron mining still provided most of the total market value of Minnesota's manufactured products. But various smaller industries already were accounting for many jobs. St. Paul was becoming a meat-packing center, railroad cars were being built in Brainerd, Minneapolis had a number of clothing factories, and printing was becoming significant in both Minneapolis and St. Paul. Companies like General Mills and Pillsbury were diversifying from flour to the manufacture of other food products.

This trend toward economic diversity continued through the 1930s, although the Great Depression was a staggering economic blow for Minnesota industry and agriculture. Unemployment increased at an alarming rate — by 1932, 70 percent of iron range workers were jobless. The prices of farm products fell until farmers didn't bother to harvest their crops. Grasshopper plagues and drought added to the farmers' distress. Many could not pay their debts, lost their farms and ended up as unemployed workers in the cities.

The state's political parties responded to the dire economic conditions with innovative ideas for reform. The Farmer-Labor Party of Minnesota, which grew out of the Nonpartisan League, had been organized during World War I and captured the governorship in 1930 with the election of Floyd B. Olson. Under Olson the state enacted programs for old age pensions, state highway expansion, welfare, state income tax for school support, and the creation and conservation of state forests. In response to agricultural problems, the state created relief programs and resettlement plans for farmers. Banking reforms also were enacted.

The Farmer-Laborites stayed in power until 1938, when Republican Harold Stassen became governor. Stassen, an advocate of "enlightened capitalism," saw all of his proposed social reforms carried into law. State government was reorganized, social security benefits were improved, and anti-loan-shark laws and a labor relations act were passed. The state debt was reduced, child welfare was strengthened, and old age assistance was liberalized. Meanwhile, the Farmer-Laborites merged with the Democatic Party in 1944 under the leadership of Hubert H. Humphrey.

A revitalized Minnesota economy was the result of the demand for grain, iron and other goods required to fight World War II. The state's resources were tapped to their utmost. During the war years Minnesota farmers produced record crops. The American productive "miracle" was evident also at Minnesota manufacturing plants, where an accelerated industrial effort was underway. General Mills manufactured gun sights and torpedoes in addition to huge quantities of flour and other food products. Minnesota Mining and Manufacturing Company (3M) of St. Paul produced vast amounts of tape used for sheeting on airplane wings and many other purposes. Honeywell helped to perfect airplane controls and to develop the proximity bomb. Minneapolis Moline produced artillery shells, and International Harvester in St. Paul made aircraft glues and spare parts. On the Iron Range, the wartime demand for military equipment required record amounts of ore. In 1943, the region produced 83 million tons, the largest single year's tonnage in its history.

Industrialization and urbanization progressed unabated after World War II. In 1948, the value of manufactured products exceeded cash farm receipts for the first time. Business concentrated in the Twin Cities as a result of its rail network and its strategic location at the hub of the Middle West. As a network of freeways neared completion, the Twin Cities became a trucking center as well.

Minneapolis remained one of the principal grain milling centers in the country. Food processing grew out of this industry and eventually overtook it in production. Pillsbury, which began grinding flour at St. Anthony Falls in 1869, became a manufacturer of convenience goods such as cake mixes, and diversified into restaurant chains and frozen foods. General Mills followed suit. Cargill, another Minnesota food-based firm, began as a grain-trading business in the Midwest in 1865 but expanded its operations to animal feeds, chemical products and other commodities.

Minneapolis had 1,400 manufacturing plants by the end of the 1950s. Industrial products included clothing, farm implements, paint, boats, heavy machinery, beer, bags and paper boxes, seeds and linseed oil. St. Paul, a wholesaling center, was home to many manufacturing concerns and large insurance companies.

Agriculture also followed the trend towards diversification. Farm population decreased, as did the number of farms. But production remained high. Minnesota continued to produce such traditional crops as wheat, oats, barley and feed corn. Soybeans became a major crop, and sweet corn, peas and other vegetables also became important to the agricultural economy.

One-fourth of Minnesota's crop production was concentrated in the southwestern part of the state. It was an important region for cattle and hogs, with meat-packing plants growing up nearby at Austin and South St. Paul.

In northern Minnesota's soft pulpwood forests, which had grown over the cut-over or burned-over acreage where white pine once stood, the forestry industry dominated. About one of every three acres in Minnesota remained forested, despite the heavy cuttings early in the state's history and the clearing of tree stands for agriculture. Pulpwood created a surge in the industry as it was harvested for the manufacture of paper and other wood-fiber products.

Iron ore production and shipping remained at record levels though the postwar years, as the United States became the world's largest steel producer and Minnesota the nation's leading iron-mining center. But eventually it was all too apparent that the war had severely depleted the high- grade hematite ore on the Mesabi, and many mines closed. The industry began mining low-grade ore, or taconite, to supply the mills. The taconite industry, involving both mining and manufacturing, gave new life to northeastern Minnesota in the 1960s.

Although lumber, wheat, and iron ore continued to be major factors in Minnesota's economy, the state increased its dependence on high technology and a skilled labor force. The electronics industry began to compete with the more traditional industries for prominence in Minnesota business.

Minnesota was not only a place but a process. Every generation had put its hand on it, leaving a mark, devising new ways to use the state's resources. When it entered the second half of the twentieth century, it did so with a backdrop of steady growth in an economy that had developed a balance among agriculture, manufacturing, trade and services. It looked forward to the modern era with many unspent resources in its rich domain and the inexhaustible capacities of a diverse people.

QUALITY OF LIFE IN MINNESOTA

In the mellifluous language of the Dakota Indians, Minnesota means ''water tinted like the sky.'' Surely it must have seemed so to the first Europeans who traveled west 335 years ago and found sprawling prairies, abundant pine and hardwood forests, and more fresh water than any other American territory. After a century of urbanization and industrialization, much of Minnesota remains wilderness and farmland. Its water is still pure and its air is among the cleanest in the nation. While other American regions face ecological and industrial crises, Minnesota's stewardship of its land and industry has brought economic stability and a harmonious coexistence between man and nature.

Quality of life studies consistently rank Minnesota as one of the best places to live in the country. ''A state that works,'' was the theme of a *Time* magazine cover story on Minnesota. The article noted: ''If the American good life has anywhere survived in some intelligent equilibrium, it may be in Minnesota...a state where a residual American secret seems to operate. Some of the nation's most agreeable qualities are evident here: courtesy and fairness, honesty, innovation, hard work, responsibility and intellectual adventurism.''

The notoriously proud Minnesotans maintain that all of these attributes are true, and not by accident. Quality of life is constantly monitored here. Having made one of the world's fiercest climates livable, Minnesotans ask probing questions of all technological, legislative and economic developments to ensure that short-term prosperity doesn't result in long-term instability and decline.

Quality of life takes on a unique dimension in Minnesota. True to the northern European heritage of many Minnesotans, the state combines a mix of social liberalism that demands an efficient and vigorous public service sector, and philosophic conservatism that is skeptical of change for its own sake. Those from other parts of the country may find Minnesotans a bit provincial on first meeting, but further acquaintance reveals the horse-sense pragmaticism for which Midwesterners are known.

A sense of balance and moderation makes Minnesota's quality of life enviable. With one of the country's lowest poverty and crime rates, it is apparent that the state's population is deeply concerned about Minnesota's standard of living and has carefully monitored growth and development in the region.

Population

Minnesota has 4,100,000 inhabitants, the majority of whom are of German or Scandinavian descent. The median age of the population is increasing, from 26.8 years in 1970 to 28.2 years currently. Two of every three Minnesotans live in the cities, a statistic that has remained stable since World War II.

Minnesota's first inhabitants and its oldest minority group are the Chippewa and Sioux Indians. There are about 40,000 Chippewa Indians in Minnesota, many living on three large reservations at Leech Lake, Red Lake and White Earth. About 5,000 Sioux live in Minnesota, some on small reservations in the southern part of the state.

There are about 60,000 blacks in Minnesota, the state's largest minority group. About 94 percent live in the seven-county metropolitan area. Minnesota's Hispanics number about 52,000, and unlike other minorities, many live outside the Twin Cities. Minnesota's newest minority is Asian, largely Indo-Chinese, who immigrated after the Vietnam War. Many are Hmong Cambodians. St. Paul has one of the largest Hmong populations in the country, numbering more than 9,000.

Most urban experts agree that Minnesota is a good place for minorities to live. It has the nation's highest non-white median school year completion rate, and unemployment is extremely low by national standards.

Education

Minnesota's educational system is the envy of the nation. State high schools see 96.7 percent of their students graduate, first in the nation, and 77 percent of those graduates go on to some type of post-secondary education. Minnesota ranks second in U.S. college entrance exam scores and is a consistent national leader in educational expenditures. State and local governments traditionally spend one-third of their budgets on education. In 1983, the legislature voted to make computer literacy a goal for students in kindergarten through 12th grade. Student access to computers in Minnesota is third best in the country.

The Minnesota State University system is the largest public university system in the nation. There are seven state universities, five branches of the University of Minnesota, and 33 state-supported vocational-technical schools. The University of Minnesota-Minneapolis/St. Paul has the largest urban campus in the country. There are 24 private colleges, with Carleton, Macalester, St. Olaf, St. Thomas and St. Catherine's among the most respected liberal arts colleges in the nation. Minnesota's post-secondary educational system attracts one-third of its students from outside the state. High numbers go on to earn advanced degrees.

The University of Minnesota Law School is considered one of the country's best. The Minnesota Institute of Technology's department of chemical engineering is considered the finest in the nation and the department of mechanical engineering is ranked fifth in the nation. Seven University of Minnesota graduates have won the Nobel Prize.

There is a strong link between Minnesota business and education. Companies choose to locate in Minnesota because they are assured of an intelligent workforce able to learn complex and technical jobs quickly. The high percentage of Minnesota-educated business leaders — 59 percent of Minnesota's chief executive officers are University of Minnesota graduates — ensures a constant and productive dialogue between business and education.

Economics

Minnesota's business climate is vigorous, competitive and healthy. Its employment rate between 1972 and 1983 exceeded the national average by more than four percentage points. It ranks fourth in the nation in the number of fastest-growing businesses. Fourteen Fortune 500 companies have their headquarters here: 3M, Honeywell, General Mills, Control Data, Pillsbury, Land O'Lakes, Farmers Union, Hormel, International

Multifoods, Bemis, Economics Laboratory, Deluxe Check Printers, M.E.I., and American Hoist and Derrick. Minnesota is second in the nation in non-fuel mineral production, third in high-tech manufacturing, fifth in cash farm income, tenth in tourism expenditures and thirteenth in commercial forestry.

While other northern tier states suffer continued recession, Minnesota has grown through its ability to anticipate economic trends. The state is recognized as the undisputed super-computer capital of the world, the home of Control Data, Honeywell, CPT and Cray Research, as well as 2,100 other high-tech companies.

''There is a rare synergism among Minnesota's high-technology companies that inspires innovation,'' says John Rollwagen, chairman and chief executive of Cray Research. ''This synergism is created by companies like Control Data, Honeywell, Data 100, CPT Corporation and our own company. Our competitors have become some of our greatest technological allies.''

Control Data's William Norris explains why businesses are attracted to Minnesota: ''The people here have the skills we need. They like to work, and the University of Minnesota and secondary schools provide high quality education. There are fewer labor problems here, we've got good government and a sense of cooperation between government and industry that is rarely found.''

Entrepreneurs are integral to the state's business climate. Minnesota's Venture Capital Pool contains almost $370 million, among the top ten states in venture capital resources. This reflects the confidence investors have in the health of Minnesota's economy, and the state's exemplary labor force. One such organization is the privately owned Small Business Investment Company, which provides equity and working capital to businesses with assets under $9 million, and average income after taxes of not more than $400,000. Women, who are forming new companies at a rate five times faster than men, have been especially successful in Minnesota.

The Farmer's Home Administration offers guaranteed and insured loans and grants to rural organizations and individuals to help improve, develop or finance business, industry and employment. Private businesses in rural areas with a population of less than 50,000 are eligible.

Business in Minnesota succeeds because of the reciprocal commitments of Minnesota's political, educational, industrial and citizen sectors. Business is drawn to enlightened government and an intelligent, hard-working labor force. Labor is motivated by management's fair and competent administration. Corporate philanthropy to civic and cultural organizations is generous and wide-ranging, topping $63 million in a recent year.

Transportation

As the twelfth-largest state in the country, with 184,068 square miles, efficient land and water transportation is essential to Minnesota's economic health.

Minnesota has more than 150 airports serving every area of the state. The largest is the Minneapolis/St. Paul International Airport, acclaimed as one of the five safest in the world, with more than 400 arrivals and departures per day. Eleven Minnesota cities are served by certified air carriers on a scheduled basis. Two airlines, Northwest and Republic, have their headquarters in Minneapolis.

The Mississippi River and Lake Superior, Minnesota's two most prominent waterways, serve as key transportation links to major American and international markets. The Mississippi River winds its way for 1,770 miles from Minneapolis to the Gulf of Mexico. It is 2,340 miles from the Lake Superior port of Duluth/Superior through the Great Lakes to the Atlantic Ocean.

The Port of Duluth/Superior is one of the busiest ports in the country due to its proximity to rich agricultural and mining areas. Typical cargoes include taconite from the Iron Range, coal, oil and petroleum products, newsprint, paper and lumber products, and grain and other commodities.

Minnesota has more than 128,000 miles of streets and highways, offering more travel routes than all other states except Kansas, California, Illinois and Texas. Ninety-one percent of the state's trunk highway system is surfaced.

Freight transportation trucking is the major user for the highway network. Minnesota is the third-largest trucking center in the country. An estimated 37.5 percent of all Minnesota communities depend entirely on trucks to meet their transportation needs. Agricultural products are the most important commodities in the state's trucking operations.

Resources

Iron ore mining accounts for 90 percent of the value of all minerals produced in Minnesota. Historically, ore has been extracted from three iron areas: the Vermilion, Mesabi and Cuyuna ranges.

Since the late 1970s, iron ore has no longer been mined from the underground deposits of the Vermilion range, or from the open pits of Cuyuna or Mesabi. The Iron Range has faced economic hardship as pure ore deposits have been depleted. University of Minnesota scientist Edward Davis worked for almost 50 years on a process to extract iron from the much harder and leaner taconite rock. Today Minnesota supplies two-thirds of the country's taconite ore.

At the time of the first permanent white settlement, about 40 percent of Minnesota was cloaked in pine, spruce and fir forests. Another quarter of the state was covered by hardwoods such as maple, oak, elm and basswood. Homesteading farmers cleared the forests to plant crops, and the state's dairy region now comprises much of the former hardwood belt.

In 1977, commercial forests covered 27 percent of Minnesota's total land area, a 30.4 percent drop from 1962. The timber stock on commercial forest lands was valued at approximately $253 million.

Energy

In comparison with other states, energy costs for commerce and industry are very low. Oil, natural gas, coal and electricity are available statewide through an extensive network of pipelines, powerlines, highways, railways and waterways. The energy that fuels Minnesota's economy is derived primarily from oil, secondarily from gas and coal and to a lesser extent from nuclear power and other sources.

Commerce and industry consume 30 percent of the primary fuels used in Minnesota. Another 28 percent is used in generating electricity. Transportation accounts for 27 percent and residential needs for 15 percent of the state's fuel consumption.

With an eye to the future, Minnesota has been looking to alternative energy sources to meet long-term demands. One promising fuel source is peat, which is found in greater abundance in Minnesota than in any other state. Lying 5 to 20 feet deep, Minnesota has 7.2 million acres of peat, half the nation's supply.

Minnesota's surplus of aspen, birch and oak, averaging 2 million cords a year, is viewed as another alternative fuel source. A half-cord of wood is equivilant to a barrel of oil in heating value. Wood pellets are more efficient than coal in providing energy for institutional buildings and light manufacturing.

Human Resources

Because no single industry dominates, Minnesota's economy is extremely stable. Work stoppages, lost work hours, employee absenteeism and employee turnover are among the lowest in the nation. Even in periods of economic recession, Minnesota's unemployment rate has been below the national average. Three out of four Minnesotans own their own home, a statistic well above the national average.

The average yearly income in Twin Cities area households is $32,907, which is 17 and 15 percent above the state and national averages, $28,021 and $28,600 respectively.

Agriculture

Minnesota's largest industry is agriculture and agribusiness. Only four other states have more farms than Minnesota, and Minnesota farmers are among the most productive and successful in the world. Minnesota is first in the nation in the production of sweet corn; second in oats, hay and sugarbeets; third in sunflowers and soybeans and fifth in corn production.

While the number of farmers has been shrinking in the last five years, the size of Minnesota farms is growing. Between 1969 and 1978, the average Minnesota farm grew seven percent to 279 acres.

The 1980 census produced a picture of Minnesota which varies along a diagonal line drawn across the state from northwest to southeast. South of the line, farms are big and getting bigger as smaller units are absorbed into larger ones. Most of the state's crops and livestock are produced here, land is more valuable and average farm income is higher. Farms to the north are smaller, with many operated by part-time farmers who earn most of their income off the farm.

Soybeans have replaced corn as the number one cash crop and account for about 18 percent of the state's farm income, with corn providing about 13 percent.

Wild rice is North America's only native grain. Minnesota grows almost three million pounds annually on about 16,000 acres, 95 percent of the country's supply. Widespread demand for wild rice began in the 1950s, resulting in the creation of many man-made paddies. Wild rice thrives in swampland where no other crop can be grown and provides an excellent breeding ground and habitat for waterfowl.

Minnesota is sixth in the nation in red meat production, and tenth in cattle and calves. The state raises about 3.5 million cows at a total cash value of about $1.6 billion. The state is ranked fourth in the nation in hog production with a cash value of about $311 million. Minnesota is the country's second-leading turkey producer, earning about $8.9 million from 447,000 turkeys.

Minnesota is the nation's second-largest dairy producer. Only Wisconsin produces more cheese and butter. The state is fourth in milk production.

The home of General Mills, Pillsbury and Hormel, Minnesota is one of the food-processing capitals of the world. Betty Crocker, The Green Giant and the Pillsbury Doughboy are all staunch Minnesotans. Both General

Mills and Pillsbury are Fortune 100 companies with revenues exceeding $4 billion. What began as milling, canning and packing factories have become sophisticated food-processing giants, with international reputations for quality and value.

Environment

It is no accident that Minnesota's air and water is among the cleanest in the country. Minnesota spends an average of $12 per person to protect the environment, by far the highest such figure in the country. Through astute conservation and rigorous legislation, the state has become a national model of resource protection and management. A recent study by the The Conservation Fund placed Minnesota's enviromental policy first in the country.

Recreation

This respect for the land and environment is due in large part to the statewide obsession with outdoor recreation. Every season has its own sport, and virtually everyone participates in some kind of outdoor activity. Despite the severity of the climate, or perhaps because of it, Minnesotans are outdoor people. At least 50 percent vacation within their own state.

The diversity of Minnesota's terrain makes it a microcosm of America's topography. The flat, glacier-carved farmland in the south gives way to the jagged granite cliffs of the northwest. The regions of the Boundary Waters and North Shore of Lake Superior contrast with the rolling hills and bluffs of the Mississippi Valley. Then there are the lakes — 11,842 to be exact. No other state in the country comes close to having as much water as Minnesota. Lakes cover 5 percent of the state and 90 percent of all Minnesotans live within two miles of a lake. Minneapolis alone has 21 lakes within its city limits.

The Boundary Waters offer an experience almost extinct in American life, an opportunity to experience some of the most unspoiled wilderness south of Alaska. Nothing is allowed to disturb this pristine wilderness. No motorized vehicles are allowed into much of the park, and even planes are forbidden to fly overhead. Strict entry regulations limit the number of visitors. The primary mode of transportation is canoe, often requiring long portages over land between the lakes, stream and rivers. It is a critical habitat for many endangered and dwindling animal species. Bear, moose, wolves, even bald eagles, can be seen throughout the Boundary Waters region.

The vast majority of the lakes are clean and stocked with some of America's finest game fish. There are 2.6 million acres of fishing water in Minnesota, and more than 150 species of fish.

The variety of Minnesota's topography makes the state a hunter's paradise. After decades of uncontrolled trapping and hunting in Minnesota's early days, wildlife populations are now closely monitored and controlled. For the conscientious hunter, the state offers a season for everything from ruffed grouse to moose and black bear. People from all over the world come to Minnesota to hunt on its more than 11 million acres of public hunting land.

In the summer, Minnesota's 59 state parks, totalling 171,000 acres and 3,550 miles of lake and river routes, provide access to every kind of camping and fishing. Water-skiing was invented by Minnesotan Ralph S. Samuelson in 1922 and remains a popular warm-weather pastime.

In winter there is cross-country and downhill skiing, skating and tobogganing. Hockey is a statewide mania, reaching its peak in early spring with the state high school tournament and the North Stars' race for a place in the National Hockey League playoffs.

Weather

Refusing to be bullied by winter's ferocity or summer's inferno, Minnesotans play along with nature, good-naturedly chiding its challenges of extremes. Still, it takes a sturdy constitution to live in Minnesota, and despite the high quality of life, the population will never be large precisely because of the weather. It is not unusual for there to be a 130-degree difference between the coldest and hottest days of the year. True to their Scandinavian ancestry, most Minnesotans are stoic about the weather. "It builds character," is a common reaction, and probably an accurate one. Minnesotans' unique relationship to nature comes from the clear delineation of the seasons. Winter fast instills humility into a person caught outside in a raging blizzard with a windchill temperature of -75. Cooperation among neighbors is another gift of winter. Everyone's car needs a push at some time, and a divine rule operates that those who help will also be helped.

The all-time record low for Minnesota was an air temperture of -59 on February 16, 1903. The warmest day was July 6, 1936 when it reached 114. Minnesota's annual precipitation averages between 20 inches in the northwest and 30 inches near Duluth. The average snowfall in Duluth is 77.6 inches (131.6 is the record) and between 33 and 58 inches in the rest of the state. Scattered frost is likely in August along the Iron Range, while just 250 miles south, the first frost usually holds off until the first week of October.

Culture

Currently one of America's cultural hotspots, artists from New York, Boston, Chicago, and Los Angeles come to the Twin Cities to create and perform. The sophistication of local audiences has long been known. During the last few years, national attention has been focused on the Walker Art Center, the Ordway Theater and the Guthrie Theater, drawing an increasing number of world-class artists to the area.

The St. Paul Chamber Orchestra is the only full-time Chamber Orchestra in the United States. Pinchas Zuckerman, musical directer and conductor, has built an international reputation for the orchestra, which performs about 80 concerts a year in the Twin Cities and tours nationally and internationally.

The Minnesota Orchestra, which records on major labels and tours around the world, increased its world-class stature in the early '80s under renowned conductor Neville Marriner. Dutch conductor Edo de Waart has been named the Orchestra's musical director for the 1986-87 season.

Minnesota has the third-highest theater attendance record in the country. There are more theaters per capita in the Twin Cities than in any other city in the United States. The Guthrie Theater is a nationally respected repertory theater.

The Walker Art Center is dedicated to promoting and preserving contemporary art, music, film, dance and theater, both nationally and locally. It was the first museum in the country to present the Picasso Legacy exhibition, one of the most important retrospectives of the last 10 years. The Walker also developed a major De Stijl show featuring paintings, furniture and design from this vital Dutch intellectual and artistic movement of the mid-twentieth century.

The Minneapolis Institute of Arts has a superb permanent collection of both eastern and western art representing every artistic period. It is home to ''Lucretia,'' perhaps the finest work by Rembrandt in the nation, superb works by Max Beckmann and Francis Bacon, and two excellent paintings by Titian.

The Children's Theater is widely considered the country's most famous and innovative acting academy for children. Gifted children from around the country come to participate in productions of incredible sophistication and accomplishment.

The Minneapolis College of Art and Design is a nationally recognized visual arts school. Its graduates are involved in everything from rock videos to *Sesame Street,* to creating visual artifacts that alter the way we see and understand shape and space.

Twin Cities architecture also boasts a national reputation. The IDS Tower, designed by Phillip Johnson, is perhaps the consummate achievement in the ''International Style,'' which has dominated post-war commercial architecture. Historic Summit Avenue in St. Paul, once the neighborhood of F. Scott Fitzgerald, has one of the nation's best-preserved stretches of Victorian architecture.

Minnesota's culture isn't confined to the Twin Cities. Robert Bly, an internationally respected poet and translator, lives in a small community in northern Minnesota. There are countless wildlife painters, photographers and essayists who quietly capture the artistry of life outside the city's eye. Sigurd Olson was a beloved Minnesotan whose tranquil ruminations on nature and rural Minnesota life soothed many spirits yearning for an existence closer to the land. His warnings of what would happen if civilization and technology were to grow unchecked have been wisely heeded by Minnesota conservationists.

Minnesotans know that their quality of life depends on a balance between urban and rural, culture and commerce, progressive and conservative, corn and computers. They scorn fads and extremes, insisting that balance and diversity are the foundation of their prosperity. It is the average Minnesota citizen who is truly responsible for the state's high quality of life.

Fiscal Facts About Minnesota

Minnesota Agricultural Production

COMMODITY	NUMBER	RANK WITHIN UNITED STATES
cattle	3,550,000	10th
hogs	4,300,000	12th
horses (1984 est.)	213,000	—
turkeys	447,000	2nd

Source: Minnesota Agriculture Statistics 1985

COMMODITY	DOLLAR VALUE	RANK WITHIN UNITED STAES
wheat	414,596,000	7th
corn	1,722,700,000	5th
oats	1,244,800,000	2nd
barley	129,675,000	4th
soybeans	976,998,000	3rd
sunflower	35,380,000	3rd
sugar beets	165,035,000	2nd
potatoes	78,519,000	9th
milk	1,127,153,000	4th
butter	221,251,000	3rd
eggs	123,627,000	—
rye	11,638,000	2nd
bay	459,980,000	2nd
sweet corn (for processing)	41,095,000	1st

Employment and State Debt

1983 Non-Agricultural Employment Minnesota. 1,714,000 persons equal to 1.9% of U.S. work force.

EMPLOYMENT BY INDUSTRY
Minnesota 1983

	# of Establishments	% of Total	# Employees	% Total
Agriculture (Non-Farm)	1,800	2	10,000	.6
Mining	194	.2	8,000	.5
Contract Construction	10,000	11	45,000	3
Manufacturing	7,000	7	333,000	21
Transportation	4,700	5	80,000	5
Trade	36,000	36	410,000	26
Finance, Insurance & Real Estate	8,700	9	96,000	6
Services	27,000	27	352,000	22
Government	3,600	4	265,000	17
All Industry Total	99,000	100%	1,600,000	100%

(1) Total Employment Variation 1,600,000 to 1,714,000 explained by seasonal and part-time employment variables.

STATE AND LOCAL GOVERNMENT EMPLOYMENT BY MAJOR FUNCTION
Minnesota 1983
(in thousands)

	Educational	Hospital	Welfare	Highways	Fire & Police	Other
1973	99	18	6	13	10	36
1983	97	20	11	11	10	45

	State Total	Local Total	Grand Total
1973	46	135	182
1983	54	140	194

PUBLIC EMPLOYMENT: STATE AND LOCAL—1983
PER 10,000 population

State	State Employees	Rank	Local	Rank	Total	Rank
Minnesota	130	38	338	14	468	29
Wisconsin	121	41	330	21	451	36
Louisiana	101	49	337	16	438	41
Illinois	100	50	321	27	421	48
North Carolina	144	31	331	20	476	26
Texas	115	45	358	9	473	28
Ohio	107	46	322	26	428	47
U.S. Average	133		332		465	

TOTAL STATE DEBT
(in dollars)

	Total Minnesota		Per Capita MN	
Year	Nominal	Adjusted for Inflation	Nominal	Adjusted for Inflation
1967	286,000,000	Base Year	78	Base Year
1970	394,000,000	335,000,000	103	88
1980	880,000,000	355,000,000	216	87
1984	1,072,000,000	342,000,000	268 (est)	86

Income Taxes

MINNESOTA PER CAPITA INCOME—1983
(in dollars)

11,913   U.S. Average: 11,658   U.S. Rank: 18

TOTAL MN PERSONAL INCOME—1983
(in dollars)

49,400,000,000 or 1.81% of U.S. Total   U.S. Rank: 19

1983 PER CAPITA DISPOSABLE INCOME
(Gross, Less Taxes and Schools Costs—in dollars)

9,942   U.S. Rank: 22

STATE AND LOCAL TAXES COLLECTED PER CAPITA—1983
(in dollars)

1,473   U.S. Average: 1,216   U.S. Rank: 5
WI: 1,425   CA: 1,337   IL: 1,255   OH: 1,100   NC: 911

CHANGES IN PER CAPITA TAXES FOR SELECTED YEARS
(in dollars)

YEAR	NOMINAL	ADJUSTED FOR INFLATION
1967	357	357 (Base)
1970	442	376
1980	1,125	954
1983	1,473	970

MAJOR SOURCES OF STATE INCOME
(Taxes!) 1984
(in $ millions)

Personal Income Tax	2,316
Sales Tax	1,253
Gasoline Tax	332
Corporate Income Tax	276
Motor Vehicle Tax	198
Sale Tax Automobile	179
Iron Ore & Taconite	94
Tobacco	84
Gross Earnings	71
Insurance Premium	71
Alcoholic Bev.	54
Bank Tax	30
Gift & Inheritance	18
Other	100 (est)
TOTAL STATE TAXES	5,176
Plus Property Taxes (local)	2,164
GRAND TOTAL	7,340

PROPERTY TAXES PER CAPITA—1983
(in dollars)

		U.S. Rank
Minnesota	413	19
Wisconsin	536	11
California	347	27
Illinois	507	14
North Carolina	213	41
Texas	381	23
Ohio	379	25
U.S. Average	381	

INCOME TAX BY STATE PER CAPITA—1983 / SALES TAX BY STATE—1983
(in dollars)

	INCOME TAX	U.S. Rank	SALES TAX	U.S. Rank
Minnesota	477	2	239	17
Wisconsin	365	6	255	13
California	304	9	309	9
Illinois	192	25	208	26
North Carolina	255	13	136	42
Texas	0	45-50	211	25
Ohio	184	27	187	38
U.S. Average	248		255	

MINNESOTA PER CAPITA INCOME TAX FOR SELECTED YEARS
(in dollars)

YEAR	NOMINAL	ADJUSTED TO INFLATION
1967	69	69 (Base Year)
1970	91	80
1980	310	125
1983	477	192

MINNESOTA TOTAL INCOME TAX COLLECTIONS FOR SELECTED YEARS
(in dollars)

YEAR	INDIVIDUAL	CORPORATE
1968	272 Million	58 Million
1970	346 Million	70 Million
1980	1,272 Million	345 Million
1984	2,316 Million	276 Million

Expenditures

PER CAPITA STATE & LOCAL EXPENDITURES—1983 (in dollars)

STATE	TOTAL GENERAL	(RANK)	HIGHER EDUCATION	LOCAL SCHOOL	HEALTH	WELFARE	HIGHWAY
Minnesota	2,404	(6)	207 (23)	576 (7)	207 (14)	356 (7)	241 (11)
Wisconsin	2,154	(16)	276 (7)	514 (17)	206 (15)	262 (16)	199 (18)
California	2,218	(12)	232 (17)	470 (28)	202 (16)	356 (8)	102 (50)
Illinois	1,897	(28)	163 (37)	465 (30)	122 (43)	281 (13)	159 (31)
North Carolina	1,497	(47)	205 (24)	395 (45)	168 (27)	150 (42)	114 (47)
Texas	1,731	(37)	216 (20)	525 (13)	171 (25)	126 (48)	158 (33)
Ohio	1,797	(31)	179 (30)	470 (29)	187 (20)	268 (14)	128 (43)
U.S. Average	1,986		187	483	189	251	157

PER CAPITA STATE AND LOCAL EXPENDITURES SELECTED YEARS
(in dollars)

YEAR	NOMINAL	INFLATION ADJUST (1)	U.S. AVG. NOMINAL	ADJUSTED (1)
1967	547	547	474	474
1970	728	620	646	550
1980	1894	764	1622	654
1983	2404	768	1986	639

(1) Adjusted Twin City CPI

NOTE: Source: Fiscal facts for Minnesotans, 1985. Minnesota Taxpayers Assoc. Figures have been rounded off for ease in reading. Adjustment for inflation: the consumer price index for Twin Cities.

MINNESOTA'S HISTORIC AND GEOLOGIC MARKERS AND MONUMENTS (by county)

Numerical coding after county name refers directly to area map section.

AITKIN, 50-C4, Highway 65
American Fur Post
Historic Fur Post located here in 1830.

AITKIN, 60-G1, Savanna State Park
Savanna Portage
Historic fur trade route.

ANOKA, 34-G4, Highway 61
Itasca Village Townsite
The ghost town of Itasca. Open to public.

ANOKA, 34-G4, Highway 169, Anoka
Mouth of the Rum River
History of the area.

ANOKA, Highway 10
Oliver Hudson Kelley Homestead
Home of Oliver Kelley, who founded the
National Grange in 1867.

BECKER, 46-A4, Highway 10, Detroit Lakes
The Lakes of Minnesota
Geological history of the area.

BECKER, 55-D4, White Earth
Chief White Cloud Monument
Chief of the White Earth Chippewa Band.

BELTRAMI, 69-D2, Puposky
Count Beltrami Monument
Explorer for the source of the Mississippi.

BELTRAMI, 69-F2, County Road 15
Giacomo C. Beltrami
Italian explorer's search for the source of the
Mississippi River.

BIG STONE, 29-B4, Highway 28
Graceville
Irish colonists established a settlement here in
1878.

BIG STONE, 29-E4, Highway 12, Ortonville
Ortonville Region
Geological history of the area.

BLUE EARTH, 15-F2, Lake Crystal
Lake Crystal and the Railroad
Story of the coming of the railroad to Lake
Crystal.

**BLUE EARTH, 15-F3, Highway 68, Minneopa
St. Park**
Seppman Mill
1864 wind-driven grist mill. Open to public with
picnic area.

BLUE EARTH, 15-F4, Highway 22
Victory Highway
Naming of the highway.

BLUE EARTH, 15-F4, Mankato
Dakota Memorial 1862
Commemorating victims of the 1862 Sioux
Uprising.

**BLUE EARTH, 15-G5, County Road 138, St.
Clair**
The Winnebago Agency
1855 Indian Agency for the Winnebago Indians.

BLUE EARTH, 5-B4, Highway 22, Mapleton
Cradle of Curling
Birthplace of curling in Minnesota.

BROWN, 14-D3, Highway 14, Sleepy Eye
Chief Sleepy Eyes
Historic Chief of the Sisseton Dakota.

BROWN, 14-D3, Sleepy Eye
Chief Sleepy Eyes Monument
Historic Dakota Chief. Museum nearby.

BROWN, 14-D4, County Road 29, Essig
Milford Monument
Casualties of the Sioux Uprising.

BROWN, 14-D5, Highway 14, New Ulm
Charles E. Flanbrau
Defender of New Ulm during the 1862 Sioux
Uprising.

BROWN, 14-D5, Highway 15
Two Battles of New Ulm
1862 attack on the defense of New Ulm.

BROWN, 14-D5, New Ulm
Defenders' Monument
Monument to the defenders of New Ulm.

BROWN, 14-D5, New Ulm
Hermann Monument
German hero against the Romans. Picnic area.

BROWN, 14-D5, New Ulm
John Lind Home
Home of one of Minnesota's Governors.

BROWN, 14-F5, County Road 20, Hanska
Lake Hanska
1862 frontier fort. Located in county park.

CARLTON, 51-E4, Highway 71, Moose Lake
Moose Lake Region
Geological history of the area.

CARLTON, 51-E4, Moose Lake
Moose Lake Monument
Victims of the 1918 forest fire.

CARLTON, 52-B1, Highway 33, Cloquet
Cloquet Fire
The town of Cloquet was destroyed by fire in
1918.

CARLTON, 52-C2, Highway 23
Fond du Lac
Early history surrounding this mid-1800s city.

**CARLTON, 52-C2, Highway 210, Jay Cooke
State Park**
Jay Cooke State Park
Geological history of the area.

CARVER, 26-E2, Highway 212, Chaska
Little Rapids Fur Post
Site of 1824 fur post.

CASS, 58-E4, Highway 200
Sugar Point Battle
1898 battle with the Chippewa Indians.

CHIPPEWA, 22-D5, County Road 15 and 9
Farther and Gay Castle
1861 home of Joseph R. Brown, fur trader,
Indian agent, inventor and journalist.
Open to public.

**CHIPPEWA, 22-B3, County Road, Lac qui
Parle State Park**
Joseph Renville
Fur post site established in 1825 by Joseph
Renville.

**CHIPPEWA, 22-B3, County Road, Lac qui
Parle State Park**
Lac qui Parle Mission Site
1835 Indian Mission established for the Dakota.
Picnic area.

CHIPPEWA, 22-C5, Highway 212, Montevideo
Camp Release Monument
Release of the captives of the Sioux Uprising.
Picnic area.

CHISAGO, 35-B5, Taylors Falls
Folsom House
Historic 1854 home of independent logger
William Henry Carmen Folsom; first
frame building in Taylors Falls. Open to public.

CHISAGO, 35-D5, Taylors Falls
Taylors Falls Region
Geological history of the area.

CLAY, 54-F2, Highway 75, Moorhead
St. John's Episcopal Church
1899 Episcopal church. Open to public.

CLAY, 54-F2, Moorhead
Solomon G. Comstock House
Home of early Red River Valley entrepreneur.
Open to public.

CLAY, 54-G2, Moorhead Rest Area
Red River Valley and Bonanza Farming
History of Red River Valley and large scale
farms of the area.

CLAY, 54-G5, Highway 10, Hawley
Lake Agassiz
Geological history of the area.

CLAY, 55-D1, Highway 32, Ulen
Viking Sword
Possible Viking sword found here.

**CLEARWATER, 56-C4, Highway 92, Itasca
State Park**
Search for the Mississippi Source
Exploration for the source of the Mississippi
River. Interpretive center.

CLEARWATER, 56-C4, Itasca State Park
Geology of Minnesota
Geological history of the area.

CLEARWATER, 68-F3, Highway 92
Jacob V. Brower
Marker commemorating the first commissioner
of Itasca State Park.

CLEARWATER, 68-F3, Highway 92
Old Northwest Territory
Marker commemorating the Old Northwest
Territory established in 1787.

COOK, 76-B3, Highway 61, Grand Marais
Good Harbor Bay
Geological history of the area.

COOK, 76-B3, Highway 61, Grand Marais
Grand Marais
Geological history of the area.

COOK, 76-B3, Highway 61, Grand Marais
Indian Church
Historic Indian church.

COOK, 76-G1, Highway 61
Judge C.R. Magney
Early Minnesota environmentalist.

23

COOK, 76-G1, Highway 61
Old Dog Trail
Mail carrying by dog sled.

COOK, 88-E1, North and South Lakes
Height of Land Portage
Important continental divide.

COOK, 88-G1, County Roads 4 and 7
Eagle Mountain
Highest point of land in Minnesota.

COTTONWOOD, 3-B4, County Road 2
Cottonwood County Petroglyphs
Prehistoric Indian carvings. Interpretive center.

CROW WING, 41-B1, Highway 371
Fort Ripley
1848 frontier fort.

CROW WING, 49-G3, Highway 371, Long
Lake
Brainerd Region
Geological history of the area.

CROW WING, 49-G5, Highway 169, Garrison
Mille Lacs Lake
Famous Minnesota lake.

CROW WING, 49-G5, Highway 169, Garrison
Mille Lacs Lake
Geological history of the area.

DAKOTA, 27-D1, Mendota
St. Peter's Church
Historic Catholic church. Open to public.

DAKOTA, 27-E3, Highway 55, Hastings
Dakota County Region
Geological history of the area. Located in park.

DAKOTA, 27-E3, Highway 61, Hastings
Hastings
History of the establishment of the city.

DAKOTA, 27-E5, Hastings
Ignatius Donnelly's Nininger City Home
Home of Ignatius Donnelly, famous author and
politician.

DAKOTA, 27-F2, Highway 52
Pine Bend Village
Site of 1838 Dakota Indian village.

DODGE, 17-G3, Highway 14, Dodge Center
Plowville
First National Plow Matches in Minnesota in
1952.

DODGE, 17-G4, County Road 16, Wasioja
Wasioja Seminary
1858 Baptist seminary.

DOUGLAS, 39-E2, Alexandria
Knute Nelson House
Home of famous Minnesota politician. Open to
public.

FILLMORE, 8-C4, Highway 52
Chatfield
Location of government land office from 1856
to 1861.

FILLMORE, 8-E4, Forestville State Park
Meighen Store
1856 store and the ghost town of Forestville.
Open to public.

FREEBORN, 6-E4, Albert Lea Rest Area
Minnesota's Highways
The development of Minnesota's roads.

GOODHUE, 17-B3, Highway 19, Cannon Falls
William Colville Monument
Hero of the Battle of Gettysburg.

GOODHUE, 17-D5, Highway 52
Zumbrota
History of the town and its covered bridge.

GOODHUE, 17-E5, Highway 52
Gold Discovery
1858 discovery of gold. Located in county park.

GOODHUE, 18-A1, Highway 61, Red Wing
William Colville
Hero at the Battle of Gettysburg. Located in city
park.

GOODHUE, 18-A1, Red Wing
Red Wing Region
Geological history of the area.

GOODHUE, 18-A3, Highway 61
Fort Beaubarnois
1727 location of French fort and mission.
Located in state park.

HENNEPIN, 26-C2, Mound
Lake Minnetonka
History of lake and map.

HENNEPIN, 26-C5, Lake Harriet/Minneapolis
Como-Harriet Trolley Line
History of the Twin Cities trolley line. Trolley
in service.

HENNEPIN, 26-C5, Minneapolis
Ard Godfrey House
Home of early St. Anthony pioneer. Open to
public.

HENNEPIN, 26-C5, Minneapolis
Father Louis Hennepin's Exploration in 1860
The history of Father Hennepin's visit to
Minnesota.

HENNEPIN, 26-C5, Minneapolis
Lake Harriet Region
Geological history of the area.

HENNEPIN, 26-C5, Minneapolis
Minnehaha Depot
1870 railroad depot. Open Sundays.

HENNEPIN, 26-C5, Minneapolis
Nicollet Baseball Park
Home of the Minneapolis Millers Triple A
baseball team.

HENNEPIN, 26-D2, County Road 19, Excelsior
Peter M. Gideon and the Wealthy Apple
Development of the Wealthy Apple, a well-
known apple variety.

HENNEPIN, 26-D2, Highway 7, Excelsior
Lake Minnetonka Region
Geological history of the area.

HENNEPIN, 26-D3, Highway 169, Eden
Prairie
Minnesota Valley
Geological history of the valley.

HENNEPIN, 26-G5, Minneapolis
Minnehaha Falls
Geological history of the falls.

JACKSON, 3-E5, Jackson
Jackson Monument
Casualties of the 1862 Sioux Uprising. Picnic
area.

KANDIYOHI, 23-A5, North of Highway 12,
Willmar
Guri Endreson Rosseland Monument
Heroine of the 1862 Sioux Uprising.

KANDIYOHI, 23-A5, Willmar
Willmar Area
Geological history of the area.

KANDIYOHI, 32-E1, Highway 23, New
London
Lundborg-Broberg Monument
Casualties of the Sioux Uprising.

KOOCHICHING, 95-F3, Highway 71,
International Falls
Route of the Voyageurs
History of the voyageurs.

LAKE OF THE WOODS, 93-E4, Highway 72,
Baudette
Great Fire of 1910
Baudette was destroyed by a forest fire in 1910.
Located in city park.

LAKE OF THE WOODS, 93-E4, Highway 72,
Baudette
Massacre Island
Site of 1732 massacre on Lake of the Woods.

LAKE OF THE WOODS, 97-D2, Magnuson
Island
Pierre Gaultier de Varennes, Sieur de la
Verendrye
History of this early French explorer.

LAKE OF THE WOODS, 93-E4, Baudette
1910 Fire Victims
Burial place of victims of 1910 forest fire.

LAKE, 62-C4, Highway 61, Gooseberry State
Park
Gooseberry Park Region
Geological history of the area.

LAKE, 62-C5, Highway 61, Split Rock State
Park
Split Rock Region
Geological history of the area.

LAKE, 62-E3, Highway 61
Buchanan
Ghost town location, named for President
Buchanan.

LE SUEUR, 15-D5, County Road 15
Geldner Sawmill & Big Woods
Restored steam-driven sawmill; history of
Minnesota's vegetation at the time of
the first settlers. Open to public.

LE SUEUR, 15-B5, Highway 169
Le Sueur
Town named for Pierre Charles Le Sueur, the
French explorer.

LE SUEUR, 15-B5, Le Sueur
Dr. William W. Mayo House
The 1859 home of the founder of the Mayo
Clinic. Open to public.

LYON, 12-A2, Minneota
The First Settlement of Icelanders in Minnesota
Settlement of area by immigrants from Iceland.

MAHNOMEN, 55-B4, White Earth Indian
Reservation
St. Columba Mission
History of the mission and the first Indian
ordained by the Episcopal Church.

MARTIN, 4-E5, Fairmont
Fort Fairmont
1863 fortification during the Sioux Uprising.

MCLEOD, 25-D1, Hutchinson
Hutchinson Stockade
1862 fortification during the Sioux Uprising.

MCLEOD, 25-E3, Highway 212
Glencoe Fort
1862 fort established because of the Sioux
Uprising.

MEEKER, 24-A4, County Road 58, Litchfield
Ness Lutheran Cemetery Monument
First casualties of the 1862 Sioux Uprising.

MEEKER, 24-A4, County Road 58, Litchfield
Ness Lutheran Church and Cemetery.
Historic church and cemetery of the 1870s.

MEEKER, 24-A4, Highway 4 and 12
The Acton Incident
The start of the 1862 Sioux Uprising.

MEEKER, 24-A4, Litchfield
G.A.R. Hall
1883 Grand Army of the Republic Hall.
Museum and park.

MEEKER, 32-G3, Highway 4, Grove City
Acton Monument
Site of the start of the 1862 Sioux Uprising.

MILLE LACS, 42-B1, Highway 169, Vineland
Battle of Kathio
Historic battle between the Dakota and
Chippewa Indians. Interpretive center.

MILLE LACS, 42-C2, Highway 169
Izatys
1679 location of Dakota Indian village.

MORRISON, 41-C1, Highway 371
Old Crow Wing
Site of 1826 trading post and later village.

MORRISON, 41-D1, County Road 52, Little
Falls
Lindbergh House
Boyhood home of Charles Lindbergh Jr. Open
to public.

MURRAY, 12-F4, Lake Shetek State Park
Lake Shetek Monument
Casualties of the Sioux Uprising.

MURRAY, 2-A5, Highway 59
Avoca
This town was established by Irish colonists in 1878.

NICOLLET, 14-B3, Highway 4
Fort Ridgely
Location of 1853 military post. Open to public.

NICOLLET, 15-D4, Highway 169, St. Peter
Traverse des Sioux
Site of 1851 Indian treaty. Picnic area.

NICOLLET, 15-D4, Highway 169, St. Peter
Traverse des Sioux Monument
Historic treaty signing. Picnic area.

NICOLLET, 15-D4, St. Peter
E. St. Julien Cox House
Home of the famous judge and Sioux Uprising hero. Open to public.

NICOLLET, 15-D4, St. Peter
The Asylum for the Dangerously Insane
Site of 1911 hospital for the mentally ill. Museum.

NICOLLET, 15-F4, Highway 14, Mankato
Mankato Region
Geological history of the area.

OLMSTED, 8-A2, County Road D, Rochester
Mayowood
Home of the co-founder of the Mayo Clinic. Open to public.

OLMSTED, 8-A2, Rochester
Geology of Minnesota
Geological history of the area.

OTTER TAIL, 46-D2, Highway 59,
Minnesota Woman
Discovery of prehistoric skeleton. Picnic area.

OTTER TAIL, 47-E1, Highway 78
Craigie Flour Mill
Location of 1872 grist mill.

OTTER TAIL, 47-E1, Highway 108
Leaf City
Historic trading post in 1857, located on the Red River ox cart trail.

OTTER TAIL, 47-E1, Highway 78
Otter Tail City
Fur post and county seat.

OTTER TAIL, 47-G1, Highway 210
Old Clitherall
1865 settlement established by Latter Day Saints.

PINE, 43-B3, Highway 61, Sandstone
Sandstone Fire
This town was destroyed by a forest fire in 1894.

PINE, 43-D1, County Road 26, Brook Park
Brook Park Fire Monument
Victims of the 1894 forest fire.

PINE, 43-D3, Highway 61
Hinckley Fire
This town was destroyed by a forest fire in 1894.

PINE, 43-D3, Highway 48, Hinckley
Hinckley Fire Monument
Victims of the 1894 Hinckley Fire.

PINE, 43-F2, Highway 61
Pine City
History of this city, platted in 1869.

PINE, 43-F2, Highway 61, Pine City
Pokegama Mission
Site of 1836 Protestant mission and school.

POPE, 31-A3, Highway 55, Glenwood
Glenwood Region
Geological history of the area.

POPE, 31-D4, Highway 104
Fort Lake Johanna
Frontier fort during the Sioux Uprising.

RAMSEY, 27-B1, Little Canada
St. John's Church of Little Canada
French-Canadian Settlement in St. Paul.

RAMSEY, 27-B2, White Bear Lake
Fillebrown House
Architecturally significant lake home. Open to public.

RAMSEY, 27-C1, Shepard Road, St. Paul
Fountain Cave
Famous cave in St. Paul.

RAMSEY, 27-C2, Highway 5, Fort Snelling
Historic River Crossing
Historic crossing of the Mississippi between St. Paul and Minneapolis.

RAMSEY, 27-C2, St. Paul
Alexander Ramsey House
Home of Minnesota's first territorial Governor. Open to public.

RAMSEY, 27-C2, St. Paul
Burbank-Livingston-Griggs House
Historic 1862 mansion.

RAMSEY, 27-C2, St. Paul
Carver's Cave
Famous St. Paul cave.

RAMSEY, 27-C2, St. Paul
Early Crossroads
Marks the Red River ox cart trail.

RAMSEY, 27-C2, St. Paul
Fort Snelling
Historic fort of the Northwest Territory. Open to public.

RAMSEY, 27-C2, St. Paul
Indian Mound Park
Geological history of the area.

RAMSEY, 27-C2, St. Paul
Lower Landing
Steamboat landing since 1827.

RAMSEY, 27-C2, St. Paul
Mattock School
1871 limestone school.

RAMSEY, 27-C2, St. Paul
Minnesota Historical Society
Oldest institution in Minnesota. Open to public.

RAMSEY, 27-C2, St. Paul
Old Federal Courts Building
1898 St. Paul landmark. Open to public.

RAMSEY, 27-C2, St. Paul
Old Muskego Church
First church of the Norwegian Lutheran Church.

RAMSEY, 27-C2, St. Paul
Rice Park
Historic park in downtown St. Paul.

RAMSEY, 27-C2, St. Paul
St. Joseph's Academy
Oldest Catholic educational institution in Minnesota, built in 1851.

RAMSEY, 27-C2, St. Paul
The Red River Ox Cart Trail
The trail and history of the Red River Ox Cart Trail.

RAMSEY, 27-D2, Highway 56, South St. Paul
Kaposia Village
Site of Dakota Indian village 1839-1852.

RED LAKE, 67-A1, County Road 11
Old Crossing Memorial Park
Site of 1863 Indian treaty. Picnic area.

REDWOOD, 13-A4, Highway 71
Battle of Birch Coulee
Location of 1862 battle during the Sioux Uprising.

REDWOOD, 13-A4, Highway 19, Redwood Falls
Camp Pope
Headquarters for the Sibley Expedition against the Sioux in 1863.

REDWOOD, 13-A4, Redwood Falls
Redwood Falls Area
Geological history of the area.

RENVILLE, 13-A4, Highway 19
Redwood Ferry
First battle of the 1862 Sioux Uprising.

RENVILLE, 14-A1, Highway 19, Morton
Birch Coulee Monument
Veterans of the Battle of Birch Coulee.

RENVILLE, 14-A1, Morton
Sioux Indian Monument
Indians honored for their service in the 1862 Sioux Uprising.

RENVILLE, 14-B2, Highway 4
Battle of Fort Ridgely
Details of the 1862 attack on the fort.

RENVILLE, 23-E4, County Road 15, Renville
Schwandt Monument
Casualties of the Sioux Uprising.

RENVILLE, 23-F3, Highway 212
Camp Release
Prisoners of the Sioux Uprising were released here in 1862.

RENVILLE/NICOLLET, 14-B3, Fort Ridgely State Park
Chief Mouzoomaunee Monument
Chippewa allies of the Sioux Uprising.

RENVILLE/NICOLLET, 14-B3, Fort Ridgely State Park
Fort Ridgely Monument
Veterans of the Siege of Fort Ridgely.

RENVILLE/NICOLLET, 14-B3, Fort Ridgley State Park
John S. Marsh Monument
Casualties of the 1862 Sioux Uprising.

RENVILLE/NICOLLET, 14-B3, Fort Ridgley State Park
Mrs. Eliza Miller Monument
Heroine of the 1862 Sioux Uprising.

RICE, 16-D5, Faribault
Alexander Faribault House
Early Minnesota fur trader's home. Open to public.

RICE, 16-D5, Faribault
Seabury Divinity School
Historic early seminary.

ROCK, 1-E3, Beaver Creek Rest Area
Sioux Quartzite and Pipestone
Geology of red/pink stone and pipestone found in area and history of their use.

ROSEAU, 92-C4, Highway 11, Warroad
Warroad Fur Post
Site of 1820 fur post.

ROSEAU, 92-C4, Warroad
Fort St. Charles
History of the 1732 French fort. Accessible by boat.

ROSEAU, 92-C4, Warroad
Warroad
History of the name for this city.

SCOTT, 26-E5, Highway 101, Shakopee
Pond Mission
Site of 1847 Presbyterian mission to the Dakota.

SHERBURNE, 33-B2, Highway 10, St. Cloud
First Granite Quarry
Location of the first commercial granite quarry, started in Minnesota in 1868.

SHERBURNE, 34-E2, Highway 10, Elk River
Babcock Memorial
Homesite of Charles M. Babcock, Commissioner of Highways.

SIBLEY, 15-A5, Henderson
Joseph R. Brown Monument
The founder of Henderson.

ST. LOUIS, 52-A4, Duluth
Minnesota's Oldest Concrete Pavement
1909 concrete pavement.

ST. LOUIS, 52-A4, Thompson Hill Information Center
Duluth Harbor
Geological history of the area.

ST. LOUIS, 60-F3, Highway 2
Floodwood
Early history of this city.

ST. LOUIS, 62-G1, Highway 61, French River
Clifton-French River
Early history of the ghost town of Clifton.

ST. LOUIS, 72-B3, Highway 1
Old Vermillion Trail and Winston City
Early historic trail and ghost town.

ST. LOUIS, 72-B4, Highway 1
First Iron Mine
From this pit the first shipment of iron ore was made in 1884.

ST. LOUIS, 72-B4, Highway 53, Cook
Wak-Em-Up Portage
Early portage used by the Indians and fur traders.

ST. LOUIS, 72-E5, Highway 169, Mountain Iron
Mesabi Range Ore Discovery
The discovery of iron ore in Minnesota took place in Mountain Iron in 1890.

ST. LOUIS, 72-E5, Highway 169, Mountain Iron
Mountain Iron Mine
A National Historic Landmark.

ST. LOUIS, 72-F3, Highway 169, Chisholm
Miners Lookout
Mesabi iron ore mine.

ST. LOUIS, 72-G2, Hibbing
Mesabi Region
Geological history of the area.

ST. LOUIS, 73-B3, Highway 169, Soudan
The Soudan Mine
1884 iron mine. Open to public.

ST. LOUIS, 73-B3, Highway 169
Tower
Early history of this Iron Range city.

ST. LOUIS, 73-C5, County Road 21, Babbitt
The First Test Pit on the Mesabi
Site of the first test pit for iron ore on the Mesabi Range.

STEARNS, 33-B1, Highway 52, St. Joseph
St. Joseph Blockhouse
Blockhouse erected in 1862.

STEARNS, 33-B1, Interstate 94, Collegeville
St. John's Abbey
Historic Catholic abbey. Open to public.

STEARNS, 33-E1, Highway 15, Maine Prairie
Maine Prairie Corners
History of the area.

STEARNS, 40-G1, Sauk Centre
Sinclair Lewis Boyhood Home
Boyhood home of author Sinclair Lewis. Open to public.

STEELE, 16-G5, Owatonna
Northwestern Bank of Owatonna
Outstanding bank architecture. Open to public.

TODD, 39-E4, Highway 52, Osakis
Osakis Stage Station
1859 stagecoach stop.

TRAVERSE, 29-B1, Browns Valley
Browns Valley Man
Earliest known inhabitant of Minnesota.

TRAVERSE, 29-B1, Browns Valley
Samuel J. Brown Monument
The Paul Revere of the Northwest frontier. Museum and picnic area.

TRAVERSE, 29-B1, Highway 28, Browns Valley
Continental Divide
Western Minnesota continental watershed.

TRAVERSE, 29-B1, Highway 28, Browns Valley

Wadsworth Trail
Historic trail in western Minnestoa.

WABASHA, 18-B3, Highway 61, Lake City
Birthplace of Water-skiing
Ralph Samuelson invented water-skiing here in 1922.

WABASHA, 18-B3, Highway 61
Maiden Rock
The legend of Winona, a Dakota maiden. Located in park with picnic area.

WABASHA, 18-C5, Highway 61, Wabasha
Lake Pepin
Geological history of the area.

WADENA, 47-E5, Wadena
The Red River Trail
History of the Red River ox cart trail. Located in park.

WASHINGTON, 27-A4, Highway 95
St. Croix Boom Site
Major center for lumbering activities in the last half of the 1800s.

WASHINGTON, 27-B4, Highway 95, Stillwater
Indian Battleground
Site of Indian battle in 1839.

WASHINGTON, 27-B4, Highway 95
Marine Mill
Location of 1857 grist mill.

WASHINGTON, 27-B4, Highway 95, Stillwater
Stillwater Region
Geological history of the area.

WASHINGTON, 27-B4, Highway 95, Stillwater
Tamarack House
Site of first capitol building in Minnesota.

WASHINGTON, 27-B4, Stillwater
Washington County Courthouse
Oldest county courthouse in Minnesota. Open to public.

WASHINGTON, 27-D4, Highway 95, Afton
Bolles Flour Mill
First commercial flour mill in Minnesota established in 1843.

WASHINGTON, 35-G4, Highway 95, Marine on the St. Croix
Marine Sawmill
Location of first commercial sawmill in Minnesota, 1838.

WASHINGTON, 35-G4, Marine on the St. Croix
Marine Mill
Early grist mill on the St. Croix River.

WASHINGTON, 35-G4, Marine on the St. Croix
Marine Township Hall
Historic 1872 town hall and jail. Open to public.

WATONWAN, 14-G5, Madelia
To the Citizenry of Madelia
Commemorates the capture of the Younger gang after the Northfield raid.

WATONWAN, 14-G5, Highway 60, Madelia
Fort Cox
1862 Sioux Uprising fortification.

WILKIN, 45-E2, Highway 75
Fort Abercrombie
Location of the U.S. Army fort in 1857.

WILKIN, 45-G3, Highway 75
Breckenridge
Early history of this city.

WINONA, 10-C2, Dresbach Rest Area
The Fashionable Tour
History of nineteenth-century vacations to Minnesota by upper class.

WINONA, 18-G5, Highway 74, Whitewater State Park

Whitewater State Park
Geological history of the area.

WINONA, 19-G4, Highway 61, Winona
Garvin Heights
History of the city of Winona.

WINONA, 19-G4, Highway 61,
Mississippi River
Geological history of the area.

WINONA, 19-G4, Winona
Julius C. Wilkie
A Mississippi River steamboat. Open to public.

WINONA, 19-G5, Highway 61, Homer
The Bunnell House
1850s home of Willard E. Bunnell. Open to public.

WRIGHT, 25-B2, Highway 12
The Dustin Massacre
Victims of the Sioux Uprising.

YELLOW MEDICINE, 23-E2, Highway 67
Upper (or Yellow Medicine) Sioux Agency
1854 Indian Agency for the Dakota Indians. Located in state park with interpretive center and picnic area.

YELLOW MEDICINE, 23-E1, Granite Falls
Andrew J. Volstead House
Home of the legislator responsible for the establishment of co-ops. Open to public.

YELLOW MEDICINE, 23-F1, Upper Sioux Agency State Park
Agency Homes
Agency personnel's homes. Picnic area.

YELLOW MEDICINE, 23-F1, Upper Sioux Agency State Park
Annuity Center
1859 Indian agency headquarters.

YELLOW MEDICINE, 23-E1, Highway 67, 12 miles east of Granite Falls
Battle of Wood Lake
Location of the final battle of the 1862 Sioux Uprising.

YELLOW MEDICINE, 23-F1, Upper Sioux Agency State Park
Employees' Duplex 1
1859 structure is first duplex built in Minnesota. Interpretive center.

YELLOW MEDICINE, 23-F1, Upper Sioux Agency State Park
Employees' Duplex 2
Employees' home at Upper Sioux Indian Agency.

YELLOW MEDICINE, 23-E1, Granite Falls
Henry Hill 1829-1879
Early settler in Yellow Medicine County. Museum.

YELLOW MEDICINE, 23-F1, Upper Sioux Agency State Park
Manual Labor School
Education center for Indian agency.

YELLOW MEDICINE, 23-F1, Highway 67, Upper Sioux Agency State Park
Mazomani
Historic Dakota Indian Chief. Picnic area.

YELLOW MEDICINE, 23-F1, Highway 67
Wood Lake Monument
Casualties of the 1862 Battle of Wood Lake.

YELLOW MEDICINE, 23-E1, Granite Falls
World's Oldest Rock
Rocks in area are 3.8 billion years old. Museum.

YELLOW MEDICINE, 23-F1, Highway 67, Upper Sioux Agency State Park
Yellow Medicine City
Early county seat of Yellow Medicine County. Museum.

CALENDAR OF EVENTS

Early January
BEMIDJI

Annual Paul Bunyan Sled Dog Races
Two-day race; more than 150 teams from across the U.S., Alaska and Canada compete for prize money in 5 classes and weight pull. Contact: Sled Dog Race Committee, Box 806, Bemidji, MN 56601, (218) 751-3541.

DULUTH

John Beargrease Sled Dog Race
430-mile sled dog race begins in Duluth along the North Shore of Lake Superior, travels to Grand Marais and returns to Duluth. Contact: David Williams, Race Director, Box 635, Grand Marais, MN 55604, (218) 387-1371.

ELY

Annual Ely All-American Championship Sled Dog Races
North America's best dog teams compete. Contact: Stuart J. Osthoff, Ely Chamber of Commerce, 1600 E. Sheridan St., Ely, MN 55731, (218) 365-6123.

FINLAND

John Beargrease Races Celebration
Bonfire, smoosh ski races, volleyball in the snow, snowshoe races, cross-country ski races, sled dog races and games. Contact: Bonnie Ttikkanen, Heart of the Arrowhead Association, P.O. Box 578, Finland, MN 55603, (218) 353-7359.

GRAND MARAIS

Curling Bonspiels
Mixed doubles and men's curling bonspiels. Contact: Bob Spry, Grand Marais Curling Club, Grand Marais, MN 55604, (218) 387-1180.

SHIELDSVILLE

Annual Monster Vigil
On the ice of Lake Mazaska; scheduled appearances by the monster, ice fishing contest, continuous prize drawings, concessions, snowmobile races, softball and more. Contact: Don Burmeister, Chairman, Lake Mazaska Monsters, Inc., Rt. 4, Faribault, MN 55021, (507) 334-9918.

Late January
ST. PAUL

Annual Ski Jumping Tournament
45-meter ski jumping. Contact: Bill Mahre, St. Paul Ski Club, 1737 Clarence St., St. Paul, MN 55109, (612) 455-6634.

ST. PAUL

Winter Carnival
More than 100 indoor/outdoor events include fun fair, softball on ice, ice-fishing contest, sleigh and pony rides, car racing on ice, snow sculptures and four parades. Contact: St. Paul Winter Carnival Association, 339 Bremer Building, St. Paul, MN 55101, (612) 222-4416.

Early February
ELY

Ely to Tower Wilderness Trek and Loppet
Cross-country ski marathon; 48-km trek and 23.5-km loppet along the Taconite Trail; USAA sanctioned, member of Central Marathon Series. Contact: Irene DeLaby, 1600 E. Sheridan St., Ely, MN 55731, (218) 365-5855.

MORA

Vasaloppet Cross Country Ski Race
Includes two separate courses — 32 km and 58 km; USSA sanctioned. Contact: Glen Johnstone, Rt. 1, Box 22, Mora, MN 55051, (612) 679-2500.

Mid February
MINNEAPOLIS

Greater Northwestern Vacation, Camping and Touring Show
Exhibitors of motorhomes, travel trailers, vans, tents, backpacking, canoeing, outfitters, resorts, campgrounds, airlines; Minneapolis Auditorium. Contact: Don Urban, 6700 Penn Ave. S., Minneapolis, MN 55423, (612) 861-4193 or (612) 944-6645.

ST. PAUL

Auto-Rama
Display of custom autos, vans, trucks, cycles, and more. Contact: St. Paul Civic Center Promotions, 143 W. Fourth St., St. Paul, MN 55102, (612) 224-7361.

ST. PAUL

Junior Olympics Ski Jumping Try-outs
14- and 15-year-old ski jumpers compete for an opportunity to participate in National Junior Olympics. Contact: Ken Perry, St. Paul Ski Club, 2081 Richard Ave., White Bear Lake, MN 55110, (612) 639-4545.

Late February
DULUTH

Annual Depot Hobby Fair
Hobbyists and collectors from the Duluth area; features antique dolls, miniatures, model trains and planes, woodcarving and a variety of crafts. Contact: Depot Community Services, 506 W. Michigan St., Duluth, MN 55802, (218) 727-8025.

ST. PAUL

Minnesota State High School Wrestling Tournament
Contact: St. Paul Civic Center, 143 West 4th St., St. Paul, MN 55102, (612) 224-7361.

Early March
BEMIDJI

Minnesota Finlandia Ski Marathon
60-km event; starts and ends at Buena Vista ski ara. Contact: Duane C. Payne, Minnesota Finlandia, Box 771, Bemidji, MN 56601, (218) 751-0041.

ST. PAUL

Minnesota State High School League Hockey Tournament
Contact: St. Paul Civic Center, 143 West 4th St., St. Paul, MN 55102, (612) 224-7361.

Mid March

Northern Lights Juried Art Show
Five-state art show of selected artists; artists are invited to submit artwork to be judged. Contact: Eliza Ellerd, 4935 Johnson Ave., White Bear Lake, MN 55110, (612) 426-5218.

ST. PAUL

St. Patrick's Day Parade
Nation's third-largest St. Patrick's Day celebration; Irish descendents of various clans parade down streets of St. Paul — more than 200,000 participants. Contact: Stewart Loper, 360 Wabasha, St. Paul, MN 55102, (612) 298-1950.

Late March
ST. PAUL

Minnesota State High School League Basketball Tournaments
Boys and girls tournaments. Contact: St. Paul Civic Center, 143 West 4th St., St. Paul, MN 55102, (612) 224-7361.

Early April
MANKATO

Annual Mankato State University Fishing Institute
Features prominent fishing experts and sessions on fishing techniques. Contact: Art Ollrich, (507) 389-6214.

MINNEAPOLIS

Annual Northwest Sportshow
Displays on travel, camping, boating, fishing, held in the Minneapolis Auditorium. Contact: Phil Perkins, Minneapolis, MN 55408, (612) 827-5833.

ROCHESTER

Annual KROC Home and Vacation Show
More than 150 exhibitors show and sell their products at the Olmsted County Fairgrounds. Contact: Rosanne Rybak, KROC Radio, 122 Fourth St. S.W., Rochester, MN 55902, (507) 286-1010.

Late April
MINNEAPOLIS

Annual Minnesota Ironman
Minnesota's largest bicycle tour, 62 or 100 miles from Wirth Park to Delano and back. Contact: American Youth Hostels, 30 S. Ninth St., Minneapolis, MN 55402, (612) 375-1904.

ST. CLOUD

Annual Arts and Crafts Show
More than 70 booths in the Crossroads Center with home made items for sale. Contact: Wanda Koski, Crossroads, 41st and Division St., St. Cloud, MN 56301, (612) 252-2856.

ST. PAUL

Annual Minnesota Quarter Horse Show
Biggest quarter horse show in the state, held at the State Fairgrounds; NRHA reining; free admission. Contact: Minnesota State Fair, St. Paul, MN 55108, (612) 642-2200.

Early May
ST. PAUL

Festival of Nations
More than 55 ethnic groups present food, folk dancing, cultural exhibits, bazaars and art from around the world, at the St. Paul Civic Center. Contact: John Gundale, International Institute, 1694 Como Ave., St. Paul, MN 55108, (612) 647-0191.

ST. PAUL

Northland Antique Toy Show

One of the top 10 toy shows in the U.S.; more than 150 toy dealers from 10 states displaying and selling rare and unusual old toys, held in Dairy Building at the State Fairgrounds. Contact John Moore, 2062 Sloan St., St. Paul, MN 55117, (612) 774-4214.

ST. PAUL

Scottish Country Fair

Highland dancers and pipers come to compete; also features Scottish memorabilia, foods, theater, games arts and crafts; held at Macalester College. Contact: Eunice Sandeen, Macalester College, 1600 Grand Ave., St. Paul, MN 55105, (612) 696-6067.

Mid May

BLUE EARTH

Sytende Mai

Norwegian music, parade, arts and crafts, and dancing. Contact: Jody Holland, 111 N. Main, Blue Earth, MN 56013, (507) 526-2961.

MINNEAPOLIS

Sytende Mai

Celebration on the Nicollet Mall with a parade, music, dancing, arts, crafts and food. Contact: Jim Johnson, Scandia Imports, 40 S. Seventh St., Minneapolis, MN 55402, (612) 339-6339.

MONTICELLO

Annual Sytende Mai

Norwegian dancing, foods and crafts in the 1870 Little Mountain Settlement. Contact: Marion Jameson, Buffalo, MN 55313, (612) 682-3900, ext. 291.

SPRING GROVE

Sytende Mai Fest

A celebration of the Norwegian heritage, with arts festival, folkemarsj trail, music, food, parade and more. Contact: Arnold Munkel, Sytende Mai, Inc., Spring Grove, MN 55974, (507) 498-5269.

STILLWATER

Rivertown Arts Festival

Designer crafts and fine arts by 150 artists who gather at Lowell Park on the St. Croix River to display and sell thei work. Contact: 101 W. Pine, Stillwater, MN 55082, (612) 439-7700.

Late May

PERHAM

Perham Turtle Races

Turtle owners compete in heat races and championship through late August. Contact: Jane Aschnewitz, 155 E. Main St., Perham, MN 56573, (218) 346-7710.

PRINCETON

Rum River Festival

Festival with parade, tournaments, races and fireworks. Contact: Rum River Citizens League, 606 First St., Princeton, MN 55371, (612) 389-4432.

Early June

EDINA

Annual Art Fair

Outdoor show and concessions along 50th and France. Contact: 50th and France Business Association, Box 24122, Edina, MN 55424,

MINNEAPOLIS

University of Minnesota Centennial Showboat

Theater performances aboard a real sternwheel riverboat moored on the Mississippi River; open through August. Contact: Centennial Showboat, 330 21st Ave. S., Minneapolis, MN 55455, (612) 373-2337.

ST. CLOUD

Minnesota State High School Boys Baseball

Tournament

Contact: Minnesota State High School League, Box 672, 2621 Fair Oak Ave., Anoka, MN 55303, (612) 427-5250.

ST. PAUL

Grand Old Days

Grand Avenue festival includes art fair, parade, entertainment, food stands and bike race with national par ticipants. Contact: Irene De Vinny, 2142 St. Anthony Ave., St. Paul, MN 55104, (612) 644-2948.

ST. PAUL

Minnesota Arabian Horse Show

Oldest and largest Arabian horse show in the state; held at the State Fairgrounds Coliseum. Contact: Minnesota State Fair, St. Paul, MN 55108, (612) 642-2200.

ST. PAUL

Minnesota Special Olympics Chapter Games

Athletic competition for mentally retarded children and adults. Contact: Randy Westerham, 625 Fourth Ave. S., 1430, Minneapolis, MN 55415, (612) 333-0999.

STATEWIDE

State Park Open House

Free admission to any of Minnesota's 64 state parks. Contact: DNR Information, 500 Lafayette Rd., St. Paul, MN 55146, (612) 296-4776.

Mid June

DULUTH

Grandma's Marathon

Running marathon which starts at Two Harbors and finishes at Grandma's Saloon and Deli in Duluth; participants from all 50 states. Contact: Scott Keenan, Box 6234, Duluth, MN 55806, (218) 727-0947.

MOUNDSVIEW

Minnesota State Music Festival

Bands from upper Midwest make music during this week- long festival. Contact: Bel Rae Ballroom, Moundsview, MN 55112, (612) 786-4630.

NISSWA

Turtle Races

Bring your own turtle or buy or rent one to race in this annual week of races. Contact: Howard Wallentine, Nisswa, MN 56468, (218) 963-2521.

SOUTH ST. PAUL

Professional (PRCA) Rodeo

Amateur and professional competition among top rodeo cowboys and cowgirls. Contact: Richard Olsen, 217 Livestock Exchange Bldg., South St. Paul, MN 55075, (612) 451-2266.

Late June

ALEXANDRIA

American Legion Baseball Tournament

Eight teams from Minnesota participate. Contact: Lee Backhaus, Box 801, Alexandria, MN 56308, (612) 762-2141.

BARNESVILLE

Clay County Fair

Contact: Bradley Field, Barnesville, MN 56514, (218) 354-2201.

COON RAPIDS

Minnesota Carp Festival

Features carp fishing contest, coloring contest, demonstrations, displays, arts, crafts, games and food; held at the Coon Rapids Dam Regional Park. Contact: Karen Kobey, Coon Rapids Dam Regional Park, 9750 Egret Blvd., Coon Rapids, MN 55433, (612) 757-4700.

DULUTH

Annual Park Point Art Fair

Features 125 exhibitors from eight states; held at the end of Park Point on the shore of Lake

Superior. Contact: Charles Simonette, Park Point Community Club, 2400 Minnesota Ave., Duluth, MN 55802, (218) 624-4481.

WACONIA

Annual Flags Over Minnesota

High school marching band competition with units from several states. Contact: Joan Eder, 24 S. Walnut, Waconia, MN 55387, (612) 442-5211.

Early July

BEMIDJI

Annual Jaycee Water Carnival

Five days of entertainment including water-ski show, fireworks, games, rides and more. Contact: Tom Schwartz, 519 Minnesota Ave., Bemidji, MN 56601, (218) 751-3159.

CANNON FALLS

Cannon Valley Fair

Contact: Kay Gysbers, 205 N. Fourth St., Cannon Falls, MN 55009, (507) 263-4442.

NISSWA

Breezy Point Island Run Sailboard Regatta

Sailboard race with various divisions. Contact: Roger Mondale, Wildblown, 515 Wedgewood Lane, Plymouth, MN 55441, (612) 546-6646.

ST. PAUL

Independence Day

Recreation of a traditional celebration at a frontier military post in the 1820s, at Historic Fort Snelling. Contact: Sandra Ledo, Fort Snelling History Center, St. Paul, MN 55111, (612) 726-1171.

ST. PAUL

Minnesota's Most Spectacular Fireworks

The state's largest, longest and loudest fireworks show; in front of the State Fair Grandstand. Contact: Bob Klepperich, 25 W. Fourth St., St. Paul, MN 55102, (612) 292-7400.

ST. PAUL

Taste of Minnesota

Five-day free festival of food, music and fireworks at the State Capitol grounds. Contact Bob Kren, 445 Minnesota St., St. Paul, MN 55101, (612) 222-5561.

Mid July

BAUDETTE

Lake of the Woods County Fair

Contact: Roger Krause, Rt. 1, Box 275, Baudette, MN 56623, (218) 634-1691.

BLOOMINGTON

Kaiser Roll

A 5-km and 10-km road race for able-bodied, handicapped and visually impared athletes. Contact: Betty Craig, Kaiser Roll Foundation, Box 20181, Bloomington, MN 55420, (612) 830-3581.

CAMBRIDGE

Isanti County Fair

Contact: Shirley M. Eklund, Stanchfield, MN 55080, (612) 689-1456.

ELK RIVER

Sherburne County Fair

Contact: Marge Kampa, 13915-24th Ave. N.W., Elk River, MN 55330, (612) 441-1366.

FERTILE

Polk County Fair

Contact: Reynold Erickson, Box 556, Fertile, MN 56540, (218) 945-6402.

HALLOCK

Kittson County Fair

Contact: Willis Lilliquist, Box 174, Kennedy, MN 56733, (218) 674-4123.

HOPKINS

Raspberry Festival

Nine-day festival with family activities. Contact: Hopkins Raspberry Festival, Hopkins, MN 55343, (612) 935-7688.

ST. JAMES
Watonwan County Fair
Contact: Dale Lange, St. James, MN 56081, (507) 375-4966.

WABASHA
Wabasha County Fair
Contact: Deb Smith, 611 E. Tenth St., Wabasha, MN 55981, (612) 565-4859.

WADENA
Wadena County Fair
Contact: Don Brown, 619 Fourth N.W., Wadena, MN 56482, (218) 631-2953.

WARREN
Marshall County Fair
Contact: Harvey Maruska, Warren, MN 56762.

Late July

ALBERT LEA
Freeborn County Fair
Contact: Howard Recknor, Freeborn County Fair, Hartland, MN 56042, (507) 373-6965.

BLUE EARTH
Faribault County Fair
Contact: Roger Oldfather, Faribault County Fair, Blue Earth, MN 56013.

BRAINERD
Crow Wing County Fair
Contact: Ruth Gilbertson, Rt. 1, Brainerd, MN 56401, (218) 829-8181.

CANBY
Yellow Medicine County Fair
Contact: Harold Pearson, Canby, MN 56220.

GLENWOOD
Glenwood Waterama
Minnesota's second-largest water celebration, held on Lake Minnewaska. Contact: Dee Holstad, Chamber of Commerce, 137 E. Minnesota Ave., Glenwood, MN 56334, (612) 634-3636.

HIBBING
St. Louis County Fair
Contact: Sulo Ojakangos, 515 E. 23rd St., Hibbing, MN 55746, (218) 263-9758.

JACKSON
Jackson County Fair
Contact: Kenneth Bargfrede, Jackson County Fair Association, 305 Second St., Jackson, MN 56143, (507) 847-3891.

LONG PRAIRIE
Todd County Fair
Contact: Richard Brand, Long Prairie, MN 56347.

LUVERNE
Rock County Fair
Contact: Bob Zinnel, W. Hwy. 17, Luverne, MN 56156, (507) 283-9536.

MINNEAPOLIS
Aquatennial
A 10-day civic celebration with more than 250 free entertainment, arts and sporting events. Contact: Fred Dresser, 702 Wayzata Blvd., Minneapolis, MN 55403, (612) 377-4621.

MINNEAPOLIS
Minnesota Orchestra's Viennese Sommerfest
A four-week music festival celebrating the music and culture of Vienna; concerts at Orchestra Hall and food, dancing and displays outside. Contact: Orchestra Hall, 1111 Nicollet Mall, Minneapolis, MN 55403, (612) 371-5656.

MONTGOMERY
Annual Bohemian Kolacky Heritage Days
Four-day celebration of Czechoslavakian-American heritage. Contact: Dr. Geoffrey A. Iverson, Box 46, Montgomery, MN 56069, (612) 364-7424.

PERHAM
East Otter Tail County Fair

Contact: Al Priebe, County Fair Board, Box 152, Perham, MN 56573, (218) 346-4383.

PINE RIVER
Cass County Fair
Contact: Vi Fenton, Star Route, Box 125, Backus, MN 56435.

PIPESTONE
The Song of Hiawatha Pageant
Cast of 200 presents the ''Song of Hiawatha'' pageant in a three-acre natural amphitheater; several weekends. Contact: Song of Hiawatha Pageant, Box 551, Pipestone, MN 56164, (507) 825-3316.

PRESTON
Fillmore County Free Gate Fair
Contact: Leslie Hellickson, Lanesboro, MN 55949, (507) 765-2238.

ROCHESTER
Olmsted County Free Fair
Contact: Ray Aune, 211 N.W. Second St., 1305, Rochester, MN 55901, (507) 289-4182.

ROSEAU
Roseau County Fair
Contact: Yvonne Magnusson, Rt. C., Roseau, MN 56751, (218) 463-2374.

ST. PAUL
Ramsey County Fair
Contact: Frank Young, 2702 Reardon Place, North St. Paul, MN 55109, (612) 777-2330.

SAUK CENTRE
Stearns County Free Gate Fair
Contact: Rictor Schwinghamer, Sauk Centre, MN 56378, (612) 352-6817.

Early August

ARLINGTON
Sibley County Fair
Contact: John Paulmann, Rt. 1, Box 91, Gaylord, MN 55334, (612) 964-5543.

AUSTIN
Mower County Fair
Contact: Ella Lausen, Box 426, Austin, MN 55912, (507) 433-1868.

BAGLEY
Clearwater County Fair
Contact: John Arneson, Shevlin, MN 56676, (218) 785-2229.

BEMIDJI
Beltrami County Fair
Contact: Bill Schulke, Rt. 6, Box 530, Bemidji, MN 56601, (218) 751-2739.

FARMINGTON
Dakota County Fair
Contact: E. W. Ahlberg, Box 73, Farmington, MN 55024, (612) 463-8818.

GLENWOOD
Pope County Fair
Contact: Marjorie Engebretson, Rt. 2, Box 223, Glenwood, MN 56334, (612) 634-4652.

LAKE ELMO
Washington County Fair
Contact: Raymond Swanson, Box F, Lake Elmo, MN 55042, (612) 777-7493.

LITCHFIELD
Meeker County Fair
Contact: Jean Holm, Dassel, MN 55325.

LITTLE FALLS
Morrison County Fair
Contact: Larry Hartwig, Fair Secretary, Rt. 2, Little Falls, MN 56345, (612) 632-5461.

MARSHALL
Annual International Rolle Bolle Tournament
More than 400 participants from several states and Canada test their skills at this traditional Belgian game. Contact: Tom Tourville, Fifth and Main, Marshall, MN 56258, (507) 532-4484.

NEVIS
Minnesota State Chili Cookoff

Winners eligible to participate in International Chili Cookoff. Contact: Crystle Mortensen, Minnesota Chili Cookoff, Box C, Nevis, MN 56467, (218) 652-4201.

NORTHOME
Koochiching County Fair
Contact: Duane Graham, Koochiching County Fair, Northome, MN 56661.

PIPESTONE
Pipestone County Fair
Contact: Willian Thies, Rt. 4, Pipestone, MN 56164, (507) 825-3931.

PRINCETON
Mille Lacs County Fair
Contact: Emma Volker, Rt. 1, Princeton, MN 55371, (612) 389-2518.

PROCTOR
South St. Louis County Fair
Contact: James White, 3912 Maple Grove Rd., Duluth, MN 55810, (218) 729-7080.

ST. PETER
Nicollet County Fair
Contact: Richard B. Johnson, Rt. 1, Box 205, St. Peter, MN 56082, (507) 931-1412.

SAUK RAPIDS
Benton County Fair
Contact: Philip Pederson, Benton County Ag. Society, Box 166, Sauk Rapids, MN 56379, (612) 253-5649.

WACONIA
Carver County Fair
Contact: Janice Albrecht, 5325 County Road 10 N., Watertown, MN 55388, (612) 442-2333.

WEST CONCORD
Annual Berne Swiss Fest
Festival with Swiss foods, imports, programs, games, yodeling and music concerts. Contact: Alice Agerter, Box 36, West Concord, MN 55985, (507)527-2730.

WILLMAR
Kandiyohi County Fair
Contact: Maggie Schwingler, Rt. 2, Atwater, MN 56209, (612) 974-8431.

WINDOM
Cottonwood County Fair
Contact: Herman Vossen, Rt. 2, Windom, MN 56101, (507) 831-2134.

Mid August

ALEXANDRIA
Douglas County Fair
Contact: Harold Johnson, 827 Westwood Drive, Alexandria, MN 56301, (612) 763-3755.

BARNUM
Carlton County Fair
Contact: Faye Hurst, Barnum, MN 55707.

CALEDONIA
Houston County Fair
Contact: Paul Plager, Caledonia, MN 55921.

FAIRMONT
Martin County Fair
Contact: Marland Austin, Rt. 3, Box 21, Fairmont, MN 56031, (507) 235-9576.

GARDEN CITY
Blue Earth County Fair
Contact: Richard Keenan, Rt. 4, Box 215, Mankato, MN 56001, (507) 625-7595.

GRAND MARAIS
Cook County Fair
Contact: Eleanor Waha, Star Rt. 3, Box 592, Grand Marais, MN 55604, (218) 387-2271.

GRAND RAPIDS
Itasca County Fair
Contact: James E. Johnson, 3652 Hwy. 2E, Grand Rapids, MN 55744, (218) 326-6270.

LE CENTER
LeSueur County Fair
Contact: Russell Baker, Box 124, 341 W. Sharon, Le Center, MN 56057.

OWATONNA
Steele County Fair
Contact: Dr. Louis Allgeyer, Box 650,
Owatonna, MN 55060, (507) 451-5305.

WORTHINGTON
Nobles County Fair
Contact: Dennis Selberg, Rt. 2, Box 247,
Worthington, MN 56187, (507) 376-5391.

Late August
BIRD ISLAND
Renville County Fair
Contact: Inez Kienholz, Box 148, Bird Island,
MN 55310, (612) 365-4585.

ST. PAUL
Minnesota State Fair
Contact: Jerry Hammer, State Fairgrounds,
St. Paul, MN 55108, (612) 642-2251.

SHAKOPEE
Minnesota Renaissance Festival
16th-century village setting with artisans,
performers, food and games for six weekends
in August and September. Contact: Marilyn
Ruedy, 3525-145th St. W., Shakopee, MN
55379, (612) 445-7361.

Early September
FALCON HEIGHTS
Labor Day Weekend Family Picnic
Gibbs Farm Museum open for tours and
picnics on the grounds. Contact: Kendra
Dillard, Gibbs Farm Museum, 2097 W.
Larpenteur, Falcon Heights, MN 55113, (612)
646-8629.

MINNEAPOLIS
Minnesota Jam to Preserve the Arts
A marathon of arts activities for all ages,
including singers, actors, poets, dancers,
painters, weavers, jugglers and more, at the
Minneapolis Auditorium. Contact: Marion
Angelica, Metropolitan Regional Arts
Council, 300 Metro Square Building, St.
Paul, MN 55101, (612) 291-6571.

MINNEAPOLIS
Tri-State 300 Bicycle Challenge
300-mile, three-day bicycle ride through

Minnesota, Wisconsin and Iowa. Contact:
Bonnie Hanlon, American Lung Association,
1829 Portland Ave., Minneapolis, MN 55404,
(612) 871-7332.

NORTHFIELD
Defeat of Jesse James Days
Four-day event celebrating the defeat of Jesse
James' bank robbery attempt with
reenactments, parade, rodeo, music and art
fair. Contact: Northfield Chamber of
Commerce, Jesse James Days, 22 Bridge
Square, Box 198, Northfield, MN 55057,
(507) 645-5604.

ST. CHARLES
Whitewater Marathon
26.2-mile race through Whitewater State Park
and Wildlife Management Area. Contact:
Chris Carl, St. Charles Chamber of
Commerce, P.O. Box 558, St. Charles, MN
55972, (507) 932-5538.

Late September
BLOOMINGTON
Minnesota Germanfest
An authentic German festival featuring
dancers, bands and choirs from throughout the
U.S. and Germany. Food and activities for
children. Adjacent to Met Center. Contact:
Mindy Erickson, Minnesota Germanfest
Association, Inc., Box 300, 1600 Arboretum
Blvd., Victoria, MN 55386, (612) 443-2620.

BRAINERD
Paul Bunyan Festival
Bike, running and hot air balloon races,
shows, music and more, at Brainerd
International Raceway. Contact: Area
Chamber of Commerce, 6th and Washington
Sts., Brainerd, MN 56401, (218) 829-0097.

MINNEAPOLIS/ST. PAUL
The Twin Cities Marathon
About 8,000 runners, including national-class
athletes, race throughout the Twin Cities for a
$150,000 purse. Contact: Jack Moran, Box
24193, Minneapolis, MN 55424, (612)
373-2165.

Early October
NEW ULM
Oktoberfest
A three-day festival with German food, crafts
and enter tainment, at the Holiday Inn, New
Ulm. Contact: Cameron Johnson, Holiday
Inn-New Ulm, 2101 S. Broadway, New Ulm,
MN 56073, (507) 359-2941.

Mid October
ST. CLOUD
Downtown St. Cloud's Annual Octoberfest
Special events including apple strudel-baking
contest, German folk dancers, music and food
stands on the Mall Germain. Contact: Mary
Stevens, Downtown Association, P.O. Box
535, St. Cloud, MN 56302, (612) 251-2940.

Early November
RED WING
Annual Craft Fair
Arts and crafts at the St. James Hotel.
Contact: Merchants' Promotion Director,
Merchants' Association, 406 Main St., St.
James Hotel, Red Wing, MN 55066, (612)
388-2846, or Twin Cities toll-free (800)
227-1800.

Mid November
ST. PAUL
Annual Holiday Arts and Craft Show
St. Paul Civic Center Arena. Contact: Civic
Center Arena, 143 West 4th St., St. Paul, MN
55102, (612) 224-7631.

Early December
ST. PAUL
Great American Train Show
10,000 manned and operated miniature trains
on display, sale and swap, workshops and
movies, at the St. Paul Civic Center. Contact:
St. Paul Civic Center, 143 W. 4th St., St.
Paul, MN 55102, (612) 224-7361.

MINNESOTA TRAVEL INFORMATION

Minnesota Travel Information Center

240 Bremer Building
419 N. Robert St.
St. Paul, MN 55101
(612) 296-5029
(800) 652-9747 toll-free in Minnesota
(800) 328-1461 toll-free in continental U.S.

Statewide fall color or snow conditions:
(612) 296-5029 in Twin Cities
(800) 652-9747 toll-free in Minnesota
(800) 328-1461 toll-free in continental U.S.
Statewide road conditions: (612) 296-3076

CITY, COUNTY & CIVIC CAMPGROUNDS

ADRIAN
Adrian Community Recreation Area
(507) 483-2820
Fee: Yes
Res: Yes

ANNANDALE
Schroeder County Park
(612) 274-8870
Fee: Yes
Res: Yes

ATWATER
Kandiyohi County Park
(612) 974-8520
Fee: Yes
Res: No

BAGLEY
Bagley Municipal Park
(218) 694-2865
Fee: Yes
Res: No

BAGLEY
Clearwater County Long Lake Park
(218) 694-6183
Fee: Yes
Res: No

BLUE EARTH
Blue Earth Fairgrounds Park
(507) 526-2916
Fee: No
Res: No

BROWNS VALLEY
Browns Valley City Park
(612) 695-2110
Fee: No
Res: Yes

BROWNS VALLEY
Traverse County Public Park
(612) 563-4242
Fee: No
Res: No

BUTTERFIELD
Voss Park Campground
(507) 956-2241
Fee: Yes
Res: Yes

CLOQUET
Spafford park
(218) 879-3347
Fee: Yes
Res: No

CROOKSTON
Crookston Central Park
No phone
Fee: Yes
Res: No

CROOKSTON
Roholt Park
No phone
Fee: Yes
Res: No

CROSBY
Crosby Memorial Park
No phone
Fee: Yes
Res: No

DETROIT LAKES
American Legion Campground
(218) 847-3759
Fee: Yes
Res: Yes

DULUTH
Indian Point Campground
(218) 624-5637
Fee: Yes
Res: Yes

FAIRFAX
Franklin CS Park
No phone
Fee: No
Res: No

FERGUS FALLS
De Lagoon Park & Campground
(218) 739-3205
Fee: Yes
Res: Yes

FOSSTON
Fosston Campsite
(218) 435-1959
Fee: Yes
Res: Yes

GLENWOOD
Chalet Campsite
(612) 634-3282
Fee: Yes
Res: No

GRAND MARAIS
Grand Marais Recreation Area
(218) 387-1712
Fee: Yes
Res: No

GRANITE FALLS
Memorial Park
(612) 564-2432
Fee: Yes
Res: No

HALLOCK
Gilbert Olson Park
(218) 843-2737
Fee: Yes
Res: No

HALLOCK
Hallock Horseshoe Park
(218) 843-2737
Fee: Yes
Res: No

HERMAN
Niemackl Lake Park
No phone
Fee: Yes
Res: No

HILL CITY
Hill City Park
No phone
Fee: Yes
Res: No

HOYT LAKES
Fisherman's Point
(218) 225-2344
Fee: Yes
Res: Yes

IVANHOE
Lake Hendricks Park
(507) 275-3323
Fee: Yes
Res: No

JACKSON
Brown Campground
(507) 847-2240
Fee: Yes
Res: No

KELLIHER
Paul Bunyan Memorial Park
No phone
Fee: Yes
Res: No

LANCASTER
Lancaster Roadside Park
(218) 762-4090
Fee: No
Res: No

LITTLEFORK
Lofgren Park
(218) 278-4262
Fee: Yes
Res: Yes

MELROSE
Sauk River Campsite
(612) 256-3659
Fee: Yes
Res: No

MENAHGA
Menahga Memorial Forest Park
(218) 564-4557
Fee: Yes
Res: No

MINNEAPOLIS
Baker Park Reserve
(612) 479-2258
Fee: Yes
Res: Yes

MONTEVIDEO
Lagoon Park
(612) 269-6575
Fee: Yes
Res: No

MOOSEHEAD LAKE
Moose Lake City Park
(218) 485-4010
Fee: Yes
Res: No

PELICAN RAPIDS
Sherin Memorial Park
(218) 863-6571
Fee: Yes
Res: No

ROCHESTER
Oronoco County Park
(507) 367-4526
Fee: Yes
Res: No

ROCHESTER
Oxbow County Park
(507) 775-2451
Fee: Yes
Res: No

ROSEAU
Roseau Tent & Trailer Park
No phone
Fee: Yes
Res: No

SEBEKA
Sebeka Village Park
No phone
Fee: Yes
Res: No

SLEEPY EYE
Sportman's Park
(507) 794-3731
Fee: Yes
Res: No

ST. HILAIRE
St. Hilaire Village Park
(218) 964-5257
Fee: Yes
Res: Yes

THIEF RIVER FALLS
Riverside Park
No phone
Fee: Yes
Res: No

TOWER
Hoodoo Point Campground
(218) 753-6868
Fee: Yes
Res: Yes

WADENA
Sunnybrook Park
(218) 631-2884
Fee: Yes
Res: Yes

WARROAD
Warroad Municipal Park
(218) 386-1454
Fee: Yes
Res: Yes

WORTHINGTON
Olson Park
No phone
Fee: Yes
Res: No

CORPS OF ENGINEERS CAMPGROUNDS

The U.S. Army Corps of Engineers maintains six year-round recreation areas in Minnesota. No reservations are accepted at these campgrounds.

BRAINERD
Cross Lake Recreation Area
(218) 692-4488
Fee: Yes

BRAINERD
Gull Lake Recreation Area
(218) 829-3334
Fee: Yes

GRAND RAPIDS
Lake Winnibigoshish Recreation Area
(218) 246-8107
Fee: Yes

GRAND RAPIDS
Leech Lake Recreation Area
(218) 654-3145
Fee: Yes

GRAND RAPIDS
Pokegama Recreation Area
(218) 326-6128
Fee: Yes

MCGREGOR
Sandy Lake Recreation Area
(218) 426-3482
Fee: Yes

NATIONAL PARK CAMPGROUNDS

Voyageurs National Park, the only national park in Minnesota, sits on the border between the United States and Canada east of International Falls. The park is one of the nation's largest unaltered wilderness areas, with 30 lakes, 1,600 islands, interconnected waterways and conifer forests. Many areas are accessible only by boat. The park maintains approximately 100 primitive campsites. Camping also is allowed at undeveloped sites. No entry permit is required, and no reservations are accepted at campgrounds.

NATIONAL PARKS - No Reservations

VOYAGEUR NATIONAL PARK
(218) 283-9821
CRANE LAKE
Voyageurs One
Fee: No

CRANE LAKE
Voyageurs Two
Fee: No

NATIONAL FOREST CAMPGROUNDS

The U.S. Forest Service manages two national forests in Minnesota. Superior and Chippewa National Forests, located in northern Minnesota, encompass three million acres of forest, lakes, streams, bogs and marshes. Campsites are available throughout the forests.

NATIONAL FORESTS - No Reservations

CHIPPEWA NATIONAL FOREST
BENA
Richards Townsite
(218) 335-2283
Fee: No

BENA
Six Mile
(218) 246-2123
Fee: Yes

BENA
Tamarack Point
(218) 246-2123
Fee: No

BLACKDUCK
Webster Lake
(218) 835-4291
Fee: Yes

CASS LAKE
Cass Lake Campground
(218) 335-2283
Fee: No

CASS LAKE
Knutson Dam
(218) 335-2283
Fee: Yes

CASS LAKE
Norway Beach
(218) 335-2283
Fee: Yes

CASS LAKE
Ojibway
(218) 335-2283
Fee: No

CASS LAKE
South Pike Bay
(218) 335-2283
Fee: No

CASS LAKE
Wanaki
(218) 335-2283
Fee: No

CASS LAKE
Winnie
(218) 335-2283
Fee: Yes

DEER RIVER
Deer Lake
(218) 246-2123
Fee: No

DEER RIVER
East Seelye Bay
(216) 246-2123
Fee: No

DEER RIVER
Fur Farm Overflow
(218) 246-2123
Fee: Yes

DEER RIVER
Mosomo Point
(218) 246-2123
Fee: No

DEER RIVER
O-Ne-Gum-E
(218) 246-2123
Fee: No

DEER RIVER
Plug Hat Point
(218) 246-2123
Fee: Yes

DEER RIVER
West Seelye
(218) 246-2123
Fee: Yes

DEER RIVER
West Seelye Overflow
(218) 246-2123
Fee: Yes

DEER RIVER
Wiliams Narrows
(218) 246-2123
Fee: No

MARCELL
Clubhouse Lake
(218) 832-3161
Fee: No

MARCELL
Northstar
(218) 832-3161
Fee: No

REMER
Mabel Lake
(218) 547-1044
Fee: No

WALKER
Horseshoe Bay
(218) 547-1044
Fee: Yes

WALKER
Stony Point
(218) 547-1047
Fee: No

WIRT
Noma Lake
(218) 835-4291
Fee: Yes

SUPERIOR NATIONAL FOREST
BRIMSON
Cadotte Lake
(218) 229-3371
Fee: Yes

BUYCK
Lake Jeanette
(218) 666-5251
Fee: Yes

ELY
Birch Lake
(218) 365-6185
Fee: Yes

ELY
Fall Lake - North Loop
(218) 365-6185
Fee: Yes

ELY
Fall Lake - South Loop
(218) 365-6185
Fee: Yes

ELY
Fall Lake - West Loop
(218) 365-6185
Fee: Yes

ELY
Fenske Lake
(218) 365-6185
Fee: Yes

ELY
South Kawishiwi
(218) 365-6185
Fee: Yes

GRAND MARAIS
Devie Track Lake
(218) 387-1750
Fee: Yes

GRAND MARAIS
East Bearskin Lake
(218) 387-1750
Fee: Yes

GRAND MARAIS
Flour Lake
(218) 387-1750
Fee: Yes

GRAND MARAIS
Iron Lake
(218) 387-1750
Fee: Yes

GRAND MARAIS
Kimball Lake
(218) 387-1750
Fee: Yes

GRAND MARAIS
Trails End
(218) 387-1750
Fee: Yes

GRAND MARAIS
Two Island Lake
(218) 387-1750
Fee: Yes

ISABELLA
Isabella River
(218) 323-7722
Fee: Yes

ISABELLA
McDougal Lake
(218) 323-7722
Fee: Yes

SCHROEDER
Nine Mile Lake
(218) 663-7981
Fee: Yes

TOFTE
Baker Lake
(218) 663-7981
Fee: Yes

TOFTE
Crescent Lake
(218) 663-7981
Fee: Yes

TOFTE
Kawishiwi Lake
(218) 663-7981
Fee: Yes

TOFTE
Sawbill Lake
(218) 663-7981
Fee: Yes

TOFTE
Temperance River
(218) 663-7981
Fee: Yes

VIRGINIA
Pfeiffer Lake
(218) 741-5736
Fee: Yes

PRIVATE CAMPGROUNDS

(Note: all have fees)

ALEXANDRIA
Berndt's Kamp Kappy
(612) 524-2225
Res: Yes

ALEXANDRIA
Big Horn Bay Resort & Campground
(612) 834-2514
Res: Yes

ALEXANDRIA
Birchwood Park & Campground
(612) 852-7110
Res: Yes

ALEXANDRIA
Broken Arrow Resort
(612) 763-4646
Res: Yes

ALEXANDRIA
Camp Omaha Resort & Campground
(612) 834-2594
Res: Yes

ALEXANDRIA
Cottage Grove Resort & Campground
(612) 762-1336
Res: Yes

ALEXANDRIA
Cozy Nook
(612) 846-3055
Res: Yes

ALEXANDRIA
Hillcrest RV Park & Resort
(612) 763-6330
Res: Yes

ALEXANDRIA
KOA Alexandria
(612) 834-2345
Res: Yes

ALEXANDRIA
Lake Andrew Resort
(612) 763-7366
Res: Yes

ALEXANDRIA
Lucky Acres Campground
(218) 267-2881
Res: Yes

ALEXANDRIA
Mill Lake Resort
(612) 886-5381
Res: Yes

ALEXANDRIA
Sun Valley Resort & Campground
(612) 886-5417
Res: Yes

ALEXANDRIA
Sunset Camping
(612) 763-7606
Res: Yes

ALEXANDRIA
Tamarac Bay Camping Area
(218) 943-5401
Res: Yes

ALEXANDRIA
Wildridge Campground
(612) 886-5370
Res: Yes

ANNANDALE
Clearwater Landing
(612) 274-5291
Res: Yes

ASHBY
Ten Mile Lake Resort

(218) 589-8845
Res: Yes

AUDUBON
Campers' Cove
(218) 439-6837
Res: Yes

AUSTIN
Beaver Trails Campground
(507) 584-6611
Res: Yes

AUSTIN
Nelson's Wheel Estates
(507) 433-3134
Res: Yes

AUSTIN
River Bend Campground
(507) 325-4637
Res: Yes

AVON
El Rancho Manana
(612) 597-2740
Res: Yes

AVON
Pelican Lake Resort
(612) 845-2432
Res: Yes

BACKUS
Lindsey Lake Campground
(218) 947-4728
Res: Yes

BALKUS
Pine Mountain
(218) 947-4730
Res: Yes

BARNUM
Bent Trout Lake Campground
(218) 389-6322
Res: Yes

BARRETT
Redmans Resort & Campground
(612) 528-2598
Res: Yes

BATTLE LAKE
Otter Tail Lake Campground
(218) 864-5848
Res: Yes

BATTLE LAKE
Rossi's Ridge
(218) 864-5001
Res: Yes

BATTLE LAKE
Twin Lake Landing
(218) 495-3447
Res: Yes

BATTLE LAKE
Woodland Beach Resort &
Campground
(218) 864-5851
Res: Yes

BAUDETTE
Adrian's Resort Campground
(218) 634-1985
Res: Yes

BAUDETTE
Bayview Lodge
(218) 634-2194
Res: Yes

BAUDETTE
KOA Lake of the Woods

(218) 634-1694
Res: Yes

BECKER
Riverwood Campland
(612) 261-5268
Res: Yes

BEMIDJI
Balsam Beach Resort Campground
(218) 751-5057
Res: Yes

BEMIDJI
Gull Lake Campground
(218) 586-2842
Res: Yes

BEMIDJI
Hamilton's Campground
(218) 586-2231
Res: Yes

BEMIDJI
KOA Bemidji
(218) 751-1792
Res: Yes

BEMIDJI
Southview Terrace
(218) 751-3328
Res: Yes

BEMIDJI
Stony Point Resort
(218) 335-6311
Res: Yes

BENA
Four Seasons Resort & Trailer Park
(218) 665-2231
Res: Yes

BIG LAKE
Shady River Campground
(612) 263-3705
Res: Yes

BLOOMING PRAIRIE
Brookside Campground
(507) 583-2979
Res: Yes

BRAINERD
Creger's Ojibwa Campground
(218) 963-2576
Res: Yes

BRAINERD
Don & Mayva's Crow Wing
Campground
(218) 829-6468
Res: Yes

BRAINERD
Donneybrook Farm Camping &
Cabin
(218) 829-0788
Res: Yes

BRAINERD
Gull & Love Lake Marina
Campground
(218) 829-8130
Res: Yes

BRAINERD
Little Pine Resort and Campground
(218) 829-3441
Res: Yes

BRAINERD
Shing-Wako Resort & Campground
(218) 765-3226
Res: Yes

BRAINERD
Sullivan's Resort & RV Park
(218) 829-5697
Res: Yes

CALEDONIA
Dunromin' Park
(507) 724-2514
Res: Yes

CAMBRIDGE
Buckhorn Resort
(612) 689-2776
Res: Yes

CANNON FALLS
KOA Cannon Falls
(507) 263-3145
Res: Yes

CASS LAKE
Marclay Point Campground
(218) 335-6589
Res: Yes

CASS LAKE
Ottertail Point Tent & Trailer Camp
(218) 654-5061
Res: Yes

CHISHOLM
Iron Range Campground
(218) 254-3635
Res: Yes

CLEARWATER
A-J Acres Campground
(612) 558-2847
Res: Yes

CLEVELAND
Beaver Dam Resort
(507) 931-5650
Res: Yes

CLOQUET
KOA Cloquet-Duluth
(218) 879-5726
Res: Yes

COKATO
Cokato Lake Country Campground
(612) 286-5779
Res: Yes

COLD SPRING
Larson's Resort & Campground
(612) 685-3377
Res: Yes

COTTONWOOD
Lindsay Mobile Court
(507) 423-6386
Res: Yes

CROMWELL
Island Lake Campground
(218) 644-3543
Res: Yes

DETROIT LAKES
Christian Retreat
(218) 983-3217
Res: Yes

DETROIT LAKES
Hilmer's Haven Resort &
Campground
(218) 847-5851
Res: Yes

DETROIT LAKES
Lake Lind Campground
No phone
Res: Yes

DETROIT LAKES
Little Toad Lake Campground
(218) 334-5742
Res: Yes

DETROIT LAKES
Long Lake Campsite
(218) 847-8920
Res: Yes

DETROIT LAKES
The Village
(218) 847-8923
Res: Yes

DETROIT LAKES
Whaley's Resort & Campsite
(218) 573-3610
Res: Yes

DETROIT LAKES
Woodland Trails Resort &
Campground
(218) 983-3230
Res: Yes

DILWORTH
Dilworth Trailer Park
(218) 287-2504
Res: Yes

DULUTH
Birch Knoll Campground
(218) 496-5722
Res: Yes

DULUTH
Buffalo Valley Camping
(218) 624-7970
Res: Yes

DULUTH
Duluth Tent & Trailer Camp
(218) 525-1350
Res: Yes

DULUTH
Helen's Campground
(218) 834-5044
Res: Yes

DULUTH
Heron Bay Campground
(218) 721-3355
Res: Yes

DULUTH
Skyline Court Motel
(218) 727-1563
Res: Yes

DUQUETTE
Hoffman's Oak Lake Campground &
Resort
(218) 496-5678
Res: Yes

EDEN VALLEY
Brown's Lake Resort
(612) 453-2126
Res: Yes

EFFIE
Hide-Away Campground
(218) 653-2661
Res: Yes

ELK RIVER
Wapiti Park Campground
(612) 441-1396
Res: Yes

ELY
Ojibway Resort & Campground
(218) 365-4106
Res: Yes

ELY
Silver Rapids Lodge
(218) 365-4877
Res: Yes

ELYSIAN
Clarke's Cabins & Campground
(507) 267-4598
Res: Yes

ERSKINE
Lake Shore Camp

(218) 687-2442
Res: Yes

FAIRMONT
Dawson's Lakeside Campground
(507) 235-5753
Res: Yes

Flying Goose Campground
(507) 235-3458
Res: Yes

Four & Ninety Campground
(507) 764-2400
Res: Yes

FAIRMONT
Meyers Campground
(507) 728-8542
Res: Yes

FARIBAULT
Camp Fairbo
(507) 332-8453
Res: Yes

FARIBAULT
Roberd's Lake Resort & Campground
(507) 332-8978
Res: Yes

FARIBAULT
Willing Campground
(507) 685-4240
Res: Yes

FERGUS FALLS
River'N Woods Campground
(218) 739-9927
Res: Yes

FERGUS FALLS
Swan Lake Resort & Campground
(218) 736-4626
Res: Yes

FINLAND
Wildhurst Campground
(218) 353-7337
Res: Yes

GARRISON
Bill's Resort & Campground
(218) 927-3841
Res: Yes

GARRISON
Birchwood Resort & Trailer Court
(612) 692-4312
Res: Yes

GARRISON
Bob's Trailer Park & Camping
(612) 692-4342
Res: Yes

GARRISON
Camp Holiday
(218) 678-2495
Res: Yes

GARRISON
Dalois RV-Camper-Trailer Park
(218) 678-2203
Res: Yes

GARRISON
Pirate's Cove Resort
(612) 532-4421
Res: Yes

GLENWOOD
Green Valley Resort
(612) 634-4010
Res: Yes

GLENWOOD
Inlet Resort Campground
(612) 634-4218
Res: Yes

GLENWOOD
Woodlawn Resort & Campground
(612) 634-3619
Res: Yes

GRAND MARAIS
Gunflint Pines
(218) 388-4454
Res: Yes

GRAND MARAIS
Okontoe Family Campsite
(218) 388-2285
Res: Yes

GRAND MARAIS
The Outpost
(218) 387-1833
Res: Yes

GRAND MARAIS
Voyageur Canoe Outfitter
(218) 388-2224
Res: Yes

GRAND PORTAGE
Hallow Rock Resort
(218) 475-2272
Res: Yes

GRAND RAPIDS
Birch Cove Resort & Campground
(218) 326-8754
Res: Yes

GRAND RAPIDS
Get Together Chalet
(218) 326-4507
Res: Yes

GRAND RAPIDS
Jake & Flossie's Campground
(218) 492-4297
Res: Yes

GRAND RAPIDS
Prairie Lake Campground
(218) 326-8486
Res: Yes

GRAND RAPIDS
Spider Shres Resort
(218) 326-2031
Res: Yes

GREY EAGLE
Big Swan Lake Resort &
Campground
(612) 732-6065
Res: Yes

GREY EAGLE
Ishnala
(612) 285-2525
Res: Yes

HACKENSACK
Abraham's Tent & Trailer Camp
(218) 675-6240
Res: Yes

HACKENSACK
Mascot Resort
(218) 682-2428
Res: Yes

HACKENSACK
Nies' Camsites
(218) 675-6389
Res: Yes

HACKENSACK
Perrault's Tent & Trailor
(218) 682-2628
Res: Yes

HACKENSACK
Wheel In Campground
(218) 675-6319
Res: Yes

HASTINGS
Hastings Mobile Home Terrace
(612) 437-3060
Res: No

HAYWARD
Camp Hiawatha
(507) 373-9794
Res: Yes

HAYWARD
KOA Austin-Albert Lea
(507) 373-5170
Res: Yes

HENNING
Linden Park Resort & Campground
(218) 583-2581
Res: Yes

HENNING
Middle Leaf Resort & Campground
(218) 583-2749
Res: Yes

HILL CITY
Quadna Mountain Resort &
Campground
(218) 697-2324
Res: Yes

HILL CITY
Shorewood Campground
(218) 697-2675
Res: Yes

HINCKLEY
Fleming Campground
(612) 384-7255
Res: Yes

HINCKLEY
Kettle River Camping Park
(612) 384-7387
Res: No

HOUSTON
Money Creek Haven Campground
(507) 896-3544
Res: Yes

INTERNATIONAL FALLS
Birch Point Camp
(218) 286-3414
Res: Yes

INTERNATIONAL FALLS
Mike's Park
(218) 283-3158
Res: Yes

INTERNATIONAL FALLS
Riverside Trailer Court
(218) 283-3474
Res: Yes

ISLE
Orr's Camping
(612) 684-2380
Res: Yes

JACKSON
Jackson Campground
(507) 847-5325
Res: Yes

KELLIHER
Rogers' Campground
(218) 647-8262
Res: Yes

KNIFE RIVER
Big Blaze Camp & Trailer Park
(218) 834-5077
Res: Yes

LAKE BENTON
Hamer's Mobile Estate &
Campground
(507) 368-9574
Res: Yes

LAKE CITY
Lake Pepin Camping & Trailer Park
(612) 345-2909
Res: Yes

LAKE LILLIAN
Tilhenger Campground
(612) 995-6479
Res: No

LESUEUR
Peaceful Valley Campsite
(612) 665-3042
Res: Yes

LINDSTROM
Blue Waters Camping Area
(612) 257-2426
Res: No

LINDSTROM
Whispering Bay Camping Area
(612) 257-1784
Res: Yes

LITTLE FALLS
Fletcher Creek Campground

(612) 632-9868
Res: Yes

LONGVILLE
All Seasons Resort
(218) 363-2030
Res: Yes

LONGVILLE
Austin's Swamp
(218) 363-2610
Res: Yes

LONGVILLE
Girl Lake Resort & Campground
(218) 363-2371
Res: Yes

LONGVILLE
Holiday Haven Resort
(218) 363-2473
Res: Yes

LONGVILLE
Little Boy Resort & Campground
(218) 363-2188
Res: Yes

LUVERNE
Bellman Trailer Park
(507) 283-8119
Res: Yes

MAHNOMEN
Pinehurst Resort & Campground
(218) 935-5745
Res: No

MANKATO
Cedar Grove Campground
(507) 546-3598
Res: Yes

MANKATO
Lone Pine Inn
(507) 243-3874
Res: Yes

MCGREGOR
Aitkin Lake Resort & Campground
(218) 426-3483
Res: Yes

MCGREGOR
Point North
(218) 426-3666
Res: Yes

MERRIFIELD
High View Campground
(218) 543-4526
Res: Yes

MERRIFIELD
Mission Beach Resort & Campground
(218) 765-3447
Res: Yes

MERRIFIELD
Sunset Bay Resort
(218) 765-3442
Res: Yes

MILACA
The Holly Tree
(612) 983-6915
Res: Yes

MINNEAPOLIS
Krestwood Motorhome Park
(612) 881-8218
Res: Yes

MINNEAPOLIS
Lowry Grove
(612) 781-3148
Res: Yes

MINNEAPOLIS
Town & Country Campground
(612) 445-1756
Res: Yes

MONTICELLO
River Terrace Park
(612) 295-2264
Res: Yes

MOORHEAD
KOA Fargo-Moorhead
(218) 233-0671
Res: Yes

MORA
Crow's Nest
(612) 679-4774
Res: Yes

MOTLEY
Auger's Resort
(218) 575-2100
Res: Yes

NEVIS
Campers' Paradise
No phone
Res: Yes

NEVIS
Drayer's Spider Lake Resort
(218) 652-3016
Res: Yes

NEVIS
Hidden Paradise Resort &
Campground
(218) 652-4303
Res: Yes

NIMROD
Gloege's Crow Wing Campground
(218) 472-3250
Res: Yes

NISSWA
Fritz's Resort & Trailer Park
(218) 568-8988
Res: Yes

NISSWA
Upper Cullen Resort & Campground
(218) 963-2249
Res: Yes

NISSWA
Wilderness Point Resort &
Campground
(218) 568-5642
Res: Yes

NORTH BRANCH
Kozy Oaks Kamp
(612) 674-8862
Res: Yes

NORTHOME
Sleepy Hollow Resort
(218) 897-5234
Res: Yes

ORR
Beddow's Campground
(218) 993-2389
Res: Yes

ORR
Pine Acres Resort & Trailer
(218) 757-3144
Res: Yes

ORR
Sunset Resort & Campground
(218) 374-3161
Res: Yes

ORTONVILLE
Rustling Elms Resort
(612) 839-3845
Res: Yes

ORTONVILLE
Sioux Historic Campground
(612) 839-3877
Res: Yes

OSAKIS
Ahlbrecht's Trailer Park &
Campground
(612) 859-2134
Res: Yes

OSAKIS
Black's Crescent Beach Resort
(612) 859-2127
Res: Yes

OSAKIS
Ironwood Resort & Campground
(612) 859-2505
Res: Yes

OSAKIS
Midway Beach Resort

(612) 859-4410
Res: Yes

OSAKIS
Smith Lake Resort & Campground
(612) 859-2501
Res: Yes

OWATONNA
Hope Oak Knoll Campground
(507) 451-2998
Res: Yes

OWATONNA
KOA Owatonna
(507) 451-8050
Res: Yes

PARK RAPIDS
Breeze Campground
(218) 732-5888
Res: Yes

PARK RAPIDS
Jemstar Wilderness Campground
(218) 652-4450
Res: Yes

PARK RAPIDS
Spruce Hill Campground
(218) 732-3292
Res: Yes

PARK RAPIDS
Timberlost Resort & Campgrounds
(218) 652-4365
Res: Yes

PAYNESVILLE
Beachside Trailer Park
(612) 243-4353
Res: Yes

PELICAN RAPIDS
Johnson's Resort & Campground
(218) 863-5456
Res: Yes

PEQUOT LAKES
Hurry's Vi-Lu Resort & RV Park
(218) 568-8811
Res: Yes

PEQUOT LAKES
Tall Timbers Campground
(218) 568-8250
Res: Yes

PERHAM
Jungle Shores
(218) 346-3085
Res: Yes

PERHAM
Rush Lake Tent & Trailer Park
(218) 385-3400
Res: Yes

PINE CITY
Pokegama Creek Campground
(612) 629-6552
Res: Yes

PRESTON
Hidden Valley
(507) 765-2467
Res: Yes

RAY
Cedar Cove Campsites & Resort
(218) 875-3851
Res: Yes

RAY
Pokorny's Resort & Campground
(218) 875-2481
Res: Yes

REMER
Graves Lake Resort & Campground
(218) 566-2362
Res: Yes

REMER
Little Sand
(218) 566-2324
Res: Yes

REMER
McBride's Campground

(218) 566-2851
Res: Yes

RICHMOND
Lakeview Resort
(612) 597-2478
Res: Yes

RICHMOND
Your Haven Resort
(612) 597-2450
Res: Yes

ROCHESTER
KOA Rochester
(507) 288-0785
Res: Yes

ROCHESTER
Van's Trailer Ranch
(507) 282-1414
Res: Yes

ROCHESTER
Wazionja Campground
(507) 356-8594
Res: Yes

ROGERS
KOA Minneapolis NW I-94
(612) 420-2255
Res: Yes

ROUND LAKE
Eastside Acres
(507) 945-8900
Res: Yes

ROUND LAKE
Hilltop Camping
(507) 945-8484
Res: Yes

ROYALTON
Two Rivers Park
(612) 584-5125
Res: Yes

RUSH CITY
Rush Lake Resort & Campground
(612) 358-4427
Res: Yes

SAUK CENTRE
Shady Rest Resort & Campground
(612) 554-2017
Res: Yes

SHAKOPEE
KOA Twins
(612) 492-6440
Res: Yes

SILVER BAY
Barebones Park
(218) 226-4712
Res: No

SLEEPY EYE
Golden Gate to Fun Campground
(507) 794-7459
Res: Yes

SPICER
Riverside Campground & Trailer
Park
(612) 796-5347
Res: Yes

SPICER
Ye Old Mill Inn
(612) 796-2212
Res: Yes

SPRING VALLEY
Five J's Campground
(507) 346-2342
Res: Yes

ST. CHARLES
Lazy D Campground
(507) 932-3098
Res: Yes

ST. CLOUD
KOA Clearwater
(612) 558-2876
Res: Yes

ST. CLOUD
Sherburne Oaks Campground
(612) 261-4252
Res: Yes

ST. PAUL
KOA St. Paul East
(612) 436-6436
Res: Yes

ST. PAUL
Landfall Terrace
(612) 739-8284
Res: No

ST. PAUL
St. Paul Trailer Park
(612) 771-2515
Res: No

STANCHFIELD
Springvale Campground
(612) 689-3208
Res: Yes

STEWARTVILLE
Serendipity Campground
(507) 533-8636
Res: Yes

STURGEON LAKE
Timberline Campground
(218) 372-3272
Res: Yes

TAYLORS FALLS
Wildwood Campground
(612) 465-7161
Res: Yes

TWO HARBORS
Penmarallter Campsite
(218) 834-4603
Res: Yes

TWO HARBORS
Star Harbor Cabins & Camping
(218) 834-3796
Res: Yes

TWO HARBORS
Wagon Wheel Campsite
(218) 834-4901
Res: Yes

UNDERWOOD
Big Island Campsite
(218) 826-6174
Res: Yes

UNDERWOOD
South Turtle Lake Resort
(218) 826-6913
Res: Yes

WABASHA
Big Sioux Campground
(612) 565-4507
Res: Yes

WALKER
Acorn Hill Resort & RV
(218) 547-1015
Res: Yes

WALKER
Agency Bay Resort
(218) 547-9755
Res: Yes

WALKER
Bayview Resort & Campground
(218) 547-1595
Res: Yes

WALKER
Camp at Spring Bay Farm
(218) 652-2597
Res: Yes

WALKER
Shores of Leech Lake RV
Campground
(218) 547-1819
Res: Yes

WALKER
Sun Bay Trailer Park
(218) 547-1555
Res: Yes

WALKER
The Wedgewood Campground
(218) 547-1443
Res: Yes

WALKER
Travel Trailer Terrace
(218) 547-1584
Res: Yes

WALKER
Wolf's Trail-in Resort
(218) 547-1323
Res: Yes

WARROAD
Springsteel Resort
(218) 386-1000
Res: No

WASECA
Kiesler's Clear Lake Campground
(507) 835-3179
Res: Yes

WATERVILLE
Cannon Gate Camp
(507) 362-8832
Res: Yes

WATERVILLE
Kamp Dels
(507) 362-8616
Res: Yes

WILLIAMS
Zippel Bay Resort
(218) 783-6235
Res: Yes

WILLMAR
Point Lake Campground
(612) 235-3315
Res: No

WINONA
KOA Winona
(507) 454-2851
Res: Yes

WINONA
Stockton Valley Camping Area
(507) 689-2654
Res: Yes

WORTHINGTON
East Acres Trailer Park
(507) 376-6919
Res: Yes

ZIMMERMAN
Camp in the Woods
(612) 389-2516
Res: Yes

ZIMMERMAN
Ridgewood Bay Resort
(612) 389-3818
Res: Yes

ZUMBRO FALLS
Bluff Valley Campground
(507) 753-2955
Res: Yes

ZUMBROTA
Shades of Sherwood Campground
(507) 732-7102
Res: Yes

STATE PARK AND RECREATION AREA CAMPGROUNDS

Minnesota has 64 state parks and recreation areas covering about 2000,000 acres. The parks offer campsites, picnic areas, swimming beaches, canoe trails, hiking trails and boat landings. Permits are required for all vehicles entering state parks and recreation areas. An annual permit allows use of all 64 parks for a calendar year, daily permits are also available. Permits can be purchased at any state park and recreation area or at the Minnesota Department of Natural Resources, (612) 296-4776.

ALBERT LEA
Helmer Myre
(507) 373-5084
Fee: Yes
Res: Yes

ALEXANDRIA
Lake Carlos
(612) 852-7200
Fee: Yes
Res: Yes

BEMIDJI
Lake Bemidji
(218) 751-1472
Fee: Yes
Res: Yes

BIGFORK
Scenic
(218) 743-3362
Fee: Yes
Res: No

BIRCHDALE
Franz Jevne
No phone
Fee: Yes
Res: No

BRAINERD
Crow Wing
(218) 829-8022
Fee: Yes
Res: No

CALEDONIA
Beaver Creek Valley
(507) 724-2107
Fee: Yes
Res: No

CARLTON
Jay Cooke
(218) 384-4610
Fee: Yes
Res: Yes

FAIRFAX
Fort Ridgely
(507) 426-7840
Fee: Yes
Res: No

GRAND MARAIS
Cascade River
(218) 387-1543
Fee: Yes
Res: No

GRAND MARAIS
Judge C. R. Magney
(218) 387-2929
Fee: Yes
Res: No

GRAND MARAIS
Temperance River
(218) 663-7476
Fee: Yes
Res: No

GRAND RAPIDS
Schoolcraft
(218) 566-2383
Fee: Yes
Res: No

HIBBING
McCarthy Beach
(218) 254-2411
Fee: Yes
Res: No

HINCKLEY
St. Croix
(612) 384-6591
Fee: Yes
Res: Yes

ISLE
Father Hennepin
(612) 676-8763
Fee: Yes
Res: No

JACKSON
Kilen Woods
(507) 662-6258
Fee: Yes
Res: No

KELLOGG
Carley
(507) 534-3400
Fee: Yes
Res: No

LAKE BRONSON
Lake Bronson
(218) 754-2200
Fee: Yes
Res: No

LAKE CITY
Frontenac
(612) 345-3401
Fee: Yes
Res: No

LE ROY
Lake Louise
(507) 324-5249
Fee: Yes
Res: No

LITTLE FALLS
Charles A. Lindberg
(612) 632-9050
Fee: Yes
Res: No

LUVERNE
Blue Mounds
(507) 283-4892
Fee: Yes
Res: No

MANKATO
Minneopa
(507) 625-4388
Fee: Yes
Res: No

MARSHALL
Camden
(507) 865-4530
Fee: Yes
Res: No

MCGREGOR
Savanna Portage
(218) 426-3271
Fee: Yes
Res: No

MONTEVIDEO
Lac Qui Parle
(612) 752-4736
Fee: Yes
Res: No

MOORHEAD
Buffalo River
(218) 498-2124
Fee: Yes
Res: No

MOOSE LAKE
Moose Lake
(218) 485-4059
Fee: Yes
Res: No

NEW ULM
Flandrau
(507) 354-3519
Fee: Yes
Res: No

NORTH BRANCH
St. Croix Wild River
(612) 583-2125
Fee: Yes
Res: Yes

NORTHFIELD
Nerstrand Woods
(507) 334-8848
Fee: Yes
Res: No

ONAMIA
Mille Lacs Kathio
(612) 532-3523
Fee: Yes
Res: No

ORTONVILLE
Big Stone Lake
(612) 839-3663
Fee: Yes
Res: No

OWATONNA
Rice Lake
(507) 451-7406
Fee: Yes
Res: No

PARK RAPIDS
Itasca
(218) 266-3656
Fee: Yes
Res: Yes

PELICAN RAPIDS
Maplewood
(218) 863-8383
Fee: Yes
Res: No

PIPESTONE
Split Rock Creek
(507) 348-7908
Fee: No
Res: Yes

ROSEAU
Hayes Lake
(218) 425-7504
Fee: Yes
Res: No

SANDSTONE
Banning
(612) 245-2668
Fee: Yes
Res: No

SLAYTON
Lake Shetak
(507) 763-3256
Fee: Yes
Res: No

SPRING VALLEY
Forestville
(507) 352-5111
Fee: Yes
Res: No

ST. CHARLES
Whitewater
(507) 932-3007
Fee: Yes
Res: Yes

STARBUCK
Glacial Lakes
(612) 239-2860
Fee: Yes
Res: No

STILLWATER
William O'Brien
(612) 433-2421
Fee: Yes
Res: Yes

TAYLORS FALLS
Interstate
(612) 465-5711
Fee: Yes
Res: No

TOWER
Bear Head Lake
(218) 365-4253
Fee: Yes
Res: No

TWO HARBORS
Gooseberry Falls
(218) 834-3787
Fee: Yes
Res: Yes

WARREN
Old Mill
(218) 437-8174
Fee: Yes
Res: No

WATERVILLE
Sakatah Lake
(507) 362-4438
Fee: Yes
Res: No

WAUBUN
Little Elbow Lake
(218) 734-2233
Fee: Yes
Res: No

WILLIAMS
Zipple Bay
(218) 783-6252
Fee: Yes
Res: No

WILLMAR
Sibley
(612) 354-2055
Fee: Yes
Res: Yes

WINONA
John A. Latsch
No phone
Fee: Yes
Res: No

WINONA
O.L. Kipp
(507) 643-6849
Fee: Yes
Res: No

STATE FOREST CAMPGROUNDS

Minnesota has 55 state forests covering more than three million acres of land. The forests are used for timber production but are available for camping and other recreational activities. State forest campgrounds offer only primitive campsites designed to furnish basic needs. No reservations are accepted.

BELTRAMI ISLAND STATE FOREST
Warroad
Bemis Hill Campground
(218) 634-2172
Fee: No

Williams
Blueberry Hill
No phone
Fee: No

BIG FORK STATE FOREST
Talmoon
Long Lake
(218) 246-8343
Fee: No

BIRCH LAKE STATE FOREST
Melrose
Birch Lake Campground
(612) 689-2832
Fee: Yes

BOWSTRING STATE FOREST
Deer River
Cottonwood Lake
(218) 246-8343
Fee: Yes

CHENGWATANA STATE FOREST
Pine City
Snake River
(218) 485-4474
Fee: Yes

CLOQUET VALLEY STATE FOREST
Brimson
Cedar Bay
(218) 723-4669
Fee: Yes

Wales
Indian Lake
(218) 723-4669
Fee: Yes

CROW WING STATE FOREST
Crosby
Greer Lake
(218) 828-2565
Fee: Yes

D.A.R. STATE FOREST
Askov
D.A.R. Campground
(218) 485-4474
Fee: Yes

DORER MEMORIAL HARDWOOD FOREST
Wabasha
Kruger Recreation Area
(612) 345-3216
Fee: Yes

(cont. next page)

FINLAND STATE FOREST
Finland
Eckbeck
(218) 723-4669
Fee: Yes

Finland
Finland Campground
(218) 723-4669
Fee: Yes

Two Harbors
Sullivan lake
(218) 723-4669
Fee: Yes

GENERAL ANDREWS STATE FOREST
Willow River
Willow River
(218) 485-4474
Fee: Yes

GEORGE WASHINGTON STATE FOREST
Bigfork
Lost Lake
(218) 262-6760
Fee: Yes

Bigfork
Owen Lake
(218) 262-6760
Fee: Yes

Effie
Larson Lake
(218) 246-8343
Fee: Yes

Hibbing
Beatrice Lake
(218) 262-6760
Fee: Yes

Nashwauk
Bear Lake
(218) 262-6760
Fee: Yes

Togo
Button Box Lake
(218) 246-8343
Fee: Yes

Togo
Thistledew Lake
(218) 246-8343
Fee: Yes

HUNTERSVILLE STATE FOREST
Menahga
Big Bend Landing
(218) 947-3232
Fee: Yes

Menahga
Huntersville Forest Landing
(218) 947-3232
Fee: Yes

Menahga
Shell City Landing
(218) 947-3232
Fee: Yes

KABETOGAMA STATE FOREST
Cook
Wakemeys Bay
(218) 757-3274
Fee: Yes

Coor
Hinsdale Island Campground
(218) 757-3274
Fee: No

Orr
Ash River
(218) 757-3274
Fee: Yes

Orr
Woodenfrog
(218) 757-3272
Fee: Yes

LAND O'LAKES STATE FOREST
Outing
Clint Cenverse Memorial
Campground
(218) 947-3232
Fee: Yes

MOOSE LAKE STATE FOREST
Deer River
Moose Lake Campground
(218) 246-8343
Fee: Yes

NEMADJI STATE FOREST
Nickerson
Gafvert
(218) 485-4474
Fee: Yes

PAUL BUNYAN STATE FOREST
Lake George
Gulch Lakes Recreation Area
(218) 755-2890

Park Rapids
Mantrap Lake
(218) 732-3309
Fee: Yes

PILLSBURY STATE FOREST
Brainerd
Rock Lake
(218) 828-2565
Fee: Yes

SAND DUNES STATE FOREST
Elk River
Ann Lake
(612) 689-2832
Fee: Yes

SAVANNA STATE FOREST
Jacobson
Hay Lake
(218) 697-2476
Fee: Yes

ST. CROIX STATE FOREST
Sandstone
Boneder Campground
(218) 485-4474
Fee: Yes

TWO INLETS STATE FOREST
Park Rapids
Hungry Man Lake
(218) 732-3309
Fee: Yes

WASKISH STATE FOREST
Waskish
Waskish Campground
(218) 835-6684
Fee: Yes

WHITE EARTH STATE FOREST
Park Rapids
Arrow Point
(218) 732-3309
Fee: No

MINNESOTA FISHING

Minnesotans and others fish about 2.6 million acres of water, bringing in 10 million pounds of non-game fish annually. Persons between the ages of 16 and 65 must have appropriate license(s) with them while fishing. Those over the age of 65 need only have proper identification. Resident licenses are issued on a seasonal basis; non-resident licenses are available for the entire season, a week or a day. Additional licenses and stamps may be required for certain kinds of fishing. Licenses are issued by county license agents or by the Department of Natural Resources. Contact them for complete information on special restrictions, current seasons, catch limits and exceptions.

Open Season and Limits

Species	Open Season	Limits
Northern Pike	Saturday nearest May 15 through Feb. 15 of the next year	3
Walleye Pike	Saturday nearest May 15 through Feb. 15 of the next year	6
Muskellunge	Early June through Feb. 15	1
Large- and smallmouth black bass	Early June through Feb. 15	6
Crappies	Continuous	15
Sunfish, Bluegills, Rock and White Bass	Contunious	30
Perch and Bullheads	Continuous	100
Catfish	Continuous	5
Whitefish, rough fish or smelt	Continuous	none
Sturgeon (only from tributaries)	Late June through late Oct. to the St. Croix River	1
Salmon	Continuous	10
Paddlefish	No open season	

RECORD FISH

Record Fish Caught in Minnesota

Walleye Pike ....17 lbs., 8 oz.	Lake Trout ....43 lbs., 8 oz.
Sauger......................................6 lbs., 2 oz.	Perch ....3 lbs., 4 oz.
Muskellunge....................................54 lbs.	Flathead Catfish................................70 lbs.
Northern Pike ....45 lbs., 12 oz.	Channel Catfish ....38 lbs.
Largemouth Bass.........................9 lbs., 4 oz.	Coho Salmon ....10 lbs., 6 oz.
Smallmouth Bass.................................8 lbs.	Chinook Salmon ....25 lbs., 8 oz.
Black Crappie...................................5 lbs.	Pink Salmon ....3 lbs., 14 oz.
Bluegill ....2 lbs., 13 oz.	Atlantic Salmon ....12 lbs., 8 oz.
Brown Trout ....16 lbs., 8 oz.	Shortnose Gar ....4 lbs, 9.6 oz.
Rainbow Trout ....17 lbs., 6 oz.	Green Sunfish ....1 lb., 2.7 oz.
Brook Trout ....6 lbs., 2 oz.	Sturgeon ....91 lbs., 8 oz.

MINNESOTA HUNTING

Small Game Hunting

All persons, age 16 and up, must have licenses to hunt small game in Minnesota. Restrictions apply to those under the age of 16. All non-residents, regardless of age must have appropriate licenses. Licenses are issued by county license agents and the Department of Natural Resources. Contact them for more detailed information as to seasons, catch limits and exceptions.

Open Seasons and Limits
(Shooting times vary)

Species	Open Season	Daily Limit
Mammals including: Cottontail Rabbit	Mid Sept. to late Feb.	10
Jack Rabbit/Snowshoe Hare		20
Gray and Fox Squirrel		7
Non-migratory birds including:		
Ruffed and Spruce Grouse	Mid Sept. to late Dec.	5
Sharp-tailed Grouse	Mid Sept. to late Nov.	3
Hungarian Partridge	Mid Sept. to late Dec.	5
Pheasant	Mid Oct. to early Dec.	2 cocks
Migratory birds including:	Early Sept. to early Nov.	
Woodcock		5
Sora and Virginia Rail		25
Common Snipe		8
Raccoon	Late Oct. to late Dec.	none*
Badger	Late Oct. to late Feb.	none
Red and Gray Fox	Late Oct. to late Feb.	none*
Bobcat	Early Dec. to mid-Jan.	5

* NOTE: Some species have different limits for non-residents.

Waterfowl Hunting

A small game license also entitles the holder to hunt waterfowl. A waterfowl hunter may need additional stamps and/or licenses. Shooting hours for waterfowl are one-half hour before sunrise to late afternoon for the first half of the season; those hours are extended until sunset thereafter. More detailed information is available where licenses are sold.

Open Season and Limits

Species	Open Season	Daily Limit
Ducks	Late Sept. to mid-Nov.	5
Coots and Gallinules	Late Sept. to mid-Nov.	15
Geese	Late Sept. to mid-Nov.	5

Deer Hunting

Deer hunters need licenses regardless of age. Children age 12 and under may not hunt deer. Hunters choose the dates of their season and area when purchasing license. Deer hunting limits are one deer per person per calendar year. Shooting hours are one-half hour before sunrise to sunset. County license agents and the Department of Natural Resources issue deer hunting licenses and have all the necessary information for the season. In general, deer hunting seasons are as follows.

	Season
Regular firearms	Early Nov. to early Dec.
Special Muzzleloader	Late Nov. to early Dec.

Bow Hunting

The season varies by zone. Check DNR.
In general:

Southwest Minnesota	Sept 14–Nov 30.
Northern Minnesota	Sept 14–Dec 8.
Southeastern Minnesota	Sept 14–Dec 31.

CANOE OUTFITTERS

This is a list of full-service outfitters—businesses that offer a full range of services to those taking canoe trips in Minnesota, ranging from complete trip planning to canoe and equipment rental. Available services include route planning and mapping, menu planning and food supplies, canoe and camping equipment rental, and instruction in canoe camping skills. All of the outfitters have brochures and rate information available on request.

Outfitters in the Ely area serve western entry points to the Boundary Waters Canoe Area (BWCA). Those in the Grand Marais and Tofte area, including the Sawbill and Gunflint trails, serve entry points on the eastern side of the BWCA. Crane Lake outfitters serve Voyageurs National Park as well as the BWCA. Other outfitters serve Lake of the Woods and several rivers in northern Minnesota.

CRANE LAKE

ANDERSON OUTFITTERS
Rt. 3, Box 126, Main Road, Crane Lake, MN 55725
(218) 993-2287
Bob Anderson, owner

Complete and partial outfitting for BWCA and Quetico Park. Ultra-light equipment and food. Personalized trip planning with complete instructions for beginners. Overnight accommodations, showers, free parking. Fly-in, and tow service to Lac La Croix (U.S. and Canadian customs available). General store, including bait and tackle. Group rates.

CRANE LAKE BASE CAMP
Rt. 3, Box 122T, Crane Lake, MN 55725
(218) 993-2396
Jeff & Joni Wartchow, owners

Complete and partial outfitting services for BWCA and Quetico canoe trips, boat camping in Voyageurs National Park, fly-in fishing trips. Shuttle and tow service, guide service, modern accommodations, showers, sauna, general store, free parking, trip planning and orientation.

OLSON'S BORDERLAND LODGE AND OUTFITTERS
Box M-89, Crane Lake, MN 55725
(218) 993-2233
Larry & Joan Olson, owners

Complete and partial outfitting for BWCA, Voyageurs National Park, Quetico Park. Overnight accommodations in lodge or cabins with restaurant, grocery store, laundromat, sauna, tackle shop, bait, license, and parking. Tow service and guide service available with personalized trip planning. Father-son camping a specialty.

ELY

BELAND'S WILDERNESS CANOE TRIPS
(218) 365-5811
Don Beland, owner

Complete and partial outfitting for BWCA and Quetico Park. Ultra-light equipment and food. Personalized trip planning. Overnight accommodations, showers, free parking. Fly-in and tow service. Guide service. Bait and tackle. Group rates.

BILL ROM'S CANOE COUNTRY OUTFITTERS
Box 30, 629 E. Sheridan St., Ely, MN 55731
(218) 365-4046
Bob Olson, owner

Complete and partial ultra-lightweight outfitting for BWCA-Quetico Park wilderness. Downtown

Ely base. Moose Lake campground and housekeeping units. Basswood Lake boat fishing trips. Fly-in canoe trips. Motel, bunkhouse, shuttle and tow service, showers, retail store, personalized trip routing. Families, fishermen, organized groups welcome.

BORDER LAKES OUTFITTERS
Box 8, Fall Lake, Winton, MN 55796
(218) 365-3783
Jack Niemi & Bonnie Farkas, owners

Complete and partial outfitting for BWCA and Quetico Park. Quality ultra-light equipment and food. Personalized trip planning. Overnight accommodations, showers, free parking. Outfitting canoeists since 1929. Group rates.

BOUNDARY WATERS CANOE OUTFITTERS
Box 447, 1323 E. Sheridan St., Ely, MN 55731
(218) 365-3201
Marty & Nancy Lakner, owners

Located in downtown Ely, with access to all parts of the BWCA and Quetico Park. Complete and partial outfitting. Ultra-light equipment and food. Personalized trip planning with orientation. Motel, showers, transportation. Fly-in and tow service available. Gift shop and sporting good store includes bait and tackle. Group rates.

CANADIAN BORDER OUTFITTERS
Box 117, Moose Lake, Ely, MN 55731
(218) 365-5847
Tom & Pat Harristhal

Complete or partial outfitting for BWCA or Quetico Park canoe trips from convenient location on Moose Lake. Motel and bunkhouse accommodations, meals, bait & tackle, tow service, van shuttle service, complete routing service, canoe instruction, safe parking. Group rates available.

CANADIAN WATERS 111 E. Sheridan St., Ely, MN 55731
(218) 365-3202
Dan & Jon Waters

Complete and partial outfitting for BWCA and Quetico Park. Deluxe ultra-light equipment (including Old Town canoes) and food. Individual personal trip planning. Complete instructions for beginners. Overnight accommodations, tiled showers, saunas, free parking. Fly-in trips, tow service, transportation. Complete sports store, clothing, tackle, bait, maps. Group rates. Phone collect.

CLIFF WOLD'S CANOE TRIP OUTFITTING CO.
1731 E. Sheridan, Ely, MN 55731 (218) 365-3267

Cliff Wold, Sr., & Cliff Wold, Jr., owners

Complete ultra-lightweight equipment, lightweight Grumman canoes. Special custom-packed lightweight food. Experienced staff to assist in planning and routing. Delivery to all landings. Bunkrooms and campgrounds, saunas and showers. Twenty-four years under same owner and manager. Group rates.

DUANE'S OUTFITTERS
Hwy. 21, Babbitt, MN 55706
(218) 827-2710
Duane Arvola, owner

Complete and partial outfitting for BWCA and Quetico Park. Ultra-light equipment and food. Personalized trip planning with complete instructions for beginners. Overnight accommodations, showers, sauna, free parking. General store, including bait and tackle. Group rates.

KAWISHIWI LODGE AND OUTFITTERS
Box 480, on Lake One, Ely, MN 55731
(218) 365-5487
Frank T. Udovich, owner

Complete and partial outfitting for BWCA starting at Lake One or Snowbank Lake. Regular, light and ultra-light equipment. Personalized trip planning, overnight accommodations, showers, parking. Small store in lodge for groceries, bait and tackle. Video games and pool table in lodge.

NORTH COUNTRY CANOE OUTFITTERS
Star Rt. 1, Box 3000, White Iron Lake, Ely, MN 55731
(218) 365-5581
John Shiefelbein, owner

Complete and partial outfitting. Paddle access to three BWCA entry points from White Iron Lake (six miles from Ely). Use ultra-light food and equipment exclusively. Detailed mapping and training session. Fly-ins, tow services, land transportation, lodging, trading post. Boat and motor wilderness fishing camps. Group and youth discounts. Scouting discount package.

NORTHWIND CANOE OUTFITTERS
Box 690, Fernberg Road, Ely, MN 55731
(218) 365-5489
Joe & Bernie Baltich, owners

Contemporary outfitting in the voyageur tradition. Complete and partial outfitting for BWCA-Quetico Personalized trip planning and routing by professional staff wilderness guides, with complete instructions for beginners. Field-tested, ultra-light equipment, good food. Guide service available, trading post, overnight accommodations, free guarded parking, showers, sauna.

OUTDOOR ADVENTURE CANOE OUTFITTERS

Box 576, on White Iron Lake, Ely, MN 55731
(218) 365-3466
Winters to 5/10: 963 Old Lincoln Hwy.,
Scherervlle, IN 46375
(219) 865-1665
Doug Jordan, owner

Complete and partial outfitting for BWCA and Quetico Park. Ultra-light equipment and food. Guaranteed one to two hours for personal routing before your canoe trip. Transportation to all outlying enty points available. Supper, overnight accommodations, and breakfast free with complete outfitting. Group rates available. Free showers and parking.

PIPESTONE CANOE OUTFITTING CO.

Box 780-EM85, Ely, MN 55731
(218) 365-3788
Jack & Toni Dulinsky, owners

Complete ultra-light outfitting, personalized service into the BWCA and Quetico. Includes: Grumman canoes, Eureka tents, foam pads, fresh laundered sleeping bags, cooking and eating gear, complete food provisions, life preservers and all packsacks. Overnight accommodations, showers, sauna, free parking. Partial outfitting also available. Personalized routing, maps and transportation.

TOM & WOODS' MOOSE LAKE WILDERNESS CANOE TRIPS

Box 358, Ely, MN 55731
(218) 365-5837
Tom Ware & Woods Davis, owners

BWCA and Quetico Park three to 30-day canoe tips. Fly-in, paddle out trips, base camp fishing trips, nature discovery trips. Ultra-light equipment, facilities and service for canoe trips. Group and individual outfitting at reasonable prices. Call collect.

WILDERNESS OUTFITTERS

One E. Camp St., Ely, MN 55731
(218) 365-3211, 365-4785
Jim Pascoe & Rick Nystrom, owners

Complete and partial outfitting for canoe trips in the BWCA, Quetico Park and southern Ontario, Canada. Ultra-lightweight equipment and food packages. Grumman and Alumacraft canoes. Complete instruction and accommodations. Also fly-in Canadian outpost cabins and a remote Canadian fishing resort. Serving the sportsman since 1921.

GRAND MARAIS/TOFTE

BEAR TRACK OUTFITTING CO.

Box 51, Hwy. 61, Grand Marais, MN 55604
(218) 387-1162
David & Cathi Williams, owners

Complete and partial outfitting for BWCA, Quetico Park, and Isle Royale. Ultra-Light equipment and food, Mad River canoes. Solo canoe specialists. Owner-operated with personalized service for beginning to advanced canoeists and backpackers. Overnight accommodations, rustic cabins, sauna, shuttle service. Retail store including bait, tackle. Group rates.

GUNFLINT NORTHWOODS OUTFITTERS

Box 100-GT, Gunflint Trail, Grand Marais, MN 55604 (800) 328-3362 (toll-free in Minnesota); (800) 328-3325 (toll-free outside Minnesota)
Bruce & Sue Kerfoot, owners

Over 50 years experience outfitting for the BWCA and Quetico Park. A full-service outfitter: complete and partial outfitting, trip routing, bunkhouse, cabins, showers, sauna, trading post meals, guide service, group rates. Open May-Oct. Special fall and spring packages.

JOCKO'S CLEARWATER CANOE OUTFITTERS Box 31, Gunflint Trail, Grand Marais, MN 55604 Oct. 1 - May 1: 8624 Kell Ave. S., Bloomington, MN 55437
(218) 388-2254
Lee Nelson, owner

Canoe trips to the BWCA-Quetico Park from a historic log lodge nestled among virgin white pines. Base on Clearwater Lake provides access to a variety of routes and fishing along the Gunflint Trail. Family-owned for 21 years. Service and equipment for complete and partial outfitting. Group rates.

SAGANAGA CANOE OUTFITTERS

Box 148, Gunflint Trail, Grand Marais, MN 55604
(218) 388-2217 Oct. - April: 371 Millwood Ave., St. Paul, MN 55113, (612) 483-2177
Carole & Don Germain, owners

Endmost point beyond northern tip of Gunflint Trail. Immediate BWCA access and nearest outfitter to Canada's Quetico Park. Complete and partial outfitting featuring quality ultra-light equipment, meals, personalized route planning, permits, instruction. Overnight accommodations, showers, free parking. Fly-in and tow service. Boat and motor rentals. Group rates.

SAWBILL CANOE OUTFITTERS

Box 2127, Sawbill Trail, Tofte, MN 55615
(218) 387-1360
William, Frank & Mary Alice Hansen, owners

Serving the ''paddle only'' zone of the BWCA wilderness. More than 25 years of friendly service. Complete or partial outfitting with state-of-the-art lightweight equipment. Personalized menu planning. Route planning. Fishing and canoeing instruction. General store sells tackle, bait, camping accessories, etc. Showers and wood-fired sauna. Free parking.

SUPERIOR NORTH CANOE OUTFITTERS

Box 141-E, Gunflint Trail, Grand Marais, MN 55604
(218) 388-4416; 10/16-4/30: (612) 421-4053
Jerry Mark, owner

Complete and partial outfitting into BWCA and Quetico Park. On Saganaga Lake at end of Gunflint Trail. Canoe, boat/motor, and fly-in packages with quality equipment and food. Personalized trip planning, special help for beginners. Launch service, private bunkhouse accommodations, showers, free parking. Store sells bait, tackle, groceries, gifts. Group rates.

TIP OF THE TRAIL OUTFITTERS

Box 147, Gunflint Trail, Grand Marais, MN 55604
(218) 388-2225
Bill & Sue Douglas, owners

Professional outfitters serving the BWCA and Quetico Park from the end of the Gunflint Trail. Specializing in ultra-light provisions (47-lb. canoe). Thorough trip-planning and instruction. Overnight accommodations, sauna and showers. Tow service, fly-ins. Personal, friendly service.

TUSCARORA CANOE OUTFITTERS

Box 110, Gunflint Trail, Grand Marais, MN 55604
(218) 388-2221
Kerry Leeds, owner

On Round Lake. Complete or partial outfitting for trips into the BWCA and Quetico Park. Large menu selection, expert routing, special attention for beginners, ultra-lightweight equipment. Dining room; store sells groceries, licenses, ice, bait, tackle. Bunkhouses and showers. Group rates.

WAY OF THE WILDERNESS

Box 131, Gunflint Trail, Grand Marais, MN 55604
(218) 388-2212
9/15 - 5/15: 833 Pin Oak Lane, University Park, IL 60466 (312) 534-0557
Bud Darling, owner

Complete and partial outfitting for BWCA and Quetico Park. Ideal circle route location, access to both Seagull and Saganaga lakes. Adjacent to U.S. Forest Service Trails End Campground. Overnight accommodations, hot showers, parking, shuttle service, and general store including: bait, tackle, trail food and camping supplies. Group rates.

WILDERNESS WATERS OUTFITTERS

Box 1007-M, W. Hwy. 61, Grand Marais, MN 55604
(218) 387-2525
Paul Redmond, owner

Located in Grand Marais, serves many BWCA entry points, also Isle Royale backpacking services. Complete and partial outfitting, transportation, ultra-light equipment and food. Personalized trip planning maps, camping supplies and food, tackle. Group discount for parties over seven. Near lodging, restaurants, pool and camping.

LAKE-OF-THE-WOODS
LAKE OF THE WOODS WILDERNESS OUTFITTERS

Box 16, Warroad, MN 56763
(218) 386-1436, 386-1606
Dick & Lynda Myers, owners

Located in the sheltered waters of the 14,000 islands of Lake of the Woods on the Canadian border. Complete or partial outfitting for canoers or boat and motor campers. No portages, no food restrictions. Fresh foods a specialty.

RIVER-BASED OUTFITTERS
HUNTERSVILLE CANOE & HORSEBACK OUTFITTERS

Rt. 4, Box 308, Menahga, MN 56464 (218) 564-4279
Turk & Dorothy Kennelly, owners

Headquarters at historic Huntersville in the middle of Huntersville State Forest. Complete or partial outfitting on the beautiful, Crow Wing and Shell rivers. Instruction available on request. Combination canoe/horseback riding trips. Wrangler/guide included with horses.

IRV FUNK CANOE OUTFITTERS

Rt. 2, Box 51, Sebeka, MN 56477
(218) 472-3272
Marlyn & Grace Horton, owners

Complete or partial outfitting and shuttle service for the 75-mile Crow Wing River Canoe Trail, served by primitive public campsites with well water. No guide necessary; some gentle rapids. Supplies available at four convenient points en route. Day trips, overnighters, or up to five days. Personal service, free parking, map, and basic instruction available.

PAPOOSE BAY LODGE AND OUTFITTERS

Niawa Star Route, Park Rapids, MN 56470
(218) 732-3065
Les Lassila, owner

Canoe outfitters for Mississippi headwaters rivers, ranging from family rivers to whitewater, following the routes of the Indians and fur trappers. No portages. Primitive to deluxe campgrounds, swimming and fishing. Canoes, camping gear, coolers, food, transportation, full resort accommodations, lunches, recreation room, and sauna; store sells bait and maps. Group rates, student discounts.

MINNESOTA SKI AREAS CROSS COUNTRY

Northeast:

Aitken:
Brown Lake Ski Trail
218-927-2102
9.2 km marked and groomed
Long Lake Conservation Center
218-927-2102
9.7 km marked and groomed
North Aitken County Trail
218-927-2102
14.5 km marked and groomed

Big Fork:
Jingo Lake Hunter-Walk Trail
218-832-3161
8.0 km marked and ungroomed
Scenic State Park
218-743-3362
16.9 km marked and groomed
Spur Lake Hunter-Walk Trail
218-832-3161
12.9 km marked and ungroomed

Cambridge:
Isanti Co. Ski Trail
612-689-2680
9.7 km marked and groomed

Carlton:
Jay Cooke State Park
218-384-4610
57.1 km marked and groomed

Cloquet:
Pine Valley Park
218-879-3347
4.0 km marked and groomed

Crane Lake:
Ash River State Forest Ski Trail
218-757-3489
20.1 km marked and groomed
Baylis-Herriman Trail
218-666-5251
14.2 km unmarked and ungroomed
Mukooda Hike-Ski Trail
218-283-9821
12.2 km marked and ungroomed

Cromwell:
Fond Du Lac Ski Trail
218-327-1709
18.2 km marked and groomed

Deer River:
Blueberry Hills Ski Trail
218-246-8195
15.8 km marked and groomed
Cut Foot Sioux Ski Trail
218-246-2123
35.4 marked and ungroomed
Simpson Creek Recreation Area
218-246-2123
24.1 km marked and ungroomed

Duluth:
Chester Municipal Park
218-724-9832
3.1 km marked and groomed
Hartley Ski Trail
218-723-3337
3.7 km marked and groomed
Lester-Amity Ski Trail
218-723-3337
18.0 km marked and groomed
Magney-Snively Ski Trail
218-723-3337
10.0 km marked and groomed
Piedmont Ski Trail
218-723-3337
4.0 km marked and groomed

Spirit Mountain
218-628-2891
20.1 km marked and groomed

Effie:
Thistledew Hike-Ski Trail
218-246-8343
32.3 km marked and ungroomed

Ely:
Angleworm Trail
218-365-6185
15.8 km unmarked and ungroomed
Bass Lake Trail
218-365-6185
8.8 km marked and ungroomed
Big Moose Trail
218-666-5251
2.9 km unmarked and ungroomed
Birch Lake Trail
218-365-6185
4.0 km marked and ungroomed
Hegman Lakes Trail
218-365-6185
6.4 km marked and ungroomed
Hidden Valley Recreation Area
218-365-6123
18.0 km marked and groomed
Northwind Lodge
218-365-5489
8.0 km unmarked and groomed
Norway Trail
218-666-5251
5.6 km unmarked and ungroomed
Secret-Blackstone Trail
218-365-6185
13.4 km marked and groomed
Sioux-Hustler Trail
218-666-5251
43.4 km marked and ungroomed
Slim Lake Trail
218-365-6185
6.4 km unmarked and groomed
Stuart Lake Trail
218-365-6185
12.4 km marked and ungroomed

Finland:
George H. Crosby Manitou State Park
218-226-4492
17.7 km marked and ungroomed

Grand Marais:
Banadad Artery Trail
218-388-2233
40.2 km marked and groomed
Border Route Trail
218-475-2210
61.6 km marked and ungroomed
Cascade River State Park
218-387-1543
27.4 km marked and groomed
Central Gunflint Trail System
218-388-2292
48.3 km marked and groomed
George Washington Pines
218-387-1750
2.4 km unmarked and ungroomed
Gunflint Lake Trail System
218-388-2233
89.9 km marked and groomed
Pincushion Mountain Trail
218-387-2524
14.0 km marked and groomed
Grand Portage National Monument
218-387-2788
13.7 km marked and ungroomed
Grand Portage Trail

218-475-2401
70.8 km marked and groomed

Grand Rapids:
Amen Lake County Trail
218-326-9288
6.4 km marked and groomed
Big Ridge Ski-Hike Trail
218-326-9288
10.0 km marked and groomed
Camp Mishawaka
218-326-5667
14.0 km marked and groomed
Cross River State Wayside
218-663-7476
5.8 km marked and groomed
Golden Anniversary State Forest
218-246-8343
10.5 km marked and groomed
Mount Itasca Ski Trails
218-245-1250
4.8 km marked and groomed
Sugar Hills Lodge Resort
218-326-0535
80.5 km marked and groomed
Suomi Hills Trail
218-832-3161
45.4 km marked and groomed
Wabana County Trail
218-326-9288
9.7 km marked and groomed

Hibbing:
Bennett Municipal Park
218-263-8851
1.6 km marked and groomed
Carey Lake Trails
218-263-8851
5.5 km marked and groomed
McCarthy Beach State Park
218-254-2411
13.5 km marked and groomed
North Dark River Trail
218-741-5736
2.6 km unmarked and ungroomed
Sturgeon River Hike-Ski Trail
218-741-5736
29.9 km marked and groomed

Hill City:
Quadna Mountain Resort
218-697-2324
20.9 km marked and groomed

Hinckley:
St. Croix State Park
612-384-6591
33.8 km marked and groomed

International Falls:
Black Bay Ski Trail
218-283-9821
14.0 km marked and ungroomed

Isabella:
Flathorn-Gegoka Ski Trail
218-323-7676
46.7 km marked and groomed
Hogback Lake Trail
218-323-7722
6.4 km marked and ungroomed

Lutsen:
Deer Yard Lake Trail
218-387-1112
28.8 km marked and groomed
Lutsen Mountains
218-663-7281
48.3 km marked and groomed
North Shore Mountains Trail

218-663-7566
120.7 km marked and groomed

Marcell:
North Star Lake Resort
218-832-3131
4.8 km marked and groomed

McGregor:
Remote Lake Solitude Area
218-426-3271
18.7 km marked and groomed
Savanna Portage State Park
218-426-3271
25.7 km marked and groomed

Moose Lake:
Moose Lake State Recreation Area
218-485-4059
6.4 km marked and groomed

North Branch:
St. Croix Wild River State Park
612-583-2125
72.4 km marked and groomed

Pine City:
Chengwatana State Forest
218-485-4744
11.3 km marked and groomed

Sandstone:
Banning State Park
612-245-2668
16.1 km marked and groomed

Schroeder:
Temperance River State Park
218-663-7476
7.6 km marked and groomed

Silver Bay:
Mariner Mountain Picnic Area
218-226-4214
1.6 km unmarked and ungroomed
Silver Bay/Northwoods Trails
218-226-4436
13.7 km marked and groomed
Tettegouche State Park
218-353-7386
14.5 km marked and ungroomed

Tower:
Bear Head Lake State Park
218-365-4253
23.3 km marked and groomed

Two Harbors:
Gooseberry Falls State Park
218-834-3855
25.7 km marked and groomed
Split Rock Lighthouse State Park
218-226-3065
8.0 km marked and groomed
Two Harbors City Trail
218-834-2689
10.5 km marked and groomed

Virginia:
Big Aspen Trail
218-741-5736
22.5 km marked and groomed
Bird Lake Trail
218-229-3371
16.9 km marked and ungroomed
Giant's Ridge Recreation Area
218-865-4620
40.2 km marked and groomed
Lookout Mountain Ski Trail
218-741-5736
30.6 km marked and groomed

North Central:

Akeley:
Earthome Resort
612-933-8939
11.3 km marked and ungroomed

Bemidji:
Bemidji City Park Trail
218-751-5610
2.1 km marked and groomed
Buena Vista Ski Area
218-751-5530
25.7 km marked and groomed
Carter Lake Trail
218-835-4291
5.5 km marked and ungroomed
Heartland State Trail
218-652-4054
45.1 km marked and ungroomed
Lake Bemidji State Park
218-755-3844
12.9 km marked and groomed
Meadow Lake Trail
218-835-4291
15.3 km marked and ungroomed
Minnesota Finlandia-Movil Maze
218-737-0041
13.7 km marked and ungroomed
Tower Lake Trail
218-335-2283
8.2 km marked and ungroomed
Wolf Lake Resort
218-751-5749
15.9 km marked and groomed

Blackduck:
Camp Rabideau-CCC Trail
218-835-4291
1.6 km marked and ungroomed
Webster Lake Trail
218-335-4291
3.2 km marked and ungroomed

Brainerd:
Acorn Trail
218-829-8770
11.3 km marked and groomed
Crow Wing State Park
218-829-8022
12.6 km unmarked and groomed
French Rapids County Park
218-829-7472
16.1 km marked and groomed
Pine Beach Trail
218-829-5226
24.1 km marked and groomed
Rock Lake Solitude Area
218-828-2565
14.5 km marked and groomed

Cass Lake:
Cass Lake Fitness Trail
218-335-2283
2.4 km marked and ungroomed
Star Island Hiking Trail
218-335-2283
8.8 km marked and ungroomed

Emily:
Washburn Lake Trail
218-947-3232
24.1 km marked and groomed

Hackensack:
Bakker County Trail
612-682-2325
6.0 km marked and groomed
Cut Lake Cross-Country Trail
218-682-2325
16.1 km marked and groomed

Little Falls:
Charles Lindbergh State Park
612-632-9050
8.0 km marked and groomed

Long Prairie:
Eagle Mountain Resort
612-285-4567
9.7 km marked and groomed

Milaca:
Father Hennepin State Park

612-676-8763
4.0 km marked and groomed

Oak Island:
Bonnie Brae Resort
218-386-1894
3.2 km unmarked and ungroomed

Onamia:
Mille Lacs Kathio State Park
612-532-3523
29.0 km marked and groomed

Park Rapids:
Itascatur Trail
218-732-3342
20.9 km marked and groomed
Long Pines Trail
218-732-9680
13.0 km marked and groomed
Papoose Bay Lodge
218-732-3065
3.2 km marked and groomed

Pine River:
Goose Lake Trail
218-682-2325
19.0 marked and groomed
Spider Lake Hike-Ski Trail
218-828-2610
24.1 km marked and groomed

Remer:
Thunder Lake Lodge
218-566-2378
11.3 km marked and groomed

Roseau:
Hayes Lake State Park
218-425-7504
8.0 km marked and groomed

St. Cloud:
Fitzharris/Pirates Cove Ski Trail
612-251-2844
22.5 km marked and groomed
Heritage Park Trail
612-255-7216
4.0 km marked and groomed
Mississippi River County Park
612-255-6172
5.6 km marked and groomed
Riverside Park Trail
612-255-7216
1.9 km marked and groomed
Tokle County Trail
612-255-6172
7.2 km marked and groomed
Whitney Memorial Park
612-255-7216
2.4 km unmarked and ungroomed

Walker:
Borde-du-lac Lodge
218-224-2384
3.2 km marked and groomed
Cedar Springs County Trail
218-682-2325
5.6 km marked and groomed
Cedar Springs Lodge
218-836-2248
4.8 km marked and ungroomed
Co. 50 Hunter-Walk Trail
218-547-1044
11.3 km marked and ungroomed
Deep-Portage Conservation Reserve
218-682-2325
22.5 km marked and groomed
Howard Lake Ski Trail
218-682-2325
4.0 km marked and groomed
North Country National Trail
218-547-1044
95.7 km marked and ungroomed
Shingobee Recreation Area
218-547-1044
9.7 km marked and ungroomed
Tower County Trail
218-682-2325
9.7 km marked and groomed

Williams:
Zippel Bay State Recreation Area

218-755-3976
3.2 km marked and groomed

Zimmerman:
Blue Hill Trail
612-389-3323
8.8 km marked and ungroomed
Mahnomen Trail
612-389-3323
4.8 km marked and ungroomed

Southeast:

Albert Lea:
Helmer Myre State Park
507-373-5084
11.3 km marked and groomed

Austin:
Jay C. Hormel Nature Center
507-437-2162
12.1 km marked and groomed

Caledonia:
Beaver Creek Valley State Park
507-724-2107
4.3 km marked and groomed

Faribault:
Cannon River Wilderness Area
507-334-2281
7.2 km marked and ungroomed
Nerstrand Woods State Park
507-334-8848
12.9 marked and groomed
River Bend Nature Center
507-332-7151
10.0 km unmarked and groomed

Houston:
Oak Ridge Recreation Center
507-523-2183
14.2 km unmarked and ungroomed

Lake City:
Frontenac State Park
612-345-3401
9.7 km marked and groomed
Zumbro Bottoms Trail
612-345-3216
6.4 km unmarked and ungroomed

Owatonna:
Kaplan Woods Municipal Park
507-455-0800
9.7 km marked and groomed
Mineral Springs Municipal Park
507-455-0800
3.7 km marked and groomed
Rice Lake State Park
507-451-7406
5.0 km marked and groomed

Pine Island:
Douglas State Trail
507-285-7176
19.3 km marked and ungroomed

Plainview:
Carley State Park
507-285-7432
5.6 km marked and groomed

Preston:
Forestville State Park
507-352-5111
8.5 km marked and groomed

Red Wing:
Hay Creek Trail
612-345-3216
14.5 km marked and groomed
Memorial Park-Sorin Bluff
612-388-6796
12.1 marked and ungroomed
Mount Frontenac Ski Area
no phone
8,0 km marked and groomed

Rochester:
Oxbow County Park
507-775-2451
6.4 km unmarked and ungroomed
Silver Creek Ski Trail
507-286-9445
5.1 marked and groomed

Spring Valley:
Lake Louise State Park
507-324-5249
3.2 km marked and ungroomed

St. Charles:
Jessen's Park
507-932-3020
2.9 unmarked and ungroomed
Whitewater State Park
507-932-3007
2.1 marked and ungroomed

Stewartville:
Bear Cave County Park
507-285-8231
3.2 km unmarked and ungroomed

Wabasha:
Kruger Recreation Trail
612-345-3216
4.8 marked and ungroomed
Snake Creek Trail
612-345-3216
4.0 km marked and groomed

Waseca:
Courthouse County Park
507-835-5600
4.5 km unmarked and groomed

Winona:
O.L. Kipp State Park
507-643-6849
14.5 km marked and groomed

Twin Cities:

Annandale:
N. Stanley Eddy Memorial County Park
612-682-3900
4.8 km marked and groomed
S. Stanley Eddy Memorial County Park
612-682-3900
1.9 km marked and groomed

Apple Valley:
Minnesota Zoological Gardens
612-432-9010
10.0 km marked and groomed
Valleywood golf Course and Trails
612-423-2171
5.6 km marked and groomed

Belle Plaine:
Lawrence Wayside
612-492-6400
6.4 km marked and groomed

Bloomington:
Girard Lake Municipal Park
612-881-5811
1.8 unmarked and groomed
Hyland-Bush-Anderson Park Reserve
612-941-7993
13.0 km marked and groomed
Mt. Normandale Lake Park
612-881-5811
5.3 km marked and groomed

Burnsville:
Alimagnet Municipal Park
612-890-4100
10.0 km marked and groomed
Civic Center Municipal Park
612-890-4100
2.6 km marked and groomed
Murphy Hanrehan Park Reserve
612-941-7993
15.0 km marked and groomed
Terrace Oaks Trail
612-431-7575
15.0 km marked and groomed

Chanhassen:
City of Chanhassen Trail
612-937-1900
1.6 marked and ungroomed

Cokato:
Collinwood County Park
612-286-2801
5.0 km marked and groomed

Coon Rapids:
Bunker Hills Trail
612-757-3920
29.0 km
marked and groomed
Sand Creek City Trail
612-755-2880
3.7 km marked and ungroomed

Cottage Grove:
Oakwood City Park
612-437-6608
1.6 km marked and ungroomed
South Washington Regional Park
612-439-6058
8.5 km marked and groomed
Valleywood Trail
612-437-6608
8.0 km marked and ungroomed
Woodridge City Park
612-458-2828
1.6 km marked and ungroomed

Eagan:
Fort Snelling State Park
612-727-1961
30.6 km marked and groomed
Lebanon Hills Regional Park
612-437-6608
15.8 km marked and groomed

Golden Valley:
Theodore Wirth City Park
612-348-2248
10.5 km unmarked and groomed

Hastings:
Spring Lake Park Reserve
612-437-6608
4.8 km marked and groomed

Hopkins:
Big Willow Municipal Park
612-938-1431
1.6 km marked and groomed
Meadow Park
612-938-1431
2.4 km marked and groomed
Purgatory Creek Park
612-938-1431
3.4 km marked and groomed

Jordan:
Carver Rapids Wayside
no phone
11.3 marked and groomed

Lake Elmo:
Lake Elmo Regional Park
612-439-6058
19.3 km marked and groomed
Sunfish Lake City Park
612-777-5510
8.2 km marked and groomed

Lakeland:
Afton State Park
612-436-5391
29.0 marked and groomed

Lakeville:
Bracketts Crossing
612-435-7600
35.1 km unmarked and groomed
Ritter Farm Municipal Park
612-469-4431
18.0 km marked and groomed

Maple Grove:
Boundary Creek Neighborhood Park
612-420-4000
2.9 km unmarked and ungroomed
Fish Lake Trails
612-420-4000
3.5 km unmarked and ungroomed
Rice Lake Trails
612-420-4000
2.9 unmarked and ungroomed

Maple Plain:
Clifton E. French Regional Park
612-472-4911
5.1 km unmarked and groomed
Coon Rapids Dam Regional Park
612-424-5511

6.4 km marked and groomed
Morris T. Baker Park Reserve
612-472-4911
12.6 km marked and groomed

Maplewood:
Battle Creek Regional Park
612-777-1361
3.2 km marked and groomed

Marine On St. Croix:
William O'Brien State Park
612-433-2421
16.9 km marked and groomed

Minneapolis:
Bassett Creek Municipal Park
612-537-8421
2.4 km unmarked and ungroomed
Columbia Municipal Park
612-789-2248
2.3 km unmarked and groomed
Hiawatha Municipal Golf
612-724-7715
3.1 km unmarked and groomed
M.A.C. Municipal Park
612-537-8421
1.9 km unmarked and ungroomed

Minnetonka:
Lone Lake City Park
612-938-1431
4.0 km marked and groomed

Monticello:
Harry Larson Memorial Forest
612-682-3900
4.0 km marked and groomed
Lake Maria State Park
612-878-2325
19.3 km marked and groomed
Manitou Lakes Trail
612-536-5707
35.4 km marked and groomed

Oakdale:
Oakdale City Park
612-739-5086
7.2 km marked and groomed

Osseo:
Elm Creek Park Reserve
612-424-5511
20.1 km marked and groomed
North Hennepin Regional Trail Corridor
612-424-5511
9.7 km marked and groomed

Prior Lake:
Carver Park Reserve
612-472-4911
32.2 km marked and groomed
Cleary Lake Regional Park
612-941-7993
9.0 km marked and groomed

Richfield:
Black Dog Lake/Long Meadow Lake Units
612-725-4148
1.6 km marked and groomed
Rich Acres Golf Course
612-861-7144
6.4 km marked and groomed

Rockford:
Lake Rebecca Park Reserve
612-472-4911
15.4 km marked and groomed

Shakopee:
Louisville Swamp Unit
612-725-4148
9.7 unmarked and groomed

St. Michael:
Crow-Hassan Park Reserve
612-424-5511
24.1 km marked and groomed

St. Paul:
Friendly Hills Municipal Park
612-452-1850
7.2 km unmarked and ungroomed
Hidden Falles/Crosby Farm
612-292-7400
8.0 km marked and groomed

Highland Municipal Park-Golf
612-292-7400
1.6 km unmarked and groomed
Interstate Valley Park
612-452-1850
1.6 km unmarked and ungroomed
Marydale Municipal Park
612-292-7400
1.6 km marked and ungroomed
Phalen-Keller Regional Park
612-292-7400
8.0 km marked and groomed

Stillwater:
Pine Point County Park
612-439-6058
8.0 km marked and groomed

Watertown:
Luce Line State Trail
612-296-9115
10.5 km marked and groomed

Southwest:

Granite Falls:
Upper Sioux Agency State Park
612-564-4777
4.8 km marked and ungroomed

Hutchinson:
Lake Marion County Park
612-864-5551
6.4 km marked and groomed
Piepenburg County Park
612-864-5551
8.0 km marked and groomed
Stahls Lake County Park
612-864-5551
1.6 km marked and groomed
Swan Lake County Park
612-864-5551
3.2 km marked and groomed

Lakefield:
Kilen Woods State Park
507-662-6258
2.4 km marked and groomed

Le Center:
Richter Wood Coutny Park
612-357-2251
2.4 km marked and ungroomed

Luverne:
Blue Mounds State Park
507-283-4892
4.8 km marked and groomed

Mankato:
Bray County Park
507-625-3281
4.8 km unmarked and ungroomed
Daly County Park
507-625-3281
4.5 km unmarked and ungroomed
Minneopa State Park
507-625-4388
5.6 km marked and groomed

Marshall:
Camden State Park
507-865-4530
8.0 km marked and groomed

Montevideo:
Lac Qui Parle State Recreation Area
612-752-4736
6.4 km marked and groomed
Wildwood Nature Center
612-269-5026
1.6 km unmarked and ungroomed

New Ulm:
Flandrau State Park
507-354-3519
9.7 km marked and groomed
Fort Ridgely State Park
507-426-7840
4.8 km marked and groomed
Lake Hanska County Park
507-359-7900
4.8 km unmarked and ungroomed

Pipestone:
Split Rock State Park
507-348-7908
2.4 km marked and groomed

Slayton:
Lake Shetek State Park
507-763-3256
2.4 km marked and groomed

Sleepy Eye:
Golden Gate to Fun Campground
507-794-6586
1.6 km unmarked and ungroomed

St. James:
Eagles Nest County Park
507-375-3341
1.9 km marked and ungroomed

St. Peter:
Riverside Park
507-931-4840
2.4 km marked and ungroomed
Seven Mile Creek County Park
507-931-1760
2.6 km marked and ungroomed
Traverse de Sioux City Park
507-931-3265
6.4 km marked and groomed

Waterville:
Sakatah Lake State Park
507-362-4438
6.4 km marked and groomed

Willmar:
Sibley State Park
612-354-2055
16.1 km marked and groomed
Willmar X-Country Ski Trail
612-235-1854
4.8 km marked and groomed

Winsted:
Maple County Park
612-864-5551
3.2 km unmarked and ungroomed

Northwest:

Alexandria:
Andes Tower Hill Ski Area
612-965-2455
16.1 km marked and groomed
Kensington Runestone County Park
612-965-2365
12.1 km marked and groomed
Lake Carlos State Park
612-852-7200
8.0 km marked and groomed
Radisson Resort Arrowhead
612-762-1124
6.4 km marked and groomed
Spruce Hill County Park
612-965-2365
3.2 km marked and ungroomed
Spruce Hill Wetlands Trail
612-763-3161
8.0 km unmarked and ungroomed

Detroit Lakes:
Booth Lake Trail
218-847-2641
4.2 km marked and ungroomed
Detroit Mountain Trail
218-847-3938
10.1 km marked and groomed
Dunton Lock Trail
218-847-3939
8.0 km marked and groomed
East Frazee Trail
218-847-8464
16.1 km marked and groomed
Maplelag Trail
218-375-2986
42.6 km marked and groomed
Old Indian Trail
218-847-2641
3.2 km marked and ungroomed
Pine Lake Trails
218-847-2641

12.1 km marked and groomed
Tamarac Trail
218-847-2641
1.6 km marked and ungroomed

East Grand Forks:
River Heights Park
218-773-1181
4.8 km marked and groomed

Fergus Falls:
Spidahl Ski Gard Trail
218-736-5097
32.2 km unmarked and groomed

Glenwood:
Glacial Lakes State Park
612-239-2860
6.4 km marked and groomed

Hallock:
Lake Bronson State Park
218-754-2200
4.8 km marked and groomed

Lake Itasca:
Itasca State Park
218-266-3656
36.8 km marked and groomed

Mahnomen:
Hoot Owl Resort
218-734-2245
4.8 km marked and groomed

Moorhead:
Buffalo River State Park
218-498-2124
19.3 km marked and groomed
Riverfront Park
218-299-5340
2.7 km marked and groomed
Ulen Municipal Park
218-596-8351

2.4 marked and ungroomed

Pelican Rapids:
Maplewood State Park
218-863-8383
21.2 km marked and groomed

Red Lake Falls:
Red Lake Falls Club Trail
218-253-2171
19.3 km unmarked and groomed

Warren:
Old Mill State Park
218-437-8174
5.6 km marked and groomed

DOWNHILL

Northeast:
Duluth:
Spirit Mountain
5 lifts, 5 chairs, 14 runs
218-628-2891

Ely:
Hidden Valley Recreation Area
3 lifts, 4 runs
218-365-3224

Grand Rapids:
Mount Itasca Ski Trails
2 lifts, 6 runs
218-245-1250

Sugar Hills Lodge Resort
6 lifts, 2 chairs, 3 T-bars, 18 runs
218-326-0535

Hill City:
Quadna Mountain Resort
4 lifts, 1 chair, 2 T-bars, 15 runs
218-697-2324

Lutsen:
Lutsen Mountains
5 lifts, 3 chairs, 1 T-bar, 14 runs
218-663-7281

North Branch:
Wild Mountain Ski Area
6 lifts, 4 chairs, 1 T-bar, 18 runs
612-465-6365

Virginia:
Giant's Ridge Recreation Area
2 lifts, 2 chairs, 7 runs
218-865-4620

North Central:
Bemidji:
Buena Vista Ski Area
4 lifts, 4 chairs, 1 run
218-751-5530

Brainerd:
Ski Gull Ski Area
4 lifts, 1 T-bar, 7 runs
218-963-4353

Long Prairie:
Eagle Mountain Resort
5 lifts, 2 T-bars, 11 runs
612-285-4567

St. Cloud:
Powder Ridge Ski Area
6 lifts, 2 chairs, 1 T-bar, 12 runs
612-398-7200

Southeast:
Red Wing:
Mount Frontenac Ski Area
5 lifts, 1 chair, 2 T-bars, 12 runs
612-388-5826

Welch Village Ski Area
9 lifts, 5 chairs, 2 T-bars, 30 runs
612-222-7079

Wabasha:
Coffee Mill
3 chairs, 1 handle tow, 13 runs
612-565-4561

Twin Cities:
Blaine:
Lochness Ski Area
3 runs
612-784-6700

Bloomington:
Hyland-Bush-Anderson Park Reserve
6 lifts, 2 chairs, 8 runs
612-941-7993

Burnsville:
Buck Hill Ski Area
9 lifts, 4 chairs, 1 T-bar, 10 runs
612-435-7187

Hastings:
Afton Alps Ski Area
18 lifts, 18 chairs, 36 runs
612-436-5245

St. Paul:
Como Park
612-292-7400

Southwest:
Mankato:
Mt. Kato
8 chairs, 18 runs
507-625-3363

Sleepy Eye:
Golden Gate to Fun Campground
2 lifts, 5 runs
507-794-6586

Northwest:
Alexandria:
Andes Tower Hill Ski Area
4 lifts, 1 chair, 3 T-bars, 11 runs
612-965-2455

Fergus Falls:
Old Smokey Ski Area
1 lift, 4 runs
218-739-2251

Viking Valley Recreation Area
6 lifts, 8 runs
218-747-2542

MINNESOTA GOLF COURSES

Albany Golf Club
500 Church Avenue
Albany, MN 56307
(612) 845-2505
Public, 9 Par 36

Albert Lea Golf Club
P.O. Box 168
Albert Lea, MN 56007
(507) 377-1683
Private, 9 Par 35

Alexandria Golf Club
P.O. Box 206
Alexandria, MN 56308
(612) 763-3605
Semi-Private, 18 Par 72

Anoka-Greenhaven Golf Club
Box 244
Anoka, MN 55303
(612) 427-3180
Public, 18 Par 71

Appleton Golf Club
326 East Ronning
Appleton, MN 56208
(612) 289-1454
Private, 9 Par 36

Arrowwood Golf Club (Radisson)
Lake Darling
Alexandria, MN 56308
(612) 762-1124
Public, 18 Par 68

Austin Country Club
P.O. Box 474
Austin, MN 55912
(507) 437-7631
Private, 18 Par 72

Babbitt Golf Club
Box 280
Babbitt, MN 55706
(218)827-2603
Semi-Private, 9 Par 35

Baker Park Golf Course
3800 County Road 24
Maple Plain, MN 55359
(612) 473-7418
Public, 9 Par 36 Reg.
9 Par 30 Exec.

Bellwood Oaks Golf Course
P.O. Box 306
Hastings, MN 55033
(612) 437-9944
Public, 18 Par 73

Bemidji Town & Country Club
Box 622
Bemidji, MN 56601
(218) 751-4535
Semi-Private, 18 Par 72

Benson Golf Club
2222 Atlantic Avenue
Benson, MN 56215
(612) 842-7901
Semi-Private, 18 Par 72

Birch Bay Golf Club
Route 6, Box 305
Brainerd, MN 56401
(218) 963-4488
Semi-Private, 9 Par 36

Birchwood Golf Course
Box 328
Pelican Rapids, MN 56572
(218) 863-6486
Semi-Private, 9 Par 34

Blackduck Golf Club
Blackduck, MN 56630
(218) 835-4872
Public, 9 Par 36

Blooming Prairie Country Club
Highway 218 North
Blooming Prairie, MN 55917
(507) 583-2887
Semi-Private, 9 Par 36

Blueberry Hills Country Club
Box 241
Deer River, MN 56636
(218) 246-8411
Public, 9 Par 36

Bluff Creek Golf Club
1025 Creekwood
Chaska, MN 55318
(612) 445-9969
Public, 18 Par 70

Bois De Sioux Golf Club
Box 720
Breckenridge, MN 56520
(701) 642-3673
Semi-Private, 18 Par 72

Brackett's Crossing
17976 Judicial Road
Lakeville, MN 55044
(612) 435-7600
Semi-Private, 18 Par 71

Braemar Golf Course
6364 Dewey Hill Road
Edina, MN 55435
(612) 941-2072
Public, 18 Par 72

Brainerd Golf & Country Club
Box 772
Brainerd, MN 56401
(218) 829-5733
Semi-Private, 18 Par 71

Breezy Point Golf Course
Breezy Point, MN 56472
(218) 562-7811
Public, 18 Par 68

Brightwood Hills
1975 Silver Lake Road
New Brighton, MN 55112
(612) 633-7776
Public, 9 Par 30

Brookview Golf Club
8200 Wayzata Boulevard
Golden Valley, MN 55426
(612) 544-8446
Public, 18 Par 72

Buffalo Heights Golf Club
R.R. 1, Box 3
Buffalo, MN 55313
(612) 682-9931
Public, 9 Par 36

Burl Country Club
5400 North Arm Drive
Mound, MN 55364
(612) 472-4909
Private, 18 Par 72

Canby Golf Club
Box 7
Canby, MN 56220
(507) 223-5259
Private, 9 Par 36

Cannon Country Club
P.O. Box 12

Cannon Falls, MN 55009
(507) 263-3126
Private, 9 Par 35

Carriage Hills Country Club
3535 Wescott Hills Drive
St. Paul, MN 55123
(612) 454-9881
Public, 18 Par 71

Castle Highlands Golf Club
Route 5, Box 328
Bemidji, MN 56601
(218) 586-2681
Semi-Private, 18 Par 71

Castlewood Golf Course
(Location: Forest Lake 55164)
P.O. Box 43360
St. Paul, MN 55164
(612) 777-8321
Public, 9 Par 36

Cedar River Country Club
Box 311
Adams, MN 55909
(507) 582-3595
Semi-Private, 18 Par 72

Chisago Lakes Golf Club
Box 529
Lindstrom, MN 55045
(612) 257-1484
Public, 9 Par 36

Chomonix Golf Club
550 Bunker Lake Blvd.
Anoka, MN 55303
(612) 757-3920
Public, 9 Par 36

Chosen Valley Golf Club
Box 506
Chatfield, MN 55923
(507) 867-4305
Semi-Private, 9 Par 35

Cleary Lake Golf Course
18106 Texas Avenue
Prior Lake, MN 55372
(612) 447-2171
Public, 9 Par 30

Cloquet Country Club
400 Country Club Drive
P.O. Box 331
Cloquet, MN 55720
Private, 9 Par 36

Coffee Mill Golf Course
Box 6
Wabasha, MN 55981
Semi-Private, 9 Par 36

Cokato Town & Country Club
Highway 12 West
Cokato, MN 55321
(612) 286-2007
Semi-Private, 9 Par 36

Columbia Golf Club
3300 Central Avenue N.E.
Minneapolis, MN 55418
(612) 789-2627
Public, 18 Par 71

Como Golf Course
1306 West Arlington Avenue
St. Paul, MN 55108
(612) 489-1804
Public, 18 Par 69

Coon Rapids Bunker Hills G.C.
Highway 242 & Bunker Hill Drive
P.O. Box 33081
Coon Rapids, MN 55433
(612) 755-4140
Public, 18 Par 72

Cottonwood Country Club
Cottonwood, MN 56229
(507) 423-6335
Private, 9 Par 36

Country Hills Golf Club
Route 2, Box 792
Shakopee, MN 55379
(612) 445-3575
Public, 9 Par 30

Countryside Golf Club
Minneota, MN 56264
(507) 872-9925
Semi-Private, 9 Par 36

Crow Greens Public Golf Course
Route 1, Box 294
Watertown, MN 55388
(612) 955-2354
Public, 9 Par 36

Crow River Country Club
P.O. Box 9
Hutchinson, MN 55350
(612) 587-3070
Private, 18 Par 71

Cuyuna Country Club
Box 96
Deerwood, MN 56444
(218) 534-3489
Semi-Private, 9 Par 35

Dahlgreen Golf Club
R.R. 2 Box 139
Chaska, MN 55318
(612) 445-4393
Semi-Private, 18 Par 72

Dawson Golf Association
Dawson, MN 56232
Public, 9 Par 35

Daytona Golf Course
14740 Lawndale Lane
Dayton, MN 55327
(612) 427-6110
Public, 18 Par 72

Dellwood Hills Golf Club
29 Highway 96 East
White Bear Lake, MN 55110
(612) 426-3218
Private, 18 Par 72

Detroit Country Club
Route 5
Detroit Lakes, MN 56501
(218) 847-5790
Public, 36 Par 71-64

Dodge Country Club
Box 429
Dodge Center, MN 55927
(507) 374-2374
Semi-Private, 9 Par 36

Dwan Golf Club
3301 West 110th Street
Bloomington, MN 55431
(612) 887-9602
Public, 18 Par 68

Eagle View Golf Course
Itasca Star Route

Park Rapids, MN 56470
(218) 732-3056
Public, 18 Par 64

Eastwood Golf Club
Eastwood Road S.E.
Rochester, MN 55901
(507) 288-2110
Public, 18 Par 70

Edenvale Golf Club
14500 Valley View Road
Eden Prairie, MN 55344
(612) 937-9347
Public, 18 Par 70

Edina Country Club
5100 Wooddale Avenue
Edina, MN 55424
(612) 927-7151
Private, 18 Par 72

Elk River Country Club
20015 Elk Lake Road
P.O. Box 17
Elk River, MN 55330
(612) 441-4111
Semi-Private, 18 Par 71

Enger Park Golf Course
1801 West Skyline Blvd.
Duluth, MN 55811
(218) 722-5044
Public, 18 Par 72

Eshquaguma Country Club
Box 527
Virginia, MN 55792
(218) 865-9986
Private, 9 Par 36

Eveleth Municipal Golf Course
P.O. Box 649
Eveleth, MN 55734
(218) 741-1577
Public, 9 Par 36

Falls Country Club
Box 283
International Falls, MN 56649
(218) 283-4491
Private, 9 Par 35

Faribault Golf & Country Club
P.O. Box 833
Faribault, MN 55021
(507) 334-5559
Private, 18 Par 72

Farmers Golf and Health Club
Box 33
Sanborn, MN 56083
(507) 648-3629
Public, 9 Par 36

Ferndale Country Club
Rushford, MN 55971
(507) 864-7626
Public, 9 Par 36

Forest Hills Golf Club
7530 210th Street North
Forest Lake, MN 55025
(612) 464-3097
Private, 18 Par 72

Fort Snelling Golf Club
(Location: St. Paul)
Box 20515
Bloomington, MN 55420
(612) 726-9331
Public, 9 Par 35

Fosston Golf Club
Box 502
Fosston, MN 56542
(218) 435-6535
Semi-Private, 9 Par 36

Fountain Valley Golf Club
2830 220th Street West
Box 97
Farmington, MN 55024
(612) 463-2121
Semi-Private, 18 Par 72

Fox Lake Golf Club
Sherburn, MN 56171
(507) 764-8381
Semi-Private, 9 Par 33

Frazee Golf Club
Box 236
Frazee, MN 56544
(218) 334-3831
Public, 9 Par 35

Glencoe Country Club
Box 187
Glencoe, MN 55336
(612) 864-5007
Semi-Private, 9 Par 36

Golden Valley Country Club
7001 Golden Valley Road
Minneapolis, MN 55427
(612) 545-2511
Private, 18 Par 73

Goodrich Golf Coursee
1820 VanDyke Avenue
St. Paul, MN 55109
(612) 777-7355
Public, 18 Par 70

Graceville Golf Club
Graceville, MN 56240
(612) 748-7403
Private, 9 Par 36

Grandy Nine Golf Course
Route 2
Stanchfield, MN 55080
(612) 689-1417
Public, 9 Par 35

Granite Falls Golf Club
Highway 67 South
Granite Falls, MN 56241
(612) 564-4141
Semi-Private, 9 Par 36

Green Lea Golf Course
Richway Drive
Albert Lea, MN 56007
(507) 373-9973
Public, 18 Par 73

Francis A. Gross Golf Course
2200 St. Anthony Blvd.
Minneapolis, MN 55418
(612) 789-2542
Public, 18 Par 71

Hampton Hills Golf Course
5313 North Juneau Lane
Plymouth, MN 55441
(612) 559-9800
Public, 18 Par 72

Harmony Golf Club
Box 385
Harmony, MN 55939
(507) 886-5622
Private, 9 Par 33

Hastings Country Club
P.O. Box 337
Hastings, MN 55033
(612) 437-6483
Private, 18 Par 72

Hawley Golf & Country Club
Box 734
Hawley, MN 56549
(218) 483-4808
Public, 18 Par 70

Hayden Hills Golf Club
618 West Hayden Lake Road
Champlin, MN 55316
Public, 9 Par 30

Hazeltine National Golf Club
1900 Hazeltine Blvd.
Chaska, MN 55318
(612) 448-4929
Private, 18 Par 72

Headwaters Country Club
Lake George Road, Box 9
Park Rapids, MN 56470
(218) 732-4832
Public, 18 Par 72

Heart of the Valley Golf Club
Ada, MN 56510
(218) 784-4746
Public, 9 Par 37

Hendricks Golf Club
Hendricks, MN 56136
(507) 275-3852
Semi-Private, 9 Par 36

Henry's Orchard Gardens
19059 Junelle Path
Burnsville, MN 55337
(612) 435-5771
Public, 9 Par 27

Hiawatha Golf Course
4553 Longfellow Avenue
Minneapolis, MN 55417
(612) 724-7715
Public, 18 Par 73

Hibbing Municipal Golf Course
Hibbing, MN 55746
(218) 263-4230
Public, 9 Par 34

Hidden Greens Golf Course
12977 200th Street
Hastings, MN 55033
(612) 437-3085
Public, 9 Par 36

Highland Park Golf Course
1856 Highland Parkway
St. Paul, MN 55116
(612) 698-7335
Public, 18 Par 72

Hillcrest Country Club
2200 East Larpenteur Avenue
St. Paul, MN 55109
(612) 774-6088
Private, 18 Par 71

Hollydale Golf Club
4710 Holly Lane
Plymouth, MN 55446
(612) 559-9847
Public, 18 Par 71

Hoyt Lakes Country Club
Hoyt Lakes, MN 55750
(218) 225-2841
Public, 9 Par 36

Indian Hills Golf Club
6667 Keats Avenue North
Stillwater, MN 55082
(612) 770-2366
Private, 18 Par 72

Interlachen Country Club
6200 Interlachen Blvd.
Edina, MN 55436
(612) 929-1661
Private, 18 Par 73

Interlaken Golf Club
277 Amber Lake Drive
Fairmont, MN 56031
(507) 235-5145
Private, 18 Par 72

Ironwood Golf Club
Route 6 Box 52
Mankato, MN 56001
(507) 625-4105
Public, 9 Par 32

Island View Country Club
P.O. Box 93
Waconia, MN 55387
(612) 448-5335
Semi-Private, 18 Par 72

Jackson Golf Club
North Highway 16 & 71
Jackson, MN 56143
(507) 847-2660
Semi-Private

Keller Golf Course
2166 Maplewood Drive
St. Paul, MN 55109
(612) 484-3011
Public, 18 Par 72

Kenyon Country Club
Highway 56 North
Kenyon, MN 55946
(507) 789-6307
Semi-Private, 9 Par 34

Kimball Golf Club
Box 188
Kimball, MN 55353
(612) 398-2285
Public, 9 Par 36

Koronis Hills Golf Club
Box 55
Paynesville, MN 56362
(612) 243-4111
Semi-Private, 9 Par 36

Lafayette Club
2800 Northview Road
Minnetonka Beach, MN 55361
(612) 471-8493
Private, 9 Par 31

Lake City Country Club
P.O. Box 119
Lake City, MN 55041
(612) 345-3543
Private, 9 Par 36

Lake Miltona Golf Club
Box 72
Miltona, MN 56354
(218) 943-2901
Semi-Private, 9 Par 36

Lakeview Golf Of Minnetonka
710 North Shore Drive West
Mound, MN 55364
(612) 472-3459
Public, 18 Par 69

Lakeview-Two Harbors Golf Club
Two Harbors, MN 55616
(218) 834-2255
Public, 9 Par 36

Lakeway Golf Course
R.R. 1
Dalton, MN 56324
(218) 589-8591
Public, 9 Par 35

Lanesboro Golf Club
Box 10
Lanesboro, MN 55949
(507) 467-3742
Semi-Private, 9 Par 35

Lebanon Hills Golf Course
4851 West 125th Street West
Apple Valley, MN 55124
(612) 423-2171
Public, 18 Par 71

Lester Park-Lakeview Golf Club
1860 Lester River Road
Duluth, MN 55804
(218) 525-1400
Public, 18 Par 72

LeSueur Country Club
P.O. Box 36
LeSueur, MN 56058
(612) 665-2291
Private, 18 Par 71

Lewiston Golf Association, Inc.
Box 100
Lewiston, MN 55952
(507) 523-9094
Public, 9 Par 35

Litchfield Golf Club
Lake Ripley
Litchfield, MN 55355
(612) 693-6425
Public, 18 Par 70

Little Crow Country Club
Box 217
Spicer, MN 56288
(612) 354-2224
Semi-Private, 18 Par 72

Little Falls Country Club
Golf Road & Edgewater Drive

Little Falls, MN 56345
(612) 632-9927
Public, 18 Par 72

Long Prairie Country Club
405 6th Street S.E.
Long Prairie, MN 56347
(612) 732-3312
Semi-Private, 9 Par 36

Loon Lake Golf Club
Route 3
Jackson, MN 56143
(507) 847-4036
Semi-Private, 9 Par 36

Lost Spur Country Club
2750 Sibley Highway
St. Paul, MN 55121
(612) 454-2330
Private, 9 Par 34

Luverne Country Club
Box 353
Luverne, MN 56156
(507) 283-4383
Private, 9 Par 35

Ma-Cal-Grove Country Club
R.R. 1
Caledonia, MN 55921
(507) 724-2733
Semi-Private, 9 Par 36

Madden's Pine Beach Golf Course
Box 387
Brainerd, MN 56401
(218) 829-2811
Public, 18 Par 72

Madison Country Club
P.O. Box 154
Madison, MN 56256
(612) 598-7587
Semi-Private, 9 Par 35

Mahnomen Country Club
Box 164
Mahnomen, MN 56557
(218) 935-5188
Semi-Private, 9 Par 36

Majestic Oaks Country Club
701 Bunker Lake Road N.E.
Ham Lake, MN 55303
(612) 755-2140
Public, 27 Par 72

Manitou Ridge Golf Club
3200 McKnight Road North
White Bear Lake, MN 55110
(612) 777-2987
Public, 18 Par 70

Mankato Golf Club
Box 3122
Mankato, MN 56001
(507) 387-5676
Private, 18 Par 71

Maple Hills Golf Club
Route 4, Box 433
Frazee, MN 56544
(218) 847-9532
Public, 9 Par 36

Maple Valley Golf & Country Club
R.R. 3
Rochester, MN 55901
(507) 285-9100
Semi-Private, 18 Par 72

Marshall Golf Club
Box 502
Marshall, MN 56258
(507) 532-2277
Private, 18 Par 72

Mayflower Country Club
Fairfax, MN 55332
(507) 426-9964
Semi-Private, 9 Par 35

Meadowbrook Golf Club
201 Meadowbrook Road
Hopkins, MN 55343
(612) 929-2077
Public, 18 Par 72

Meadowlark Country Club
403 1st Street S.W.
Melrose, MN 56352
(612) 256-4937
Public, 9 Par 35

Mendakota Country Club
2075 Dodd Road
St. Paul, MN 55120
(612) 454-2822
Private, 18 Par 72

Mesaba Country Club
Box 157
Hibbing, MN 55746
(218) 262-2851
Private, 9 Par 36

Midland Hills Country Club
2001 Fulham Street
St. Paul, MN 55113
(612) 631-0440
Private, 18 Par 72

Milaca Country Club
Milaca, MN 56353
(612) 983-9889
Public, 9 Par 35

Mille Lacs Lake Country Club
Star Route
Garrison, MN 56450
Public, 18 Par 71

Miller's Crestwood Golf Course
Route 6, Box 211
Alexandria, MN 56308
(612) 762-8223
Public, 9 Par 36

Minakwa Country Club
P.O. Box 633
Crookston, MN 56716
(218) 281-1773
Private, 9 Par 36

Minikahda Club
Excelsior Bllvd. & West 32nd St.
Minneapolis, MN 55416
(612) 926-1601
Private, 18 Par 73

Minneapolis Golf Club
2001 Flag Avenue
Minneapolis, MN 55426
(612) 544-4471
Private, 18 Par 72

Minneapolis Golf Club
Route 9, Box 133
Mankato, MN 56001
(507) 625-5777
Public, 9 Par 33

Minnesota Valley Club
6300 Auto Club Road
Bloomington, MN 55438
(612) 884-2409
Private, 18 Par 73

Minnetonka Country Club
P.O.. Box J
Excelsior, MN 55331
(612) 474-5222
Private, 18 Par 71

Minnewaska Golf Club
Box D
Glenwood, MN 56334
(612) 634-9902
Semi-Private, 9 Par 36

Minniowa Golf Club
Highway 169 North
Elmore, MN 56027
(507) 943-3149
Public, 9 Par 35

Montevideo Country Club
P.O. Box 321
Montevideo, MN 56265
(612) 269-8600
Private, 9 Par 36

Montgomery Golf Club
P.O. Box 64

Montgomery, MN 56069
(612) 364-5602
Public, 9 Par 36

Monticello Country Club
Route 4
Monticello, MN 55362
(612) 295-9991
Public, 9 Par 35

Moorhead Country Club
Box 98
Moorhead, MN 56560
(218) 236-0100
Private, 18 Par 72

Moorhead Village Green Golf Course
3420 Village Green Blvd.
Moorhead, MN 56560
(218) 299-5366
Public, 9 Par 36

Moose Lake Golf Club
Moose Lake, MN 55767
(218) 485-4886
Public, 9 Par 34

Mora Country Club
Route 1
Mora, MN 55051
(612) 679-2317
Public, 9 Par 36

Mountain Lake Golf Club
Box 227
Mountain Lake, MN 56159
(507) 427-3869
Private, 9 Par 36

New Hope Village Golf Course
4401 Xylon Avenue North
New Hope, MN 55428
(612) 537-1149
Public, 9 Par 27

New Prague Golf Club
Box 107
New Prague, MN 56071
(612) 758-3126
Semi-Private, 18 Par 72

New Ulm Country Club
New Ulm, MN 56073
(507) 354-8896
Semi-Private, 18 Par 71

North Branch Golf Association
Box 387
North Branch, MN 55056
(612) 674-9981
Public, 9 Par 32

North Oaks Golf Club
54 East Oaks Road
St. Paul, MN 55110
(612) 484-6311
Private, 18 Par 71

Northern Hills Golf Club
4805 41st Avenue N.W.
Rochester, MN 55901
(507) 285-0318
Public, 18 Par 72

Northfield Golf Club
707 Prairie Avenue N.E.
Northfield, MN 55057
(507) 645-7694
Semi-Private, 18 Par 69

Northland Country Club
3901 East Superior Street
Duluth, MN 55804
(218) 525-1941
Private, 18 Par 72

Oak Glen Country Club
305 South Greeley Street
Stillwater, MN 55082
(612) 439-6981
Private, 27 Holes

Oak Harbor Golf Club
P.O. Box 626
Baudette, MN 56623
(218) 634-9939
Public, 9 Par 36

Oak Knolls Golf Club
P.O. Box 208
Red Lake Falls, MN 56750
(218) 253-4423
Public, 9 Par 36

Oak Ridge Country Club
700 County Road 18
Hopkins, MN 55343
(612) 935-7721
Private, 18 Par 70

Oak Ridge Golf Club
Box 475
Hallock, MN 56728
(218) 843-2155
Public, 9 Par 36

Oak View Golf Course
Box 123
Freeborn, MN 56032
(507) 863-2288
Public, 9 Par 36

Oakcrest Golf Club
P.O. Box 69
Roseau, MM 56751
(218) 463-3999
Public, 9 Par 36

Oakdale Country Club
Buffalo Lake, MN 55314
(612) 833-5518
Private, 9 Par 35

Oaks Country Club
Box 86
Hayfield, MN 55940
(507) 477-3115
Public, 18 Par 72

Oakwood Golf Course
R.R. 2, Box 176
Henning, MN 56551
(218) 583-2127
Public, 9 Par 36

Olivia Golf Club
512 South 6th Street
Olivia, MN 56277
(612) 523-9967
Semi-Private, 9 Par 36

Olympic Hills Golf Club
9520 Franlo Road
Eden Prairie, MN 55344
(612) 941-6262
Private, 18 Par 73

Orono Golf Course
265 Orono Orchard Road
Wayzata, MN 55391
(612) 473-0876
Public, 9 Par 33

Ortonville Municipal Golf Course
315 Maddison Avenue
Ortonville, MN 56278
Public, 18 Par 72

Osakis Country Club
Osakis, MN 56360
(612) 859-2140
Semi-Private, 9 Par 36

Owatonna Country Club
P.O. Box 446
Owatonna, MN 55060
(507) 451-6120
Private, 18 Par 71

Owatonna Municipal Brooktree G.C.
1131 Sumac
Owatonna, MN 55060
(507) 451-0730
Public, 18 Par 72

Parkview Golf Club
1310 Cliff Road
Eagan, MN 55123
(612) 454-9884
Public, 18 Par 62

Pebble Lake Golf Club
P.O. Box 772
Fergus Falls, MN 56537
(218) 736-7404
Public, 18 Par 72

Perham Lakeside Country Club
P.O. Box 313
Perham, MN 56573
(218) 346-6070
Public, 9 Par 35

Pezhekee Golf Course
Peters Sunset Beach
Glenwood, MN 56334
(612) 634-4502
Public, 9 Par 35

Phalen Golf Course
1772 Lafond Avenue
St. Paul, MN 55104
(612) 644-2106
Public, 18 Par 70

Pierz Municipal Golf Course
Route 3, Box 93
Pierz, MN 56364
(612) 468-6270
Public, 9 Par 35

Pine City Country Club
Pine City, MN 55063
(612) 629-3848
Semi-Private, 9 Par 36

Pine River Country Club
Box 196
Pine River, MN 56474
(218) 587-4774
Public, 9 Par 36

Pinewood Estates Golf Course
Elk River, MN 55330
(612) 441-1081
Public, 9 Par 30

Piper Hills Golf Club
P.O. Box 276
Plainview, MN 55964
(507) 534-3161
Public, 9 Par 36

Pipestone Country Club
Box 463
Pipestone, MN 56164
(507) 825-9991
Semi-Private, 9 Par 36

Pokegama Country Club
3910 Golf Course Road
Grand Rapids, MN 55744
(218) 326-0785
Public, 18 Par 72

Pomme De Terre Golf Club
4 South Court
Morris, MN 56267
(612) 589-9925
Private, 9 Par 35

Preston Golf Club
Preston, MN 55965
(507) 765-4485
Public, 9 Par 35

Purple Hawk Golf Club
Box 528
Cambridge, MN 55008
(612) 689-3800
Semi-Private, 18 Par 72

Quadna Golf Club
South Star Route, Box 405
Hill City, MN 55748
(218) 697-2324
Public, 9 Par 35

Ramsey Golf Club
R.R. 1, Box 83
Austin, MN 55912
(507) 433-9098
Public, 18 Par 71

Red Wing Country Club
1311 West 6th Street
Red Wing, MN 55066
(612) 388-9524
Private, 9 Par 36

Redwood Falls Golf Club
P.O. Box 384
Redwood Falls, MN 56283
(507) 637-9975
Private, 9 Par 36

Rich-Acres Golf Course
6700 Portland Avenue South
Richfield, MN 55423
(612) 861-7144
Public, 18 Par 71

Rich-Spring Golf Club
R.R. 1
Cold Spring, MN 56320
(612) 685-9901
Public, 9 Par 36

Ridgeview Country Club
West Redwing Street
Duluth, MN 55803
(218) 724-0370
Private, 18 Par 70

Riverside Golf Club
Box 387
Stephen, MN 56757
(218) 478-2735
Public, 9 Par 35

Riverside Town & Country Club
Winnebago, MN 56098
(507) 526-2764
Private, 9 Par 36

Rochester Golf & Country Club
P.O. Box 6877
Rochester, MN 55901
(507) 282-2708
Private, 18 Par 71

Rolling Green Country Club
400 Evergreen Road
Hamel, MN 55340
(612) 478-6021
Private, 18 Par 72

Rolling Green Fairways
2556 Stella Street
Fairmont, MN 56031
(507) 235-9533
Public, 9 Par 27

Rolling Hills Golf Club
Westbrook, MN 56183
(507) 274-5166
Public, 9 Par 36

Root River Country Club
RFD
Spring Valley, MN 55975
(507) 346-2501
Private, 9 Par 36

Rose Lake Golf Club
P.O. Box 202
Fairmont, MN 56031
(507) 235-5274
Semi-Private, 9 Par 36

Rum River Golf Club
Box 326
Princeton, MN 55371
(612) 389-5109
Semi-Private, 9 Par 35

Ruttger's Golf Course
Ruttger's Bay Lake Lodge
Deerwood, MN 56444
(218) 678-2885
Semi-Private, 9 Par 35

Sartell Golf Club
Box 363
Sartell, MN 56377
(612) 259-0551
Public, 9 Par 36

Sauk Centre Country Club
Box 173
Sauk Centre, MN 56378
(612) 352-3860
Semi-Private, 9 Par 37

Savanna Golf Club
Route 4
McGregor, MN 55760
(218) 426-3117
Public, 9 Par 36

Scottdale Golf Club
19400 Natchez Avenue
Prior Lake, MN 55372

(612) 435-7182
Public, 9 Par 36

Shamrock Golf Club
19625 Larkin Road
Corcoran, MN 55340
(612) 478-9977
Public, 18 Par 72

Shoreland Country Club
Box 516
St. Peter, MN 56082
(507) 931-4400
Private, 9 Par 35

Silver Bay Country Club
Box 38
Silver Bay, MN 55614
(218) 226-9977
Private, 9 Par 36

Silver Springs Golf Club
P.O. Box 246
Monticello, MN 55362
(612) 338-2207
Public, 18 Par 72

Slayton Country Club
Box 182
Slayton, MN 56172
(507) 794-7105
Semi-Private, 9 Par 35

Sleepy Eye Golf Club, Inc.
Highway 14 West
Sleepy Eye, MN 56085
(507) 794-7105
Semi-Private, 9 Par 36

Soldiers Memorial Golf Course
Box 1102
Rochester, MN 55901
(507) 282-1525
Public, 18 Par 70

Somerset Country Club
1416 Dodd Road
St. Paul, MN 55118
(612) 457-1416
Private, 18 Par 72

Southview Country Club
239 East Mendota Road
West St. Paul, MN 55118
(612) 451-6856
Private, 18 Par 71

Springfield Golf Club
Box 74
Springfield, MN 56087
(507) 723-5888
Semi-Private, 9 Par 36

St. Cloud Country Club
Box 1064
St. Cloud, MN 56302
(612) 253-1331
Private, 18 Par 72

Stillwater Country Club
North 4th Street
Stillwater, MN 55082
(612) 439-7979
Private, 18 Par 72

Sugar Lodge
Box 369
Grand Rapids, MN 55744
(218) 326-3473
Public, 9 Par 34

Sundance Golf Club
15240 113th Avenue North
Osseo, MN 55369
(612) 425-5757
Public, 18 Par 71

Swan Lake Country Club
Box 308
Pengilly, MN 55775
(218) 885-9970
Private, 9 Par 36

Tartan Park Golf Club
11455 20th Street North
Lake Elmo, MN 55042
(612) 733-3475
Private, 18 Par 71

Terrace Golf Club
Box 26
Staples, MN 56479
(218) 894-9907
Public, 9 Par 36

Terrace View Golf Course
420 Holly Lane 20
Mankato, MN 56001
(507) 625-6370
Public: 9 Par 36 Reg.
9 Par 27 Exec.

Thief River Golf Club
P.O. Box 481, Rt. 2
Thief River Falls, MN 56701
(218) 681-2955
Semi-Private, 9 Par 36

Tianna Country Club
Walker, MN 56484
(218) 547-1712
Semi-Private, 18 Par 72

Tipsinah Mounds Country Club
Elbow Lake, MN 56531
(218) 685-4180
Public, 9 Par 35

Town and Country Club
2279 Marshall Avenue
St. Paul, MN 55104
(612) 646-7121
Private, 18 Par 72

Tracy Country Club
Highway 14
Tracy, MN 56175
(507) 629-9950
Private, 9 Par 35

Travelers Country Club on
the Mississippi
Clear Lake, MN 55319
9 Par 31

Twin Pines Golf Course
Box 564
Bagley, MN 56621
(218) 694-2454
Public, 9 Par 36

Tyler Community Golf Club
Box 447
Tyler, MN 56178
(507) 247-3242
Public, 9 Par 36

University of Minnesota Golf Club
Larpenteur at Fulham
St. Paul, MN 55113
(612) 373-1645
Public, 18 Par 71

Vallebrook Golf Club
P.O. Box 807
Lakefield, MN 56150
(507) 662-6308
Public, 9 Par 36

Valley Golf Association
P.O. Box 461
East Grand Forks, MN 56721
(218) 773-1207
Public, 9 Par 36

Valley Golf Course
Route 4, Box 318
Willmar, MN 56201
(612) 235-6790
Public, 9 Par 35

Valley High Country Club
Route 2
Houston, MN 55943
(507) 894-4444
Semi-Private, 9 Par 36

Vermilion Fairways Golf Club
County Road 24
Cook, MN 55723
(218) 666-2679
Public, 9 Par 36

Victoria Hills Golf Course
11177 McKusick Road North
Stillwater, MN 55082
(612) 439-0033
Public, 9 Par 37

Virginia Municipal Golf Course
Virginia, MN 55792
(218) 741-4366
Public, 18 Par 70

Wadena Country Club
P.O. Box 446
Wadena, MN 56482
(218) 631-4010
Public, 9 Par 36

Wapicada Golf Course
Box 73
St. Cloud, MN 56301
(612) 251-7804
Semi-Private, 18 Par 72

War-Road Estates Golf Course
War-Road Estates
Warroad, MN 56763
(218) 386-2200
Public, 18 Par 72

Waseca Lakeside Golf Club
Box 187
Waseca, MN 56093
(507) 835-1983
Private, 18 Par 71

Watona Park and Golf Course
116 West Main
Madelia, MN 56062
(507) 642-3245
Public, 9 Par 36

Watonwan Country Club
Box 147
St. James, MN 56081
(507) 375-3849
Private, 9 Par 34

Wayzata Country Club
Box 151
Wayzata, MN 55391
(612) 473-8846
Private, 18 Par 72

Wells Golf Club
P.O. Box 236
Wells, MN 56097
(507) 553-3313
Public, 9 Par 30

Westfield Golf Club
P.O. Box 324
Winona, MN 55987
(507) 452-6901
Public, 9 Par 36

Wheaton Country Club
Wheaton, MN 56296
(612) 563-4928
Public, 9 Par 36

White Bear Yacht Club
P.O. Box 8696
White Bear Lake, MN 55110
(612) 429-5002
Private, 18 Par 72

Whitefish Golf Club
Route 1, Box 111-B
Pequot Lakes, MN 56472
(218) 543-4900
Public, 9 Par 36

Willmar Golf & Country Club
Box 344
Willmar, MN 56201
(612) 235-1166
Private, 18 Par 72

Willow Creek Golf
P.O. Box 68
Rochester, MN 55901
(507) 285-0305
Public, 18 Par 71

Willow Creek Golf Club
Route 1
Barnesville, MN 56514
(218) 493-4486
Semi-Private, 9 Par 36

Windom Country Club
Box 74
Windom, MN 56101
(507) 831-3489
Private, 9 Par 36

Winona Country Club
Pleasant Valley
Winona, MN 55987
(507) 452-3535
Private, 18 Par 71

Winthrop Golf Club
P.O. Box 544
Winthrop, MN 55396
(507) 647-5828
Semi-Private, 9 Par 36

Theodore Wirth Golf Club
Glenwood Pkwy. & Plymouth North
Minneapolis, MN 55422
(612) 522-4584
Public, 18 Par 72

Woodhill Country Club
200 Woodhill Road
Wayzata, MN 55391
(612) 473-7333
Private, 18 Par 70

Wedgewood Valley Golf Club
9372 Bailey Rd.
Woodbury, MN 55125
(612) 459-0288
Semi-Private, 18 Par 72

Worthington Country Club
Box 306
Worthington, MN 56187
(507) 376-5142
Private, 18 Par 71

Zumbro Valley Golf Club
Box 76
Kasson, MN 55944
(507) 635-2821
Semi-Private, 9 Par 36

Zumbrota Golf Club
Zumbrota, MN 55992
(507) 732-5817
Semi-Private, 9 Par 34

MINNESOTA HOSPITALS

ADA
Ada Municipal Hospital
405 E. Second Ave.
(218) 784-2561

ADRIAN
Arnold Memorial Hospital
601 Louisiana Ave., Box 279
(507) 483-2668

AITKIN
Aitkin Community Hospital
301 Minnesota Ave. S.
(218) 927-2121

ALBANY
Albany Community Hospital
Box 370
(612) 845-2121

ALBERT LEA
Naeve Hospital
404 Fountain St.
(507) 373-2384

ALEXANDRIA
Douglas County Hospital
111 17th Ave. E.
(612) 762-1511

APPLETON
Appleton Municipal Hospital
30 S. Behl St.
(612) 289-2422

ARLINGTON
Arlington Municipal Hospital
601 W. Chandler St.
(612) 964-2271

AURORA
White Community Hospital
320 Hwy. 110 E.
(218) 229-2211

AUSTIN
St. Olaf Hospital
300 N.W. Eighth Ave.
(507) 437-4551

BAGLEY
Clearwater County Memorial
Hospital
505 N. Bagley Ave., Box P
(218) 694-6501

BAUDETTE
Trinity Hospital
Main Ave. & Fifth St., Box E
(218) 634-2120

BEMIDJI
North Country Hospital
1100 W. 38th St.
(218) 751-5430

BENSON
Swift County-Benson Hospital
1815 Wisconsin Ave.
(612) 843-4232

BERTHA
Memorial Community Hospital
(218) 924-2700

BIGFORK
Northern Itasca District Hospital
(218) 743-3177

BLUE EARTH
United Hospital District
515 S. Moore St.
(507) 526-3273

BRAINERD
St. Joseph's Hospital

523 N. Third St.
(218) 829-2861

BRECKENRIDGE
St. Francis Hospital
415 Oak St.
(218) 643-6641

BROWERVILLE
St. John's Hospital
(612) 594-2204

BUFFALO
Buffalo Memorial hospital
303 Catlin St.
(612) 682-1212

CALEDONIA
Caledonia Community Hospital
425 N. Badger
(507) 724-3351

CAMBRIDGE
Memorial Hospital
725 S. Dellwood St.
(612) 689-1500

CANBY
Canby Community Hospital District
One
112 St. Olaf Ave.
(507) 223-7277

CANNON FALLS
Community Hospital
1116 W. Mill St.
(507) 263-4221

CASS LAKE
U.S. Public Health Service Indian
Hospital
Third Ave. W. & Seventh St.
(218) 335-2293

CHISAGO CITY
Chisago Lakes Hospital
(612) 257-2500

CLARKFIELD
Community Memorial Hospital
(612) 669-4421

CLOQUET
Community Memorial Hospital
Skyline Blvd.
(218) 879-4641

COMFREY
Comfrey Hospital
(507) 877-3211

COOK
Cook Community Hospital
Third St. & Cedar Ave.
(218) 666-5945

COON RAPIDS
Mercy Medical Center
4050 Coon Rapids Blvd.
(612) 427-2200

CROOKSTON
Riverview Hospital Association
323 S. Minnesota St.
(218) 281-4682

CROSBY
Cuyuna Range District Hospital
(218) 546-5147

DAWSON
Johnson Memorial Hospital
Walnut St. & Memorial Pl.
(612) 769-4323

DEER RIVER
Community Memorial Hospital of

Deer River
Box 488
(218) 246-8245

DETROIT LAKES
St. Mary's Hospital
1014 Lincoln Ave.
(218) 847-5611

DULUTH
● Miller-Dwan Hospital and Medical
Center
502 E. Second St.
(218) 727-8762
● St. Luke's Hospital
915 E. First St.
(218) 726-5555
● St. Mary's Hospital
407 E. Third St.
(218) 726-4000

ELBOW LAKE
Grant County Hospital
Box 5052
(218) 885-4462

ELY
Ely-Bloomenson Community
Hospital
328 W. Conan St.
(218) 365-3271

EVELETH
Eveleth Fitzgerald Community
Hospital
227 McKinley Ave.
(218) 744-1950

FAIRMONT
Fairmont Community Hospital
835 Johnson St.
(507) 238-4254

FARIBAULT
Rice County District One Hospital
631 S.E. First St.
(507) 334-6451

FARMINGTON
Sanford Memorial Hospital
913 Main St.
(612) 463-7825

FERGUS FALLS
Lake Region Hospital
712 S. Cascade St.
(218) 736-5475

FOREST LAKE
District Memorial Hospital
246 11th Ave. S.E.
(612) 464-3341

FOSSTON
Fosston Municipal Hospital
900 S. Hilligoss Blvd. E.
(218) 435-1133

FRIDLEY
Unity Medical Center
550 Osborne Rd. N.E.
(612) 786-2200

GAYLORD
Gaylord Community Hospital
640 Third St., Box 386
(612) 237-2905

GLENCOE
Glencoe Municipal Hospital
705 E. 18th St.
(612) 864-3121

GLENWOOD
Glacial Ridge Hospital

10 Fourth Ave S.E.
(612) 634-4521

GOLDEN VALLEY
Golden Valley Health Center
4101 Golden Valley Rd.
(612) 588-2771

GRACEVILLE
Holy Trinity Hospital
115 W. Second St.
(612) 748-7223

GRAND MARAIS
Cook County North Shore Hospital
(218) 387-1500

GRAND RAPIDS
Itasca Memorial Hospital
126 First Ave S.E.
(218) 326-3401

GRANITE FALLS
Granite Falls Municipal Hospital
345 Tenth Ave.
(612) 564-3111

GREENBUSH
Greenbush Community Hospital
(218) 782-2131

HALLOCK
Kittson Memorial Hospital
(218) 843-3612

HARMONY
Harmony Community Hospital
815 S. Main Ave., Rte. 1, Box 173
(507) 886-6544

HASTINGS
Regina Memorial Hospital
Nininger Rd.
(612) 437-3121

HENDRICKS
Hendricks Community Hospital
E. Lincoln St.
(507) 275-3134

HERON LAKE
Heron Lake Municipal Hospital
(507) 793-2346

HIBBING
Central Mesabi Medical Center
750 E. 34th St.
(218) 262-4881

HUTCHINSON
Hutchinson Community Hospital
Century Ave.
(612) 896-1665

INTERNATIONAL FALLS
International Falls Memorial Hospital
1800 Third St.
(218) 283-4481

IVANHOE
Divine Providence Hospital
(507) 694-1414

JACKSON
Jackson Municipal Hospital
North Hwy.
(507) 847-2420

KARLSTAD
Karlstad Memorial Hospital
(218) 436-2141

LAKE CITY
Lake City Hospital
904 S. Lakeshore Dr.
(612) 345-3321

LAKEFIELD
Lakefield Municipal Hospital
Second Ave. & Milwaukee St.
(507) 662-5295

LESUEUR
Minnesota Valley Memorial Hospital
621 S. Fourth St.
(612) 665-3375

LITCHFIELD
Meeker County Memorial Hospital
612 S. Sibley Ave.
(612) 693-3242

LITTLE FALLS
St. Gabriel's Hospital
815 Second St. S.E.
(612) 632-5441

LITTLEFORK
Littlefork Municipal Hospital
(218) 278-6634

LONG PRAIRIE
Long Prairie Memorial Hospital
20 Ninth St. S.E.
(612) 732-2141

LUVERNE
Community Hospital
305 E. Luverne St.
(507) 283-2321

MADELIA
Madelia Community Hospital
121 Drew Ave. S.E.
(507) 642-3255

MADISON
Madison Hospital
820 Third Ave.
(612) 598-7556

MAHNOMEN
Mahnomen County and Village
Hospital
Box 396
(218) 935-2511

MANKATO
Immanuel-St. Joseph's Hospital
325 Garden Blvd.
(507) 625-4031

MARSHALL
Weiner Memorial Medical Center
300 S. Bruce St.
(507) 532-9661

MELROSE
Melrose Hospital
11 N. Fifth Ave. W.
(612) 256-4231

MILACA
Milaca Area District Hospital
150 N.W. Tenth St.
(612) 983-3131

MINNEAPOLIS
- Abbott-Northwestern Hospital
  800 E. 28th St. at Chicago Ave.
  (612) 874-4000
- Eitel Hospital
  1375 Willow St.
  (612) 870-1122
- Fairview Deaconess Hospital
  1400 24th Ave. S.
  (612) 721-9100
- Fairview Hospital
  2312 S. Sixth St.
  (612) 371-6300
- Fairview-Southdale Hospital
  6401 France Ave. S.
  (612) 924-5000
- Hennepin County Medical Center
  701 Park Ave. S.
  (612) 347-2338
- Methodist Hospital
  6500 Excelsior Blvd.
  (612) 932-5000
- Metropolitan Medical Center
  900 S. Eighth St.
  (612) 347-4444
- Minneapolis Children's Medical
  Center

2525 Chicago Ave.
(612) 874-6122
- Mount Sinai Hospital
  2215 Park Ave.
  (612) 871-3700
- North Memorial Medical Center
  See Robbinsdale
- Shriners Hospital for Crippled
  Children
  2025 E. River Rd.
  (612) 339-6711
- St. Mary's Hospital
  2414 S. Seventh St.
  (612) 338-2229
- University of Minnesota Hospitals
  and Clinics
  420 Delaware St. S.E.
  (612) 373-8484
- Veterans Administration Medical
  Center
  54th St. & 48th Ave. S.
  (612) 725-6767

MONTEVIDEO
Chippewa County Montevideo
Hospital
824 N. 11th St.
(612) 269-8878

MONTICELLO
Monticello-Big Lake Community
Hospital
1013 Hart Blvd., Box 480
(612) 295-2945

MOORHEAD
St. Ansgar Hospital
715 N. 11th St.
(218) 299-2200

MOOSE LAKE
Mercy Hospital
(218) 485-4481

MORA
Kanabec Hospital
300 Clark St.
(612) 679-1212

MORRIS
Stevens County Memorial Hospital
400 E. First St.
(612) 589-1313

MOUNTAIN LAKE
Mountain Lake Community Hospital
801 Third Ave.
(507) 427-2511

NEW PRAGUE
Queen of Peace Hospital
301 Second St. N.E.
(612) 758-4431

NEW ULM
Sioux Valley Hospital
- North Unit
  1324 Fifth St. N.
  (507) 354-4124
- South Unit
  Seventh St. S. & Broadway
  (507) 354-2111

NORTHFIELD
Northfield City Hospital
800 W. Second St.
(507) 645-6661

OLIVIA
Renville County Hospital
300 S. Seventh St.
(612) 523-1261

ONAMIA
Community Mercy Hospital
(612) 532-3154

ORTONVILLE
Ortonville Area Health Services
750 Eastvold Ave.
(612) 839-2525

OWATONNA
Owatonna City Hospital
828 S. Cedar St.
(507) 451-3850

PARK RAPIDS
St. Joseph's Hospital
600 Pleasant Ave.
(218) 732-3311

PARKERS PRAIRIE
Parkers Prairie District Hospital
(218) 338-4011

PAYNESVILLE
Paynesville Community Hospital
200 First St. W.
(612) 243-3767

PELICAN RAPIDS
Pelican Valley Health Center
211 E. Mill St.
(218) 863-3111

PERHAM
Memorial Hospital
665 Third St. S.W.
(218) 346-4500

PIPESTONE
Pipestone County Hospital
911 Fifth Ave. S.W.
(507) 825-5811

PRINCETON
Fairview-Princeton Hospital
704 First St.
(612) 389-1313

RED LAKE FALLS
St. John's Hospital
(218) 253-2131

RED WING
St. John's Hospital
1407 W. Fourth St.
(612) 388-6721

REDLAKE
U.S. Public Health Service Indian
Hospital
(218) 679-3912

REDWOOD FALLS
Redwood Falls Municipal Hospital
100 Fallwood Rd.
(507) 637-2907

ROBBINSDALE
North Memorial Medical Center
3300 Oakdale Ave. N.
(612) 520-5200

ROCHESTER
- Olmsted Community Hospital
  1650 Fourth St. S.E.
  (507) 285-8485
- Rochester Methodist Hospital
  201 W. Center St.
  (507) 286-7890
- St. Mary's Hospital
  1216 Second St. S.W.
  (507) 285-5123

ROSEAU
Roseau Area Hospital
715 Third Ave S.E.
(218) 463-2500

RUSH CITY
Rush City Hospital
(612) 358-4708

SANDSTONE
Sandstone Area Hospital and Nursing
Home
317 Court St.
(612) 245-2212

SHAKOPEE
St. Francis Regional Medical Center
325 W. Fifth Ave.
(612) 445-2322

SLAYTON
Murray County Memorial Hospital
2042 Juniper Ave.
(507) 836-6111

SLEEPY EYE
Sleepy Eye Municipal Hospital
400 Fourth Ave. N.W.
(507) 794-3571

SOUTH ST. PAUL
Divine Redeemer Memorial Hospital
724 19th Ave. N.
(612) 450-4500

SPRING GROVE
Tweeten Memorial Hospital
125 Fifth Ave. S.E., Box 158
(507) 498-3211

SPRING VALLEY
Community Memorial Hospital
800 Memorial Dr.
(507) 346-7381

SPRINGFIELD
Springfield Community Hospital
625 N. Jackson, Box 146
(507) 723-4215

ST. CLOUD
- St. Cloud Hospital
  1406 Sixth Ave. N.
  (612) 251-2700
- Veterans Administration Medical
  Center
  (612) 252-1670

ST. JAMES
Watonwan Memorial Hospital
1207 Sixth Ave. S.
(507) 375-3261

ST. PAUL
- Bethesda Lutheran Medical Center
  559 Capitol Blvd.
  (612) 221-2200
- Children's Hospital
  345 N. Smith Ave.
  (612) 298-8666
- Gillette Children's Hospital
  200 University Ave. E.
  (612) 291-2848
- Midway Hospital
  1700 University Ave.
  (612) 641-5500
- Mounds Park Hospital
  200 Earl St.
  (612) 774-5901
- Samaritan Hospital
  1515 Charles Ave.
  (612) 645-9111
- St. John's Hospital
  403 Maria Ave.
  (612) 228-3600
- St. Joseph's Hospital
  69 W. Exchange St.
  (612) 291-3000
- St. Paul-Ramsey Medical Center
  640 Jackson St.
  (612) 221-3456
- United Hospitals
  333 N. Smith St.
  (612) 298-8888

ST. PETER
Community Hospital
618 W. Broadway
(507) 931-2200

STAPLES
United District Hospital
401 Prairie Ave. N.
(218) 894-1515

STARBUCK
Minnewaska District Hospital
610 W. Sixth St.
(612) 239-2201

STILLWATER
Lakeview Memorial Hospital
919 W. Anderson St.
(612) 439-5330

THIEF RIVER FALLS
Northwestern Hospital Services
120 LaBree Ave. S.
(218) 681-4240

TRACY
Tracy Municipal Hospital
Fifth St. E.
(507) 629-3200

TRIMONT
Trimont Community Hospital
Box H
(507) 639-2911

TWO HARBORS
Lake View Memorial Hospital
11th Ave. & Fourth St.
(218) 834-2211

TYLER
A.L. Vadheim Memorial Hospital
240 Willow St.
(507) 247-5521

VIRGINIA
Virginia Regional Hospital
901 Ninth St. N.
(218) 741-3340

WABASHA
St. Elizabeth Hospital
1200 Fifth Grant Blvd. W.
(612) 565-4531

WACONIA
Waconia Ridgeview Hospital
500 S. Maple St.
(612) 442-2191

WADENA
Tri-County Hospital
418 Jefferson St. N.
(218) 631-3510

WARREN
Warren Community Hospital
109 S. Minnesota St.
(218) 745-4211

WASECA
Waseca Area Memorial Hospital
100 Fifth Ave. N.W.
(507) 835-1210

WELLS
Wells Municipal Hospital
400 Fourth Ave. S.W.
(507) 553-3111

WESTBROOK
Dr. Henry Schmidt Memorial
Hospital
920 Bell Ave.
(507) 274-6121

WHEATON
Wheaton Community Hospital
(612) 563-8226

WILLMAR
Rice Memorial Hospital
301 Becker Ave. S.W.
(612) 235-4543

WINDOM
Windom Area Hospital
Highways 60 & 71 N., Box 339
(507) 831-2400

WINONA
Community Memorial Hospital
855 Mankato Ave.
(507) 454-3650

WINSTED
St. Mary's Hospital and Home
551 Fourth St. N.
(612) 485-2151

WORTHINGTON
Worthington Regional Hospital
1018 Sixth Ave.
(507) 372-2941

ZUMBROTA
Zumbrota Community Hospital
383 W. Fifth St.
(507) 732-5131

FOR FURTHER READING

Good books to read –
Minnesota by William E. Lass
Paperback – W.W. Norton & Company

Minnesota Travel Companion by Richard Olsenius
A unique guide to history along Minnesota highways
Many illustrations – Bluestem Productions

The Thirty Second State – A Pictorial History of Minnesota
By Bertha L. Heilbron – MHS Press
Profusely illustrated

Minnesota by Theodore Blegen
Publisher – University of Minnesota
Very complete history – hard bound

Minnesota Guide – Dorn Books
Much valuable information, especially on
accommodations and dining

Twin Cities Guide – Dorn Books
Detailed information, including entertainment,
accommodations, and dining

The Minnesota Almanac – John L. Brekke and sons
A great reference book on the state

Weights and Measures

Lineal Measure

FEET	=	METERS OR FEET	=	METERS
3.281	=	1	=	.305
6.562	=	2	=	.610
9.843	=	3	=	.914
13.123	=	4	=	1.219
16.404	=	5	=	1.524
19.685	=	6	=	1.829
22.966	=	7	=	2.134
26.247	=	8	=	2.438
29.528	=	9	=	2.743
32.808	=	10	=	3.048
65.617	=	20	=	6.096
82.021	=	25	=	7.620
164.042	=	50	=	15.240
328.048	=	100	=	30.480

MILES	=	KM OR MILES	=	KM
.621	=	1	=	1.609
1.243	=	2	=	3.219
2.486	=	4	=	6.437
3.107	=	5	=	8.047
6.214	=	10	=	16.093
15.534	=	25	=	40.234
31.069	=	50	=	80.467
62.137	=	100	=	160.934

LINEAL MEASURE
1 Inch = 2.54 Centimeters
12 Inches = 1 Foot = 30.48 Centimeters
3 Feet = 1 Yard = .9144 Meter
1 Meter = 39.37 Inches
5½ Yards = 1 Rod
40 Rods = ⅛ mile = 1 Furlong
5,280 Feet = 1 Mile = 1.6093 Kilometers
3 Miles = 1 League
1 Furlong = 660 Feet
8 Furlongs = 5,280 Feet or 1 Mile
1 Nautical Mile = 1.1516 Statute Miles or 6,080 Feet
60 Nautical Miles = 1 Degree = 69.169 Statute Miles

MIXING GAS & OIL (16 FLUID OZ = 1 PINT) = APPROX. MEASURE

Gal	1/16 Mix	1/25 Mix	1/50 Mix
1	½ pt	5 oz	2½ oz
2	1 pt	10 oz	5 oz
3	1½ pt	15 oz	7½ oz
5	2½ pt	1 pt, 9 oz	13 oz
6	3 pt	1 pt, 14 oz	1 pt
10	5 pt	3 pt	1 pt, 9 oz
12	6 pt	3 pt, 12 oz	1 qt

Square Measure

160 Square Rods = 1 Acre
640 Square Acres = 1 Square Mile
640 Acres = 1 Section
36 Sections = 1 Township

Wood Measure

144 Cubic Inches = 1 Board Feet = 1″ x 1 ft x 1″
16 Cubic Feet = 1 Cord Foot = 4 ft x 4 ft x 1 ft
8 Cord Feet = 1 Cord = 4 ft x 4 ft x 8 ft

Liquid Measure

8 Fluid Drams = 1 Ounce = 3.699 Ml (Milliliter)
16 Fluid Ounces = 1 Pint = .4732 L (Litre)
8 Pints = 1 Gallon = 3.7853 L (Litre)
1 Barrel = 31.5 Gallons = 119.24 L (Litre)
1 Barrel (Oil) = 42 Gallons = 158.98 L (Litre)
1 Teaspoon = ⅙ Fluid Ounce
3 Teaspoons = 1 Tablespoon = ½ Ounce
16 Tablespoons = 1 Cup = 8 Ounce
2 Cups = 1 Pint
1.2 U.S. Quart = 1 Imperial Quart
1.201 U.S. Gallon = 1 Imperial Gallon
1 Litre = 1.057 Quarts
1 Quart = .9463 Litre

Weights

POUNDS	=	KG OR LBS	=	KILOGRAMS
2.205	=	1	=	.454
11.023	=	5	=	2.268
22.046	=	10	=	4.536
55.116	=	25	=	11.340
110.231	=	50	=	22.680
220.462	=	100	=	45.359

Temperature

CENTIGRADE	=	FAHRENHEIT
−100°	=	−148°
−50°	=	−58°
−30°	=	−22°
−20°	=	−4°
−10°	=	+14°
−5°	=	23°
0°	=	32°
+5°	=	41°
10°	=	50°
15°	=	59°
20°	=	68°
25°	=	77°
30°	=	86°
35°	=	95°
40°	=	104°
45°	=	113°
100°	=	212°

$C = 5/9 (F − 32)$ $F = 9/5 C + 32$

ALL DISTANCES COMPUTED VIA TRUNK HIGHWAYS FROM CENTER TO CENTER OF CITIES

One mile equals 1.6093 kilometers

City	Distances
Albert Lea	224 22 402 309 220 231 380 293 245 403 338 61 49 268 399 271 286 123 387 122 144 192 150 58 163 97 179 324 223 87 63 472 34 171 99 63 161 99 69 88 117 388 289 33 168 106 103 11_
Alexandria	229 235 133 86 183 163 79 199 186 275 192 179 52 352 168 203 101 245 273 80 55 188 165 118 131 80 107 45 144 171 256 195 163 185 214 68 142 158 141 151 174 229 192 64 159 249 18_
Austin	404 311 223 232 385 295 246 409 339 80 51 274 399 273 288 141 389 100 161 194 168 76 181 100 196 330 241 104 65 474 33 190 85 41 163 100 87 97 114 390 290 49 186 125 80 13_
Baudette	102 199 202 165 194 213 175 188 394 355 239 341 131 166 303 69 444 293 220 423 368 353 305 315 234 280 346 345 148 369 398 356 387 252 310 360 317 317 122 168 373 290 386 420 41_
Bemidji	97 139 88 92 150 113 173 292 262 136 301 69 104 201 112 356 191 117 320 266 251 214 213 134 178 244 254 176 277 295 267 297 150 221 258 224 231 91 130 279 188 283 331 31_
Brainerd	98 182 92 113 207 189 205 173 96 267 83 117 114 194 267 104 31 256 179 188 125 154 137 123 157 165 271 188 231 178 208 63 132 171 135 142 187 143 190 116 211 242 21_
Cloquet	227 189 19 252 107 264 182 194 172 70 71 178 156 265 168 128 328 212 259 135 225 232 221 221 168 315 199 303 177 210 127 132 201 157 133 230 58 209 187 278 240 19_
Crookston	90 238 25 259 348 335 113 390 157 192 257 198 429 236 190 305 322 257 287 220 70 165 301 327 92 351 280 340 370 224 295 315 297 304 44 218 349 221 316 404 32_
Detroit Lakes	199 115 238 269 245 46 350 131 166 178 204 339 157 100 247 243 190 197 153 45 98 221 237 179 261 222 250 280 133 205 235 207 214 95 192 262 143 292 314 25_
Duluth	263 113 278 196 210 153 81 76 192 163 279 182 144 342 227 274 149 239 244 236 235 183 326 213 317 191 224 141 117 215 171 147 242 64 223 201 238 255 17_
East Grand Forks	283 367 359 135 414 182 216 280 222 454 259 215 319 345 273 310 236 79 181 322 351 92 374 294 365 394 248 319 337 321 328 59 242 371 237 332 429 33_
Ely	370 288 283 153 107 72 285 119 372 275 220 434 319 366 242 332 282 313 328 275 323 306 409 283 316 233 239 307 264 240 239 49 315 294 385 347 41_
Fairmont	94 236 431 285 315 91 399 179 112 174 92 51 118 129 137 288 185 48 107 441 91 114 144 120 142 135 63 107 154 363 321 78 130 49 160 6_
Faribault	224 349 223 239 94 339 122 111 145 171 43 144 50 155 280 194 68 13 424 17 172 50 54 114 49 40 47 68 340 239 27 138 109 100 13_
Fergus Falls	363 176 211 145 249 318 124 105 202 210 145 176 108 56 53 189 216 205 239 177 230 259 114 187 203 186 196 139 237 237 109 204 294 20_
Grand Portage (Port of Entry)	233 226 345 272 432 336 297 495 380 427 302 392 395 389 388 336 477 366 470 344 377 294 300 368 324 300 393 202 376 354 446 408 47_
Grand Rapids	35 194 116 313 185 113 339 242 270 173 236 175 206 238 214 244 238 314 224 256 143 179 230 186 185 160 61 241 198 293 288 32_
Hibbing	225 101 321 215 147 373 266 305 189 271 209 240 268 225 279 254 348 233 266 173 189 254 210 189 195 26 263 232 328 297 36_
Hutchinson	308 197 21 83 167 65 99 58 69 201 103 43 87 350 106 143 108 135 51 65 57 47 84 273 235 91 48 105 172 13_
International Falls	421 299 225 433 358 363 289 325 246 290 351 325 217 355 408 333 366 257 289 346 302 289 179 99 358 301 396 397 41_
La Crescent	208 238 268 152 257 143 266 374 290 180 125 518 109 283 89 68 208 134 162 149 139 434 323 125 235 218 26 33_
Litchfield	74 168 86 99 66 65 180 82 65 105 329 127 143 119 149 42 75 78 68 92 252 226 113 27 116 183 16_
Little Falls	226 148 157 96 123 145 93 126 137 280 160 201 150 180 33 104 141 106 113 196 174 162 85 180 214 21_
Luverne	128 70 205 108 239 149 124 183 397 169 26 220 209 201 212 139 183 230 340 385 154 141 62 249 33_
Mankato	105 77 120 266 165 28 56 415 42 131 92 83 115 84 12 56 102 338 270 27 110 66 130 9_
Marshall	146 39 194 92 77 142 349 146 45 178 188 133 154 105 128 172 284 317 132 72 69 235 63_
Minneapolis	127 231 149 89 40 376 65 189 54 83 65 9 66 22 26 292 193 75 93 143 118 174_
Montevideo	157 54 92 151 312 162 83 177 204 98 135 117 116 153 246 283 147 38 97 241 10_
Moorhead	102 243 272 162 295 215 285 315 169 241 258 242 252 113 235 292 158 254 349 257_
Morris	140 187 258 207 124 202 231 94 158 158 150 174 192 266 192 55 151 266 155_
New Ulm	79 393 70 104 115 112 94 97 28 71 115 317 279 55 85 62 158 92_
Northfield	416 30 183 37 58 105 36 50 40 55 332 226 40 132 121 101 152_
Noyes	440 372 430 459 313 384 407 386 393 84 303 441 313 408 494 412_
Owatonna	173 67 41 128 66 52 62 85 355 256 15 152 107 87 138_
Pipestone	220 215 176 197 132 171 216 315 360 158 116 65 259 59_
Red Wing	46 119 46 87 61 50 346 234 77 146 158 64 189_
Rochester	148 77 94 88 88 375 267 57 176 149 46 178_
St. Cloud	73 108 75 83 229 184 131 60 156 183 186_
St. Paul	72 28 18 300 190 76 102 150 110 180_
St. Peter	44 91 330 258 37 103 77 140 9_
Shakopee	47 302 214 55 95 121 125 152_
Stillwater	309 191 95 119 188 114 199_
Thief River Falls	219 358 238 333 409 346_
Virginia	266 245 336 298 367_
Waseca	137 92 103 123_
Willmar	95 210 126_
Windom	195 31_
Winona	218_
Worthington	

EXAMPLE:

International Falls to St. Paul - 289 miles

58

MAP PAGE INDEX

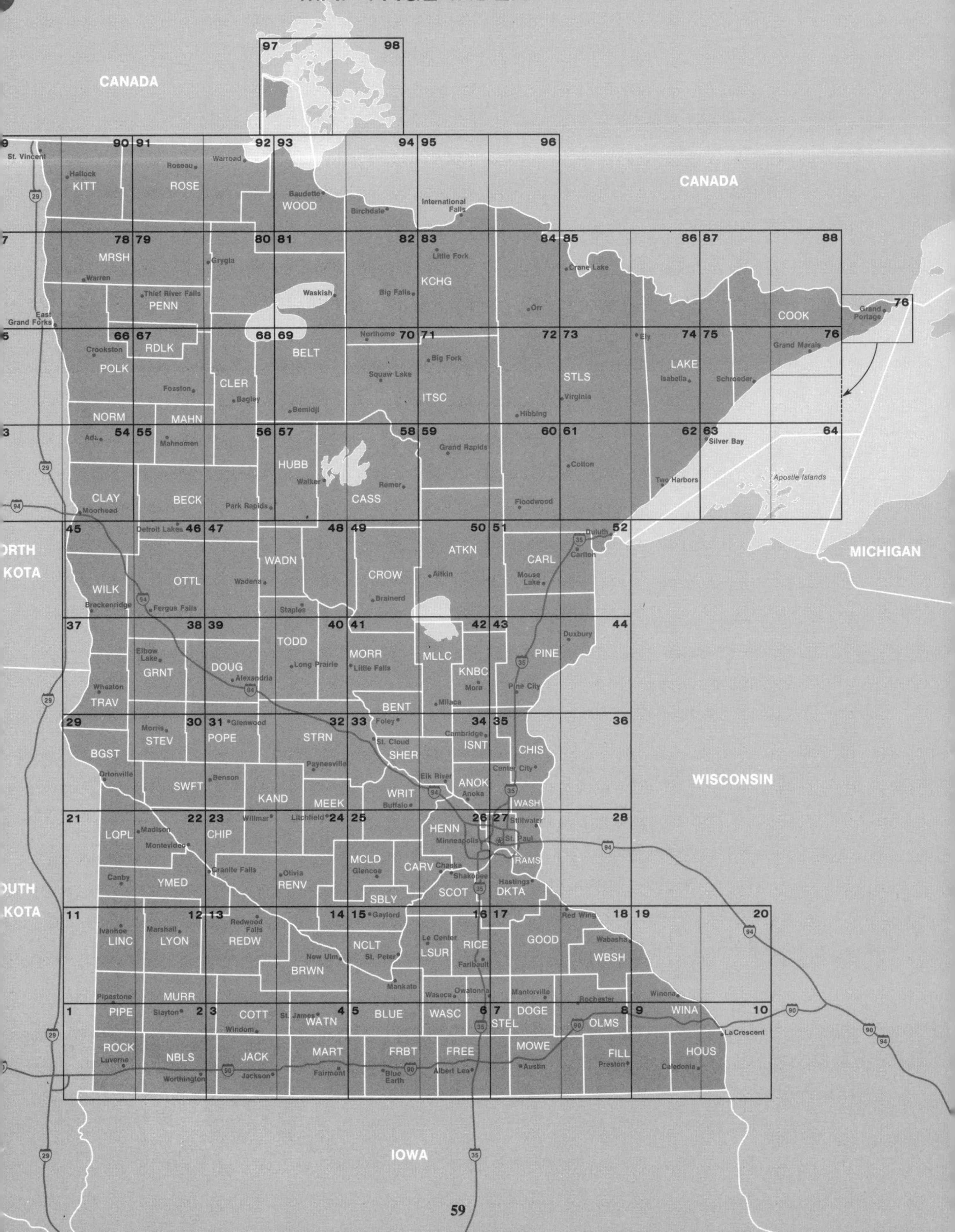

EXPLANATION OF MAP INFORMATION

ROADS AND HIGHWAYS

▬▬▬ Interstate Highway

═══ Limited Access Divided Highway

━━━ Primary Highway

─── Secondary Highway

─── Other Paved Road

═══ Unpaved Road

(35) Interstate

(52) U.S. Highway

(96) State Highway

[59] County Highway

✳ Great River Road

┿ Interchange

╟─1─╢ Red numbers show mileage between red markers

BOUNDARIES

▬ ▬ ▬ International

▬·▬·▬ State

Martin County

L Y L E Township

TOWNS AND CITIES (1980 Census Data)

Wright○ Place with population less than 200 and/or unincorporated

Bethel● Population 200–1,000

Byron● Population 1,000–5,000

Morris● Population 5,000–10,000

Duluth Population more than 10,000

Olivia County Seat

○ Central Business District

OTHER FEATURES

∿ River

IC RR Railroad

─── State Trail, Complete

- - - - State Trail, Planned

▨ Forest

▨ Swamp or Marsh

▨ Open Water

+1526 FT. Hills/Spot Elevation

▨ ● County or State Park or Recreation Site

▨ Indian Reservation

▨ Military Reservation

▨ Wildlife Area

▨ State Forest

▨ National Forest

▨ Boundary Waters Canoe Area

⬥ Airport

�֎ Border Crossing

■ College, University or State Institution

▲ Point of Interest

▲ Wayside or Rest Area

Public Water Access:
(In BWCA by Permit Only)

◆ Ramp

◆ Portage

(20) Page on which adjacent area is mapped

MAP PAGE INDEX

To find the page on which an area of interest is mapped, see Map Page Index, page 59.

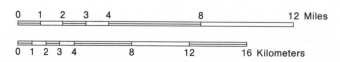

Representative Fraction for all maps 1:250,000

Map Symbols

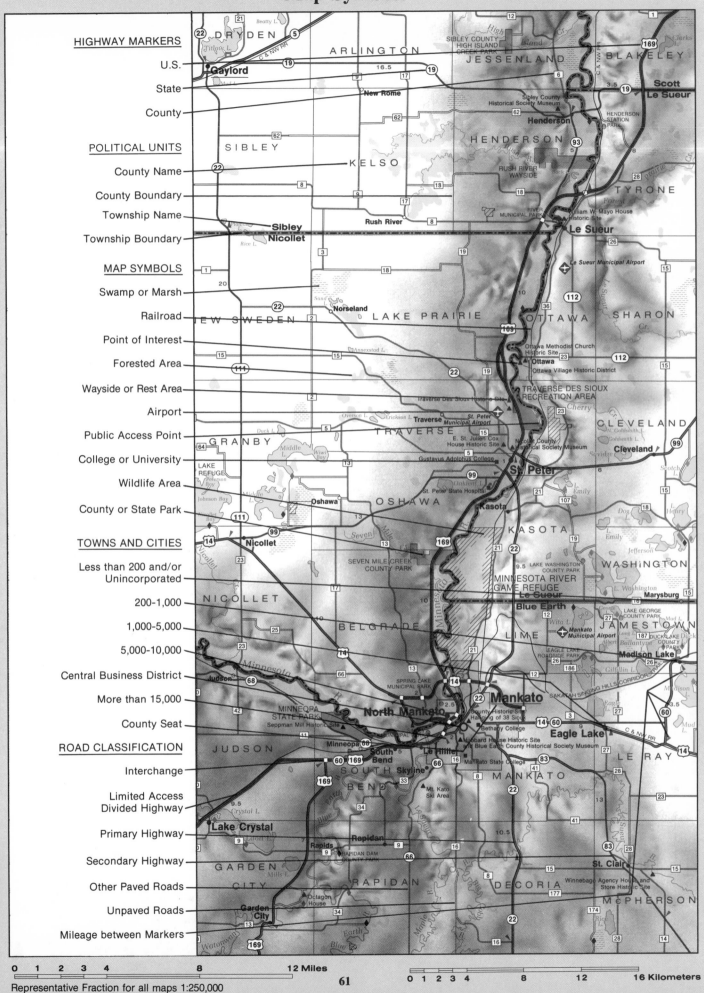

HIGHLIGHT MARKERS

U.S.

State

County

POLITICAL UNITS

County Name

County Boundary

Township Name

Township Boundary

MAP SYMBOLS

Swamp or Marsh

Railroad

Point of Interest

Forested Area

Wayside or Rest Area

Airport

Public Access Point

College or University

Wildlife Area

County or State Park

TOWNS AND CITIES

Less than 200 and/or
Unincorporated

200-1,000

1,000-5,000

5,000-10,000

Central Business District

More than 15,000

County Seat

ROAD CLASSIFICATION

Interchange

Limited Access
Divided Highway

Primary Highway

Secondary Highway

Other Paved Roads

Unpaved Roads

Mileage between Markers

0 1 2 3 4   8   12 Miles

0 1 2 3 4   8   12   16 Kilometers

Representative Fraction for all maps 1:250,000

61

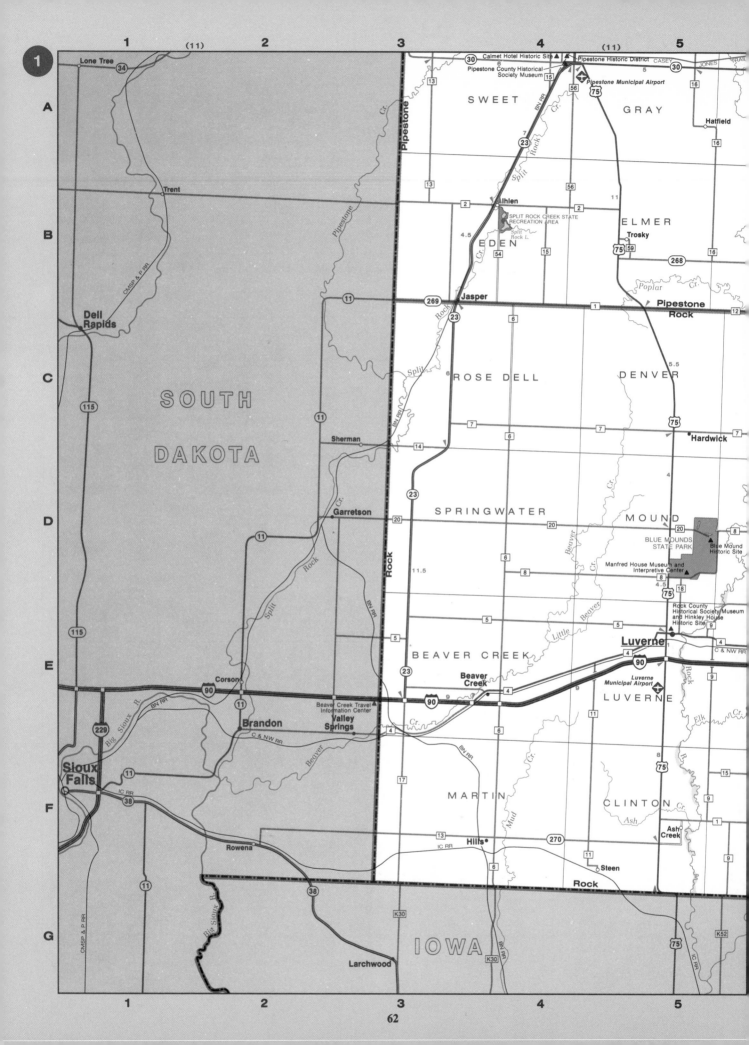

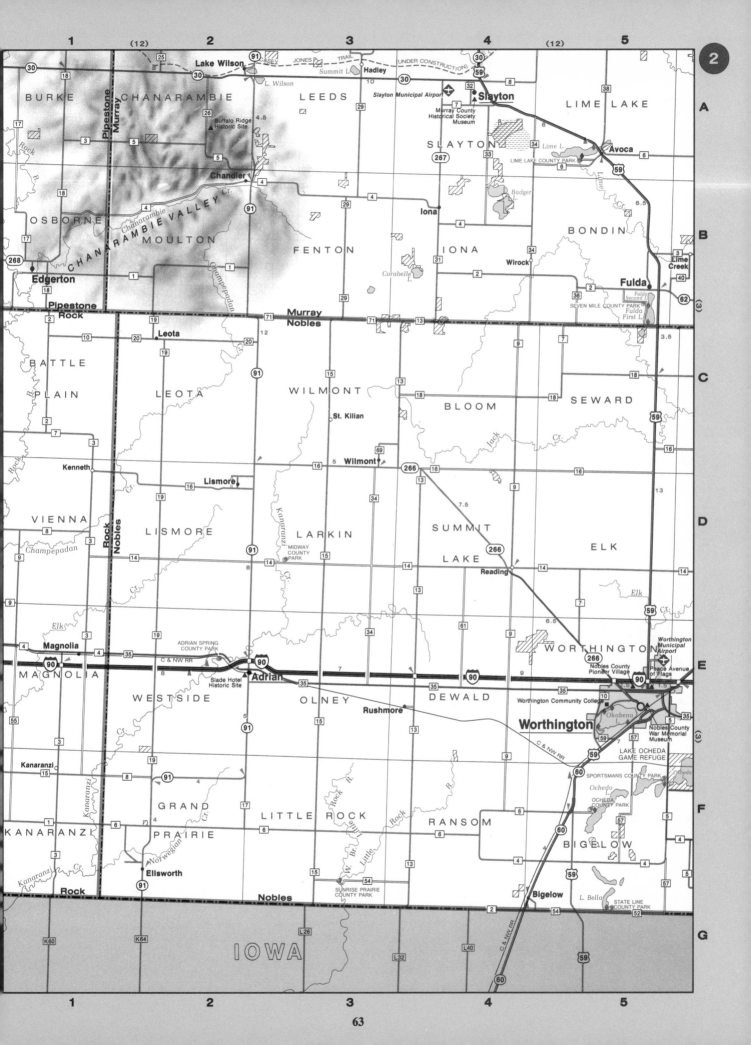

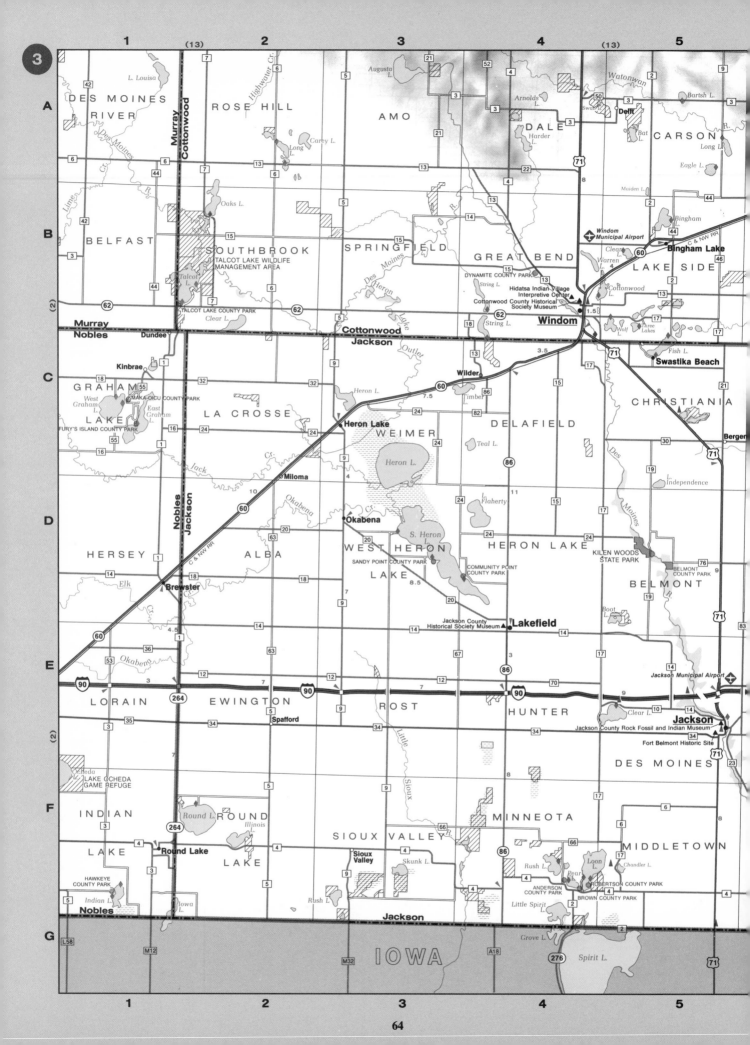

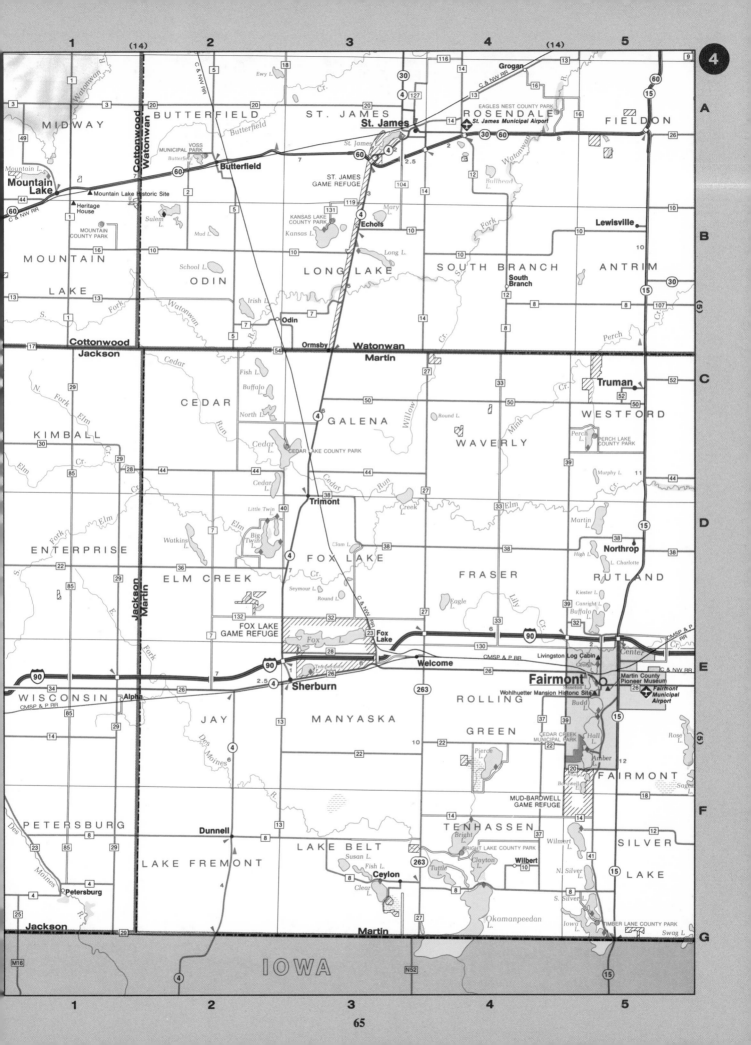

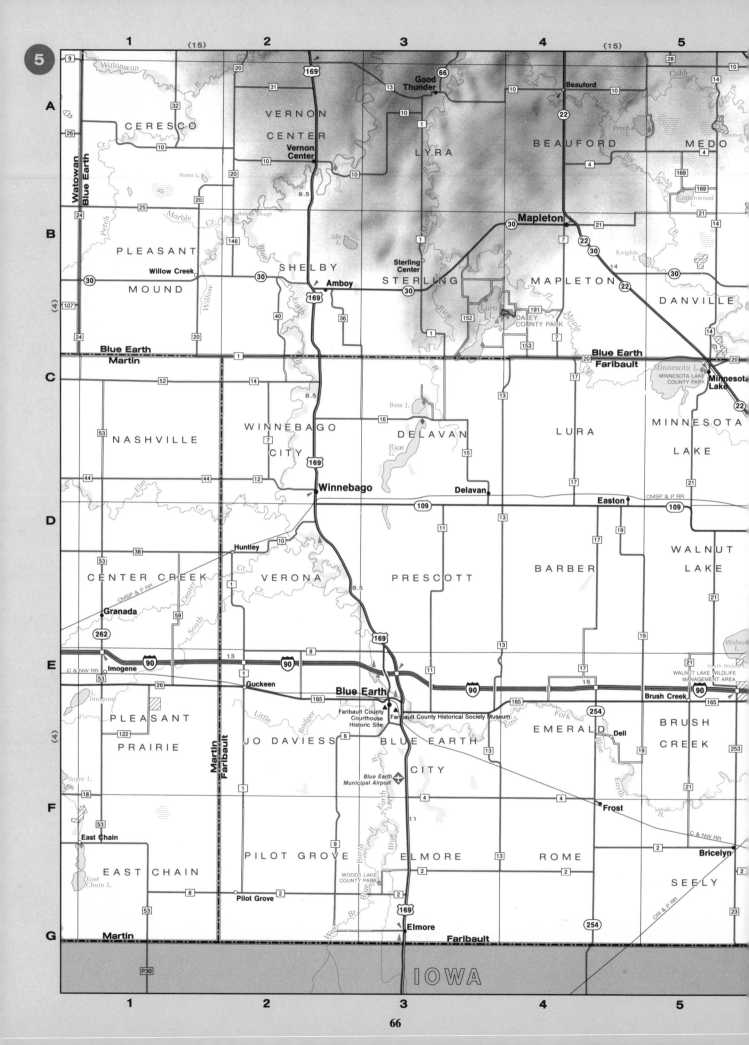

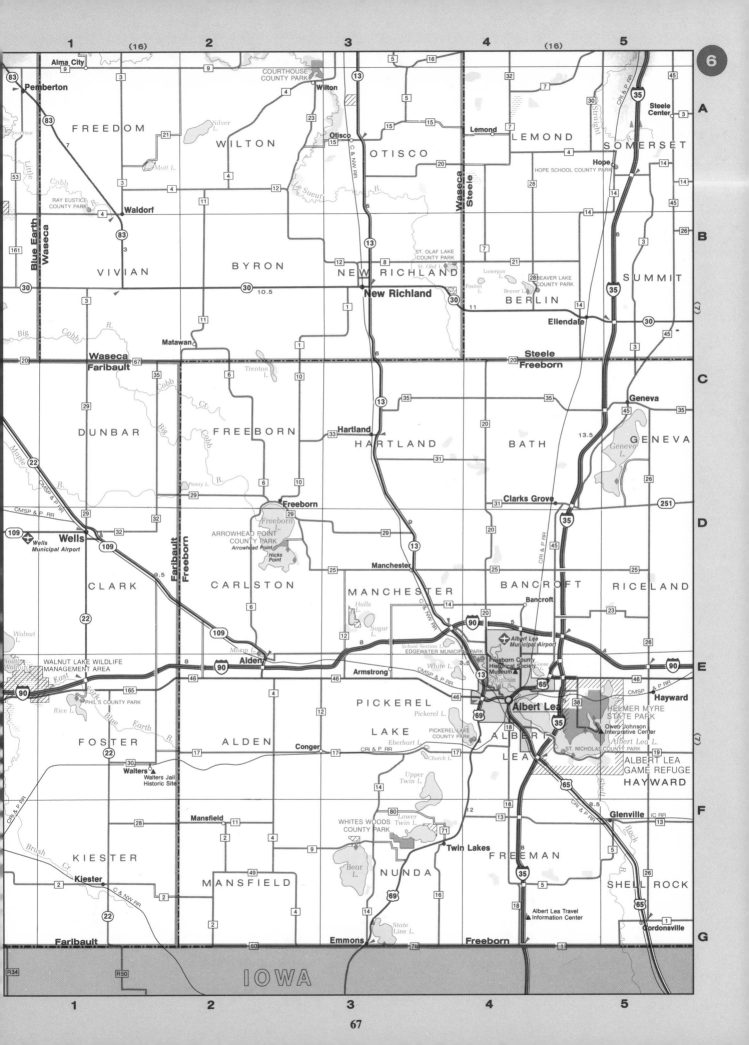

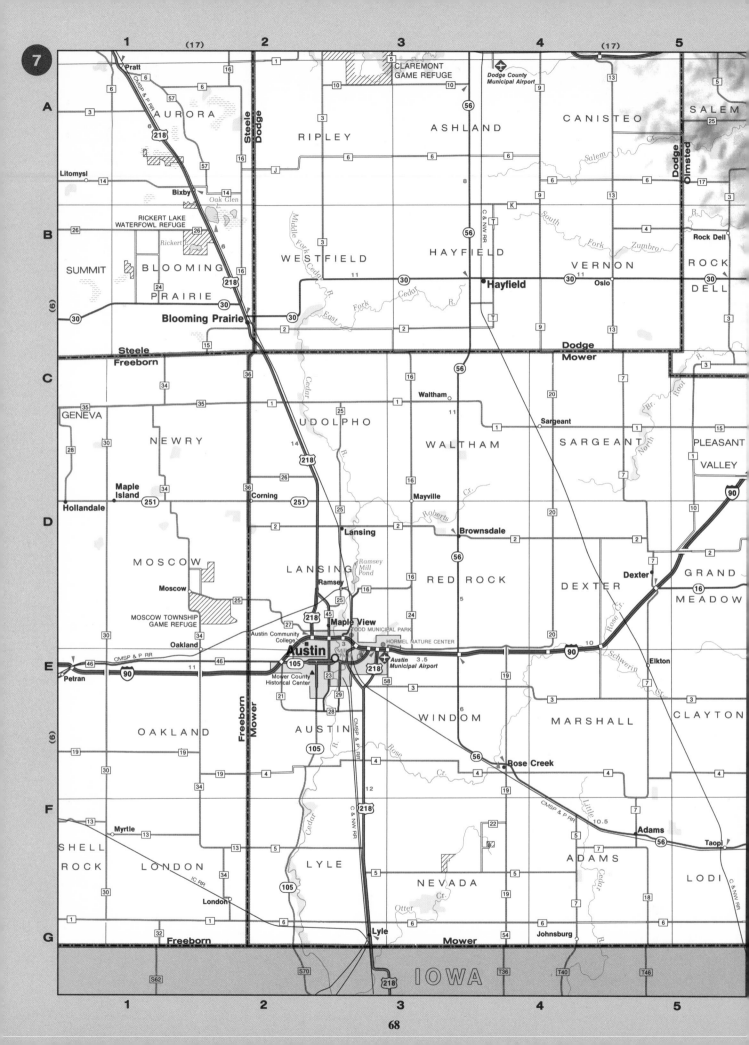

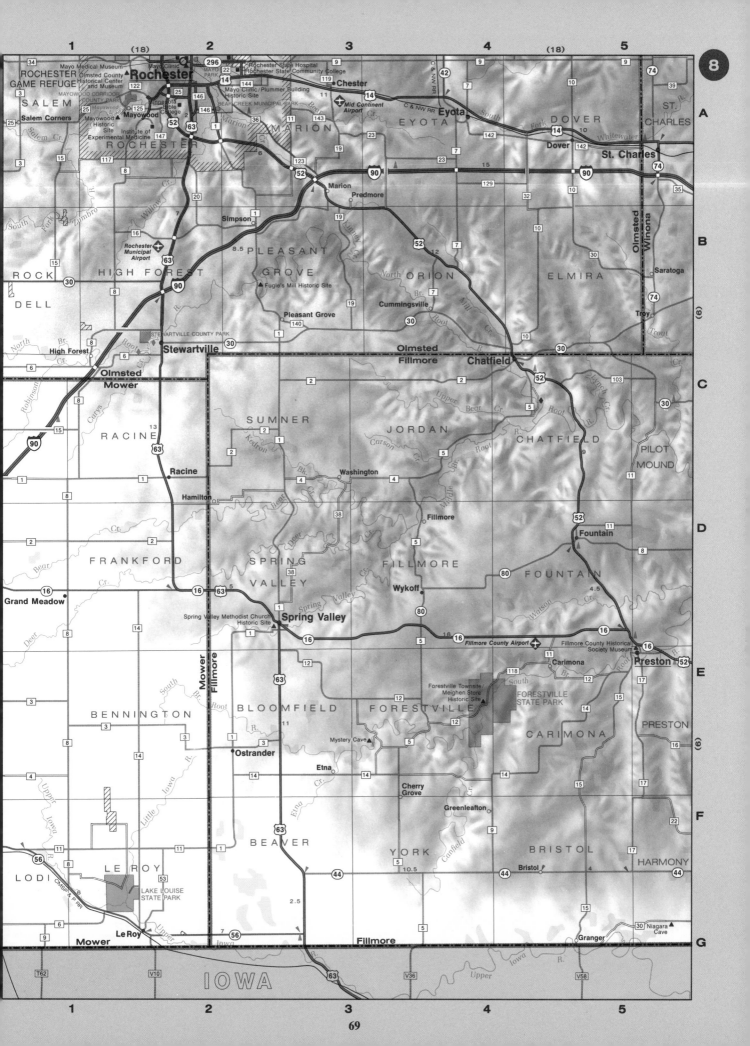

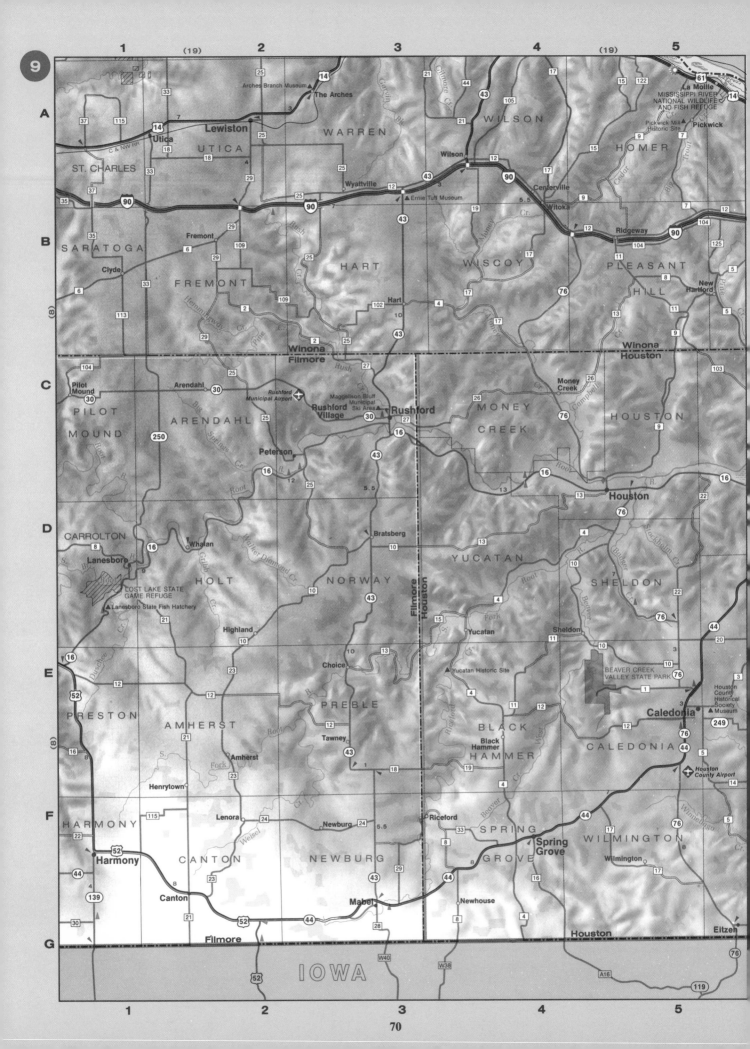

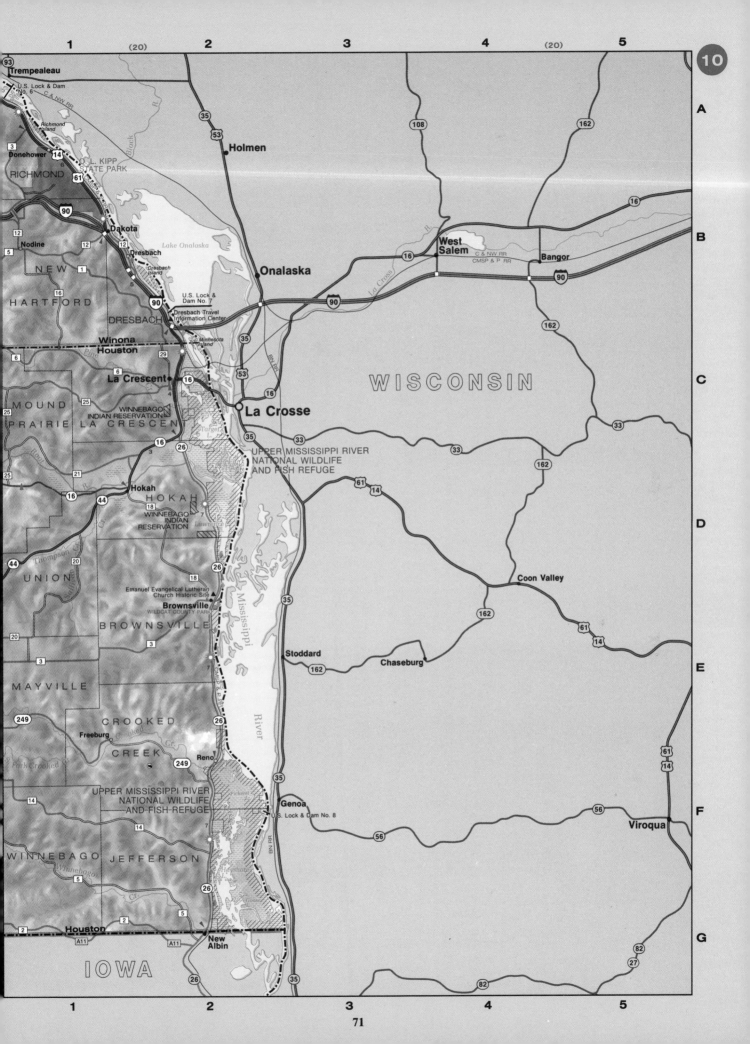

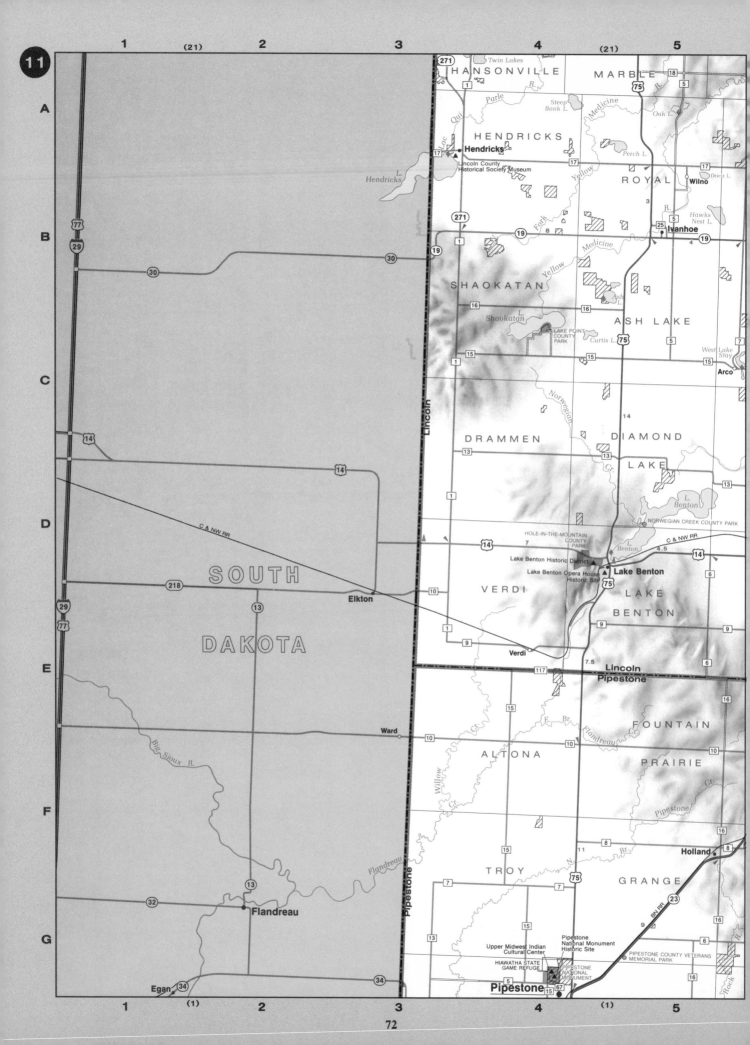

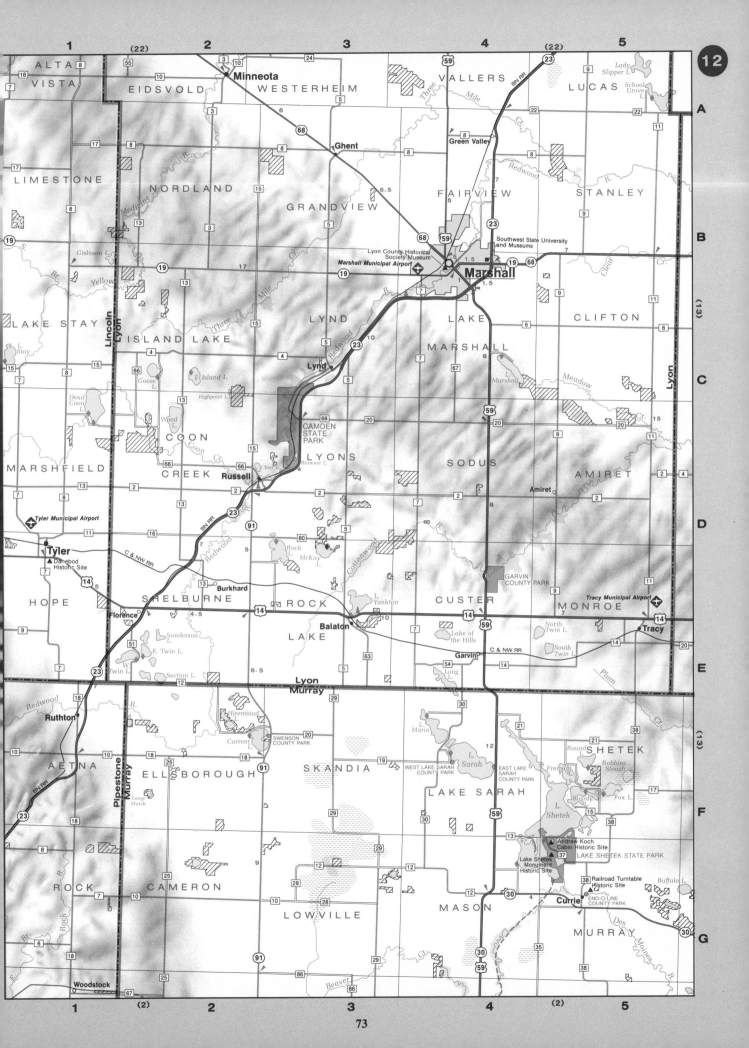

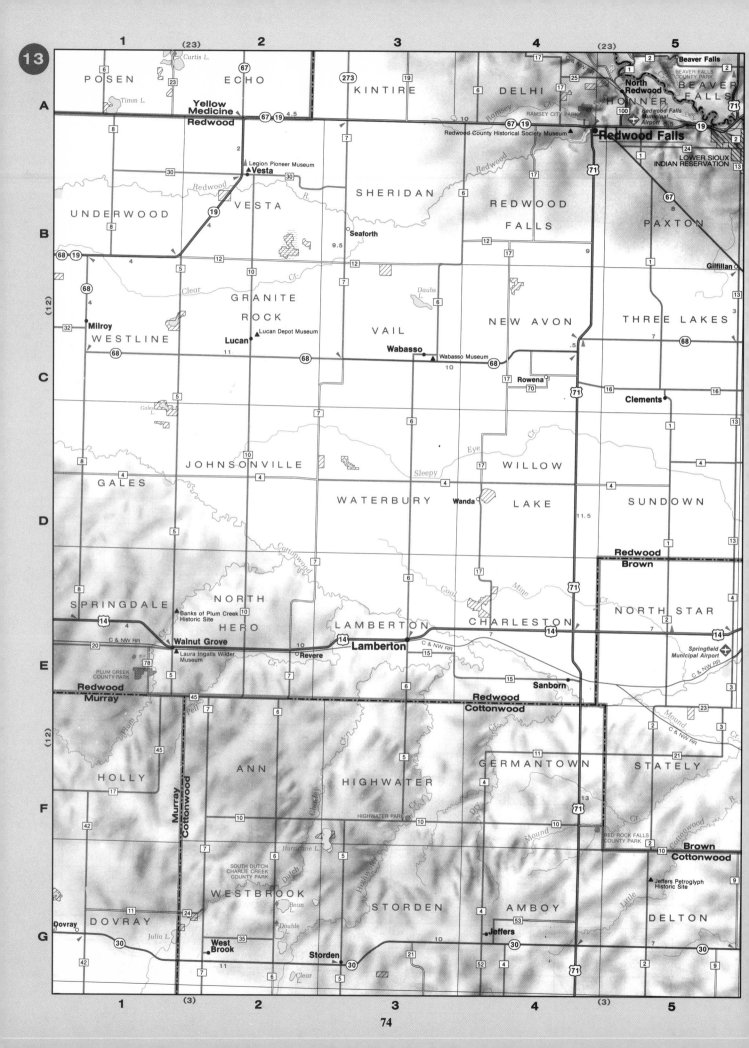

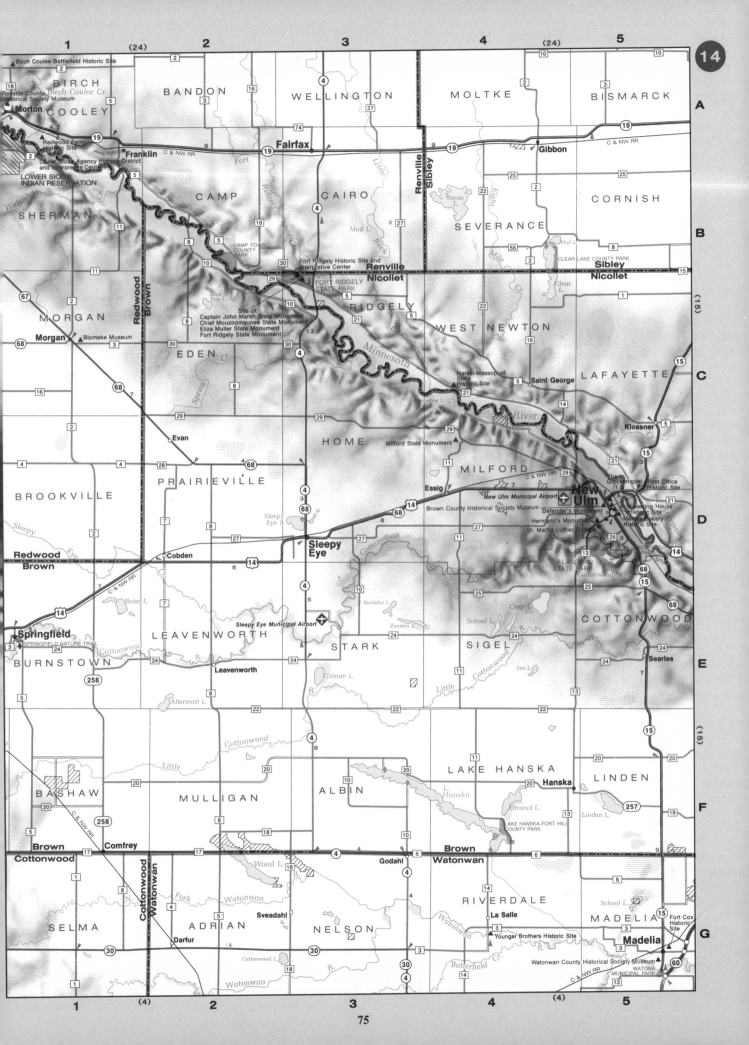

1 (24) **2** **3** **4** (24) **5**

BIRCH COULEE BATTLEFIELD HISTORIC SITE

Birch Coulee Battlefield Historic Site

BIRCH

Renville County Birch Coulee Cr.
Historical Society Museum

COOLEY **Morton**

BANDON

WELLINGTON

MOLTKE

BISMARCK

A

Redwood Ferry
Historic Site

Fairfax **Gibbon**

C & NW RR

Franklin

Lower Sioux Agency Historic District
and Interpretive Center

**LOWER SIOUX
INDIAN RESERVATION**

CAMP

CAIRO

SEVERANCE

CORNISH

SHERMAN

Camp Town County Park

Fort Ridgely Historic Site and
Interpretive Center

Renville
Nicollet

Sibley
Nicollet

B

FORT RIDGELY STATE PARK

Clear Lake County Park

MORGAN

Site of:
Captain John Marsh State Monument
Chief Mouzzomaunee State Monument
Eliza Muller State Monument
Fort Ridgely State Monument

RIDGELY

WEST NEWTON

Harkin-Massopust
Store Historic Site

Saint George

LAFAYETTE

Morgan

Blomeke Museum

EDEN

Klossner

C

Redwood
Brown

Evan

HOME

Milford State Monument

MILFORD

Essig

The Glockenspiel Post Office Historic Site

New Ulm

Kiesling House Historic Site
Meidl Bakery Historic Site

BROOKVILLE

PRAIRIEVILLE

New Ulm Municipal Airport

Brown County Historical Society Museum

Defender's Monument

Hermann's Monument

Dr. Martin Luther College

D

Redwood
Brown

Cobden

Sleepy
Eye

FLANDRAU STATE PARK

COTTONWOOD

Springfield

SPRINGFIELD NATURE TRAIL

LEAVENWORTH

Sleepy Eye Municipal Airport

STARK

SIGEL

Searles

E

BURNSTOWN

Leavenworth

BASHAW

MULLIGAN

ALBIN

LAKE HANSKA

Hanska

LINDEN

F

Lake Hanska-Fort Hill
County Park

Brown
Cottonwood

Comfrey

Godahl

Brown
Watonwan

SELMA

ADRIAN

Darfur

Sveadahl

NELSON

RIVERDALE

La Salle

MADELIA

Fort Cox
Historic Site

Madelia

Younger Brothers Historic Site

Watonwan County Historical Society Museum

WATONA MUNICIPAL PARK

G

1 (4) **2** **3** **4** (4) **5**

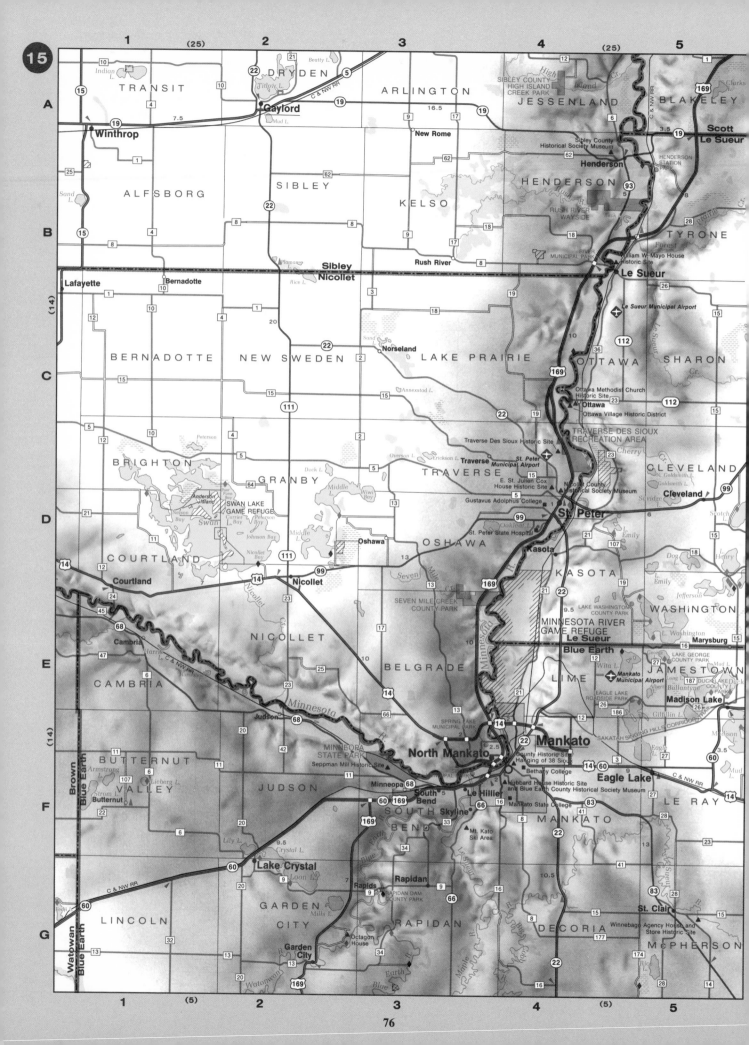

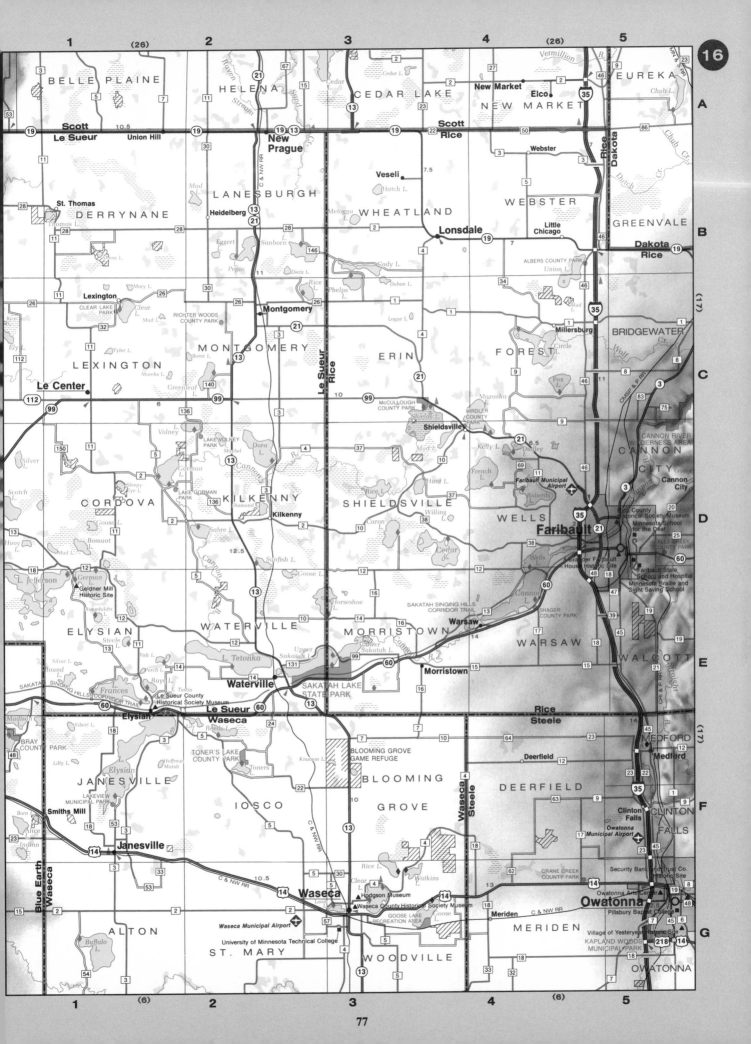

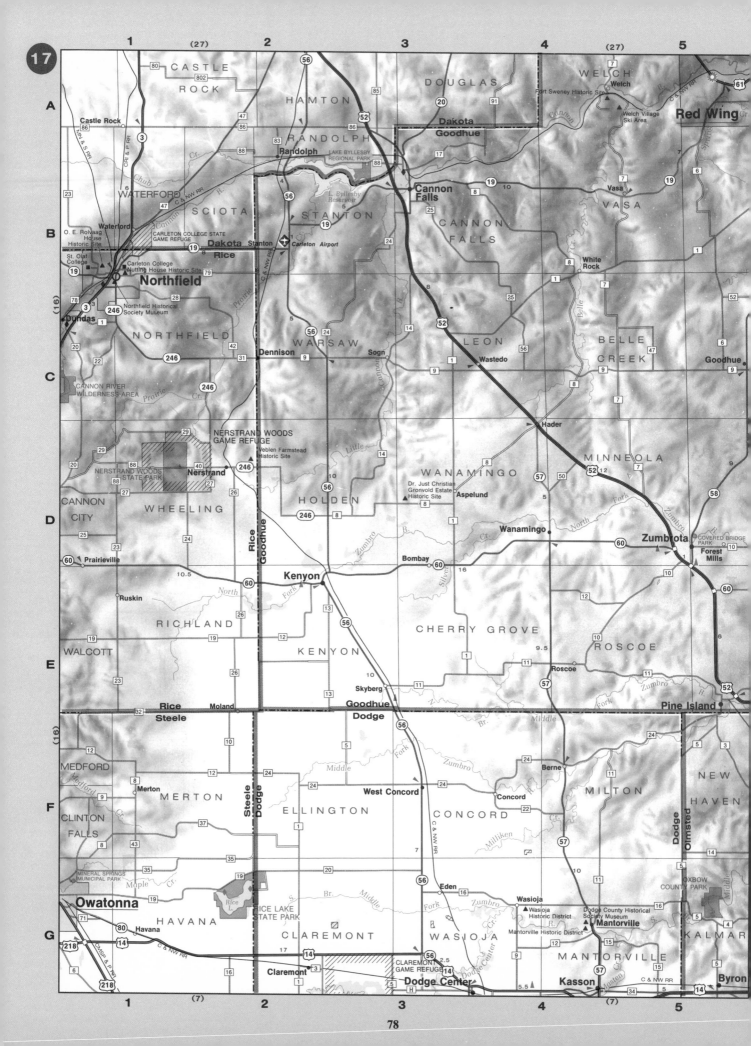

1 (27) **2** **3** **4** (27) **5**

A

80 CASTLE
ROCK
802
HAMTON
DOUGLAS
85 WELCH 7
Fort Sweney Historic Site Welch
52 20 Welch Village
Ski Area
91 Red Wing
Castle Rock
86 DAKOTA
86 RANDOLPH Goodhue 61
23 47 Randolph LAKE BYLLESBY
REGIONAL PARK 88 17 VASA
WATERFORD 88 19 10 Vasa 7 19
Cr. 4
B
SCIOTA 56 STANTON 25 7
O. E. Rolvaag CARLETON COLLEGE STATE
House GAME REFUGE 19 Dakota Stanton 24 CANNON 6
Historic Site 19 Carleton Airport FALLS 8 White
St. Olaf Rice 52 Rock
College 79 8 1 1
19 Carleton College Nutting House Historic Site 28 8 25 7 BELLE
Northfield 56 24 1 47 CREEK
3 Northfield Historical LEON 56 Goodhue
16 78 246 Society Museum 14 6
Dundas 42 31 WARSAW Sogn 1 9 9
C 20 NORTHFIELD Dennison 9 Wastedo 8 7
22 246
CANNON RIVER 246 Hader
WILDERNESS AREA Cr. 29 MINNEOLA
NERSTRAND WOODS 40 246 Little 14 WANAMINGO 57 50 52 12 58
GAME REFUGE Veblen Farmstead Dr. Just Christian 5
29 Historic Site Gronvold Estate 7
20 88 Nerstrand 10 Historic Site Aspelund 5
NERSTRAND WOODS 26 56 8
88 STATE PARK 27 246 HOLDEN 8 Wanamingo COVERED BRIDGE
D 27 WHEELING 8 North Fork Zumbrota PARK
CANNON 246 1 60 Forest
CITY Rice 60 Mills
25 24 Goodhue Bombay 60 16 10
23 Zumbro 60
60 Prairieville 10.5 North Fork Kenyon 56 10
Ruskin 13 CHERRY GROVE ROSCOE 60
19 RICHLAND 26 12 9.5 11
E 19 12 11 Roscoe 11 52
WALCOTT KENYON 57
23 26 10 13 Skyberg 11 Pine Island
Rice Moland Goodhue 52
32 Steele Dodge 56
F 16 MEDFORD 10 5 24 Berne
12 12 24 11 NEW
Medford 8 24 West Concord 24 Concord MILTON HAVEN
9 Merton MERTON Steele Dodge 22 57
CLINTON ELLINGTON CONCORD Milliken 14
FALLS 37 1 7 11
8 43 35 Eden 16 OXBOW
MINERAL SPRINGS 35 20 56 11 COUNTY PARK
MUNICIPAL PARK Maple Cr. 19 Rice L. Wasioja Dodge County Historical 16
G Owatonna 19 HAVANA RICE LAKE Wasioja Society Museum 5
71 STATE PARK Historic District Mantorville KALMAR
80 Havana CLAREMONT Mantorville Historic District MANTORVILLE
218 14 17 WASIOJA 9 15
14 Claremont CLAREMONT 56 2.5 Kasson 57 15
6 16 GAME REFUGE 14 5.5 34 Byron
218 1 Dodge Center 218 14

1 (7) **2** **3** (7) **4** **5**

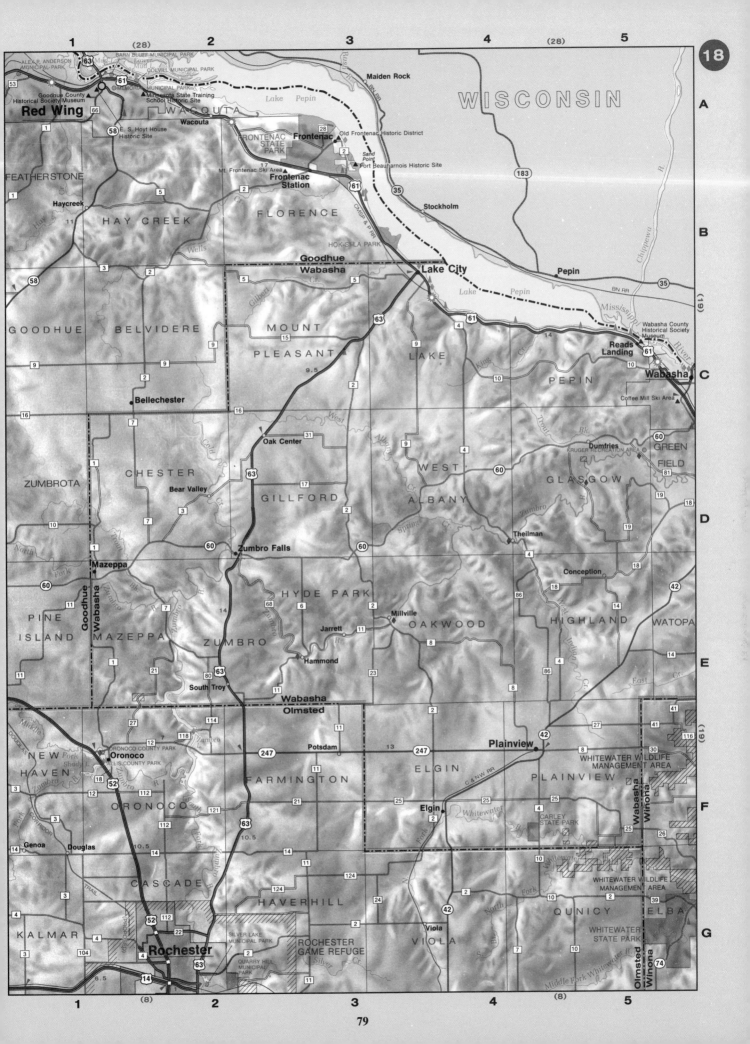

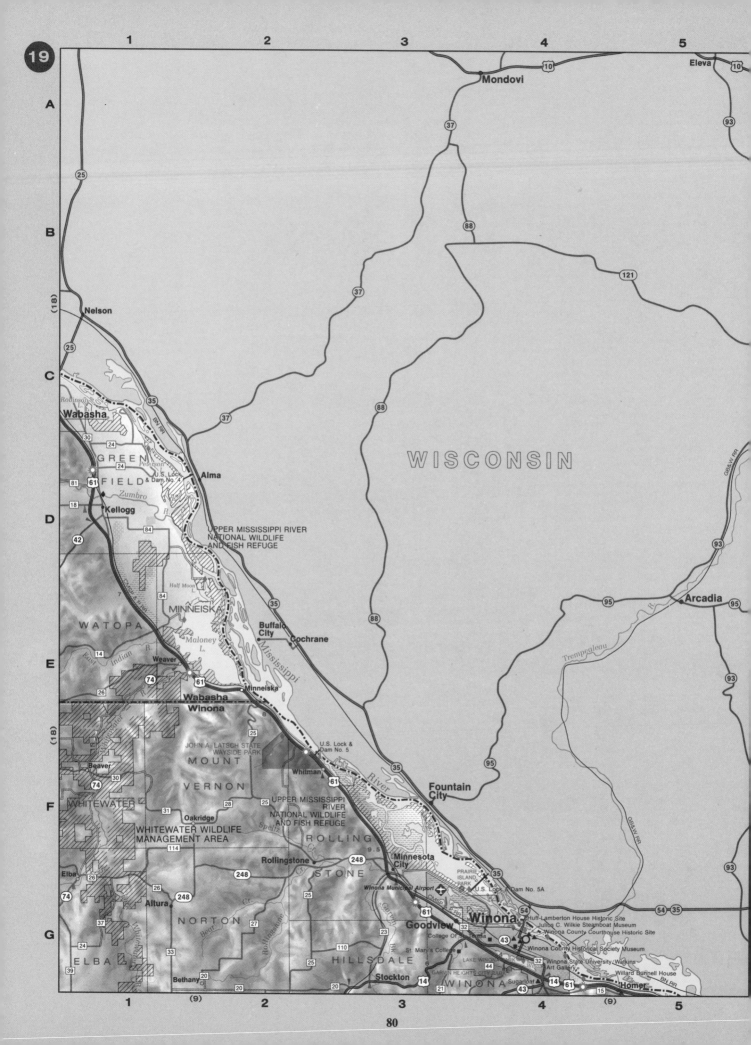

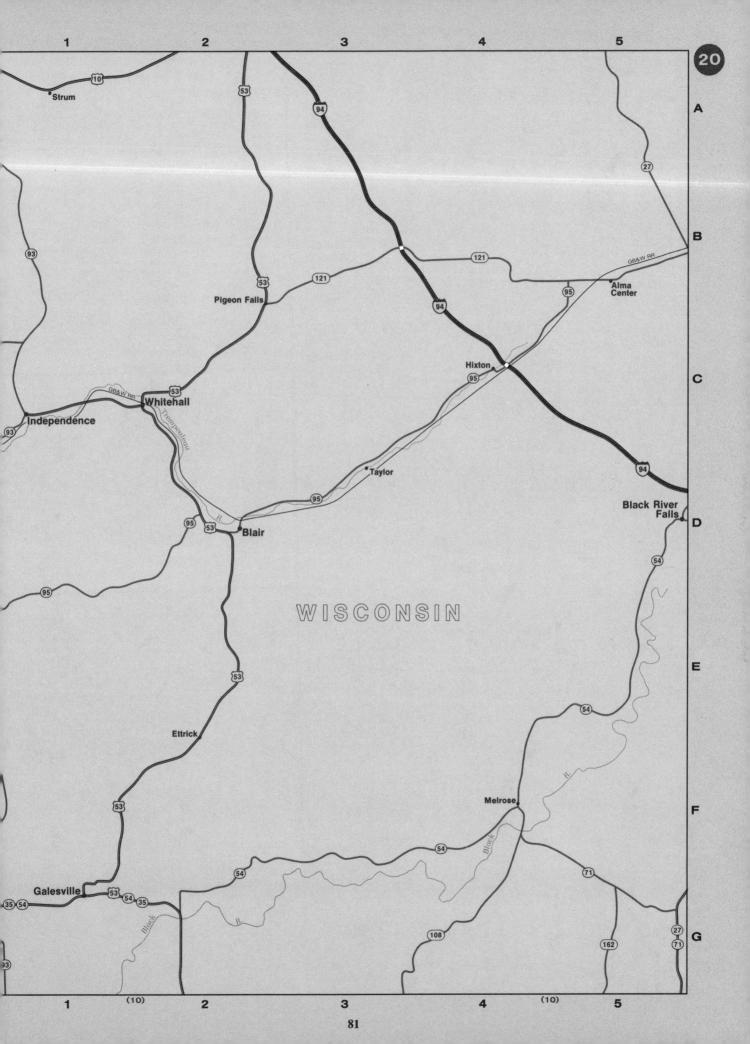

A

B

C

D

E

F

G

1 2 3 4 5

10

Strum

53

94

27

93

121

53

Pigeon Falls

121

94

95

Alma Center

GB&W RR

Hixton

95

53

GB&W RR

Whitehall

Independence

93

Trempealeau

Taylor

95

94

Black River Falls

95

53

Blair

R.

54

95

WISCONSIN

53

54

Ettrick

54

Melrose

53

Black

54

71

Galesville

35 54

53 54 35

Black

R.

54

108

71

27

162

71

93

(10)

(10)

1 2 3 4 5

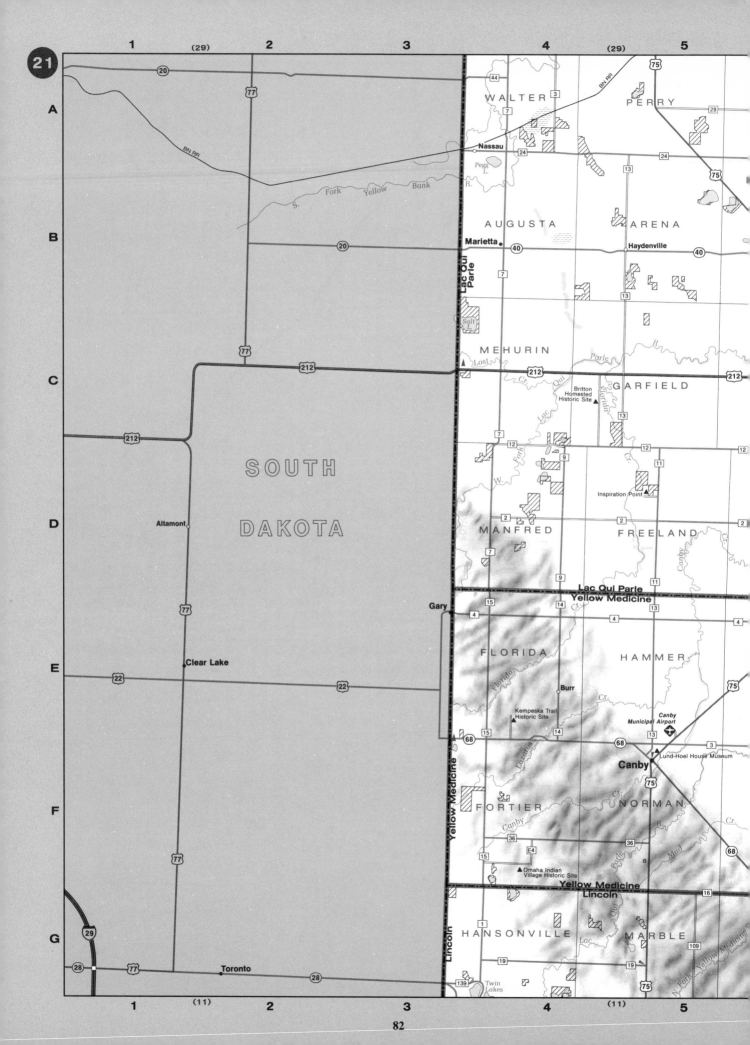

SOUTH

DAKOTA

WALTER

PERRY

Nassau

AUGUSTA

ARENA

Marietta

Haydenville

Lac Qui Parle

MEHURIN

GARFIELD

Britton
Homestead
Historic Site

MANFRED

FREELAND

Inspiration Point

Altamont

Lac Qui Parle
Yellow Medicine

Gary

FLORIDA

HAMMER

Clear Lake

Burr

Kempeska Trail
Historic Site

Canby
Municipal Airport

Lund-Hoel House Museum

Canby

Yellow Medicine

FORTIER

NORMAN

Omaha Indian
Village Historic Site

Yellow Medicine
Lincoln

Toronto

HANSONVILLE

MARBLE

Twin
Lakes

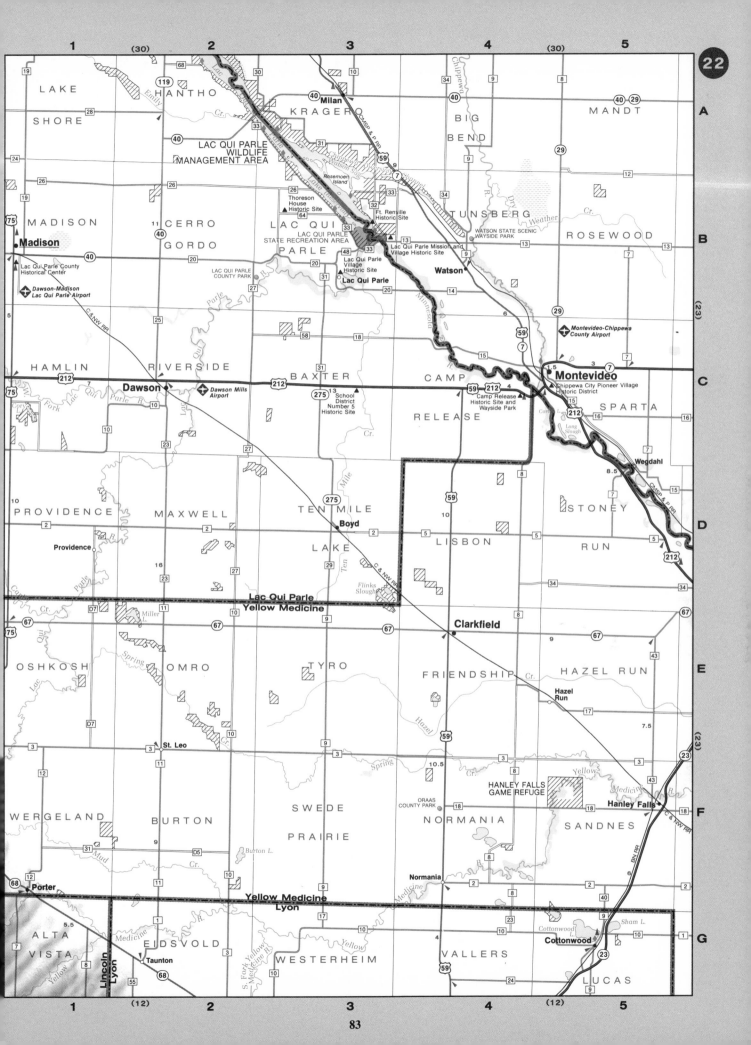

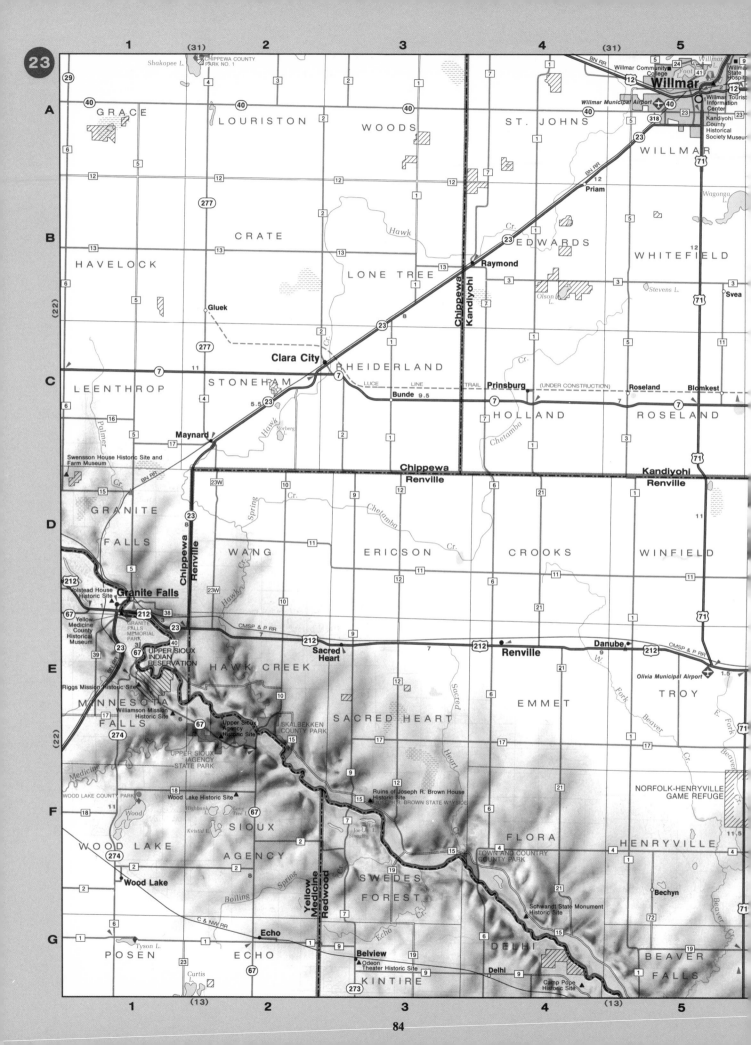

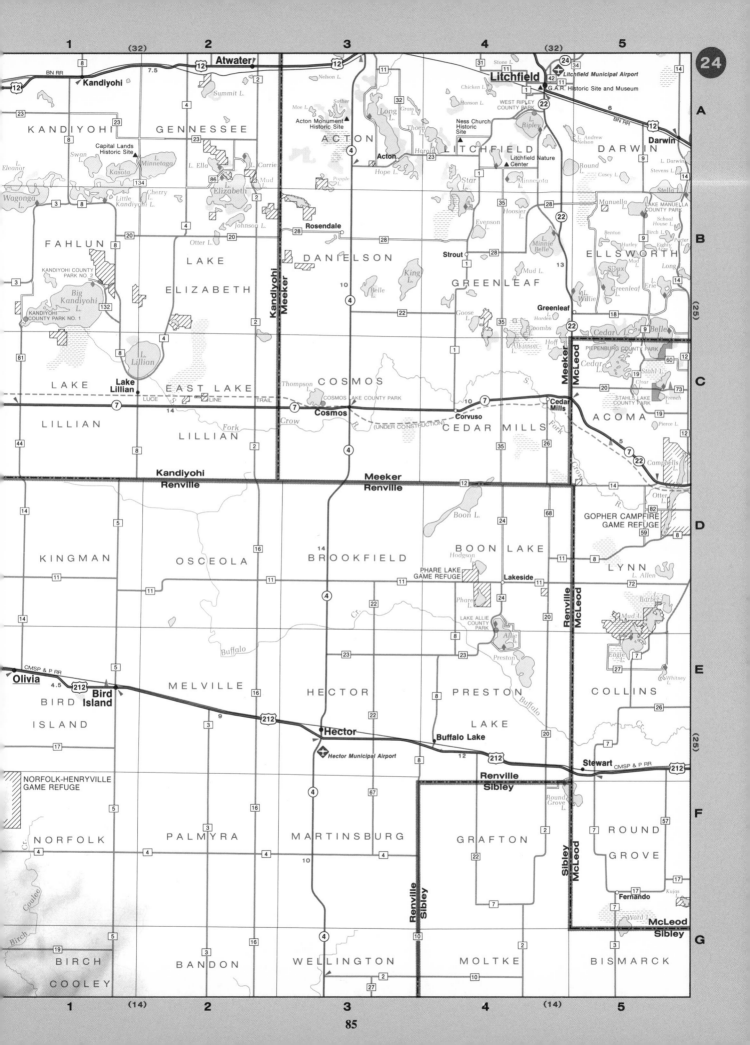

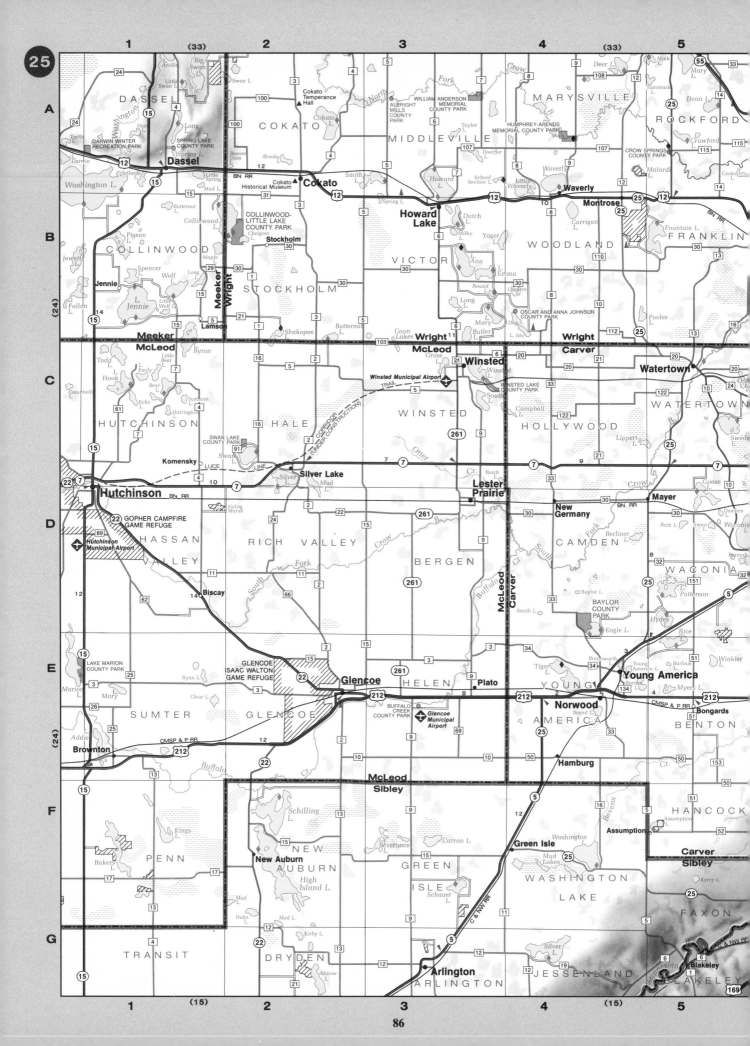

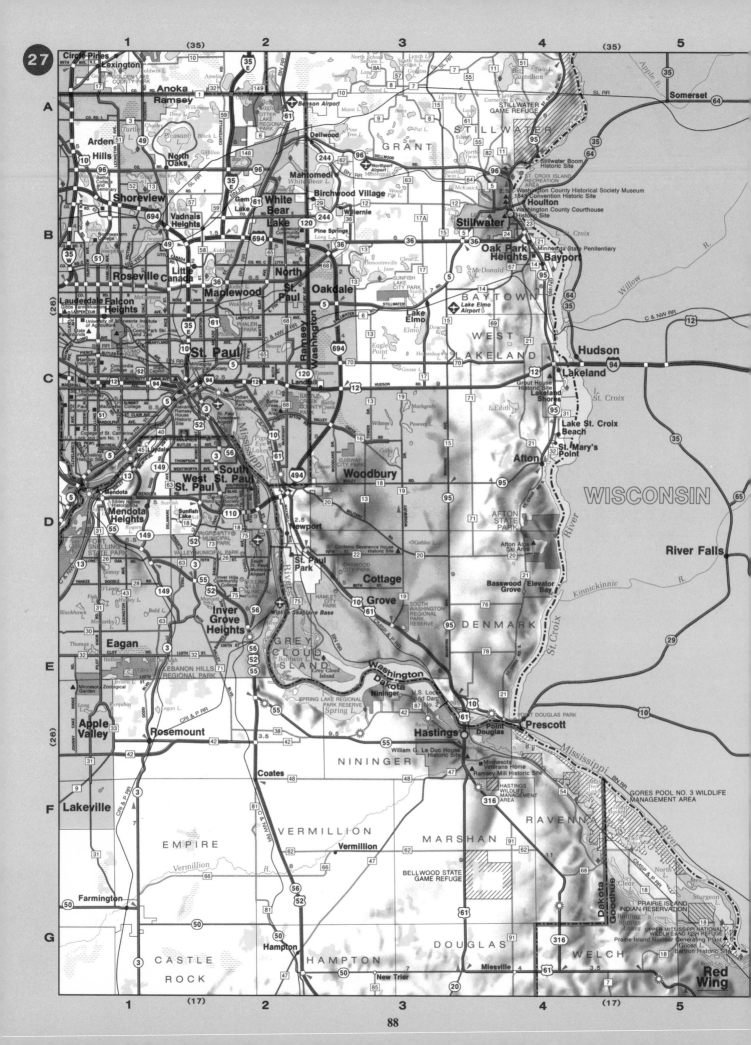

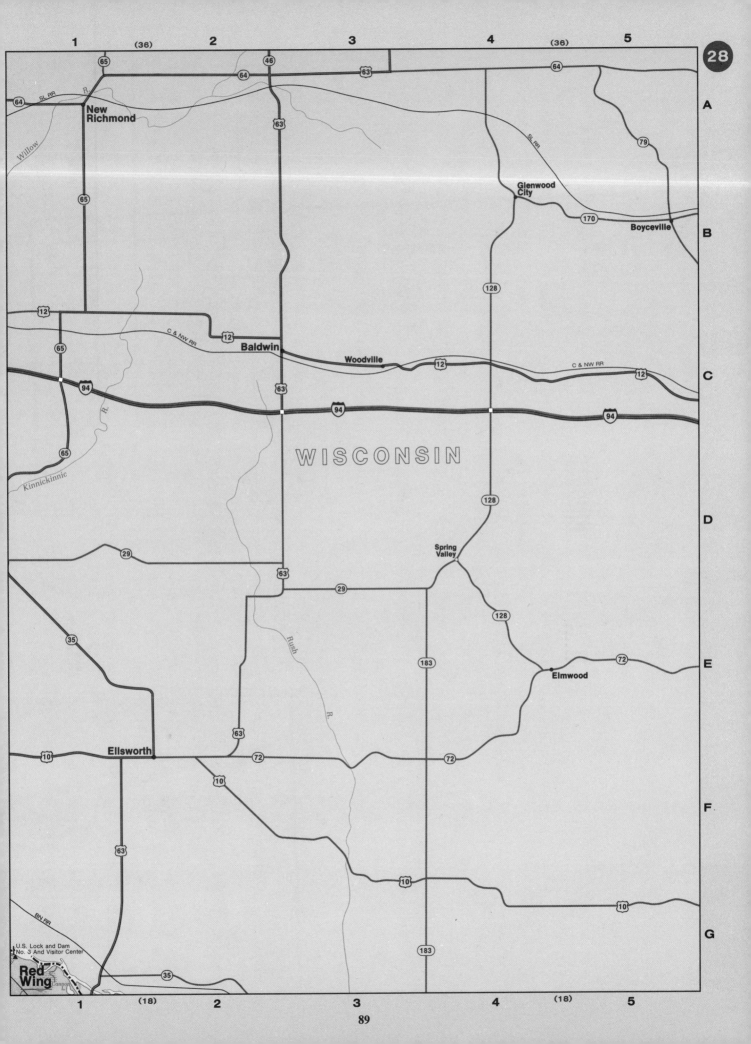

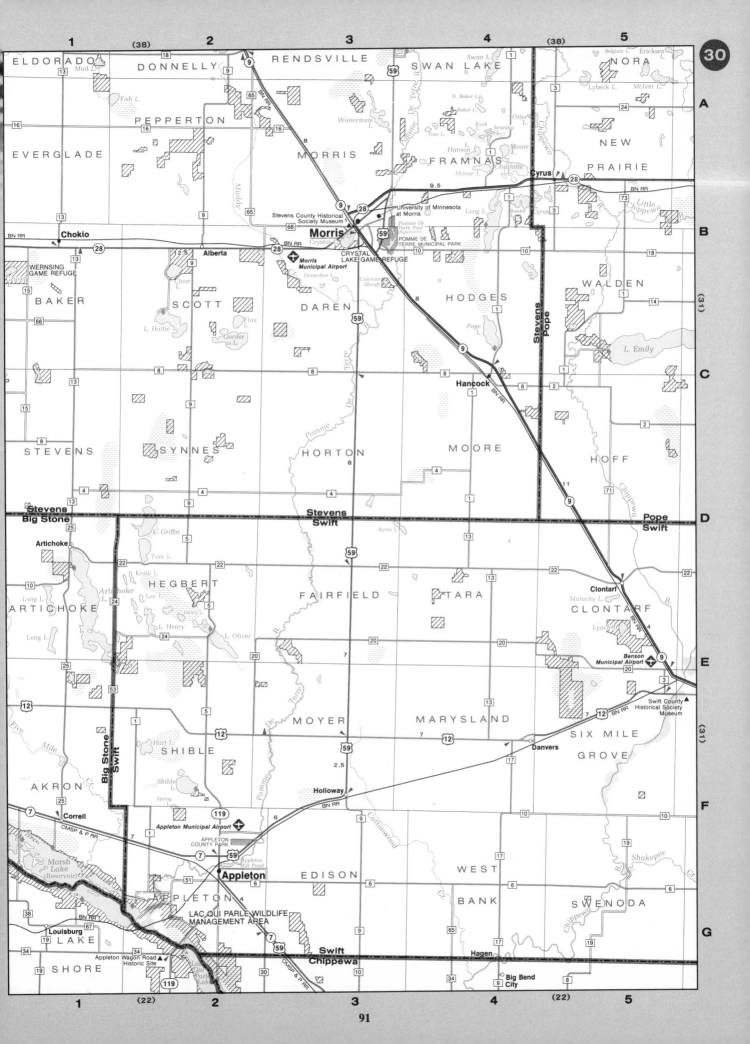

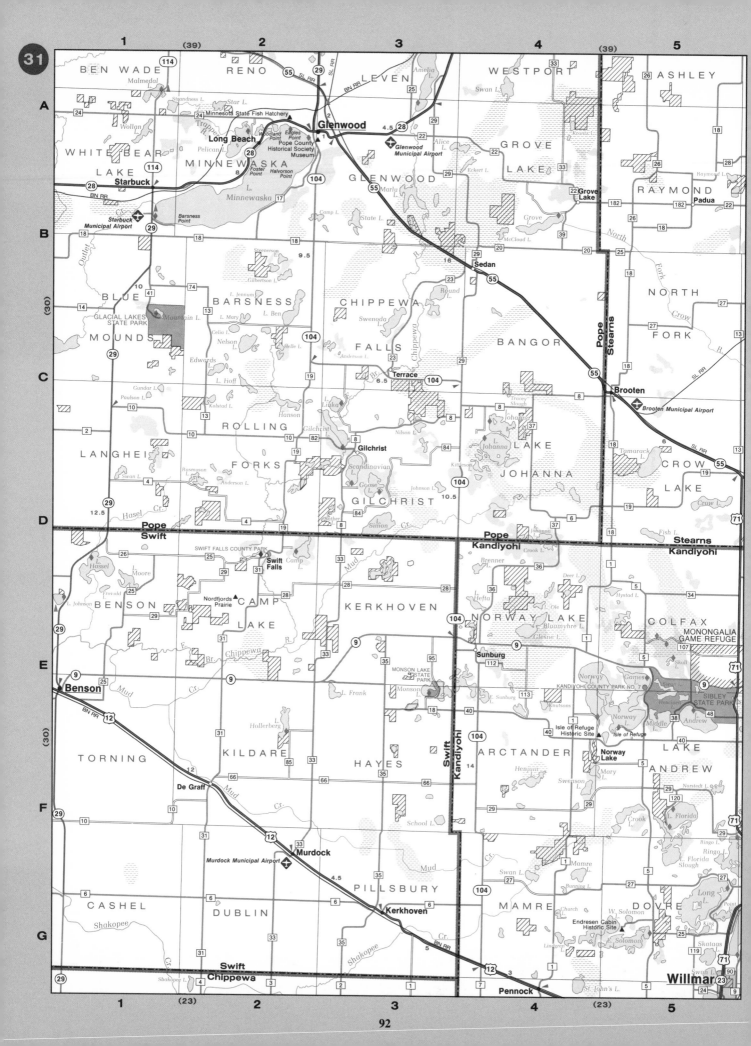

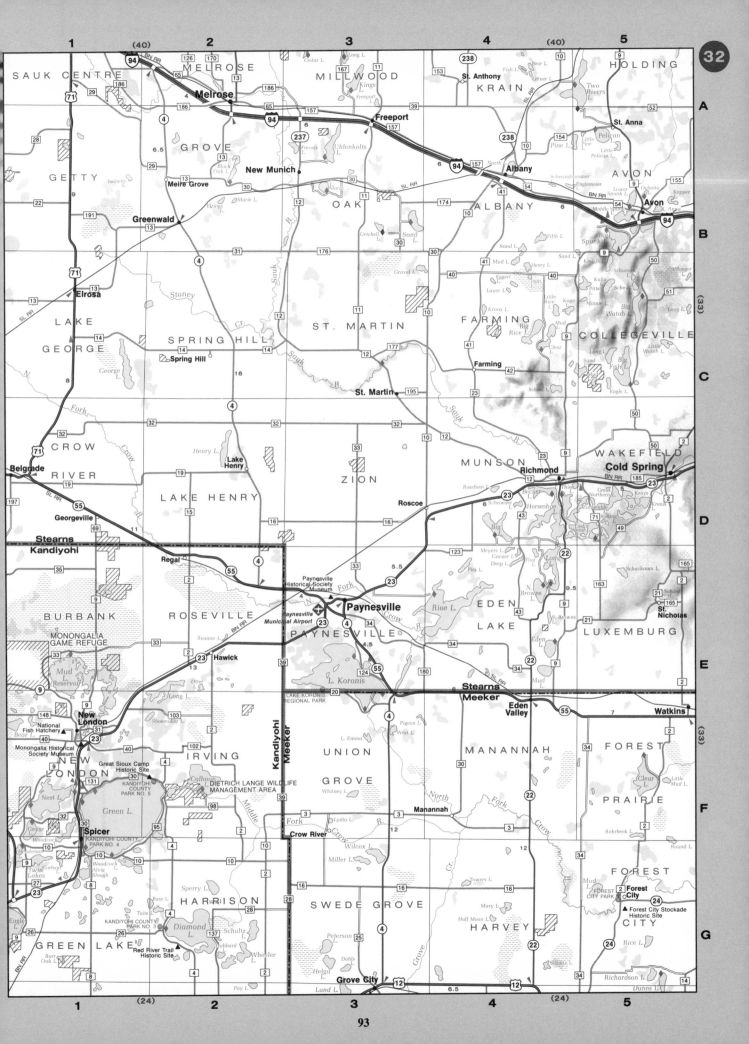

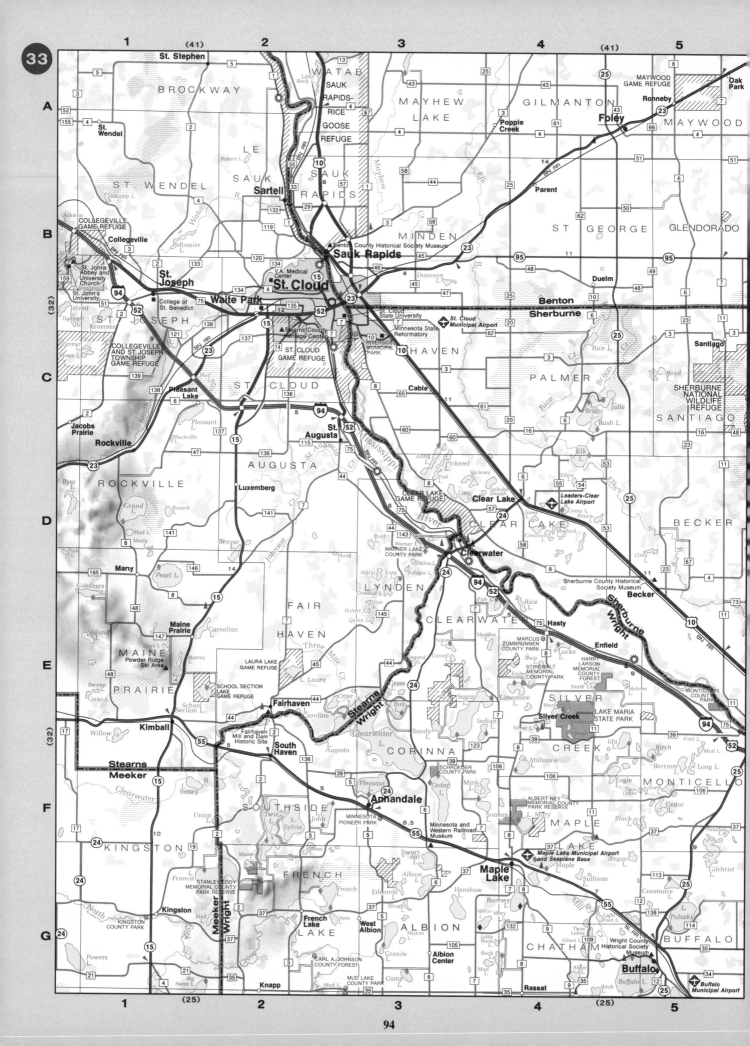

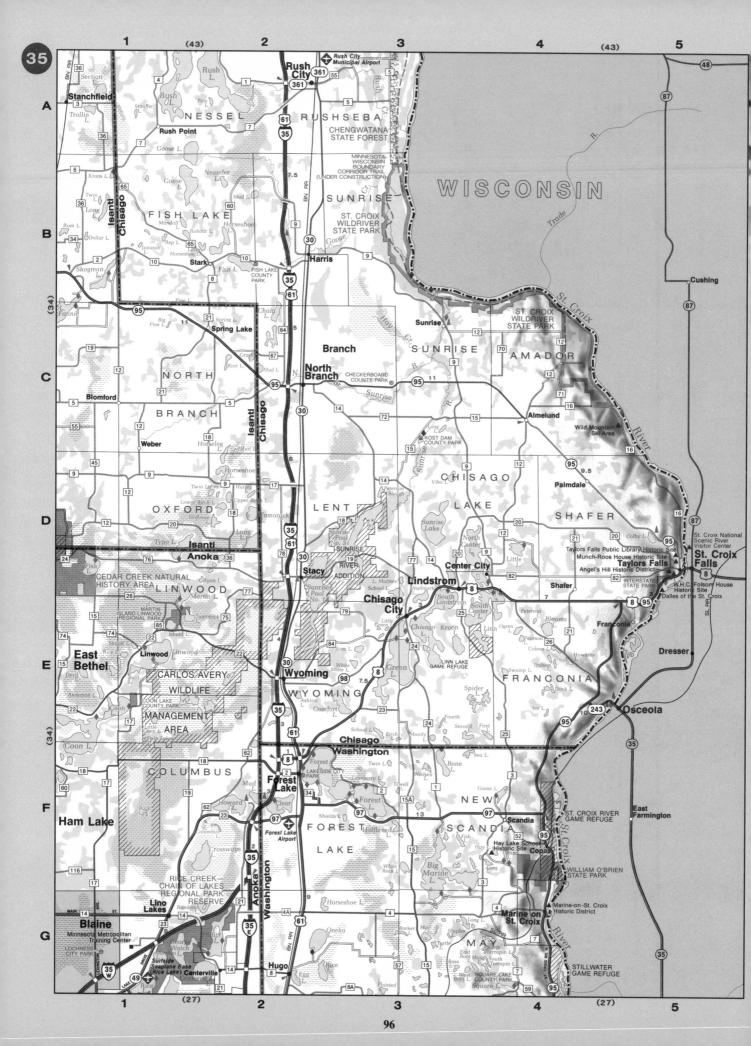

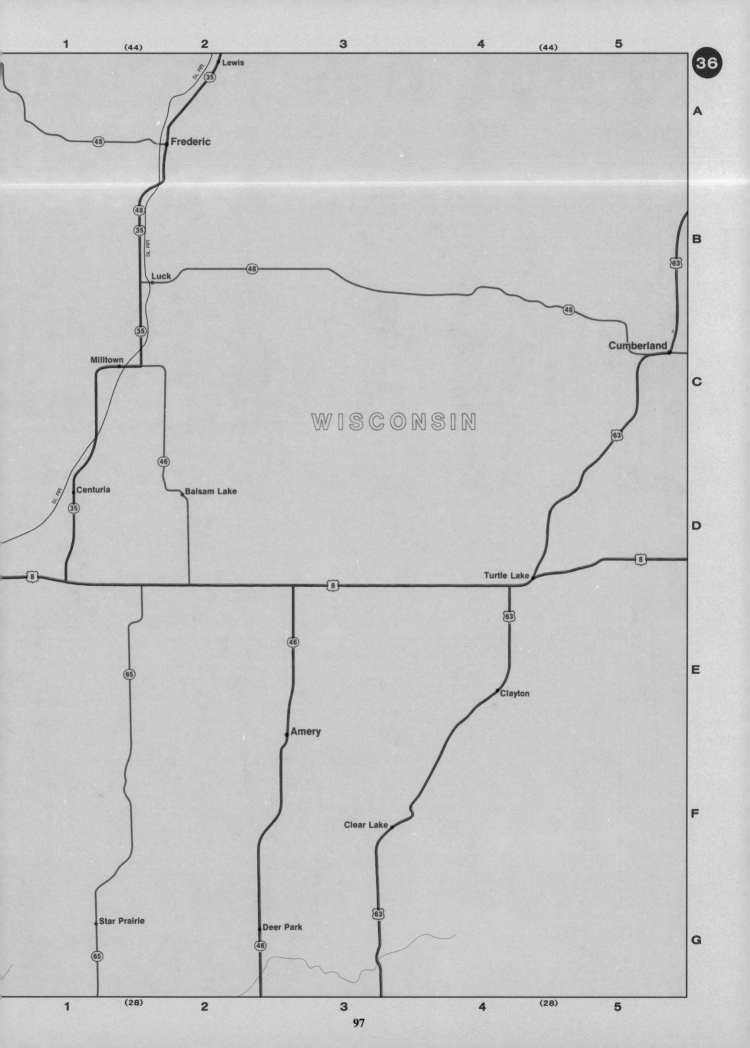

WISCONSIN

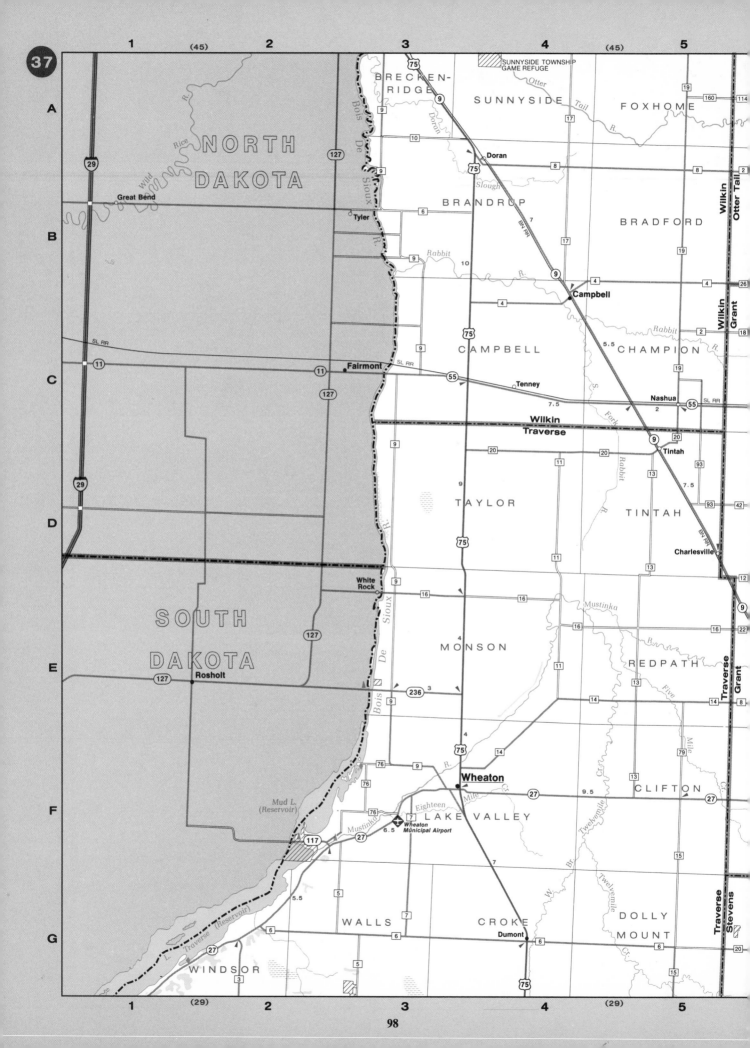

1 (45) 2 3 4 (45) 5

A
B
C
D
E
F
G

NORTH DAKOTA

Rice R.
Wild R.

Great Bend

Tyler

(29)

(11)

(127)

Fairmont

SL RR

SOUTH DAKOTA

Rosholt

(127)

Mud L. (Reservoir)

(117)

L. Traverse (Reservoir)

WINDSOR

(27)

(3)

Bois De Sioux R.

De Sioux R.

White Rock

Bois De Sioux R.

Mustinka R.

Wheaton Municipal Airport

Eighteen Mile

WALLS

LAKE VALLEY

CROKE

Dumont

(75)

BRECKEN-RIDGE

SUNNYSIDE TOWNSHIP GAME REFUGE

SUNNYSIDE

FOXHOME

Otter Tail R.

Doran

Doran

Slough

BRANDRUP

BRADFORD

Rabbit R.

Campbell

CAMPBELL

CHAMPION

Rabbit R.

Tenney

Nashua

SL RR

Wilkin
Traverse

Tintah

S. Fork R.

TAYLOR

TINTAH

Charlesville

Mustinka R.

MONSON

REDPATH

Five Mile Cr.

Wheaton

CLIFTON

Twelvemile Cr.

DOLLY MOUNT

Twelvemile Cr.

W. Br.

Twelvemile Cr.

Wilkin
Otter Tail

Wilkin
Grant

Traverse
Grant

Traverse
Stevens

1 (29) 2 3 4 (29) 5

98

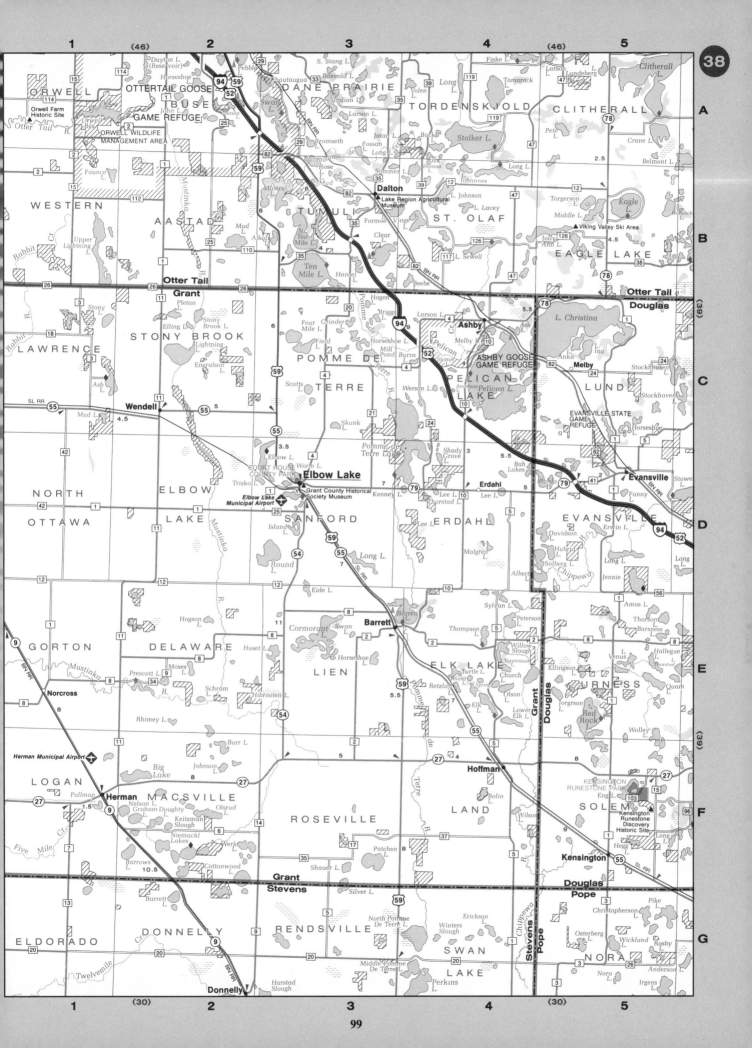

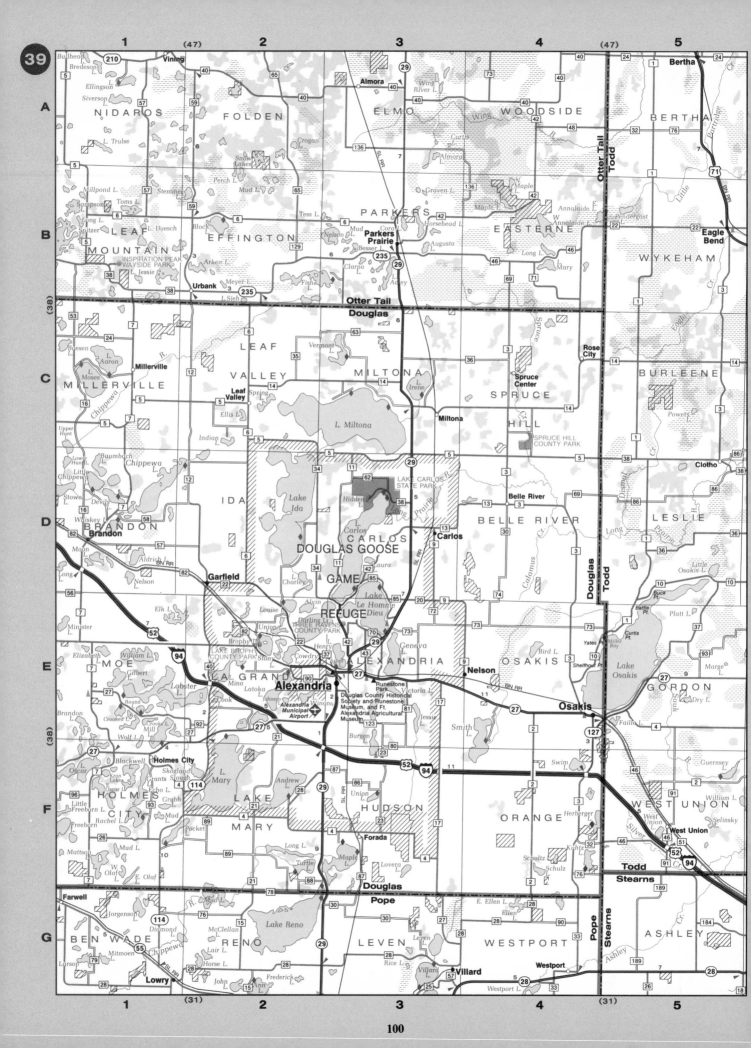

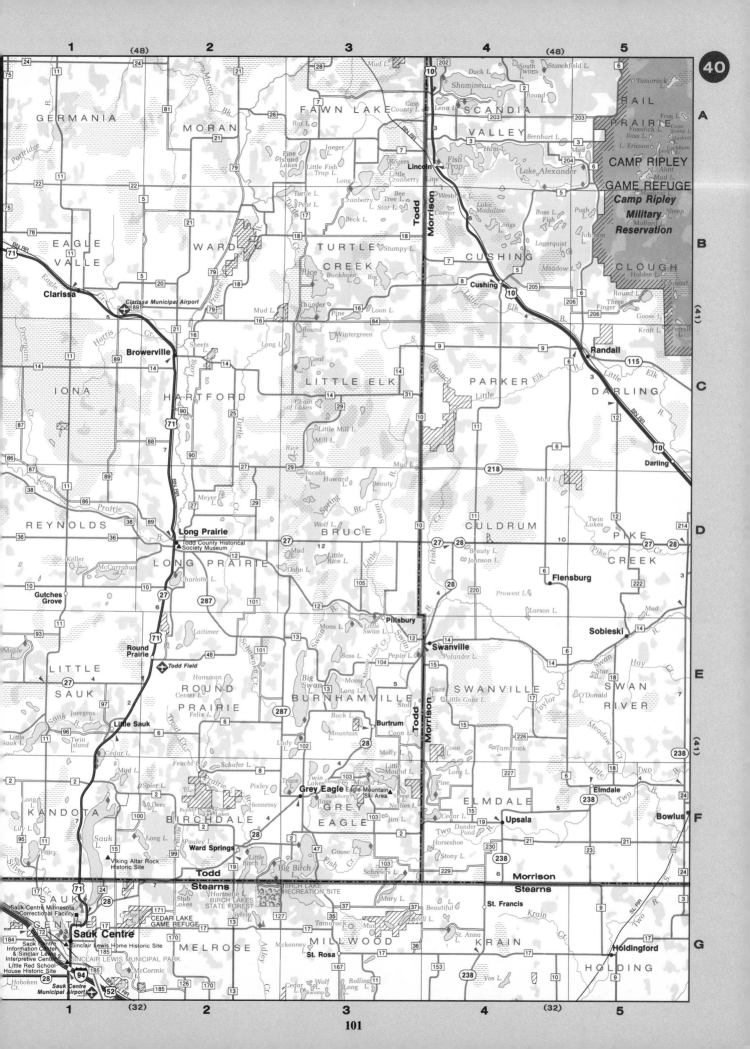

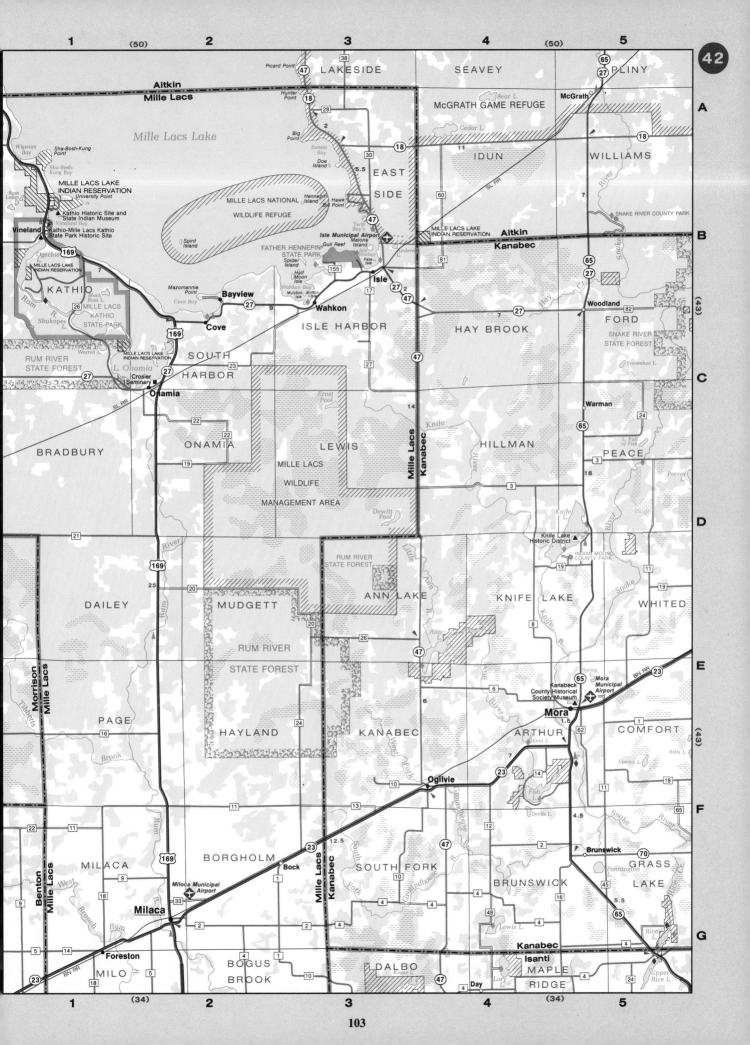

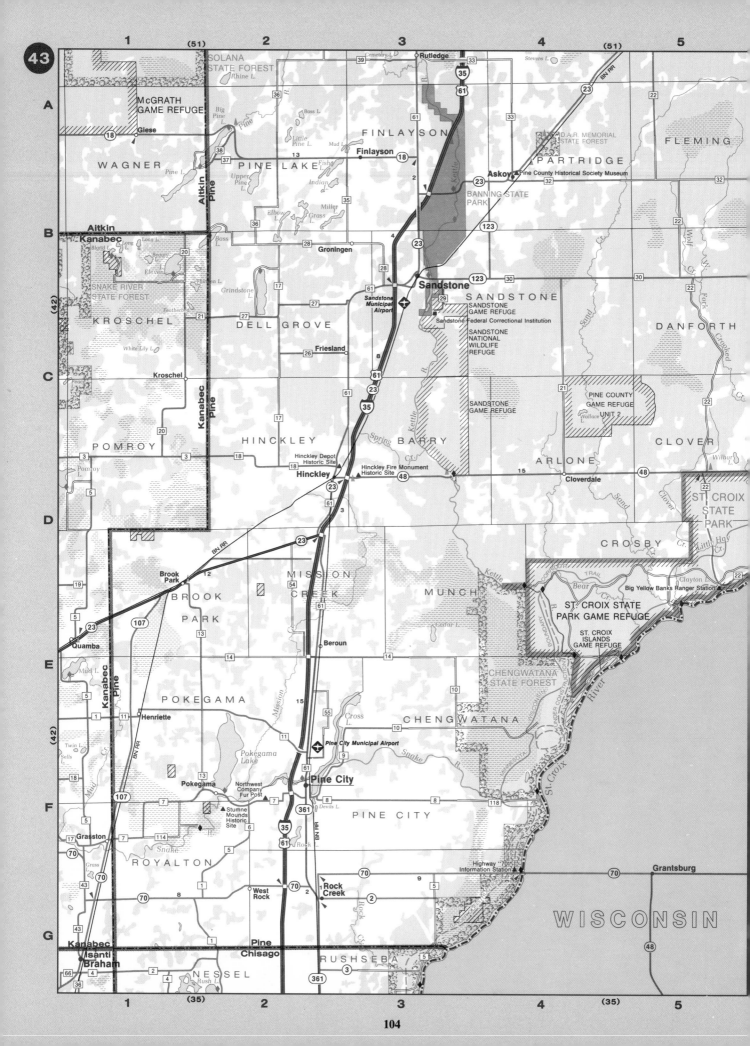

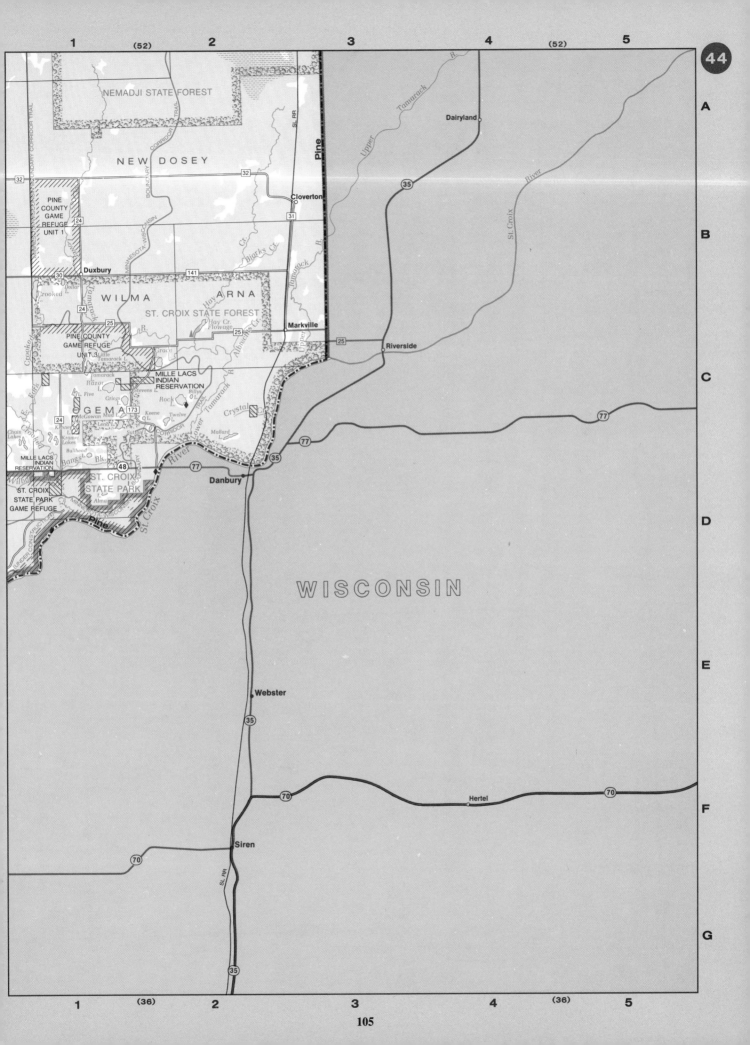

1 (52) **2** **3** **4** (52) **5**

A

NEMADJI STATE FOREST

Dairyland

NEW DOSEY

32 32

Cloverton

Upper Tamarack R.

35

B

PINE COUNTY GAME REFUGE UNIT 1

24

31

St. Croix River

Duxbury

30 141

WILMA ARNA

Crooked L. Dollar L.

ST. CROIX STATE FOREST

24 Tamarack R.

Bjorks Ck.

25 Hay Cr. Flowage

Markville

PINE COUNTY GAME REFUGE UNIT 3

25 25

Riverside

C

Razor L. Tamarack L. Little Tamarack L.

Grace

Stevens

MILLE LACS INDIAN RESERVATION

Five L. Griggs

Billys

Crooked L.

Rock

Keene L. Twelve L.

Albrahns Cr.

Upper Tamarack R.

Crystal Cr.

77

OGEMA 173 24 McGowan Mud L.

Leon L. Kanabec L. Kramer Lakes

Sutley

Ballhead

CORRIDOR TRAIL

Mallard

77 77

Chain Lakes

Bangs Bk.

48

St. Croix River

35

MILLE LACS INDIAN RESERVATION

Wilbot

77

Danbury

ST. CROIX STATE PARK

Alma

ST. CROIX STATE PARK GAME REFUGE

Pine

St. Croix

D

UNDER CONSTRUCTION

WISCONSIN

E

Webster

35

F

70 70

Hertel

70

Siren

70

SL RR

G

35

1 (36) **2** **3** **4** (36) **5**

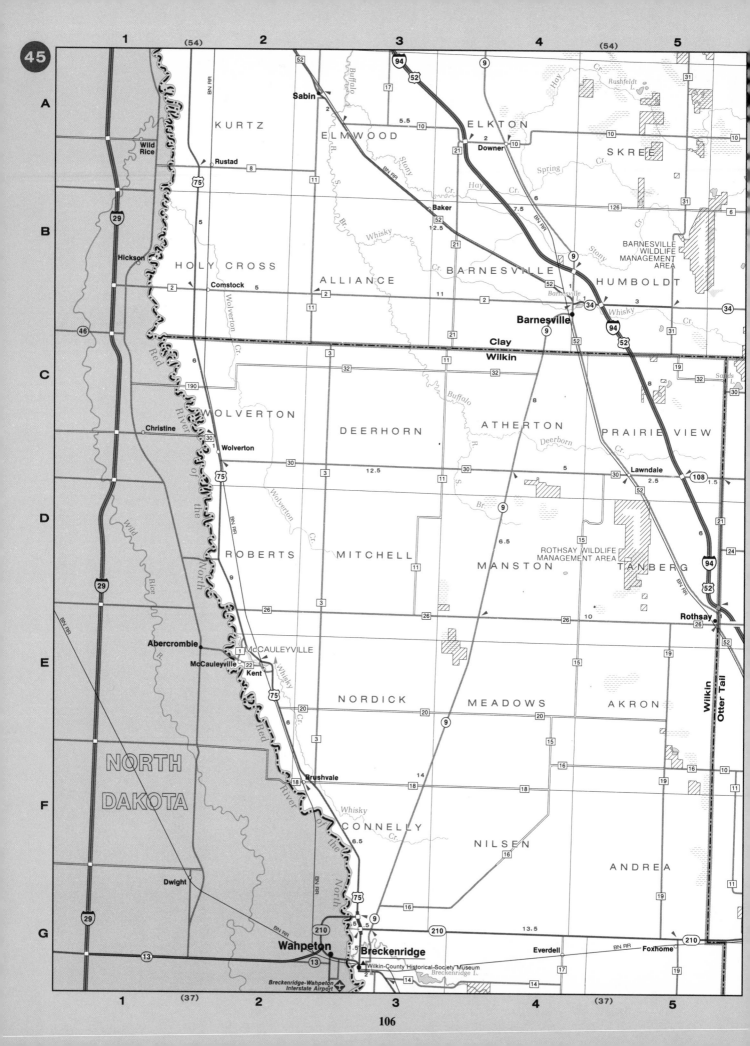

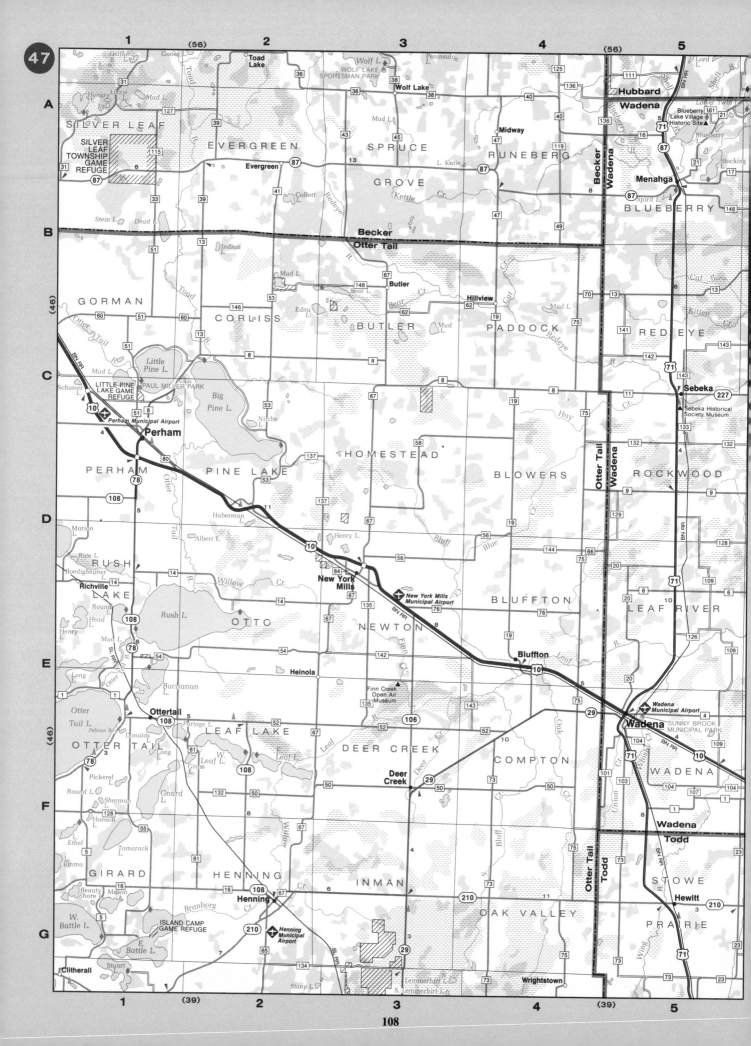

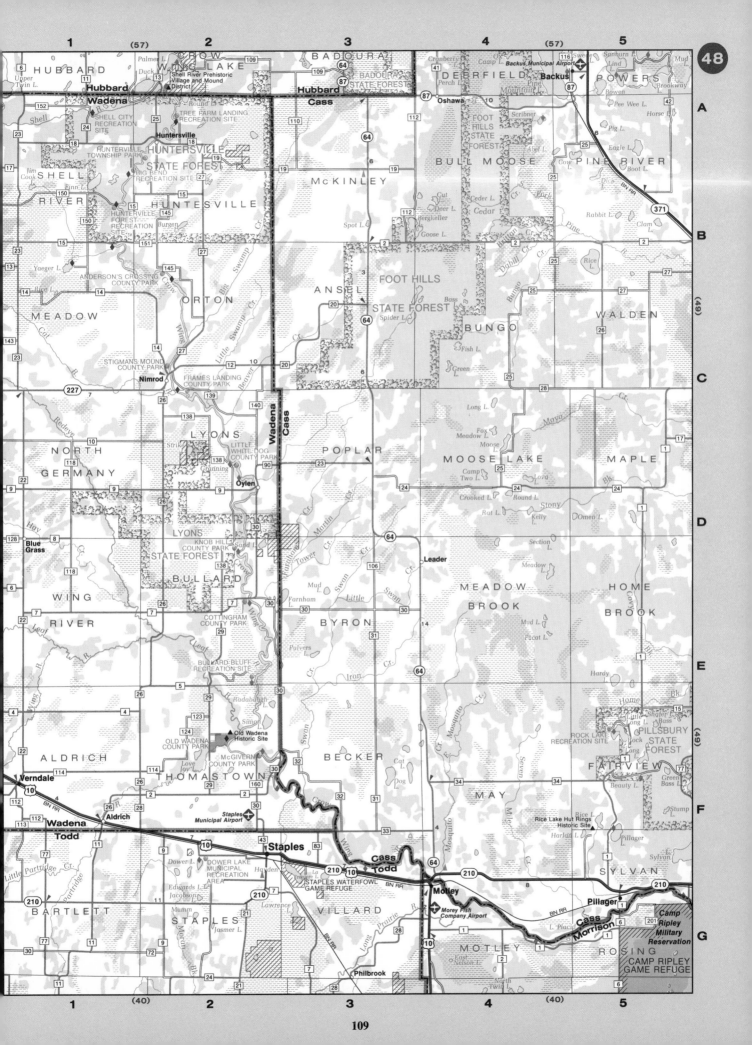

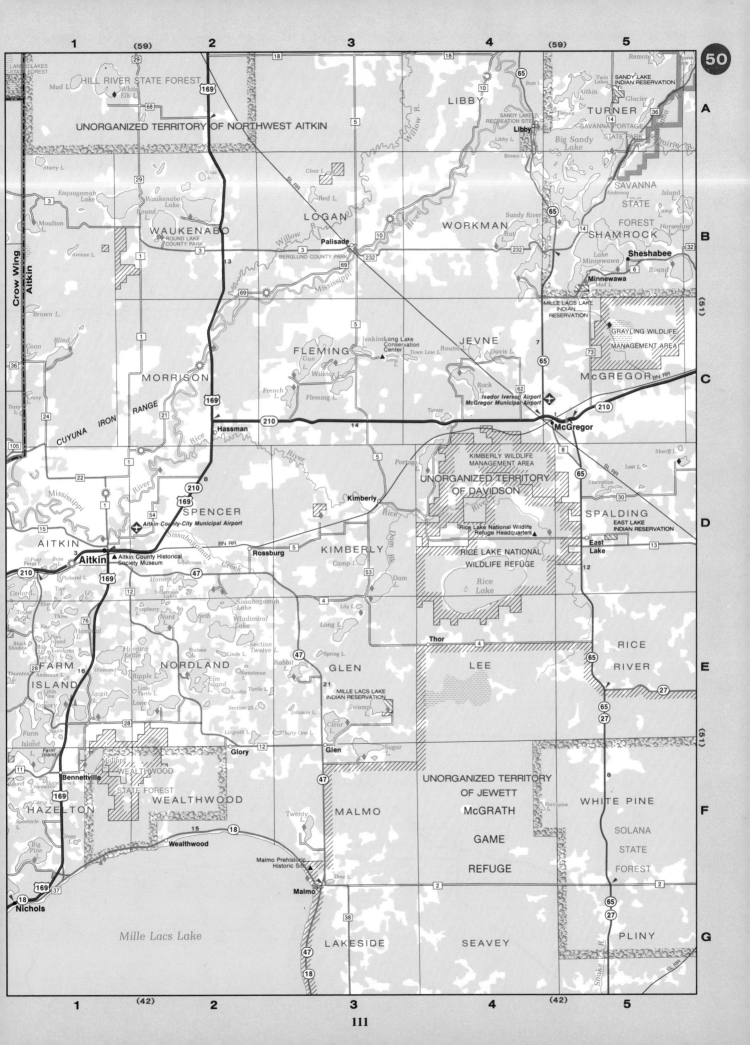

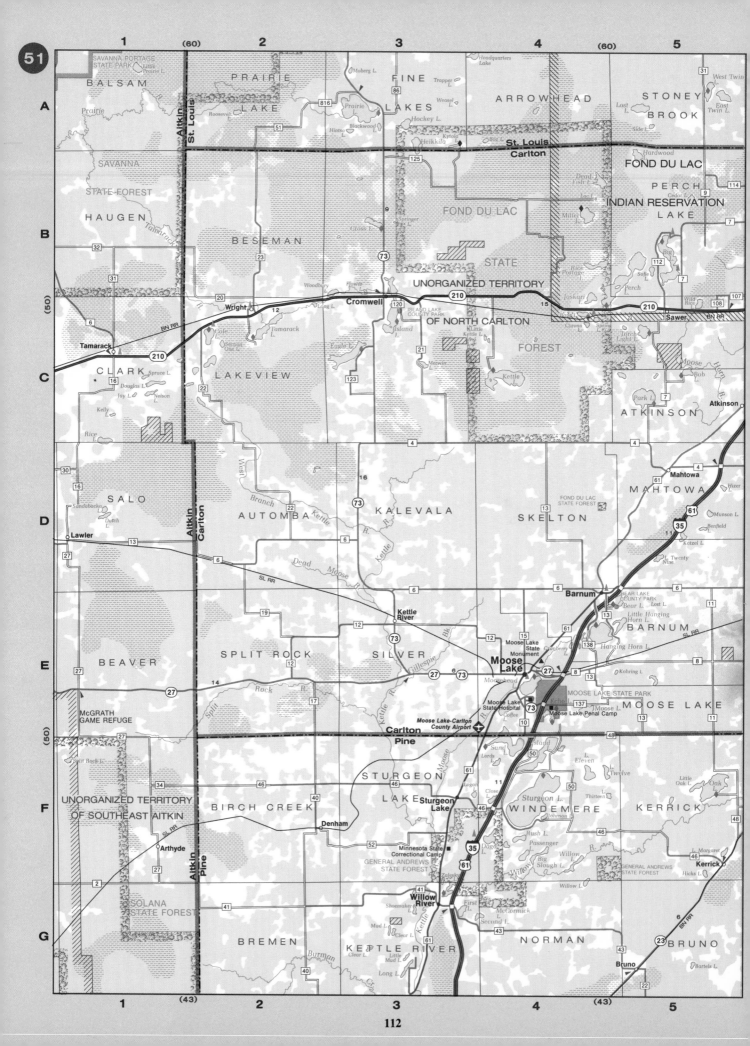

1 (65) 2 3 4 (65) 5

A
B
C
D
E
F
G

Blanchard

Kelso

18

81
29

Grandin

Hunter

NORTH DAKOTA

Gardner

Arthur

18

BN RR

Rush

BN RR

81
29
Argusvill

Rush
R.

BN RR

18

BN RR

Maple

Casselton

94
18
94
West Fargo
94

BN RR
BN RR
18
BN RR

Elm

R.

Elm

R.

1 2 3 4 5

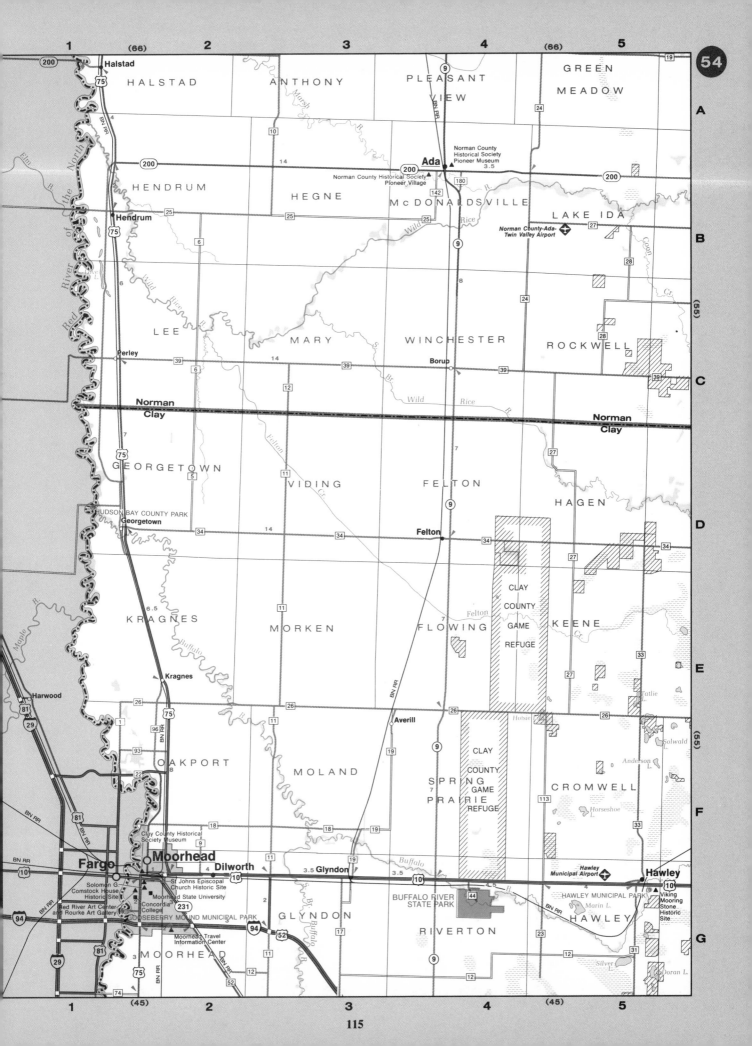

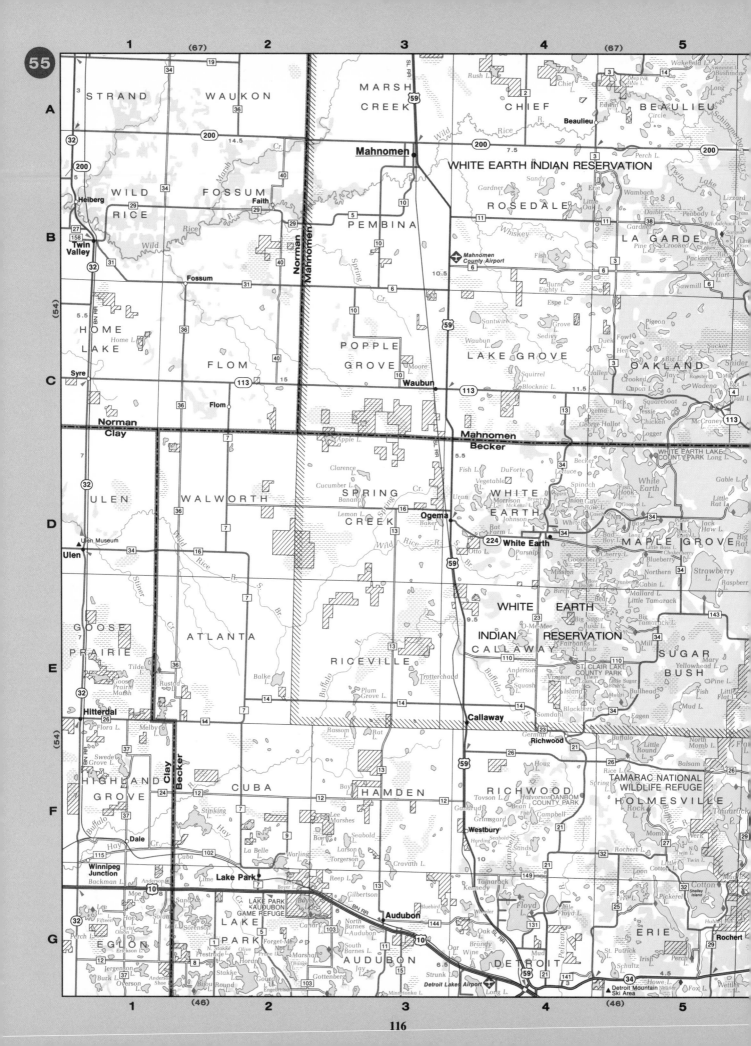

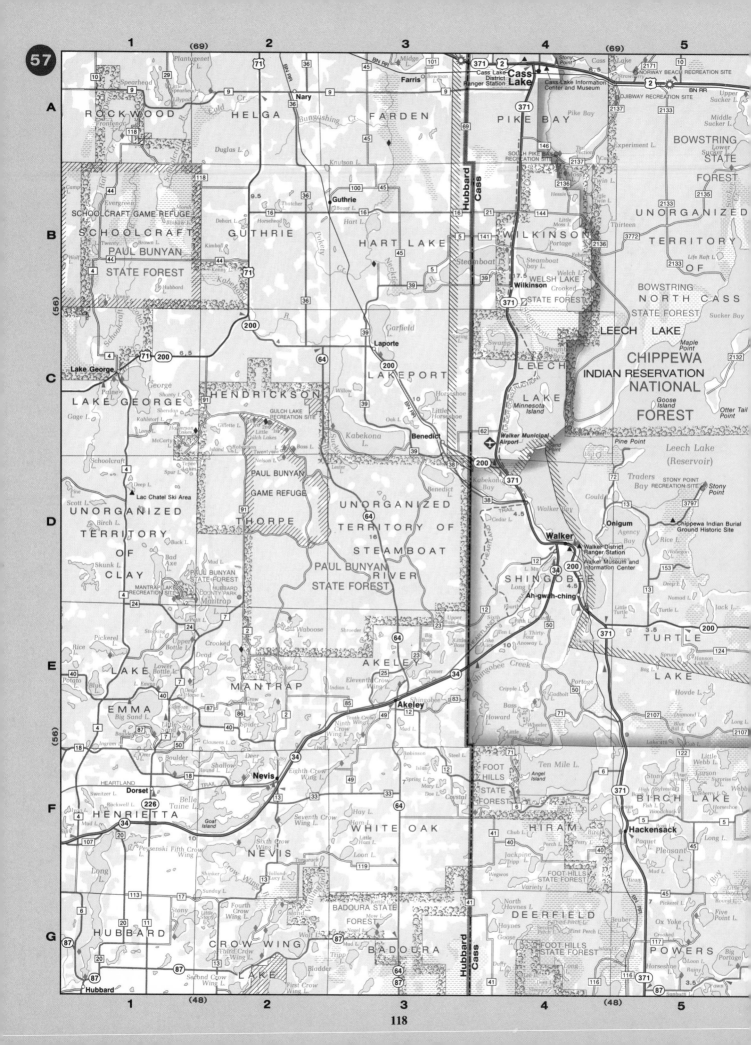

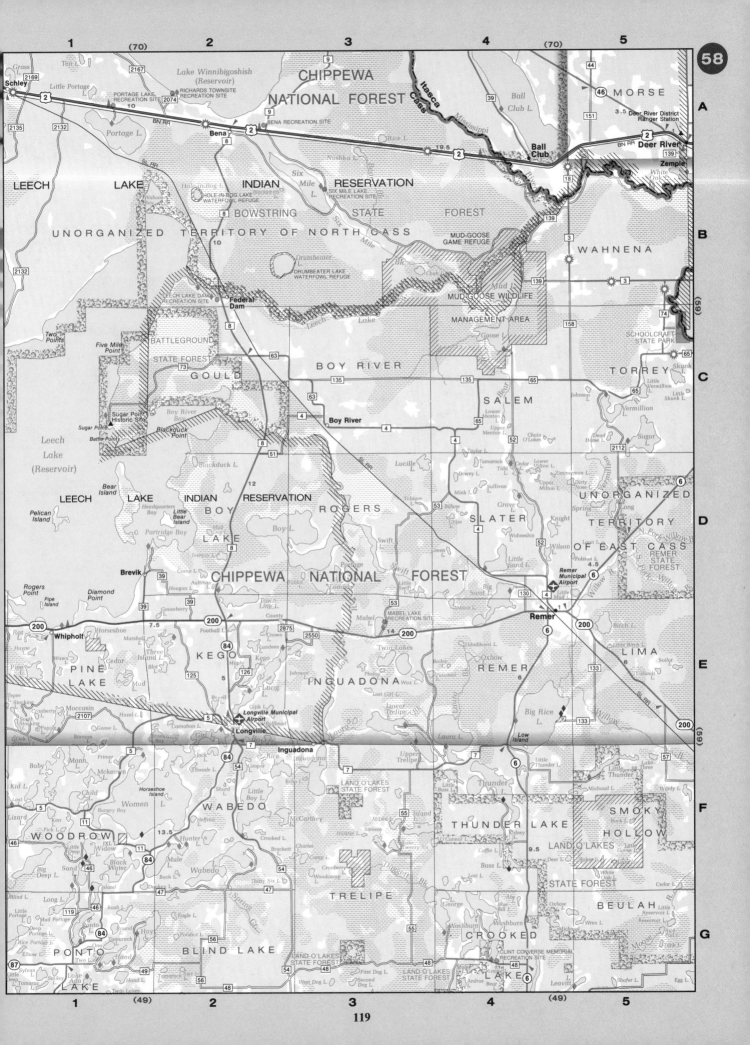

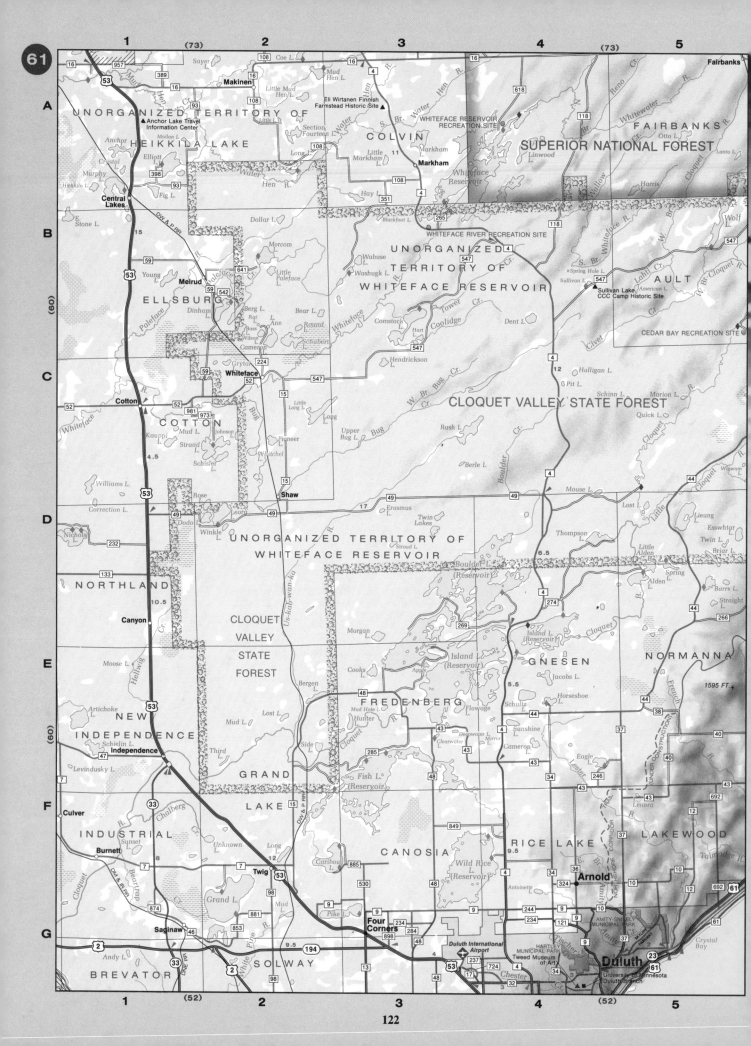

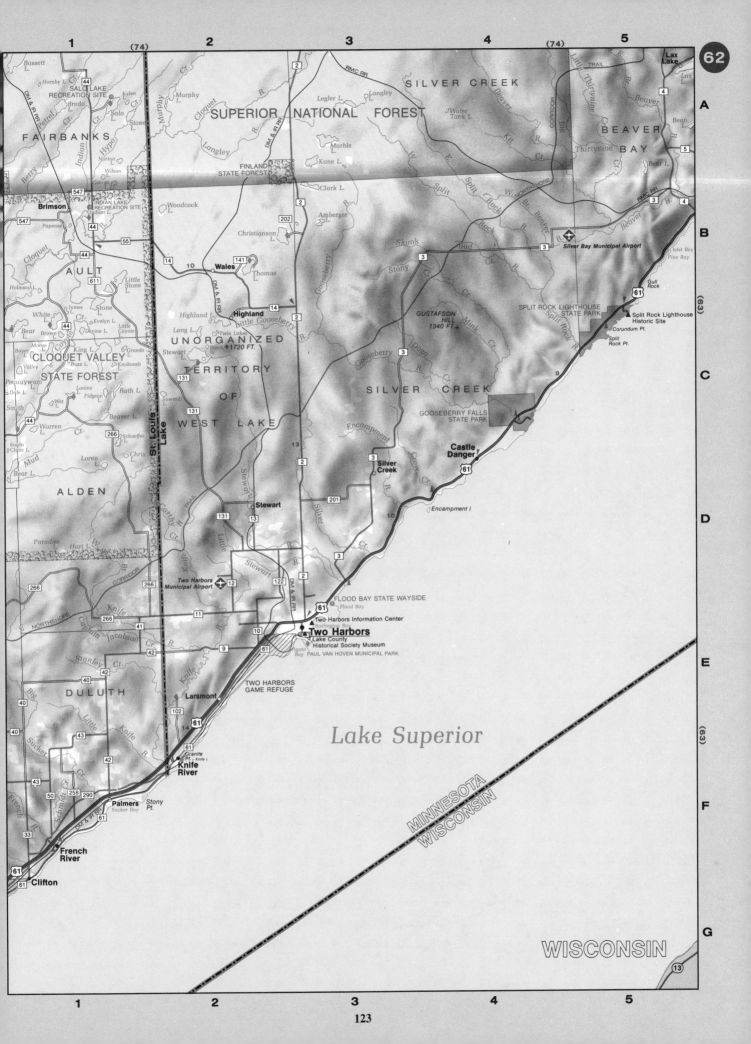

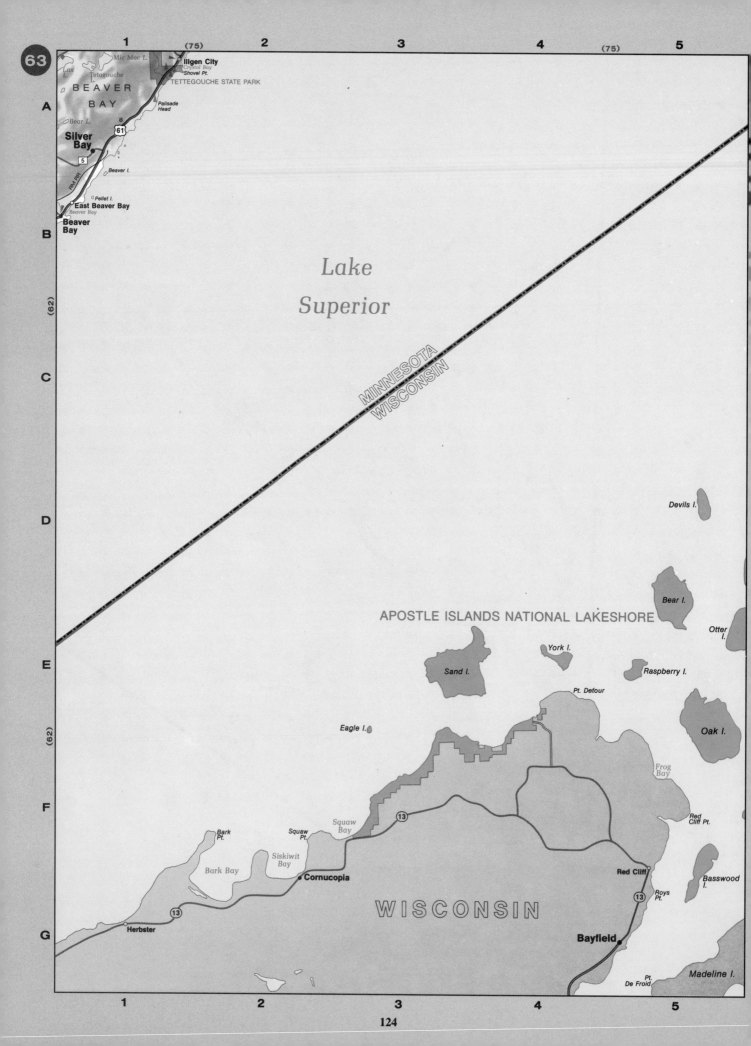

63

1 (75) 2 3 4 (75) 5

A

Mic Mac L.
Lax I.
Tetagouche L.
BEAVER BAY
Bear I.

Illgen City
Crystal Bay
Shovel Pt.
TETTEGOUCHE STATE PARK

Palisade Head

8
61

Silver Bay

5

FM RR

Beaver I.

Pellet I.

East Beaver Bay
Beaver Bay

B

Beaver Bay

Lake

Superior

(62)

MINNESOTA
WISCONSIN

C

D

Devils I.

E

Bear I.

APOSTLE ISLANDS NATIONAL LAKESHORE

Otter I.

Sand I.

York I.

Raspberry I.

Pt. Defour

Oak I.

Eagle I.

Frog Bay

(62)

F

Bark Pt.

Squaw Pt.

Squaw Bay

13

Red Cliff Pt.

Siskiwit Bay

Bark Bay

Cornucopia

Red Cliff

Basswood I.

13

Roys Pt.

W I S C O N S I N

13

G

Herbster

Bayfield

Pt. De Froid

Madeline I.

1 2 3 4 5

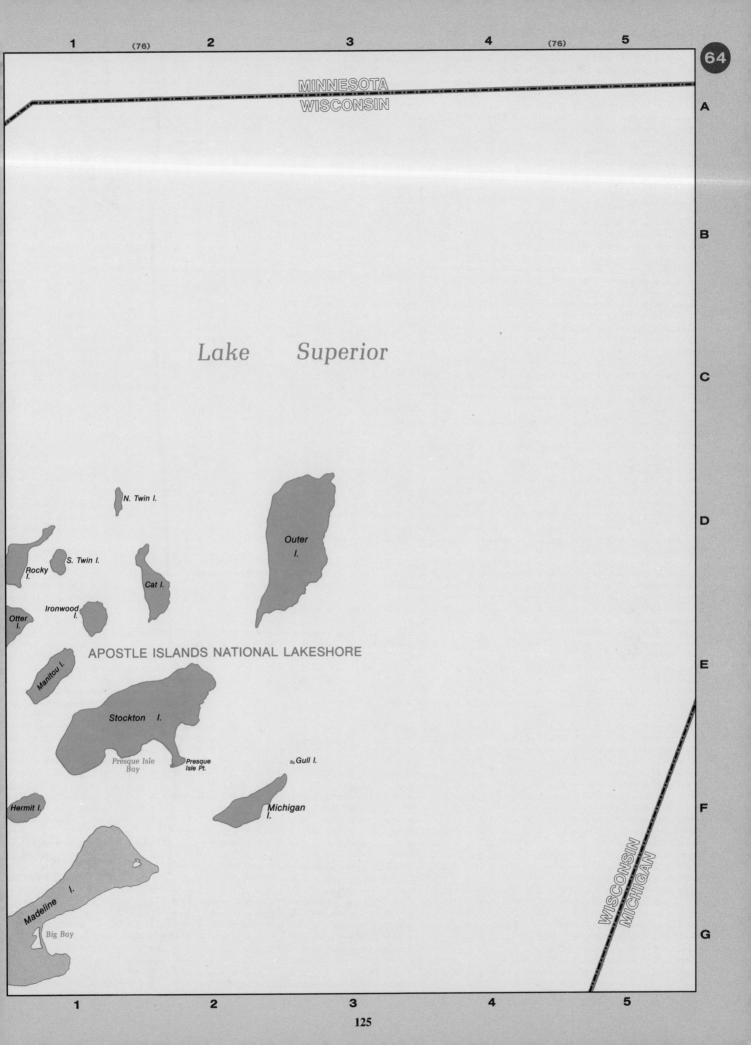

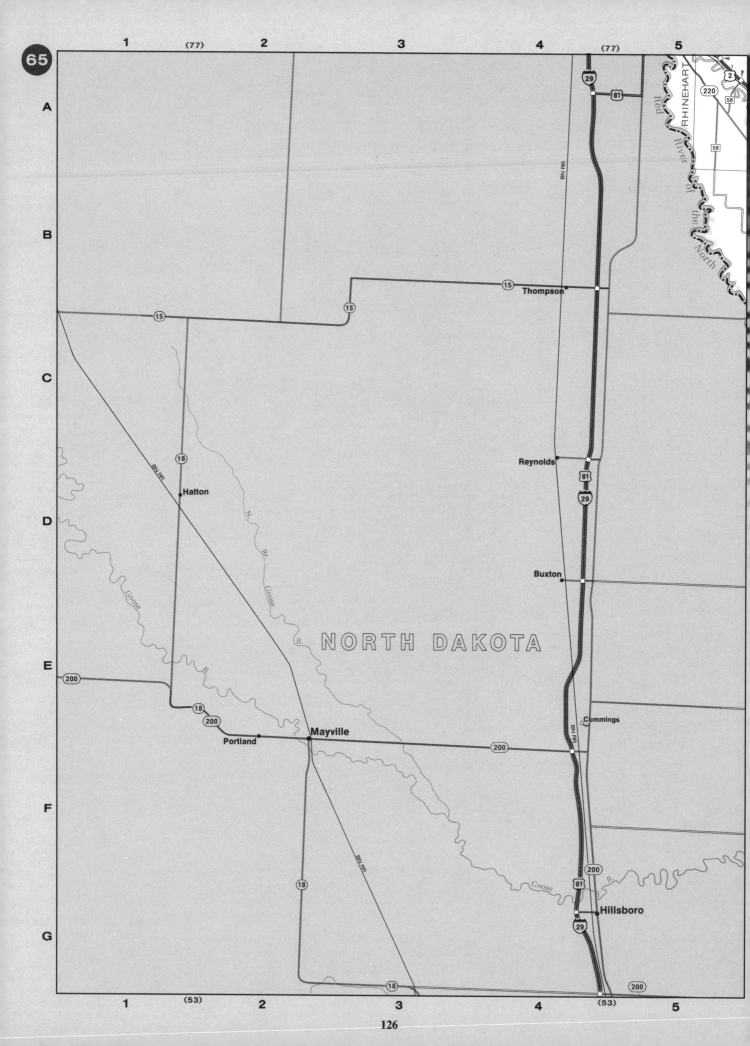

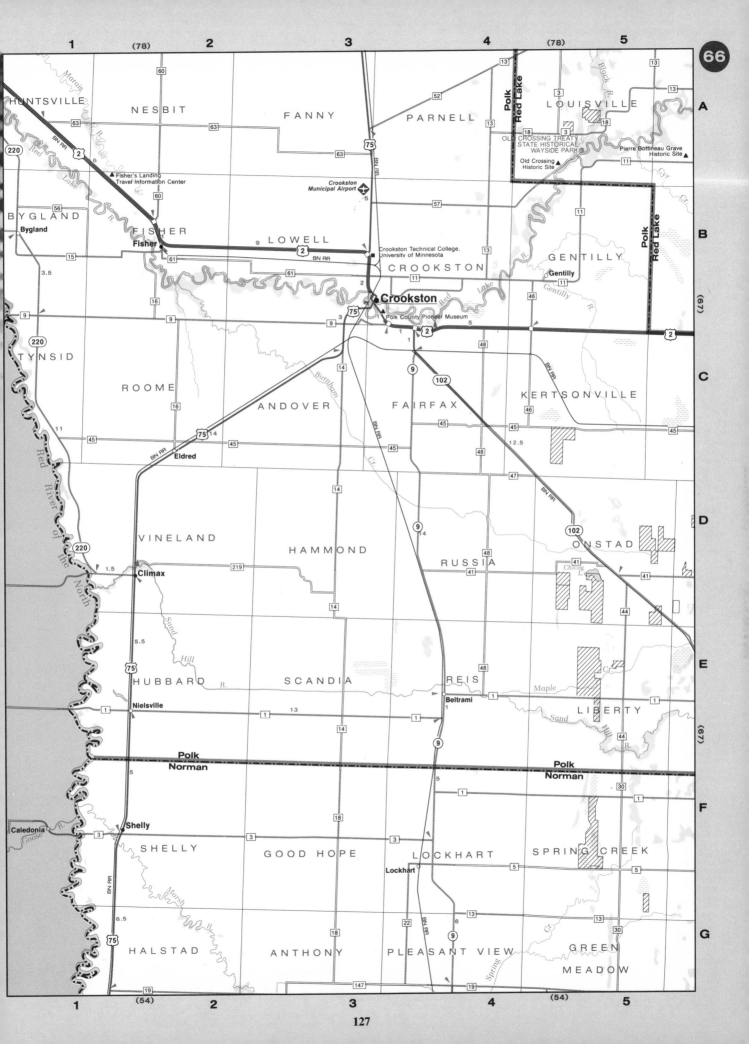

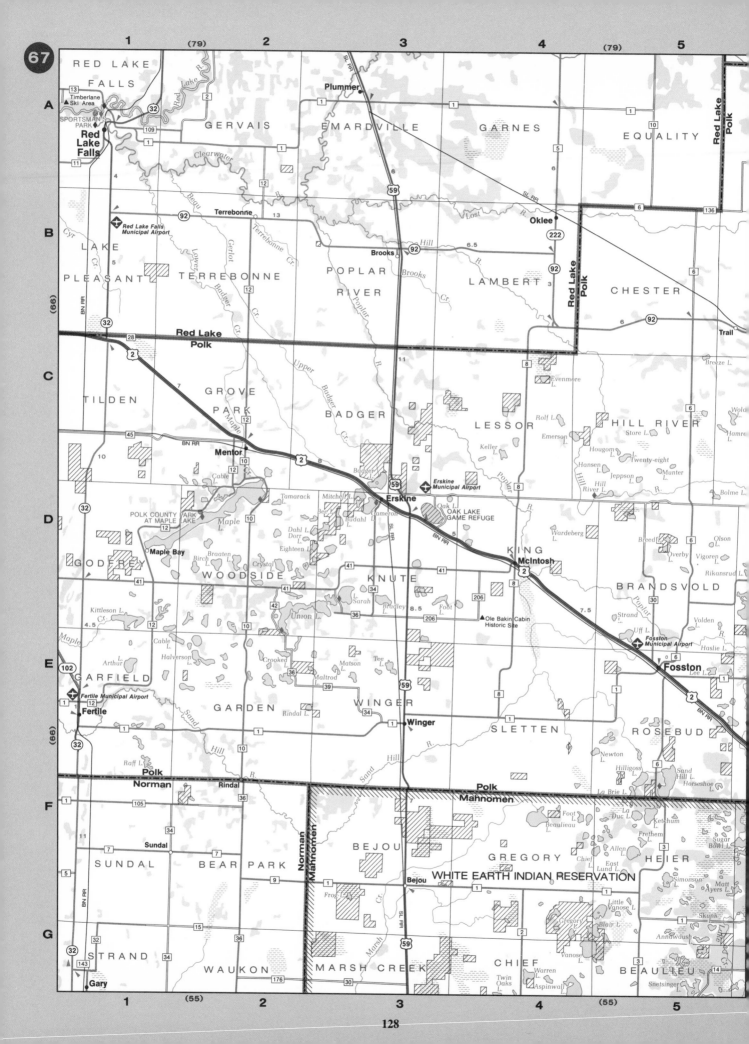

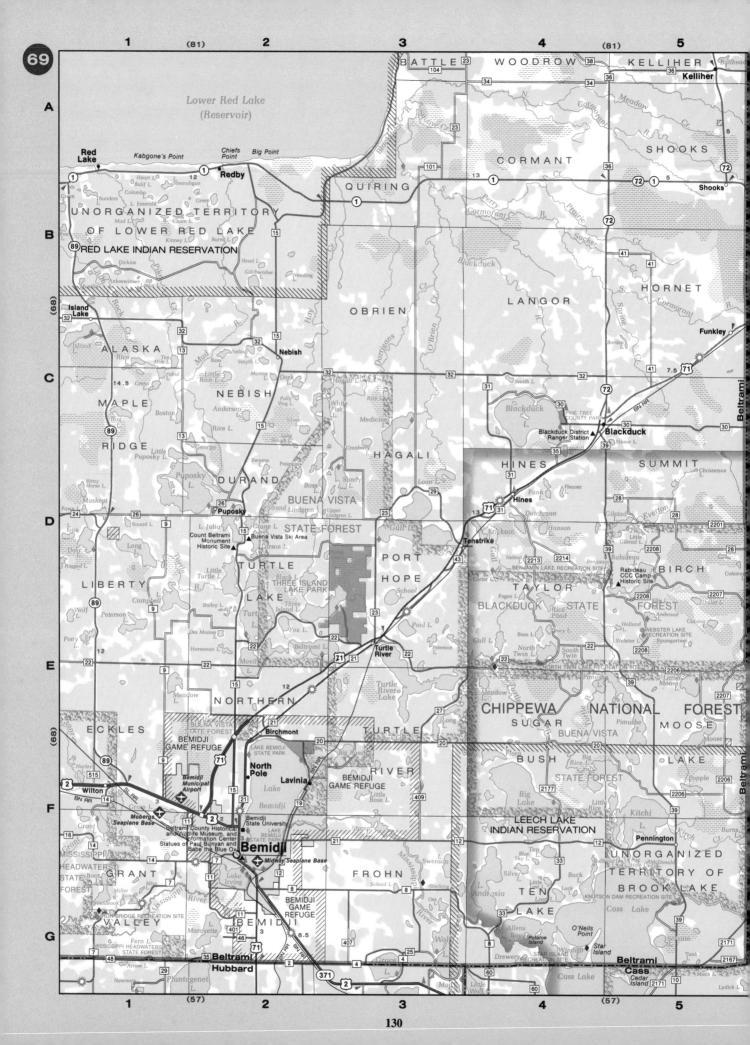

Lower Red Lake
(Reservoir)

BATTLE | 23 | WOODROW | 38 | KELLIHER | Bullhead

104 | | | | Kelliher

34 | 34 36 | 36

CORMANT | Meadow | SHOOKS

Kabgone's Point | Chiefs Point | Big Point

Red Lake

12

Redby

QUIRING | 101 | | 36

13 | 1 | 72 | 1 | 5 | Shooks | 72

1

UNORGANIZED TERRITORY

OF LOWER RED LAKE

15

HORNET

89 RED LAKE INDIAN RESERVATION

41 | 41

Head L.

Gibibwisher

Wending

OBRIEN | LANGOR

Funkley

Island Lake

32 | ALASKA | 32 | 13 | 512 | Nebish | 32

41 | 7.5 | 71

Nebish

MAPLE | NEBISH | 32 | 32 | 32 | 72 | BN RR | Beltrami

14.5 | | | | | 31 | Smith L. | 30

Blackduck | PINE TREE COUNTY PARK | 30

RIDGE | 13 | 15 | HAGALI | | Rice Lake | Blackduck District Ranger Station | Blackduck | 30

DURAND | 26 | BUENA VISTA | 23 | 29 | Loon L. | HINES | 35 | 39 | Stoner L.

24 | 26 | Puposky | | | 31 | SUMMIT

9 | STATE FOREST | 13 | 71 | Hines | 28

Count Beltrami Monument Historic Site | 15 | Buena Vista Ski Area | Gull L. | Dutchman | 28 | 2201

LIBERTY | TURTLE | PORT | 43 | Erickson | Hanson | 2213 | 2214 | 39 | BIRCH | 2208

89 | 9 | LAKE | HOPE | BENJAMIN LAKE RECREATION SITE | Rabideau | Rabideau CCC Camp Historic Site | 2208 | 2207

THREE ISLAND LAKE PARK | School L. | 23 | TAYLOR | STATE | 2208

22 | Three Island L. | BLACKDUCK | Rice Pond | WEBSTER LAKE RECREATION SITE

12 | 22 | 9 | 22 | 22 | Pool L. | 23 | Gull L. | North Twin | South Twin | FOREST | 2208

71 | 21 | Turtle River | 22 | NORTH TWIN LAKE RECREATION SITE | 2206

Meadow | 12 | Turtle River Lake | CHIPPEWA | NATIONAL | FOREST | 2207

27 | SUGAR | Pimushe | MOOSE

NORTHERN | TURTLE | Long L. | BUENA VISTA | 2206

ECKLES | BUENA VISTA STATE FOREST | 21 | Birchmont | 20 | 20 | BUSH | LAKE

89 | BEMIDJI GAME REFUGE | 9 | LAKE BEMIDJI STATE PARK | RIVER | Big Bass L. | 20 | STATE FOREST | 2177 | 2206

2 | Wilton | 515 | 71 | North Pole | Lavinia | BEMIDJI GAME REFUGE | 409 | Big Rice L. | 2206

14 | BN RR | Bemidji Municipal Airport | 15 | 21 | 19 | LEECH LAKE INDIAN RESERVATION | Kitchi | 39

16 | Mobergs Seaplane Base | 11 | 2 | Bemidji State University | 21 | 12 | Pennington | 12

MISSISSIPPI HEADWATERS STATE FOREST | Bemidji County Historical and Wildlife Museum, and Information Center Statues of Paul Bunyan and Babe the Blue Ox | BEMIDJI STATE PARK | Bemidji | 7 | Midway Seaplane Base | 33 | UNORGANIZED TERRITORY OF BROOK LAKE

14 | GRANT | 7 | 12 | FROHN | School L. | 8 | TEN | 33 | KNUTSON DAM RECREATION SITE

VALLEY | 11 | Lake Irving | 8 | LAKE | Andrusia | O'Neils Point | 39

IRON BRIDGE RECREATION SITE | 401 | 46 | 407 | 8 | Star Island | 2171

48 | 35 | Beltrami | 71 | 25 | Drewery | STAR ISLAND RECREATION SITE | Beltrami Cass | Cedar Island | 10

29 | Hubbard | 371 | 4 | 60 | Cass Lake | 2167

57 | 2 | 60 | Lydick L.

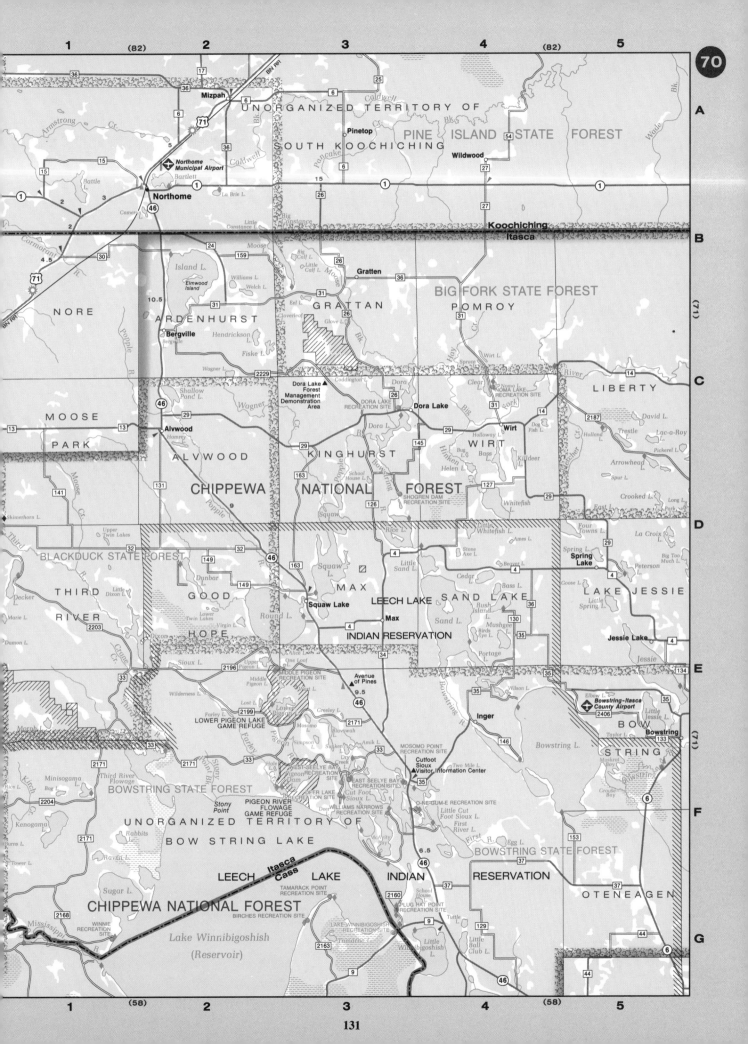

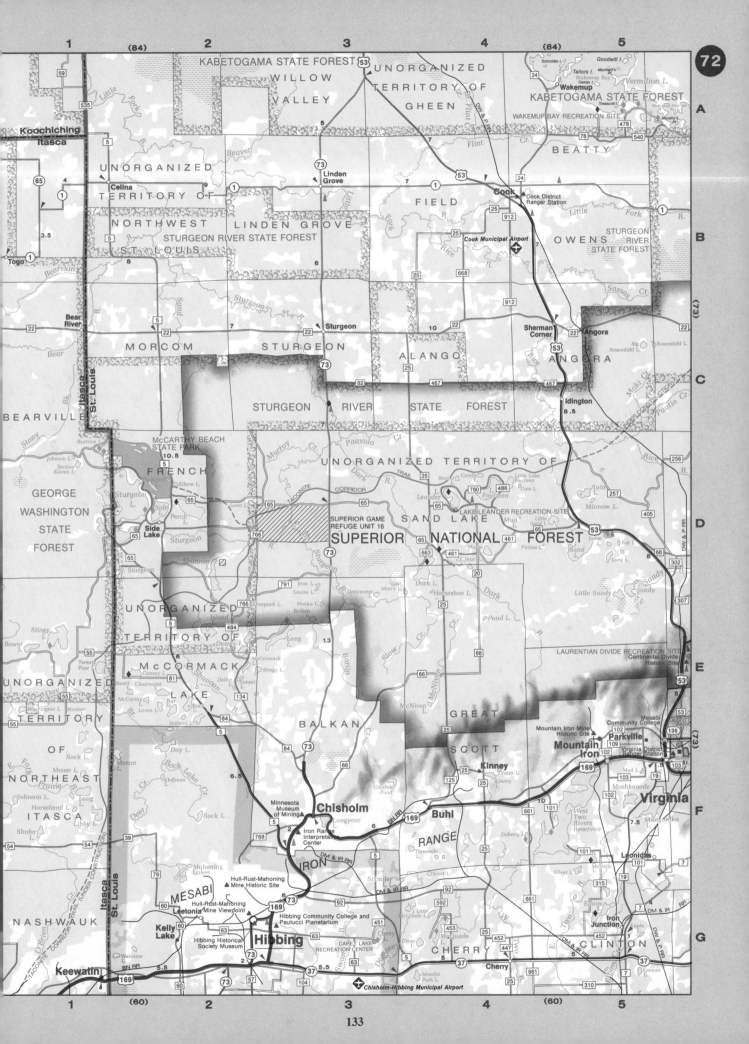

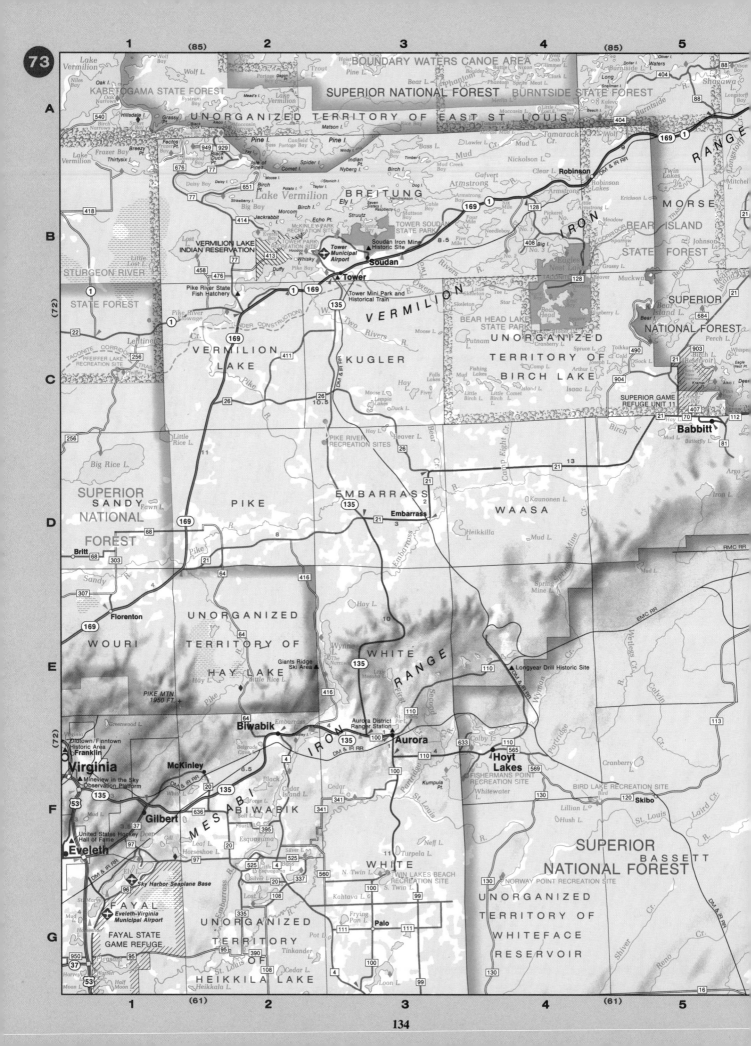

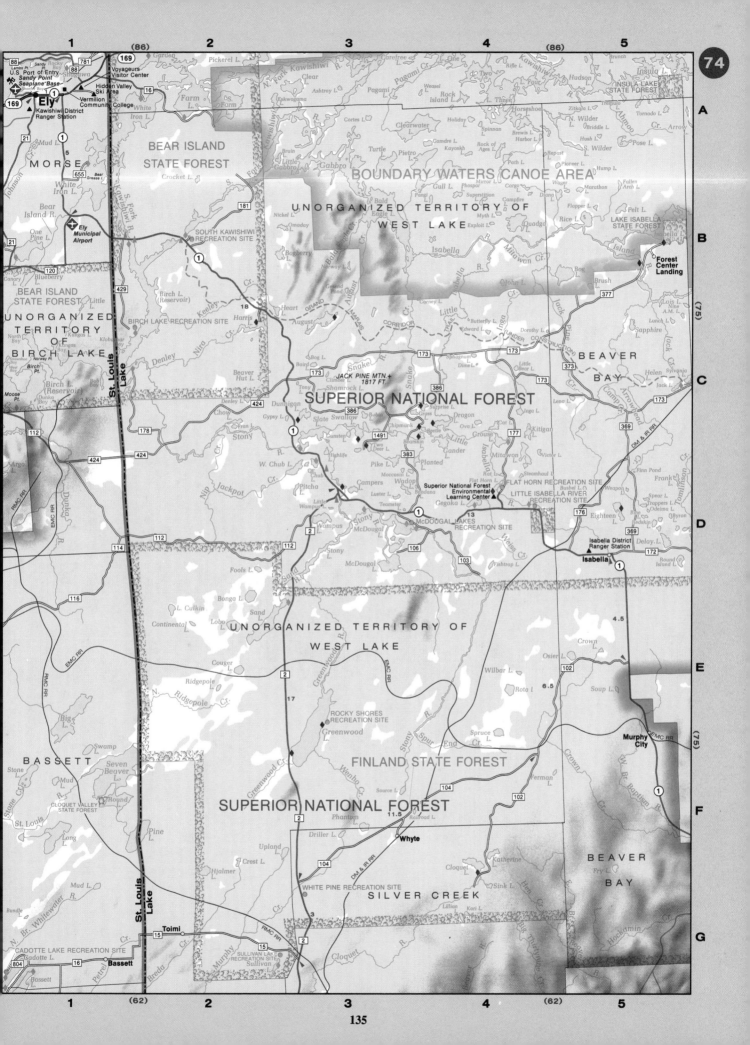

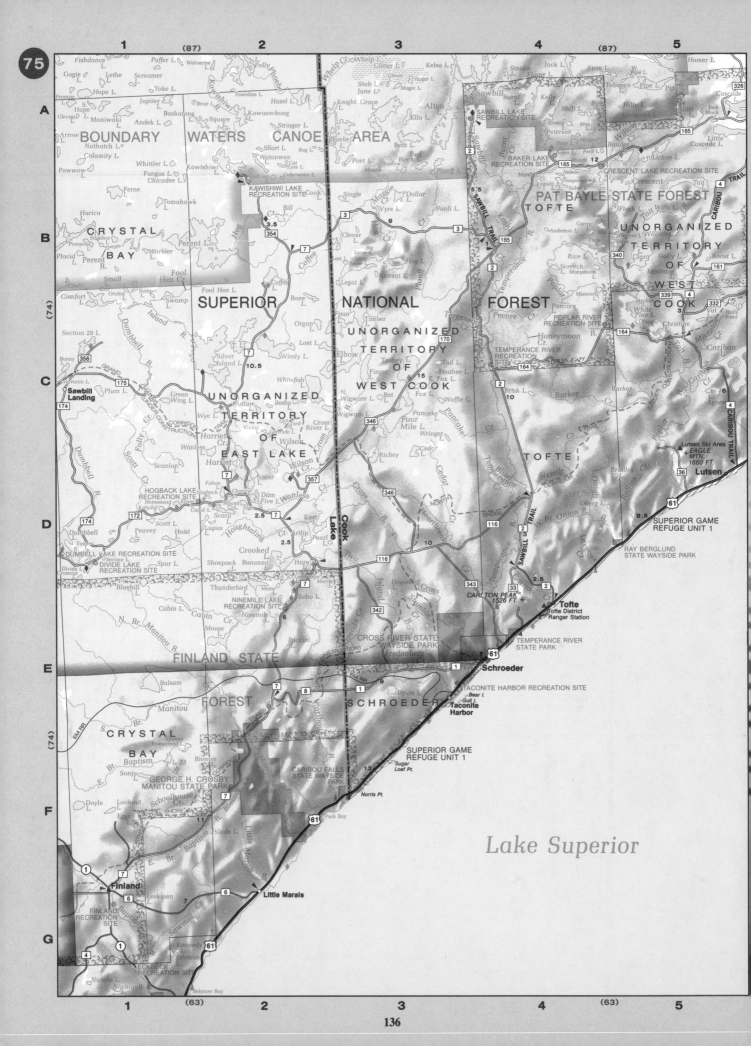

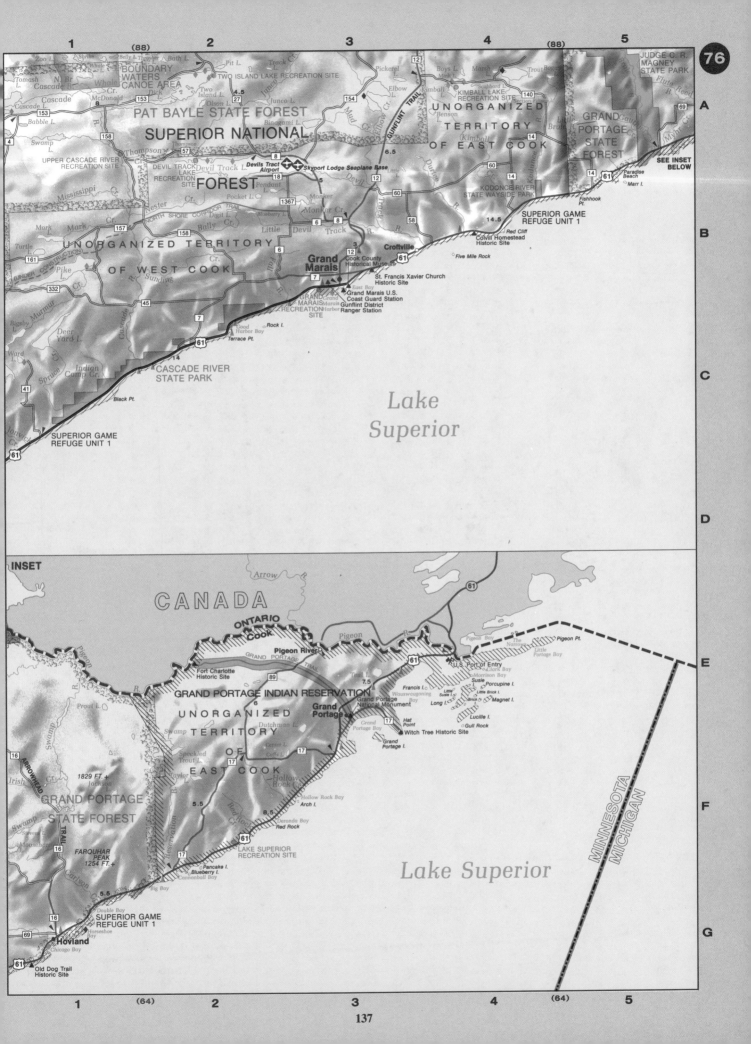

1 (88) **2** **3** **4** (88) **5**

Zoo L.
Shrike
Belly L.
Thunder
Bath L.
BOUNDARY
WATERS
CANOE AREA
Whale
N. Br.
Cascade
Tomash
Pit L.
Two Island L.
Cr.
TWO ISLAND LAKE RECREATION SITE
Pickerel
Boys L.
Mink L.
Marsh
Trout
12
JUDGE C. R.
MAGNEY
STATE PARK

A

Cascade
Cascade L.
McDonald
153
Dick
Whale L.
4.5
Olson L.
Two Island L.
27
Junco L.
154
Mud
Cr.
Elbow
Kimball
Scabbard L.
KIMBALL LAKE
RECREATION SITE
140
GRAND
PORTAGE
STATE
FOREST
Babble L.
Cascade
153
Cr.
Binogami L.
Kimball L.
69

PAT BAYLE STATE FOREST
SUPERIOR NATIONAL
UNORGANIZED
TERRITORY
OF EAST COOK

158
Swamp
Thompson
Thompson L.
57
6.5
14
SEE INSET
BELOW

4
Mississippi
UPPER CASCADE RIVER
RECREATION SITE
Vester
Cr.
DEVIL TRACK
LAKE
RECREATION
SITE
Devil Track L.
DEVILS TRACT
AIRPORT
8
18
Skyport Lodge Seaplane Base
5
12
Little
Devil
60
Duran
KODONCE RIVER
STATE WAYSIDE PARK
60
14
14
Paradise
Beach
61
Fishhook
Pt.
Marr I.

FOREST
Pocket L.
1367
Pendant
Monker
Cr.
Tr.
Track

B

Mark
Mark L.
157
Little
Bally
Blueberry L.
Cr.
6
8
Devil
R.
58
14.5
SUPERIOR GAME
REFUGE UNIT 1
Red Cliff
Colvill Homestead
Historic Site
161
158
Cr.
6
Track

Turtle
L.
UNORGANIZED TERRITORY
OF WEST COOK
Cr.
12
Croftville
Cook County
Historical Museum
61
Five Mile Rock
332
Pike
Cr.
7
Grand
Marais
3
St. Francis Xavier Church
Historic Site
East Bay
Grand Marais U.S.
Coast Guard Station
Gunflint District
Ranger Station
45
GRAND
MARAIS
RECREATION
SITE
Grand
Marais
Harbor

C

41
Sunding
R.
7
Good
Harbor Bay
Rock I.
Deer
Yard L.
Bigsby
Murmur
Cr.
Spruce
Cr.
61
14
Terrace Pt.
CASCADE RIVER
STATE PARK
Ward
L.
Indian
Camp Cr.
Black Pt.

Lake
Superior

Ionvet
Cr.
SUPERIOR GAME
REFUGE UNIT 1
61

D

INSET

Arrow
61
CANADA

E

Pigeon
ONTARIO
Cook
Pigeon River
Pigeon
R.
Pigeon Bay
The
Narrows
Pigeon Pt.
Little
Portage Bay
Pigeon Pt.
Fort Charlotte
Historic Site
GRAND
PORTAGE
TRAIL
89
7.5
61
U.S Port of Entry
Clark Bay
Morrison Bay
Susie
Porcupine I.
R.
GRAND PORTAGE INDIAN RESERVATION
UNORGANIZED
TERRITORY
OF
EAST COOK
6
Dutchman L.
Grand
Portage
Francis I.
Wauswaugoning
Bay
Little
Susie I.
Long I.
Little Brick I.
Brick I.
Magnet I.
Grand Portage
National Monument
17
Hat Point
Lucille I.
Gull Rock

Swamp
Pigeon
R.
Prout L.
Speckled
Trout L.
17
Center L.
Cliffs L.
Taylor L.
17
Hollow
Rock Cr.
Grand
Portage Bay
Grand
Portage I.
Witch Tree Historic Site

F

16
ARROWHEAD
TRAIL
Irish
Swamp
1829 FT. +
Jackson
5.5
Red Rock
Cr.
Hollow Rock Bay
Arch I.
Deronda Bay
Red Rock
GRAND PORTAGE
STATE FOREST
Steven L.
16
Moosehau
FARQUHAR
PEAK
1254 FT. +
17
61
LAKE SUPERIOR
RECREATION SITE
MINNESOTA
MICHIGAN

Carlson
Cr.
5.5
Big Bay
Pancake I.
Blueberry I.
Cannonball Bay
Double Bay

G

16
Horseshoe
Bay
SUPERIOR GAME
REFUGE UNIT 1
69
Hovland
61
Old Dog Trail
Historic Site
Chicago Bay

Lake Superior

1 (64) **2** **3** **4** (64) **5**

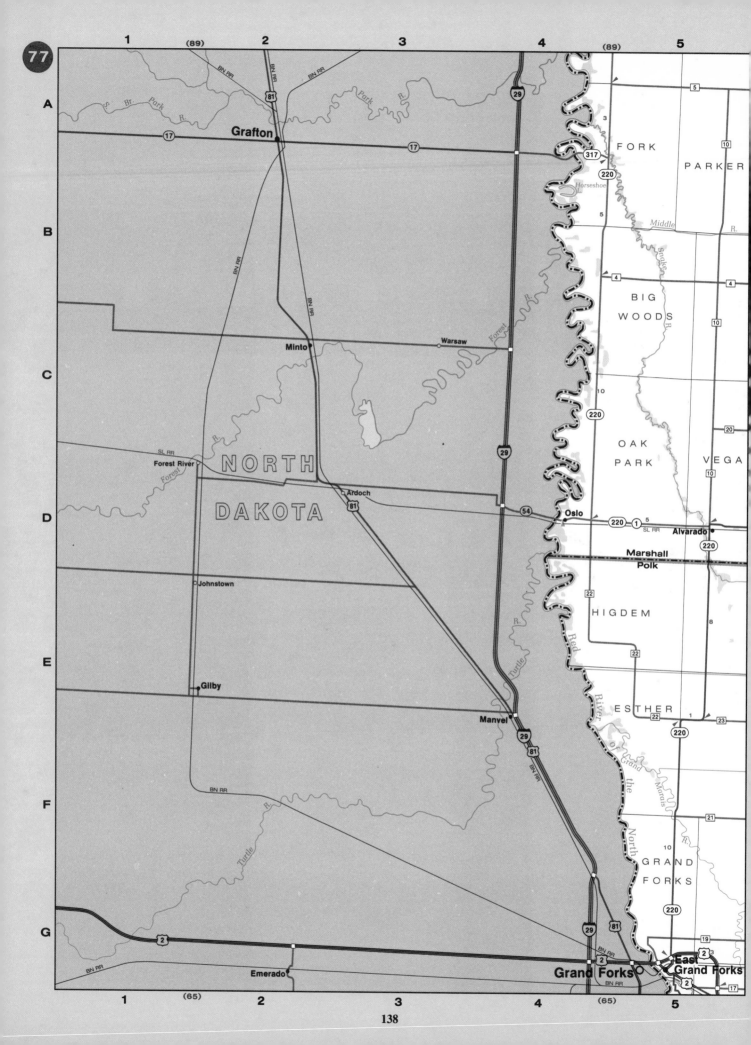

1 (89) 2 3 4 (89) 5

A

B

C

D

E

F

G

BN RR
BN RR
BN RR
81
29

17
Grafton
17
317
220
FORK
5
PARKER
10
Horseshoe L.
220
4
4
BIG
WOODS
10
Minto
Warsaw
Forest R.
Snake R.
SL RR
220
10
NORTH
220
OAK
20
Forest River
PARK
VEGA
Forest R.
Ardoch
29
10
DAKOTA
81
54
Oslo
220 1 5
SL RR
Alvarado
220
Marshall
Polk
Johnstown
22
HIGDEM
8
22
Gilby
Turtle R.
22
ESTHER
1
23
Manvel
220
29
81
BN RR
Red River
Marais
of
21
BN RR
the
10
GRAND
Turtle R.
North
FORKS
220
29 81
19
2
29
2 3
BN RR
East
Grand Forks
Grand Forks
17
Emerado
2
BN RR
2

1 (65) 2 3 4 (65) 5

138

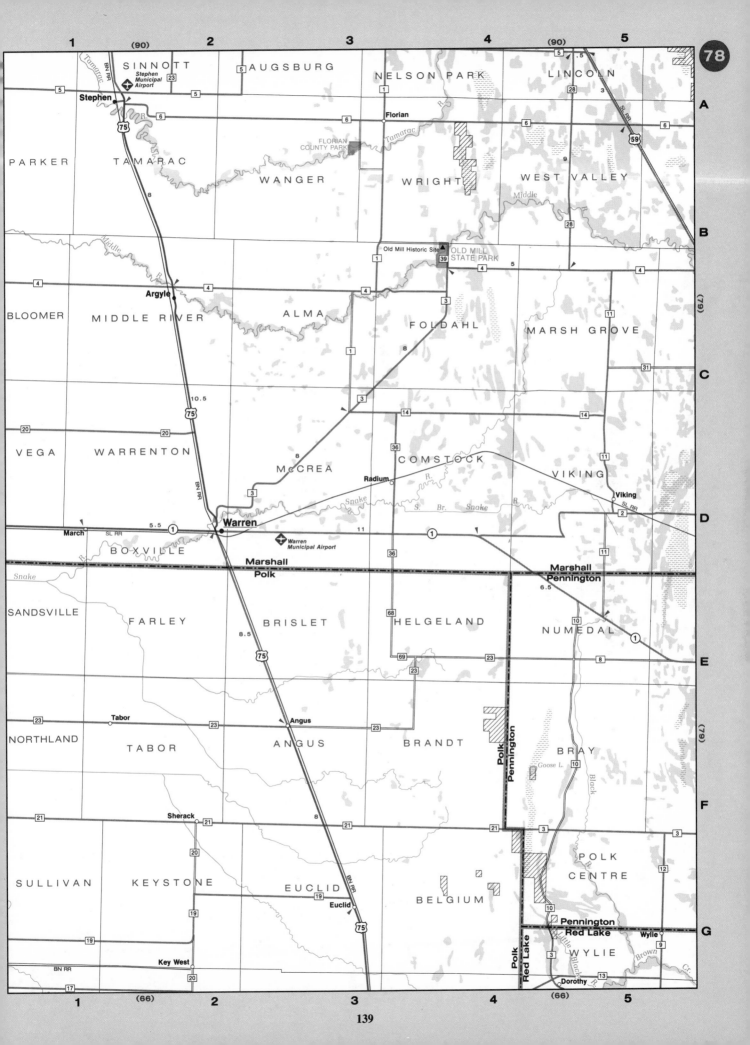

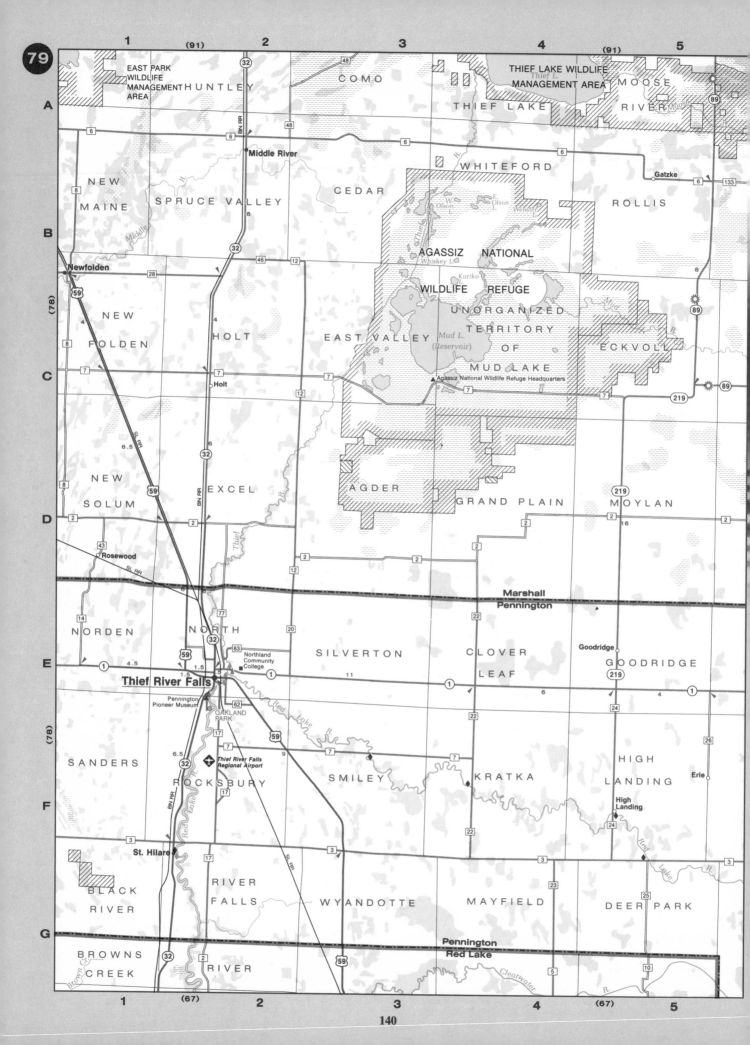

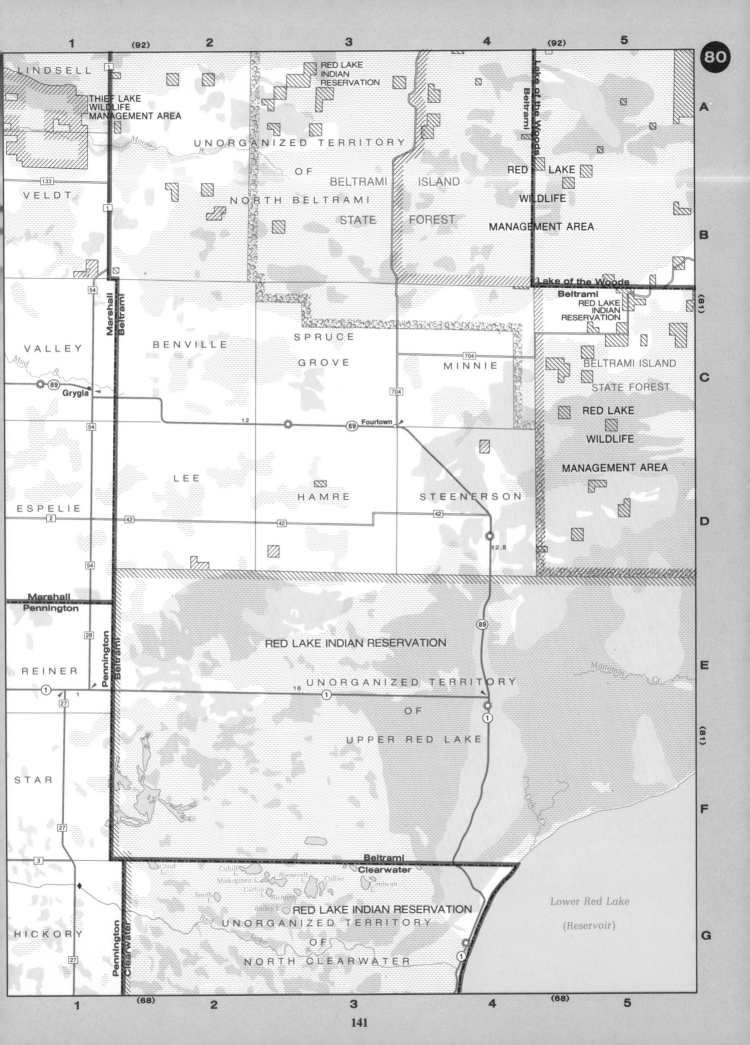

1 (93) **2** **3** **4** (93) **5**

A

RED LAKE INDIAN
RESERVATION

BELTRAMI ISLAND
STATE FOREST

RED LAKE INDIAN
RESERVATION

Carp

UNORGANIZED TERRITORY

OF RAINY RIVER

UNORGANIZED TERRITORY

OF BELTRAMI FOREST

RED LAKE INDIAN
RESERVATION

Rapid

Bk.

Chase Cr.

Thomson Cr.

Troy

77

77

Lake of the Woods

B

RED LAKE WILDLIFE

MANAGEMENT AREA

Rapid R.

Miller Cr.

S. Br.

Lake of the Woods

Beltrami

19.5

72

Beltrami

C

BELTRAMI ISLAND

STATE

FOREST

UNORGANIZED TERRITORY

OF

UPPER RED LAKE

RED LAKE INDIAN
RESERVATION

RED LAKE WILDLIFE

MANAGEMENT AREA

Hilman L.

RED LAKE INDIAN
RESERVATION

D

RED LAKE WILDLIFE MANAGEMENT AREA

RED LAKE INDIAN
RESERVATION

Poplar

72

72

WASKISH

40

E

RED LAKE INDIAN

RESERVATION

Big Point

Tamarac R.

Wild Rice

Upper Red Lake

(Reservoir)

WASKISH
RECREATION SITE

Waskish

Washkish Municipal Airport

Norman L.

RED LAKE

STATE FOREST

Larson L.

Dumas Cr.

5

4

72

F

SHOTLEY

Shotley Bk.

23

23

Sand Cliff Point

Rabbit Point

Halfway Point

Pelican
Point

Uninhabited
Point

Elm Point

108

108

UNORGANIZED TERRITORY OF

LOWER RED LAKE

RED LAKE INDIAN RESERVATION

Ponemah

Sucker Cr.

Shotley

111

11

G

Lower Red Lake

(Reservoir)

Saum
Saum Schools
Historic Site

BATTLE

106

N. Br.

Battle R.

23

23

WOODROW

S. Br. Battle R.

38

RED LAKE STATE FOREST

KELLIHER

72

Beltrami

1 (69) **2** **3** **4** (69) **5**

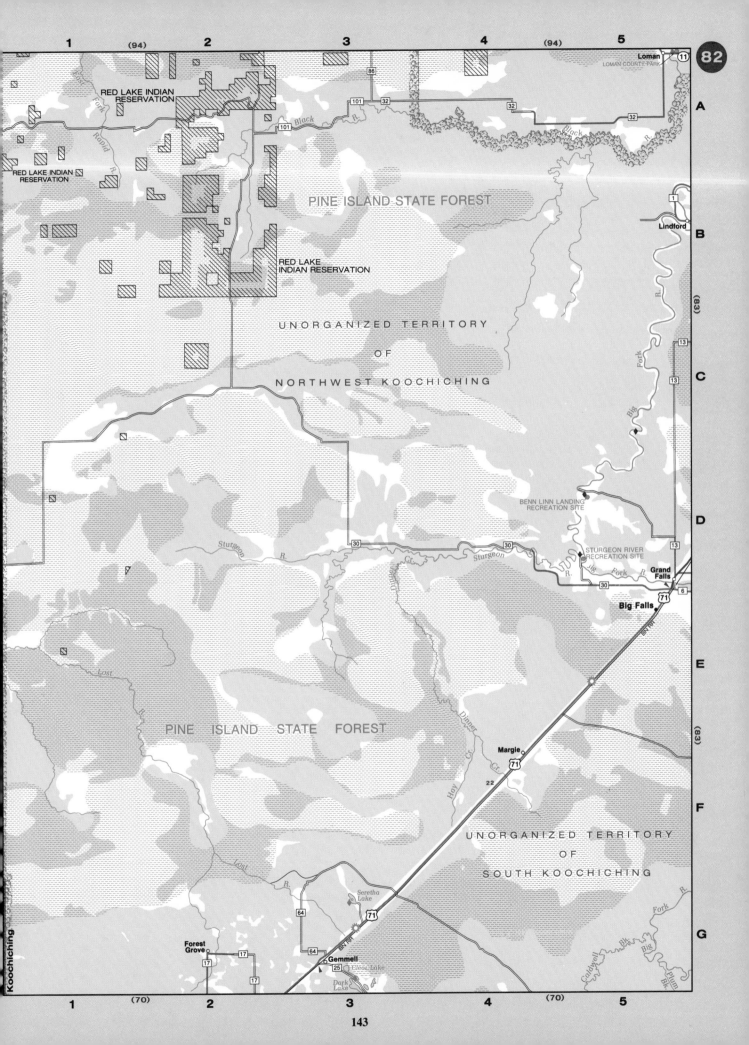

Loman
LOMAN COUNTY PARK

RED LAKE INDIAN
RESERVATION

RED LAKE INDIAN
RESERVATION

PINE ISLAND STATE FOREST

Lindford

RED LAKE
INDIAN RESERVATION

UNORGANIZED TERRITORY

OF

NORTHWEST KOOCHICHING

BENN LINN LANDING
RECREATION SITE

STURGEON RIVER
RECREATION SITE

Grand
Falls

Big Falls

PINE ISLAND STATE FOREST

Margie

UNORGANIZED TERRITORY

OF

SOUTH KOOCHICHING

Seretha
Lake

Forest
Grove

Gemmell

Clear Lake

Dark
Lake

Koochiching

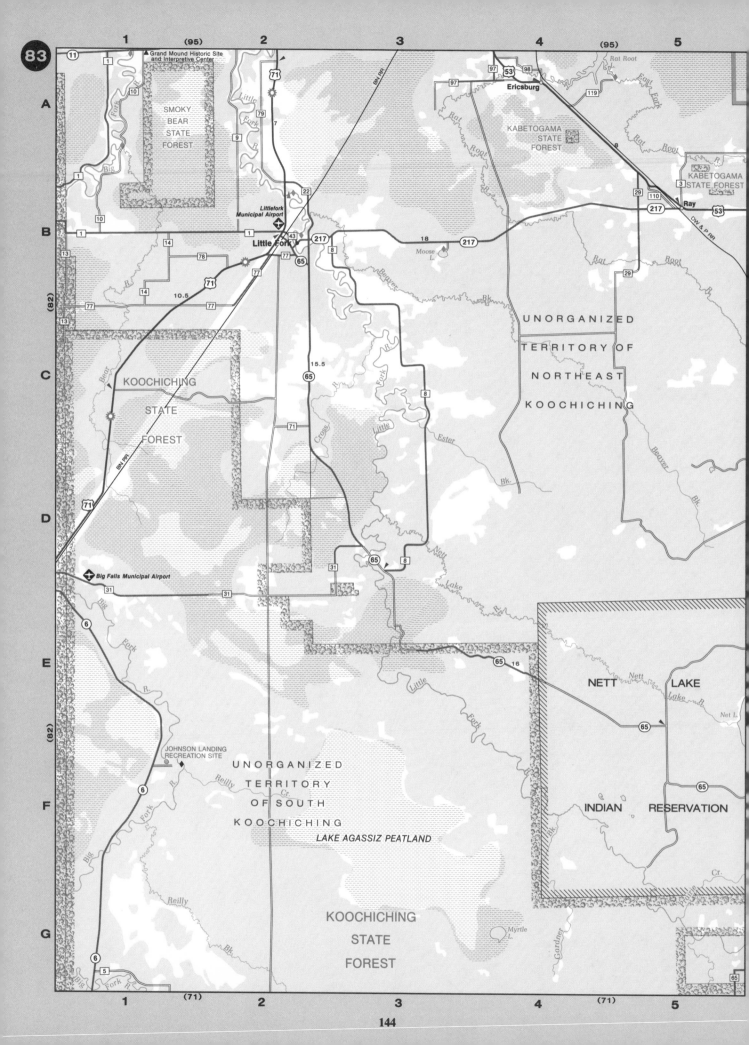

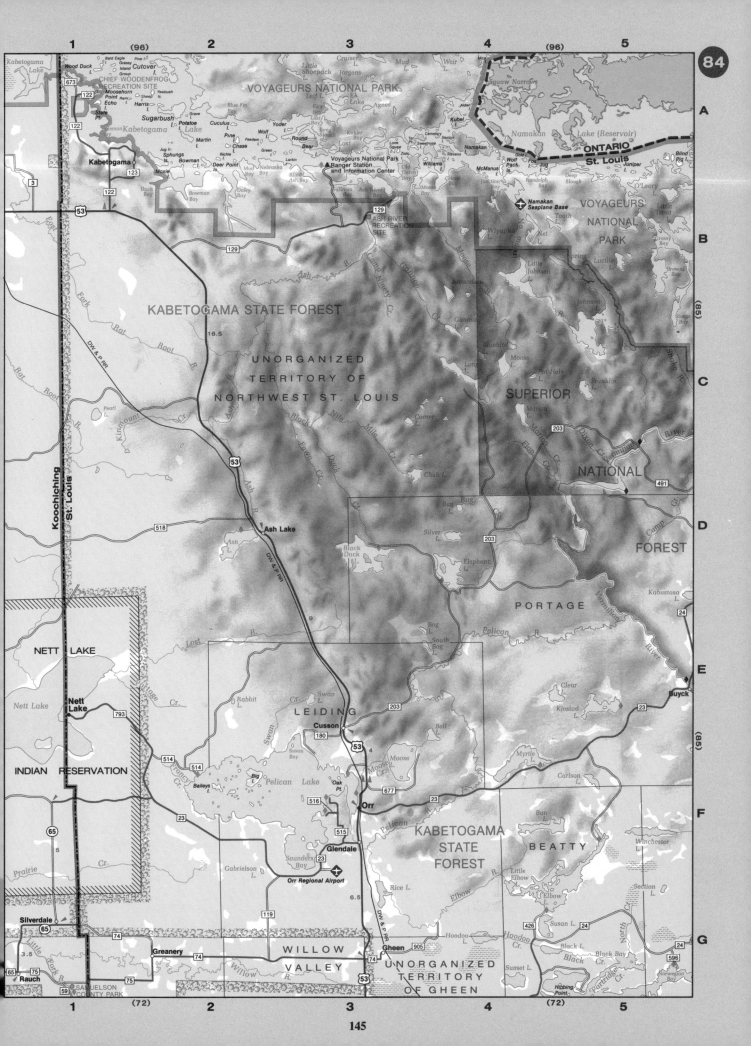

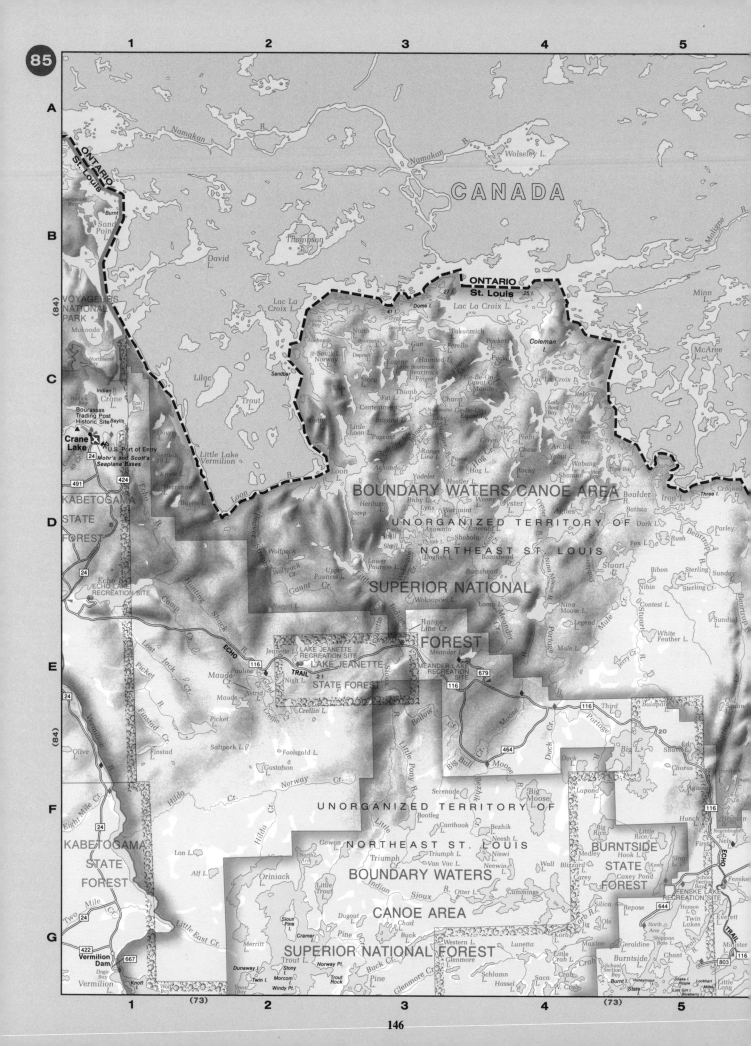

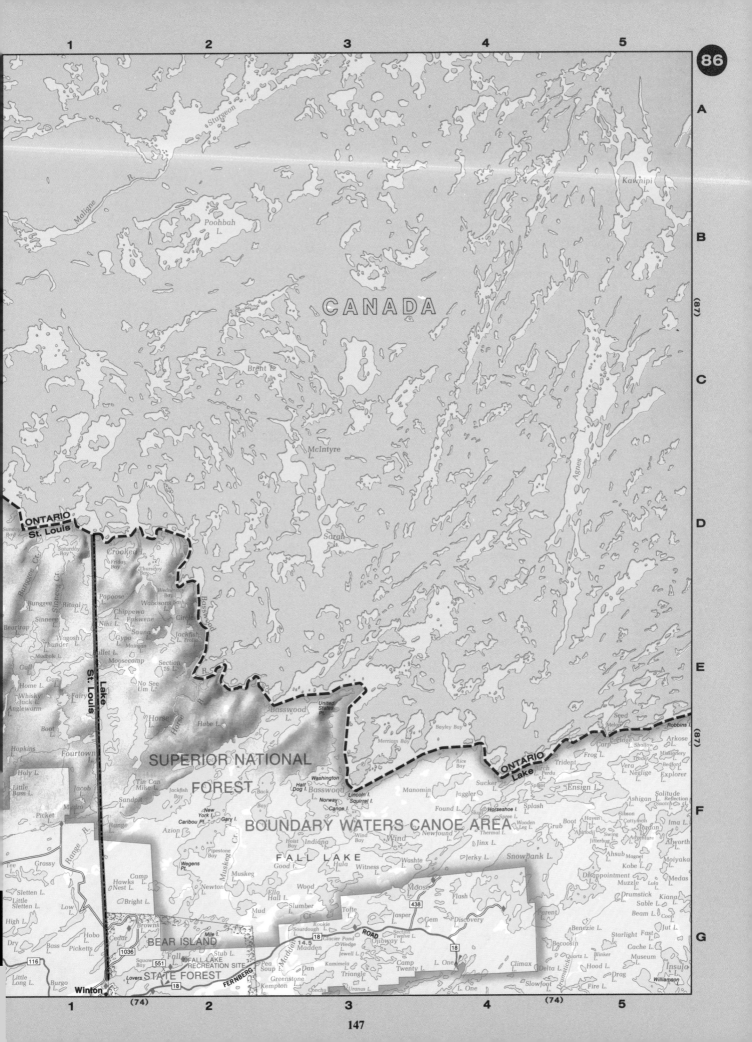

CANADA

SUPERIOR NATIONAL FOREST

BOUNDARY WATERS CANOE AREA

FALL LAKE

BEAR ISLAND

STATE FOREST

Winton

1   2   3   4   5

A

B

CANADA

Titmarsh L.

Weikwabinonaw L.

Nelson

Weikwabinonaw L.

Northern
Light L.

C

Sandstone L.

Mackies

588

Whitefish L.

D

Arrow L.

Arrow

Little
Gunflint L.
Little
North
Susana
North

ONTARIO
Cook

Rose L.

Watap

Mountain

Mountain

Fan
Vaseux

ONTARIO
Cook

N. Fowl Lake

E

Height of Land
Portage
Historic Site

Rat

Dunn Partridge

Daniels L.

Clearwater

BOUNDARY WATERS
CANOE AREA

Pemmican
Canoe

Moss

John L.

Little
John L.

IRON LAKE RECREATION
SITE

Mayhew

Iron L.

Birch L.

12

Duncan

W. Bearskin

FLOUR LAKE
RECREATION
SITE

Flour

Deer

Moon

Ivory Rocky Canoe
Puddle

Table L.

Alders

Pine L.

W. Pike L.

E. Pike L.

Spaulding

Sawbill

Long L.

Stump L.

McFarland

74

Royal

Fowl
Lake

(76)

Portage L.

5

65

Leo L.

Spen L.

66

Aspen

EAST BEARSKIN RECREATION SITE

Rudy L.

Crystal L.

Piers

Kiowa

Bronco L.

Beaver L.

Fault L.

16

Rush L.

Skipper

Poplar

Prune L.

Lizz L.

Ruby

Trap

Ditty L.

Strawberry
Parsnip
Kraut

Bean

Puff L. Pea

Mirage

Tittle L.

Loft L.

R.

Alpha Moon L.

Meeda

Swamp

Caribou

Allen L.

Gore

Dot

Swamper

Cucumber
Onion

Melon L.

Bean
Turnip Celery

Carrot L.
Potato

N. Shady

Nisula

Highlander L.

16

Swallow

Horseshoe

315

Jim L.

UNORGANIZED TERRITORY

Devil
Fish L.

Otter

Hensen

Gaskin

Jump L.

Snack

Marie L.

Helen L.

Jacket Morgan

Jim L.

Little
Jim L.

Shoe L.

Yawke

Greenwood

141

Sunfish Edith

Chester

Portage

ARROWHEAD TRAIL

Larsen

Winchell L.

Lux L.

Carl L.

OF EAST COOK

Esther

Otto
Lakes

Vista

Spud L.

152

Lima

Brule

Woodpile Cr.

Woodpecker

Squaw L.

Powers

GRAND PORTAGE

16

UNORGANIZED TERRITORY

Trimble L.

Redeye L.

State

Lantern
Globe

Misquah L.

Lullaby L.

Spark L.

309

Cyprinid

STATE FOREST

Rug L.

Whitaker L.

Trout L.

Little

Paddle

Irish

OF WEST COOK

Sledge

Riddle

Sere L.

Paige L.

Section
Ten L.

Cr.

Bell

Vonce L.

BOUNDARY WATERS

Disillusion

Lullaby L.

Stony L.

325

Pistol

Twelve L.

Redcoat

Cr.

Echo L.

Vernon

Swan

Rum

Dugout

Iota

PAT BAYLE STATE FOREST

4,5

Logged L.

Chase L.

Paine L.

Tom

Marshall

152

South

Brule R.

Mergansr

SEE INSET
ON PAGE 76

Bull L.

Calf L.

CANOE AREA

SUPERIOR

152

NATIONAL

Muckwa
Musquash

FOREST

Mumo

12

Merganser

Lost L.

Mons Cr.

F

G

Fishhook L.

Goose

Trine

Craw

Bull Club

Spray

Talus

154

Pine
Mountain

Northern
Light L.

Swamp R.

Eagle L.

Cascade R.

Eagle Mountain Historic Site
and Highest Point in
Minnesota / El. 2301 ft.

323

Thrush

Kemo

Pine

Mush

Makada

JUDGE C.R.
MAGEY
STATE PARK

1   (76)   2   3   4   (76)   5

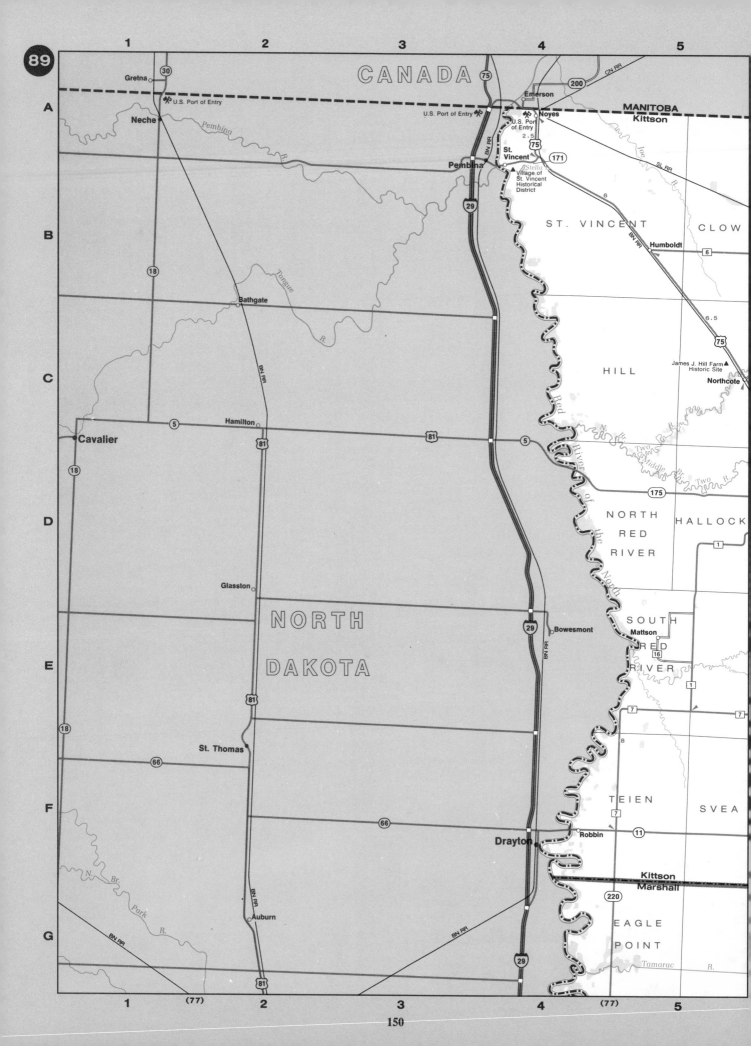

CANADA

MANITOBA

Gretna

30

75

200

CN RR

Emerson

U.S. Port of Entry

Noyes

U.S. Port of Entry

Kittson

A

Neche

Pembina R.

U.S. Port
of Entry

2.5

75

St. Vincent

171

Pembina

Village of
St. Vincent
Historical
District

ST. VINCENT

CLOW

B

Tongue

18

BN RR

Humboldt

6

29

R.

Joe SL RR

Bathgate

James J. Hill Farm
Historic Site

HILL

6.5

75

C

BN RR

R.

Northcote

Hamilton

81

5

Cavalier

5

Red

River

N. Br.

Two

Middle Br.

Br.

175

18

81

of

the

Two

R.

NORTH

RED

RIVER

HALLOCK

1

D

Glasston

North

NORTH

SOUTH

Mattson

RED

16

Bowesmont

E

DAKOTA

29

BN RR

1

RIVER

7

7

St. Thomas

81

8

66

TEIEN

SVEA

7

F

66

11

Robbin

Drayton

Kittson

Park

N. Br.

Marshall

220

R.

Auburn

EAGLE

G

BN RR

BN RR

81

29

POINT

Tamarac R.

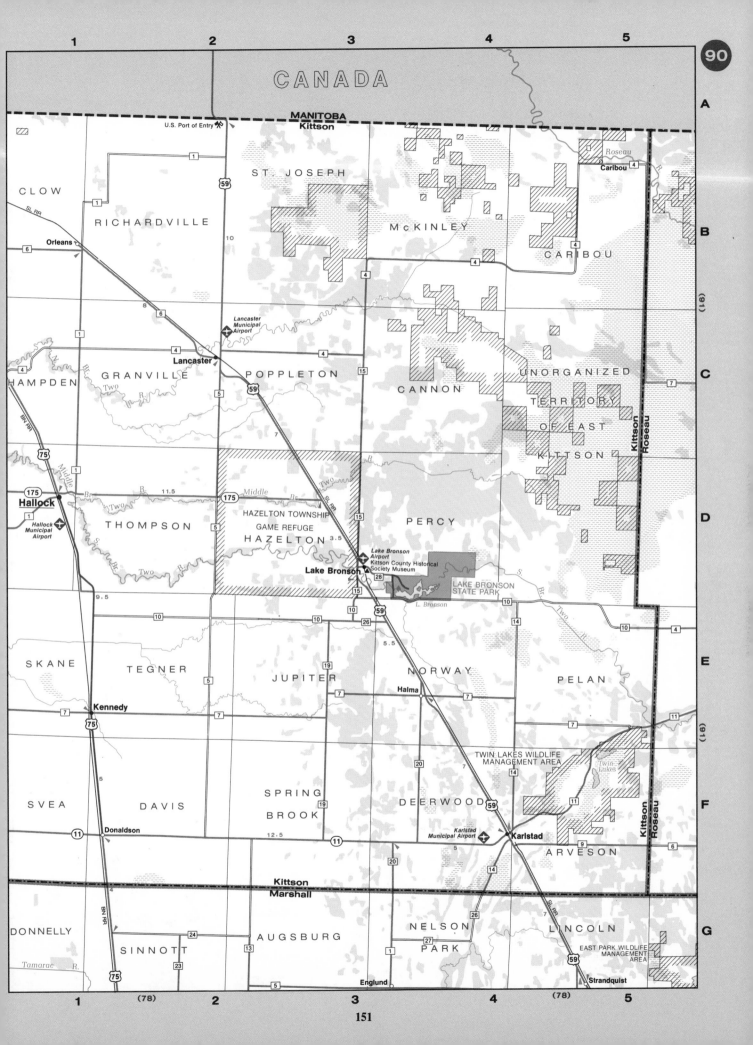

CANADA

MANITOBA

Kittson

U.S. Port of Entry

CLOW

RICHARDVILLE

ST. JOSEPH

McKINLEY

Roseau

Caribou

CARIBOU

Orleans

Lancaster Municipal Airport

HAMPDEN

GRANVILLE

POPPLETON

CANNON

UNORGANIZED

TERRITORY

OF EAST

KITTSON

Lancaster

Two R.

Middle

Hallock

Hallock Municipal Airport

THOMPSON

HAZELTON TOWNSHIP GAME REFUGE

HAZELTON

PERCY

Lake Bronson Airport
Kittson County Historical Society Museum

Lake Bronson

LAKE BRONSON STATE PARK

L. Bronson

SKANE

TEGNER

JUPITER

NORWAY

PELAN

Kennedy

Halma

TWIN LAKES WILDLIFE MANAGEMENT AREA

Twin Lakes

SVEA

DAVIS

SPRING BROOK

DEERWOOD

Karlstad Municipal Airport

Karlstad

ARVESON

Donaldson

Kittson

Marshall

DONNELLY

SINNOTT

AUGSBURG

NELSON

PARK

LINCOLN

EAST PARK WILDLIFE MANAGEMENT AREA

Tamarac R.

Englund

Strandquist

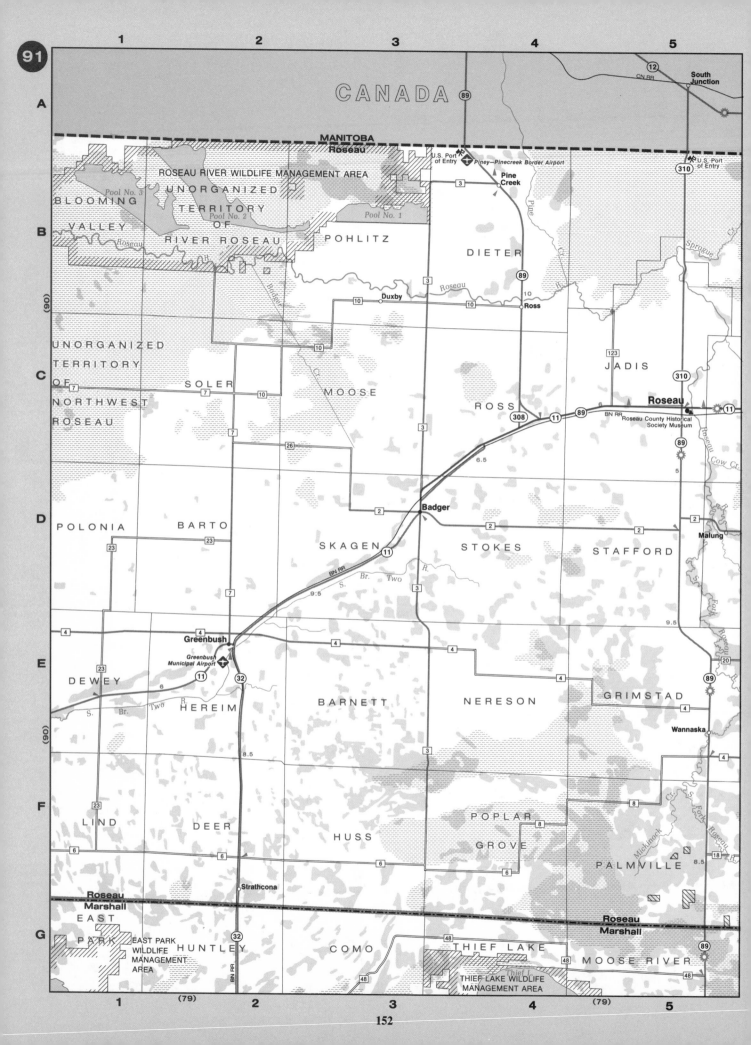

CANADA (89)

South
Junction

CN RR

12

MANITOBA
Roseau

ROSEAU RIVER WILDLIFE MANAGEMENT AREA

U.S. Port
of Entry

Piney—Pinecreek Border Airport

U.S. Port
of Entry

310

UNORGANIZED

Pool No. 3

BLOOMING

TERRITORY

Pool No. 2

Pine
Creek

3

DIETER

Pohlitz

Pine

VALLEY

OF

Pool No. 1

Sprague

Roseau

RIVER ROSEAU

POHLITZ

Roseau R.

89

10

Sprague Cr.

(90)

3

Duxby

10

Ross

10

UNORGANIZED

10

123

JADIS

310

TERRITORY

7

SOLER

MOOSE

ROSS

6

Roseau

Roseau

11

OF

7

10

308

89

Roseau County Historical
Society Museum

BN RR

11

Cow Cr.

NORTHWEST

3

5

89

ROSEAU

7

26

6.5

POLONIA

BARTO

2

Badger

STOKES

2

2

STAFFORD

Malung

2

23

23

SKAGEN

11

9.5

4

4

DEWEY

23

Greenbush

4

4

Greenbush
Municipal Airport

11

32

HEREIM

BN RR

9.5

S.   Br.   Two   R.

3

BARNETT

NERESON

GRIMSTAD

89

20

S.   Br.   Two   R.

4

Wannaska

4

(90)

8.5

3

4

LIND

DEER

HUSS

POPLAR

8

F

23

GROVE

8

PALMVILLE

8.5

6

6

6

Mickinock Cr.

18

S. Fork Roseau R.

6

Strathcona

Roseau
Marshall

Roseau
Marshall

EAST

48

89

PARK

EAST PARK
WILDLIFE
MANAGEMENT
AREA

32

HUNTLEY

COMO

THIEF LAKE

MOOSE RIVER

48

Thief L.

48

BN RR

48

THIEF LAKE WILDLIFE
MANAGEMENT AREA

89

1   (79)   2   3   4   (79)   5

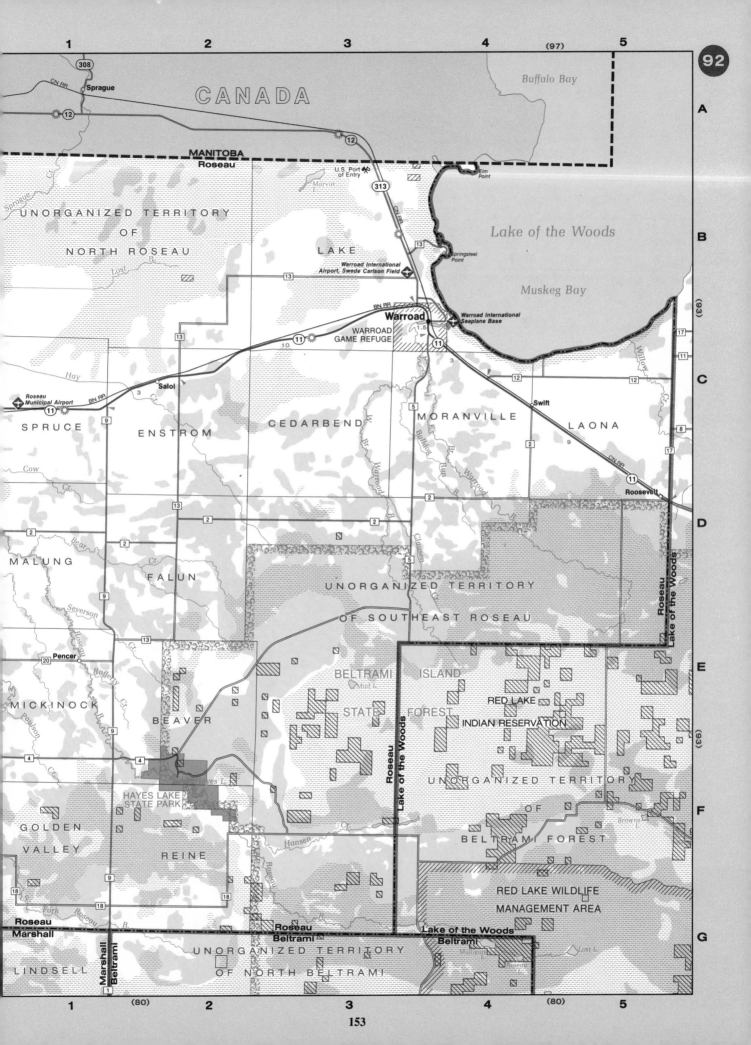

CANADA

Buffalo Bay

MANITOBA
Roseau

UNORGANIZED TERRITORY

OF

NORTH ROSEAU

LAKE

U.S. Port
of Entry

Marvin

Elm
Point

Lake of the Woods

Springsteel
Point

Warroad International
Airport, Swede Carlson Field

Muskeg Bay

Warroad

WARROAD
GAME REFUGE

Warroad International
Seaplane Base

Sprague

CN RR

Roseau
Municipal Airport

SPRUCE

ENSTROM

Salol

Swift

LAONA

MORANVILLE

CEDARBEND

Roosevelt

Hay

Cow

Cr.

MALUNG

FALUN

UNORGANIZED TERRITORY

OF SOUTHEAST ROSEAU

Roseau Lake of the Woods

Severson

Pencer

MICKINOCK

BEAVER

BELTRAMI ISLAND

Mud L.

STATE FOREST

RED LAKE

INDIAN RESERVATION

Lake of the Woods

UNORGANIZED TERRITORY

OF

HAYES LAKE
STATE PARK

Hayes L.

BELTRAMI FOREST

Browns

GOLDEN

VALLEY

REINE

RED LAKE WILDLIFE

MANAGEMENT AREA

Roseau
Marshall

LINDSELL

Marshall Beltrami

Roseau
Beltrami

Beltrami

Lake of the Woods

UNORGANIZED TERRITORY

OF NORTH BELTRAMI

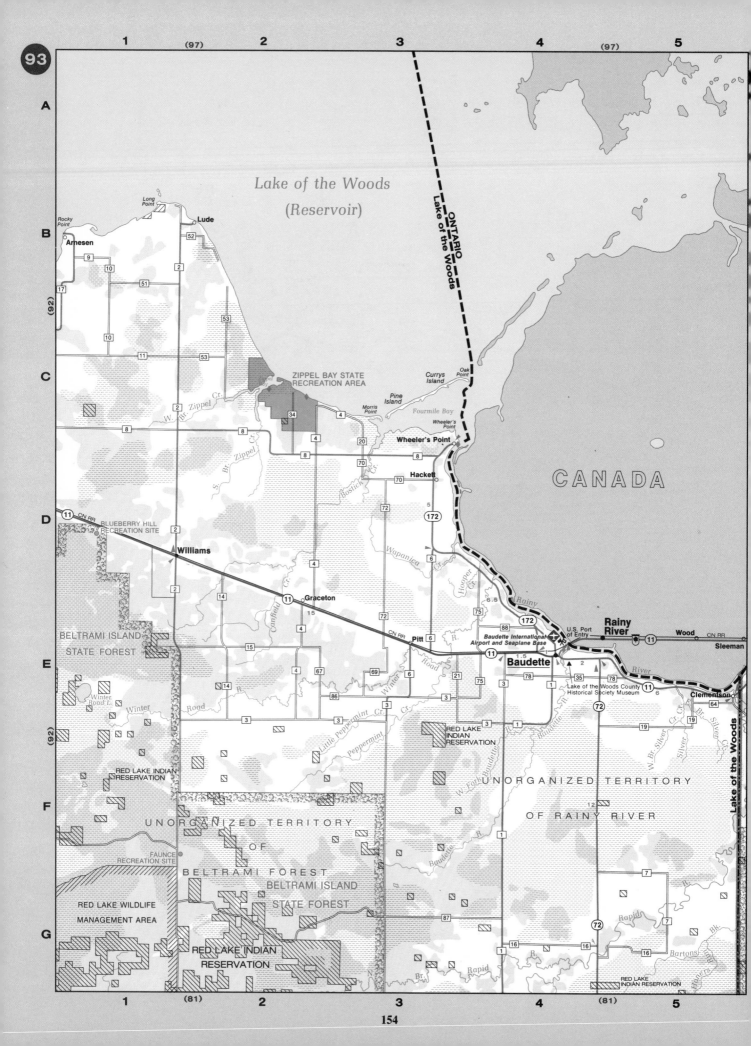

Lake of the Woods

(Reservoir)

ONTARIO
Lake of the Woods

Long Point

Rocky Point

Lude

Arnesen

CANADA

Currys Island

Oak Point

Pine Island

Morris Point

Fourmile Bay

ZIPPEL BAY STATE RECREATION AREA

Wheeler's Point

Wheeler's Point

Hackett

Williams

BLUEBERRY HILL RECREATION SITE

Graceton

Pitt

Baudette International Airport and Seaplane Base

U.S. Port of Entry

Rainy River

Wood

Sleeman

BELTRAMI ISLAND STATE FOREST

Baudette

Lake of the Woods County Historical Society Museum

Clementson

Winter Road L.

RED LAKE INDIAN RESERVATION

RED LAKE INDIAN RESERVATION

Little Peppermint

Peppermint

UNORGANIZED TERRITORY OF RAINY RIVER

FAUNCE RECREATION SITE

UNORGANIZED TERRITORY OF BELTRAMI FOREST

RED LAKE WILDLIFE MANAGEMENT AREA

BELTRAMI ISLAND STATE FOREST

RED LAKE INDIAN RESERVATION

Rapid

Rapid

RED LAKE INDIAN RESERVATION

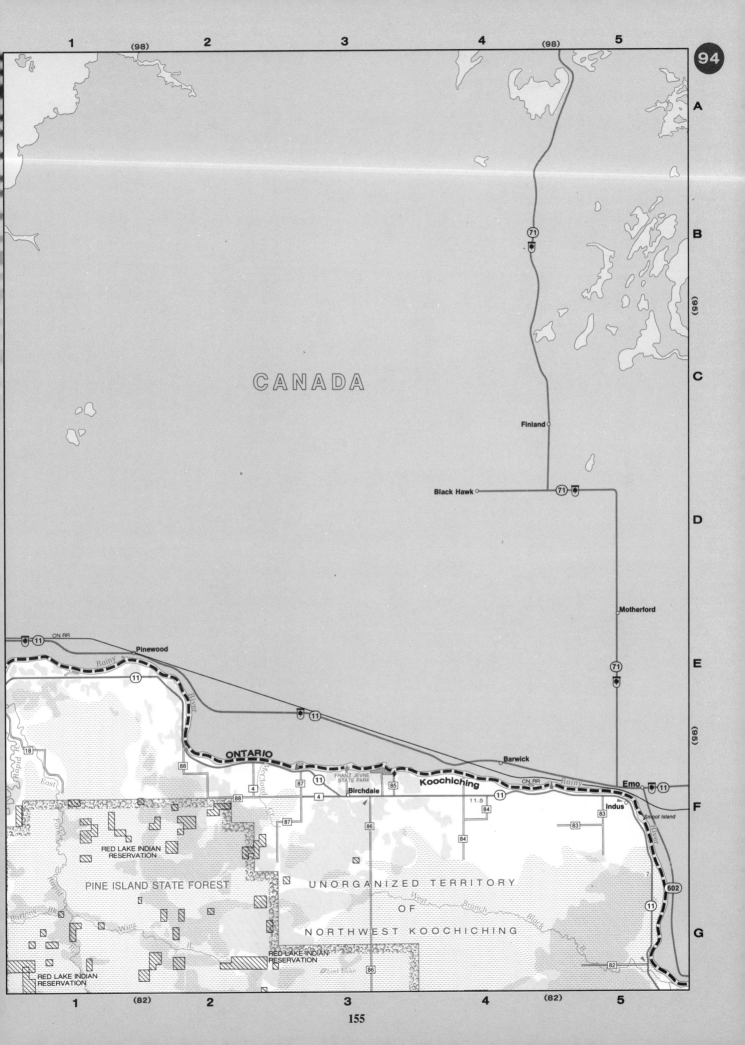

CANADA

71

Finland

Black Hawk   71

Motherford

71

CN RR
11   71
Pinewood
11

11

18
ONTARIO   Barwick
88   Emo   11
McCloud Cr.   87   11   Koochiching   CN RR   Rainy
88   4   85   11   Indus
RED LAKE INDIAN   87   11.5   83   Smoot Island
RESERVATION   86   84   84
84   River
PINE ISLAND STATE FOREST   U N O R G A N I Z E D   T E R R I T O R Y   7
602
RED LAKE INDIAN   West   Branch   Black   11
RESERVATION   O F
N O R T H W E S T   K O O C H I C H I N G
RED LAKE INDIAN   Lost Lake   86   82
RESERVATION

FRANZ JEVNE
STATE PARK
Birchdale

Rapid R.
East
Rainy River
Burtons Bk.
Rapid R.
Wing R.

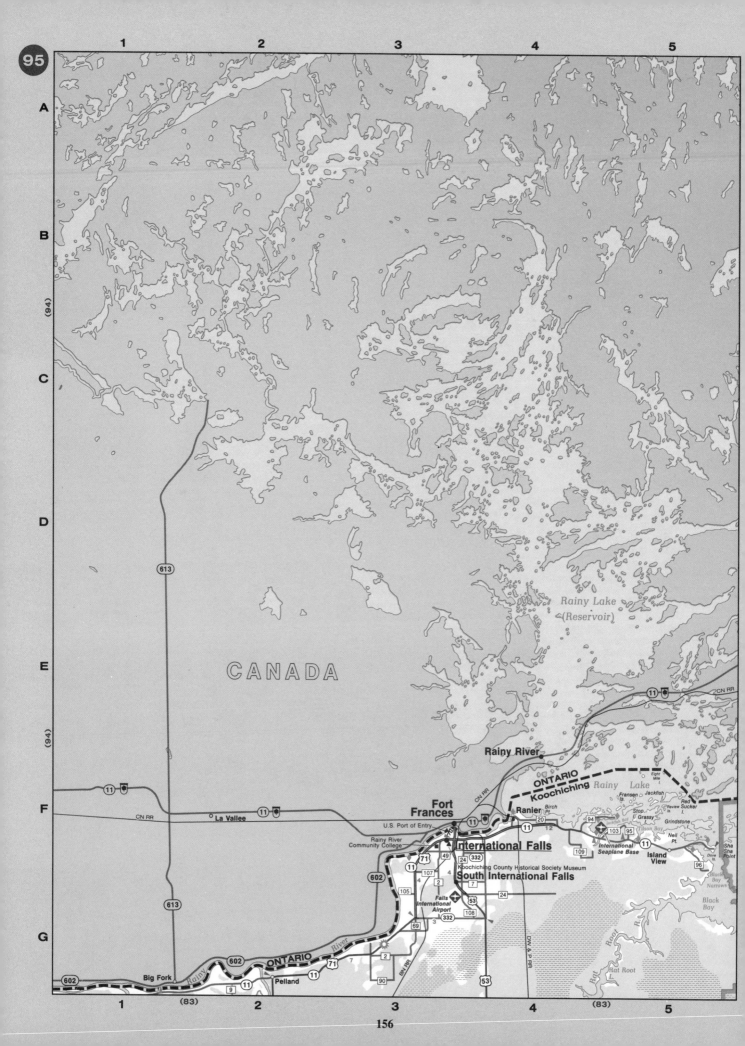

CANADA

Mine Centre

CN RR

11

11

11

CN RR

CN RR

Swell Bay

ONTARIO
St. Louis

Fox I.

Powder

Drywood

Steamboat

Dryweed

Cranberry

Harbor

Cranberry
Bay

Olson
Bay

Lost
Bay

Bruce
Narrows

Soldier Pt.

Duckfoot

Rainy Lake
(Reservoir)

Finlander

Finlander
Bay

Nelson

Saginaw
Bay

Marion
Bay

Three Sisters
Island

Pine

Shelland

Norway

Dove
Bay

Cranberry Cr.

VOYAGEURS NATIONAL PARK
War Club

Hitchcock
Bay

Hitchcock

Kawawia

Emerald

Cape
Rudolph

Blueberry

Black
Bay

Big I.

Locator L.

Quill

Kempton
Bay

Lyman

Browns
Bay

Peary

Sandbay

Rabbit

Koochiching
St. Louis

Black Bay
Portage

Moose
Bay

Loiten

Kempton
Channel

Anderson
Bay

Smith

Kettle
Channel

Kabetogama
Lake

Chief Wooden

Browns

Fishmouth

Oslo

Brown

Ernst

Rottenwood

Frogs Is.

Three
Sister

Camel
Back L.

Shoepack

Mica
Bay

Squirrel
Narrows

Cemetery

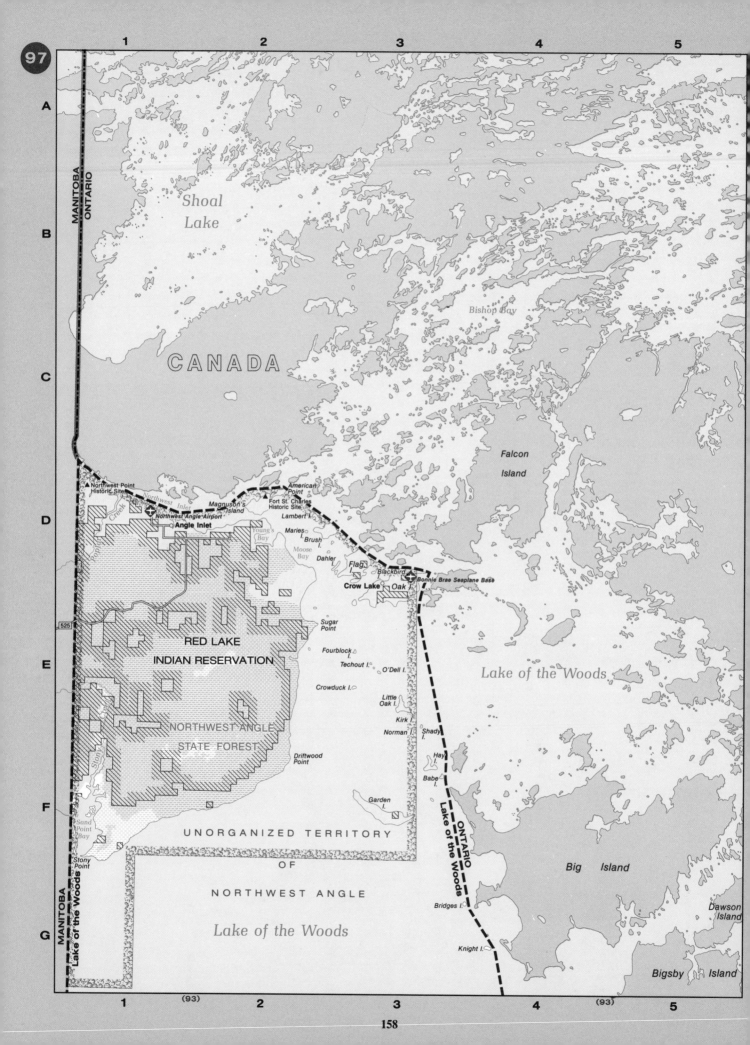

1   2   3   4   5

A

MANITOBA
ONTARIO

Shoal
Lake

B

Bishop Bay

C A N A D A

C

Falcon
Island

Northwest Point
Historic Site
Northwest Inlet
Magnuson's
Island
Northwest Angle Airport
Angle Inlet
American
Point
Fort St. Charles
Historic Site.
Lambert I.

D

Maries
I. Brush
I.
Young's
Bay
Moose
Bay
Dahler
I.
Flag
Blackbird
Crow Lake
Oak I.
Bonnie Brae Seaplane Base

525

Sugar
Point

RED LAKE
INDIAN RESERVATION

Fourblock
I.
Techout I.
O'Dell I.

Lake of the Woods

E

Crowduck I.

Little
Oak I.

NORTHWEST ANGLE

Kirk I.

STATE FOREST

Norman I.
Shady
I.

Driftwood
Point

Hay
I.

Stony

Babe
I.

F

Garden
I.

Sand
Point
Bay

U N O R G A N I Z E D   T E R R I T O R Y

Stony Point

O F

N O R T H W E S T   A N G L E

ONTARIO
Lake of the Woods

Big   Island

MANITOBA
Lake of the Woods

Bridges I.

Dawson
Island

G

Lake of the Woods

Knight I.

Bigsby   Island

1   (93)   2   3   4   (93)   5

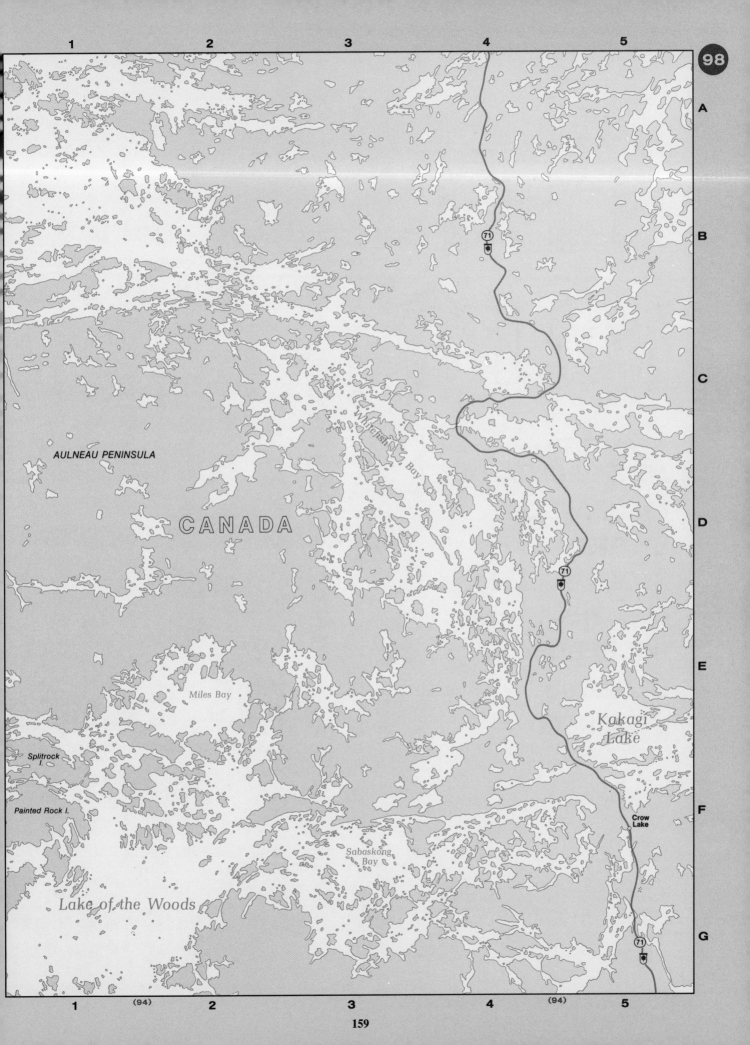

AULNEAU PENINSULA

Whitefish Bay

CANADA

Miles Bay

Splitrock I.

Painted Rock I.

Kakagi Lake

Crow Lake

Sabaskong Bay

Lake of the Woods

(94)

(94)

CITY MAPS

TWIN CITY METROPOLITAN AREA
MINNEAPOLIS
ST. PAUL
BLOOMINGTON
DULUTH
ROCHESTER
ST. CLOUD
MOORHEAD

MINNEAPOLIS INDEX

COMMERCIAL

1 Builders Exchange B6
2 Butler Square B4
3 City Center B5
4 Control Data Bus. Tech. Ctr. D9
Cray Research C5
6 Dain Tower B5
7 Dayton's C5
8 Donaldson's C5
F&M Marquette Bank B5
10 First Bank Place C6
11 Foshay Tower C5
12 Grain Exchange B7
13 Hyatt Merchandise Mart D3
14 IBM B6
15 IDS C5
16 International Market Center B1
17 Lumber Exchange Bldg. B5
18 Lutheran Brotherhood C6/C5
19 Milwaukee RR Station B7
20 Multifoods Tower B5
21 NSP B5
22 Northwestern Bell B6
23 Northwestern Nat'l Life A6
24 Northwestern Operations Center B6
25 100 Washington Square A6
26 Peavey Bldg. C5
Penney's B5
28 Pillsbury Center C6
29 Piper, Jaffray & Hopwood C5
30 Riverplace A8
31 St. Anthony Main A9
32 608 Building C6
33 Soo Line Railroad B6

EDUCATION

34 Dunwoody Institute D1
35 Mpls. Comm. College D2
36 Mpls. Tech. Inst. D2
37 North Central Bible Coll. E7

ENTERTAINMENT/ARTS/RECREATION

38 Cricket Theatre B4
39 Dudley Riggs Theatres F1/D10
40 Guthrie Theatre E1
41 Henn. Center for the Arts B4
42 Metrodome C8
43 Mpls. Aud. & Conv. Hall E4
44 Mpls. Planetarium B5
45 Mixed Blood Theatre E10
46 Nicollet Island A7
47 Orchestra Hall D4
48 Orpheum Theatre C4
49 Parade Stadium D1
50 Walker Art Center E1
51 YMCA/YWCA C4/D4

GOVERNMENT

52 Federal Courts B6
53 Federal Reserve Bank B6
54 Henn. Cty. Govt. Center C6
55 Mpls. City Hall B6
56 Post Office A7
57 Public Health Ctr. B6

HISTORICAL POINTS OF INTERESTS

58 Father Hennepin Statue D1
59 James J. Hill RR Bridge B9
St. Anthony Falls A8

HOSPITALS

61 Henn. Cty. Med. Ctr. D7
62 Metropolitan Med. Ctr. D7

HOTELS

Amfac Hotel B5
64 Guest House Motel C6
65 Holiday Inn E4
66 Hyatt Regency D4
67 Leamington ...
68 Leamington Motor Inn D6
Marquette C5
70 Mpls. Plaza B6
71 Normandy Inn C6
72 Northstar Inn C6
73 Radisson Metrodome C10
74 Regency Plaza C3

MISCELLANEOUS

75 Basilica of St. Mary D2
76 Bus Depot C4
77 Henn. Methodist Church E1
78 Mpls. Athletic Club C5
Mpls. Chamber of Commerce B5
80 Minneapolis Club C5
81 St. Mark's Cathedral E1
Visitor Information Ctr. C5

PARKS

Loring Park E3
84 Elliot Park D8

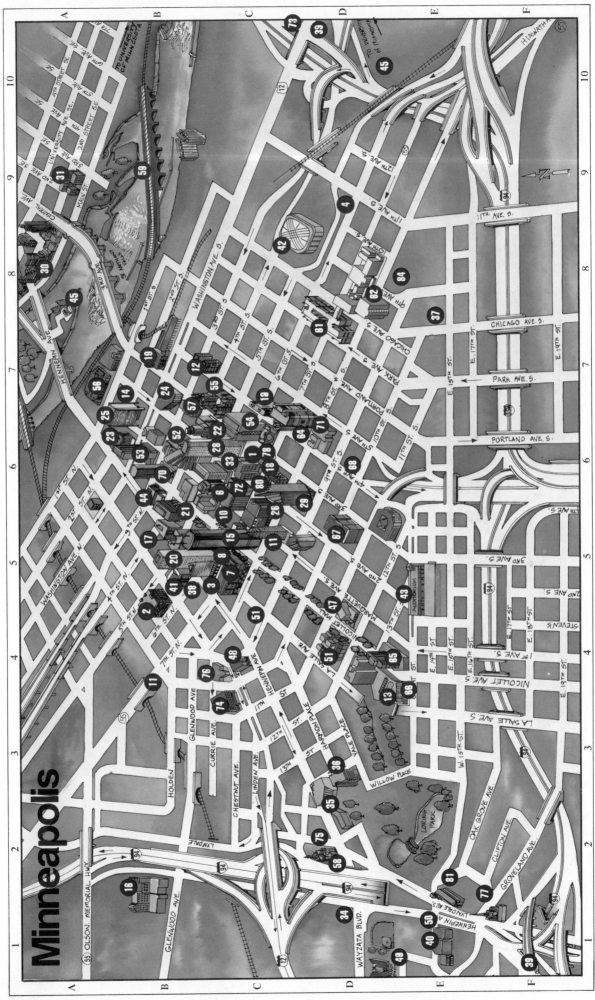

Minneapolis

Bloomington

BLOOMINGTON INDEX

ST. PAUL INDEX

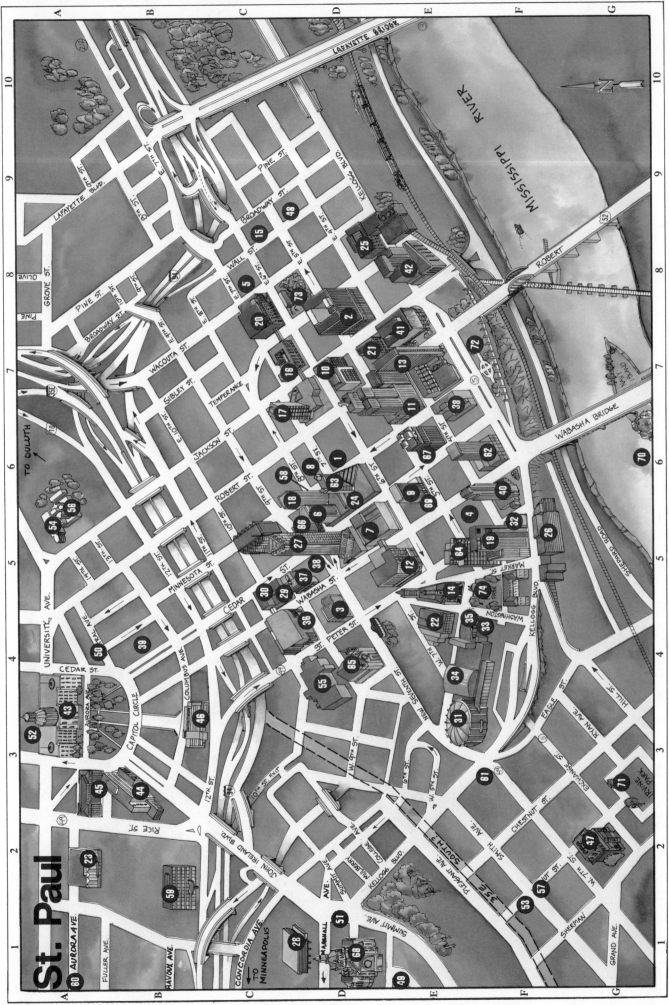

St. Paul

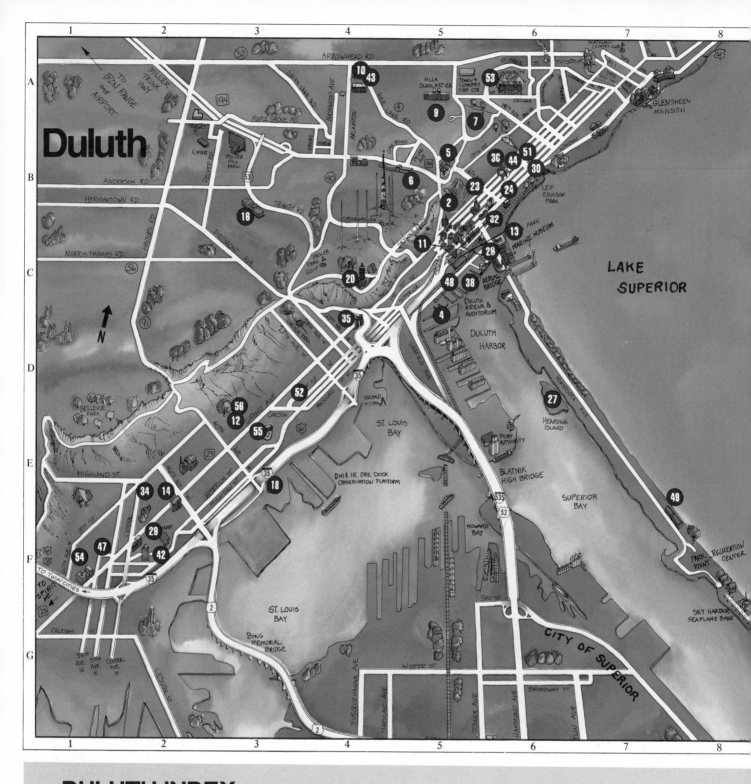

Duluth

LAKE SUPERIOR

DULUTH INDEX

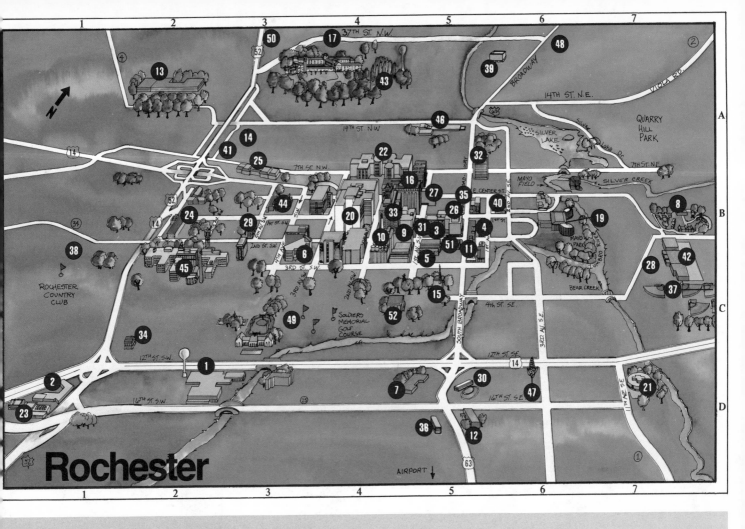

Rochester

ROCHESTER INDEX

Twin Cities Metropolitan Area

TWIN CITY METROPOLITAN AREA INDEX

169

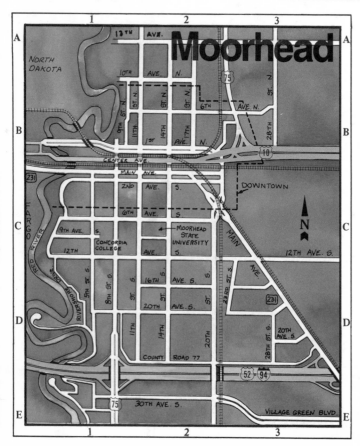

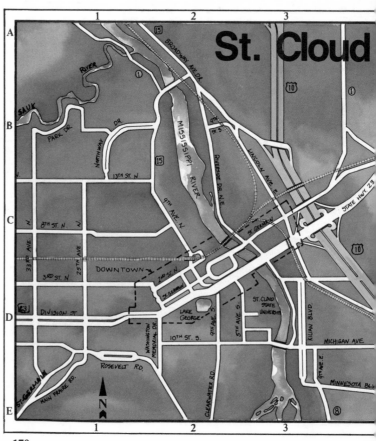

INDEX TO MINNESOTA PLACE-NAMES

There are approximately 15,000 place-names shown on the maps in the *Atlas,* and they are all listed alphabetically in this index. Named features include populated places, lakes, rivers, townships, counties and a variety of other cultural and physical features and points of interest.

Each index entry includes the following information:

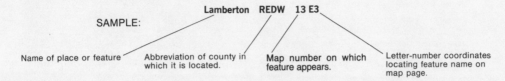

SAMPLE:

Name of place or feature   Abbreviation of county in which it is located.   Map number on which feature appears.   Letter-number coordinates locating feature name on map page.

Standard abbreviations for county names used throughout this index are shown below:

ATKN	Aitkin	FILL	Fillmore	MART	Martin	ROCK	Rock
ANOK	Anoka	FREE	Freeborn	MCLD	McLeod	ROSE	Roseau
BECK	Becker	GOOD	Goodhue	MEEK	Meeker	STLS	St. Louis
BELT	Beltrami	GRNT	Grant	MLLC	Mille Lacs	SCOT	Scott
BENT	Benton	HENN	Hennepin	MORR	Morrison	SHER	Sherburne
BGST	Big Stone	HOUS	Houston	MOWE	Mower	SBLY	Sibley
BLUE	Blue Earth	HUBB	Hubbard	MURR	Murray	STRN	Stearns
BRWN	Brown	ISNT	Isanti	NCLT	Nicollet	STEL	Steele
CARL	Carlton	ITSC	Itasca	NBLS	Nobles	STEV	Stevens
CARV	Carver	JACK	Jackson	NORM	Norman	SWFT	Swift
CASS	Cass	KNBC	Kanabec	OLMS	Olmsted	TODD	Todd
CHIP	Chippewa	KAND	Kandiyohi	OTTL	Otter Tail	TRAV	Traverse
CHIS	Chisago	KITT	Kittson	PENN	Pennington	WBSH	Wabasha
CLAY	Clay	KCHG	Koochiching	PINE	Pine	WADN	Wadena
CLER	Clearwater	LOPL	Lac Qui Parle	PIPE	Pipestone	WASC	Waseca
COOK	Cook	LAKE	Lake	POLK	Polk	WASH	Washington
COTT	Cottonwood	WOOD	Lake of the Woods	POPE	Pope	WATN	Watonwan
CROW	Crow Wing	LSUR	Le Sueur	RAMS	Ramsey	WILK	Wilkin
DKTA	Dakota	LINC	Lincoln	RDLK	Red Lake	WINA	Winona
DOGE	Dodge	LYON	Lyon	REDW	Redwood	WRIT	Wright
DOUG	Douglas	MAHN	Mahnomen	RENV	Renville	YMED	Yellow Medicine
FRBT	Faribault	MRSH	Marshall	RICE	Rice		

Abbreviations used in this index include:

Bk.	Brook	Cr.	Creek	L.	Lake	R.	River
Br.	Branch	I.	Island	Pt.	Point	Twp.	Township

Railroad abbreviations used on the maps are as follows:

BN RR	Burlington Northern Inc.
CN RR	Canadian National Railway
C & NW RR	Chicago and North Western Railway
CM St P & P RR	Chicago, Milwaukee, St. Paul and Pacific Railroad
CRI & P RR	Chicago, Rock Island and Pacific Railroad
DNE RR	Duluth, Northeastern Railroad
DM & IR RR	Duluth, Missabe and Iron Range Railway
DW & P RR	Duluth, Winnipeg & Pacific Railway
EM RR	Erie Mining Co. Railroad
IC RR	Illinois Central Railroad
MN & S RR	Minneapolis, Northfield and Southern Railway
MT RR	Minnesota Transfer Railway Co.
RM RR	Reserve Mining Co. Railroad
SL RR	Soo Line Railroad

Certain principles have been followed in creating this place-name index; the most important of these are described below, with examples when these help to illustrate the point.

1. General alphabetical order of place-names is letter-by-letter, for the entire subject name.

2. Many lakes have the same name. They are alphabetized on the basis of the name of the county in which they are located.

3. Generally the word "Lake" follows a specific lake name, so it does not affect significantly the feature alphabetization. If, however, "Lake" precedes the specific name (e.g. "Lake Oscar"), the name will appear in the index wherever the specific part of the feature name falls ("O", for "Oscar"), *not* under "L".

4. All directional components of place-names, e.g., *"North Fork Spring Creek"*, are spelled out and alphabetized on that basis, as part of the name.

5. When "St." (Saint) is part of a place-name, it is alphabetized as if it were spelled-out. "St. Paul" therefore follows "Sailor" and preceeds "Sakatah" in the index.

6. Some place-names and features appear on many map pages (e.g. Mississippi River). The name appears in the index only once, generally with the page number on which the feature is mapped most prominently. Extensions or continuations of the feature can be found by using the adjacent page location information included on all edges of each map (brown type, in parentheses).

7. On maps of the Minneapolis-St. Paul metropolitan area, some street names are included. These are alphabetized separately at the end of the main place-name index.

1st Little Gulch L. HUBB 57 C2
2nd Little Gulch L. HUBB 57 C2
3rd Little Gulch L. HUBB 57 C2
4th Little Gulch L. HUBB 57 C2
L. 23 LAKE 75 F1
25 I. STLS 85 B4
27 I. STLS 85 B3
41 I. STLS 85 B3
L. 418 CASS 57 E5
1848 Convention Historic Site WASH 27 B4
L. Aaron DOUG 39 C1
Aastad Twp OTTL 38 B2
L. Abbey BECK 46 A4
Abbie L. WRIT 33 G4
Abe L. CASS 58 G4
Abel L. CASS 48 A4
Abinodji L. LAKE 86 F5
Abita L. COOK 88 G2
Abners L. BECK 56 D4
Abrahamson L. CLAY 46 A1
Achman L. STRN 33 B1
Achundo L. STLS 85 D3
Acoma Twp MCLD 24 C5
Acorn L. BECK 46 B5
Acorn L. COOK 87 E3
Acton MEEK 24 A3
Acton Monument Historic Site MEEK 24 A3
Acton Twp MEEK 24 A3
Ada Bk. CASS 49 A1
L. Ada CASS 58 G1
Ada L. COOK 87 G4
Adams MOWE 7 F5
Adams L. ISNT 34 A5
Adams L. LAKE 87 F2
Adams Twp MOWE 7 F4
Ada NORM 54 A4
L. Addie MCLD 25 F1
Adele L. ITSC 71 F2
Adley Cr. STRN 40 G2
L. Adley OTTL 39 B3
Adney L. CROW 49 C4
Adrian NBLS 2 E2
Adrian Spring County Park NBLS 2 E2
Adrian Twp WATN 14 G2
Adventure L. LAKE 86 F5
Aerial Lift Bridge STLS 52 A4
Aerie L. STLS 60 E5
Aetna Twp PIPE 12 F1
Afton WASH 27 D4
Afton Alps Ski Area WASH 27 D4
Afton L. COOK 87 F3
Afton State Park WASH 27 D4
Agamok L. LAKE 87 E2
Agassa L. STLS 85 F5
Agassiz National Wildlife Refuge Headquarters MRSH 79 C3
Agassiz National Wildlife Refuge MRSH 79 B3
Agassiz Twp LQPL 29 F5
Agate Bay LAKE 62 E3
Agate L. CASS 49 E1
Agate L. CROW 49 E4
Agawato L. STLS 85 D3
Agder Twp MRSH 79 D3
Agency Bay CASS 57 D5
L. Agnes COOK 75 C5
Agnes L. DOUG 39 E3
Agnes L. STLS 84 A3
L. Agnes STLS 85 D4
Agram Twp MORR 41 D2
Ahgoday L. COOK 87 F4
Ah-gwah-ching CASS 57 D4
Ahlin L. BELT 68 B5
Ahlswede L. SCOT 26 F2
Ahmakose L. LAKE 87 F1
Ahmoo Cr. LAKE 74 A5
Ahsebun L. CASS 59 F1
Ahsub L. LAKE 86 F5
Aikio I. STLS 73 C5
Airlake Industrial Park Airport DKTA 26 G5
AITKIN — 50 —
Aitkin ATKN 50 D1
Aitkin County-City Municipal Airport ATKN 50 D1
Aitkin County Historical Society Museum ATKN 50 D1
Aitkin L. BELT 50 A5
Aitkin Twp ATKN 50 D1
Akeley HUBB 57 E3
Akeley Twp HUBB 57 E3
Akron Twp BGST 30 F1
Akron Twp WILK 45 E5
Alango Twp STLS 72 C4
Alaska L. BELT 68 B5
Alaska Twp BELT 68 C5
Albany STRN 32 B4
Albany Twp STRN 32 B4
Alba Twp JACK 3 D2
Albers County Park RICE 16 B5
Alberta STEV 30 B2
Alberta Twp BENT 41 G4
Albert Kordiak County Park ANOK 26 B5
Albert L. BLUE 15 E5
Albert L. DOUG 38 D4
Albert Lea FREE 6 E4
Albert Lea Game Refuge FREE 6 F5
Albert Lea L. FREE 6 F5
Albert Lea Municipal Airport FREE 6 E4
Albert Lea Travel Information Center FREE 6 G4
Albert Lea Twp FREE 6 F4
Albert L. OTTL 47 D2
Albert L. WRIT 33 G4
Albert Ney Memorial County Park Reserve WRIT 33 F4
Albertson L. OTTL 46 B5
Albertville WRIT 34 F2
Albin Twp BRWN 14 F3
Albion Center WRIT 33 G3
Albion L. WRIT 33 F3
Albion Twp WRIT 33 G3
Alborn STLS 60 F5
Alborn Twp STLS 60 E5
Albrechts Cr. PINE 44 C2
Albright Mills County Park WRIT 25 A3
Alcohol Cr. HUBB 57 C1
Alcove L. COOK 87 G3
Alden FREE 6 E3
Alden I. STLS 84 A4
Alden L. STLS 61 D5
Alden Twp FREE 6 E2
Alden Twp STLS 62 D1
Alder L. COOK 88 E3
Aldrich WADN 48 F1
Aldrich L. DOUG 39 D1
Aldrich Twp WADN 48 F1
Alepo I. STLS 73 A2
L. Alexander MORR 40 B4
Alexander Faribault House Historic Site RICE 16 D5
Alexander Ramsey House Historic Site RAMS 27 C1
Alexandria DOUG 39 E2
Alexandria Municipal Airport DOUG 39 E2
Alexandria Twp DOUG 39 E3
Alex L. ITSC 71 G1
Alex P. Anderson Municipal Park GOOD 18 A1
Alf L. STLS 85 F2
L. Alfred OTTL 46 C1
Alfsborg Twp SBLY 15 B1
Alger L. LAKE 75 D2
L. Alice CASS 57 E4
L. Alice WASH 35 F4
Alice L. BELT 69 E2
Alice L. BLUE 16 F1
Alice L. HUBB 56 C5
Alice L. ITSC 70 E3
Alice L. LAKE 87 G1
Alice L. OTTL 46 C4
Alice L. OTTL 46 E5
Alice L. POPE 31 A3
Alida CLER 56 A4
Alimagnet L. DKTA 26 E5
Alimagnet Municipal Park DKTA 26 E5
Alkali L. OTTL 38 B2
L. Allen MCLD 24 D5
Allen L. CLER 56 C4
Allen L. COOK 88 F1
Allen L. CROW 49 A4
Allen L. ITSC 71 E3
Allen L. MAHN 67 F5
Allen L. STLS 60 A5
Allens Bay BELT 69 G4
Alliance Twp CLAY 45 B3
Allie L. RENV 24 E4
Allis County Park OLMS 18 F1
Alma City WASC 6 A1
L. Alma PINE 44 D1
Alma Twp MRSH 78 C3
Almelund CHIS 35 C4
Almond Twp BGST 29 C4
Almora OTTL 39 A3
Almora L. OTTL 39 A3
L. Alott MORR 40 B5
Alpha JACK 4 E1
Alpha L. COOK 88 F1
Alpine L. COOK 87 E3
Alp L. ITSC 71 F1
Alta Vista Twp LINC 22 G1
Altermatt L. BRWN 14 E2
Altnow L. SBLY 25 G2
Altona Twp PIPE 11 F4
Alton L. COOK 75 A3
Alton Twp WASC 16 G1
Altura WINA 19 G1
Alvarado MRSH 77 D5
Alvig Slough KAND 32 F1
Alvin L. BECK 56 G1
Alvin L. DOUG 39 E2
Alvwood ITSC 70 C2
Alvwood Twp ITSC 70 D2
Alworth L. LAKE 86 F5
Amador Twp CHIS 35 C4
Amberger L. LAKE 62 B3
Amber L. LAKE 87 G1
Amber L. MART 4 F5
Amboy BLUE 5 B2
Amboy Twp COTT 13 G4
Ambush L. COOK 87 D4
Amelia L. ANOK 27 A2
Amelia L. POPE 31 A3
Amenda Cr. COOK 75 E3
Amen L. ITSC 71 G2
American L. STLS 61 B5
American Point COOK 87 D3
American Point WOOD 97 D2
Ames L. ITSC 70 D4
Amherst FILL 9 F2
Amherst Twp FILL 9 E2
Amik L. ITSC 70 F3
Amimi L. LAKE 87 F2
Amiret LYON 12 D4
Amiret Twp LYON 12 D5
Amity Cr. STLS 61 G5
Amity-Snively Municipal Park STLS 61 G5
Amoeber L. LAKE 87 E1
Amor L. OTTL 46 E5
Amor OTTL 46 E5
Amor Twp OTTL 46 E5
Amos L. DOUG 38 E5
Amo Twp COTT 3 A3
Amundsen L. STLS 84 B4
Anchor L. STLS 61 A1
Anchor Lake Travel Information Center and Rest Area STLS 61 A1
Andek L. LAKE 75 A1
Anderson Bay STLS 96 G4
Anderson County Park JACK 3 G4
Anderson Cr. CARL 52 E1
Anderson Island NCLT 15 D2
Anderson L. ANOK 35 E1
Anderson L. ATKN 50 B5
Anderson L. ATKN 50 E1
Anderson L. BECK 55 E4
Anderson L. BECK 55 F1
Anderson L. BELT 69 C2
Anderson L. BELT 69 E5
Anderson L. CLAY 54 F5
Anderson L. CLER 56 B3
Anderson L. CLER 68 C2
Anderson L. COOK 75 B4
Anderson L. GRNT 38 C4
Anderson L. HENN 26 D4
Anderson L. ITSC 71 D3
Anderson L. MLLC 42 B3
Anderson L. OTTL 46 E3
Anderson L. POPE 31 C3
Anderson L. POPE 31 D2
Anderson L. POPE 38 G5
Anderson's Crossing County Park WADN 48 B2
Anderson Shoe L. BECK 55 G1
Andover ANOK 34 F4
Andover Twp POLK 66 C3
Andrea Twp WILK 45 F5
L. Andrew KAND 31 E5
Andrew Koch Cabin Historic Site MURR 12 F5
Andrew L. DOUG 39 F2
L. Andrew Nelson MEEK 24 A5
Andrews L. CLER 56 C2
Andrews L. CROW 49 B4
L. Andrusia BELT 69 G4
Andrus L. CASS 58 G4
Andy L. STLS 61 G1
Anfinson L. CLAY 46 A1
Angel Island CASS 57 F4
Angel's Hill Historic District CHIS 35 D5
Angle Inlet (city) WOOD 97 D1
Angleworm L. STLS 86 E1
Angora STLS 72 C5
Angora Twp STLS 72 C5
Angus POLK 78 E3
Angus L. CLER 56 C2
Angus L. WRIT 33 F5
Angus Twp POLK 78 F3
Anit L. LAKE 87 F2
L. Anka DOUG 38 C5
Ankeewinsee L. BELT 69 B1
L. Anna STRN 32 B5
Anna L. CROW 49 A4
Anna L. OTTL 46 F4
Annandale WRIT 33 F3
Annawaush L. MAHN 67 G5
Annexstad L. NCLT 15 C3
Annie Battle L. OTTL 46 G5
Annie L. LAKE 87 E2
L. Annie OTTL 46 D1
L. Annie OTTL 46 G3
L. Ann CARV 26 D3
L. Ann SHER 34 D1
L. Ann STLS 61 C2
L. Ann WRIT 25 B3
Ann L. CROW 49 E5
Ann L. ITSC 71 D3
Ann L. KNBC 42 E4
Ann L. POPE 39 G2
Ann Lake Recreation Site SHER 34 D1
Ann Lake Twp KNBC 42 E3
Ann R. KNBC 42 E4
Ann Twp COTT 13 F2
ANOKA — 34 —
Anoka ANOK 34 G4
Anoka County-Blaine-Janes Airport ANOK 26 A5
Anoka County Historical Society Museum ANOK 34 G4
Anoka Ramsey Community College ANOK 34 G4
Anoka State Hospital ANOK 34 G4
Anoway L. CASS 57 E4
Ansel Twp CASS 48 C3
Anthony Twp NORM 66 G3
Antler L. ITSC 71 D3
Antoinette L. STLS 61 G4
Antrim Twp WATN 4 B5
Apple L. ATKN 50 E1
Apple L. BECK 55 C2
Apple L. STLS 61 E3
Appleton SWFT 30 F2
Appleton County Park SWFT 30 F2
Appleton Mill Pond SWFT 30 F2
Appleton Municipal Airport SWFT 30 F2
Appleton Twp SWFT 30 G2
Appleton Wagon Road Historic Site LQPL 30 G2
Apple Valley DKTA 26 F5
Aqua Park Aquarium HUBB 56 F5
Arago Twp HUBB 56 E5
Arbo L. ITSC 59 A3
Arbo Twp ITSC 59 A3
Arches Branch Museum WINA 9 A2
Arch I. COOK 76 F3
Arch L. STLS 85 C4
Arc L. COOK 87 E3
Arco LINC 11 C5
Arctander Twp KAND 31 F4
Arctic L. COOK 87 G4
Arden Hills RAMS 27 A1
Ardenhurst Twp ITSC 70 C2
L. Ardmore HENN 26 B2
Arena L. COOK 88 G1
Arena Twp LQPL 21 B5
Arendahl FILL 9 C2
Arendahl Twp FILL 9 C2
Argo L. STLS 74 D1
Argyle MRSH 78 B2
Aria L. COOK 87 G4
Arken L. OTTL 39 B2
Arkose L. LAKE 86 E5
Arlington SBLY 25 G3
Arlington Twp SBLY 25 G3
Arlone Twp PINE 43 D4
Armstrong FREE 6 E3
Armstrong Bay STLS 73 B3
Armstrong Cr. KCHG 70 A1
Armstrong L. BLUE 15 F1
Armstrong L. CLER 68 C3
Armstrong L. STLS 73 B4
Armstrong R. STLS 73 B4
Arna Twp PINE 44 B2
Arnesen WOOD 93 B1
Arnold STLS 61 G3
Arnolds L. COTT 3 A4
Arrowhead Cr. LAKE 74 C5
Arrowhead L. CROW 49 B2
Arrowhead L. ITSC 70 D5
Arrowhead L. ITSC 71 G3
Arrowhead Point County Park FREE 6 D2
Arrowhead Point FREE 6 D2
Arrowhead Trail COOK 76 F1
Arrowhead Twp STLS 60 G4
Arrow L. HUBB 69 G1
Arrow L. LAKE 74 A5
Arrow L. LAKE 75 A1
L. Arthur POLK 67 E1
Arthur L. STLS 73 C4
Arthur Twp KNBC 42 F4
Arthur Twp TRAV 29 A2
Arthyde ATKN 51 F1
Artichoke BGST 30 D1
Artichoke L. BGST 30 E1
Artichoke L. STLS 61 E1
Artichoke R. STLS 60 F5
Artichoke Twp BGST 30 E1
Art L. CROW 49 C3
Artlip L. LAKE 75 D2
Arveson Twp KITT 90 F5
L. Arville MEEK 25 A1
Ashby Goose Game Refuge GRNT 38 C4
Ashby GRNT 38 C4
Ash Creek (city) ROCK 1 F5
Ash Cr. ROCK 1 F5
Ashdick L. LAKE 87 D2
Ashigan L. LAKE 86 F5
Ash L. COOK 87 F4
Ash L. GRNT 38 C1
Ash L. LINC 11 B5
Ash L. STLS 84 D2
Ash Lake (city) STLS 84 D2
Ash Lake Twp LINC 11 C5
Ashland Twp DOGE 7 A3
Ashley Cr. STRN 39 G5
Ashley Twp STRN 39 G5
Ash R. STLS 84 B3
Ash River Bay STLS 84 B3
Ash River Recreation Site STLS 84 B3
Ashton L. CHIS 35 E2
Ashtray L. LAKE 74 A3
Ask L. GRNT 38 C4
Askov PINE 43 B4
Aspelund GOOD 17 D3
Aspen L. COOK 88 F2
Aspen L. ITSC 71 C2
Aspinwall L. BECK 56 E2
Aspinwall L. MAHN 67 G4
Asp L. CHIS 35 B1
Assawa L. HUBB 56 B5
Assawan L. LAKE 87 G1
Assinika Cr. COOK 88 F3
Assumption CARV 25 F5
Assumption L. CARV 25 F5
Astrid Cr. STLS 85 E2
Astrid L. STLS 85 E2
Athens Twp ISNT 34 D5
Atherton Twp WILK 45 C4
Atkinson CARL 51 C5
Atkinson L. MEEK 24 C4
Atkinson Twp CARL 51 C5
Atlanta Twp BECK 55 E2
Atwater KAND 24 A2
L. Auburn CARV 26 D1
Auchagah L. STLS 85 C2
Audubon BECK 55 G3
Audubon L. BECK 55 G3
Audubon Twp BECK 55 G3
Aue L. CARV 26 E1
Auganaush Cr. CLER 56 A2
Augsburg College HENN 26 C5
Augsburg Twp MRSH 90 G3
Augusta CARV 26 E1
Augusta L. COTT 3 A3
Augusta L. DKTA 27 D1
Augusta L. OTTL 39 B3
Augusta Twp LQPL 21 B4
Augusta Twp STRN 33 D2
L. Augusta WRIT 33 F2
August Cr. LAKE 74 B3
August L. LAKE 74 C3
Auk L. COOK 87 F4
Aultman L. CASS 58 D2
Ault Twp STLS 61 B5
Aurdal Twp OTTL 46 F3
Aure BELT 68 D5
Aurora District Ranger Station STLS 73 E3
Aurora STLS 73 E3
Aurora Twp STEL 7 A1
Austin MOWE 7 E2
Austin Community College MOWE 7 E2
Austin L. ITSC 59 D4
Austin Municipal Airport MOWE 7 E3
Austin Twp MOWE 7 E2
Auto L. STLS 72 D5
Automba Twp CARL 51 D2
Avenue L. ATKN 50 B1
Avenue of Pines ITSC 70 E3
Averill CLAY 54 E3
Avoca MURR 2 A5
Avon STRN 32 B5
Avon Twp STRN 32 B5
Axe L. COOK 87 G5
Ayer Mission Historic Site MORR 41 C1
Azion L. LAKE 86 F2
Babbitt STLS 73 C5
Babble L. COOK 76 A1
Babe I. WOOD 97 F3
Baby L. CASS 58 F1
Bachelor L. BRWN 14 E3
Back Bay LAKE 86 F2
Back L. COOK 75 A4
Back L. OTTL 38 A4
Backman L. CLAY 55 F1
Backus CASS 48 A5
Backus Municipal Airport CASS 48 A5
Bad Axe L. HUBB 57 D1
Badboy Cr. MAHN 56 B1
Bad Boy L. BECK 55 D4
Badger ROSE 91 D3
Badger Cr. HOUS 9 D5
Badger Cr. ROSE 91 B2
Badger L. MURR 2 B4
Badger L. POLK 67 D3
Badger Twp POLK 67 C3
Bad Medicine L. BECK 56 D3
Badoura State Forest HUBB 57 G3
Badoura Twp HUBB 57 G3
Bag L. CASS 57 E5
Bag L. LAKE 75 A2
Bag L. STLS 51 A4
Bagley CLER 68 F3
Bagley Game Refuge CLER 68 F2
Bagley L. CLER 68 C4
Bagley Municipal Airport CLER 68 F3
Bagley Slough CLER 56 A3
Bah Lakes GRNT 38 D4
Bailey L. BELT 69 E2
Bailey L. CASS 58 E4
Bailey L. CLER 80 G2
Baileys I. STLS 84 F2
Baird L. LAKE 74 C3
Bakekana L. LAKE 87 F1
Baker CLAY 45 B3
Baker County Park Reserve HENN 26 B2
Baker L. BECK 55 D3
Baker L. CASS 58 F5
Baker L. COOK 75 A4
Baker L. STEV 30 A4
Baker Lake Recreation Site COOK 75 A4
Bakers L. MCLD 25 F1
Bakers L. STRN 33 A2
Baker Twp STEV 30 B1
Balaton LYON 12 E3
Bald Eagle Cr. LAKE 74 B3
Bald Eagle I. STLS 84 A1
Bald Eagle L. LAKE 74 B3
Bald Eagle L. RAMS 27 A2
Bald L. DKTA 27 D2
Baldpate L. STLS 85 E5
Baldwin L. ANOK 27 A1
Baldwin L. WASH 27 E2
Baldwin Twp SHER 34 C2
Baldy L. ITSC 71 F2
Balif L. BELT 69 B1
Balkan Twp STLS 72 E3
Balke L. BECK 55 E2
Balken L. STLS 72 E3
Ballantyne L. BLUE 15 E5
Ballard L. BECK 56 G1

Ball Bluff ATKN 59 F5
Ball Bluff L. ATKN 59 F5
Ball Bluff Twp ATKN 59 E5
Ball Club ITSC 58 A4
Ball Club Cr. COOK 88 G1
Ball Club L. COOK 88 G2
Ball Club L. ITSC 58 A4
Balloon L. ITSC 71 F2
Bally Cr. COOK 76 B2
Ballyhoo L. COOK 87 F3
Balm L. BELT 68 C5
Balmoral OTTL 46 F5
Balmy L. LAKE 87 F1
Balsam Cr. ITSC 71 F4
Balsam L. BECK 55 F5
Balsam L. ITSC 71 F3
Balsam L. LAKE 75 E1
Balsam Twp ATKN 51 A1
Balsam Twp ITSC 71 F3
Baltic L. LAKE 87 D2
Banadad Cr. COOK 87 F5
Banadad L. COOK 87 F5
Banana L. BECK 55 D3
Bancroft FREE 6 E4
Bancroft Twp FREE 6 D4
Bandana L. LAKE 74 D4
Bandon Twp RENV 14 A2
Bang L. CARL 51 C4
Bangor Twp POPE 31 C4
Bangs Bk. PINE 44 D1
Banks of Plum Creek Historic Site REDW 13 E1
Ban L. STLS 84 F4
Bannick L. COOK 88 G1
Banning State Park PINE 43 B3
Baptism R. LAKE 75 G1
L. Barber MCLD 24 D5
Barber Twp FRBT 5 D4
Barbour L. CROW 41 A5
Barclay Twp CASS 49 B1
Bardon's Peak Municipal Forest STLS 52 B3
Bardwell L. MART 4 F5
Barker Cr. COOK 75 C4
Barker L. COOK 75 C5
Barker L. WASH 35 G3
Barlous L. CARV 25 E5
Barn Bluff Municipal Park GOOD 18 A1
Barnes L. CARV 25 E5
Barnesville CLAY 45 C4
Barnesville Twp CLAY 45 B4
Barnesville Wildlife Management Area CLAY 45 B5
Barnett Twp ROSE 91 E3
Barney Lakes MAHN 55 B5
Barney L. ITSC 71 F1
Barnum CARL 51 D4
Barnum L. CASS 58 F1
Barnum Twp CARL 51 E5
Barrett GRNT 38 E3
Barrett L. GRNT 38 E3
Barrett L. STEV 38 G2
Barr L. BELT 68 C5
Barrows CROW 49 G2
Barrows L. GRNT 38 F1
Barrs L. STLS 61 D5
Barry BGST 29 B3
Barry L. BGST 29 B3
Barry Twp PINE 43 C3
Barsness L. DOUG 38 E5
Barsness Point POPE 31 B1
Barsness Twp POPE 31 B2
Bartels L. PINE 51 G5
Barter L. LAKE 87 E2
Bartlet L. ITSC 71 D4
Bartlett L. KCHG 70 B2
Bartlett Twp TODD 48 G1
Barto Cr. LAKE 87 G2
Barto L. COOK 87 G3
Bartons Bk. WOOD 93 G5
Barto Twp ROSE 91 D2
Bartron Historic Site GOOD 27 G5
Bartsh L. COTT 3 A5
Barwise L. ITSC 71 E3
Bashaw Twp BRWN 14 F1
Baskatong L. LAKE 75 A2
Bass Bay STLS 73 A3
Bass Brook Twp ITSC 59 B2
Bassett STLS 74 G1
Bassett L. STLS 74 G1
Bassett Slough BGST 29 D4
Bassett Twp STLS 73 F5
Bass L. ANOK 34 E3
Bass L. ATKN 50 A4
Bass L. ATKN 50 D1
Bass L. ATKN 59 G1
Bass L. BECK 46 A3
Bass L. BECK 55 D5
Bass L. BECK 56 D3
Bass L. BECK 56 F2
Bass L. BELT 68 B5
Bass L. BELT 69 C2
Bass L. BELT 69 E4
Bass L. CASS 48 B4
Bass L. CASS 48 E5
Bass L. CASS 49 A1
Bass L. CASS 49 F1
Bass L. CASS 57 E4
Bass L. CASS 58 F4
Bass L. CROW 41 B5
Bass L. CROW 49 B3
Bass L. CROW 49 B5
Bass L. CROW 49 C2
Bass L. CROW 49 C4
Bass L. CROW 49 D3
Bass L. CROW 49 E2
Bass L. CROW 49 E3
Bass L. CROW 49 F5
Bass L. CROW 49 G1
Bass L. FRBT 5 C3
Bass L. HENN 26 B4
Bass L. HUBB 57 C2
Bass L. ITSC 59 A1
Bass L. ITSC 59 B2
Bass L. ITSC 59 B4
Bass L. ITSC 59 C4
Bass L. ITSC 70 D4
Bass L. ITSC 71 B4
Bass L. ITSC 71 C4
Bass L. ITSC 71 D4
Bass L. ITSC 71 G4
Bass L. KAND 32 G2
Bass L. MAHN 56 C1
Bass L. MLLC 42 B1
Bass L. MORR 40 A5
Bass L. MORR 40 B4
Bass L. OTTL 46 B3
Bass L. OTTL 46 D3
Bass L. OTTL 46 G3
Bass L. PINE 43 A2
Bass L. PINE 43 B2
Bass L. STLS 61 C2
Bass L. STLS 73 A2
Bass L. STLS 73 A3
Bass L. STLS 73 F2
Bass L. STLS 86 G1
Bass L. TODD 40 E3
Bass L. TODD 40 F3
Bass L. WASH 35 G3
Bass L. WRIT 33 E3
Basswood OTTL 46 E5
Basswood Cr. BECK 56 D4
Basswood Grove WASH 27 D4
Basswood L. LAKE 86 F3
Basswood R. LAKE 86 E2
Bates L. OTTL 46 E3
Bath L. COOK 76 A2
Bath Twp FREE 6 C4
Batista L. STLS 85 D5
Bat L. COOK 75 C3
Bat L. COOK 87 E3
Bat L. COTT 3 A5
Batson L. ITSC 71 D2
Battle Bk. SHER 34 C2
Battle Creek County Park RAMS 27 C2
Battle Creek L. WASH 27 C2
Battle Creek Ski Area RAMS 27 C2
Battleground State Forest CASS 58 C2
Battle L. ITSC 71 B4
Battle L. KCHG 70 B1
Battle L. OTTL 46 E5
Battle L. STLS 73 A4
Battle Lake (city) OTTL 46 G5
Battle Lake Municipal Airport OTTL 46 G5
Battle Plain Twp ROCK 2 C1
Battle Point (city) CASS 58 C1
Battle Pt. TODD 39 E5
Battle R. RAMS 27 C2
Battle Twp BELT 81 G3
Baudette WOOD 93 E4
Baudette International Airport and Seaplane Base WOOD 93 E4
Baudette R. WOOD 93 E4
Bauer L. HUBB 57 B2
Baumbach L. DOUG 39 D1
Baumgartner L. BELT 69 E5
L. Bavaria CARV 26 D2
Baxter CROW 49 F2
Baxter L. ISNT 34 C3
Baxter Twp LQPL 22 C3
Bay L. ATKN 59 F5
Bay L. BECK 55 F3
Bay L. CROW 49 F5
Bay Lake (city) CROW 49 F5
Bay Lake Twp CROW 49 F5
Bayley Bay LAKE 86 E4
Baylis I. STLS 85 C1
Baylis L. STLS 85 D1
Baylor County Park CARV 25 E4
Baylor L. CARV 25 D4
Bay L. STLS 60 B1
Bayport WASH 27 B4
Baytown Twp WASH 27 B4
Bayview MLLC 42 B2
Beach I. STLS 73 A4
Beam L. LAKE 86 G5
Bean L. BECK 55 F4
Bean L. COOK 88 F4
Bean L. COTT 13 G2
Bean L. LAKE 62 A5
Bear Bk. CASS 58 B3
Bear Cr. BECK 56 D2
Bear Cr. CLER 56 A4
Bear Cr. MOWE 8 D1
Bear Cr. OLMS 8 A3
Bear Cr. OTTL 47 B3
Bear Cr. PINE 43 D4
Bear Cr. ROSE 92 D1
Bear Cr. STLS 73 C3
Bear Cr. WINA 19 G2
Bear Creek Municipal Park OLMS 8 A2
Bear Creek Twp CLER 56 A4
Bear Cub L. COOK 88 F2
Bear Den Landing Recreation Site BELT 68 G5
Beardsley BGST 29 B1
Bear Grease I. STLS 74 B1
Bear Head Lake State Park STLS 73 B4
Bear Head L. STLS 73 C4
Bear I. COOK 75 E3
Bear I. STLS 73 C5
Bear Island CASS 58 D1
Bear Island L. STLS 73 C5
Bear Island R. STLS 73 B5
Bear Island State Forest STLS 73 B5
Bear L. ANOK 34 E3
Bear L. ATKN 42 A4
Bear L. BECK 55 E4
Bear L. CARL 51 E5
Bear L. CARL 52 D1
Bear L. CASS 58 G4
Bear L. FREE 6 F3
Bear L. ISNT 34 B3
Bear L. ITSC 71 D5
Bear L. KAND 32 E1
Bear L. LAKE 75 A1
Bear L. MCLD 25 C1
Bear L. OTTL 47 B3
Bear L. STLS 61 C2
Bear L. STLS 62 C1
Bear L. STLS 62 D1
Bear L. STLS 73 A3
Bear L. STRN 32 A4
Bear Lake County Park CARL 51 E5
Bear Park Twp NORM 67 F2
Bear R. CASS 58 C4
Bear R. ITSC 71 C5
Bear R. KCHG 83 C1
Bear River (city) ITSC 72 C1
Bearskin L. LAKE 74 C4
Bearskin R. STLS 72 B1
Beartrack L. STLS 85 C3
Beartrap Cr. STLS 61 G1
Beartrap L. STLS 86 E1
Beartrap R. STLS 85 D5
Bear Valley (city) WBSH 18 D2
Bearville Twp ITSC 72 C1
Beast L. STLS 96 G4
Beatrice L. ITSC 72 C1
Beatty L. SBLY 15 A2
Beatty L. STLS 85 C2
Beatty Twp STLS 84 F4
Beauford BLUE 5 A4
Beauford Twp BLUE 5 A4
Beau Gerlot Cr. RDLK 67 B2
Beaulieu MAHN 55 A4
Beaulieu L. MAHN 67 F4
Beaulieu Twp MAHN 55 A5
L. Beautiful STRN 40 G4
Beauty L. CASS 48 F5
Beauty L. HUBB 56 B5
Beauty L. HUBB 56 C5
Beauty L. ITSC 60 B1
Beauty L. KNBC 43 B1
Beauty L. MORR 40 D4
Beauty L. TODD 40 D3
Beauty Shore L. OTTL 47 G1
Beaver WINA 19 F1
Beaver Bay (city) LAKE 63 B1
Beaver Bay Twp LAKE 74 E5
Beaver Bk. ITSC 71 A1
Beaver Bk. KCHG 83 B3
Beaver Cr. HOUS 9 E4
Beaver Cr. MURR 12 G3
Beaver Cr. RENV 13 A5
Beaver Cr. RENV 23 G5
Beaver Cr. ROCK 1 D4
Beaver Cr. STLS 72 A2
Beaver Cr. WADN 48 C2
Beaver Creek (city) ROCK 1 E4
Beaver Creek Travel Information Center ROCK 1 E3
Beaver Creek Twp ROCK 1 E3
Beaver Creek Valley State Park HOUS 9 E4
Beaver Cr. West HOUS 9 F4
Beaverdam Cr. COOK 88 F5
Beaver Dam L. WRIT 25 A2
Beaver Falls RENV 13 A5
Beaver Falls County Park RENV 13 A5
Beaver Falls Twp RENV 13 A5
Beaver Hut L. LAKE 74 C2
Beaver I. LAKE 63 B1
Beaver L. BECK 56 D2
Beaver L. COOK 88 E4
Beaver L. ITSC 70 D4
Beaver L. ITSC 71 C4
Beaver L. ITSC 71 D2
Beaver L. ITSC 71 D3
Beaver L. ITSC 71 E3
Beaver L. ITSC 71 F2
Beaver L. ITSC 71 G2
Beaver L. LAKE 87 F1
Beaver L. RAMS 27 C2
Beaver L. STEL 6 B4
Beaver L. STLS 62 C1
Beaver L. STLS 72 D4
Beaver L. STLS 73 B4
Beaver L. STLS 73 C3
Beaver L. STRN 33 D2
Beaver Lake County Park STEL 6 B4
Beaver R. LAKE 62 B5
Beaver R. STLS 73 B5
Beaver Stream STLS 85 D2
Beavertail L. ITSC 71 F3
Beaver Twp ATKN 51 E1
Beaver Twp FILL 8 F2
Beaver Twp ROSE 92 E2
Bebow L. CASS 58 D4
Bechyn RENV 23 G5
Becida HUBB 56 A5
BECKER — 46 —
Becker SHER 33 D5
Becker County Historical Society Museum BECK 46 A4
Becker L. BECK 55 D4
Becker L. STRN 32 D4
Becker Twp CASS 48 F3
Becker Twp SHER 33 D5
Beck L. TODD 40 B3
Becks L. OTTL 46 C1
Becoosin L. LAKE 86 G4
Beden L. HUBB 56 E5
Bedew L. COOK 87 F5
Bedford L. LAKE 86 F5
Beebe L. OTTL 38 B3
Beebe L. WRIT 34 G1
Beebe Lake County Park WRIT 34 G1
Beeber L. BECK 46 A1
Bee Cee L. ITSC 71 F3
Bee L. POLK 67 D2
Beers L. OTTL 46 D3
Beetle L. LAKE 74 C4
Bee Tree L. TODD 40 B3
Beiningen L. OTTL 46 D3
Bejou MAHN 67 G3
Bejou Twp MAHN 67 F3
Belfast Twp MURR 3 B1
Belgium L. POPE 30 A5
Belgium Twp POLK 78 G4
Belgrade STRN 32 D1
Belgrade Cave L. STLS 73 F2
Belgrade Twp NCLT 15 E3
L. Bella NBLS 2 G5
Bellechester GOOD 18 C1
Belle Cr. GOOD 17 B4
Belle Creek Twp GOOD 17 C4
Belle L. MCLD 24 C5
Belle L. MEEK 24 B3
Belle Plaine SCOT 26 G1
Belle Plaine Airport SBLY 26 F1
Belle Plaine Twp SCOT 26 G1
Belle Prairie (city) MORR 41 D1
Belle Prairie Twp MORR 41 C2
Belle Prairie Village Historic Site MORR 41 D1
Belle River (City) DOUG 39 D4
Belle River Twp DOUG 39 D4
Belle Taine L. HUBB 57 F1
Bellevue Twp MORR 41 E2
Bellingham LQPL 29 G5
Bell L. STLS 84 E4
Bello L. ITSC 71 D1
Bellow Cr. STLS 85 E3
Bellwood State Game Refuge DKTA 27 F4
Belly L. COOK 76 A1
Belmont County Park JACK 3 D5
Belmont L. OTTL 38 A5
Belmont Twp JACK 3 D5
Belmore Bay LAKE 75 G2
BELTRAMI — 69 —
Beltrami POLK 66 E4
Beltrami County Historical and Wildlife Museum BELT 69 F2
Beltrami County Information Center BELT 69 F2
Beltrami Island State Forest ROSE 92 E3
Beltrami L. BELT 69 E2
Belvidere Twp GOOD 18 C1
Belview REDW 23 G3
Bemidji BELT 69 F2
L. Bemidji BELT 69 F2
Bemidji Game Refuge BELT 69 F3
Bemidji Municipal Airport BELT 69 F1
Bemidji State University BELT 69 F2
Bemidji Twp BELT 69 G2
L. Ben POPE 31 C2
Bena CASS 58 A2
Bena Recreation Site CASS 58 A2
Bench L. COOK 88 E4
Bender L. CLER 68 B4
Benedict HUBB 57 C3
Benedict L. HUBB 57 D3
Benezie L. LAKE 86 G5
Benfield L. CARL 51 D5
Bengal L. ITSC 61 B1
Benjamin L. ANOK 34 E4
Benjamin L. BELT 69 D4
Benjamin Lake Recreation Site BELT 69 D4
Bennettville ATKN 50 F1
Benning L. COOK 87 E5
Bennington Twp MOWE 8 E1
Benn Linn Landing Recreation Site KCHG 82 D5
Bensen L. LAKE 75 F2
Benson SWFT 31 E1
Benson Airport RAMS 27 A2
Benson L. COOK 76 A4
Benson Municipal Airport SWFT 30 E5
Benson Twp SWFT 31 E1
BENTON — 33 —
Benton Beach County Park BENT 41 G2
Benton County Historical Society Museum BENT 33 B3
L. Benton LINC 11 D5
Benton L. MEEK 24 B5
Benton Twp CARV 25 E5
Bentsen L. BGST 29 D4
Benville Twp BELT 80 C2
Ben Wade Twp POPE 39 G1
Benz L. WASH 27 A3
Berend L. OTTL 46 C4
Bergen JACK 3 C5
Bergen L. STLS 61 E2
Bergen Twp MCLD 25 D3
Berger L. OTTL 46 C5
Bergerson L. BECK 46 A2
Bergkeller L. CASS 48 B4
Berg L. CLER 68 F4
Berg L. STLS 61 C2
Berglund County Park ATKN 50 A4
Bergville ITSC 70 C2
Bergville L. ITSC 70 C2
Berle L. STLS 61 D3
Berliner L. CARV 25 D5
Berlin Twp STEL 6 B4
Bernadotte NCLT 15 B1
Bernadotte Twp NCLT 15 C1
Berne DOGE 17 F4
Berner CLER 68 B2
Bernhart L. MORR 40 A4
Beroun PINE 43 E2
Berry Cr. STLS 62 A1
Berseth L. BECK 46 A3
Bertha TODD 39 A5
Bertha L. CROW 49 C2
Bertha Twp TODD 39 A5
Bertram L. WRIT 33 F5
Beseman Twp CARL 51 B2
Besho L. LAKE 75 C2
Besser L. OTTL 39 B3
Beta L. COOK 88 F1
Bethany WINA 19 G1
Bethany College BLUE 15 F4
Bethel ANOK 34 D5
Bethel College and Seminary RAMS 27 B1
Beth L. COOK 75 A3
Bet L. COOK 88 F1
L. Betsey MEEK 33 F2
Beuber L. CASS 57 G5
Beulah Twp CASS 58 G5
Bevens Cr. CARV 26 E1
Bevo L. ITSC 71 D2
Bewon L. LAKE 87 F2
Bezhik Cr. STLS 85 F3
Bezhik L. STLS 85 F4
Biavswah L. ITSC 70 E3
Bibon L. STLS 85 D5
Biesner L. LAKE 75 F2
Big Bass L. BELT 69 F3
Big Bass L. HUBB 57 E3
Big Basswood L. BECK 56 D3
Big Bay COOK 76 G2
Big Bay STLS 73 B2
Big Bend City CHIP 30 G4
Big Bend Recreation Site WADN 48 B1
Big Bend Twp CHIP 22 A4
Big Birch L. TODD 40 F3
Big Bird L. CROW 49 C3
Big Bull Cr. STLS 85 F3
Big Calf L. ITSC 70 B3
Big Carnelian L. WASH 27 A4
Big Cobb R. BLUE 5 B5
Big Constance L. ITSC 70 B3
Big Cranberry L. CASS 49 A2
Big Crow L. OTTL 46 C3
Big Deep L. CASS 58 F1
Big Diamond L. ITSC 59 A4
Big Dick L. ITSC 71 E2
Bigelow NBLS 2 G4
Bigelow Twp NBLS 2 F5
Big Falls (city) KCHG 82 E5
Big Falls Municipal Airport KCHG 83 D1
Big Fish L. STRN 32 C5
Bigfork ITSC 71 C2
Bigfork Municipal Airport ITSC 71 C2
Big Fork R. ITSC 71 C2
Big Fork R. KCHG 82 C5
Big Fork State Forest KCHG 70 B4
Bigfork Twp ITSC 71 C1
Big Green L. ITSC 71 G1
Big Horn L. ITSC 71 G2
Big I. MORR 40 A4
Big I. STLS 73 B4
Big I. STLS 84 F2
Big I. STLS 96 G3
Big Island HENN 26 C3
Big Island L. ITSC 71 E2
Big Jack L. ITSC 71 F2
Big Kandiyohi L. KAND 24 B1
Big L. BELT 69 F4
Big L. CARL 51 B5
Big L. GRNT 38 F2
Big L. MAHN 55 C5
Big L. SHER 34 E1
Big L. STLS 74 E1
Big L. STLS 85 F5
Big L. STRN 32 D4
Big L. TODD 40 B3
Big Lake (city) SHER 34 E1
Big Lake Twp SHER 34 E1
Big La Salle L. CLER 56 B5
Big Marine L. WASH 35 F3
Big McCarthy L. ITSC 71 G5
Big McDonald L. OTTL 46 D4
Big Mink Cr. MORR 41 D3

Big Moose L. STLS 85 F4
Big Mud L. SHER 34 D1
Big Ole L. ITSC 71 E2
Big Pine L. ATKN 50 F1
Big Pine L. ISNT 35 C1
Big Pine L. OTTL 47 C2
Big Pine L. PINE 43 A2
Big Point BELT 69 A2
Big Point BELT 81 E2
Big Point MLLC 42 A3
Big Portage L. CASS 57 G5
Big Rat L. BECK 55 D5
Big Rice L. BELT 69 F4
Big Rice L. CASS 58 E4
Big Rice L. STLS 73 D1
Big Rice L. STLS 85 F4
Big Rice L. STRN 32 C4
Big Rock L. BECK 46 A5
Big Rose L. ITSC 71 D1
Big Rosendahl L. STLS 72 C5
Big Rush L. BECK 56 E2
Big Sand L. CASS 58 E4
Big Sand L. HUBB 57 E1
Big Sandy L. ATKN 50 A5
Bigsby L. COOK 76 C1
Big Slough L. PINE 51 F4
Big Snow L. COOK 75 B3
Big Springs Cr. FILL 9 C2
Big Spunk L. STRN 32 B5
BIG STONE — 29 —
Big Stone Colony (Hutterite Community) BGST 29 B3
Big Stone L. CROW 49 A3
Big Stone L. OTTL 46 E3
Big Stone L. (Reservoir) BGST 29 D3
Big Stone Lake State Park — 29 D3
Big Stone National Wildlife Refuge Area LQPL 29 F4
Big Stone National Wildlife Refuge Interpretive Area LQPL 29 F4
Big Stone Twp BGST 29 D4
Big Sucker Cr. STLS 62 E1
Big Sugar Bush L. BECK 55 E4
Big Swamp Cr. WADN 48 B2
Big Swan L. MEEK 25 A2
Big Swan L. TODD 40 E3
Big Tamarack L. BECK 55 E5
Big Thirtynine Cr. LAKE 62 A5
Big Too Much L. ITSC 71 D1
Big Trout Cr. WINA 9 A5
Big Trout L. CROW 49 B3
Big Twin L. MART 4 D2
Big Watab L. STRN 32 C5
Big Woods Twp MRSH 77 B5
Big Yellow Banks Ranger Station PINE 43 D5
Bijou L. BECK 55 G2
Bill L. LAKE 75 B2
Billo L. ITSC 71 D2
Billys L. PINE 44 C2
Binagami L. COOK 76 A3
Bine L. LAKE 74 D5
Bingham L. COTT 3 B5
Bingham Lake (city) COTT 3 B5
Bingshick L. COOK 87 E3
Birch Cooley Twp RENV 14 A1
Birch Coulee Battlefield Historic Site RENV 14 A1
Birch Coulee Cr. RENV 24 G1
Birch Creek Twp PINE 51 F2
Birchdale KCHG 94 F3
Birchdale L. CROW 49 B5
Birchdale Twp TODD 40 F2
Birches Recreation Site CASS 70 G3
Birch I. STLS 73 B2
Birch I. STLS 73 B3
Birch Island L. HENN 26 D3
Birch L. BECK 55 D4
Birch L. CASS 57 F4
Birch L. CASS 58 E5
Birch L. CHIS 35 E3
Birch L. COOK 88 E1
Birch L. CROW 49 F5
Birch L. GOOD 27 G5
Birch L. HUBB 57 D1
Birch L. ITSC 71 E3
Birch L. ITSC 71 G3
Birch L. LAKE 86 F4
Birch L. MEEK 24 B5
Birch L. POLK 67 D2
Birch L. RAMS 27 A2
Birch L. (Reservoir) STLS 73 C5
Birch L. SHER 34 E2
Birch L. WRIT 33 F5
Birch L. WRIT 33 G4
Birch Lake Recreation Site LAKE 74 C2
Birch Lake Recreation Site STRN 40 G3
Birch Lakes State Forest STRN 40 G2
Birch Lake Twp CASS 57 F5
Birchmont BELT 69 E2
Birch Narrows STLS 73 A1
Birch Pt. KCHG 95 F4
Birch Pt. STLS 73 B2
Birch Pt. STLS 74 C1
Birch R. STLS 73 C5
Birch River Narrows STLS 73 C5
Birch Twp BELT 69 D5
Birchwood Village WASH 27 B2
Bird Island (city) RENV 24 E1
Bird Island Twp RENV 24 E1
Bird L. DOUG 39 E4
Bird L. STLS 73 F4
Bird Lake Recreation Site STLS 73 F4
Birds Eye L. ITSC 70 E4
Birl L. LAKE 87 F2
Biscay MCLD 25 D2
Bismarck Twp SBLY 14 A5
Biwabik STLS 73 E2
Biwabik Twp STLS 73 F2
Bixby STEL 7 B1
Bjorkland L. WRIT 33 E4
Bjork L. STEV 30 A4
Bjorks Cr. PINE 44 B2
Blaamyhre L. KAND 31 E4
Black Bass L. MLLC 42 B1
Black Bay KCHG 95 G5
Black Bay STLS 84 G5
Black Bay Narrows KCHG 95 F5
Black Bay Portage STLS 96 G1
Black Bear L. CROW 49 E3
Blackberry ITSC 59 C4
Blackberry L. BECK 55 E4
Blackberry L. ITSC 59 C4
Blackberry Twp ITSC 59 C4
Blackbird I. WOOD 97 D3
Blackbird L. BECK 56 F1
Black Cr. STLS 84 G5
Black Dog L. DKTA 26 E5
Blackduck BELT 69 C4
Black Duck Bay STLS 73 A2
Black Duck Cr. STLS 84 C3
Blackduck District Ranger Station BELT 69 C4
Black Duck I. STLS 73 A1
Blackduck L. BELT 69 C4
Blackduck L. CASS 58 D2
Black Duck L. STLS 84 D3
Blackduck Pt. CASS 58 C2
Black Duck Pt. STLS 73 A2
Blackduck R. BELT 69 B3
Blackduck State Forest ITSC 70 D1
Black Earth L. BECK 55 D5
Blackface L. ATKN 59 F5
Blackfoot L. STLS 61 B3
Black Hammer HOUS 9 E4
Black Hammer Twp HOUS 9 E4
Blackhawk L. DKTA 27 D2
Blackhoof Cr. CARL 52 D1
Blackhoof L. CARL 52 D1
Blackhoof L. CROW 49 E4
Black Hoof Twp CARL 52 D1
Black Island L. ITSC 71 F3
Black L. BELT 69 D2
Black L. CROW 49 E5
Black L. HENN 26 C2
Black L. LAKE 62 C2
Black L. RAMS 27 A2
Black L. STLS 73 F2
Black L. STLS 84 G5
Black L. WRIT 33 F5
Black Oak L. STRN 32 B2
Black Pt. COOK 76 C1
Black R. KCHG 82 A4
Black R. RDLK 66 A5
Black River Twp PENN 79 G1
Black Shadow L. ATKN 50 E1
Blacksmith L. CASS 58 B3
Blacksmith L. HUBB 56 D5
Blackwater L. ATKN 59 G1
Black Water L. CASS 58 F1
Blackwater L. ITSC 59 B2
Blackwell L. DOUG 39 F1
Blackwood L. STLS 51 A3
Bladder L. HUBB 57 G2
Blaine ANOK 34 G5
Blair L. MAHN 67 G4
Blake L. BELT 68 B5
Blakeley SCOT 25 G5
Blakeley Twp SCOT 15 A5
L. Blanche OTTL 46 F5
Blandin L. ITSC 71 E3
Bland L. KNBC 43 B1
Blesner Cr. LAKE 75 F2
Blind Ash Bay STLS 84 B3
Blind L. ATKN 50 C1
Blind L. CASS 49 A2
Blind L. CASS 58 G1
Blind L. ITSC 71 F2
Blind Lake Twp CASS 58 G2
Blind Pete L. ITSC 71 C4
Blind Pig I. STLS 84 A5
Blind Temperance Cr. COOK 75 D4
Blinker L. LAKE 86 G5
Blissful L. LAKE 87 G1
Blizzard L. STLS 85 F4
Block L. OTTL 39 B2
Blocknic L. MAHN 55 C4
Blomeke Museum REDW 14 C1
Blomford ISNT 35 C1
Blomkest KAND 23 C5
Bloody L. MURR 12 F5
Bloomer Twp MRSH 78 C1
Bloomfield Twp FILL 8 E2
Blooming Grove Game Refuge WASC 16 F3
Blooming Grove Twp WASC 16 F3
Blooming Prairie (city) STEL 7 C2
Blooming Prairie Twp STEL 7 B1
Bloomington HENN 26 E4
Bloomington Historical Society Museum HENN 26 E4
Blooming Valley Twp ROSE 91 B1
Bloom L. ITSC 71 D3
Blooms L. CHIS 35 E4
Bloom Twp NBLS 2 C4
Blot L. CASS 58 E2
Blowers Twp OTTL 47 D4
Blueberry Hill Recreation Site WOOD 93 D1
Blueberry I. COOK 76 F2
Blueberry I. STLS 85 G5
Blueberry I. STLS 96 G3
Blueberry L. BECK 55 D5
Blueberry L. BECK 56 G4
Blueberry L. CASS 57 F5
Blueberry L. COOK 76 B2
Blueberry L. STLS 73 C4
Blueberry L. STLS 74 B1
Blueberry L. WADN 47 A5
Blueberry Lake Village Historic Site WADN 47 A5
Blueberry R. WADN 47 A5
Blueberry Twp WADN 47 B5
Blue Bill L. CASS 57 E5
Blue Bill L. CASS 58 G4
Bluebill L. ITSC 71 E4
Bluebill L. LAKE 75 D1
Bluebill L. STLS 60 A5
Bluebird L. BECK 55 G3
Bluebird L. STLS 84 C4
Blue Cr. OTTL 47 D4
BLUE EARTH — 15 —
Blue Earth FRBT 5 E3
Blue Earth City Twp FRBT 5 E3
Blue Earth County Historical Society Museum BLUE 15 F4
Blue Earth Municipal Airport FRBT 5 F3
Blue Earth R. BLUE 15 G3
Blue Fin Bay STLS 84 A2
Blue Grass WADN 48 D1
Blue Hill Twp SHER 34 C1
Blue Jay L. LAKE 87 G2
Blue L. ATKN 50 E1
Blue L. CROW 49 A4
Blue L. CROW 49 E5
Blue L. HUBB 57 E1
Blue L. ISNT 34 C3
Blue L. SCOT 26 E4
Blue Mound Historic Site ROCK 1 D5
Blue Mounds State Park ROCK 1 D5
Blue Mounds Twp POPE 31 C1
Blue Sky L. BELT 69 F4
Blue Snow L. COOK 87 E4
Bluewater L. ITSC 71 G2
Blue Wing L. LAKE 87 G2
Bluff Cr. COOK 88 G2
Bluff Cr. OTTL 47 D3
Bluffton OTTL 47 E4
Bluffton Twp OTTL 47 E4
Bob Bay STLS 74 C1
Bob L. CARL 51 C5
Bock MLLC 42 F3
Bodum ISNT 34 C5
Boedigheimer L. OTTL 47 D1
Boe L. BECK 55 F2
Boesen L. DOUG 39 C1
Bogberry L. LAKE 74 B3
Bogenho L. COOK 88 E2
Boggy L. ITSC 71 D1
Bog L. BECK 56 F4
Bog L. BELT 69 C1
Bog L. ITSC 59 D5
Bog L. ITSC 70 F1
Bog L. ITSC 71 F3
Bog L. LAKE 74 B5
Bog L. LAKE 74 C3
Bog L. STLS 84 E4
Bogus Brook Twp MLLC 34 A2
Bogus L. CLER 56 C4
Bogus L. COOK 76 A4
Bohall L. CLER 56 C4
Boiler L. CASS 49 A3
Boiling Spring Cr. YMED 23 G2
Bois De Sioux R. TRAV 37 E3
Boise L. BRWN 14 E1
Bolme L. POLK 67 D5
Bologna L. COOK 87 F4
Bolting L. STRN 32 D5
Bolton L. OTTL 46 D5
Bombay GOOD 17 D3
Bonanza Grove BGST 29 C1
Bonanza L. LAKE 75 D2
Bondin Twp MURR 2 B5
Bond L. HUBB 56 B5
Bone L. LAKE 75 B2
Bone L. WASH 35 F3
Bonga L. LAKE 74 E2
Bongards CARV 25 E5
Bonita L. COOK 87 F3
Bon L. OTTL 46 E3
Bonnie Brae Seaplane Base WOOD 97 D3
Bonnie L. CROW 49 D3
Bonnie L. LAKE 87 E1
Boogun L. BECK 56 D4
Boon L. RENV 24 D4
Boon Lake Twp RENV 24 D4
Boos L. OTTL 46 D5
Booth L. BECK 56 F1
Boot L. ANOK 35 E1
Boot L. ATKN 59 G5
Boot L. BECK 46 B5
Boot L. BECK 56 D4
Boot L. BELT 69 F1
Boot L. CASS 48 B5
Boot L. JACK 3 E4
Boot L. LAKE 86 F5
Boot L. STLS 86 E1
Bootleg L. STLS 85 F3
Borden L. BELT 69 C5
Borden L. CROW 49 G5
Borer L. LSUR 16 C2
Borgholm Twp MLLC 42 F2
Borg L. CLER 68 C4
Borg L. STLS 60 A5
Boriin Cr. STLS 72 E3
Born L. BLUE 16 F1
Borup NORM 54 C4
Bosley L. ITSC 71 G2
Boss L. CASS 57 F5
Bossuot L. LSUR 16 D1
Bostick Cr. WOOD 93 D3
Boston L. BELT 69 C1
Bouder L. COOK 75 A5
Boulder Bay STLS 85 D4
Boulder Cr. STLS 61 D4
Boulder L. HUBB 57 F1
Boulder L. LAKE 87 F2
Boulder L. (Reservoir) STLS 61 D3
Boulder L. STLS 73 A4
Boulder R. STLS 85 D4
Boundary Waters Canoe Area STLS 74 B4
Bourassa L. STLS 85 C3
Bourassas Trading Post Historic Site STLS 85 C1
Bovey ITSC 59 B4
Bow Dodge L. BECK 55 D4
Bowen L. CASS 48 A5
Bower L. ITSC 72 E1
Bowerman Bk. ITSC 71 A1
Bow L. COOK 88 F2
Bow L. LAKE 87 G1
Bowlus MORR 40 F5
Bowman Bay STLS 84 B2
Bowman I. STLS 84 A2
Bowman L. HUBB 57 A3
Bowstring ITSC 70 E5
Bowstring Itasca County Airport ITSC 70 E5
Bowstring L. ITSC 70 F5
Bowstring L. LAKE 87 G2
Bowstring R. ITSC 70 E4
Bowstring State Forest CASS 58 B2
Bow String Twp ITSC 70 E5
Boxell L. CASS 58 E2
Boxville Twp MRSH 78 D1
Boyd LQPL 22 D3
Boyd L. SHER 33 C5
Boyer L. BECK 55 G2
Boyer L. STLS 62 C1
Boy L. CASS 58 D3
Boy L. ITSC 71 F1
Boy Lake Twp CASS 58 D2
Boy R. CASS 58 E3
Boy River (city) CASS 58 C3
Boy River Bay CASS 58 C2
Boy River Twp CASS 58 C3
Boys L. COOK 76 A4
Boze L. LAKE 87 G2
Braas L. BELT 68 D5
Braaten L. POLK 67 D2
Bracket L. OTTL 46 E3
Brackett L. CASS 58 F2
Bradbury Homestead Historic Site OTTL 46 B4
Bradbury L. OTTL 46 B4
Bradbury Twp MLLC 42 D1
Bradford Twp ISNT 34 C4
Bradford Twp WILK 37 B5
Bradfort ISNT 34 C4
Bradley I. STLS 73 E2
Bradley L. COOK 75 D5
Bradley L. POLK 67 E3
Braham ISNT 43 G1
Brainerd CROW 49 F2
Brainerd Community College CROW 49 F2
Brainerd-Crow Wing County Airport CROW 49 F3
Brainerd International Raceway CROW 49 F2
Brainerd State Hospital CROW 49 F3
Branborg Cr. OTTL 47 G2
Branch CHIS 35 C2
Branch L. BECK 56 G3
Brand L. CARV 25 E4
Brandon DOUG 39 D1
Brandon L. DOUG 39 E1
Brandon Twp DOUG 39 D1
Brandrup Twp WILK 37 B3
Brandsvold Twp POLK 67 D5
Brandt Twp POLK 78 F4
Brandy L. BECK 55 G4
Brannigan L. BECK 46 A2
Brant L. COOK 87 E4
Bratsberg FILL 9 D3
Braunworth L. CARV 25 E5
Brawner L. LYON 12 D3
Bray County Park BLUE 16 E1
Bray L. ITSC 71 F5
Bray L. OTTL 46 E3
Bray Twp PENN 78 F5
Breamar Park HENN 26 D4
Breckenridge WILK 45 G3
Breckenridge L. WILK 45 G3
Breckenridge Twp WILK 37 A3
Breckenridge-Wahpeton Interstate Airport WILK 45 G2
Breda L. STLS 62 A1
Bredeson L. OTTL 39 A1
Breed L. POLK 67 D5
Breeze L. POLK 67 C5
Breezy Point (city) CROW 49 D2
Breezy Point Airport CROW 49 C2
Breezy Pt. STLS 73 A1
Breitung Twp STLS 73 B3
Brekke L. OTTL 46 F3
Bremen Twp PINE 51 G2
Brenner L. KAND 31 D4
Brennyville BENT 41 F5
Brenum L. BECK 56 F2
Brevator Twp STLS 52 A1
Brevik CASS 58 D2
Brewer L. GOOD 27 F5
Brewis L. LAKE 74 A4
Brewster NBLS 3 D1
Briar L. LAKE 75 A2
Briar L. STLS 61 D5
Bricelyn FRBT 5 F5
Brick I. COOK 76 E4
Briddle L. LAKE 74 A5
Bridges I. WOOD 97 G3
Bridgewater Twp RICE 16 C5
Brigand L. STLS 85 C3
Briggs Cr. SHER 33 C5
Briggs L. GRNT 38 C3
L. Briggs SHER 33 C4
Bright L. LAKE 86 G1
Bright L. MART 4 F4
Bright Lake County Park MART 4 F4
Brighton Twp NCLT 15 D1
Brimson STLS 62 B1
Brislet Twp POLK 78 E3
Bristol FILL 8 F4
Bristol Twp FILL 8 F4
Britt STLS 73 D1
Brittan Cr. CASS 48 B4
Britton Homested Historic Site LQPL 21 C4
Britton Isle MLLC 42 B3
Broadwater Bay CASS 58 E2
Brockway Twp STRN 41 G1
Brokaw L. HUBB 57 B1
Bromseth L. OTTL 38 A3
Bronco L. COOK 88 E4
L. Bronson KITT 90 E3
Brookfield Twp RENV 24 D3
Brooklyn Center HENN 26 B4
Brooklyn Park (city) HENN 26 A4
Brook Park (city) PINE 43 D1
Brook Park Twp PINE 43 E1
Brooks RDLK 67 B3
Brooks Cr. RDLK 67 B3
Brooks L. WRIT 25 A2
Brookston STLS 60 G5
Brookville Twp REDW 14 D1
Brookway L. CASS 48 A5
Brookway Twp STRN 33 A1
Brooten STRN 31 C5
Brooten Municipal Airport STRN 31 C5
Brophy L. DOUG 39 E2
Browerville TODD 40 C2
BROWN — 14 —
Brown County Historical Society Museum BRWN 14 D4
Brown County Park JACK 3 G4
Brown Cr. RDLK 78 G5
Brown L. ATKN 50 A4
Brown L. ATKN 50 C1
Brown L. BECK 55 D4
Brown L. HUBB 57 B1
Brown L. ITSC 71 E3
Brown L. ITSC 71 F3
Brown L. OTTL 46 F4
Brown L. STLS 62 C1
Brown L. STLS 96 G3
Browns Bay HENN 26 C3
Browns Bay STLS 84 B5
Browns Bay STLS 96 G3
Browns Creek Twp RDLK 79 G1
Brownsdale MOWE 7 D3
Browns I. STLS 96 G1
Browns L. LAKE 86 G2
Browns L. SCOT 26 G1
Browns L. WOOD 92 F5
Browns Valley (city) TRAV 29 B1
Browns Valley Man Historic Site TRAV 29 B1
Browns Valley Park TRAV 29 B1
Browns Valley Twp BGST 29 B1
Brownsville HOUS 10 E2
Brownsville Twp HOUS 10 E2
Brownton MCLD 25 F1
Bruce Cr. ITSC 59 D5
Bruce Twp TODD 40 D3
Bruin L. LAKE 74 A3
Brule Bay COOK 88 G1
Brule L. COOK 87 G5

175

Chain of Lakes TODD 40 C3
Chain O'Lakes CASS 58 C4
Chalberg Cr. STLS 61 F1
Chamberlin L. ATKN 59 E2
Champepadan Cr. NBLS 2 D1
Champion Twp WILK 37 C5
Champlin HENN 34 G4
Chanarambie Cr. NBLS 2 B1
Chanarambie Twp MURR 2 A2
Chanarambie Valley MURR 2 B1
Chandler MURR 2 B2
Chandler L. CROW 49 G5
Chandler L. JACK 3 F5
Chanhassen CARV 26 D3
Chant L. STLS 85 G5
Charity L. LAKE 75 D2
Charles A. Lindbergh House Historic Site MORR 41 D1
Charles A. Lindbergh State Memorial Park MORR 41 D1
Charles Babcock Memorial Historic Site SHER 34 F2
Charles L. CASS 58 F3
Charleston Twp REDW 13 E4
Charlesville TRAV 37 D5
Charles Weyerhaeuser Memorial Museum MORR 41 E1
L. Charley DOUG 39 D2
Charley L. RAMS 27 A1
Charlie L. ITSC 71 F2
L. Charlotte ITSC 59 A2
L. Charlotte MART 4 D5
L. Charlotte WRIT 34 G1
Charlotte L. STEV 30 B4
Charlotte L. TODD 40 D2
Charm L. STLS 85 C3
Chase Bk. WOOD 81 B3
Chase I. STLS 84 A2
Chase L. COOK 87 F4
Chase L. COOK 88 G4
Chase L. ITSC 59 A1
Chase L. STLS 85 D4
Chase Meadow Wildlife Management Area ATKN 59 F3
Chaser L. COOK 87 G3
Chaska CARV 26 E2
Chaska L. CARV 26 E2
Chaska Twp CARV 26 E2
Chatfield FILL 8 C4
Chatfield Twp FILL 8 C4
Chatham Twp WRIT 33 G4
Chautaugua L. OTTL 38 A2
Checkerboard County Park CHIS 35 C3
Chelgren L. WRIT 25 B2
Chengwatana State Forest PINE 43 E4
Chengwatana Twp PINE 43 E3
Cherokee L. COOK 87 G4
Cherry STLS 72 G4
Cherry Cr. LSUR 15 C5
Cherry Grove FILL 8 F3
Cherry Grove Twp GOOD 17 E3
Cherry L. BECK 55 D4
Cherry L. KAND 24 B2
Cherry L. LAKE 87 E2
Cherry Twp STLS 72 G4
Chester Cr. STLS 61 G4
Chester L. COOK 88 F5
Chester Municipal Park STLS 52 A4
Chester OLMS 8 A3
Chester Twp POLK 67 B5
Chester Twp WBSH 18 D1
Chetamba Cr. RENV 23 D3
Chicadee L. LAKE 75 B1
Chicago Bay COOK 76 G1
Chickamaw Beach (city) CASS 49 B1
Chicken L. MAHN 55 C5
Chicken L. MEEK 24 A4
Chicog L. POLK 66 D5
Chief L. MAHN 55 A4
Chief L. MAHN 67 F4
Chief Mouzoomaunee State Monument NCLT 14 B3
Chiefs Point BELT 69 A2
Chief Twp MAHN 55 A4
Chief Wooden Frogs Is. STLS 96 G1
Child L. CASS 58 F1
Chilton County Park BECK 56 F2
Chilton L. BECK 46 B5
Chip L. COOK 87 E3
Chipmunk L. LAKE 74 C3
CHIPPEWA — 22 —
Chippewa Agency Historic District CASS 49 G1
Chippewa City Pioneer Village Historic District CHIP 22 C4
Chippewa County Park No. 1 CHIP 23 A2
Chippewa Diversion Channel CHIP 22 A3
Chippewa Falls Twp POPE 31 B3
Chippewa Indian Burial Ground Historic Site CASS 57 D5
Chippewa L. BECK 56 F1
Chippewa L. DOUG 39 D1
Chippewa L. LAKE 86 E1
Chippewa National Forest CASS 58 C3
Chippewa R. SWFT 30 G5
CHISAGO — 35 —
Chisago City CHIS 35 E3
Chisago Lake Twp CHIS 35 D3
Chisago L. CHIS 35 E3
Chisholm STLS 72 F3
Chisholm-Hibbing Municipal Airport STLS 72 G3
Chisholm Pt. ITSC 59 C2
Chloupek L. CLER 56 C2
Choice FILL 9 E3
Chokecherry L. BECK 55 D5
Choker L. COOK 87 G4
Chokio STEV 30 B1
Chorus L. STLS 85 F5
Chow L. LAKE 74 C2
Chris L. STLS 62 D1
Christerson L. BELT 69 D5
Christiania Twp JACK 3 C5
Christianson L. LAKE 62 B2
L. Christina DOUG 38 C5
Christine L. COOK 75 C5
Christmas L. HENN 26 D3
Christmas L. ITSC 71 F4
Christmas L. MORR 41 C5
Christ Olson L. CLAY 55 G1
Christopherson L. OTTL 46 E1
Christopherson L. POPE 38 G5
Chrysler L. CROW 49 G4
Chub Cr. DKTA 17 B1
Chub Lake County Park CARL 52 C1
Chub L. CARL 52 C1
Chub L. CASS 57 F4
Chub L. CASS 58 B4
Chub L. COOK 87 E4
Chub L. DKTA 16 A5
Chub L. LAKE 87 G1
Chub L. STLS 84 D4
Chuck L. COOK 87 F3
Church L. FREE 6 F4
Church L. GRNT 38 E4
Church L. KAND 31 G4
Churn L. LAKE 87 F2
Circle L. COOK 88 G3
Circle L. ITSC 71 F2
Circle L. LAKE 86 E2
Circle L. MAHN 55 A5
Circle L. RICE 16 C5
Circle Pines ANOK 27 A1
Civet Cr. STLS 61 C5
Clam L. CASS 48 B5
Clam L. COOK 87 G4
Clam L. LAKE 87 E2
Clam L. MART 4 D3
Clamshell L. CROW 49 C2
Clara City CHIP 23 C2
L. Clara COOK 75 B5
Claremont DOGE 17 G2
Claremont Game Refuge DOGE 17 G3
Claremont Twp DOGE 17 G2
Clarence L. BECK 55 D3
Clarissa TODD 40 B1
Clarissa Municipal Airport TODD 40 B1
Clark Bay COOK 76 E4
Clarke L. CLER 56 C4
Clarke L. ITSC 59 A2
Clarkfield YMED 22 E4
Clark L. CROW 49 D2
Clark L. LAKE 62 B3
Clark L. STLS 73 A4
Clarks Grove FREE 6 D4
Clarks L. SCOT 15 A5
Clark Twp ATKN 51 C1
Clark Twp FRBT 6 D1
Clarno L. OTTL 39 B3
L. Classen HENN 26 C2
Clausen Cr. ROSE 92 D3
Clausens L. HUBB 57 F2
CLAY — 54 —
Clay County Game Refuge CLAY 54 E4
Clay County Historical Society Museum CLAY 54 F2
Clayson County Park BECK 55 G4
Clayton L. MART 4 F4
Clayton L. PINE 43 D5
Clayton Twp MOWE 7 E5
Clearbrook CLER 68 D3
Clearbrook Game Refuge CLER 68 C2
Clearbrook L. CLER 68 D3
Clear Cr. CARL 52 E1
Clear Cr. LYON 12 B5
Clear Cr. REDW 13 B2
Clear L. ATKN 50 B3
Clear L. ATKN 50 E3
Clear L. BRWN 14 E4
Clear L. COTT 13 G2
Clear L. COTT 3 B5
Clear L. COTT 3 C2
Clear L. CROW 49 C2
Clear L. GOOD 27 G5
Clear L. ITSC 70 C4
Clear L. JACK 3 E5
Clear L. KCHG 82 G3
Clear L. LAKE 74 A3
Clear L. LSUR 16 C1
Clear L. LYON 12 D2
Clear L. MART 4 G3
Clear L. MCLD 24 C5
Clear L. MCLD 25 E2
Clear L. MEEK 32 F5
Clear L. OTTL 38 B3
Clear L. PINE 51 G3
Clear L. SBLY 14 B5
Clear L. SHER 33 D3
Clear L. STEV 30 B2
Clear L. STLS 72 D4
Clear L. STLS 73 B4
Clear L. STLS 84 E5
Clear L. STRN 32 C4
Clear L. WASC 16 G3
Clear L. WASH 35 F2
Clear Lake (city) SHER 33 D4
Clear Lake County Park SBLY 14 B5
Clear Lake Game Refuge SHER 33 D3
Clear Lake Park LSUR 16 C1
Clear Lake Twp SHER 33 D4
Clears L. CROW 49 A3
CLEARWATER — 68 —
Clearwater WRIT 33 D3
Clearwater County Historical Society Museum CLER 68 F3
Clearwater L. BELT 68 C5
Clearwater L. COOK 88 E3
Clearwater L. CROW 49 F5
Clearwater L. ITSC 59 C4
Clearwater L. ITSC 71 G3
Clearwater L. LAKE 74 A4
Clearwater L. STLS 61 E3
Clearwater L. STLS 72 E2
Clearwater L. WRIT 33 F3
Clearwater R. CLER 68 E3
Clearwater R. STRN 33 F1
Clearwater Twp WRIT 33 E3
Cleary Lake Regional Park SCOT 26 F4
Cleary L. SCOT 26 F4
Cleaver L. COOK 88 G1
Cleft L. COOK 87 F4
Clementson WOOD 93 E5
Clements REDW 13 C5
Cleveland LSUR 15 D5
Cleveland Twp LSUR 15 D5
Clevise L. LAKE 75 A1
Cliff L. COOK 87 F5
Cliff Rd. DKTA 26 E5
Clifton STLS 62 G1
Clifton Twp LYON 12 C5
Clifton Twp TRAV 37 F5
Climax POLK 66 D1
Climax L. LAKE 86 G4
Climber L. LAKE 74 C3
Clinker L. CROW 49 D4
Clint Converse Memorial Recreation Site CASS 58 G4
Clinton BGST 29 C4
Clinton Falls STEL 16 F5
Clinton Falls Twp STEL 16 F5
Clinton Twp ROCK 1 F5
Clinton Twp STLS 72 G5
Clitherall OTTL 47 G1
Clitherall L. OTTL 38 A5
Clitherall Twp OTTL 38 A5
Clitty L. SHER 33 D5
Clontarf SWFT 30 D5
Clontarf Twp SWFT 30 E5
Cloquet CARL 52 B1
Cloquet-Carlton County Airport CARL 52 B1
Cloquet Forest Game Refuge CARL 52 B1
Cloquet Forestry Center, University of Minnesota CARL 52 B1
Cloquet L. LAKE 74 F4
Cloquet R. STLS 61 C5
Cloquet Valley State Forest STLS 61 C4
Close L. PINE 51 F4
Clotho TODD 39 D5
Clough Island STLS 52 B4
Clough L. CROW 49 A1
Clough Twp MORR 40 B5
Clove L. COOK 87 E4
Clover Cr. PINE 43 D5
Cloverdale PINE 43 D4
Clover L. COOK 75 B3
Cloverleaf L. CROW 49 D2
Cloverleaf L. ITSC 70 C3
Clover Leaf Twp PENN 79 E4
Clover L. STLS 60 A5
Cloverton PINE 44 B3
Clover Twp CLER 68 C4
Clover Twp HUBB 56 D5
Clover Twp MAHN 56 A1
Clover Twp PINE 43 C5
Clow Twp KITT 90 B1
Clubhouse L. ITSC 71 E2
Clubhouse Lake Recreation Site ITSC 71 E2
Club L. OTTL 46 D4
Clyde WINA 9 B1
Coal L. TODD 40 C3
Coal Mine Cr. BRWN 13 D4
Coates DKTA 27 F2
Cobb Cr. BLUE 6 C2
Cobden BRWN 14 D2
Cockburn L. MORR 40 A5
Coddington L. ITSC 70 C3
Cody L. RICE 16 B3
Coe L. STLS 61 A2
Coffee Cr. LAKE 75 B2
Coffee L. CARL 51 E4
Coffee L. LAKE 75 B2
Coffee L. OTTL 46 C4
Coffee Mill Ski Area WBSH 18 C5
Coffin L. CASS 58 F4
Cohasset ITSC 59 B2
Cokato WRIT 25 B2
Cokato Historical Museum WRIT 25 B2
Cokato L. WRIT 25 A2
Cokato Temperance Hall WRIT 25 A2
Cokato Twp WRIT 25 A2
Colby L. CHIS 35 D5
Colby L. STLS 73 E4
Colby L. WASH 27 D3
Cold Cr. HUBB 57 A2
Cold Cr. WBSH 18 D2
Cold L. STLS 73 C5
Cold Spring STRN 32 D5
Coleen L. CHIS 35 E4
Cole L. CARL 51 C2
Cole L. CROW 49 D4
Coleman I. STLS 85 C4
Coleman L. BECK 56 E3
Coleman L. BELT 69 D5
Coleman Slough STEV 30 B3
Coleraine ITSC 59 B3
Colfax Twp KAND 31 E5
College of St. Benedict STRN 33 B1
College of St. Catherine RAMS 27 C1
College of St. Scholastica STLS 52 A4
College of St. Teresa WINA 19 G4
Collegeville STRN 33 B1
Collegeville and St. Joseph Township Game Refuge STRN 33 C1
Collegeville Game Refuge STRN 33 B1
Collegeville Twp STRN 32 C5
Collett L. BECK 47 B2
Collier L. CLER 80 G3
Collins Twp MCLD 24 E5
Collinwood-Little Lake County Park WRIT 25 B2
Collinwood L. WRIT 25 B2
Collinwood Twp MEEK 25 B1
Collis TRAV 29 A4
L. Colness OTTL 46 D1
Cologne CARV 26 E1
Colombo L. BELT 69 B1
Columbia Heights ANOK 26 B5
Columbia Twp POLK 68 E1
Columbus L. ANOK 35 F2
Columbus Twp ANOK 35 F1
Colvill Homestead Historic Site COOK 76 B4
Colvill Municipal Park GOOD 18 A2
Colvin Cr. STLS 73 E5
Colvin Twp STLS 61 A3
Comet I. STLS 73 A2
Comet L. STLS 73 C4
Comfort L. CHIS 35 E3
Comfort L. LAKE 75 B1
Comfort Twp KNBC 42 E5
Comfrey BRWN 14 F1
Community Point County Park JACK 3 D4
Como Park RAMS 27 C1
Como Park Ski Area and Zoo RAMS 27 C1
L. Como RAMS 27 C1
Como Twp MRSH 91 G3
Compton Twp OTTL 47 F4
Comstock CLAY 45 B2
Comstock L. STLS 61 C3
Comstock Twp MRSH 78 D4
Conception WBSH 18 D5
Conchu L. LAKE 86 G3
Concord DOGE 17 F4
Concordia College CLAY 54 G2
Concordia College RAMS 27 C1
Concord Twp DOGE 17 F3
Cone Bay COOK 87 G5
Coney Island CARV 26 D1
Coney Island of the West Historic Site CARV 26 D1
Conger FREE 6 F3
Conic L. LAKE 87 E2
Connelly Twp WILK 45 F3
Conners I. COOK 87 C4
Connors L. ITSC 71 C2
Constance L. WRIT 33 G5
Contentment L. STLS 85 C3
Contest L. COOK 87 F4
Contest L. STLS 85 E5
Continental Divide Historic Site STLS 72 E5
Continental Divides Historic Site TRAV 29 B1
Continental L. LAKE 74 E2
COOK — 75 —
Cook STLS 72 B4
Cook County Historical Museum COOK 76 B3
Cook District Ranger Station STLS 72 B4
Cook L. DOUG 39 E2
Cook L. HENN 26 A3
Cook L. ITSC 59 D3
Cook L. LAKE 75 B2
Cook L. LAKE 87 E2
Cook L. WRIT 25 B5
Cook Municipal Airport STLS 72 B4
Cookoosh L. LAKE 87 F2
Cooks Bay HENN 26 C2
Cooks L. OTTL 46 B4
Cooks L. STLS 61 E3
Coolidge Cr. STLS 61 C3
Coo L. STLS 73 A4
Coombs L. MEEK 24 C4
Coon Creek Twp LYON 12 D2
Coon Cr. ITSC 71 C2
Coon Cr. LYON 12 C2
Coon Cr. NORM 54 B5
Coon L. ANOK 35 E1
Coon L. ATKN 50 C1
Coon L. BECK 56 D3
Coon L. HUBB 56 D5
Coon L. HUBB 57 E2
Coon L. ITSC 71 C2
Coon L. ITSC 71 C4
Coon L. LAKE 86 G5
Coon L. MORR 40 F4
Coon L. MORR 41 E3
Coon L. STLS 60 B2
Coon L. TODD 40 E3
Coon Lake County Park ANOK 35 E1
Coon Lakes WRIT 25 C3
Coon Rapids (city) ANOK 34 G4
Coon Rapids Dam Regional Park ANOK 26 A4
Coon Stump L. MORR 40 A5
Cooper I. COOK 87 D3
Cooper L. CASS 58 F2
Coopers L. ANOK 34 D5
Coot L. LAKE 87 G2
Copas WASH 35 F4
Copenhagen L. ITSC 71 E2
Copley Twp CLER 68 E3
Copper L. COOK 87 F4
Corabelle L. MURR 2 B3
Cora L. OTTL 39 B3
Corcoran HENN 26 A3
Cordenio Severence House Historic Site WASH 27 D3
Cordova Twp LSUR 16 D1
Corinna Twp WRIT 33 F3
Corliss Twp OTTL 47 C2
Cormorant BECK 46 B2
Cormant Twp BELT 69 A4
Cormorant L. BECK 46 A2
Cormorant L. GRNT 38 E3
Cormorant R. ITSC 70 B1
Cormorant Twp BECK 46 A2
L. Cornelia HENN 26 D4
Cornell L. WRIT 33 E3
Corner L. MORR 40 B4
Corner L. STLS 84 C3
Corning MOWE 7 D2
Cornish Twp ATKN 59 F5
Cornish Twp SBLY 14 B5
Corny L. COOK 75 B4
Corona L. CARL 51 C4
Correction L. STLS 61 D1
Correll BGST 30 F1
Cortes L. LAKE 74 A3
Corundum Pt. LAKE 62 C5
Corvuso MEEK 24 C4
Cory L. LQPL 22 C1
Cosmos MEEK 24 C3
Cosmos Lake County Park MEEK 24 C3
Cosmos Twp MEEK 24 C3
Cottage Grove WASH 27 D3
Cottage L. BECK 46 B4
Cottingham County Park WADN 48 E2
Cotton STLS 61 C1
Cotton L. BECK 55 G5
Cotton Twp STLS 61 C2
COTTONWOOD — 3 —
Cottonwood LYON 22 G5
L. Cottonwood BRWN 14 D5
Cottonwood County Historical Society Museum COTT 3 B4
Cottonwood Cr. SWFT 30 F3
Cottonwood L. BLUE 5 B5
Cottonwood L. COTT 3 B4
Cottonwood L. GRNT 38 F2
Cottonwood L. ITSC 71 G1
Cottonwood L. LYON 22 G5
Cottonwood L. WATN 14 G2
Cottonwood R. BRWN 14 D3
Cottonwood Twp BRWN 14 E5
Couger L. LAKE 74 E2
Count Beltrami Monument Historic Site BELT 69 D2
County L. COOK 87 E2
Courthouse County Park GRNT 38 D3
Courthouse County Park WASC 6 A3
Courtland NCLT 15 D1
Courtland Twp NCLT 15 D1
Courtney L. ITSC 71 E3
Courty L. CASS 58 E3
Cove MLLC 42 C2
Cove Bay MLLC 42 B2
Covered Bridge Park GOOD 17 D5
Covy Bk. CASS 48 E5
Cowan L. LAKE 87 F2
Cow Cr. ROSE 92 D1
Cowdry L. DOUG 39 E2
Cowhorn L. ITSC 59 D3
Cow L. CASS 48 A5
Cow L. COOK 88 G1
Cowley L. HENN 34 G2
Coxey Pond STLS 85 F5
Cox L. CLER 56 C3
Coyote Cr. STLS 62 C1

Crab Cr. STLS 85 G4
Crab L. COOK 87 E5
Crab L. STLS 85 G4
Cracker L. CROW 49 E4
Crag L. COOK 87 E3
Craig L. CASS 58 E2
Craigville KCHG 71 A2
Cramer Homestead L. LAKE 75 F1
Cramer I. STLS 85 G2
Cramer L. HUBB 57 E3
Cranberry Bay STLS 96 F1
Cranberry Cr. STLS 96 G1
Cranberry I. STLS 96 F1
Cranberry L. ATKN 50 F1
Cranberry L. ATKN 59 E1
Cranberry L. BECK 55 D4
Cranberry L. BELT 69 C3
Cranberry L. CARL 51 E4
Cranberry L. CASS 48 A4
Cranberry L. CASS 58 E1
Cranberry L. CASS 58 F3
Cranberry L. HUBB 56 C5
Cranberry L. ITSC 71 G1
Cranberry L. PINE 52 F2
Cranberry L. STLS 73 C4
Cranberry L. STLS 73 F5
Cranberry L. TODD 40 B3
Cranberry L. WASH 35 F3
Crandall L. BELT 69 C4
Crane Cr. ITSC 70 E1
Crane Creek County Park STEL 16 G5
Crane L. BELT 69 D2
Crane L. ITSC 71 G2
Crane L. OTTL 38 A5
Crane L. STLS 85 C1
Crane Lake (city) STLS 85 C1
Crate Twp CHIP 23 B2
Crato L. CROW 49 E4
Cravath L. BECK 55 F3
Crawford I. ITSC 59 A1
Crawford L. WRIT 25 A5
Cream L. COOK 87 G4
Credit R. SCOT 26 F4
Credit River (city) SCOT 26 F4
Credit River Twp SCOT 26 F4
Creek L. MART 4 D3
Creeper L. COOK 88 F1
Crellin Cr. STLS 85 E2
Crellin L. STLS 85 E2
Crescent L. COOK 75 B5
Crescent L. ITSC 71 D3
Crescent L. SHER 33 D4
Crescent Lake Recreation Site COOK 75 B5
Crest L. LAKE 74 F2
Crippled Deer L. ITSC 71 D1
Cripple L. CASS 57 E4
Crocket L. LAKE 74 B2
Crocodile L. COOK 88 F3
Crocodile R. COOK 88 F3
Croftville COOK 76 B3
Crogan L. OTTL 39 A2
Croke Twp TRAV 37 G4
Cromwell CARL 51 B3
Cromwell Twp CLAY 54 F5
Crooked Cr. HOUS 10 F2
Crooked Cr. PINE 44 D1
Crooked Creek Twp HOUS 10 E1
Crooked L. ANOK 34 G4
Crooked L. BELT 68 B5
Crooked L. CASS 48 D4
Crooked L. CASS 57 B4
Crooked L. CASS 57 G5
Crooked L. CASS 58 F2
Crooked L. COOK 87 F3
Crooked L. CROW 49 F5
Crooked L. DOUG 39 E1
Crooked L. HUBB 57 E2
Crooked L. ITSC 70 D5
Crooked L. ITSC 71 E2
Crooked L. ITSC 71 G4
Crooked L. LAKE 75 D2
Crooked L. LAKE 86 D1
Crooked L. MAHN 55 B5
Crooked L. MAHN 55 C5
Crooked L. OTTL 46 F4
Crooked L. PINE 44 B1
Crooked L. POLK 67 E2
Crooked L. STLS 60 E5
Crooked L. STRN 33 D3
Crooked Lake Twp CASS 58 G4
Crook L. KAND 31 D4
Crook L. KAND 31 F5
Crooks L. DOUG 39 E1
Crookston POLK 66 B3
Crookston Airport POLK 66 B3
Crookston Technical College, University of Minnesota POLK 66 B3
Crookston Twp POLK 66 B4
Crooks Twp RENV 23 D4
Cropless L. ITSC 60 C1
Crosby CROW 49 E4
Crosby Beach (city) CROW 49 E4
Crosby L. DKTA 27 D1
Crosby Twp PINE 43 D5
Crosier Seminary MLLC 42 C2
Cross Bay L. COOK 87 F4
Crosscut L. LAKE 75 D1
Cross L. CARL 51 B3
Cross L. CROW 49 C3
Cross L. PINE 43 E3
Cross L. POLK 68 D1
Cross Lake (city) CROW 49 C3
Cross Lake Game Refuge CROW 49 C3
Cross R. COOK 75 D3
Cross R. COOK 87 E4
Cross R. KCHG 83 C2
Cross River L. LAKE 75 C2
Cross River State Wayside Park COOK 75 E3
Crossways L. ANOK 35 F2
Crow Cr. LAKE 62 D3
Crowduck I. WOOD 97 E3
Crow-Hassen County Park Reserve HENN 34 G2
Crow L. COOK 88 G1
Crow L. STRN 31 D5
Crow Lake Twp STRN 31 D5
Crown ISNT 34 D3
Crown Cr. LAKE 74 F5
Crown L. CASS 58 E2
Crown L. LAKE 74 E5
Crow River MEEK 32 F3
Crow River (city) WRIT 26 B1
Crow River Twp STRN 32 D1
Crow Springs County Park WRIT 25 A5
CROW WING — 49 —
Crow Wing CROW 49 G1
Crow Wing County Historical Society Museum CROW 49 F2
Crow Wing L. CROW 41 A1
Crow Wing L. HUBB 57 E2
Crow Wing Lake Twp HUBB 57 G2
Crow Wing R. TODD 48 F3
Crow Wing State Forest CROW 49 C4
Crow Wing State Park CROW 41 A1
Crow Wing Twp CROW 49 G2
Croxton Pond STLS 72 F3
Cruiser L. STLS 84 A3
Crystal HENN 26 B4
Crystal Airport HENN 26 B4
Crystal Bay HENN 26 C2
Crystal Bay LAKE 63 A1
Crystal Bay STLS 61 G5
Crystal Bay Twp LAKE 75 E1
Crystal Cr. PINE 44 C2
Crystal L. BLUE 15 F2
Crystal L. CASS 57 F3
Crystal L. COOK 88 E4
Crystal L. CROW 49 E3
Crystal L. DKTA 26 F5
Crystal L. HENN 26 B4
Crystal L. HUBB 68 G5
Crystal L. OTTL 46 C3
Crystal L. OTTL 46 E3
Crystal L. POLK 67 D2
Crystal L. RICE 16 D5
Crystal L. SCOT 26 F4
Crystal L. STEV 30 B3
Crystal L. STLS 61 B1
Crystal Lake Game Refuge STEV 30 B3
Cuba L. BECK 46 A1
Cuba L. BECK 55 F1
Cuba Twp BECK 55 F2
Cub L. CASS 57 E5
Cuckoo L. COOK 87 F5
Cuculus I. STLS 84 A2
Cucumber L. BECK 55 D3
Cucumber L. COOK 88 F3
Cuffs L. COOK 76 F3
Culdrum Twp MORR 40 D4
L. Culkin LAKE 74 E2
Culp L. ITSC 59 D5
Culver STLS 61 F1
Culver Twp STLS 60 F5
Cummings L. STLS 85 G4
Cummingsville OLMS 8 B4
Cupid L. COOK 87 D3
Cup L. BGST 29 C4
Cup L. LAKE 87 E2
Curran L. SBLY 25 F3
Current L. MURR 12 E2
Currie MURR 12 G5
Currier Bay NCLT 15 D2
Currys Island WOOD 93 C3
Curtis L. LINC 11 C4
Curtis L. OTTL 39 A3
Curtis L. YMED 13 A1
Curtis Pt. TODD 39 E5
Curtus L. CLER 80 G2
Cushing MORR 40 B4
Cushing Twp MORR 40 B4
Cusson STLS 84 E3
Custer Twp LYON 12 E4
Cutaway L. ATKN 59 G5
Cutaway L. ITSC 71 F3
Cut Foot Sioux L. ITSC 70 F3
Cut Foot Sioux Visitor Information Center ITSC 70 F3
Cut L. CASS 48 B4
Cut-Off L. ITSC 59 B2
Cutover I. STLS 84 A2
Cuyuna CROW 49 D4
Cuyuna Iron Range CROW 49 D5
Cuyuna Range Historical Society Museum CROW 49 E4
Cynthia L. SCOT 26 G3
Cypress L. LAKE 87 D2
Cyprinid L. COOK 88 F4
Cyr Cr. RDLK 66 B5
Cyrus POPE 30 B4
L. Cyrus STEV 30 B4
Dabill Cr. CASS 48 B4
Dade L. CASS 49 F1
Daggett Bk. CASS 58 F3
Daggett Bk. CROW 49 B3
Daggett Brook Twp CROW 41 B3
Daggett L. CROW 49 B3
Dagle L. ATKN 59 F2
Dago Bay STLS 85 G1
Dago Cr. LAKE 62 C4
Dago L. PINE 51 F4
Dahlberg L. CLER 68 F4
Dahler I. WOOD 97 D3
Dahler L. CROW 49 B4
Dahlgren R. STLS 85 D4
Dahlgren Twp CARV 26 E1
Dahl L. POLK 67 D2
Dahls L. MEEK 32 G3
Daible L. MAHN 55 B5
Dailey Twp MLLC 42 E1
Daisy Bay STLS 73 B2
Daisy I. STLS 73 B2
Daisy L. HUBB 57 F2
DAKOTA — 27 —
Dakota WINA 10 B1
Dakota County Historical Society Museum DKTA 27 D2
Dalbec L. COOK 87 G4
Dalbo ISNT 34 A4
Dalbo Twp ISNT 34 A3
Dale CLAY 55 F1
Dale L. STLS G2 C1
Dale Twp COTT 3 A4
Daley Bay STLS 84 B2
Daley County Park BLUE 5 C4
Dallas L. STRN 33 D3
Dallas of the St. Croix CHIS 35 D5
Dalton OTTL 38 B3
Dalton L. ITSC 71 G1
Dam Bk. ATKN 50 D3
Dam Five L. LAKE 75 D2
Dam L. ATKN 50 D3
Damon L. ITSC 70 E1
Danbom County Park BECK 55 F4
Danebod Historic Site LINC 12 D1
Dane L. COOK 88 G2
Dane L. OTTL 46 G4
Dane Prairie Twp OTTL 38 A3
Danforth Twp PINE 43 C5
Daniel L. CLER 68 F4
Daniels L. COOK 88 E2
Danielson Twp MEEK 24 B3
Dan L. LAKE 86 G3
Dans L. WRIT 33 G3
Danube RENV 23 E5
Danvers SWFT 30 F4
Danville Twp BLUE 5 B5
Daren Twp STEV 30 B3
Darfur WATN 14 G2
Dark L. BELT 69 C2
Dark L. KCHG 82 G3
Dark L. STLS 72 D4
Dark L. STLS 85 D5
Dark R. STLS 72 E4
Darlet L. LAKE 87 F2
Darling MORR 40 D5
Darling L. DOUG 39 E2
Darling Twp MORR 40 C5
D.A.R. Memorial State Forest PINE 43 A4
Darrigans Cr. BELT 69 C3
Dart L. BECK 46 A3
Darwin MEEK 24 A5
L. Darwin MEEK 24 A5
Darwin Twp MEEK 24 A5
Darwin Winter Recreation Park MEEK 25 A1
Dassel MEEK 25 A1
Dassel Twp MEEK 25 A1
Daubs L. REDW 13 B3
David L. ITSC 70 C5
Davidson L. DOUG 38 D4
Davies L. OTTL 46 E5
Davis L. ATKN 50 C4
Davis L. COOK 87 F5
Davis L. CROW 49 B4
Davis Twp KITT 90 F2
Dawkins Cr. COOK 87 E4
Dawkins L. COOK 87 F4
Dawson LQPL 22 C2
Dawson-Madison Lac Qui Parle Airport LQPL 22 B1
Dawson Mills Airport LQPL 22 C2
Day ISNT 42 G4
Day Bk. ITSC 71 E5
Day L. ITSC 71 F2
Day L. STLS 72 F2
Days L. STRN 33 E1
Dayton HENN 34 F3
Dayton L. (Reservoir) OTTL 38 A2
Dead Beaver L. CLER 56 C4
Dead Coon L. LINC 12 C1
Dead Cr. HUBB 57 A1
Dead Fish L. CARL 51 B4
Dead Horse L. CASS 58 C5
Dead Horse L. HUBB 57 E1
Dead Horse L. ITSC 59 C1
Dead Horse L. ITSC 71 F1
Dead Horse L. ITSC 71 G2
Dead L. BECK 47 B1
Dead L. HUBB 57 E2
Dead L. OTTL 46 E5
Dead Lake Twp OTTL 46 E5
Deadmans L. CROW 49 D4
Dead Moose R. CARL 51 D2
Dead R. STLS 85 G5
Deadwood L. OTTL 46 D3
Dean L. CROW 49 C5
Dean L. SCOT 26 E3
Dean L. WRIT 25 A5
Dean Lake Twp CROW 49 C5
Debs BELT 68 C5
Decker L. ITSC 70 D1
Decoria Twp BLUE 15 G4
Deephaven HENN 26 C3
Deep L. CASS 57 D5
Deep L. CLER 68 D3
Deep L. HUBB 57 D1
Deep L. RAMS 27 A1
Deep L. STLS 73 F1
Deep L. STRN 32 D4
Deep Portage L. CASS 58 G1
Deep Pot Hole L. MAHN 55 A5
Deep Slough STLS 84 B5
Deepwater L. STLS 61 E3
Deepwater L. STLS 72 D3
Deerborn Cr. WILK 45 C4
Deer Cr. CARL 52 D2
Deer Cr. ITSC 71 B3
Deer Cr. MOWE 8 E1
Deer Cr. OTTL 47 F3
Deer Cr. STLS 72 F2
Deer Creek (city) OTTL 47 F3
Deer Creek Twp OTTL 47 F3
Deerfield STEL 16 F4
Deerfield Twp CASS 57 G4
Deerfield Twp STEL 16 F4
Deerhorn Twp WILK 45 C3
Deer I. STLS 73 C5
Deer L. ANOK 34 E5
Deer L. ATKN 50 F3
Deer L. BELT 69 D1
Deer L. CASS 48 B4
Deer L. CASS 57 G4
Deer L. CASS 58 F5
Deer L. COOK 88 E3
Deer L. CROW 49 C1
Deer L. CROW 49 D5
Deer L. HUBB 57 F1
Deer L. HUBB 57 F2
Deer L. ITSC 59 A1
Deer L. ITSC 70 F3
Deer L. ITSC 71 B4
Deer L. KAND 31 D4
Deer L. OTTL 46 F4
Deer L. TODD 40 F2
Deer L. WRIT 25 A5
Deer Lake Lookout ITSC 59 A2
Deer Lake Recreation Site ITSC 70 F3
Deer Park L. CLER 56 C4
Deer Park Twp PENN 79 G5
Deer Point Is. STLS 84 A2
Deer R. ITSC 59 A1
Deer River (city) ITSC 58 A5
Deer River District Ranger Station ITSC 58 A5
Deer River Twp ITSC 71 G1
Deer Town HUBB 56 F5
Deer Twp ROSE 91 F2
Deerwood CROW 49 E5
Deerwood Twp CROW 49 E5
Deerwood Twp KITT 90 F4
Deer Yard L. COOK 76 C1
Defender's Monument BRWN 14 D5
De Graff SWFT 31 F2
Dehart L. HUBB 57 B2
Delafield Twp JACK 3 C4
De Lagoon Municipal Park OTTL 46 G2
Delano WRIT 26 B1
Delavan FRBT 5 D4
Delavan Twp FRBT 5 C3
Delaware Twp GRNT 38 E2
Delay L. LAKE 74 D5
Delft COTT 3 A5
Delhi REDW 23 G4
Delhi Twp REDW 23 G4
Dell FRBT 5 E4
Dell Grove Twp PINE 43 C2
Dellwater L. BELT 68 C5
Dellwood WASH 27 A2
DeLong L. PINE 52 F1
Delta L. LAKE 86 G4
Delton Twp COTT 13 G5
Demning L. CLER 56 C4
L. Demontreville WASH 27 B3
Dempsey Cr. STLS 72 G3
Denger L. MORR 41 D3
Denham PINE 51 F2
Denley L. LAKE 74 C2
Denley Nira Cr. LAKE 74 C2
Denmark Twp WASH 27 E4
Dennison GOOD 17 C2
Dent OTTL 46 D5
Dent L. COOK 87 G3
Dent L. STLS 61 C4
Denver Twp ROCK 1 C5
Deposit L. STLS 85 C3
Deronda Bay COOK 76 F2
Derrynane Twp LSUR 16 B1
Des Moines L. BELT 69 E2
Des Moines R. JACK 3 D5
Des Moines R. MURR 12 G5
Des Moines River Twp MURR 3 A1
Des Moines Twp JACK 3 F5
Dethloff Slough ITSC 59 A2
Detroit L. BECK 46 A4
Detroit Lakes (city) BECK 46 A4
Detroit Lakes Airport BECK 55 G4
Detroit Mountain Ski Area BECK 55 G5
Detroit Twp BECK 55 G4
Devil Fish L. COOK 88 F5
Devil L. ANOK 35 E1
Devil's Elbow L. COOK 87 D4
Devils L. DOUG 39 D1
Devils L. KNBC 42 F4
Devils L. OTTL 46 C5
Devils L. OTTL 46 F2
Devils L. PINE 43 F2
Devils Tract Airport COOK 76 B2
Devil Track L. COOK 76 B2
Devil Track Lake Recreation Site COOK 76 A2
Devil Track R. COOK 76 B3
Devine L. STLS 62 C1
Dewald Twp NBLS 2 E4
Dewey L. CASS 58 D4
Dewey L. CLAY 46 B1
Dewey L. STLS 72 E2
Dewey Twp ROSE 91 E1
Dewing L. CROW 41 B5
Dewitt Pool MLLC 42 D3
Dexter MOWE 7 D5
Dexter Twp MOWE 7 D4
Diamond L. ATKN 50 E1
Diamond L. CASS 57 E5
Diamond L. COOK 87 D3
Diamond L. HENN 26 D5
Diamond L. HENN 34 G3
Diamond L. HUBB 56 A5
Diamond L. KAND 32 G2
Diamond L. LSUR 16 D2
Diamond L. POPE 39 G1
Diamond Lake Twp LINC 11 C5
Diamond Point CASS 58 E1
Diana L. LAKE 74 B5
Diann L. SHER 34 C2
Dickeys L. HENN 26 C2
Dickins L. BELT 69 B1
Dick L. CASS 48 B5
Dick L. COOK 76 A2
Dieter Twp ROSE 91 B4
Dietrich Lange Wildlife Management Area KAND 32 F2
Dietz L. LSUR 16 B3
Digit L. COOK 76 B2
Dilworth CLAY 54 F2
Dime L. LAKE 74 C4
Dinham L. STLS 61 C2
Din L. COOK 87 F4
Dinner Cr. KCHG 82 E4
Dinner L. BECK 56 D4
Dinner Pail L. ITSC 59 E2
Dipper L. LAKE 87 E1
Dirty Mike L. ITSC 59 A3
Dirty Nose L. CASS 58 D5
Disappointment L. LAKE 86 F5
Discovery L. LAKE 86 G4
Dislocation L. COOK 88 F2
Dismal Cr. TODD 39 D5
Dismal Swamp BGST 29 C5
Ditty L. COOK 88 F3
Divide L. LAKE 75 D1
Divide Lake Recreation Site LAKE 75 D1
Dix L. LAKE 87 E1
Dixon Cr. STLS 84 C5
Dixon L. ITSC 70 E2
Doam L. ITSC 71 G2
Doan L. ITSC 71 G2
Dock L. ITSC 71 E2
Doctor L. ITSC 71 F2
Dode L. ITSC 60 B1
DODGE — 17—
Dodge Center DOGE 17 G3
Dodge Center Cr. DOGE 17 G3
Dodge County Historical Society Museum DOGE 17 G4
Dodge County Municipal Airport DOGE 7 A4
Dodo L. STLS 61 D2
Doe Island MLLC 42 B3
Doe L. COOK 87 F4
Doe L. HUBB 57 F3
Doe L. ITSC 71 E3
Doerfler L. WRIT 25 A4
Dog Fish L. ITSC 70 C4
Dogfish L. CROW 49 E5
Dogfish L. STLS 85 D3
Dog I. STLS 73 B3
Dog L. CASS 48 F3
Dog L. CROW 49 F4
Dog L. LSUR 15 D5
Dog L. WRIT 25 C4
Dogleg L. COOK 87 E4
Dogtrot L. COOK 75 B5
Dogwood L. COOK 75 D3
Doherty L. STLS 72 F4
Dohn L. TODD 40 D3
Dollar I. STLS 73 A5
Dollar L. BELT 69 E5
Dollar L. COOK 75 B3
Dollar L. ISNT 35 B1
Dollar L. ITSC 71 F5
Dollar L. PINE 44 B1
Dollar L. STLS 61 B2
Dollar L. STLS 72 E2
Dollymount Twp TRAV 37 G5
Dolney L. CROW 49 C4
Dome I. STLS 85 B3

Donalds L. OTTL 47 E1
Donaldson KITT 90 F1
Donders L. CARV 25 D5
Donehower WINA 10 A1
Donkey L. CASS 58 G2
Don L. COOK 87 F4
Donnelly STEV 38 G2
Donnelly Twp MRSH 90 G1
Donnelly Twp STEV 38 G2
Donovan L. BENT 33 B3
Dora I. ITSC 70 C3
Dora L. LSUR 16 C2
Dora L. OTTL 46 C4
Dora Lake (city) ITSC 70 C3
Dora Lake Forest Management Demonstration Area ITSC 70 C3
Dora Lake Recreation Site ITSC 70 C3
Doran WILK 37 A4
Doran L. CLAY 54 G5
Doran Slough WILK 37 A3
Dora Twp OTTL 46 D4
Dorothy RDLK 78 G5
Dorothy L. LAKE 74 C4
Dorr L. POLK 67 D2
Dorset HUBB 57 F1
Dot L. COOK 88 F2
Double Bay COOK 76 G1
Double L. COTT 13 G2
Double L. MAHN 68 F1
Doughty L. GRNT 38 F2
DOUGLAS — 39 —
Douglas OLMS 18 F1
Douglas Corridor Trail OLMS 18 F1
Douglas County Historical Society Museum DOUG 39 E3
Douglas Goose Game Refuge DOUG 39 D3
Douglas L. ATKN 51 C1
Douglas Twp DKTA 27 G3
Douse L. LAKE 87 F1
Dove Bay KCHG 96 F1
Dove Is. KCHG 95 F5
Dover OLMS 8 A5
Dover Twp OLMS 8 A4
Dovray MURR 13 G1
Dovray Twp MURR 13 G1
Dovre L. STLS 85 C1
Dovre Twp KAND 31 G5
Dower L. TODD 48 F2
Dower Lake Municipal Recreation Area TODD 48 F2
Downer CLAY 45 A4
Downs L. WASH 27 C3
Doyle L. LAKE 75 F1
Drag L. COOK 88 E4
Drag L. LAKE 86 G5
Dragon L. LAKE 74 C4
Drammen Twp LINC 11 C4
Dresbach WINA 10 B1
Dresbach Island WINA 10 B1
Dresbach Travel Information Center WINA 10 C2
Dresbach Twp WINA 10 C1
Drewery L. BELT 69 G4
Drietz L. LINC 11 B5
Driftwood Point WOOD 97 F2
Driller L. LAKE 74 F3
Dr. Just Christian Gronvold Estate Historic Site GOOD 17 D3
Dr. Martin Luther College BRWN 1 4 D5
Droff L. BECK 46 A3
Drumbeater I. ITSC 59 C2
Drumbeater L. CASS 58 B3
Drumbeater Lake Waterfowl Refuge CASS 58 B3
Drumstick Cr. LAKE 86 G5
Drumstick L. LAKE 86 G5
Drury L. BELT 69 E4
Dry Cr. COTT 13 F4
Dry Creek L. ITSC 70 F3
Dryden Twp SBLY 15 A2
Dry L. STLS 86 G1
Dry L. TODD 39 E5
Dry Weather Cr. CHIP 22 B5
Dryweed I. KCHG 96 F1
Drywood I. STLS 96 F1
Duban L. RICE 16 C3
Dublin Twp SWFT 31 G2
Duck Bay STLS 84 B2
Duck Cr. STLS 85 F4
Duckfoot I. STLS 96 F2
Duck L. BECK 56 E4
Duck L. BLUE 15 E5
Duck L. CHIS 35 E4
Duck L. COOK 87 G3
Duck L. CROW 49 B5
Duck L. CROW 49 C2
Duck L. CROW 49 D3
Duck L. HENN 26 D3
Duck L. HUBB 48 A2
Duck L. ITSC 71 C3
Duck L. ITSC 71 F2
Duck L. MAHN 55 C4
Duck L. MORR 40 A4
Duck L. NCLT 15 D2
Duck L. OTTL 46 B2
Duck L. OTTL 46 E4
Duck L. STLS 73 C3
Duck L. STLS 85 F4
Duck Lake County Park BLUE 15 E5
Dudley L. RICE 16 D4
Dudley Twp CLER 68 E4
Duelm BENT 33 B4
L. Duesch OTTL 39 B1
Duffy I. STLS 73 B2
Duffy L. CASS 57 G4
Duffy L. SHER 34 D1
DuForte L. BECK 55 D4
Duglas L. HUBB 57 A2
Dugout L. COOK 88 G2
Dugout L. STLS 85 G3
Duke L. COOK 88 G3
Dullinger L. STRN 33 C1
Duluth STLS 52 A4
Duluth Central High School Historic Site STLS 52 A4
Duluth Harbor STLS 52 A4
Duluth International Airport STLS 61 G3
Duluth Marine Museum STLS 52 A4
Duluth Municipal Zoo STLS 52 B4
Duluth Ship Canal Historic Site STLS 52 B5
Duluth Twp STLS 62 E1
Dumas Cr. BELT 81 E5
Dumbbell L. BECK 56 F2
Dumbbell L. LAKE 75 D1
Dumbbell R. LAKE 75 C1
Dumbell Lake Recreation Site LAKE 75 D1
Dumfries WBSH 18 C5
Dumont TRAV 37 G4
Dunaway I. STLS 85 G2
Dunbar L. BELT 68 B5
Dunbar L. ITSC 70 D2
Dunbar Twp FRBT 6 C1
Duncan L. CLER 68 F4
Duncan L. COOK 88 E2
Dundas RICE 17 C1
Dundee NBLS 3 C1
Dunder Pond MORR 40 F4
Dunka Bay STLS 74 C1
Dunka R. STLS 74 D1
Dunnell MART 4 F2
Dunnigan L. LAKE 74 C3
Dunning L. ITSC 59 A4
Dunn L. COOK 88 E1
Dunns L. MEEK 32 G5
Dunn Twp OTTL 46 B3
Dunton Locks County Park BECK 46 A4
Dunvilla OTTL 46 C3
Duquette PINE 52 F1
Durand Twp BELT 69 D2
Durgin Slough SHER 34 C1
Durtee R. COOK 76 B4
Duschee Cr. FILL 9 E1
Dutch Charley Cr. COTT 13 F2
Dutch Cr. DKTA 16 B5
Dutch L. ATKN 51 D1
Dutch L. HENN 26 C1
Dutch L. WRIT 25 B3
Dutchman L. BELT 69 D4
Dutchman L. COOK 76 E3
Dutton L. LAKE 87 E1
Duxbury PINE 44 B1
Duxey ROSE 91 C3
Dyers L. COOK 75 E3
Dynamite County Park COTT 3 B4
Eagan DKTA 26 E5
Eagen L. BECK 55 E5
Eagle Bend TODD 39 B5
Eagle Cr. SCOT 26 E4
Eagle Cr. TODD 40 B1
Eagle L. BECK 46 B5
Eagle L. BLUE 15 F5
Eagle L. CARL 51 C3
Eagle L. CARV 25 E4
Eagle L. CASS 48 A5
Eagle L. CASS 58 G2
Eagle L. COOK 88 G1
Eagle L. COTT 3 B5
Eagle L. CROW 49 B3
Eagle L. CROW 49 F4
Eagle L. HENN 26 B4
Eagle L. HUBB 56 E5
Eagle L. ITSC 71 E3
Eagle L. KAND 32 G1
Eagle L. MART 4 E4
Eagle L. MCLD 24 E5
Eagle L. OTTL 38 B5
Eagle L. SHER 34 D1
Eagle L. STLS 61 F4
Eagle L. STRN 32 C5
Eagle L. WRIT 33 F5
Eagle Lake (city) BLUE 15 F5
Eagle Lake Roadside Park BLUE 15 E5
Eagle Lake Twp OTTL 38 B5
Eagle Mountain Historic Site COOK 88 G1
Eagle Mountain Ski Area TODD 40 F3
Eagle Mountain COOK 88 G1
Eagle Mountain COOK 75 D5
Eagle Nest Pt. STLS 73 C5
Eagle Point L. WASH 27 C3
Eagle Point Twp MRSH 89 G5
Eagles Nest County Park WATN 4 A4
Eagles Nest Lakes STLS 73 B4
Eagles Point POPE 31 A2
Eagle Valle Twp TODD 40 B1
East Annalaide L. OTTL 39 B4
East Battle L. OTTL 47 E3
East Bay COOK 76 B3
East Bay STLS 73 B4
East Bay STLS 85 C1
East Bearskin L. COOK 88 E3
East Bearskin Recreation Site COOK 88 F2
East Beaver Bay (city) LAKE 63 A1
East Bethel ANOK 34 D5
East Boot L. WASH 35 G4
East Branch Amity Cr. STLS 61 F4
East Branch Baptism R. LAKE 75 F1
East Branch Beaver R. LAKE 62 A5
East Branch Chippewa R. SWFT 31 E2
East Branch Flandreau Cr. PIPE 11 E4
East Branch Rock R. PIPE 12 G1
East Branch Silver Cr. WOOD 93 E5
East Branch Sturgeon R. STLS 72 D3
East Branch Warroad R. ROSE 92 D4
East Chain MART 5 F1
East Chain L. MART 5 F1
East Chain Twp MART 5 F1
East Chub L. LAKE 74 D3
East Cr. WBSH 18 E5
East Cranberry L. CLER 56 C2
East Dawkins L. COOK 87 E5
East Ellen L. POPE 39 G4
Easterne Twp OTTL 39 B4
East Fork Beaver Cr. RENV 23 F5
East Fork Blue Earth R. FRBT 5 E4
East Fork Cedar R. DOGE 7 B3
East Fork Crooked Cr. PINE 44 C1
East Fork Des Moines R. MART 4 F3
East Fork Prairie R. ITSC 71 F5
East Fork Rapid R. KCHG 94 F1
East Fork Rat Root R. KCHG 83 A5
East Fork Twelve Mile Cr. TRAV 29 A5
East Four Legged L. CLER 68 D4
East Fox L. COOK 75 C3
East Fox L. CROW 49 B3
East Graham L. NBLS 3 C1
East Grand Forks POLK 77 G5
East Gull Lake (city) CASS 49 F1
East Gull Lake Municipal Airport CASS 49 F1
Eastham L. CROW 49 C4
East Indian R. WBSH 19 E1
East Johanna L. POPE 31 D4
East L. ITSC 70 D5
East L. ITSC 71 E2
East L. LAKE 75 D2
East Lake (city) ATKN 50 D5
East Lake Indian Reservation ATKN 50 D5
East Lake Lillian Twp KAND 24 C2
East Lake Sarah County Park MURR 12 F4
East Leaf L. OTTL 47 F2
East Lost L. OTTL 46 F4
East Lund L. MAHN 67 F5
East Mosquito Cr. CASS 48 F4
East Nelson L. MORR 48 G4
East Olaf L. DOUG 39 F1
East Olson L. MRSH 79 B4
Easton FRBT 5 D5
East Otter L. COOK 88 E1
East Park Twp MRSH 91 G1
East Park Wildlife Management Area MRSH 79 A1
East Pike L. COOK 88 E5
East Pipe L. COOK 75 A5
East Pope L. COOK 88 E1
East Savanna R. STLS 60 F2
East Seelye Bay Recreation Site ITSC 70 F3
East Side Twp MLLC 42 B3
East Smith L. ITSC 71 F2
East Solomon L. KAND 31 G5
East Spirit L. OTTL 46 C4
East Split Rock R. LAKE 62 B4
East Stone L. STLS 61 B1
East Sunburg L. KAND 31 E4
East Swan R. STLS 60 B3
East Toqua L. BGST 29 B4
East Twin L. COOK 88 G2
East Twin L. CROW 49 D1
East Twin L. LYON 12 E2
East Twin L. STLS 51 A5
East Twin Lake County Park ANOK 34 E3
East Two R. STLS 72 G5
East Two Rivers R. STLS 73 B3
East Union CARV 26 F2
East Valley Twp MRSH 79 C3
Eberhart L. FREE 6 F3
Ebro CLER 68 F2
Echo YMED 23 G2
Echo Cr. REDW 23 G3
Echo I. STLS 84 A1
Echo L. CARL 51 E4
Echo L. CASS 58 F3
Echo L. COOK 88 G1
Echo L. DOUG 39 F1
Echo L. LAKE 75 D2
Echo L. MCLD 25 C1
Echo L. STLS 85 D1
Echo Lake Recreation Site STLS 85 D1
Echols WATN 4 B3
Echo Pt. STLS 73 B2
Echo R. STLS 85 D1
Echo Trail STLS 85 E2
Echo Twp YMED 23 G2
Eckbeck Recreation Site LAKE 75 G1
Eckert L. POPE 31 B4
Eckles Twp BELT 69 E1
Eckvoll Twp MRSH 79 C5
Ecstasy L. COOK 87 F3
Eddy L. ANOK 34 F3
Eddy L. LAKE 87 E2
Eddy L. OTTL 46 E3
Eddy Twp CLER 68 D2
Eden DOGE 17 G3
Eden L. STRN 32 E4
Eden Lake Twp STRN 32 E4
Eden Prairie (city) HENN 26 D3
Eden Twp BRWN 14 C2
Eden Twp PIPE 1 B4
Eden Twp POLK 68 C1
Eden Valley (city) MEEK 32 E4
Edge L. LAKE 87 G2
Edgerton PIPE 2 B1
Edgewater Municipal Park FREE 6 E4
Edgewood ISNT 34 C5
Edina HENN 26 D4
L. Edina HENN 26 D4
Edison Twp SWFT 30 F3
L. Edith WASH 27 C4
Edith L. COOK 88 F4
Edmund L. ITSC 71 D2
Edna L. ATKN 59 G1
Edna L. CROW 49 D1
Edna L. OTTL 47 C2
Edna Twp OTTL 46 D5
Edquist L. ATKN 50 E1
Ed Shave L. STLS 85 F5
Edward L. CROW 49 D3
Edward L. LAKE 74 C4
Edwards L. POPE 31 C2
Edwards L. TODD 48 G2
Edwards L. WRIT 33 G3
Edwards Twp KAND 23 B4
Edwin L. MAHN 55 A4
Eel L. ITSC 70 B3
Effie ITSC 71 B2
Effington Twp OTTL 39 B2
Egge L. LAKE 75 F1
Eggers L. COOK 88 G2
Eggert L. LSUR 16 B2
Eggert L. STRN 32 B4
Egg L. CASS 58 G5
Egg L. ITSC 70 F4
Egg L. MAHN 55 C5
Egg L. WASH 35 G2
Egg R. BECK 56 E1
Eglon Twp CLAY 55 G1
Eide L. GRNT 38 D3
Eidsvold Twp LYON 12 G2
Eier L. STLS 60 E5
Eighteen L. LAKE 74 D5
Eighteen L. POLK 67 D2
Eighteen Mile Cr. TRAV 37 F3
Eighth Crow Wing L. HUBB 57 F2
Eight Mile Cr. SBLY 14 B4
Eight Mile Cr. STLS 85 F1
Eight Mile I. KCHG 95 F5
Eighty Acre L. MEEK 24 B5
Eilers L. SHER 33 D4
Eitzen HOUS 9 G5
Ek L. STLS 84 A3
Ek's Bay STLS 84 A3
Elba WINA 19 F1
Elba Twp WINA 19 G1
Elbow Cr. COOK 76 A3
Elbow Cr. STLS 72 G5
Elbow L. BECK 56 D1
Elbow L. BECK 56 F3
Elbow L. CASS 58 G1
Elbow L. COOK 75 C3
Elbow L. COOK 76 A3
Elbow L. GRNT 38 D2
Elbow L. ITSC 70 E5
Elbow L. ITSC 71 B4
Elbow L. ITSC 71 D1
Elbow L. OTTL 46 C3
Elbow L. OTTL 46 D4
Elbow L. OTTL 46 G5
Elbow L. PINE 43 B2
Elbow L. STLS 72 D2
Elbow L. STLS 72 G5
Elbow L. STLS 84 G4
Elbow Lake (city) GRNT 38 D3
Elbow Lake Municipal Airport GRNT 38 D2
Elbow Lake Twp GRNT 38 D2
Elbow R. STLS 84 G4
Eldorado Twp STEV 38 G1
Eldred POLK 66 D2
L. Eleanor KAND 24 A1
Elephant L. STLS 84 D4
Elevator Bay (city) WASH 27 D4
L. Eleven CLAY 46 A1
L. Eleven KNBC 43 B1
L. Eleven PINE 51 F4
Eleventh Crow Wing L. HUBB 57 E3
Elgin WBSH 18 F4
Elgin Twp WBSH 18 F3
Eli L. BGST 29 C4
Eli Wirtanen Finnish Farmstead Historic Site STLS 61 A3
Elixer L. LAKE 75 D2
Elizabeth OTTL 46 F2
L. Elizabeth KAND 24 B2
Elizabeth L. DOUG 39 E1
Elizabeth L. ISNT 34 B5
Elizabeth L. ITSC 71 E3
Elizabeth Twp OTTL 46 E2
Eliza Muller State Monument NCLT 14 B3
Elk Cr. NBLS 2 E1
Elk Cr. NBLS 3 D1
Elk L. CLER 56 C4
Elk L. DOUG 39 E1
Elk L. GRNT 38 E4
Elk L. LAKE 87 F1
Elk L. SHER 33 D4
Elk L. SHER 34 C2
Elk Lake Twp GRNT 38 E4
Elko SCOT 16 A5
Elk R. BENT 41 G4
Elk R. SHER 33 D5
Elk River (city) SHER 34 E2
Elkton MOWE 7 E5
Elkton Twp CLAY 45 A4
Elk Twp NBLS 2 D5
Ella Hall L. LAKE 86 G2
L. Ella KAND 24 B2
Ella L. COOK 75 A3
Ellendale STEL 6 C5
Ellen L. POPE 39 G4
Elling L. GRNT 38 C2
L. Ellingson OTTL 39 A1
Ellingson L. GRNT 38 E4
Ellington Twp DOGE 17 F2
Elliott L. STLS 61 A1
Ellis L. BELT 69 E5
Ellis L. DOUG 39 C2
Ellison L. BECK 46 A3
Ell L. COOK 87 F4
Ellquist L. COOK 87 E3
Ellsborough Twp MURR 12 F2
Ellsburg Twp STLS 61 B1
Ellstrom L. CARL 52 D1
Ellsworth NBLS 2 F2
Ellsworth Twp MEEK 24 B5
Elm Cr. HENN 26 A3
Elm Cr. MART 5 D1
Elm Creek County Park Reserve HENN 34 G3
Elm Creek Twp MART 4 D2
Elmdale MORR 40 F5
Elmdale Twp MORR 40 F4
Elmer STLS 61 D4
Elmer Twp PIPE 1 B5
Elmer Twp STLS 60 D3
Elmira Twp OLMS 8 B4
Elm Island L. ATKN 50 E2
Elm L. COOK 87 F3
Elm L. ITSC 71 D1
Elmore FRBT 5 G3
Elmore Twp FRBT 5 F3
L. Elmo WASH 27 C3
Elmo Twp OTTL 39 A3
Elm Point BELT 81 G2
Elm Point WOOD 92 B4
Elm Pt. ITSC 59 B2
Elms L. ISNT 34 C5
Elmwood Island ITSC 70 B2
Elmwood Twp CLAY 45 A3
Elrings L. STRN 32 B2
Elrosa STRN 32 B1
Elton L. LAKE 87 F2
Elusion L. COOK 87 E3
Elwell L. WASH 35 F3
Ely STLS 74 A1
Ely I. STLS 73 B3
Ely L. LSUR 16 C1
Ely L. STLS 73 F1
Ely Municipal Airport STLS 74 B1
Elysian LSUR 16 E2
Elysian Twp LSUR 16 E1
L. Elysian WASC 16 F1
Emardville Twp RDLK 67 A3
Embarrass STLS 73 D3
Embarrass L. STLS 73 E2
Embarrass R. STLS 73 D3
Embarrass Twp STLS 73 D3
Ember L. WRIT 33 E4
Embla L. LAKE 87 D2
L. Emerald BELT 69 B1
Emerald I. STLS 96 G3
Emerald L. STLS 85 D3
Emerald Twp FRBT 5 E4
Emerson L. POLK 67 C4
Emily CROW 49 B4
Emily Cr. LQPL 22 A2
L. Emily LSUR 15 D5
L. Emily MCLD 25 C1
L. Emily POPE 30 C5
Emily L. CROW 49 B4
Emily State Forest CROW 49 B5
L. Emma CLAY 46 B1
L. Emma HUBB 56 B5
L. Emma HUBB 57 E1
L. Emma MEEK 32 E3
L. Emma OTTL 46 F5
L. Emma WRIT 25 B4

Emmanuel Evangelical Lutheran Church Historic Site HOUS 10 D2
Emmet Twp RENV 23 E4
Emmons FREE 6 G3
Empire Twp DKTA 27 F1
Encampment I. LAKE 62 D4
Encampment R. LAKE 62 C3
End-O-Line County Park MURR 12 G5
Endresen Cabin Historic Site KAND 31 G5
Enfield WRIT 33 E4
L. Engebretson BECK 55 G2
Eng L. DOUG 38 F5
Englemeier L. STRN 32 B5
Englishman I. COOK 87 D3
Englund MRSH 90 G3
Engralson L. GRNT 38 C2
Ensign L. LAKE 86 F5
Enstrom Twp ROSE 92 C2
Enterprise Twp JACK 4 D1
Equality Twp RDLK 67 A5
Erasmus L. STLS 61 D3
Erdahl GRNT 38 D4
Erdahl Twp GRNT 38 D4
Erhard OTTL 46 E2
Erhard Grove Twp OTTL 46 D2
Erhards Grove Game Refuge OTTL 46 D2
L. Erick BELT 69 D1
Ericksen L. POPE 30 A5
Erickson L. BELT 69 D4
Erickson L. CLAY 55 G1
Erickson L. ITSC 71 D3
Erickson L. NCLT 15 D3
Erickson L. STEV 38 G4
Erickson L. STLS 73 B5
Ericsburg KCHG 83 A4
L. Ericson MORR 40 A5
Ericson Twp RENV 23 D3
Erie PENN 79 F5
L. Erie MEEK 24 B5
Erie L. MAHN 55 B4
Erie Twp BECK 55 G5
Erin Twp RICE 16 C3
Ernest L. COOK 87 E4
Ernie Tuff Museum WINA 9 B3
Ernst Pool MLLC 42 C3
Erskine POLK 67 D3
L. Erskine ITSC 71 B4
Erskine L. CROW 41 B5
Erskine Municipal Airport POLK 67 D3
Erwin L. DOUG 38 D5
Erwin L. ITSC 71 D3
Esden L. CROW 49 F4
E. S. Hoyt House Historic Site GOOD 18 A1
Esko CARL 52 B2
Eskwagama L. LAKE 74 A3
Espelie Twp MRSH 80 D1
Espe L. MAHN 55 B4
Esquagamah L. ATKN 50 B1
Esquagama L. STLS 73 F2
Essig BRWN 14 D4
Ess L. BELT 68 E5
Esswhtar L. STLS 61 D5
Ester Bk. KCHG 83 C3
Ester L. LAKE 87 D2
Estes Bk. MLLC 34 A1
Estes Brook (city) MLLC 34 A1
Esther L. COOK 88 F5
Esther Twp POLK 77 E5
E. St. Julien Cox House Historic Site NCLT 15 D4
L. Ethel OTTL 47 F1
Ethel L. ITSC 71 D2
Etna FILL 8 F3
Etna Cr. FILL 8 F3
Euclid POLK 78 G3
Euclid Twp POLK 78 G3
Eugene L. STLS 85 C3
L. Eunice BECK 46 B3
Eureka Twp DKTA 26 G5
Evan BRWN 14 C2
Evans L. BECK 56 F1
Evans L. OTTL 46 E3
Evansville DOUG 38 D5
Evansville State Game Refuge DOUG 38 C5
Evansville Twp DOUG 38 D5
Eveleth STLS 73 F1
Eveleth-Virginia Municipal Airport STLS 73 G1
Evelyn L. STLS 62 C1
Evenmore L. POLK 67 C4
Evenson L. MEEK 24 B4
Everdell WILK 45 G4
Everett Bay STLS 73 B2
Everett L. COOK 87 E4
Everett L. STLS 85 G5
Everglade Twp STEV 30 A1
Evergreen BECK 47 B2
Evergreen L. HUBB 57 B1
Evergreen Twp BECK 47 A2
Everton Cr. BELT 69 D5
Everts Twp OTTL 46 G5
Evey L. CLER 56 C2
Ewington Twp JACK 3 E2
Ewy L. WATN 4 A2
Excelsior HENN 26 D2
Excel Twp MRSH 79 D2
Exnell L. STLS 60 C2
Experiment L. CASS 57 A4
Exploit L. LAKE 74 B4
Explorer L. LAKE 86 F5
Extortion Cr. COOK 87 E4
Extortion L. COOK 87 E4
Eyota OLMS 8 A4
Eyota Twp OLMS 8 A3
Fable L. LAKE 87 F2
Fagen L. BELT 69 E4
Fag L. COOK 88 F2
Faherty L. CASS 57 B4
Fahlun Twp KAND 24 B1
Fahul L. BELT 69 C1
Faille L. TODD 39 E5
Fairbanks STLS 61 A5
Fairbanks L. BECK 55 E4
Fairbanks L. BELT 68 B5
Fairbanks L. MAHN 56 B1
Fairbanks Twp STLS 61 A5
Fairfax RENV 14 A3
Fairfax Twp POLK 66 C4
Fairfield Twp CROW 49 B4
Fairfield Twp SWFT 30 D3
Fairhaven STRN 33 E2
Fairhaven Mill and Dam Historic Site STRN 33 E2
Fair Haven Twp STRN 33 E2
Fairmont MART 4 E5
Fairmont Municipal Airport MART 4 E5
Fairmont Twp MART 4 E5
Fairview Twp CASS 48 F5
Fairview Twp LYON 12 B4
Fairy L. OTTL 46 B5
Fairy L. STLS 86 E1
Fairy L. TODD 40 F1
Faith NORM 55 B2
Faith L. LAKE 87 D2
Falcon Heights (city) RAMS 27 C1
Falk L. CLER 68 D4
Falk Twp CLER 68 G2
Fallen Arch L. LAKE 74 B5
Fall L. LAKE 86 G2
Fall Lake Recreation Site LAKE 86 G2
Fall Lake Twp LAKE 86 F3
Fallon L. MEEK 25 B1
Fall R. COOK 76 B3
Falls Creek County Park RICE 16 D5
Falls International Airport KCHG 95 G3
Falls Lakes STLS 73 C3
Falun Twp ROSE 92 D2
Famine L. COOK 87 G5
Fan L. COOK 88 E4
Fannie L. ISNT 35 C1
L. Fanny DOUG 38 D5
Fanny Twp POLK 66 A3
Fantail L. LAKE 87 G2
Farden Twp HUBB 57 A3
FARIBAULT — 5 —
Faribault RICE 16 D5
Faribault County Courthouse Historic Site FRBT 5 E3
Faribault County Historical Society Museum FRBT 5 E3
Faribault Municipal Airport RICE 16 D5
Faribault State School and Hospital RICE 16 D5
Farley Cr. ITSC 70 E2
Farley L. ITSC 70 E2
Farley Twp POLK 78 E2
Farming STRN 32 C4
Farmington DKTA 27 G1
Farmington Twp OLMS 18 F2
Farming Twp STRN 32 C4
Farm Island ATKN 50 F1
Farm Island L. ATKN 50 E1
Farm Island Twp ATKN 50 E1
Farm L. LAKE 74 A2
Farnham Cr. CASS 48 D3
Farnham L. WADN 48 E3
Farquhar L. DKTA 27 E1
Farquhar Peak COOK 76 F1
Farris HUBB 57 A3
Farwell POPE 39 G1
Fast L. LAKE 86 G5
Father Hennepin State Park MLLC 42 B3
Fat L. STLS 85 C3
Fault L. COOK 88 E4
Faunce L. OTTL 38 B1
Faunge Recreation Site WOOD 93 F1
Faupel L. CROW 49 D3
Fawn Cr. STLS 84 C3
Fawn L. BELT 69 D1
Fawn L. CASS 57 G5
Fawn L. COOK 87 F4
Fawn L. CROW 49 C3
Fawn L. CROW 49 D1
Fawn L. CROW 49 E3
Fawn L. ITSC 71 G1
Fawn L. STLS 73 D1
Fawn Lake County Park CROW 49 E3
Fawn Lake Twp TODD 40 A3
Faxon Twp SBLY 25 G5
Fayal State Game Refuge STLS 73 G1
Fayal Twp STLS 73 G1
Fay I. STLS 73 A2
Fay L. COOK 87 E3
Featherbed L. KNBC 43 C1
Feather L. COOK 75 C3
Featherstone Twp GOOD 18 B1
Fectos Pt. STLS 73 A1
Federal Dam (city) CASS 58 B2
Fedji L. Watowan 15 G1
Feedem I. STLS 84 A2
Feeley Twp ITSC 59 C5
Fee L. LAKE 87 F2
Feldges L. STRN 33 D3
Felix L. TODD 40 E2
Felton CLAY 54 D4
Felton Cr. CLAY 54 E4
Felton Twp CLAY 54 D4
Femling L. OTTL 46 D3
Fence L. CLER 68 C4
Fenske L. STLS 85 F5
Fenske Lake Recreation Site STLS 85 G5
Fente L. COOK 87 F3
Fenton Twp MURR 2 B3
Ferello L. STLS 85 C3
Fergus Falls (city) OTTL 46 G2
Fergus Falls Community College OTTL 46 G1
Fergus Falls Game Refuge OTTL 46 G2
Fergus Falls Municipal Airport OTTL 46 G1
Fergus Falls State Hospital OTTL 46 G2
Fergus Falls Twp OTTL 46 F2
Ferman L. LAKE 74 F4
Fernando MCLD 24 G5
Fernberg Road LAKE 86 G2
Ferne L. LAKE 75 B1
Fern L. BELT 69 G1
Fern L. COOK 87 F3
Fern Twp HUBB 56 A5
Ferrell L. MORR 40 C5
Ferret L. COOK 87 F5
Fertile POLK 67 E1
Fertile Municipal Airport POLK 67 E1
Fessland L. BELT 68 B5
Fetters L. COOK 87 F4
Feucht L. TODD 40 F2
Fiddle L. COOK 88 F2
Field L. GRNT 38 C3
Fieldon Twp WATN 4 A5
Field Twp STLS 72 B4
L. Fifteen CLAY 46 A1
L. Fifteen CLAY 55 G1
Fifth Crow Wing L. HUBB 57 F1
Fifth L. CASS 57 E4
Fifth L. CLER 68 B4
Fifth L. STRN 32 B4
Fifty Lakes (city) CROW 49 B3
Fig L. BECK 46 A2
Fig L. STLS 61 B1
Figure Eight L. ITSC 59 C1
FILLMORE — 8 —
Fillmore FILL 8 D4
Fillmore County Airport FILL 8 E4
Fillmore County Historical Society Museum FILL 8 E5
Fillmore Twp FILL 8 D3
Finberg L. STLS 60 C2
Fine Lakes Twp STLS 51 A3
Finger Cr. STLS 85 C3
Finger L. COOK 75 C3
Finger L. STLS 85 C3
Fink L. STRN 33 D1
Finks Slough LQPL 22 D3
Finland LAKE 75 G1
Finlander Bay STLS 96 G2
Finlander I. STLS 96 G2
Finland Recreation Site LAKE 75 G1
Finland State Forest LAKE 75 E2
Finlayson PINE 43 A3
Finlayson Twp PINE 43 A3
Finn Bay STLS 73 C5
Finn Cr. COOK 87 F5
Finn Cr. OTTL 47 E3
Finn Creek Open Air Museum OTTL 47 E3
Finn L. COOK 87 F5
Finn L. WADN 48 B1
Finn Pond LAKE 74 D5
Finstad Cr. STLS 85 E1
Finstad L. STLS 85 F1
Fire L. LAKE 86 G5
First Crow Wing L. HUBB 57 G2
First Cr. STLS 73 E3
First Dog L. CASS 58 G3
First L. CHIS 35 E4
First L. CLER 68 B3
First L. CLER 68 F2
First L. PINE 51 G3
First L. STLS 85 F5
First L. WRIT 33 F5
First Perch L. CASS 57 G4
First R. ITSC 70 F4
First River L. ITSC 70 F4
Fish Cr. BECK 56 F2
Fish Cr. BGST 29 C2
Fish Cr. TODD 40 F3
Fishdance L. LAKE 75 A1
Fisher POLK 66 B2
Fisher L. LAKE 87 G1
Fisher L. SCOT 26 E4
Fishermans Point Recreation Site STLS 73 F3
Fisher's Landing Travel Information Center POLK 66 B1
Fisher Twp POLK 66 B2
Fishgig L. COOK 87 F3
Fishhook I. COOK 87 E3
Fish Hook L. BECK 55 D5
Fishhook L. COOK 88 G1
Fish Hook L. HUBB 56 F5
Fishhook L. ITSC 71 E2
Fishhook Pt. COOK 76 B5
Fish Hook R. HUBB 56 G5
Fish House Bay ITSC 59 A2
Fishing Lakes STLS 73 C4
Fish L. ANOK 35 D1
Fish L. BECK 46 A3
Fish L. BECK 55 D4
Fish L. BECK 55 E5
Fish L. BECK 55 F4
Fish L. CASS 48 C4
Fish L. CASS 57 F5
Fish L. CHIS 35 B2
Fish L. COTT 3 C5
Fish L. DKTA 27 E1
Fish L. HENN 26 A3
Fish L. KNBC 42 F4
Fish L. LAKE 87 E2
Fish L. LSUR 16 E2
Fish L. MAHN 55 B4
Fish L. MART 4 C2
Fish L. MART 4 F3
Fish L. MORR 40 B5
Fish L. OTTL 39 B2
Fish L. OTTL 46 B3
Fish L. OTTL 46 F3
Fish L. PINE 43 B2
Fish L. POLK 68 C1
Fish L. (Reservoir) STLS 61 F3
Fish L. SCOT 26 G3
Fish L. SHER 33 D3
Fish L. STEV 30 A1
Fish L. STRN 31 D5
Fish L. STRN 32 A4
Fish L. WASH 35 F3
Fish L. WRIT 33 E4
Fish Lake County Park CHIS 35 B2
Fish Lake Twp CHIS 35 B1
Fishmouth L. STLS 96 G3
Fish Trap L. CROW 49 E2
Fishtrap L. LAKE 74 D4
Fish Trap L. MORR 40 A4
Fiske L. ITSC 70 C2
Fiske L. OTTL 38 A4
Five Island L. ITSC 71 B4
Five L. BECK 55 G5
Five L. CLER 68 D2
Five L. OTTL 46 B5
Five Mile Cr. BGST 30 F1
Five Mile Cr. TRAV 37 E5
Five Mile L. STLS 73 B3
Five Mile Point CASS 58 C1
Five Mile Rock COOK 76 B4
L. Five PINE 44 C1
Five Point L. CASS 57 G5
Fiver L. STLS 73 C3
Fjestad L. OTTL 46 F1
Fladmark L. OTTL 46 D3
Flag I. WOOD 97 D3
L. Flaherty JACK 3 D4
Flame L. COOK 75 A4
Flanders L. CROW 49 C3
Flandreau Cr. PIPE 11 F3
Flap Cr. STLS 84 C4
Flap L. COOK 87 E3
Flapper L. LAKE 74 B5
Flash L. LAKE 86 G4
Flat Horn L. LAKE 74 D4
Flat Horn Recreation Site LAKE 74 D4
Flat L. BECK 56 F1
Flat Lake Mounds Historic Site BECK 56 E1
Flattail L. COOK 87 G3
Flax L. STEV 30 C2
Fleck L. COOK 75 B5
Fleming L. ATKN 50 C3
Fleming Twp ATKN 50 C3
Fleming Twp PINE 43 A5
Flenner L. BELT 69 D4
Flensburg MORR 40 D4
Fletcher HENN 34 G3
Fletcher Cr. ITSC 70 C5
Fletcher Cr. MORR 41 C1
Flicker L. COOK 88 F1
Flint Cr. STLS 72 A4
Flint L. COOK 87 E3
Flint L. STRN 32 D4
Flodeen L. CARL 52 D1
Flom NORM 55 C2
Flom Twp NORM 55 C2
Flood Bay LAKE 62 E3
Flood Bay State Wayside LAKE 62 E3
Floodwood STLS 60 F3
Floodwood Game Refuge ATKN 60 F1
Floodwood L. STLS 60 C1
Floodwood R. ITSC 60 D1
Floodwood R. STLS 60 D2
Floodwood Twp STLS 60 F3
L. Flora BELT 69 F4
Flora L. CLAY 55 E1
Flora Twp RENV 23 F4
Florence LYON 12 E1
Florence L. COOK 87 F3
Florence L. ISNT 34 C5
Florence Twp GOOD 18 B2
Florenton STLS 73 E1
Florian County Park MRSH 78 A3
Florian MRSH 78 A3
Florida Cr. LQPL 21 C4
L. Florida KAND 31 F5
L. Florida Slough KAND 31 F5
Florida Twp YMED 21 E4
Flour Lake Recreation Site COOK 88 E2
Flour L. COOK 88 E2
Flowage L. STLS 61 E3
Flower L. CARL 51 B3
Flowing Twp CLAY 54 E4
Floyd L. BECK 55 G4
Flute Reed R. COOK 76 A5
Flying Cloud Airport HENN 26 E3
Flying L. COOK 87 E3
Fly L. ITSC 71 F2
Flynn Airport SHER 34 E1
Flynn L. CROW 49 D4
Fogard L. OTTL 46 E3
Fogarty L. BGST 29 B3
Fogelberg L. OTTL 46 D2
Fog L. BECK 46 A3
Fog L. MLLC 34 B2
Foldahl Twp MRSH 78 C4
Folden Twp OTTL 39 A2
Foley BENT 33 A5
Foley L. CROW 49 D4
Foley L. ITSC 71 C4
Folly Cr. LAKE 75 C1
Folsom Twp TRAV 29 A1
Folston L. CASS 58 D5
Fond Du Lac Indian Reservation CARL 51 B5
Fond Du Lac Municipal Forest STLS 52 B3
Fond Du Lac Municipal Park STLS 52 C3
Fond Du Lac State Forest CARL 51 B4
Fool Hen Cr. LAKE 75 B1
Fool Hen L. LAKE 75 B2
Fool L. COOK 87 F4
Fool L. CROW 49 D4
Foolsgold L. STLS 85 F2
Fools L. BECK 56 E4
Fools L. LAKE 74 D2
Football L. CASS 58 E2
Foot Hills State Forest CASS 48 B3
Foot L. ITSC 59 B4
Foot L. KAND 23 A5
Foot L. MAHN 67 F4
Foot L. POLK 67 E3
Footsteps L. COOK 88 F1
Forada DOUG 39 F3
Forbay L. CARL 52 C2
Forbes STLS 60 A5
Ford Twp KNBC 42 C5
Forest Center Landing LAKE 74 B5
Forest City MEEK 32 G5
Forest City Park MEEK 32 G5
Forest City Stockade Historic Site MEEK 32 G5
Forest City Twp MEEK 32 G5
Forest Grove KCHG 82 G2
Forest L. HENN 26 C2
Forest L. ITSC 59 B2
Forest L. ITSC 71 E2
Forest L. WASH 35 F2
Forest Lake (city) WASH 35 F2
Forest Lake Airport WASH 35 F2
Forest Lake Twp WASH 35 F2
Forest Mills GOOD 17 D5
Foreston MLLC 42 G1
Forest Prairie Cr. LSUR 15 B5
Forest Prairie Twp MEEK 32 F5
Forest Twp RICE 16 C4
Forestville State Park FILL 8 E4
Forestville Townsite/Meighen Store Historic Site FILL 8 E4
Forestville Twp FILL 8 E3
Forge L. STLS 73 F2
Forget-Me-Not L. BECK 55 G2
Forjer L. ITSC 71 G2
Fork Twp MRSH 77 A5
L. Formoe OTTL 38 B3
Forsythe L. ITSC 59 B2
Forth Sucker L. ITSC 71 G4
Fortier Twp YMED 21 F4
Fort Alexandria Agricultural Museum DOUG 39 E3
Fort Beauharnois Historic Site GOOD 18 B3
Fort Belmont Historic Site JACK 3 E5
Fort Charlotte Historic Site COOK 76 E2
Fort Cox Historic Site WATN 14 G5
Fort Flatmouth Mound Group Historic Site CROW 49 C3
Fort Renville Historic Site CHIP 22 B3
Fort Ridgely Cr. RENV 14 B2
Fort Ridgely Historic Site and Interpretive Center NCLT 14 B3
Fort Ridgely State Monument NCLT 14 B3
Fort Ridgely State Park NCLT 14 B3
Fort Ripley CROW 41 B1
Fort Ripley Historic Site MORR 41 C1

Fort Ripley Twp CROW 41 A1
Fort Snelling Historic Site HENN 27 D1
Fort Snelling National Cemetery HENN 26 D5
Fort Snelling State Park DKTA 27 D1
Fort St. Charles Historic Site WOOD 97 D2
Fort Sweney Historic Site GOOD 17 A4
Fositen L. STEL 6 B4
Fossan L. OTTL 38 A3
Fossdick L. MORR 40 A5
Foss L. STEV 30 A4
Foss L. STLS 73 A4
Fosston POLK 67 E5
Fosston Municipal Airport POLK 67 E5
Fossum NORM 55 B1
Fossum Twp NORM 55 B2
Foster L. WRIT 34 F2
Foster Point POPE 31 B2
Foster Twp BGST 29 C2
Foster Twp FRBT 6 E1
Foulball L. CLAY 46 A1
Found L. LAKE 86 F4
Fountain FILL 8 D5
Fountain L. FREE 6 E4
Fountain L. WRIT 25 B5
Fountain Prairie Twp PIPE 11 F5
Fountain Twp FILL 8 D4
L. Four ATKN 50 E1
L. Four LAKE 74 A4
Fourblock I. WOOD 97 E3
Four Corners STLS 61 G3
Four L. CLER 68 D2
Fourmile Bay WOOD 93 C3
Four Mile L. COOK 75 C3
Four Mile L. GRNT 38 C3
Four Mile L. STLS 73 B3
L. Fourteen CLAY 46 A1
L. Fourteen STLS 72 D4
Fourth Crow Wing L. HUBB 57 G2
Fourth L. CASS 57 E4
Fourth L. CHIS 35 E3
Fourth L. CLER 68 B3
Fourth L. STLS 73 F2
Fourtown BELT 80 C3
Fourtown L. LAKE 86 F1
Four Towns L. ITSC 70 D5
Fowl L. MAHN 55 C5
Foxhome WILK 45 G5
Foxhome Twp WILK 37 A5
Fox I. STLS 84 A4
Fox I. STLS 96 F2
Fox L. BECK 46 A3
Fox L. BECK 55 G5
Fox L. BELT 69 B1
Fox L. BELT 69 E2
Fox L. COOK 75 C3
Fox L. ITSC 71 E3
Fox L. MART 4 E3
Fox L. MURR 12 F5
Fox L. RICE 16 C4
Fox L. STLS 85 D5
Fox Lake (city) MART 4 E3
Fox Lake Game Refuge MART 4 E2
Fox Lake Twp MART 4 D3
Fox Meadow L. CASS 48 C4
Frames Landing County Park WADN 48 C2
Framnas Twp STEV 30 A4
Frances Bay COOK 88 E1
Francis I. COOK 76 E4
L. Francis ISNT 34 C4
L. Frances LSUR 16 E1
L. Francis MEEK 33 F2
Francis L. ITSC 71 F3
Francis R. SHER 34 D1
Franconia CHIS 35 E5
Franconia Twp CHIS 35 E4
Francy Cr. STLS 84 F2
Frandrau State Park BRWN 14 D5
Frankford Twp MOWE 8 D1
Frankfort Twp WRIT 34 G1
Franklin RENV 14 A1
Franklin STLS 73 F1
Franklin L. KCHG 71 A4
Franklin L. OTTL 46 C3
Franklin L. STLS 84 C5
Franklin Twp WRIT 25 B5
L. Frank SWFT 31 E3
Frank L. LAKE 74 D5
Fran L. LAKE 74 C2
Fransen Is. KCHG 95 F5
Franta L. CLER 56 B2
Franz Jevne State Park KCHG 94 F3
Fraser L. LAKE 87 F1
Fraser Twp MART 4 D4
Frazee BECK 46 B5
Frazee County Park BECK 46 B5
Frazee Waterfowl Game Refuge BECK 46 B5
Frazer Bay STLS 73 A1
Frear L. COOK 75 C3
Fredenberg Cr. COOK 75 E3
Fredenberg Twp STLS 61 E3
Frederick L. COOK 87 G3
Frederick L. POPE 39 G2
FREEBORN — 6 —
Freeborn FREE 6 D3
Freeborn County Historical Society Museum FREE 6 E4
Freeborn L. DOUG 39 F1
Freeborn L. FREE 6 D2
Freeborn Twp FREE 6 C2
Freeburg HOUS 10 E1
Freedhem MORR 41 C2
Freedom Twp WASC 6 A1
Freeland Twp LQPL 21 D5
Freemans Cr. TODD 40 C1
Freeman Twp FREE 6 F4
L. Freemont SHER 34 D2
Freeport STRN 32 A3
Freeport L. STRN 32 A3
Frellsen L. CLER 56 C3
Fremont L. MURR 12 F5
Fremont Twp WINA 9 B2
Fremont WINA 9 B2
French L. ATKN 50 C2
French L. COOK 87 E3
French L. HENN 26 C2
French L. HENN 34 G3
French L. MCLD 24 C5
French L. RICE 16 D4
French L. WRIT 33 G2
French Lake (city) WRIT 33 G2
French Lake Twp WRIT 33 G2
French Rapids County Park CROW 49 F3
French R. STLS 61 E5
French River (city) STLS 62 F1
French Twp STLS 72 D2
Frethem L. MAHN 67 F5
Frevels L. STRN 32 A3
Friberg Twp OTTL 46 F3
Friday Bay LAKE 86 D1
Fridley ANOK 26 B5
Friendship Twp YMED 22 E4
Friesland PINE 43 C3
Frieze L. MORR 41 D2
Frisk L. COOK 75 C4
Fritsche Cr. NCLT 14 C5
Frog L. LAKE 86 E5
Frog L. MAHN 67 G3
Frog L. MORR 40 A5
Frohn Twp BELT 69 F3
Frolic L. LAKE 86 E2
Frond L. LAKE 87 G2
Frontenac GOOD 18 A3
Frontenac L. HUBB 57 A1
Frontenac State Park GOOD 18 A3
Frontenac Station GOOD 18 B3
Frost FRBT 5 F4
Frost L. COOK 87 F4
Frost R. COOK 87 F3
Frovold L. SWFT 31 D1
Frying Pan L. STLS 73 G3
Fry L. LAKE 74 F5
Fucat L. CASS 48 E4
Fuchs L. CROW 41 A3
Fugle's Mill Historic Site OLMS 8 B2
Fulda MURR 2 B5
Fulda First L. MURR 2 C5
Fulda Second L. MURR 2 B5
L. Full of Fish KNBC 42 C5
Fulton L. LAKE 75 D2
Fungus L. COOK 87 F4
Fungus L. LAKE 75 B1
Funk L. BELT 69 D4
Funkley BELT 69 C5
Funkley L. BELT 68 E5
Fun L. COOK 87 F5
Fur L. COOK 87 F4
Fury's Island County Park NBLS 3 C1
Gaards L. OTTL 46 C1
Gabbro L. LAKE 74 B3
Gabimichigami L. COOK 87 E2
Gable L. BECK 55 D5
Gables L. WASH 27 D3
Gabrielson L. STLS 84 F2
Gadbolt L. CASS 57 E4
Gadwell L. COOK 88 E4
Gafvert L. STLS 73 B4
Gage L. HUBB 57 C1
Gagon Pt. STLS 73 A2
Gail Lake Twp CROW 49 B1
Gaiter L. COOK 87 E3
Gale Bk. ITSC 71 D2
Gale L. ITSC 71 D3
Galena Twp MART 4 C3
Gales L. REDW 13 C1
Gales Twp REDW 13 D1
Galpin L. HENN 26 D2
Games L. KAND 31 E5
Gander L. LAKE 74 D4
Gandrud L. BECK 55 F4
Gannon Cr. STLS 84 B3
Gannon L. STLS 84 C4
Gansey L. STLS 72 E1
Ganzer L. STRN 32 D4
Ganz L. MORR 40 E4
Garden City BLUE 15 G2
Garden City Twp BLUE 15 G2
Garden I. WOOD 97 F3
Garden L. CROW 49 D2
Garden L. LAKE 74 A2
Garden Twp POLK 67 E2
Gardner Bk. KCHG 83 G4
Gardner L. CLER 56 C3
Gardner L. MAHN 55 B4
Gardner L. MAHN 55 B5
Garfield DOUG 39 D2
Garfield L. HUBB 57 C3
Garfield Twp LQPL 21 C5
Garfield Twp POLK 67 E1
G.A.R. Historic Site and Museum MEEK 24 A1
Garnes Twp RDLK 67 A4
Garrison CROW 49 G5
Garrison Twp CROW 49 G5
Garvin LYON 12 E4
Garvin Bk. WINA 19 G3
Garvin County Park LYON 12 D4
Garvin Heights City Park WINA 19 G4
Gary I. LAKE 86 F2
Gary NORM 67 G1
Gasket L. COOK 87 F5
Gaskin L. COOK 88 F1
Gate L. STLS 72 D4
Gateway North Industrial Airport ANOK 34 F3
Gatzke MRSH 79 B5
Gaunt Cr. STLS 85 D2
Gauthier Cr. COOK 76 A5
Gay Bow L. BECK 55 D4
Gaylord SBLY 15 A2
Gaystock L. CARV 26 E2
Ge-Be-On-Equat Cr. STLS 85 C4
Ge-Be-On-Equat L. STLS 85 C4
Gebo L. BECK 46 B5
Gegoka L. LAKE 74 D4
Geis L. SCOT 26 F3
Geldner Mill Historic Site LSUR 16 D1
Gem L. LAKE 86 G4
Gem Lake (city) RAMS 27 B2
Gemmell KCHG 82 G3
General Andrews State Forest PINE 51 F3
Geneva FREE 6 C5
Geneva L. DOUG 39 E3
Geneva L. FREE 6 C5
Geneva Twp FREE 6 C5
Gennessee Twp KAND 24 A2
Genoa OLMS 18 F1
Genola MORR 41 D3
Gentilly POLK 66 B4
Gentilly R. POLK 66 B5
Gentilly Twp POLK 66 B5
George H. Crosby Manitou State Park LAKE 75 F2
L. George ANOK 34 E4
L. George HUBB 57 C1
L. George MART 4 E5
George L. BELT 69 C1
George L. BLUE 15 E5
George L. COOK 87 F5
George L. ITSC 71 E2
George L. KAND 32 F1
George L. MAHN 55 C4
George L. STLS 62 B1
George L. STRN 32 C1
Georges L. ITSC 71 E3
Georgetown CLAY 54 D1
Georgetown Twp CLAY 54 D2
Georgeville STRN 32 D1
George Washington State Forest ITSC 71 C4
George Watch L. ANOK 35 G1
Geraldine L. STLS 85 G5
Germania Twp TODD 40 A1
German L. BECK 55 E4
German L. ISNT 34 C4
German L. LSUR 16 D1
German L. OTTL 46 G4
German Lake Game Refuge ISNT 34 C4
Germantown Twp COTT 13 F4
Gertrude L. LAKE 75 C2
Gerund L. LAKE 87 F1
Gervais L. RAMS 27 B2
Gervais Twp RDLK 67 A2
Gesend Pond LAKE 74 B3
Getchell L. STRN 32 B3
Getty Twp STRN 32 B1
Gheen STLS 84 G3
Ghent LYON 12 A3
Ghost L. ITSC 71 E2
Giants Ridge Ski Area STLS 73 E2
Gibbon SBLY 14 A4
Gibbs Farm Museum RAMS 27 B1
Gibibwisher L. BELT 69 B2
Gibson L. LAKE 86 F5
Gideon Bay HENN 26 D2
Giese ATKN 43 A1
Gifford L. SCOT 26 E2
Gift L. LAKE 87 E2
Gijikiki L. LAKE 87 D2
Gijik L. CASS 58 E2
Gilbert STLS 73 F1
Gilbert Cr. WBSH 18 B2
Gilbert L. CROW 49 F2
Gilbert L. DOUG 39 E1
Gilbertson L. BECK 55 G3
Gilbertson L. POPE 31 B2
Gilchrist POPE 31 C3
Gilchrist L. POPE 31 C3
Gilchrist L. WRIT 33 F5
Gilchrist Twp POPE 31 D3
Gilfillan REDW 13 B5
Gilfillan L. BECK 56 D4
Gilfillan L. RAMS 27 A2
Gilfillin L. BLUE 15 E5
Gillespie Bk. CARL 51 E3
Gillette L. HUBB 57 C2
Gillford Twp WBSH 18 D2
Gillis L. COOK 87 F3
Gill L. CLER 56 B4
Gill L. STLS 73 F1
Gilman BENT 41 G4
Gilman L. BRWN 14 E3
Gilmanton Twp BENT 33 A4
Gilmore Cr. WINA 9 A3
Gilmore L. HUBB 57 E1
Gilstad L. BELT 69 D5
Gimiwan L. CLER 80 G3
Gimmer L. BELT 69 E5
Girard Twp OTTL 47 F1
Girl L. CASS 58 E2
Gislason L. LINC 12 B1
Glacial Lakes State Park POPE 31 C1
Glacier L. ATKN 50 A5
Glacier Pond LAKE 86 G3
Gladstone L. CROW 49 E2
Glanders L. CLER 56 C3
Glasgow Twp WBSH 18 D4
Glawe L. BECK 46 A4
Gleam L. COOK 75 A3
Gleason L. HENN 26 C3
Glee L. COOK 87 E3
Glen ATKN 50 F3
Glencoe MCLD 25 E3
Glencoe Isaac Walton Game Refuge MCLD 25 E2
Glencoe Twp MCLD 25 E2
Glenco Municipal Airport MCLD 25 E3
Glendale STLS 84 F3
Glendalough Game Farm OTTL 46 G5
Glendorado BENT 34 B1
Glendorado Twp BENT 33 B5
Glen L. HENN 26 D3
Glen L. LAKE 87 D2
Glenmore Cr. STLS 85 G3
Glenmore L. STLS 85 G3
Glenn L. COOK 88 F2
Glen Twp ATKN 50 E3
Glenville FREE 6 F5
Glenwood Municipal Airport POPE 31 A3
Glenwood POPE 31 A3
Glenwood Twp POPE 31 B3
Glesne L. KAND 31 E4
Glimmer L. STLS 73 A4
Glitter L. COOK 75 A3
Glitter L. LAKE 87 F2
Globe L. COOK 88 F1
Glory ATKN 50 F2
Glossy L. COOK 87 E3
Glove L. ITSC 70 C3
Gluek CHIP 23 B2
Glyndon CLAY 54 F3
Glyndon Twp CLAY 54 G3
Gnesen Twp STLS 61 E4
Goat Island HUBB 57 F2
Gobetween L. LAKE 75 B2
Godahl WATN 14 F3
Godfrey Twp POLK 67 D1
Gogebic L. COOK 88 E4
Goggins L. WASH 27 A3
Goggle L. CROW 49 C4
Gogie L. LAKE 75 A1
Golden Anniversary State Forest ITSC 59 D4
Goldeneye L. LAKE 75 D2
Golden Lake County Park ANOK 27 A1
Golden L. ANOK 27 A1
Golden Valley (city) HENN 26 C4
Golden Valley Lutheran College HENN 26 C4
Golden Valley Twp ROSE 92 F1
Gold I. COOK 87 D3
Gold I. STLS 84 A4
Goldsmith L. LSUR 15 D5
Gonvick CLER 68 C2
Good Harbor Bay COOK 76 C2
Good Hope Twp ITSC 70 E2
Good Hope Twp NORM 66 F3
GOODHUE — 18 —
Goodhue GOOD 17 C5
Goodhue County Historical Society Museum GOOD 18 A1
Goodhue Twp GOOD 18 C1
Good L. CLER 80 F2
Good L. LAKE 86 F3
Goodland ITSC 60 C1
Goodland Twp ITSC 60 C1
Goodners L. STRN 33 D1
Goodrich L. CROW 49 B4
Goodridge PENN 79 E5
Goodridge Twp PENN 79 E5
Good Thunder BLUE 5 A3
Goodview WINA 19 G3
Goodwill I. STLS 72 A5
Goodwin L. MAHN 56 A1
Googun L. BECK 55 D5
Gooseberry Falls State Park LAKE 62 C4
Gooseberry Island CROW 49 D2
Gooseberry L. BECK 55 D4
Gooseberry L. CASS 58 E2
Gooseberry Mound Municipal Park CLAY 54 G1
Gooseberry R. LAKE 62 C3
Goose Cr. CHIS 35 B2
Goose Island CASS 57 C5
Goose L. ANOK 34 E3
Goose L. BECK 56 G1
Goose L. BECK 56 G3
Goose L. CARV 25 D5
Goose L. CASS 48 B4
Goose L. CASS 57 G4
Goose L. CASS 58 C4
Goose L. CASS 58 E1
Goose L. CHIS 35 B1
Goose L. COOK 88 G1
Goose L. CROW 49 A5
Goose L. CROW 49 E5
Goose L. CROW 49 F5
Goose L. FREE 6 E4
Goose L. GOOD 27 G5
Goose L. HENN 34 G4
Goose L. HOUS 10 G2
Goose L. ITSC 70 D5
Goose L. LSUR 16 D1
Goose L. LSUR 16 D3
Goose L. LYON 12 C2
Goose L. MEEK 24 C4
Goose L. MORR 40 B5
Goose L. PENN 78 F4
Goose L. POPE 31 D3
Goose L. RAMS 27 B2
Goose L. SHER 34 C2
Goose L. TODD 40 F3
Goose L. WASC 16 G4
Goose L. WASH 27 C3
Goose L. WASH 35 F4
Goose L. WRIT 33 F2
Goose Lake Recreation Area WASC 16 G3
Goose Prairie Marsh CLAY 55 E1
Goose Prairie Twp CLAY 55 E1
Gopher Campfire Game Refuge MCLD 25 D1
Gorder L. STEV 30 C2
Gordon L. COOK 87 F4
Gordonsville FREE 6 G5
Gordon Twp TODD 39 E5
Gore L. COOK 88 F2
Gores Pool No. 3 Wildlife Management Area GOOD 27 F5
Gorman L. LSUR 16 D2
Gorman Twp OTTL 47 B1
Gorton Twp GRNT 38 E1
Gossip L. COOK 75 A4
Gotha CARV 26 F1
Gottenberg L. BECK 55 G3
Gould Cr. CLER 56 B4
Gould L. CASS 57 D4
Gould Twp CASS 58 C2
Gourd L. BECK 55 G2
Gourd L. OTTL 47 F1
Gowan STLS 60 G3
Gowan L. STLS 85 F3
Grace L. COOK 75 A3
Grace L. HUBB 69 G3
Grace L. PINE 44 C2
Graceton WOOD 93 E2
Grace Twp CHIP 23 A1
Graceville BGST 29 B4
Graceville Twp BGST 29 B4
Grafton Twp SBLY 24 F4
Graham L. CARL 52 E1
Graham L. GRNT 38 F1
Graham L. OTTL 46 B5
Graham Lake Twp NBLS 3 C1
Graham Twp BENT 41 F3
Granada MART 5 E1
Granby Twp NCLT 15 D2
Grande L. STLS 62 C1
Grand Falls (city) KCHG 82 D5
Grand Forks Twp POLK 77 F5
Grand L. STLS 61 G2
Grand L. STRN 33 D1
Grand Lake Twp STLS 61 F2
Grand Marais COOK 76 B3
Grand Marais Corridor Trail LAKE 75 C1
Grand Marais Harbor COOK 76 B3
Grand Marais Recreation Site COOK 76 B3
Grand Marais R. POLK 77 F5
Grand Marais U.S. Coast Guard Station COOK 76 B3
Grand Meadow MOWE 8 D1
Grand Meadow Twp MOWE 7 D5
Grand Mound Historic Site and Interpretive Center KCHG 83 A1
Grandpa L. COOK 87 D3
Grand Plain Twp MRSH 79 D4
Grand Portage COOK 76 E3
Grand Portage Bay COOK 76 E3
Grand Portage Corridor Trail COOK 76 E2
Grand Portage I. COOK 76 F3
Grand Portage Indian Reservation COOK 76 E2
Grand Portage National Monument COOK 76 E3
Grand Portage of the St. Louis River Historic Site CARL 52 C2
Grand Portage State Forest COOK 76 F1
Grand Prairie Twp NBLS 2 F2
Grand Rapids ITSC 59 C3
Grand Rapids-Itasca County Airport ITSC 59 C3
Grand Rapids Twp ITSC 59 B3
Grandrud L. OTTL 46 E2

Grandview Twp LYON 12 B3
Grandy ISNT 34 B5
Granger FILL 8 G5
Grange Twp PIPE 11 F5
Graning L. BELT 68 B5
Granite Falls (city) YMED 23 E1
Granite Falls Memorial Park YMED 23 E1
Granite Falls Twp CHIP 23 D1
Granite L. COOK 87 D4
Granite L. WRIT 33 G3
Granite Ledge Twp BENT 41 G5
Granite Pt. LAKE 62 F2
Granite R. COOK 87 D4
Granite Rock Twp REDW 13 C2
Granite Twp MORR 41 D4
Granning L. WADN 48 D2
Granrud L. OTTL 46 D1
GRANT — 38 —
Grant County Historical Society Museum GRNT 38 D3
Grant Cr. BELT 69 F1
Grant L. BELT 69 F1
Grants L. DOUG 39 F1
Grant Twp WASH 27 A3
Grant Valley Twp BELT 69 F1
Granville Twp KITT 90 C1
Grass L. ANOK 34 E5
Grass L. ANOK 34 F4
Grass L. BELT 69 F1
Grass L. CASS 58 A1
Grass L. CASS 58 D4
Grass L. CROW 49 B4
Grass L. CROW 49 C2
Grass L. HENN 26 E3
Grass L. ISNT 34 A3
Grass L. ISNT 35 C2
Grass L. ITSC 71 B2
Grass L. ITSC 71 D1
Grass L. ITSC 71 F4
Grass L. KNBC 43 F1
Grass L. LAKE 74 C4
Grass L. MAHN 55 B5
Grass L. MCLD 25 C3
Grass L. MEEK 24 A3
Grass L. OTTL 46 D3
Grass L. OTTL 47 F1
Grass L. PINE 43 B2
Grass L. STLS 72 G4
Grass L. WRIT 33 E3
Grass Lake Twp KNBC 42 F5
Grasston KNBC 43 F1
Grassy Bay STLS 84 B5
Grassy I. KCHG 95 F5
Grassy Island Group STLS 84 A1
Grassy L. COOK 87 F5
Grassy L. STLS 73 B4
Grassy L. STLS 86 F1
Grassy Point STLS 52 B4
Grassy Pt. STLS 73 A1
Gratten ITSC 70 B3
Grattan Twp ITSC 70 C3
Grave I. STLS 84 A2
Grave L. CASS 58 D4
Grave L. CROW 49 F4
Grave L. ITSC 71 F1
Gravel L. STEV 30 B1
Gravel L. STRN 32 B3
Graven L. OTTL 39 B3
Graveyard L. MAHN 68 F1
Grayling Wildlife Management Area ATKN 50 C5
Gray L. OTTL 46 B5
Grays Bay HENN 26 C3
Gray Twp PIPE 1 A5
Greanery STLS 84 G2
Great Bend Twp COTT 3 B4
Great Northern L. STRN 32 D5
Great Scott Twp STLS 72 E4
Great Sioux Camp Historic Site KAND 32 F2
Greeley L. ITSC 70 E3
Green Bass L. CASS 48 F5
Greenbush ROSE 91 E2
Greenbush Municipal Airport ROSE 91 E2
Green Bush Twp MLLC 34 B1
Greenfield HENN 26 A1
Greenfield Twp WBSH 19 D1
Green I. STLS 84 A2
Green Isle (city) SBLY 25 F4
Green Isle Twp SBLY 25 F3
Green L. ATKN 60 G1
Green L. BELT 69 B1
Green L. BELT 69 B2
Green L. CASS 48 C4
Green L. CASS 58 D4
Green L. CHIS 35 E3
Green L. CLER 56 C4
Green L. COOK 87 E3
Green L. CROW 49 E3
Green L. ISNT 34 B3
Green L. ITSC 71 G2
Green L. KAND 32 F1
Green L. STLS 85 C4
Green Lake Twp KAND 32 G1
Greenleaf MEEK 24 C5
Greenleaf L. MEEK 24 B5
Greenleaf L. LSUR 16 C2
Greenleafton FILL 8 F4
Greenleaf Twp MEEK 24 B4
Green Meadow Twp NORM 66 G5
Green Mountain L. WRIT 34 G1
Green Prairie Fish L. MORR 41 C1
Green Prairie Twp MORR 41 C1
Greenstone L. LAKE 86 G3
Greenvale Twp DKTA 16 B5
Green Valley (city) LYON 12 A4
Green Valley Twp BECK 56 G4
Greenwald STRN 32 B2
Green Water L. BECK 56 E2
Greenway Twp ITSC 59 A5
Green Wing L. LAKE 75 C1
Greenwood HENN 26 D2
Greenwood Bay STLS 73 A2
Greenwood Cr. LAKE 74 F2
Greenwood L. COOK 88 F4
Greenwood L. LAKE 74 E3
Greenwood R. COOK 88 F4
Greenwood R. LAKE 74 E3
Greenwood Twp CLER 68 C3
Greer L. CROW 49 C3
Greer L. MAHN 68 F1
Greer Lake Recreation Site CROW 49 C3
Gregg L. ATKN 50 F1
Gregory L. MAHN 67 G4
Gregory Twp MAHN 67 F4
Grena L. OTTL 46 D1
Grenn L. BELT 69 C1
Grey Cloud Island WASH 27 E2
Grey Cloud Island Twp WASH 27 E2
Grey Eagle TODD 40 F3
Grey Eagle Twp TODD 40 F3
Gribb Cr. FILL 9 D2
Griegs L. PINE 44 C1
L. Griffin SWFT 30 D2
Grimsgard L. BECK 55 F4
Grimstad Twp ROSE 91 E5
Grinder L. GRNT 38 C3
Grindstone I. KCHG 95 F5
Grindstone L. PINE 43 B2
Grogan WATN 4 A4
Groningen PINE 43 B3
Grossman Slough STEV 29 C5
Grouse Bay ITSC 70 F5
Grouse L. LAKE 74 C4
Grout House Historic Site WASH 27 C4
Grove City MEEK 32 G3
Grove Cr. MEEK 32 G4
Grove L. JACK 3 G4
Grove L. MAHN 55 C4
Grove L. OTTL 46 C1
Grove L. POLK 68 E1
Grove L. POPE 31 B4
Grove Lake (city) POPE 31 B4
Grove Lake Twp POPE 31 A4
Grove Park Twp POLK 67 C2
Grove Twp STRN 32 A2
Grubb L. DOUG 39 F1
Grub L. LAKE 86 F4
Grubstake L. LAKE 87 F1
Grunard L. OTTL 46 C5
Grunt L. COOK 87 G3
Grytal L. STLS 61 C2
Guard L. COOK 87 F4
Guckeen FRBT 5 E2
Guernsey L. TODD 39 F5
Gufstafson Hill LAKE 62 C4
Guida L. CROW 49 E2
Gulch Lake Recreation Site HUBB 57 C2
Gulf L. BELT 69 D3
Gulf L. COOK 87 D3
Gulf R. CROW 49 F1
Gull I. COOK 75 E3
Gull L. BELT 69 E4
Gull L. CASS 49 E1
Gull L. LAKE 74 B4
Gull L. MAHN 55 C5
Gull L. STLS 86 E1
Gull Lake Mounds Historic Site CASS 49 F1
Gull R. BELT 69 D4
Gull Reef MLLC 42 B3
Gull Rock COOK 76 E4
Gull Rock LAKE 62 B5
Gully POLK 68 C1
Gully Twp POLK 68 B1
Gump L. COOK 87 D3
Gun Club L. DKTA 27 D1
Gundar L. POPE 31 C1
Gunderson L. ITSC 71 D1
Gunflint District Ranger Station COOK 76 B3
Gunflint L. COOK 87 E5
Gunflint Trail COOK 76 B3
Gun L. ATKN 50 C3
Gun L. STLS 85 C3
Gun L. STLS 86 E1
Gunner L. BELT 68 B5
Gunn L. ITSC 71 E3
Gunny Sack L. ITSC 71 E4
Gunsten L. LAKE 74 C3
Gunstock L. COOK 87 F4
Gurneau L. CLER 68 B4
Gustafson L. STLS 85 F2
Gust Anderson L. CLER 68 C4
Gustavus Adolphus College NCLT 15 D4
Gust L. COOK 75 A5
Gutches Grove TODD 40 D1
Guthrie HUBB 57 B2
Guthrie Theater and Walker Art Center HENN 26 C5
Guthrie Twp HUBB 57 B2
Gwinn L. BELT 68 B5
Gyles L. BECK 56 F3
Gypo L. LAKE 86 E1
Gypsy L. LAKE 74 C3
Gyrgla MRSH 80 C1
Haberman L. OTTL 47 D2
Hackensack CASS 57 F5
Hackett WOOD 93 D3
Hack L. LAKE 87 F2
Hader GOOD 17 C4
Hadley MURR 2 A3
Hadley L. HENN 26 C3
Hafften L. HENN 26 A2
Hagali L. BELT 69 C3
Hagali Twp BELT 69 D3
Hag Cr. STLS 85 D4
Hagen CHIP 30 G4
Hagen L. GRNT 38 B3
Hagen Twp CLAY 54 D5
Haggerty L. CLER 68 C4
Hag L. STLS 85 D3
Hahn L. SBLY 25 G2
Hairy L. COOK 87 F4
Halden Twp STLS 60 F2
Hale L. ITSC 59 B2
Hale L. ITSC 59 D3
Hale L. ITSC 70 F2
Hale Twp MCLD 25 C2
Halfbreed L. WASH 35 F3
Half Dog I. LAKE 86 F3
Half Moon Isle MLLC 42 B3
Half Moon L. CROW 49 D3
Half Moon L. HENN 26 B2
Half Moon L. MEEK 32 G4
Half Moon L. STLS 73 G1
Half Moon L. WINA 19 D2
Halfway Point BELT 81 F1
Hallegue L. DOUG 38 E5
Hall L. CLER 56 C4
Hall L. MART 4 E5
Hallock KITT 90 D1
Hallock Municipal Airport KITT 90 D1
Hallock Twp KITT 89 D5
Hallot L. MAHN 55 C5
Halls L. FREE 6 E3
Halls Pond COOK 75 B5
Halma KITT 90 E3
Halstad NORM 54 A1
Halstad Twp NORM 66 G2
Halsted Bay HENN 26 C1
Halva Marsh MCLD 25 D2
Halverson L. OTTL 46 D2
Halverson L. POLK 67 E1
Halverson Lakes HUBB 57 C1
Halvorson L. BECK 55 F4
L. Halvorson OTTL 46 E1
Halvorson Point POPE 31 B2
Hamburg CARV 25 F4
Ham Cr. COOK 87 E4
Hamden Twp BECK 55 F3
Hamel HENN 26 B3
Hamilton FILL 8 D2
Ham L. ANOK 34 F5
Ham L. COOK 87 E4
Ham L. HUBB 57 F3
Ham L. MORR 40 A4
Ham Lake (city) ANOK 34 F5
Hamlet City Park WASH 27 E2
Hamlet L. CROW 49 E5
Hamline University RAMS 27 C1
Hamlin Twp LQPL 22 C1
Hammal L. ATKN 50 E1
Hammer L. STLS 60 A5
Hammer Twp YMED 21 E5
Hammond WBSH 18 E3
Hammond Twp POLK 66 D3
Hampden Twp KITT 90 C1
Hampton DKTA 27 G2
Hampton L. CROW 41 B2
Hampton Twp DKTA 27 G2
Hamre L. POLK 67 C5
Hamre Twp BELT 80 D3
Hamrey L. ITSC 70 C2
Hamton Twp DKTA 17 A2
Hancock STEV 30 C4
Hancock L. OTTL 38 B5
Hancock Twp CARV 25 F5
Hand L. CASS 58 G1
Hand L. COOK 88 G2
Hand L. OTTL 46 B3
Handle L. COOK 87 G4
Haners Run WOOD 93 G5
Hangaard Twp CLER 68 A2
Hanging Horn L. CARL 51 E4
Hanging Kettle L. ATKN 50 E1
Hanging of 38 Sioux County Historic Site BLUE 15 F4
Hank Haug Wildlife Museum CLER 68 F3
Hanks L. CROW 49 F5
Hanley Falls (city) YMED 22 F5
Hanley Falls Game Refuge YMED 22 F4
Hannah L. MORR 41 B5
Hanover WRIT 34 G2
Hanrahan L. SCOT 26 F4
Hansel L. OTTL 38 B3
Hanse L. STEV 30 B4
Hansen Cr. ROSE 92 F3
Hansen L. ATKN 50 D2
Hansen L. ITSC 71 G1
Hansen L. POLK 67 D4
Hanska BRWN 14 F5
L. Hanska BRWN 14 F4
Hansman L. TODD 40 E2
L. Hanson POPE 31 C2
L. Hanson STEV 30 A4
Hanson L. BELT 69 D4
Hanson L. BGST 29 E5
Hanson L. ITSC 71 G3
Hanson L. LAKE 87 E2
Hanson L. MEEK 24 A4
Hanson L. OTTL 38 A4
Hanson L. OTTL 47 F1
Hanson L. STLS 85 G5
Hanson Lakes CASS 57 E5
Hanson Slough BGST 29 D5
Hansonville Twp LINC 21 G4
Hantho Twp LQPL 22 A2
Happy L. CROW 49 F4
Harbor I. STLS 96 F2
Harbor L. LAKE 74 A4
L. Harden MEEK 24 C4
Harder L. COTT 3 A4
Harding MORR 41 C4
Harding L. BECK 55 F4
Hardtack L. STLS 85 F5
Hardwick ROCK 1 C5
Hardwood L. CARL 51 A5
Hardy L. CASS 48 E5
Hare L. LAKE 75 D2
Harica L. LAKE 75 B1
Harkin-Massopust Store Historic Site NCLT 14 C4
Harlan L. CASS 48 F5
Harley L. BELT 69 F1
Harmony FILL 9 F1
Harmony L. LAKE 87 F1
Harmony Twp FILL 9 F1
Harness L. LAKE 87 F2
L. Harold MEEK 24 A4
Harriet Cr. LAKE 75 C2
L. Harriet HENN 26 C5
Harriet L. CASS 49 A1
Harriet L. LAKE 75 D2
Harriet L. STLS 60 B2
Harrington L. MCLD 25 C1
Harris CHIS 35 B2
Harris Cr. TODD 40 C1
Harris I. STLS 84 A2
Harris L. BLUE 15 E1
Harris L. LAKE 74 C2
Harris L. STLS 61 B5
L. Harrison OTTL 46 B1
Harrison L. CARV 26 D2
Harrison L. ITSC 71 F5
Harrison Twp KAND 32 G2
Harris Twp ITSC 59 D3
Harry Larson Memorial County Forest WRIT 33 E4
Harstad Slough STEV 38 G2
Hart WINA 9 B3
Hartford Twp TODD 40 C2
Hartland FREE 6 C3
Hartland Twp FREE 6 C3
Hartley L. CROW 49 F1
Hartley L. ITSC 71 E4
Hartley Municipal Park STLS 61 G4
Hart L. HUBB 57 B3
Hart L. ITSC 60 B1
Hart L. MAHN 55 B5
Hart L. MEEK 25 A1
Hart L. STLS 61 C3
Hart L. STLS 62 D1
Hart L. SWFT 30 F2
Hart Lake Twp HUBB 57 B3
Hartnette L. STRN 40 G2
Hart Twp WINA 9 B3
Harvey L. STLS 73 G1
Harvey Twp MEEK 32 G4
Hasel Cr. POPE 31 D1
Haskell L. ITSC 71 F3
Haslie L. POLK 67 E5
Hassan Valley Twp MCLD 25 D1
L. Hassel SWFT 31 D1
Hassel L. STLS 85 G4
Hassen Twp HENN 34 G2
Hassman ATKN 50 C2
Hastings DKTA 27 E3
Hastings Wildlife Management Area DKTA 27 F4
Hasty WRIT 33 E4
Hatchet L. LAKE 87 F1
Hatch L. ITSC 71 D1
Hatch L. RICE 16 B3
Hatfield PIPE 1 A5
Hat L. LAKE 87 F2
Hat Point COOK 76 E3
L. Hattie CASS 49 A1
L. Hattie HUBB 56 B5
L. Hattie STEV 30 C2
Haugen Twp ATKN 51 B1
Haughey L. HENN 26 B1
Haunted L. STLS 85 C3
Havana STEL 17 G1
Havana Twp STEL 17 G1
Havelock Twp CHIP 23 B1
Haven L. LAKE 86 F5
Haven Twp SHER 33 C3
Haverhill Twp OLMS 18 G2
Hawick KAND 32 E2
Hawk Bill Point MLLC 42 B3
Hawk Creek Twp RENV 23 E2
Hawk Cr. RENV 23 E2
Hawkeye County Park NBLS 3 G1
Hawkins L. CHIS 35 E4
Hawks Nest L. LAKE 86 G1
Hawks Nest L. LINC 11 B5
Hawley CLAY 54 G5
Hawley Municipal Airport CLAY 54 F5
Hawley Municipal Park CLAY 54 G5
Hawley Twp CLAY 54 G5
Hay Brook Twp KNBC 42 C4
Hay Cr. BECK 55 F2
Hay Cr. BELT 69 C2
Hay Cr. CARL 52 A2
Hay Cr. CHIS 35 C3
Hay Cr. CLAY 45 A4
Hay Cr. GOOD 18 B1
Hay Cr. HUBB 56 E5
Hay Cr. ITSC 60 B1
Hay Cr. ITSC 70 C4
Hay Cr. KCHG 82 F4
Hay Cr. KNBC 42 B4
Hay Cr. MORR 41 E1
Hay Cr. OTTL 47 C4
Hay Cr. PINE 44 B2
Hay Cr. ROSE 92 C1
Hay Cr. WADN 48 D1
Hay Cr. Flowage PINE 44 C2
Haycreek (city) GOOD 18 B1
Hay Creek Twp GOOD 18 B1
Hayden L. HENN 34 G4
Hayden L. TODD 48 F2
Haydenville LQPL 21 B5
Hayes L. ROSE 92 F2
Hayes Lake State Park ROSE 92 F2
Hayes Twp SWFT 31 F3
Hayfield DOGE 7 B4
Hayfield Twp DOGE 7 B3
Hay I. WOOD 97 F3
Hay L. ATKN 59 F5
Hay L. CARL 52 C1
Hay L. CASS 58 G2
Hay L. CROW 49 E4
Hay L. HUBB 57 F3
Hay L. ITSC 59 A3
Hay L. ITSC 60 B1
Hay L. STLS 61 B3
Hay L. STLS 73 C3
Hay L. STLS 73 C3
Hay L. STLS 73 C5
Hay L. STLS 73 E2
Hay L. STLS 73 E3
Hay L. WASH 35 F4
Hay Lake School Historic Site WASH 35 F4
Hayland Twp MLLC 42 F2
Haymanns Cr. NCLT 14 D5
Hayne L. CASS 58 E1
Haynes L. CASS 57 G4
Haypoint ATKN 59 F2
Hayshore L. HOUS 10 F2
Hays L. CLER 56 C4
Hay Stack I. MORR 40 B4
Hayward FREE 6 F5
Hayward Twp FREE 6 E5
Hazel Cr. YMED 22 E4
Hazel L. CASS 58 E1
Hazel L. LAKE 75 A2
Hazel Run (city) YMED 22 E4
Hazel Run Twp YMED 22 E5
Hazeltine L. CARV 26 D2
Hazelton Township Game Refuge KITT 90 D2
Hazelton Twp ATKN 50 F1
Hazelton Twp KITT 90 D2
Head L. BELT 69 B2
Head L. OTTL 47 E1
Headlight L. COOK 87 G5
Headquarters Bay CASS 58 D2
Headquarters L. PINE 52 F1
Headquarters L. STLS 51 A4
Hearding Island STLS 52 A4
Heartbreak Cr. COOK 75 D3
Heartland Corridor Trail HUBB 57 F1
Heart L. BELT 69 B1
Heart L. CLER 56 B3
Heart L. LAKE 74 C3
Hector RENV 24 E3
Hector Municipal Airport RENV 24 F3
Hector Twp RENV 24 E3
Hedlund L. POLK 68 C1
Heffron L. CASS 58 F2
L. Hefta KAND 31 E4
Hegbert Twp SWFT 30 D2
Hegg L. DOUG 38 F5
Hegman L. STLS 85 F5
Hegne Twp NORM 54 B3
Hegre L. CLER 68 E2
Heiberg NORM 55 B1
Heidelberg LSUR 16 B2
Heier Twp MAHN 67 F5
Height of Land L. BECK 56 G1
Height of Land Lake County Park BECK 56 F1
Height of Land Portage Historic Site COOK 88 E1
Height of Land Twp BECK 56 F1
Heikkala L. STLS 73 G1
Heikkila L. STLS 51 A3
Heikkila L. STLS 73 D3
Heilberger L. OTTL 46 E3
Heinen L. ITSC 71 E2
Heinola OTTL 47 E2
Heir Cr. CLER 56 A3
Helena Twp SCOT 26 G2
Helene L. SHER 34 C2
Helen L. COOK 88 F2
Helen L. ITSC 60 B1
Helen L. ITSC 70 D4

Interstate Park CHIS 35 D5
Inver Grove Heights DKTA 27 E2
Inver Hills Community College DKTA 27 D2
Iona MURR 2 B4
Iona Twp MURR 2 B4
Iona Twp TODD 40 C1
Iosco Twp WASC 16 F2
Iota L. COOK 88 G2
Iowa L. COOK 75 B4
Iowa L. JACK 3 G1
Iowa L. MART 4 G5
L. Irene DOUG 39 C3
Irgens L. POPE 38 G5
Irish Cr. COOK 76 F1
Irish Cr. MORR 40 D4
Irish L. BECK 55 G5
Irish L. WATN 4 B2
Iris L. COOK 87 F4
Iron Bridge Recreation Site BELT 69 G1
Iron Cr. CASS 48 E3
Irondale Twp CROW 49 E4
Iron Hub CROW 49 D5
Iron Junction STLS 72 G5
Iron L. COOK 88 E1
Iron L. STLS 73 D5
Iron L. STLS 85 D5
Iron Lake Recreation Site COOK 88 E1
Iron Range Interpretative Center STLS 72 F3
Iron Range Twp ITSC 59 A4
Ironton CROW 49 E4
L. Irving BELT 69 F2
Irving Twp KAND 32 F2
Isaac L. ITSC 71 D2
Isaac L. STLS 73 C4
Isabella LAKE 74 D5
Isabella District Ranger Station LAKE 74 D5
Isabella L. LAKE 74 B5
Isabella R. LAKE 74 B4
L. Isabelle DKTA 27 F4
L. Isabelle STRN 32 A2
Isabelle L. STRN 32 B1
ISANTI — 34 —
Isanti ISNT 34 C5
Isanti Twp ISNT 34 C5
Isedor Iverson Airport ATKN 50 C4
Island Camp Game Refuge OTTL 47 G1
Island L. ANOK 35 E1
Island L. ATKN 50 B5
Island L. BECK 55 E4
Island L. BECK 56 F2
Island L. BECK 56 G3
Island L. BELT 69 C1
Island L. CARL 51 C3
Island L. CASS 57 G5
Island L. CASS 58 F4
Island L. CASS 58 G1
Island L. CLER 56 B2
Island L. CROW 49 B3
Island L. CROW 49 B4
Island L. CROW 49 B5
Island L. CROW 49 C2
Island L. CROW 49 D4
Island L. CROW 49 F5
Island L. CROW 49 G1
Island L. GRNT 38 D3
Island L. HUBB 56 E5
Island L. HUBB 57 D2
Island L. HUBB 57 F3
Island L. HUBB 57 G2
Island L. ITSC 59 A3
Island L. ITSC 59 A4
Island L. ITSC 70 B2
Island L. ITSC 71 A5
Island L. ITSC 71 B4
Island L. ITSC 71 G1
Island L. LYON 12 C2
Island L. MAHN 68 G1
Island L. PINE 51 F4
Island L. (Reservoir) STLS 61 E3
Island L. STLS 60 C2
Island L. STLS 72 E2
Island L. STLS 73 C4
Island L. STRN 33 C1
Island L. STRN 33 E1
Island Lake (city) BELT 69 C1
Island Lake County Park CARL 51 C3
Island Lake Twp LYON 12 C2
Island Lake Twp MAHN 68 F1
Island R. ITSC 71 G1
Island R. LAKE 74 B5
Island R. LAKE 75 C1
Island View KCHG 95 F5
Isle MLLC 42 B3
Isle Harbor MLLC 42 B3
Isle Harbor Twp MLLC 42 C3
Isle L. BELT 68 B5
Isle Municipal Airport MLLC 42 B3
Isle of Pines STLS 73 B2
Isle of Refuge KAND 31 E5
Isle of Refuge Historic Site KAND 31 E4
Islet Bay LAKE 62 B5
ITASCA — 59 —
Itasca Bison Historic Site CLER 56 C4
L. Itasca CLER 56 C4
Itasca Community College ITSC 59 B3
Itasca County Historical Society Museum ITSC 59 B2
Itasca L. ANOK 34 F3
Itasca State Park CLER 56 C4
Itasca Twp CLER 56 B4
Ivanhoe LINC 11 B5
Ivan L. HUBB 57 F1
Iverson CARL 52 C1
Iverson L. BELT 68 D5
Iverson L. CASS 58 D2
Iverson L. OTTL 38 A2
Ivis L. COOK 87 F4
Ivory L. COOK 88 E3
IXL L. CASS 58 F1
Jack Cr. JACK 3 D2
Jack Cr. LAKE 74 C5
Jackel L. COOK 88 F2
Jackfish Bay KCHG 95 F5
Jackfish Bay LAKE 86 F2
Jackfish I. KCHG 95 F5
Jackfish L. LAKE 86 E2
Jack Haw L. BECK 55 D5
Jack L. CASS 57 E5
Jack L. CASS 58 F2
Jack L. COOK 75 A4
Jack L. ITSC 71 F4
Jack L. LAKE 74 C5
Jack L. MAHN 55 C5
Jack Pine Cr. LAKE 74 C5
Jackpine L. CASS 57 F4
Jack Pine L. CROW 41 G4
Jack Pine Mountain LAKE 74 C3
Jackpot Cr. LAKE 74 D2
Jackrabbit I. STLS 73 B2
Jacks L. CROW 49 F2
JACKSON — 3 —
Jackson JACK 3 E5
Jackson County Historical Society Museum JACK 3 E4
Jackson County Rock Fossil and Indian Museum JACK 3 E5
Jackson L. CLER 56 A2
Jackson L. COOK 76 F1
Jackson Municipal Airport JACK 3 E5
Jackson Twp SCOT 26 E3
Jack The Horse L. ITSC 71 E2
Jacob L. STLS 86 F1
L. Jacobs OTTL 46 D1
Jacobs L. STLS 61 E4
Jacobs L. TODD 40 D3
Jacobson ATKN 59 E5
Jacobson County Park ATKN 60 E5
Jacobson L. TODD 48 G2
Jacobs Prairie STRN 33 C1
Jadis Twp ROSE 91 C5
Jaeger L. TODD 40 A3
Jail L. CROW 49 A1
Jakeville BENT 41 G4
James Bay COOK 87 D4
James J. Hill House Historic Site RAMS 27 C1
James L. STLS 62 B1
James L. STLS 73 D5
Jamestown Twp BLUE 15 E5
James W. Wilkie Regional Park SCOT 26 E4
Jam L. COOK 87 F3
Janesville WASC 16 F1
Janesville Twp WASC 16 F1
Janet L. STLS 60 B2
L. Jane WASH 27 B3
Jap L. COOK 87 E3
Jarrett WBSH 18 E3
Jaskari L. CARL 51 B4
Jasmer L. TODD 48 G2
Jasper PIPE 1 B3
Jasper L. COOK 87 E2
Jasper L. LAKE 86 G3
Java L. COOK 87 G4
Jay Cooke State Park CARL 52 C2
Jay Gould L. ITSC 59 B2
Jay L. ATKN 51 C1
Jay L. BECK 55 G3
Jay L. COOK 87 F4
Jay L. MAHN 55 C5
Jaynes ITSC 71 D1
Jay Twp MART 4 E2
Jeanette Cr. STLS 85 E3
Jeanette L. STLS 85 E2
Jean L. ITSC 71 D3
Jean L. STLS 72 D3
Jeffers COTT 13 G4
L. Jefferson LSUR 16 D1
Jefferson Twp HOUS 10 F2
Jeffers Petroglyph Historic Site COTT 13 F5
Jegtvig L. CLAY 46 A1
Jenkins CROW 49 C1
Jenkins L. ATKN 50 C3
Jenkins Twp CROW 49 B1
Jennie MEEK 25 B1
L. Jennie MEEK 25 B1
Jennie L. DOUG 38 D5
Jennings Bay HENN 26 C2
Jennison L. CROW 41 A5
L. Jennum POPE 31 B2
Jenny L. LAKE 87 E2
Jensen L. DKTA 27 E1
Jeppson L. POLK 67 D5
Jergenson L. CLAY 55 G1
Jerky L. LAKE 86 F4
Jerry Cr. STLS 85 E5
Jerry L. COOK 87 F3
Jessenland Twp SBLY 25 G4
L. Jessie OTTL 39 B1
Jessie L. BELT 69 F4
Jessie L. DOUG 39 E3
Jessie L. ITSC 70 E5
Jessie L. MAHN 55 C5
Jessie Lake (city) ITSC 70 E5
Jevne Twp ATKN 50 C4
Jewell L. LAKE 86 G3
Jewett L. MEEK 25 B1
Jewett L. OTTL 46 E2
Jidana City Park HENN 26 C3
Jig L. COOK 87 F3
Jig L. STLS 85 G4
Jim Cook L. WADN 48 B1
Jim L. COOK 88 F3
Jim L. CROW 49 E5
Jim L. OTTL 46 B5
Jim L. TODD 40 F3
Jimmy L. COOK 87 E3
Jingo L. ITSC 71 D1
Jink L. LAKE 86 F4
Jinks L. CROW 41 B1
Jitterbug L. LAKE 86 F5
Jock Mock Bay COOK 87 G5
Jock Mock L. COOK 75 A5
Jock Mock Point COOK 87 G5
Jo Daviess Twp FRBT 5 E2
Joel L. ITSC 71 D2
Joe R. KITT 89 A5
Joe Slough REDW 23 F3
L. Johanna POPE 31 C4
L. Johanna RAMS 27 B1
L. Johannes OTTL 38 B4
John A. Latsch State Wayside Park WINA 19 F2
John Anderson Memorial County Park ANOK 34 D5
John Ek L. LAKE 87 F2
John L. COOK 88 E5
John L. LAKE 74 B4
John L. OTTL 38 A2
John L. OTTL 46 D2
John L. OTTL 46 G4
John L. POPE 39 G2
Johnsburg MOWE 7 G4
Johnson BGST 29 B5
Johnson Bay NCLT 15 D2
Johnson Cr. STLS 74 A1
Johnson Cr. STRN 33 D2
L. Johnson OTTL 38 B4
L. Johnson SWFT 31 E1
Johnson L. ATKN 50 D2
Johnson L. ATKN 50 E3
Johnson L. BECK 46 B4
Johnson L. BECK 55 D4
Johnson L. BECK 56 D1
Johnson L. BECK 56 F1
Johnson L. BELT 68 B5
Johnson L. CARV 26 F1
Johnson L. CASS 58 C5
Johnson L. CASS 58 E3
Johnson L. CLER 68 C3
Johnson L. CROW 49 D2
Johnson L. DOUG 39 E2
Johnson L. GRNT 38 F2
Johnson L. ITSC 71 E2
Johnson L. ITSC 71 G2
Johnson L. ITSC 72 D1
Johnson L. ITSC 72 F1
Johnson L. KAND 24 B2
Johnson L. LAKE 75 G1
Johnson L. MORR 40 B5
Johnson L. MORR 40 D4
Johnson L. OTTL 46 E3
Johnson L. OTTL 46 F1
Johnson L. PINE 51 F4
Johnson L. POPE 31 D3
Johnson L. STLS 61 C2
Johnson L. STLS 73 B5
Johnson L. STLS 84 C5
Johnson Slough SHER 34 D1
Johnson Landing Recreation Site KCHG 83 F1
Johnson Twp POLK 68 A1
Johnsonville Twp REDW 13 D2
L. John WRIT 33 F2
Joki Cr. STLS 60 C5
Jolly Ann L. OTTL 38 B4
Jonason L. CHIS 35 B1
Jones L. BECK 46 A5
Jones L. BECK 56 F2
Jones L. OTTL 46 F4
Jones L. SHER 33 D4
Jones Twp BELT 68 F5
Jonvick Cr. COOK 76 C1
Jopp L. STRN 32 B4
Jordan SCOT 26 F2
Jordan L. LAKE 86 F5
Jordan Twp FILL 8 C3
Jorgens L. STLS 84 A3
Jorgenson L. POPE 39 G1
Jorgrson L. DOUG 38 E5
L. Josephine RAMS 27 B1
L. Josephine SHER 34 D1
Josephine L. CLER 56 C4
Joseph L. STLS 73 C4
Joseph R. Brown House Historic Site RENV 23 F3
Joseph R. Brown State Wayside RENV 23 F3
Jotan L. OTTL 38 A3
Joy L. ITSC 71 B4
Jubert L. HENN 26 B2
Judge C. R. Magney State Park COOK 76 A5
Judson BLUE 15 E2
Judson Twp BLUE 15 F2
Juergens L. TODD 40 E1
Juggler L. BECK 56 D2
Juggler L. LAKE 86 F4
Jug I. STLS 84 A2
Jug I. STLS 84 B4
Jug L. LAKE 87 F2
L. Julia BELT 69 D2
L. Julia SHER 33 C4
Julia L. MURR 13 G1
Julius C. Wilkie Steamboat Museum WINA 19 G4
Jump L. COOK 88 F1
Jump L. LAKE 87 F2
Junco Cr. COOK 76 A2
Junco L. COOK 76 A2
Junction Bay STLS 84 B4
June L. COOK 75 A3
June L. CROW 49 E4
Juni L. BRWN 14 E4
Juniper I. STLS 84 B5
Juniper L. COOK 87 F4
Juno L. COOK 87 G5
Jupiter L. LAKE 75 A1
Jupiter Twp KITT 90 E3
Jut L. LAKE 86 G5
Kaapoo L. LAKE 87 G1
Kabekona Bay CASS 57 D4
Kabekona L. HUBB 57 C3
Kabekona R. HUBB 57 B2
Kabetogama STLS 84 A1
Kabetogama L. STLS 84 A2
Kabetogama State Forest STLS 84 F4
Kabgone's Point BELT 69 A1
Kabustasa L. STLS 84 D5
Kadunce R. COOK 76 A4
Kahlstorf L. HUBB 57 C1
Kahtava L. STLS 73 G3
Kaiak L. LAKE 87 F2
Kale L. LAKE 87 E2
Kaleva Bay STLS 73 A4
Kalevala Twp CARL 51 D3
Kalla L. STRN 32 B5
Kallio L. LAKE 87 F2
Kalmar Twp OLMS 18 G1
Kamimela L. LAKE 86 G3
KANABEC — 42 —
Kanabec County Historical Society Museum KNBC 42 E5
Kanabec Twp KNBC 42 F3
Kanaranzi ROCK 2 F1
Kanaranzi Cr. NBLS 2 F1
Kanaranzi Twp ROCK 2 F1
KANDIYOHI — 23 —
Kandiyohi KAND 24 A1
Kandiyohi County Historical Society Museum KAND 23 A5
Kandiyohi County Park No. 1 KAND 24 C1
Kandiyohi County Park No. 2 KAND 24 B1
Kandiyohi County Park No. 3 KAND 32 G2
Kandiyohi County Park No. 4 KAND 32 F1
Kandiyohi County Park No. 5 KAND 32 F2
Kandiyohi County Park No. 7 KAND 31 E5
Kandiyohi Twp KAND 24 A1
Kandota Twp TODD 40 F1
Kane L. BECK 56 D4
Kane L. LAKE 62 A3
Kane L. SCOT 26 F4
Kangas Bay STLS 74 C1
Kangas L. ATKN 59 F2
Kangas L. STLS 74 C1
Kansas L. BECK 56 D3
Kansas L. WATN 4 B3
Kansas Lake County Park WATN 4 B3
Kapla L. STLS 72 G5
Kapland Woods Municipal Park STEL 16 G5
Kari L. LAKE 74 G4
Karl L. COOK 87 F4
Karl Slough BGST 29 D4
Karlstad KITT 90 F4
Karlstad Municipal Airport KITT 90 F4
Kasota LSUR 15 D4
L. Kasota KAND 24 B1
Kasota Twp LSUR 15 D4
Kasson DOGE 17 G4
Katherine L. LAKE 74 F4
Kathio Historic Site and State Indian Museum MLLC 42 B1
Kathio-Mille Lacs Kathio State Park Historic Site MLLC 42 B1
Kathio Twp MLLC 42 B1
L. Katie BECK 47 A3
Katrina L. HENN 26 B2
Katydid L. LAKE 75 D1
Katzel L. CARL 51 D5
Kaunonen L. STLS 73 D4
Kauppi L. STLS 61 C1
Kawasachong L. LAKE 75 A2
Kawawia I. STLS 96 G3
Kawishiwi District Ranger Station STLS 74 A1
Kawishiwi Lake Recreation Site LAKE 75 B2
Kawishiwi L. LAKE 75 B2
Kawishiwi R. LAKE 74 A4
Kawishiwi R. LAKE 75 A2
Kayoskh L. LAKE 74 A4
Kedron Bk. FILL 8 C2
Keeley Cr. LAKE 74 B2
Keenan L. STLS 72 G5
Keene L. PINE 44 C2
Keene Twp CLAY 54 E5
Keewatin ITSC 72 G1
Kegan L. DKTA 27 E1
Kego L. CASS 58 E2
Kego L. CROW 49 A3
Kego Twp CASS 58 E2
Keith L. SWFT 30 D1
Keitzman Slough GRNT 38 F2
Kekekabic L. LAKE 87 F1
Kekekabic Ponds LAKE 87 E2
Kek L. LAKE 87 E1
Keller L. POLK 67 D4
Keller L. RAMS 27 B2
Keller L. TODD 40 D1
Kelliher BELT 69 A5
Kelliher Twp BELT 69 A5
Kellogg WBSH 19 D1
Kelly L. ATKN 51 C1
Kelly L. CARV 26 F1
Kelly L. CASS 48 D4
Kelly L. COOK 75 A4
Kelly L. ITSC 71 D4
Kelly L. RICE 16 D4
Kelly Lake (city) STLS 72 G2
Kelsey STLS 60 C5
Kelsey L. STLS 85 C4
Kelsey Twp STLS 60 C5
Kelso L. COOK 75 A3
Kelso L. COOK 87 G3
Kelso R. COOK 87 G3
Kelso Twp SBLY 15 B3
Kemo L. COOK 88 G2
Kempeska Trail Historic Site YMED 21 E4
Kempton Bay STLS 96 G3
Kempton Channel STLS 96 G3
Kempton L. LAKE 86 G2
Kener L. STLS 85 F5
Kennedy KITT 90 E1
Kennedy L. BECK 55 G4
Kennedy L. ITSC 71 F5
Kennedy L. LAKE 75 G1
Kenneth ROCK 2 D1
Kenney L. CROW 49 G5
Kenney L. GRNT 38 D3
Kenney L. PINE 44 C1
Kenny L. HUBB 57 B2
Kenogama L. ITSC 70 F1
Kensington DOUG 38 F5
Kensington Runestone Discovery Historic Site DOUG 38 F5
Kent WILK 45 E2
Kent L. KNBC 42 F4
Kenyon GOOD 17 D2
Kenyon Twp GOOD 17 E2
Kepper L. STRN 32 B5
Kerfoot Lakes COOK 87 E4
Kerkhoven SWFT 31 G3
Kerkhoven Twp SWFT 31 E3
Kerrick PINE 51 F5
Kerrick Twp PINE 51 F5
Kerr L. CASS 58 F1
Kerry L. SBLY 25 F5
Kertsonville Twp POLK 66 C5
Kesagiagan L. BELT 68 B5
Ketchum L. MAHN 67 F5
Ketten L. STRN 33 C1
Kettle Channel STLS 96 G4
Kettle Cr. BECK 47 B3
Kettle L. CARL 51 C4
Kettle L. HUBB 57 G3
Kettle L. LAKE 87 E1
Kettle R. CARL 51 E3
Kettle R. PINE 43 D4
Kettle River (city) CARL 51 E3
Kettle River Twp PINE 51 G3
Keyes L. OTTL 46 B5
Keystone Twp POLK 78 G2
Key West POLK 78 G2
Kiana L. LAKE 86 G5
Kibbee L. CLER 56 C2
Kibler L. LQPL 29 G4
Kickshaw L. LAKE 87 F2
Kid L. CASS 58 F1
Kidney L. CASS 58 F4
Kieseling House Historic Site BRWN 14 D5
Kiester FRBT 6 G1
Kiester L. MART 4 D5
Kiester Twp FRBT 6 F1
Kildare Twp SWFT 31 F2
Kilen Woods State Park JACK 3 D5
Kilkenny LSUR 16 D2
Kilkenny Twp LSUR 16 D2
Killdeer L. ITSC 70 D4
Kimball STRN 33 E1
Kimball Cr. COOK 76 A4
Kimball L. COOK 76 A4
Kimball L. CROW 49 C2
Kimball L. HUBB 57 B2
Kimball Lake Recreation Site COOK 76 A4
Kimball Twp JACK 4 C1
Kimberly ATKN 50 D3
Kimberly Twp ATKN 50 D3
Kimberly Wildlife Management Area ATKN 50 D4
Kinbrae NBLS 3 C1
Kingburg L. STLS 60 G4
King Cr. WBSH 18 C4
Kingfisher L. COOK 87 E2
Kinghurst Twp ITSC 70 D3

Liberty Twp BELT 69 D1
Liberty Twp ITSC 70 C5
Liberty Twp POLK 66 E5
Lichen L. COOK 75 A5
L. Lida OTTL 46 C3
Lida Twp OTTL 46 D3
Lieberg L. BLUE 15 F1
Lien Twp GRNT 38 E3
Lieung L. STLS 61 D5
Life Raft L. CASS 57 B5
Light Foot L. WRIT 33 G4
Lightning L. GRNT 38 C2
L. Lillian KAND 24 C2
Lillian L. ITSC 59 A1
Lillian L. LAKE 74 G4
Lillian L. STLS 73 F4
Lilly L. WASC 16 F1
Lily Cr. MART 4 E4
Lilydale DKTA 27 C1
Lily L. ATKN 50 E1
Lily L. ATKN 50 E3
Lily L. BLUE 15 F2
Lily L. CASS 49 A2
Lily L. COOK 87 G5
Lily L. ITSC 59 C3
Lily L. OTTL 46 D5
Lily L. TODD 40 F1
Lily L. WASC 16 E2
Lily L. WASH 27 B4
Lily Pad L. CROW 49 B3
Lilypad L. HUBB 57 A1
Lima L. COOK 88 F2
Lima Twp CASS 58 E5
Lime Cr. MURR 2 B5
Lime Cr. MURR 3 B1
Lime Creek (city) MURR 2 B5
Lime L. BECK 55 F2
Lime L. MURR 2 A5
Lime Lake County Park MURR 2 A5
Lime Lake Twp MURR 2 A5
Limestone L. WRIT 33 E4
Limestone Twp LINC 12 B1
Lime Twp BLUE 15 E4
Linbolm L. BECK 56 F3
LINCOLN — 11 —
Lincoln MORR 40 A4
Lincoln County Historical Society Museum LINC 11 A3
Lincoln I. LAKE 86 F3
Lincoln Twp BLUE 15 G1
Lincoln Twp MRSH 90 G5
Lindberg L. CLER 68 D2
Linde L. ATKN 50 E2
Linden Grove STLS 72 B3
Linden Grove Twp STLS 72 B3
L. Linden HENN 26 D2
Linden L. BRWN 14 F5
Linden L. ITSC 71 F2
Linden Twp BRWN 14 F5
Lindford KCHG 82 B5
Lindgren L. BELT 69 D2
Lindgren L. BGST 29 D4
Lindgren L. KAND 31 G4
Lind L. BECK 46 B4
Lind L. CASS 48 A5
Lindsell Twp MRSH 80 A1
Lindstrom CHIS 35 D3
Lind Twp ROSE 91 F1
Line L. MORR 40 B4
Lingroth L. ATKN 50 E2
L. Linka POPE 31 C3
Link L. LAKE 87 D2
Linn L. CHIS 35 E4
Linn Lake Game Refuge CHIS 35 E4
Lino Lakes (city) ANOK 35 G1
Linwood ANOK 35 E1
Linwood L. ANOK 35 E1
Linwood L. STLS 61 A4
Linwood Twp ANOK 35 D1
Lions Municipal Park SCOT 26 E3
Lippert L. CARV 25 C5
Lisbon Twp YMED 22 D4
Lismore NBLS 2 D2
Lismore Twp NBLS 2 D2
Litchfield MEEK 24 A4
Litchfield Municipal Airport MEEK 24 A5
Litchfield Nature Center MEEK 24 B4
Litchfield Twp MEEK 24 A4
Litomysl STEL 7 B1
Little Alden L. STLS 61 D5
Little Anna L. OTTL 46 F4
Little Ann R. KNBC 42 D4
Little Antler L. ITSC 71 D3
Little Arm L. ITSC 71 F3
Little Armstrong L. STLS 73 B4
Little Badger Cr. FRBT 5 E2
Little Ball Bluff L. ATKN 59 F5
Little Ball Club L. ITSC 70 G4
Little Bass L. BECK 55 D5
Little Bass L. BELT 69 F3
Little Bass L. CASS 57 E4
Little Bass L. CASS 58 F4
Little Bass L. CROW 49 C4
Little Bass L. CROW 49 D3
Little Bass L. HUBB 57 E3
Little Bass L. ITSC 59 B2
Little Bass L. ITSC 71 E2
Little Bass L. STLS 86 F1
Little Basswood L. BECK 56 D3
Little Bay L. CASS 57 G5
Little Bear Island CASS 58 D2
Little Bear L. ITSC 71 D4
Little Bear L. LAKE 74 C4
Little Bear L. MCLD 25 C1
Little Beartrack L. STLS 85 C3
Little Beaver Cr. ROCK 1 E4
Little Bemidji L. BECK 56 D1
Little Birch L. CASS 58 E5
Little Birch L. STLS 73 C3
Little Birch L. STLS 73 C4
Little Birch L. TODD 40 F2
Little Blackhoof L. CROW 49 E4
Little Black R. RDLK 78 G5
Little Bowstring L. ITSC 71 F1
Little Boyer L. BECK 55 F2
Little Boy L. CASS 58 F2
Little Brick I. COOK 76 E4
Little Brule R. COOK 76 A5
Little Buck L. ITSC 71 F5
Little Buzzle L. BELT 68 E5
Little Calf L. ITSC 70 B3
Little Canada RAMS 27 B1
Little Cannon R. GOOD 17 C3
Little Caribou L. COOK 88 E3
Little Carnelian L. WASH 27 A4
Little Cascade L. COOK 75 A5
Little Cedar R. MOWE 7 F4
Little Chicago RICE 16 B5
Little Chippewa L. DOUG 39 D1
Little Chippewa R. POPE 30 B5
Little Cloquet R. STLS 61 D5
Little Cobb R. BLUE 5 A5
Little Constance L. KCHG 70 B2
Little Coon L. ANOK 35 E1
Little Coon L. ITSC 71 C3
Little Copper L. COOK 87 F4
Little Cormorant L. BECK 46 A3
Little Cotton L. BECK 55 F5
Little Cottonwood L. ITSC 71 G1
Little Cottonwood R. BRWN 14 E4
Little Cowhorn L. ITSC 59 D4
Little Coyote L. STLS 62 C1
Little Crab L. STLS 85 G4
Little Cranberry L. CROW 49 A2
Little Cranberry L. TODD 40 B3
Little Crow L. OTTL 46 C3
Little Cut Foot Sioux L. ITSC 70 F4
Little Dead Horse L. ITSC 71 F2
Little Deep L. CASS 58 F1
Little Deep L. CASS 58 G1
Little Deer L. ITSC 59 A1
Little Devil Track R. COOK 76 B3
Little Diamond L. ITSC 59 A4
Little Dick L. ITSC 71 E2
Little Dinner L. BECK 56 D4
Little Dixon L. ITSC 70 D1
Little Drum L. ITSC 59 B1
Little East Cr. STLS 85 G1
Little East L. ITSC 71 E3
Little Elbow Cr. MAHN 56 C1
Little Elbow L. MAHN 56 C1
Little Elbow L. STLS 84 F4
Little Elbow Lake State Park MAHN 56 C1
Little Elk L. CLER 56 C4
Little Elk R. MORR 40 B4
Little Elk Twp TODD 40 C3
Little Esquagama L. STLS 73 F2
Little Falls (city) MORR 41 D1
Little Falls Morrison County Airport MORR 41 E1
Little Falls Twp MORR 41 D1
Little Fish Trap L. TODD 40 A3
Little Flat L. BECK 55 E5
Little Floyd L. BECK 55 G4
Little Fork KCHG 83 B2
Little Fork Municipal Airport KCHG 83 B2
Little Fork R. KCHG 83 E3
Little Fowler L. ITSC 60 B1
Little Freeborn L. DOUG 39 F1
Little Gabbro L. LAKE 74 B3
Little Ganz L. MORR 40 E4
Little Gilstad L. BELT 69 D5
Little Gooseberry R. LAKE 62 C2
Little Goose L. CASS 58 F5
Little Green L. CHIS 35 E3
Little Gunflint L. COOK 88 E1
Little Ham L. HUBB 57 F3
Little Hanging Horn L. CARL 51 E5
Little Harriet L. STLS 60 B2
Little Hay Cr. PINE 43 D5
Little Hill R. ATKN 59 F1
Little Horn L. ITSC 71 G2
Little Horseshoe L. CHIS 35 B2
Little Horseshoe L. HUBB 57 C3
Little Indian Sioux R. STLS 85 E3
Little Inkey L. ITSC 59 A3
Little Iowa R. MOWE 8 F2
Little Iron L. COOK 87 E5
Little Isabella R. LAKE 74 C4
Little Isabella River Recreation Site LAKE 74 D4
Little Island L. ITSC 71 F3
Little Jessie L. ITSC 70 E5
Little Jim L. COOK 88 F3
Little John L. COOK 88 E5
Little Johnson L. STLS 84 B4
Little Kandiyohi L. KAND 24 B1
Little Kettle L. CARL 51 C4
Little Knife R. STLS 62 E1
Little L. BECK 56 G4
Little L. CHIS 35 D4
Little L. COOK 76 B3
Little L. OTTL 46 G3
Little L. STLS 61 A2
Little L. STLS 74 B1
Little L. Fourteen STLS 72 D4
Little L. Hubert CROW 49 E2
Little L. Vermilion STLS 85 D2
Little Leighton L. ITSC 59 C1
Little Long L. BECK 56 G4
Little Long L. CASS 48 E5
Little Long L. ITSC 71 F2
Little Long L. OTTL 46 D4
Little Long L. STLS 61 C2
Little Long L. STLS 86 G1
Little Loon L. STLS 85 C3
Little Lost L. BELT 69 F4
Little Lost L. STLS 73 A4
Little Lost L. STLS 73 B1
Little Mantrap L. BECK 56 D4
Little Marais LAKE 75 G2
Little Marais R. LAKE 75 F2
Little Markham L. STLS 61 A3
Little Mayhew L. COOK 87 E5
Little McCarthy L. ITSC 71 G5
Little McDonald L. OTTL 46 C5
Little McKinney L. ATKN 59 G1
Little McQuade L. STLS 72 G4
Little Mesaba L. STLS 73 E3
Little Mill L. TODD 40 C3
Little Minnesota R. BGST 29 B1
Little Mississippi R. BELT 68 F4
Little Moose L. BELT 69 E5
Little Moose L. ITSC 71 C5
Little Moose L. ITSC 71 D5
Little Moose L. ITSC 71 G2
Little Moss L. CASS 57 B4
Little Mound L. TODD 40 F3
Little Mud Hen L. STLS 61 A2
Little Mud L. BECK 56 E4
Little Mud L. BECK 56 G1
Little Mud L. CASS 58 D5
Little Mud L. MEEK 32 F5
Little Mud L. PINE 51 G3
Little Neck L. ITSC 71 D3
Little Net R. CARL 52 E2
Little Nokasippi R. CROW 41 B1
Little North L. COOK 88 E1
Little North Star L. ITSC 71 E1
Little Oak I. WOOD 97 E3
Little Oak L. MAHN 55 B4
Little Oak L. PINE 51 F5
Little O'Brien L. ITSC 60 A1
Little Ole L. ITSC 71 E2
Little O'Reilly L. ITSC 59 A3
Little Osakis L. TODD 39 D5
Little Otter Cr. CARL 52 C1
Little Ox L. CROW 49 B3
Little Paleface L. STLS 61 B2
Little Partridge Cr. TODD 48 F1
Little Pearl L. BECK 46 A3
Little Pelican L. CROW 49 D2
Little Pelican L. OTTL 46 B3
Little Pelican L. STRN 32 A5
Little Peppermint Cr. WOOD 93 E3
Little Pine L. ATKN 50 E1
Little Pine L. CLER 68 D2
Little Pine L. CROW 49 A5
Little Pine L. CROW 49 B3
Little Pine L. OTTL 47 C1
Little Pine L. PINE 43 A2
Little Pine L. STRN 32 A5
Little Pine Lake Game Refuge OTTL 47 C1
Little Pine R. CROW 49 C4
Little Pine Twp CROW 49 A5
Little Pony R. STLS 85 F3
Little Porky L. ITSC 71 E3
Little Portage Bay COOK 76 E4
Little Portage L. CASS 58 A1
Little Portage L. CASS 58 G1
Little Prairie L. ATKN 51 A1
Little Puposky L. BELT 69 D1
Little Rabbit L. CROW 49 E3
Little Rat L. BECK 55 D5
Little Red Horse L. ATKN 59 G5
Little Red School House Historic Site STRN 40 G1
Little Reservoir L. CASS 58 G5
Little Rice L. BECK 56 D1
Little Rice L. BELT 69 C2
Little Rice L. BELT 69 F4
Little Rice L. ITSC 59 C1
Little Rice L. MAHN 55 B5
Little Rice L. STLS 73 C1
Little Rice L. STLS 73 E2
Little Rice L. STLS 85 F5
Little Rice L. STRN 32 C4
Little Rice L. TODD 40 D3
Little Rock MORR 41 F3
Little Rock Cr. BELT 68 B5
Little Rock Cr. MORR 41 F2
Little Rock Cr. RENV 14 B3
Little Rock L. BENT 33 A2
Little Rock L. BENT 41 G3
Little Rock L. CLER 56 C2
Little Rock L. WRIT 33 G4
Little Rock Point COOK 87 E4
Little Rock R. NBLS 2 F3
Little Rock Twp NBLS 2 F3
Little Rose L. ITSC 71 D1
Little Rose L. OTTL 46 B4
Little Round L. BECK 55 F5
Little Round L. BECK 56 G4
Little Rush L. COOK 88 E1
Little Saganaga L. COOK 87 F3
Little Sand L. CASS 49 A1
Little Sand L. CASS 58 D4
Little Sand L. HUBB 57 E1
Little Sand L. ITSC 59 B4
Little Sand L. ITSC 70 D4
Little Sand L. STLS 72 D5
Little Sandy L. STLS 72 D4
Little Sauk TODD 40 E1
Little Sauk L. TODD 40 E1
Little Sauk Twp TODD 40 E1
Little Shell L. STLS 85 D3
Little Shoepack L. STLS 84 A3
Little Sioux R. JACK 3 F3
Little Siseebakwet L. ITSC 59 C1
Little Skeleton L. STLS 73 B4
Little Skunk L. CASS 58 C5
Little Sletten L. STLS 86 G1
Little Smith L. ITSC 71 E2
Little Snow L. COOK 75 B3
Little Spearhead L. HUBB 57 A1
Little Split Hand L. ITSC 59 D3
Little Spring L. ITSC 70 E5
Little Spring L. MEEK 25 B2
Little Sprit L. JACK 3 G4
Little Spruce L. ATKN 49 F5
Little Stanchfield L. ISNT 34 B5
Little Star L. CROW 49 C2
Little Stewart R. LAKE 62 D2
Little Stone L. STLS 62 B1
Little Stony Cr. COOK 88 F4
Little Stony L. HUBB 57 G2
Little Sucker L. ITSC 59 A5
Little Sugar Bush L. BECK 55 E5
Little Susie I. COOK 76 E4
Little Swamp Cr. WADN 48 C2
Little Swan STLS 60 B3
Little Swan Cr. CASS 48 E3
Little Swan L. MEEK 25 A1
Little Swan L. TODD 40 E3
Little Swan R. TODD 40 D3
Little Swift L. CASS 58 D3
Little Tamarack L. BECK 55 E5
Little Tamarack L. PINE 44 C1
Little Thirtynine Cr. LAKE 62 A5
Little Thunder L. CASS 58 F4
Little Thunder L. CASS 58 F5
Little Toad L. BECK 56 G1
Little Tony L. STLS 60 A5
Little Trout L. COOK 88 F2
Little Trout L. ITSC 71 G2
Little Trout L. STLS 84 B5
Little Trout L. STLS 85 G2
Little Trump L. COOK 87 F5
Little Turtle L. ATKN 50 E1
Little Turtle L. BELT 69 D2
Little Turtle L. CASS 57 E5
Little Turtle L. ITSC 71 E1
Little Twin L. CASS 57 B4
Little Twin L. MART 4 D2
Little Two R. MORR 40 F5
Little Vanose L. MAHN 67 G4
Little Vermillion L. CASS 58 C5
Little Wabana L. ITSC 71 G3
Little Wampus L. LAKE 74 D3
Little Wasson L. ITSC 71 D4
Little Watab L. STRN 32 C5
Little Waverly L. WRIT 25 B4
Little Webb L. CASS 57 F5
Little White Dog County Park WADN 48 D2
Little Whiteface R. STLS 60 D5
Little Whitefish L. ITSC 70 D4
Little White Oak L. ITSC 59 B1
Little Winnibigoshish L. ITSC 70 G4
Little Wolf L. CASS 69 G4
Little Wolf L. ITSC 71 F2
Little Wolf L. ITSC 71 F3
Little Wolf L. MEEK 25 C1
Littner L. STRN 32 A4
Livingston Log Cabin MART 4 E5
Livonia Twp SHER 34 D2
Lizard L. CASS 58 F1
Lizard L. COOK 87 F5
Lizard L. CROW 49 C3
Lizotte L. CASS 49 B1
Lizzard L. MAHN 55 B5
Lizzie L. BECK 47 A1
Lizzie L. CROW 49 A1
L. Lizzie OTTL 46 C3
Lizz L. COOK 88 F1
Loaine L. STLS 62 C1
Lobo L. LAKE 74 E2
Lobster L. DOUG 39 E1
Local BECK 56 G1
Locator L. STLS 96 G2
Lochness City Park ANOK 35 G1
Locke L. WRIT 33 E4
Locke Municipal Park ANOK 26 A5
Locket L. COOK 88 F3
Lockhart NORM 66 F3
Lockhart I. STLS 85 G5
Lockhart Twp NORM 66 F4
Lodemier L. MORR 41 B2
Lodi Twp MOWE 7 F5
Loft L. COOK 88 F5
Logan L. PINE 51 F4
Logan Twp ATKN 50 B3
Logan Twp GRNT 38 F1
Logger L. COOK 88 G3
Logger L. MAHN 55 C5
Logue L. RICE 16 C3
Lois L. LAKE 74 B5
Loiten L. STLS 96 G2
Loki L. LAKE 87 E2
Loman KCHG 82 A5
Loman County Park KCHG 82 A5
Lomish L. CASS 58 D3
L. Lomond CLER 68 F3
London FREE 7 G2
London Twp FREE 7 F1
Lone Cr. COOK 87 D3
Lone L. ATKN 50 E1
Lone L. CLER 68 E2
Lone L. COOK 87 D3
Lone L. HENN 26 D4
Lone L. MAHN 56 A1
Lonely L. COOK 87 E5
Lone Pine L. CROW 49 A3
Lone Pine L. OTTL 46 D5
Lone Pine Twp ITSC 60 A1
Lonergan L. STEL 6 B4
Lone Squaw I. STLS 84 A3
Lone Tree L. BRWN 14 B2
Lone Tree L. YMED 23 F2
Lone Tree Slough BGST 29 C4
Lone Tree Twp CHIP 23 B3
Long Beach (city) POPE 31 A2
Long I. COOK 76 E4
Long I. COOK 87 D3
Long I. STLS 73 A4
Long Island L. COOK 87 F4
Long L. ATKN 50 C3
Long L. ATKN 50 E1
Long L. ATKN 50 E3
Long L. ATKN 59 F5
Long L. BECK 55 D5
Long L. BECK 55 G4
Long L. BELT 68 D5
Long L. BELT 69 D1
Long L. BELT 69 E3
Long L. BGST 30 E1
Long L. BLUE 15 E5
Long L. CARL 51 B2
Long L. CARV 26 F2
Long L. CASS 48 C4
Long L. CASS 48 F5
Long L. CASS 57 D4
Long L. CASS 57 E5
Long L. CASS 57 F5
Long L. CASS 57 G4
Long L. CASS 58 D5
Long L. CASS 58 E2
Long L. CASS 58 G1
Long L. CHIS 35 C3
Long L. CLER 56 B4
Long L. CLER 68 C4
Long L. COOK 88 E4
Long L. COTT 3 A1
Long L. COTT 3 A5
Long L. CROW 41 A5
Long L. CROW 49 E5
Long L. DKTA 27 E1
Long L. DOUG 38 D5
Long L. DOUG 38 D5
Long L. DOUG 38 F5
Long L. DOUG 39 F2
Long L. GRNT 38 D3
Long L. HENN 26 C1
Long L. HENN 26 C3
Long L. HUBB 57 C1
Long L. HUBB 57 F1
Long L. ISNT 34 B5
Long L. ISNT 34 C4
Long L. ISNT 35 B1
Long L. ISNT 35 D2
Long L. ITSC 59 C2
Long L. ITSC 59 D1
Long L. ITSC 60 C1
Long L. ITSC 71 B4
Long L. ITSC 71 D1
Long L. ITSC 71 E4
Long L. ITSC 71 G2
Long L. ITSC 72 F1
Long L. KAND 31 G5
Long L. KAND 32 E2
Long L. KNBC 43 B1
Long L. LAKE 62 C2
Long L. LYON 12 E4
Long L. MAHN 55 A5
Long L. MAHN 68 F1
Long L. MEEK 24 A3
Long L. MEEK 24 B5
Long L. MEEK 25 A1
Long L. MEEK 25 B2
Long L. MORR 40 A5

Long L. MORR 40 F4
Long L. MORR 41 B5
Long L. OTTL 38 A3
Long L. OTTL 38 A4
Long L. OTTL 38 B4
Long L. OTTL 39 B1
Long L. OTTL 39 B4
Long L. OTTL 46 C5
Long L. OTTL 46 E2
Long L. OTTL 46 E3
Long L. OTTL 46 F3
Long L. OTTL 47 E1
Long L. OTTL 47 F1
Long L. PINE 51 G3
Long L. RAMS 26 B5
Long L. REDW 23 F3
Long L. SHER 33 D3
Long L. STEV 30 B4
Long L. STLS 61 A2
Long L. STLS 61 C2
Long L. STLS 61 F2
Long L. STLS 72 D5
Long L. STLS 72 E3
Long L. STLS 74 F1
Long L. STLS 84 C4
Long L. STRN 32 A3
Long L. STRN 32 C5
Long L. STRN 32 C5
Long L. STRN 32 D4
Long L. STRN 33 D3
Long L. TODD 40 B3
Long L. TODD 40 C2
Long L. TODD 40 E3
Long L. TODD 40 F1
Long L. TODD 40 F2
Long L. WASH 27 A3
Long L. WASH 27 B3
Long L. WASH 35 F4
Long L. WASH 35 G3
Long L. WATN 4 B3
Long L. WRIT 25 B3
Long L. WRIT 33 F5
Long Lake (city) HENN 26 C2
Long Lake Conservation Center Aitken 50 C3
Long Lake County Park CLER 56 B3
Long Lake Recreation Site ITSC 71 B4
Long Lake Twp CROW 49 G3
Long Lake Twp WATN 4 B3
Longleg L. COOK 87 G3
Long Lost L. CLER 56 C3
Long Meadow L. HENN 26 E5
Long Point WOOD 93 B1
Long Pond SHER 34 C2
Long Prairie TODD 40 D2
Long Prairie R. TODD 40 B2
Long Prairie Twp TODD 40 D2
Long Siding MLLC 34 B2
Longs L. MORR 40 B4
Long Slough CHIP 22 C5
Long Slough L. BELT 69 C2
Long Slough STLS 84 A3
Longstorff Bay STLS 73 A5
Longstorff Cr. STLS 73 A5
Long Tom L. BGST 29 E4
Longville CASS 58 E2
Longville Municipal Airport CASS 58 E2
Longyear Drill Historic Site STLS 73 E4
Longyear L. STLS 72 F3
Lon L. STLS 85 F1
Lonsdale RICE 16 B4
Lookout L. LAKE 75 F1
Lookout L. MORR 40 B5
Loon L. BECK 46 A3
Loon L. BECK 55 F5
Loon L. BELT 69 D3
Loon L. BLUE 15 F2
Loon L. CASS 49 D1
Loon L. CASS 57 G5
Loon L. CASS 58 D5
Loon L. CASS 58 F5
Loon L. COOK 87 E5
Loon L. CROW 49 F4
Loon L. CROW 49 F5
Loon L. HUBB 57 F3
Loon L. ITSC 59 A2
Loon L. ITSC 59 B4
Loon L. ITSC 59 C2
Loon L. JACK 3 F4
Loon L. KNBC 43 B1
Loon L. OTTL 46 C4
Loon L. OTTL 46 F3
Loon L. STLS 73 G3
Loon L. STLS 85 D2
Loon L. TODD 40 B3
Loon L. WASC 16 G3
Loon L. WASH 27 A3
Loon Lake Twp CASS 49 D1
Loon R. STLS 85 D2
Loop L. COOK 87 E3
Lorain Twp NBLS 3 E1
Lord L. HUBB 56 G5
Lords L. PINE 51 F4
Loren L. STLS 62 D1
Loretto HENN 26 B2
Lorraine L. ITSC 71 B4
Lory L. ISNT 42 G4
Lost Bay STLS 84 A3
Lost Bay STLS 96 F2
Lost Cr. LQPL 21 C4
Lost Girl I. STLS 85 G5
Lost Girl L. CASS 58 E3
Lost Jack Cr. STLS 85 E1
Lost L. ATKN 50 D5
Lost L. BELT 69 G4
Lost L. CARL 51 E5
Lost L. CARL 52 C2
Lost L. CASS 57 D4
Lost L. CASS 58 F1
Lost L. CASS 58 F4
Lost L. CLER 68 E2
Lost L. COOK 88 G5
Lost L. HUBB 56 B5
Lost L. ITSC 59 B2
Lost L. ITSC 70 E2
Lost L. ITSC 71 A5
Lost L. ITSC 71 D4
Lost L. KCHG 94 G3
Lost L. LAKE 75 C2
Lost L. STLS 51 A5
Lost L. STLS 61 D5
Lost L. STLS 61 E2
Lost L. STLS 73 B1
Lost L. STLS 73 G2
Lost L. STLS 84 A3
Lost L. WOOD 92 G5
Lost Lake Recreation Site ITSC 71 D4
Lost Lake State Game Refuge FILL 9 D1
Lost Man's L. STLS 72 D3
Lost Moose L. ITSC 71 F3
Lost R. KCHG 82 F2
Lost R. RDLK 67 B3
Lost R. ROSE 92 B1
Lost R. STLS 84 E2
Lotus L. CARV 26 D3
Lougee L. CROW 49 D3
Louisburg LQPL 30 G1
L. Louise HENN 26 C3
Louise L. CASS 49 A2
Louise L. DOUG 39 E2
Louise L. STLS 72 D3
Louise L. WASH 27 A3
L. Louise MURR 3 A1
Louisville Twp RDLK 66 A5
Louisville Twp SCOT 26 F2
Lounge L. LAKE 87 F2
Louriston Twp CHIP 23 A2
Louse L. COOK 87 G3
Louse R. LAKE 87 G2
Lova L. CASS 48 D4
Love Joy L. WADN 48 F2
Lovelace L. CLER 56 C3
Lovell L. STRN 40 G3
Love L. NORM 54 B1
Loven L. STLS 72 E2
Lovera L. DOUG 39 F3
Lovers I. LAKE 86 G1
Lowell Twp POLK 66 B3
Lower Badger Cr. RDLK 67 B2
Lower Balsam L. ITSC 71 F4
Lower Birch L. ISNT 35 D2
Lower Bottle L. HUBB 57 E1
Lower Camp L. CLER 56 C2
Lower Cone L. COOK 87 G5
Lower Cullen L. CROW 49 D2
Lower Egg L. BECK 56 E1
Lower Elk L. GRNT 38 E4
Lower George L. COOK 87 F4
Lower Gull L. CASS 49 F1
Lower Hanson L. ITSC 71 G3
Lower Hay L. CROW 49 C2
Lower Hunt L. DOUG 39 D1
Lower L. HENN 26 C2
Lower Lawrence L. ITSC 71 G4
Lower Menton L. CASS 58 C4
Lower Milton L. CASS 58 D4
Lower Mission L. CROW 49 D3
Lower Mud L. GOOD 18 A1
Lower Mud L. HUBB 56 E5
Lower Pauness L. STLS 85 D3
Lower Pigeon Lake Game Refuge ITSC 70 E3
Lower Pigeon L. ITSC 70 E3
Lower Red L. CLER 68 A4
Lower Red L. (Reservoir) BELT 81 G2
Lower Rice L. CLER 56 A2
Lower Sakatah L. RICE 16 E3
Lower Sioux Agency Historic District and Interpretive Center REDW 14 A1
Lower Sioux Indian Reservation REDW 14 A1
Lower Spring L. ITSC 71 F2
Lower Spunk L. STRN 32 B5
Lower Sucker L. CASS 57 A5
Lower Tamarack R. PINE 44 C2
Lower Trelipe L. CASS 58 E3
Lower Trout L. COOK 88 G2
Lower Twin L. FREE 6 F4
Lower Twin L. ITSC 70 E2
Lower Twin L. WADN 47 A5
Lower Whitefish L. CROW 49 B2
Low Island CASS 58 F4
Low L. STLS 86 G1
Lowry POPE 39 G1
Lows L. CROW 49 B5
Lowville Twp MURR 12 G3
L.Sieh OTTL 39 B2
L. Thirty-Four CASS 57 E4
Lucan REDW 13 C2
Lucan Depot Museum REDW 13 C2
Lucas Twp LYON 12 G5
Luce Line Corridor Trail HENN 26 C1
Lucille I. COOK 76 E4
Lucille L. CASS 58 D3
Lucille L. STLS 84 B5
Luck L. BELT 69 G4
Lucky Finn L. STLS 85 C3
Lucky L. ITSC 71 G2
Lude WOOD 93 B2
Luethi L. CLER 56 C2
Lujenida L. COOK 87 G3
Lula L. LAKE 86 G5
Lullaby Cr. COOK 88 F3
Lullaby L. COOK 88 F3
Lumbertown, U.S.A. CASS 49 F1
Lum L. COOK 88 F1
Lum L. ITSC 71 E3
Luna L. STLS 72 D1
Lunar L. LAKE 87 E2
Lunch L. LAKE 74 C5
L. Lundeberg OTTL 38 A5
Lundeen L. CASS 58 E2
Lundeen L. ITSC 71 D2
Lund-Hoel House Museum YMED 21 F5
Lund L. MEEK 32 G3
Lundquist L. CARV 26 F2
Lund Twp DOUG 38 C5
Lunetta L. STLS 85 G4
Lunker L. COOK 87 F3
Lunsten L. CARV 26 D1
Lupus L. LAKE 75 D2
Lura L. BLUE 5 C4
Lura Twp FRBT 5 C4
Luster L. LAKE 74 D3
Lutsen COOK 75 D5
Lutsen Ski Area COOK 75 C5
Luverne ROCK 1 E5
Luverne Municipal Airport ROCK 1 E5
Luverne Twp ROCK 1 E5
Luxemberg STRN 33 D2
Luxemburg Twp STRN 32 E5
Lux L. COOK 88 F2
Lybeck L. POPE 30 A5
Lydia SCOT 26 G3
Lydia L. MEEK 32 F3
Lydiard L. HENN 26 C3
Lydick L. CASS 69 G5
Lyendecker L. CLER 56 C4
Lyle MOWE 7 G3
Lyle Twp MOWE 7 F2
Lyman I. STLS 96 G3
Lynch Cr. FILL 8 C5
Lynch L. CASS 49 F1
Lynch L. CROW 49 C2
Lynch L. SWFT 30 E5
Lynch L. WASH 27 A3
Lynden Twp STRN 33 D3
Lynd LYON 12 C3
Lynd Twp LYON 12 C3
Lynix L. ITSC 71 D4
Lynn Twp MCLD 24 D5
Lynx L. STLS 85 D3
LYON — 12 —
Lyon County Historical Society Museum LYON 12 B4
Lyons State Forest WADN 48 D2
Lyons Twp LYON 12 C3
Lyons Twp WADN 48 C2
Lyra Twp BLUE 5 A3
Lyseng L. BGST 29 D4
Mabel FILL 9 G3
Mabel L. CASS 58 E3
Mabel Lake Recreation Site CASS 58 E3
Macalester College RAMS 27 C1
Macdougal Bay ITSC 59 A3
Mack L. CASS 69 G5
Macsville Twp GRNT 38 F2
Macville Twp ATKN 59 F2
L. Madaline MORR 40 B4
Madden Cr. LAKE 86 G3
Madden L. LAKE 86 G3
Mad Dog L. CASS 58 D2
Madelia WATN 14 G5
Madelia Twp WATN 14 G5
Madison LQPL 22 B1
Madison L. BLUE 15 E5
Madison Lake (city) BLUE 15 E5
Madison Twp LQPL 22 B1
Maggellson Bluff Municipal Ski Area FILL 9 C3
Maggie Cr. COOK 75 B3
Maggie L. COOK 75 B3
Magic L. COOK 75 A3
Magnetic L. COOK 87 E5
Magnet I. COOK 76 E4
Magnet L. LAKE 86 F5
Magney Municipal Forest STLS 52 B3
Magnolia ROCK 2 E1
Magnolia Twp ROCK 2 E1
Magnuson's Island WOOD 97 D2
Maheu L. PINE 52 F1
Mah Konce MAHN 56 A1
Mahla L. DOUG 38 D4
MAHNOMEN — 55 —
Mahnomen MAHN 55 A3
Mahnomen County Airport MAHN 55 B3
Mahnomen L. CROW 49 E4
Mahoning Lakes STLS 72 F2
Mahtomedi WASH 27 B2
Mahtowa CARL 51 D5
Mahtowa Twp CARL 51 D5
Maiden L. COTT 3 B5
Maine OTTL 46 E4
Maine L. OTTL 46 E4
Maine Prairie STRN 33 E1
Maine Prairie Twp STRN 33 E1
Maine Twp OTTL 46 F4
Maingan L. LAKE 86 E2
Main L. CLER 56 A1
Majestic L. STLS 72 F5
Makada L. COOK 88 G3
Maka-Oicu County Park NBLS 3 C1
Maki Cr. STLS 72 C5
Maki L. ITSC 71 F1
Makinen STLS 61 A2
Makwa L. LAKE 87 F2
Malachy L. SWFT 30 E5
Malardi L. WRIT 25 B5
Malberg L. LAKE 87 G2
Malgren L. GRNT 38 D4
Mallard L. ATKN 50 F1
Mallard L. BECK 55 D5
Mallard L. BECK 56 D1
Mallard L. BECK 56 D3
Mallard L. CLER 56 B4
Mallard L. CROW 49 B3
Mallard L. CROW 49 E2
Mallard L. ITSC 59 A2
Mallard L. MORR 40 B5
Mallard L. PINE 44 C2
Mallard L. STLS 60 A5
Malmedal L. POPE 31 A1
Malmo ATKN 50 G3
Malmo Prehistoric Historic Site ATKN 50 F3
Malmo Twp ATKN 50 F3
Malone Island MLLC 42 B3
Maloney L. WINA 19 E1
Malta Twp BGST 29 C5
Maltrod L. POLK 67 E2
Malung ROSE 91 D5
Malung Twp ROSE 92 D1
Mamre L. KAND 31 F4
Mamre Twp KAND 31 G4
Manannah MEEK 32 F4
Manannah Twp MEEK 32 F4
Manchester FREE 6 D3
Manchester Twp FREE 6 D3
Mancs Cr. STLS 85 D4
Mandall L. CHIS 35 B1
Mandt Twp CHIP 22 A5
Manfred House Museum and Interpretive Center ROCK 1 D5
Manfred Twp LQPL 21 D4
Manganika L. STLS 72 F5
Manhattan Beach (city) CROW 49 B3
Manitou R. LAKE 75 F2
Maniwaki L. LAKE 75 A1
Mankato BLUE 15 F4
Mankato Municipal Airport BLUE 15 E5
Mankato State College BLUE 15 F4
Mankato Twp BLUE 15 F4
Mankie I. ITSC 59 B3
Mann L. CASS 58 F1
Mann L. WASH 27 A3
L. Manomin BELT 68 G5
Manomin County Park ANOK 26 A5
Manomin Cr. BELT 80 E5
Manomin L. LAKE 86 F4
Mansfield FREE 6 F2
Mansfield Twp FREE 6 F2
Manston Twp WILK 45 D4
Mantle L. STLS 85 C3
Mantorville DOGE 17 G4
Mantorville Historic District DOGE 17 G4
Mantorville Twp DOGE 17 G4
Mantrap L. HUBB 57 E2
Mantrap Lake Recreation Site HUBB 57 E1
Mantrap Twp HUBB 57 E2
Manuella L. MEEK 24 B5
Many Arm L. HUBB 56 E5
Manyaska Twp MART 4 E3
Manymoon L. COOK 75 B4
Many Point L. BECK 56 D1
Mapel L. ITSC 71 D1
Maple Bay (city) POLK 67 D1
Maple Cr. POLK 66 E4
Maple Cr. STEL 17 G1
Maple Grove HENN 26 A3
Maple Grove Twp BECK 56 D1
Maple Grove Twp CROW 49 G4
Maple Island (city) FREE 7 D1
Maple L. CASS 58 E2
Maple L. CLAY 46 C1
Maple L. DOUG 39 F3
Maple L. ITSC 59 E2
Maple L. MEEK 25 B2
Maple L. POLK 67 D2
Maple L. TODD 40 E1
Maple L. WRIT 33 F4
Maple Lake (city) WRIT 33 F4
Maple Lake Municipal Airport and Seaplane Base WRIT 33 F4
Maple Lake Twp WRIT 33 F4
Maple Leaf L. STLS 60 E5
Maple Plain HENN 26 B2
Maple Point CASS 57 C5
Maple R. BLUE 5 B3
Maple Ridge Twp BELT 69 C1
Maple Ridge Twp ISNT 34 A4
Mapleton BLUE 5 B4
Mapleton Twp BLUE 5 B4
Maple Twp CASS 48 D5
Maple View MOWE 7 E3
Maplewood RAMS 27 B2
Maplewood State Park OTTL 46 D3
Maplewood Twp OTTL 46 D3
Maraboeuf L. COOK 87 D4
Marais R. POLK 66 A1
Marathon L. LAKE 74 B5
Marble ITSC 59 A4
Marble Cr. BLUE 5 B1
Marble L. ITSC 71 E3
Marble L. LAKE 62 A3
Marble L. LAKE 87 F2
Marble Twp LINC 21 G5
Marcell ITSC 71 E1
Marcell District Ranger Station ITSC 71 E1
Marcell Twp ITSC 71 E1
March MRSH 78 D1
March L. CLER 56 B2
Marcott L. DKTA 27 E2
Marcus L. BELT 69 C2
Marcus Zumbrunnen County Park WRIT 33 E4
Mareks L. LSUR 16 C2
L. Margaret CASS 49 E1
L. Margaret PINE 51 F5
Marge L. TODD 39 E5
Margie KCHG 82 F4
L. Maria MURR 12 E4
L. Maria STRN 32 B3
Maria L. CARV 26 F1
Maria L. OTTL 46 E4
Maria L. STRN 33 D3
L. Marie WRIT 33 E4
Marie L. COOK 88 F2
Marie L. ITSC 70 E1
Marie L. ITSC 71 D2
Marie L. STRN 32 B2
Maries I. WOOD 97 D2
Marietta LQPL 21 B4
Marine on St. Croix WASH 35 G4
Marine-on-St. Croix Historic District WASH 35 G4
Marin L. CLAY 54 G5
Marion OLMS 8 B3
Marion Bay STLS 96 G2
Marion Cr. OLMS 8 A2
Marion Cr. STLS 84 C4
L. Marion HENN 26 C3
Marion L. DKTA 26 F5
Marion L. MCLD 25 E1
Marion L. OTTL 47 D1
Marion L. STLS 61 C5
Marion L. STLS 84 C4
Marion Twp OLMS 8 A2
Mark Cr. COOK 76 B1
Markgrafs L. WASH 27 C3
Markham STLS 61 B3
Markham L. STLS 61 A3
Mark L. COOK 76 B1
Markville PINE 44 C3
Marlu L. POPE 31 B3
Marlyn L. ITSC 71 E4
L. Marquette BELT 69 G2
Marr I. COOK 76 B5
MARSHALL — 78 —
Marshall LYON 12 B4
L. Marshall LYON 12 C4
Marshall L. BECK 55 G2
Marshall L. CASS 58 E2
Marshall L. COOK 88 G2
Marshall Municipal Airport LYON 12 B3
Marshall Twp MOWE 7 E4
Marshan L. ANOK 35 G1
Marshan Twp DKTA 27 F3
Marsh Cr. NORM 55 B2
Marsh Creek Twp MAHN 55 A3
Marshfield Twp LINC 12 D1
Marsh Grove Twp MRSH 78 C5
Marsh L. CARV 26 D2
Marsh L. COOK 75 B4
Marsh L. COOK 76 A4
Marsh L. HUBB 57 B1
Marsh L. (Reservoir) BGST 30 F1
Marsh Lake Municipal Park-East HENN 26 D4
Marsh R. NORM 66 G2
L. Martha WRIT 26 A1
MARTIN — 4 —
Martin County Pioneer Museum MART 4 E5
Martin Cr. CASS 48 D3
Martin I. STLS 84 A2
Martin-Island-Linwood Regional Park ANOK 35 E1
Martin L. ANOK 35 E1
Martin L. MART 4 D5
Martin L. STLS 60 G4
Martin Rosen L. CLER 68 C3
Martinsburg Twp RENV 24 F3
Martin Twp ROCK 1 F3
Marty STRN 33 D1
Marty L. STRN 33 D1
Marvin L. ROSE 92 B3
L. Mary DOUG 39 F2
L. Mary MCLD 25 E1
L. Mary OTTL 39 B4
L. Mary POPE 31 C2
L. Mary WRIT 25 C4
L. Mary WRIT 33 F4

Mary L. CROW 49 B4
Mary L. HENN 26 D2
Mary L. HUBB 56 C4
Mary L. HUBB 57 F3
Mary L. ITSC 60 C1
Mary L. ITSC 71 E3
Mary L. KAND 31 F4
Mary L. LSUR 16 B1
Mary L. MEEK 32 G4
Mary L. STRN 40 G3
Mary L. WATN 4 B3
Mary L. WRIT 25 A5
Mary L. WRIT 33 G4
Marysburg LSUR 15 E5
Marysland Twp SWFT 30 E4
Marystown SCOT 26 F3
Marysville Twp WRIT 25 A4
Mary Twp NORM 54 C3
Mary Yellowhead L. BECK 55 E5
Masabi Iron Range STLS 73 F2
Masford L. SHER 33 D4
Mashkenode L. STLS 72 F5
L. Mason OTTL 46 E2
Mason L. OTTL 47 G1
Mason Twp MURR 12 G4
Masten Cr. DOGE 17 G5
L. Masterman WASH 27 B3
Matawan WASC 6 C2
Matson I. STLS 73 A3
Matson L. ISNT 34 A4
Matson L. POLK 67 E3
Matt Ayers L. MAHN 67 G5
Mattson KITT 89 E5
Mattson Bay STLS 73 B3
L. Mattson CHIS 35 D3
Mattson L. DOUG 39 F1
L. Maud BECK 46 B3
Maude Cr. STLS 85 E2
Maude L. STLS 85 E2
Mauser L. COOK 88 E5
Mavis L. COOK 87 E4
Max ITSC 70 E3
Maxfield's Pt. STLS 72 A5
Maxim L. WRIT 33 G3
Maxine L. STLS 85 G4
Max Twp ITSC 70 E3
Maxwell Bay HENN 26 C2
Maxwell Twp LQPL 22 D2
L. Maybel LSUR 16 C2
L. May CASS 57 D4
Mayer CARV 25 D5
Mayfield L. CLAY 46 A1
Mayfield Twp PENN 79 G4
Mayhew BENT 41 G3
Mayhew Cr. BENT 33 B3
Mayhew L. COOK 88 E1
Mayhew Lake Twp BENT 33 A3
May L. ITSC 71 D4
Maymay L. LAKE 87 F2
Maynard CHIP 23 C2
Mayo Clinic OLMS 8 A2
Mayo Clinic/Plummer Building Historic Site OLMS 8 A2
Mayo Cr. CASS 48 C5
Mayo L. CROW 49 D1
Mayo Medical Museum OLMS 8 A1
Mayo Park OLMS 8 A2
Mayowood OLMS 8 A1
Mayowood Corridor County Park OLMS 8 A1
Mayowood Historic Site OLMS 8 A1
Mayowood L. OLMS 8 A1
Mays L. WASH 35 G4
May Twp CASS 48 F4
May Twp WASH 35 G4
Mayville MOWE 7 D3
Mayville Twp HOUS 10 E1
Maywood Game Refuge BENT 33 A5
Maywood Twp BENT 33 A5
Mazaska L. RICE 16 C4
Maze L. LAKE 87 D2
Mazeppa WBSH 18 D1
Mazeppa Twp WBSH 18 E1
Mazomannie Point MLLC 42 B2
McAlpine L. ITSC 71 F3
McAuity L. ITSC 59 A2
McAvity Bay ITSC 70 F3
McCall L. BELT 68 B5
McCarrahan L. TODD 40 D1
McCarrons L. RAMS 27 B1
McCarthey L. CASS 58 F3
McCarthy Beach State Park STLS 72 D2
McCarthy Cr. LAKE 62 D2
McCarthy L. DKTA 27 E1
McCarthy L. STLS 72 E2
McCarty Cr. STLS 60 F3
McCarty L. HUBB 57 C1
McCauleyville WILK 45 E2
McCauleyville Twp WILK 45 E2
McClain L. CROW 49 B3
McClellan L. POPE 39 G2
McCloud Cr. KCHG 94 F2
McCloud L. POPE 31 B4
McCollum L. OTTL 46 C4
McCollum L. OTTL 46 C4
McCormack L. STLS 72 E2
McCormick L. PINE 51 G4
McCormic L. STRN 40 G1
McCoy L. BELT 68 B5
McCoy L. HENN 26 D3
McCraney L. MAHN 55 C5
McCrea Twp MRSH 78 D3
McCullough County Park RICE 16 C4
McDavitt Twp STLS 60 A5
McDonald L. BELT 69 F5
McDonald L. COOK 76 A1
McDonald L. ITSC 71 D2
McDonald L. ITSC 71 F1
McDonald L. OTTL 46 D4
McDonald L. WASH 27 B3
McDonaldsville Twp NORM 54 B4
McDonough L. DKTA 27 E1
McDougal L. LAKE 74 D3
McDougal Lakes Recreation Site LAKE 74 D4
McDougall Island MORR 41 F1
McFarland L. COOK 88 E5
L. McGinty CASS 49 A3
McGivern County Park WADN 48 F2
McGowan L. PINE 44 C1
McGrath ATKN 42 A5
McGrath Game Refuge ATKN 50 F4
McGregor ATKN 50 C4
McGregor Municipal Airport ATKN 50 C4
McGregor Twp ATKN 50 C5
McGroarty Municipal Park DKTA 27 D2
McGuire L. ITSC 59 D4
McIntosh POLK 67 D4
McIver L. POPE 30 A5
Mckay L. CLER 56 C4
McKay L. HENN 34 G5
McKay L. LYON 12 D3
McKenna L. BECK 56 D4
McKenney L. STRN 40 G3
McKenzie L. CLER 56 B2
McKenzi L. BECK 55 D4
McKeown L. CASS 58 F1
McKewen L. ITSC 71 E2
McKinley STLS 73 F2
McKinley L. ITSC 59 C3
McKinley Park Recreation Site STLS 73 B2
McKinley Twp CASS 48 B3
McKinley Twp KITT 90 B3
McKinney L. ATKN 59 G1
McKinney L. ITSC 59 B3
L. McKusick WASH 27 B4
MCLEOD — 25 —
McMahon L. SCOT 26 G4
McManus I. STLS 84 B4
McNiven Cr. STLS 72 E4
McNiven L. STLS 72 F3
McPherson Twp BLUE 15 G5
McQuade L. STLS 72 G4
Meadow Brook Twp CASS 48 E4
Meadow City Park HENN 26 C3
Meadow Cr. BELT 69 A5
Meadow Cr. LYON 12 C5
Meadow Cr. MORR 40 E5
Meadow L. BECK 46 A4
Meadow L. BELT 69 E1
Meadow L. BELT 69 E4
Meadow L. CASS 48 D4
Meadow L. MORR 40 B5
Meadow L. STLS 73 B4
Meadowlands STLS 60 D4
Meadow Lands Twp STLS 60 D4
Meadows Twp WILK 45 E4
Meadow Twp WADN 48 C1
Mead's I. STLS 73 A2
Meander Cr. STLS 85 E4
Meander L. STLS 85 E3
Meander Lake Recreation Site STLS 85 E3
Meat L. STLS 73 A4
Medas L. LAKE 86 F5
Medford Cr. STEL 17 F1
Medford STEL 16 F5
Medford Twp STEL 16 F5
Median L. LAKE 87 F2
Medicine L. BELT 69 C3
Medicine L. HENN 26 B4
Medicine Lake (city) HENN 26 C4
Medicine R. YMED 23 F1
Medina HENN 26 B2
Meditation L. COOK 87 E3
Medley L. STLS 85 F4
Medo Twp BLUE 5 A5
Meeds L. COOK 88 F1
MEEKER — 24 —
Mehurin Twp LQPL 21 C4
Meire Grove STRN 32 B2
Melby DOUG 38 C5
Melby L. CLAY 55 E1
Melby L. GRNT 38 C4
Melges Bakery Historic Site BRWN 14 D5
L. Melissa BECK 46 B3
Melon L. COOK 88 F3
Melon L. LAKE 86 E5
Melrose STRN 32 A2
Melrose L. WRIT 33 E5
Melrose Twp STRN 32 A2
Melrud STLS 61 B2
Melville Twp RENV 24 E2
Meme L. LAKE 75 D2
Memorial Municipal Park GOOD 18 A1
Memorial Park SCOT 26 E3
Menahga WADN 47 B5
Mendota DKTA 27 D1
Mendota Heights DKTA 27 D1
Mentor POLK 67 D2
Merganser L. COOK 88 G4
Meriden STEL 16 G4
Meriden Twp STEL 16 G4
Merlin L. STLS 73 A4
Merriam Bay LAKE 86 F3
Merrifield CROW 49 E2
Merrill L. STLS 60 C2
Merritt L. STLS 85 G2
Merton STEL 17 F1
Merton Twp STEL 17 F1
Merwin L. CARL 51 C3
Mesaba L. COOK 87 G3
Mesaba Park L. STLS 72 G4
Mesabi Community College STLS 72 F5
Mesabi Iron Range STLS 72 F3
Metogga L. RICE 16 B3
Metropolitan Community College HENN 26 C5
Metropolitan Sports Center HENN 26 D5
Meuwissen L. CARV 26 E1
Meyer L. CROW 49 B3
Meyer L. OTTL 39 B2
Meyer L. TODD 40 D2
Meyers L. STRN 32 D4
Mica Bay STLS 96 G4
Mica I. STLS 84 A4
Michaels L. MORR 41 B2
Michaud L. CASS 58 F5
Michaud L. CASS 58 G5
Mickinock Cr. ROSE 91 F5
Mickinock Twp ROSE 92 E1
Mic Mac L. LAKE 63 A1
Midas L. LAKE 87 E2
Mid Cone L. COOK 87 F5
Mid-Continent Airport OLMS 8 A3
Middle Branch Root R. FILL 8 D4
Middle Branch Two R. KITT 90 D1
Middle Cormorant County Park BECK 46 A2
Middle Cormorant L. BECK 46 A2
Middle Cullen L. CROW 49 D2
Middle Fork Cedar R. DOGE 7 B2
Middle Fork Crow R. MEEK 32 F3
Middle Fork Whitewater R. OLMS 18 G5
Middle Fork Zumbro R. DOGE 17 F3
Middle Hanson L. ITSC 71 G3
Middle L. KAND 31 E5
Middle L. NCLT 15 D2
Middle L. NCLT 15 D3
Middle L. OTTL 38 B5
Middle La Salle L. HUBB 56 B5
Middle Mud L. STLS 73 A4
Middle Pigeon L. ITSC 70 E2
Middle Pigeon Recreation Site ITSC 70 E3
Middle Pomme De Terre L. STEV 38 G3
Middle R. MRSH 78 B1
Middle River (city) MRSH 79 A2
Middle River Twp MRSH 78 C1
Middle Spunk L. STRN 32 B5
Middle Sucker L. CASS 57 A5
Middletown Twp JACK 3 F5
Middleville Twp WRIT 25 A3
Midge L. HUBB 57 A3
Midget L. COOK 75 A4
Midway BECK 47 A4
Midway County Park NBLS 2 D3
Midway R. CARL 52 B2
Midway Seaplane Base BELT 69 F2
Midway Twp COTT 4 A1
Midway Twp STLS 52 B3
Miesville DKTA 27 G4
Mike L. ITSC 71 D1
Mike L. MAHN 55 C5
Milaca MLLC 42 G2
Milaca Municipal Airport MLLC 42 G2
Milaca Twp MLLC 42 F1
Milan CHIP 22 A3
Mile I. LAKE 86 G2
Mile L. CASS 49 F1
Miles I. COOK 87 E3
Milford State Monument BRWN 14 C4
Milford Twp BRWN 14 D4
Milky L. WRIT 25 B3
Mill Cr. OLMS 8 B4
Mill Cr. WRIT 33 G4
MILLE LACS — 42 —
Mille Lacs County Historical Society Museum MLLC 34 B2
Mille Lacs Indian Reservation PINE 44 D1
Mille Lacs Kathio State Park MLLC 42 C1
Mille Lacs L. MLLC 42 A2
Mille Lacs National Wildlife Refuge MLLC 42 B2
Mille Lacs Wildlife Management Area MLLC 42 D3
Miller Bay TODD 39 E5
Miller Cr. STLS 52 A4
Miller Cr. WOOD 81 B3
Miller I. STLS 85 G5
Miller L. BELT 69 G1
Miller L. CARL 51 B4
Miller L. CARV 26 E1
Miller L. CROW 49 D3
Miller L. CROW 49 G5
Miller L. ITSC 59 A1
Miller L. ITSC 71 G2
Miller L. MEEK 32 F3
Miller L. PINE 43 B3
Miller L. YMED 22 E1
Millersburg RICE 16 C4
Millerville DOUG 39 C1
Millerville Twp DOUG 39 C1
Milliken Cr. DOGE 17 F4
Mill L. BECK 46 B4
Mill L. BECK 55 E5
Mill L. DOUG 39 E1
Mill L. TODD 40 C3
Mill Pond L. BENT 41 G2
Mill Pond L. GRNT 38 C3
Millpond L. OTTL 39 B1
Mill Pond MOWE 7 E3
Mill Pond SCOT 26 F2
Mills L. BLUE 15 G2
Millstone L. WRIT 33 F4
Millville WBSH 18 E3
Millwood Twp STRN 40 G3
Miloma JACK 3 D2
Milo Twp MLLC 34 A1
Milroy REDW 13 C1
Miltona DOUG 39 C3
L. Miltona DOUG 39 C3
Miltona Twp DOUG 39 C3
Milton Twp DOGE 17 F4
L. Mina DOUG 39 E2
Mina L. BELT 68 C5
Mina L. COOK 87 F3
Minard L. ANOK 34 D5
Minden Twp BENT 33 B3
Mine L. COOK 87 E4
Mineral L. OTTL 38 B2
Mineral Springs Municipal Park STEL 17 G1
Minerva L. CLER 56 A3
Minerva L. LAKE 87 F1
Minerva Twp CLER 56 A3
Mineview in the Sky Observation Platform STLS 73 F1
Minisogama L. ITSC 70 F1
Minister L. DOUG 39 E1
Minister L. STLS 85 G5
Mink Cr. LAKE 62 C4
Mink Cr. MART 4 C4
Mink L. CASS 58 D4
Mink L. CLER 56 C4
Mink L. COOK 76 A4
Mink L. ITSC 71 E3
Mink L. OTTL 46 C5
Mink L. WRIT 25 A5
Mink L. WRIT 33 F4
Minneapolis HENN 26 C5
Minneapolis College of Art and Design HENN 26 C5
Minneapolis-St. Paul International Airport HENN 26 D5
Minnehaha Cr. HENN 26 C4
Minnehaha Depot Historic Site and Minnehaha Falls HENN 26 D5
Minnehaha Municipal Park HENN 26 C5
Minneiska Twp WBSH 19 E1
Minneiska WBSH 19 E2
Minneola Twp GOOD 17 D4
Minneopa BLUE 15 F3
Minneopa State Park BLUE 15 F3
Minneota LYON 12 A2
Minneota Twp JACK 3 F4
Minnesota and Western Railroad Museum WRIT 33 F3
Minnesota Braille and Sight Saving School RICE 16 D5
Minnesota City WINA 19 F3
Minnesota Falls Twp YMED 23 E1
Minnesota Forest History Interpretive Center ITSC 59 C2
Minnesota Historical Society RAMS 27 C1
Minnesota Island CASS 57 C4
Minnesota Island HOUS 10 C2
Minnesota L. FRBT 5 C5
Minnesota L. MEEK 24 B4
Minnesota Lake (city) FRBT 5 C5
Minnesota Lake County Park FRBT 5 C5
Minnesota Lake Twp FRBT 5 C5
Minnesota Metropolitan Training Center ANOK 35 G1
Minnesota Mills Historic District HENN 26 C3
Minnesota Museum of Mining STLS 72 F3
Minnesota Pioneer Park WRIT 33 F3
Minnesota Point STLS 52 B5
Minnesota Point Lighthouse Historic Site STLS 52 B5
Minnesota Point Municipal Park STLS 52 B5
Minnesota Reformatory for Women SCOT 26 E3
Minnesota R. HENN 26 F2
Minnesota R. NCLT 15 E3
Minnesota River Game Refuge LSUR 15 E4
Minnesota School for the Deaf RICE 16 D5
Minnesota State Capitol RAMS 27 C1
Minnesota State Correctional Camp PINE 51 F3
Minnesota State Fairgrounds RAMS 27 C1
Minnesota State Fish Hatchery POPE 31 A2
Minnesota State Penitentiary WASH 27 B4
Minnesota State Reformatory SHER 33 C3
Minnesota State Training School Historic Site GOOD 18 A1
Minnesota Valley Corridor Trail SCOT 26 E2
Minnesota Valley Lawrence State Wayside SCOT 26 F1
Minnesota Valley National Wildlife Refuge and Recreation Area SCOT 26 F2
Minnesota Valley Trail Site No. 2 SCOT 26 E2
Minnesota Veterans Home DKTA 27 F4
Minnesota-Wisconsin Boundary Corridor Trail PINE 44 B2
Minnesota Woman Historic Site OTTL 46 C2
Minnesota Zoological Garden DKTA 26 E5
L. Minnetaga KAND 24 A2
Minnetonka HENN 26 C3
Minnetonka Beach (city) HENN 26 C2
Minnetonka Game Refuge CARV 26 D1
L. Minnetonka HENN 26 C3
Minnetonka L. BECK 46 A3
Minnetrista HENN 26 C1
L. Minnewashta CARV 26 D2
L. Minnewaska POPE 31 B2
Minnewaska Twp POPE 31 B2
Minnewawa ATKN 50 B5
L. Minnewawa ATKN 50 B5
L. Minnie Belle MEEK 24 B4
L. Minnie HUBB 57 B1
Minnie L. CROW 49 A4
Minnie L. STRN 32 C5
Minnie Twp BELT 80 C4
Minnitaki I. STLS 96 G4
Minnow L. CLER 68 F2
Minnow L. STLS 72 D5
Minnow L. STLS 73 C5
Mirage L. COOK 88 F4
Mirror L. ITSC 71 B5
Mirror L. LAKE 74 B4
Mirror L. STLS 61 F4
Mirth L. LAKE 87 G2
Miskogineu L. CLER 80 F2
Misplaced L. COOK 88 F1
Misquah L. COOK 88 F2
Missing Link L. COOK 87 F4
Mission Creek Twp PINE 43 D2
Mission Cr. PINE 43 E2
Missionery L. LAKE 86 F5
Mission L. BECK 55 D4
Mission Point CASS 49 F1
Mission Twp CROW 49 D3
Mississippi Cr. COOK 76 B1
Mississippi Headwaters State Forest BELT 69 F1
Mississippi Melodie Showboat ITSC 59 C2
Mississippi R. RAMS 27 C2
Mississippi River County Park MORR 41 C1
Mississippi River County Park Sterns 41 G2
Miss L. BELT 69 G1
Missouri Cr. COOK 75 B5
Missouri L. BECK 56 D3
Missouri L. COOK 75 B4
Mistletoe Cr. COOK 75 B5
Mistletoe L. COOK 75 B5
Mist L. LAKE 87 D2
Mitawan Cr. LAKE 74 B4
Mitawon L. LAKE 74 D4
L. Mitchell SHER 34 E1
Mitchell L. CROW 49 A3
Mitchell L. HENN 26 D3
Mitchell L. POLK 67 D3
Mitchell L. STLS 73 B5
Mitchell Twp WILK 45 D3
Mite L. COOK 87 G3
Mit L. COOK 88 G2
Mitmoen L. POPE 39 G1
Mitten L. CASS 58 F3
Mizpah KCHG 70 A2
Moberg L. STLS 51 A3
Mobergs Seaplane Base BELT 69 F1
Moburg L. CROW 49 E1
Moburg L. CROW 49 F1

Moccasin L. CASS 58 E1
Moccasin L. LAKE 74 D3
Moccasin L. STLS 73 A4
Moccasin Narrows STLS 73 A2
Moe L. BECK 46 A3
Moe L. CLAY 55 G1
Moe L. MEEK 24 A3
Moe L. WRIT 33 F2
Moenkedick L. OTTL 46 C5
Moe Twp DOUG 39 E1
Mogie L. STLS 52 A3
Mohr's and Scott's Seaplane Bases STLS 85 C1
Moilan L. STLS 61 A1
Moiyaka L. LAKE 86 F5
Moland RICE 17 E2
Moland Twp CLAY 54 F3
Mole L. ITSC 71 F4
Mollar L. BECK 46 A2
Mollie L. CROW 49 E2
Mollison L. BELT 68 B5
Molly L. TODD 40 F3
Molly Stark L. OTTL 46 G5
Moltke Twp SBLY 14 A4
Momb L. BECK 55 F5
Money Cr. HOUS 9 C4
Money Creek (city) HOUS 9 C4
Money Creek Twp HOUS 9 C4
Monker Cr. COOK 76 B3
Monker L. COOK 76 B3
Monongalia Game Refuge KAND 32 E1
Monongalia Historical Society Museum KAND 32 F1
Monroe Twp LYON 12 E5
Mons Cr. COOK 88 G5
Mons L. TODD 40 E3
Monson L. BECK 46 A3
Monson L. CLER 68 E2
Monson L. ITSC 72 E1
Monson L. SWFT 31 E3
Monson Lake State Park SWFT 31 E3
Monson Twp TRAV 37 E3
Montevideo CHIP 22 C5
Montevideo-Chippewa County Airport CHIP 22 C5
Montgomery LSUR 16 C2
Montgomery Twp LSUR 16 C2
Monticello WRIT 34 E1
Monticello Twp WRIT 33 F5
Montissippi County Park WRIT 33 E5
Montrose WRIT 25 B5
Moody L. CHIS 35 E3
Moody L. CROW 49 E2
Mooers L. WASH 27 E2
Mooney L. HENN 26 B3
Moon L. CASS 58 E4
Moon L. CLER 56 A3
Moon L. COOK 88 E3
Moon L. COOK 88 F1
Moon L. DOUG 39 D1
Moon L. ITSC 71 F3
Moon L. STLS 73 G1
Moonshine L. ITSC 59 A3
Moonshine L. ITSC 71 F3
Moonshine Twp BGST 29 B5
L. Moore SWFT 31 D1
Moore L. ANOK 26 B5
Moore L. CLER 56 C2
Moore L. COOK 75 B4
Moore L. ITSC 71 G2
Moore L. MAHN 55 C3
Moore L. OTTL 46 D4
Moore L. STEV 30 A4
Moore L. WRIT 26 A1
Moore L. WRIT 34 G1
Moore Twp STEV 30 C4
Moorhead CLAY 54 F2
Moorhead State University CLAY 54 G2
Moorhead Travel Information Center CLAY 54 G2
Moorhead Twp CLAY 54 G2
Moose Bay CROW 49 D2
Moose Bay STLS 84 B4
Moose Bay STLS 96 G1
Moose Bay WOOD 97 D2
Moose Bk. ITSC 70 B3
Moosecamp L. STLS 86 E1
Moose Cr. ITSC 70 D1
Moose Cr. STLS 84 F3
Moose Cr. WOOD 81 A4
Moose Creek Twp CLER 68 F4
Moosehead L. CARL 51 E4
Moosehorn L. COOK 76 F1
Moosehorn Point STLS 84 A1
Moose Horn R. CARL 51 C5
Moose I. STLS 73 B2
Moose L. ATKN 59 G2
Moose L. BELT 68 C5
Moose L. BELT 68 F4
Moose L. BELT 69 F5
Moose L. CARL 51 E4
Moose L. CASS 48 C4
Moose L. COOK 88 B5
Moose L. ITSC 60 B1
Moose L. ITSC 70 B2
Moose L. ITSC 71 F4
Moose L. ITSC 71 G1
Moose L. ITSC 71 G4
Moose L. ITSC 72 F1
Moose L. KCHG 83 B3
Moose L. LAKE 75 E2
Moose L. LAKE 86 G4
Moose L. STLS 61 E1

Moose L. STLS 62 C1
Moose L. STLS 72 D4
Moose L. STLS 73 C3
Moose L. STLS 73 C3
Moose L. STLS 84 C4
Moose L. STLS 84 F3
Moose L. TODD 40 E3
Moose L. WRIT 33 F2
Moose L. Pool ATKN 59 F3
Moose Lake (city) CARL 51 E4
Moose Lake-Carlton County Airport CARL 51 E4
Moose Lake Cr. TODD 40 E3
Moose Lake Penal Camp CARL 51 E4
Moose Lake State Hospital CARL 51 E4
Moose Lake State Monument CARL 51 E4
Moose Lake State Park CARL 51 E4
Moose Lake Twp BELT 69 E5
Moose Lake Twp CARL 51 E4
Moose Lake Twp CASS 48 D4
Moose Park Twp ITSC 70 C1
Moose Pt. STLS 74 C1
Moose R. ATKN 59 G2
Moose R. BELT 80 A2
Moose R. PINE 51 F3
Moose R. STLS 84 B4
Moose R. STLS 85 E4
Moose River Twp MRSH 91 G5
Moose Twp ROSE 91 C3
Moose-Willow Wildlife Management Area ATKN 59 F3
Mora KNBC 42 E5
Mora L. COOK 87 F3
Mora Municipal Airport KNBC 42 E5
Moran Bk. TODD 48 G2
Moran L. HUBB 56 G5
Moran L. ITSC 72 F1
Moran Twp TODD 40 A2
Moranville Twp ROSE 92 C4
Morcom I. STLS 73 B2
Morcom I. STLS 85 G2
Morcom L. STLS 61 B2
Morcom Twp STLS 72 C2
Morey Fish Company Airport MORR 48 G4
Morgan REDW 14 C1
Morgan L. COOK 88 F2
Morgan L. STLS 61 E3
Morgan Park Historic District STLS 52 B3
Morgan Twp REDW 14 C1
Morin L. FREE 6 E2
Morken Twp CLAY 54 E3
Morph L. ITSC 70 E1
Morrill MORR 41 F4
Morrill Twp MORR 41 F4
Morris STEV 30 B3
Morris L. COOK 88 E2
Morris L. LAKE 75 D2
Morris Municipal Airport STEV 30 B3
MORRISON — 41 —
Morrison Bay COOK 76 E4
Morrison Bk. ATKN 59 E2
Morrison L. BECK 55 D4
Morrison L. BECK 56 D4
Morrison L. CASS 49 A5
Morrison L. CLER 68 B4
Morrison Mounds Historic Site OTTL 46 F5
Morrison Twp ATKN 50 C2
Morris Point WOOD 93 C3
Morristown RICE 16 E4
Morristown Twp RICE 16 E3
Morris Twp STEV 30 A3
Morse Twp ITSC 58 A5
Morse Twp STLS 73 B5
Morton RENV 14 A1
Moscow FREE 7 D1
Moscow Township Game Refuge FREE 7 E2
Moscow Twp FREE 7 D1
L. Moses DOUG 39 C1
Moses L. COOK 88 G2
Moses L. GRNT 38 E2
Moska L. STLS 72 E3
Mosomo L. ITSC 70 E3
Mosomo Point Recreation Site ITSC 70 F3
Mosquito Cr. CASS 48 F4
Mosquito Cr. CLER 68 G2
Mosquito L. LAKE 87 F1
Mosquo L. BELT 68 B5
Moss L. CASS 57 B4
Moss L. COOK 88 E2
Moss L. ITSC 71 F3
Moth L. COOK 87 F4
Motley MORR 48 G4
Motley Twp MORR 48 G4
Mott L. WASC 6 A2
Moulton L. ATKN 50 B1
Moulton Twp MURR 2 B2
Mound HENN 26 C2
Mound Cr. BRWN 13 E5
Mound L. LAKE 75 D2
Mound L. TODD 40 F3
Mound Prairie Twp HOUS 10 C1
Mounds View RAMS 26 A5
Mound Twp ROCK 1 D5
Mountain Ash L. ITSC 59 E2
Mountain County Park

COTT 4 B1
Mountain Iron STLS 72 E5
Mountain Iron Mine Historic Site STLS 72 E5
Mountain L. COOK 88 E4
Mountain L. COTT 4 B1
Mountain L. POPE 31 C1
Mountain L. TODD 40 E3
Mountain Lake (city) COTT 4 B1
Mountain Lake Historic Site COTT 4 B1
Mountain Lake Twp COTT 4 B1
Mountain Ski Area STLS 52 B3
Mount Morris Twp MORR 41 E5
Mount Pleasant Twp WBSH 18 C2
Mount Vernon Twp WINA 19 F2
Mouse L. STLS 61 D4
Movil L. BELT 69 E2
MOWER — 7 —
Mower County Historical Center MOWE 7 E2
Mow L. HUBB 57 G3
Moxie I. STLS 84 B2
Moyer Twp SWFT 30 E3
Moylan Twp MRSH 79 D5
Mt. Frontenac Ski Area GOOD 18 B3
Mt. Itasca Ski Area ITSC 59 B2
Mt. Kato Ski Area BLUE 15 F4
Mt. Wirth Ski Area HENN 26 C4
Mucker L. COOK 88 E1
Muckwa L. COOK 88 G3
Muckwa L. STLS 73 B5
Mud-Bardwell Game Refuge MART 4 F5
Mud Bay LAKE 87 D2
Mud Bay STLS 84 B2
Mud Bk. CROW 49 C4
Mud Cr. COOK 76 A3
Mud Cr. KNBC 43 F1
Mud Cr. ROCK 1 F4
Mud Cr. STLS 62 C1
Mud Cr. STLS 73 A3
Mud Cr. SWFT 31 E2
Mud Cr. SWFT 31 F2
Mud Cr. YMED 22 F1
Mud Creek Bay STLS 73 A3
Muddy Cr. STEV 30 B2
Mudgett Twp MLLC 42 E2
Mud-Goose Game Refuge CASS 58 B4
Mud Hen Cr. STLS 61 A1
Mud Hen Lakes DKTA 27 F4
Mud Hen L. STLS 61 A1
Mud Hole L. STLS 61 E3
Mudhole L. STLS 86 E1
Mud L. ANOK 34 E4
Mud L. ANOK 34 E5
Mud L. ANOK 35 F2
Mud L. ATKN 50 A1
Mud L. ATKN 50 B5
Mud L. BECK 46 A3
Mud L. BECK 47 A1
Mud L. BECK 47 A3
Mud L. BECK 55 E5
Mud L. BECK 55 F5
Mud L. BECK 55 G4
Mud L. BECK 56 D4
Mud L. BECK 56 E2
Mud L. BECK 56 E4
Mud L. BECK 56 F2
Mud L. BECK 56 G1
Mud L. BECK 56 G2
Mud L. BELT 68 D5
Mud L. BELT 69 B1
Mud L. BLUE 15 F4
Mud L. BLUE 15 F5
Mud L. CARL 52 E2
Mud L. CARV 26 C1
Mud L. CASS 48 A5
Mud L. CASS 48 D3
Mud L. CASS 48 E4
Mud L. CASS 57 F5
Mud L. CASS 58 B4
Mud L. CASS 58 E1
Mud L. CHIS 35 B2
Mud L. CHIS 35 C2
Mud L. CLER 56 B3
Mud L. CLER 68 F2
Mud L. CLER 68 F3
Mud L. CLER 68 G4
Mud L. CROW 41 A1
Mud L. CROW 41 B1
Mud L. CROW 41 B5
Mud L. CROW 49 B2
Mud L. CROW 49 B5
Mud L. CROW 49 C4
Mud L. CROW 49 D2
Mud L. CROW 49 D3
Mud L. CROW 49 D4
Mud L. CROW 49 F2
Mud L. CROW 49 F3
Mud L. CROW 49 G5
Mud L. DOUG 39 F1
Mud L. GRNT 38 C1
Mud L. HENN 26 A4
Mud L. HENN 26 B3
Mud L. HENN 26 D1
Mud L. HUBB 56 F5
Mud L. HUBB 57 D2
Mud L. HUBB 57 E3

Mud L. HUBB 57 F1
Mud L. HUBB 57 F3
Mud L. HUBB 69 G3
Mud L. ISNT 34 A5
Mud L. ISNT 34 C3
Mud L. ISNT 35 C2
Mud L. ITSC 59 B4
Mud L. ITSC 59 C4
Mud L. ITSC 59 D3
Mud L. ITSC 59 E3
Mud L. ITSC 71 F2
Mud L. KAND 24 B2
Mud L. KNBC 43 E1
Mud L. LAKE 86 G2
Mud L. LSUR 16 B2
Mud L. LSUR 16 C2
Mud L. LSUR 16 D1
Mud L. MART 4 F5
Mud L. MCLD 24 E5
Mud L. MCLD 25 D2
Mud L. MEEK 24 A5
Mud L. MEEK 24 B5
Mud L. MEEK 32 G5
Mud L. MEEK 33 G2
Mud L. MORR 40 A5
Mud L. MORR 40 B5
Mud L. MORR 40 D5
Mud L. MORR 40 E5
Mud L. MORR 41 C1
Mud L. MORR 41 C4
Mud L. MORR 41 E2
Mud L. MORR 49 G1
Mud L. OTTL 38 B2
L. Mud OTTL 38 B3
Mud L. OTTL 39 B2
Mud L. OTTL 39 B3
Mud L. OTTL 46 D5
Mud L. OTTL 46 E4
Mud L. OTTL 46 F3
Mud L. OTTL 46 F4
Mud L. OTTL 47 B2
Mud L. OTTL 47 B4
Mud L. OTTL 47 C1
Mud L. OTTL 47 C3
Mud L. PINE 43 A3
Mud L. PINE 44 C1
Mud L. PINE 51 G3
Mud L. POPE 39 G2
Mud L. RENV 14 B3
Mud L. RICE 16 C5
Mud L. RICE 16 D4
Mud L. ROSE 92 E3
Mud L. SBLY 14 B5
Mud L. SBLY 15 A2
Mud L. SBLY 25 G2
Mud L. SHER 34 E2
Mud L. STEV 30 A1
Mud L. STLS 52 C3
Mud L. STLS 61 C1
Mud L. STLS 61 E2
Mud L. STLS 61 G2
Mud L. STLS 72 D4
Mud L. STLS 72 F5
Mud L. STLS 73 A4
Mud L. STLS 73 C3
Mud L. STLS 73 C5
Mud L. STLS 73 D4
Mud L. STLS 73 D5
Mud L. STLS 73 F1
Mud L. STLS 73 G1
Mud L. STLS 74 A1
Mud L. STLS 74 F1
Mud L. STLS 74 F1
Mud L. STLS 84 A3
Mud L. STRN 32 B4
Mud L. STRN 32 C4
Mud L. STRN 32 C5
Mud L. STRN 32 E4
Mud L. STRN 33 C2
Mud L. STRN 33 D1
Mud L. STRN 40 G3
Mud L. TODD 40 A3
Mud L. TODD 40 B2
Mud L. TODD 40 D3
Mud L. TODD 40 F1
Mud L. WASH 35 G3
Mud L. WATN 4 B2
Mud L. WRIT 33 F5
Mud L. WRIT 33 G3
Mud L. WRIT 33 G4
Mud L. WRIT 34 F2
Mud L. WRIT 34 G1
Mud L. (Reservoir) KAND 32 E1
Mud L. (Reservoir) MRSH 79 C3
Mud L. (Reservoir) TRAV 37 F2
Mud Lake County Park WRIT 33 G3
Mud Lakes SBLY 25 F4
Mud Portage L. CASS 58 G1
Mud R. BELT 69 C2
Mud R. MRSH 79 C5
Mudro L. STLS 86 F1
Mueller L. LAKE 87 E2
Muerlin L. BELT 69 B1
Mug L. COOK 87 G3
Mug L. STLS 85 C4
Mugwump L. LAKE 87 F2
Mukooda L. STLS 85 C1
Mule Cr. STLS 85 E4
Mule John L. POLK 68 D1
Mule L. CASS 58 F2
Mule L. CASS 58 G4
Mule L. STLS 85 E4
Mulgri L. BECK 55 E4

Mulligan L. BELT 92 G4
Mulligan L. COOK 87 G5
Mulligan Twp BRWN 14 F2
Mulybys Isle MLLC 42 B3
Muma L. COOK 88 G3
Mumm L. TODD 48 G2
Munch-Roos House Historic Site CHIS 35 D5
Munch Twp PINE 43 D3
Mund L. STRN 33 D3
Munger STLS 52 A2
Munker I. COOK 87 D3
Munson L. CARL 51 D5
Munson Twp STRN 32 D4
Munter L. POLK 67 D5
Munzer L. ITSC 59 D3
Murdock SWFT 31 F2
Murdock Municipal Airport SWFT 31 F2
Murmur Cr. COOK 76 C1
Murphy City STLS 74 E5
Murphy-Hanrahan Regional Park Reserve SCOT 26 F4
Murphy L. ITSC 71 G3
Murphy L. LAKE 62 A2
Murphy L. MART 4 D5
Murphy L. OTTL 46 B5
Murphy L. SCOT 26 F4
Murphy L. STLS 61 B1
Murphy's Landing Historic Site SCOT 26 E3
Murphy's Pt. STLS 72 A5
MURRAY — 2 —
Murray County Historical Society Museum MURR 2 A4
Murray Cr. STLS 72 C3
Murray L. STRN 33 E1
Murray Twp MURR 12 G5
Museum L. LAKE 86 G5
Mushgee L. ITSC 70 E4
Mush L. COOK 88 G3
Muskeg Bay WOOD 92 B4
Muskeg Cr. LAKE 86 F2
Muskeg Cr. ATKN 59 G1
Muskeg L. COOK 87 F5
Muskeg L. ITSC 59 D1
Muskeg L. LAKE 86 F2
Muskrat Bay ITSC 70 F5
Muskrat L. BELT 69 D1
Muskrat L. CASS 57 E4
Muskrat L. LAKE 87 F1
Muskrat L. MORR 40 A5
Muskrat L. MORR 40 B5
Muskrat L. STLS 60 F5
Musquash L. COOK 88 G3
Mustinka R. GRNT 37 E4
Muzzle L. LAKE 86 F5
Myers L. CARV 25 E5
Myhr Cr. COOK 76 G5
Myhre L. POLK 68 E1
My L. ITSC 71 F2
My L. LAKE 87 F2
Myrtle FREE 7 F1
Myrtle L. BELT 68 C5
Myrtle L. CLER 56 C4
Myrtle L. KCHG 83 G4
Myrtle L. STLS 84 F4
Mystery Cave FILL 8 E3
Mystery L. ITSC 71 F2
Myth L. COOK 87 F4
Myth L. LAKE 74 G2
Nabek L. LAKE 87 E2
Nagel L. HUBB 57 B3
Nagel L. ITSC 59 B2
Nahimana L. STLS 85 C3
Namakan I. STLS 84 A4
Namakan L. (Reservoir) STLS 84 A4
Namakan R. STLS 84 B4
Namakan Seaplane Base STLS 84 B4
Nameless L. ITSC 60 B1
The Narrows CASS 57 D4
The Narrows COOK 76 E4
The Narrows STLS 73 E2
Nary HUBB 57 A2
Nashua WILK 37 C5
Nashville Twp MART 5 C1
Nashwauk ITSC 59 A5
Nashwauk Twp ITSC 71 G5
Nashwauk L. ITSC 71 G4
Nassau LQPL 21 A4
National Fish Hatchery KAND 32 L1
Nave L. LAKE 87 E2
Nawakwa L. LAKE 87 D2
Nay Tah-Waush MAHN 56 B1
Neander L. CHIS 35 B2
Nebish BELT 69 C2
Nebish L. BELT 69 C2
Nebish Twp BELT 69 C2
Nebraska Bay STLS 84 B2
Necktie R. HUBB 57 B3
Nectar L. LAKE 87 E2
Neds L. ANOK 34 E5
Needleboy L. STLS 73 B4
Needle L. COOK 87 G3
Neesh L. STLS 85 F4
Neewin L. STLS 85 F4
Neff L. STLS 73 F3
Neglige L. LAKE 86 F5
Neill L. BELT 68 B5
Neil Pt. KCHG 95 F5
Nellies L. TODD 40 F3
Nels L. STLS 85 F5
Nels Olson L. CLER 68 C3
Nelson DOUG 39 E3

Nelson Bay CROW 49 D2
Nelson Bay NCLT 15 D1
Nelson I. STLS 96 G2
Nelson L. ATKN 51 C1
Nelson L. BECK 46 A2
Nelson L. BELT 69 D4
Nelson L. CLAY 46 A1
Nelson L. COOK 75 B4
Nelson L. CROW 49 C1
Nelson L. CROW 49 C5
Nelson L. DOUG 39 D1
Nelson L. GRNT 38 F1
Nelson L. HUBB 57 D2
Nelson L. MEEK 24 A3
Nelson L. OTTL 39 B2
Nelson L. OTTL 46 E1
Nelson L. OTTL 46 G3
Nelson L. POPE 31 C2
Nelson Park Twp MRSH 90 G4
Nelson Twp WATN 14 G3
Nemadji State Forest PINE 52 F2
Nereson Twp ROSE 91 E4
Nerstrand RICE 17 D2
Nerstrand Woods Game Refuge RICE 17 C2
Nerstrand Woods State Park RICE 17 D1
Nesbitt I. ITSC 59 C2
Nesbit Twp POLK 66 A2
Ness Church Historic Site MEEK 24 A4
Nessel Twp CHIS 35 A2
Ness L. CLAY 46 A1
Ness Twp STLS 60 E4
Nester Cr. COOK 76 B2
Nest L. KAND 32 F1
Nest L. MAHN 55 C5
Net L. BECK 55 D5
Net L. PINE 52 E2
Net L. STLS 84 B4
Net R. CARL 52 E2
L. Netta ANOK 34 F5
Nett L. KCHG 84 E1
Nett Lake (city)STLS 84 E1
Nett Lake Indian Reservation KCHG 83 E5
Nett Lake R. KCHG 83 D3
Neuner L. BECK 55 G5
Nevada Twp MOWE 7 F3
Never Fail Bay STLS 85 C4
Nevis HUBB 57 F2
Nevis Twp HUBB 57 F2
New Auburn SBLY 25 F2
New Auburn Twp SBLY 25 F2
New Avon Twp REDW 13 C4
New Brighton RAMS 26 B5
Newburg FILL 9 F2
Newburg Twp FILL 9 F3
New Dosey Twp PINE 44 A2
Newfolden MRSH 79 B1
New Folden Twp MRSH 79 C1
Newfound L. LAKE 86 F4
New Germany CARV 25 D4
New Hartford WINA 9 B5
New Hartford Twp WINA 10 B1
New Haven Twp OLMS 18 F1
New Hope HENN 26 B4
Newhouse HOUS 9 G3
New Independence Twp STLS 61 E1
New L. ITSC 60 C1
New London KAND 32 E1
New London Twp KAND 32 F1
New Maine Twp MRSH 79 B1
Newman L. HUBB 69 G1
New Market SCOT 16 A4
New Market Twp SCOT 16 A4
New Munich STRN 32 B3
Newport WASH 27 D2
New Prague LSUR 16 A2
New Prairie Twp POPE 30 A5
New Richland WASC 6 B3
New Richland Twp WASC 6 B3
New Rome SBLY 15 A3
Newry Twp FREE 7 C1
New Scandia Twp WASH 35 F4
New Solum Twp MRSH 79 D1
New Sweden Twp NCLT 15 C2
Newton L. LAKE 86 G2
Newton L. POLK 67 F4
Newton Twp OTTL 47 E3
New Trier DKTA 27 G3
New Ulm BRWN 14 D5
New Ulm Municipal Airport BRWN 14 D4
New York I. LAKE 86 F2
New York Mills OTTL 47 D3
New York Mills Municipal Airport OTTL 47 D3
Niagara Cave FILL 8 G5
Nibble L. COOK 87 G3
Nibin L. STLS 85 D5
Nicado L. LAKE 75 G1
Nichols ATKN 50 G1
Nichols L. STLS 61 D1
Nickel L. LAKE 74 B3
Nickerson PINE 52 E1
Nickerson Twp CARL 52 F2
Nickolson L. STLS 73 A4
NICOLLET — 15 —
Nicollet NCLT 15 D2
Nicollet Bay NCLT 15 D2
Nicollet County Historical Society Museum NCLT 15 D4
Nicollet Cr. NCLT 15 E2
Nicollet L. CLER 56 C4
Nicollet Twp NCLT 15 E2
Nidaros Twp OTTL 39 A1
Nielsen L. WASH 35 F3
Nielsville POLK 66 E1
Niemackl Lakes GRNT 38 F2
Niemada L. HUBB 56 D5
Nigh L. STLS 85 E2
Nighthawk L. COOK 88 F2
Night L. COOK 87 F4
Niki L. STLS 86 E1
Nile Mile Cr. STLS 84 C3
Niles Bay STLS 73 A1
Nilsen Twp WILK 45 F4
Nilson L. POPE 31 C3
Nimrod WADN 48 C2
Nina Moose L. STLS 85 E4
Nina Moose R. STLS 85 D4
Nine A.M. L. LAKE 74 C5
Nine Mile Cr. HENN 26 D4
Ninemile Lake Recreation Site LAKE 75 E2
Ninemile L. LAKE 75 E2
Nininger DKTA 27 E3
Nininger Twp DKTA 27 F3
Ninth Crow Wing L. HUBB 57 E3
Nip Cr. LAKE 74 D2
Nipisiquit L. LAKE 75 G1
Nisswa CROW 49 D1
Nisswa L. CROW 49 D1
Nisula L. COOK 88 F5
Niswi L. STLS 85 F4
Nitche L. OTTL 47 C2
Nixon L. STLS 73 A4
Nixon L. WRIT 33 E3
L. No. 1 STLS 73 B4
L. No. 2 STLS 73 B4
L. No. 3 STLS 73 B4
L. No. 4 STLS 73 B4
NOBLES — 2 —
Nobles County Pioneer Village NBLS 2 E5
Nobles County War Memorial Museum NBLS 2 E5
Nodine WINA 10 B1
Noerenberg Memorial County Park HENN 26 C2
Nokasippi R. CROW 41 B1
Nokay Lake Twp CROW 49 F4
Nokay L. CROW 49 F4
L. Nokomis HENN 26 D5
Nomad L. CASS 57 D5
Noma Lake Recreation Site ITSC 70 C4
Noma L. ITSC 70 C4
No Mans L. ITSC 71 E2
Noodle L. COOK 87 F4
Nora L. POPE 38 G5
Nora Twp CLER 68 F3
Nora Twp POPE 38 G5
Norberg L. CHIP 23 C2
Norberg L. STLS 73 B4
Norcross GRNT 38 E1
Norden Twp PENN 79 E1
Nordfjords Prairie SWFT 31 E2
Nordick Twp WILK 45 E3
Nordland Twp ATKN 50 E2
Nordland Twp LYON 12 B2
Nord L. ATKN 50 E2
Nore Twp ITSC 70 C1
Norfolk-Henryville Game Refuge RENV 24 F1
Norfolk Twp RENV 24 F1
NORMAN — 54 —
Norman County-Ada-Twin Valley Airport NORM 54 B4
Norman County Historical Society Pioneer Museum CLAY 54 B4
Norman County Historical Society Pioneer Village CLAY 54 B4
Normandale Community College HENN 26 E4
Normania YMED 22 F4
Normania Twp YMED 22 F4
Norman I. WOOD 97 E3
Norman L. BELT 81 E5
Normanna Twp STLS 61 E5
Norman Twp PINE 51 G4
Norman Twp YMED 21 F5
Norris L. ANOK 34 E4
Norris L. MAHN 56 B1
Norris Pt. COOK 75 F3
Norseland NCLT 15 C3
Norstedt L. KAND 31 F5
North Arm HENN 26 C2
North Arm STLS 85 F2
North Arm STLS 85 G5
North Baker L. STEV 30 A4
North Barnes L. BECK 55 G3
North Bay COOK 87 G5
North Bay STLS 73 B4
North Bay STLS 74 C1
North Benton BENT 41 F4
North Branch CHIS 35 C2
North Branch Battle R. BELT 81 G4
North Branch Cascade R. COOK 76 A1
North Branch Flint Cr. STLS 72 A4
North Branch Manitou R. LAKE 75 E1
North Branch Middle Fork Zumbro R. GOOD 17 E5
North Branch Rapid R. WOOD 81 A2
North Branch Root R. OLMS 8 B3
North Branch Sunrise R. CHIS 35 C3
North Branch Two R. KITT 90 C3
North Branch Twp ISNT 35 C1
North Branch Whitewater R. STLS 61 A5
North Browns L. STRN 32 D4
North Center L. CHIS 35 D4
North Cormorant R. BELT 69 A4
Northcote KITT 89 C5
North Country Museum of Art HUBB 56 F5
North Cr. STLS 84 G5
Northern L. BECK 55 D5
Northern Light L. COOK 88 G4
Northern Pacific Shops Historic Site CROW 49 F2
Northern Twp BELT 69 E2
Northfield RICE 17 B1
Northfield Historical Society Museum RICE 17 B1
Northfield Twp RICE 17 C1
North Fork Crow R. WRIT 25 A3
North Fork Elm Cr. JACK 4 C1
North Fork Kawishiwi R. LAKE 74 A3
North Fork L. CASS 59 F1
North Fork Nemadji R. CARL 52 D2
North Fork Twp STRN 31 B5
North Fork Watonwan R. WATN 14 G2
North Fork Whitewater R. WBSH 18 F4
North Fork Willow R. CASS 58 D5
North Fork Yellow Bank R. LQPL 29 F4
North Fork Yellow Medicine R. LINC 11 B4
North Fork Zumbro R. GOOD 17 D3
North Fowl L. COOK 88 E5
North Germany Twp WADN 48 D1
North Goldsmith L. LSUR 15 D5
North Haynes L. CASS 57 G4
North Hennepin Community College HENN 26 A4
North Hero Twp REDW 13 E2
North Java L. COOK 87 G4
North L. COOK 88 E1
North L. GOOD 27 F5
North L. MART 4 C2
North L. STLS 85 C3
North L. STRN 32 B4
North L. WRIT 33 E4
North L. WRIT 33 F5
Northland Community College PENN 79 E2
Northland Twp POLK 78 F1
Northland Twp STLS 61 D1
North Lemmerhirt L. OTTL 47 G3
North Long L. CROW 49 E2
North Long L. OTTL 46 D3
North Mankato NCLT 15 F4
North Maple L. OTTL 39 B4
North Momb L. BECK 55 E5
North Oaks RAMS 27 A1
Northome KCHG 70 B2
Northome L. ITSC 71 F2
Northome Municipal Airport KCHG 70 A2
North Ottawa Twp GRNT 38 D1
North Pipestone Cr. PIPE 11 F5
North Pole BELT 69 F2
North Pomme De Terre L. STEV 38 G3
Northport Airport WASH 27 A3
North Prairie (city) MORR 41 F1
North Red River Twp KITT 89 D5
North Redwood REDW 13 A5
North Rice L. OTTL 46 D5
North Ridgepole Cr. LAKE 74 E2
Northrop MART 4 D5
North Rothwell L. BGST 29 C4
North School Section L. WASH 27 A3
North Shady L. COOK 88 F4
North Shore Corridor Trail LAKE 62 B4
North Silver L. MART 4 F5
North Stakke L. BECK 55 G2
North Stanchfield L. ISNT 34 A3
North Stang L. OTTL 46 G3
North Star L. ITSC 71 E2
North Star Recreation Site ITSC 71 E2
North Star Twp BRWN 13 E5
North St. Paul RAMS 27 B2
North Temperance L. COOK 87 G4
North Ten Mile L. OTTL 38 B3
North Terrapin L. WASH 35 G4
North Turtle L. OTTL 46 G4
North Turtle R. BELT 69 E4
North Twin L. BECK 55 F5
North Twin L. BECK 56 G1
North Twin L. BELT 69 E4
North Twin L. CLER 56 C4
North Twin L. LYON 12 E4
North Twin L. MAHN 56 B1
North Twin L. MORR 48 G4
North Twin L. STLS 73 F3
North Twin L. WASH 27 A3
North Twin Lake Recreation Site BELT 69 E4
North Twp PENN 79 E2
Northwest Angle Airport WOOD 97 D1
Northwest Angle State Forest WOOD 97 E1
Northwest Bay STLS 85 C1
Northwest Company Fur Post PINE 43 F2
Northwestern College RAMS 27 B1
Northwest Inlet WOOD 97 D1
Northwest Point Historic Site WOOD 97 D1
North Wigwam L. COOK 75 C3
North Wilder L. LAKE 74 A5
Norton L. STLS 62 A1
Norton Twp WINA 19 G2
Norway Beach Recreation Site CASS 57 A5
Norway Cr. STLS 85 F2
Norway I. LAKE 86 F3
Norway I. STLS 96 G3
Norway L. CASS 49 B1
Norway L. KAND 31 E4
Norway L. LAKE 74 B3
Norway L. OTTL 46 G3
Norway L. STLS 85 C2
Norway Lake (city) KAND 31 F4
Norway Lake Twp KAND 31 E4
Norway Point Recreation Site STLS 73 F4
Norway Pt. STLS 74 C1
Norway Pt. STLS 85 G2
Norway Twp FILL 9 D3
Norway Twp KITT 90 E4
Norwegian Bay STLS 84 G5
Norwegian Cr. LINC 11 C4
Norwegian Cr. NBLS 2 F2
Norwegian Creek County Park LINC 11 D5
Norwegian Grove Twp OTTL 46 C1
Norwood CARV 25 E4
No See Um L. LAKE 86 E1
Nose L. ITSC 71 F3
No Sleep L. COOK 87 G4
No-Ta-She-Bun L. ITSC 59 C1
Nottage L. BECK 46 B4
Nowthen ANOK 34 E3
Noyes KITT 89 A4
Nugget L. STLS 85 E2
Numedal Twp PENN 78 E5
Nunda Twp FREE 6 F3
Nushka L. CASS 58 A3
Nuthatch L. LAKE 75 A1
Nutting House Historic Site RICE 17 B1
Nyberg I. STLS 73 B3
Oak Center WBSH 18 C2
Oak Cr. BELT 80 F4
Oak Cr. OTTL 47 E4
Oakdale WASH 27 B3
Oak Glen L. STEL 7 B2
Oak Grove Twp ANOK 34 E4
Oak I. STLS 73 A1
Oak I. WOOD 97 D3
Oak Island (city) WOOD 97 D3
Oak L. BECK 55 G3
Oak L. CARV 25 C5
Oak L. CASS 58 E1
Oak L. HUBB 57 C3
Oak L. ITSC 71 E3
Oak L. LINC 11 A5
Oak L. PINE 51 F5
Oak L. POLK 67 D3
Oak Lake Game Refuge POLK 67 D3
Oakland County Park PENN 79 E2
Oakland FREE 7 E1
Oakland Twp FREE 7 E1
Oakland Twp MAHN 55 C5
Oak Lawn Twp CROW 49 F3
Oakleaf L. NCLT 15 D4
Oak Narrows STLS 73 A1
Oak Park (city) BENT 33 A5
Oak Park Heights WASH 27 B4
Oak Park Twp MRSH 77 C5
Oak Point WOOD 93 C4
Oakport Twp CLAY 54 F2
Oak Pt. STLS 84 F3
Oakridge WINA 19 F2
Oaks L. COTT 3 B2
Oak Twp STRN 32 B3
Oak Valley Twp OTTL 47 G4
Oakwood City Park WASH 27 D3
Oakwood Twp WBSH 18 E4
Oar L. BECK 55 G4
Oar L. ITSC 71 E3
Oberg L. COOK 75 D4
O'Brien Cr. BELT 69 C3
O'Brien Cr. ITSC 60 A1
O'Brien L. CROW 49 C3
O'Brien L. DKTA 27 E1
O'Brien L. ITSC 60 A1
Obrien Twp BELT 69 C3
Ocheda County Park NBLS 2 F5
Ocheda L. NBLS 2 F5
Ochotto L. STRN 32 B5
O'Connor L. CASS 58 F4
Octagon House BLUE 15 G3
Octopus L. COOK 87 F4
Odeima L. LAKE 74 D5
O'Dell I. WOOD 97 E3
Odeon Theater Historic Site REDW 23 G3
Odessa BGST 29 F4
Odessa Twp BGST 29 E5
Odin WATN 4 C3
Odin Twp WATN 4 B2
Ododikossi L. CASS 58 E4
O'Donald L. MORR 40 E5
O'Donnell L. ITSC 71 D4
O'Dowd L. SCOT 26 E3
Oelfke L. BECK 47 A1
O. E. Rolvaag House Historic Site RICE 17 B1
Ogechie L. MLLC 42 B1
Ogema BECK 55 D3
Ogema L. MAHN 55 C4
Ogema Twp PINE 44 C1
Ogilvie KNBC 42 F4
Ogishkemuncie L. LAKE 87 E2
Ogle L. COOK 87 F3
Ogren L. CHIS 35 E4
Ojibway City Park WASH 27 D3
Ojibway L. LAKE 86 G3
Ojibway Recreation Site BELT 69 E4
Okabena JACK 3 D3
Okabena Cr. JACK 3 D2
Okabena L. NBLS 2 E5
Okamanpeedan L. MART 4 G4
Oketo L. COOK 87 G3
Oklee RDLK 67 B4
L. Olaf OTTL 46 C1
Olander L. CROW 49 E4
Olcott Park STLS 72 F5
Old Crossing Historic Site RDLK 66 B4
Old Crossing Treaty State Historical Wayside Park RDLK 66 A5
Old Crow Wing Historic Site CROW 49 G1
Old Dog Trail Historic Site COOK 76 G1
Old Dutch Bay STLS 84 B3
Old Frontenac Historic District GOOD 18 A3
Old Mill Historic Site MRSH 78 B4
Old Mill State Park MRSH 78 B4
Olds L. ATKN 59 G1
Old Squaw L. STLS 85 E5
Oldtown/Finntown Historic Area STLS 73 F1
Old Wadena County Park WADN 48 F2
Old Wadena Historic Site WADN 48 E2
O'Leary L. DKTA 27 D1
O'Leary L. ITSC 71 E5
O'Leary L. STLS 84 B5
Ole Bakin Cabin Historic Site POLK 67 E4
L. Ole KAND 31 E4
Ole L. STLS 85 G4
Olga POLK 68 D1
Olio L. COOK 87 G4
Olive L. BECK 55 G2
Olive L. STLS 85 F1
Oliver H. Kelley Homestead Historic Site SHER 34 F3
Oliver I. STLS 73 A5
L. Oliver SWFT 30 E2
Olivia RENV 24 E1
Olivia Municipal Airport RENV 23 E5
O. L. Kipp State Park WINA 10 B1
OLMSTED — 8 —
Olmsted County Historical Center and Museum OLMS 8 A1
Olney Twp NBLS 2 E3
Olson Bay STLS 73 A5
Olson Bay STLS 96 F1
Olson L. BGST 29 D4
Olson L. COOK 76 A2
Olson L. CROW 49 C5
Olson L. GRNT 38 E4
Olson L. KAND 23 B4
Olson L. POLK 67 D5
Olsrud L. GRNT 38 F2
Omaday L. LAKE 74 B3
Omaha Indian Village Historic Site YMED 21 F4
Omega L. COOK 87 F5
O-Me-Mee L. BECK 55 E4
Omen L. CASS 48 D5
Omro Twp YMED 22 E2
Omsrud L. BRWN 14 F4
L. Onalaska WINA 10 B2
Onamia MLLC 42 C2
L. Onamia MLLC 42 C1
Onamia Twp MLLC 42 D2
O-Ne-Gum-E Recreation Site ITSC 70 F4

O'Neils Point BELT 69 G4
One Island L. COOK 88 E1
Oneka L. WASH 35 G2
L. One LAKE 86 G4
One L. CASS 58 G1
One L. CLER 68 C2
One Loaf L. ITSC 70 E3
One Mile L. OTTL 46 G2
One Pine L. STLS 74 B1
One Tool L. COOK 87 G4
Onigum CASS 57 D4
Onion L. BECK 55 D4
Onion L. COOK 88 F3
Onion R. COOK 75 D4
Onstad L. OTTL 46 G4
Onstad Twp POLK 66 D5
Opole STRN 41 G1
Oraas County Park YMED 22 F4
Orange L. BECK 55 G2
Orange L. ITSC 71 G2
Orange Twp DOUG 39 F4
Orchard L. DKTA 26 F5
Orchid L. LAKE 75 B1
O'Reilly L. ITSC 59 A3
Oreland L. CROW 49 E4
Organ L. LAKE 75 C2
Oriniack L. STLS 85 F2
Oriole L. COOK 87 G3
Orion Twp OLMS 8 B3
Orleans KITT 90 B1
Ormsby WATN 4 C3
Orono HENN 26 C3
Oronoco OLMS 18 F1
Oronoco County Park OLMS 18 F1
Oronoco Twp OLMS 18 F1
Orono L. SHER 34 E2
Orr STLS 84 F3
Orrock SHER 34 D1
Orrock Twp SHER 34 D1
Orr Regional Airport STLS 84 F3
Ortman L. MORR 41 C3
Orton Twp WADN 48 B2
Ortonville BGST 29 E4
Ortonville Municipal Airport BGST 29 E4
Ortonville Twp BGST 29 E4
Orwell Farm Historic Site OTTL 38 A1
Orwell Reservoir OTTL 38 A1
Orwell Twp OTTL 38 A1
Orwell Wildlife Management Area OTTL 38 A1
Osage BECK 56 F4
Osage Twp BECK 56 F4
Osakis DOUG 39 E4
L. Osakis TODD 39 E5
Osakis Twp DOUG 39 E4
Osborne Twp PIPE 2 B1
Oscar And Anna Johnson County Park WRIT 25 C4
L. Oscar DOUG 39 F1
L. Oscar OTTL 46 F1
Oscar Twp OTTL 46 E1
Osceola Twp RENV 24 D2
Ose L. BELT 69 G3
Oshawa CASS 48 A4
Oshawa NCLT 15 D3
Oshawa Twp NCLT 15 D3
Oshkosh Twp YMED 22 E1
Osier L. LAKE 74 E5
Oskenonton I. COOK 87 C4
Oslo DOGE 7 B5
Oslo MRSH 77 D4
Oslo L. STLS 96 G3
Osprey L. COOK 88 G2
Ossawinnamakee L. CROW 49 C2
Osseo HENN 26 A4
Osterberg L. POPE 38 G5
Ostrander FILL 8 F2
Oteneagen Twp ITSC 70 G5
Otisco WASC 6 A3
Otisco Twp WASC 6 A3
Otrey L. BGST 29 E4
Otrey Twp BGST 29 D5
Otsego WRIT 34 F2
Otsego Twp WRIT 34 F2
Ottawa LSUR 15 C4
Ottawa Methodist Church Historic Site LSUR 15 C4
Ottawa Twp LSUR 15 C4
Ottawa Village Historic District LSUR 15 C4
Otter Cr. CARL 52 B1
Otter Cr. MCLD 25 D3
Otter Cr. MOWE 7 G3
Otter L. ATKN 59 G1
Otter L. BECK 56 G3
Otter L. COOK 88 F5
Otter L. ITSC 71 D4
Otter L. ITSC 71 G2
Otter L. KAND 24 B2
Otter L. KAND 32 E2
Otter L. MCLD 24 D5
Otter L. OTTL 46 C3
Otter L. RAMS 27 A2
Otter L. STEV 30 A4
Otter L. STLS 85 G3
Otter L. STRN 33 E3
Otter Lake Regional Park RAMS 27 A2
OTTER TAIL — 46 —
Ottertail OTTL 47 E1
Otter Tail County Historical Society Museum OTTL 46 G2
Ottertail Goose Game Refuge OTTL 46 F2
Otter Tail L. OTTL 46 F5
Otter Tail Point CASS 57 C5
Otter Tail R. BECK 46 A5
Otter Tail R. BECK 56 E1
Otter Tail R. OTTL 47 D1
Otter Tail R. WILK 37 A4
Otter Tail Twp OTTL 47 F1
Ott L. COOK 88 F1
Otto L. BECK 55 D3
Otto L. STLS 61 A5
Otto Lakes COOK 88 F1
Otto Twp OTTL 47 E2
Outing CASS 49 A4
Outlaw L. LAKE 75 C2
Outlet Cr. POPE 31 B1
Ova L. LAKE 74 C4
Overby L. POLK 67 D5
Overson L. CLAY 55 G1
Overson L. NCLT 15 D3
L. Owasso RAMS 27 B1
Owatonna Arts Center STEL 16 G5
Owatonna Municipal Airport STEL 16 F5
Owatonna STEL 16 G5
Owatonna Twp STEL 16 G5
Owen Johnson Interpretive Center FREE 6 E5
Owen L. ITSC 71 D4
Owen Lake Recreation Site ITSC 71 D4
Owens Cr. STLS 73 B3
Owens Twp STLS 72 B5
Owl L. COOK 87 F3
Owl L. HUBB 57 F2
Oxbow County Park OLMS 17 G5
Oxbow L. ATKN 59 G4
Oxbow L. CASS 58 E4
Oxbow L. CASS 58 G5
Ox Camp L. CASS 48 A4
Oxford Twp ISNT 35 D1
Ox Hide L. ITSC 59 A5
Ox L. CROW 49 B3
Oxlip ISNT 34 C4
Ox Yoke L. CASS 57 G5
Ox Yoke L. HENN 26 C1
Oylen WADN 48 D2
Oyster L. STLS 85 D4
Oyster R. STLS 85 D4
Ozada L. COOK 88 G1
Paavola Cr. STLS 72 C3
Paccini L. LAKE 75 E2
Pace L. LAKE 87 F2
Packard L. MAHN 55 B5
Paco L. LAKE 87 E2
Paddle L. COOK 88 E3
Paddock Twp OTTL 47 C4
Padua STRN 31 B5
Pagami Cr. LAKE 74 A3
Pagami L. LAKE 74 A3
Pageant Cr. STLS 85 D3
Pageant L. STLS 85 C3
Page L. STEV 30 C4
Page Twp MLLC 42 E1
Pagoda L. COOK 75 B4
Paine L. COOK 88 G4
Paine L. HUBB 57 C1
Pakwene L. LAKE 86 E1
Paleface R. STLS 61 C1
Palisade ATKN 50 B3
Palisade Head LAKE 63 A1
Palkie Grist Mill Historic Site CARL 52 B2
Palmdale CHIS 35 D4
Palmer Cr. CHIP 23 C1
Palmer L. HENN 26 B5
Palmer L. HUBB 48 A2
Palmers STLS 62 F1
Palmer Twp SHER 33 C4
Palmville Twp ROSE 91 F5
Palmyra Twp RENV 24 F2
Palo STLS 73 G3
Panasa L. ITSC 59 B5
Pancake Cr. COOK 75 C3
Pancake Cr. KCHG 70 A3
Pancake I. COOK 76 F2
Pancake L. COOK 75 C3
Pancake L. ITSC 60 D1
Pancore L. COOK 75 C4
Pangi L. LAKE 74 B4
Panhandle L. LAKE 87 F2
Pan L. LAKE 87 F2
Paoli L. COOK 75 B3
Paper Mill Reservoir ITSC 59 C2
Papoose L. CROW 49 A4
Papoose L. STLS 62 B1
Papoose L. STLS 86 E1
Paquet L. CASS 57 F5
Paradise Beach COOK 76 B5
Paradise L. STLS 62 D1
Paradise L. WRIT 33 F5
Parent BENT 33 B4
Parent L. LAKE 86 G4
Parkers L. HENN 26 C3
Parkers Prairie OTTL 39 B3
Parkers Twp OTTL 39 B3
Parker Twp MORR 40 C4
Parker Twp MRSH 78 A1
Parke Twp CLAY 46 A1
Park L. CARL 51 C5
Park L. ITSC 70 D5
Park Rapids (city) HUBB 56 F5
Park Rapids Municipal Airport HUBB 56 G5
Park Rapids Tourist Information Center HUBB 56 F5
Park Twp CARL 52 G1
Parkville STLS 72 E5
Parley L. CARV 26 D1
Parley L. STLS 85 D5
Parnell Twp POLK 66 A4
Parnell Twp TRAV 29 A3
Parsnip L. BECK 55 D4
Parsnip L. COOK 88 F3
Partridge Bay CASS 58 D2
Partridge Cr. STLS 84 G5
Partridge L. COOK 88 E2
Partridge L. CROW 49 F5
Partridge R. STLS 73 F3
Partridge R. TODD 48 G1
Partridge Twp PINE 43 A4
Party L. COOK 87 D3
Pascoe L. CROW 49 E4
Passenger L. PINE 51 F4
Pat Bayle State Forest COOK 76 B4
Patchen L. GRNT 38 F3
Path L. LAKE 74 A4
Pat Kapaun Airport BGST 29 B4
Pat L. COOK 87 G3
Pat L. WASH 27 A3
L. Patterson CARV 25 D5
Paul Bunyan Arboretum CROW 42 F2
Paul Bunyan Game Refuge HUBB 57 D2
Paul Bunyan State Forest HUBB 57 D2
Pauley L. TODD 40 F2
Pauline L. STLS 85 E2
Paul L. OTTL 46 C5
Paul Miller Park OTTL 47 C1
Paulson Cr. ROSE 92 E1
Paulson L. POPE 31 C1
Paulson Mine Historic Site COOK 87 E4
Paulucci Planetarium STLS 72 B4
Paul Van Hoven Municipal Park LAKE 62 E3
Pavelgrit L. CASS 49 A4
Paxton Twp REDW 13 B5
Pay L. KAND 32 G2
Payne STLS 60 D5
Paynesville STRN 32 E3
Paynesville Historical Society Museum STRN 32 D3
Paynesville Municipal Airport STRN 32 E3
Paynesville Twp STRN 32 E3
Payne Twp STLS 60 D5
Peabody L. MAHN 55 B5
Peace Avenue of Flags NBLS 2 E5
Peace L. KNBC 43 C1
Peace Twp KNBC 42 D5
Peach L. BECK 46 A2
Pea L. COOK 88 F4
Peanut L. COOK 88 F3
Pearce L. BECK 46 A5
Pear L. ITSC 71 E2
Pear L. LAKE 87 E2
Pearl L. BECK 46 A3
Pearl L. JACK 3 F4
Pearl L. LAKE 75 D2
Pearl L. STLS 84 C1
Pearl L. STRN 33 D1
Pearson L. CHIS 35 E4
Peary L. STLS 96 G3
Pease MLLC 34 A2
Pea Soup L. LAKE 86 G2
Peat L. TODD 40 B3
Peavey L. HENN 26 C3
Peavey L. LAKE 75 D1
Peavy L. MORR 41 B5
Pebble L. OTTL 38 A2
Pecore Cr. COOK 75 C4
Pee Wee L. CASS 48 A5
Pegg L. LQPL 21 A4
Pekan L. STLS 85 C4
Pelan Twp KITT 90 E5
Pelewski L. OTTL 46 D5
Pelican Bay OTTL 47 E1
Pelican Bk. CROW 49 C3
Pelican Cr. GRNT 38 C4
Pelican Island CASS 58 D1
Pelican L. CROW 49 D2
Pelican L. GRNT 38 C4
Pelican L. OTTL 46 B2
Pelican L. POPE 31 A2
Pelican L. STLS 84 F3
Pelican L. STRN 32 A5
Pelican L. WRIT 34 F1
Pelican Lake Twp GRNT 38 C4
Pelican Point BELT 81 F1
Pelican R. OTTL 46 E2
Pelican R. STLS 84 E4
Pelican Rapids (city) OTTL 46 D2
Pelican Rapids Municipal Airport OTTL 46 C2
Pelican Twp CROW 49 D2
Pelican Twp OTTL 46 C2
Pelkey L. MORR 41 D2
Pelland KCHG 95 G2
Pell Cr. REDW 13 E2
Pellet I. LAKE 63 B1
Pellet L. COOK 87 E4
Peltier L. ANOK 35 G2
Pelt L. LAKE 74 B5
Pelton L. ITSC 71 D1
Pemberton BLUE 6 A1
Pembina Twp MAHN 55 B3
Pemmican L. COOK 88 E4
Pencer ROSE 92 E1
Pencil L. COOK 87 F4
Pendant L. COOK 76 B2
Pendergast L. TODD 39 B5
Pengar L. COOK 75 C5
Pengilly ITSC 59 A5
Peninsula L. BECK 47 A3
Peninsula L. BECK 56 G3
PENNINGTON — 79 —
Pennington BELT 69 F5
Pennington L. KNBC 42 F5
Pennington Pioneer Museum PENN 79 E2
Penn L. HENN 26 D5
Pennock KAND 31 G4
Penn Twp MCLD 25 F1
Penny L. FREE 6 D2
L. Pepin GOOD 18 A3
L. Pepin LSUR 16 B2
Pepin L. TODD 40 E3
Pepin Twp WBSH 18 C5
Peppermint Cr. WOOD 93 E3
Pepperton Twp STEV 30 A2
Pequaywam L. STLS 62 C1
Pequot Lakes (city) CROW 49 C1
Perch Cr. BLUE 5 B1
Perch L. BECK 55 G5
Perch L. BELT 68 D5
Perch L. BLUE 5 A5
Perch L. CARL 51 B5
Perch L. CASS 48 A4
Perch L. CASS 57 F4
Perch L. CLAY 55 G1
Perch L. CLER 56 A2
Perch L. CROW 49 D3
Perch L. CROW 49 G1
Perch L. LINC 11 A5
Perch L. LSUR 16 E2
Perch L. MAHN 55 A5
Perch L. MART 4 C5
Perch L. OTTL 39 B2
Perch L. POLK 68 C1
Perch L. POLK 68 D1
Perch L. STLS 60 B5
Perch L. STLS 72 D2
Perch L. STLS 73 C5
Perch Lake County Park MART 4 C5
Perch Lake Twp CARL 51 B5
Percy Twp KITT 90 D4
Perdu L. LAKE 86 F4
Perent L. LAKE 75 B2
Perent R. LAKE 75 B1
Perham OTTL 47 C1
Perham Municipal Airport OTTL 47 C1
Perham Twp OTTL 47 D1
Perkins L. STEV 38 G4
Perley NORM 54 C1
Peron L. LAKE 87 F2
Perry Cr. BELT 69 B4
Perry L. ATKN 59 E1
Perry L. CASS 57 F4
Perry L. CROW 49 C4
Perry Lake Twp CROW 49 D4
Perry Twp LQPL 21 A5
Pete Isle MLLC 42 B3
Pete L. OTTL 38 A4
Pete L. OTTL 46 C1
Peter Gideon Homestead Historic Site HENN 26 D2
Peter L. COOK 87 E3
Peter L. HENN 26 B2
Petersburg JACK 4 G1
Petersburg Twp JACK 4 F1
Peterson FILL 9 C2
Peterson Bay NCLT 15 D2
Peterson Bay STLS 84 A1
Peterson L. BELT 69 D2
Peterson L. BELT 69 E1
Peterson L. BELT 69 E3
Peterson L. BGST 29 E4
Peterson L. CASS 49 A2
Peterson L. CASS 57 F5
Peterson L. CASS 58 E4
Peterson L. CHIS 35 E4
Peterson L. CLER 68 D3
Peterson L. COOK 75 A4
Peterson L. GRNT 38 E4
Peterson L. ITSC 70 D5
Peterson L. MEEK 32 G3
Peterson L. NCLT 15 C2
Peterson L. OTTL 46 E4
Peterson L. WBSH 19 D1
Peterson Slough CHIS 35 D3
Petit L. COOK 75 A4
Petit L. HUBB 57 E1
Petran FREE 7 E1
Petrel Cr. STLS 62 A1
Peysenski L. HUBB 57 F1
Pfeiffer L. STLS 73 C1
Pfeiffer Lake Recreation Site STLS 73 C1
Pflueger L. STRN 32 B5
Phalanx L. COOK 87 F5
Phalen Park RAMS 27 C2
L. Phalen RAMS 27 C2
Phantom Cr. STLS 73 A3
Phantom L. LAKE 74 F3
Phantom L. STLS 73 A4
Phare Lake Game Refuge RENV 24 D4
Phare L. RENV 24 E4
Phelon L. CASS 58 E3
Phelps OTTL 46 F4
Phelps Bay HENN 26 C2
Phelps L. RICE 16 B3
Phelps Mill County Park OTTL 46 F4
Phelps Mill Historic Site OTTL 46 F4
Philbrook TODD 48 G3
Phil's County Park FRBT 6 E1
Phoebe L. COOK 75 A3
Phoebe R. LAKE 75 A2
Phospor L. LAKE 74 B4
Picard Point ATKN 42 A3
Pickard L. CLER 56 C4
Pickerel L. ANOK 34 E3
Pickerel L. ATKN 50 D1
Pickerel L. BECK 55 G5
Pickerel L. BECK 56 G3
Pickerel L. CASS 57 G5
Pickerel L. CLER 56 C2
Pickerel L. CLER 68 C4
Pickerel L. COOK 76 A3
Pickerel L. CROW 49 B4
Pickerel L. CROW 49 C5
Pickerel L. CROW 49 E3
Pickerel L. FREE 6 E4
Pickerel L. HOUS 10 F2
Pickerel L. HUBB 57 E1
Pickerel L. ITSC 70 C5
Pickerel L. ITSC 71 B4
Pickerel L. ITSC 71 F2
Pickerel L. ITSC 71 G1
Pickerel L. LAKE 74 A2
Pickerel L. OTTL 46 D5
Pickerel L. OTTL 46 E4
Pickerel L. OTTL 47 F1
Pickerel L. PINE 52 F2
Pickerel L. SHER 33 D3
Pickerel L. STLS 72 D1
Pickerel L. STLS 73 B4
Pickerel Lake County Park FREE 6 E4
Pickerel Lake Recreation Site ITSC 71 B4
Pickerel Lake Twp FREE 6 E3
Picket L. STLS 85 E2
Picket L. STLS 86 F1
Picket R. STLS 85 E1
Picketts L. STLS 86 G1
Pick L. CASS 58 F1
Pickle L. BECK 55 D5
Pickle L. LAKE 87 E1
Pickles L. STLS 72 D4
Pickwick WINA 9 A5
Pickwick Mill Historic Site WINA 9 A5
Picnic I. ITSC 59 A1
Pidgeon L. STLS 62 C1
Pie L. COOK 87 G3
Piepenburg County Park MCLD 24 C5
Pierce L. MART 4 F4
Pierce L. MCLD 24 C5
Pierre Bottineau Gravsite Historic Site RDLK 66 A5
Pierson L. CARV 26 D1
Pierz MORR 41 D3
Pierz L. COOK 88 E3
Pierz L. MORR 41 D3
Pierz Twp MORR 41 E3
Pietro L. LAKE 74 A4
Pigeon Bay COOK 76 E4
Pigeon Dam L. ITSC 70 F3
Pigeon L. MAHN 55 C5
Pigeon L. MEEK 25 B1
Pigeon L. MEEK 32 E3
Pigeon Pt. COOK 76 E4
Pigeon R. COOK 76 E2
Pigeon R. ITSC 70 F3
Pigeon River (city) COOK 76 E3
Pigeon River Flowage Game Refuge ITSC 70 F3
Pig L. CASS 48 A5
Pig L. CROW 49 C2
Pigs Eye L. RAMS 27 C2
Pike Bay CASS 57 A4
Pike Bay STLS 73 B2
Pike Bay Twp CASS 57 A4
Pike Cr. BELT 69 B1
Pike Cr. MORR 40 D5
Pike Creek Twp MORR 40 D5
Pike L. BECK 56 D2
Pike L. CLER 68 D2
Pike L. COOK 76 B1
Pike L. HENN 26 B4
Pike L. ITSC 71 F1
Pike L. LAKE 74 D3
Pike L. POPE 38 G5
Pike L. SCOT 26 E4
Pike L. STLS 61 G3
Pike Mountain STLS 73 E1
Pike R. STLS 73 C2
Pike River Flowage STLS 73 C2
Pike River Recreation Sites STLS 73 C2
Pike River State Fish Hatchery STLS 73 B2
Pike's Fort Historic Site MORR 41 E1
Pike Twp STLS 73 D2
Pillager CASS 48 G5
Pillager L. CASS 48 F5
Pillsberry L. COOK 88 F1
Pillsbury TODD 40 E3
Pillsbury Baptist College STEL 16 G5

Pillsbury State Forest CASS 48 F5
Pillsbury Twp SWFT 31 F3
Pilot Grove FRBT 5 G2
Pilot Grove Twp FRBT 5 F2
Pilot Mound FILL 9 C1
Pilot Mound Twp FILL 9 C1
Pimushe L. BELT 69 E5
Pinch L. COOK 87 G3
PINE — 43 —
Pine Bay LAKE 62 B5
Pine Center CROW 41 A4
Pine City PINE 43 F2
Pine City Municipal Airport PINE 43 F2
Pine City Twp PINE 43 F3
Pine County Game Refuge Unit 1 PINE 44 B1
Pine County Game Refuge Unit 2 PINE 43 C4
Pine County Game Refuge Unit 3 PINE 44 C1
Pine County Historical Society Museum PINE 43 B4
Pine Cr. HOUS 10 C1
Pine Cr. ROSE 91 B4
Pine Cr. STLS 85 G3
Pine Cr. WINA 9 C2
Pine Creek (city) ROSE 91 B4
Pine Grove Park and Zoo MORR 41 D1
Pine I. STLS 73 A2
Pine I. STLS 84 A2
Pine I. STLS 84 A2
Pine I. STLS 96 G3
Pine Island (city) GOOD 17 E5
Pine Island WOOD 93 C3
Pine Island L. ATKN 50 E1
Pine Island L. BECK 56 D2
Pine Island L. BELT 68 B5
Pine Island L. TODD 40 A3
Pine Island State Forest KCHG 82 E3
Pine Island Twp GOOD 18 E1
Pine L. ATKN 43 B1
Pine L. BECK 55 E5
Pine L. BECK 56 F1
Pine L. CASS 58 E1
Pine L. CHIS 35 A2
Pine L. COOK 88 E4
Pine L. COOK 88 G2
Pine L. CROW 49 C3
Pine L. CROW 49 F5
Pine L. HUBB 57 D1
Pine L. ITSC 71 C2
Pine L. ITSC 71 E2
Pine L. MAHN 55 B5
Pine L. MORR 40 F4
Pine L. OTTL 46 D4
Pine L. OTTL 46 D5
Pine L. STLS 74 F1
Pine L. STLS 85 G3
Pine L. STRN 32 A5
Pine Lake Twp CASS 58 E1
Pine Lake Twp CLER 68 C2
Pine Lake Twp OTTL 47 D2
Pine Lake Twp PINE 43 B2
Pine Mountain L. CASS 48 A4
Pine Mountain L. COOK 88 G3
Pine Point CASS 57 C5
Pine Point Twp BECK 56 E3
Pine R. CASS 49 C3
Pine R. CASS 57 F4
Pine R. COOK 88 E5
Pine R. PINE 43 A2
Pine River (city) CASS 49 B1
Pine River Twp CASS 48 B5
Pine Springs (city) WASH 27 B3
Pinetop KCHG 70 A3
Pine Tree County Park BELT 69 C4
Pine Tree L. WASH 27 A3
Pine Valley Ski Area CARL 52 B1
Pinewood BELT 68 E5
Piney-Pinecreek Border Airport ROSE 91 A4
Pinnakers L. ANOK 34 E4
Pioneer City Park ANOK 34 G5
Pioneer L. LAKE 74 B5
Pioneer L. STLS 61 C2
Pipe Island CASS 58 E1
Pipe L. COOK 75 A5
PIPESTONE — 11 —
PIPESTONE PIPE 11 G4
Pipestone Bay LAKE 86 F2
Pipestone County Historical Society Museum PIPE 1 A4
Pipestone County Veterans Memorial Park PIPE 11 G5
Pipestone Cr. PIPE 1 A3
Pipestone Historic District PIPE 1 A4
Pipestone Municipal Airport PIPE 1 A4
Pipestone National Monument Historic Site PIPE 11 G4
Pipestone National Monument PIPE 11 G4
Pirz L. STRN 32 D4
Pistol L. CASS 49 A3
Pistol L. COOK 88 G3
Pitcha L. LAKE 74 D3
Pitcher L. COOK 88 F3
Pitfall L. LAKE 87 E2
Pit L. COOK 76 A2
Pit L. STLS 61 C4
Pitt WOOD 93 E3
Pitts L. STRN 32 B5
Pixley L. TODD 40 F2
L. Placid CASS 48 G5
Placid L. LAKE 75 B1
Plainview WBSH 18 F4
Plainview Twp WBSH 18 F4
L. Plaisted WASH 35 G3
Plaman L. SBLY 15 B2
Plantagenet L. HUBB 69 G1
Plantation L. ITSC 71 F3
Planted L. LAKE 74 D4
Plato MCLD 25 E4
Platte L. CROW 41 B4
Platte Lake Twp CROW 41 B4
Platte R. MORR 41 C3
Platte Twp MORR 41 C3
Platt L. TODD 39 E5
Pleasant Grove OLMS 8 C3
Pleasant Grove Twp OLMS 8 B2
Pleasant Hill Twp WINA 9 B5
Pleasant L. CASS 57 F5
Pleasant L. CROW 49 C3
Pleasant L. OTTL 46 D4
Pleasant L. OTTL 46 F3
Pleasant L. RAMS 27 A1
Pleasant L. SCOT 26 G2
Pleasant L. STLS 73 G1
Pleasant L. STRN 33 C1
Pleasant L. WRIT 33 F3
Pleasant Lake (city) STRN 33 C2
Pleasant Mound Twp BLUE 5 B1
Pleasant Prairie Twp MART 5 E1
Pleasant Valley Twp MOWE 7 C5
Pleasant View Twp NORM 66 G4
Pletan L. GRNT 38 B2
Pliny Twp ATKN 50 G5
Plouff Cr. COOK 75 B3
Plouff L. COOK 75 A3
Plug Hat Point Recreation Site ITSC 70 G3
Plug L. COOK 87 F4
Plum Bk. KCHG 82 G5
Plum Creek Park REDW 13 E1
Plum Cr. REDW 13 E1
Plume L. LAKE 87 D2
Plum Grove L. BECK 55 E3
Plum L. ITSC 71 E2
Plum L. LAKE 75 C1
Plummer RDLK 67 A3
Plymouth HENN 26 B3
Pocket Cr. STLS 85 C4
Pocket L. COOK 76 B2
Pocket L. DOUG 39 F1
Pocket L. STLS 85 C4
Pocquette L. ITSC 71 A4
Poe L. COOK 87 G3
Poet L. COOK 75 A3
Pogo L. COOK 87 E4
Pohlitz Twp ROSE 91 B3
Pohl L. WRIT 34 G1
Point Douglas WASH 27 E4
Point Douglas Park WASH 27 E4
Pointer L. COOK 87 F2
Point L. KAND 31 G5
Pointon L. CROW 49 F4
Pokegama PINE 43 F2
Pokegama L. PINE 43 F2
Pokegama L. (Reservoir) ITSC 59 C2
Pokegama Recreation Site ITSC 59 B2
Pokegama Twp PINE 43 E2
Pokety Cr. HUBB 57 B2
Polander L. MORR 40 E4
POLK — 66 —
Polk Centre Twp PENN 78 F5
Polk-Clearwater Game Refuge POLK 68 B1
Polk County Park at Cross Lake POLK 68 D1
Polk County Park at Maple Lake POLK 67 D2
Polk County Pioneer Museum POLK 66 C3
L. Polly LAKE 75 A2
Polly Wog L. BELT 69 C2
Pollywog L. CASS 58 E1
Polonia Twp ROSE 91 D1
Pomerleau L. HENN 26 B3
Pomme de Terre L. GRNT 38 C3
Pomme De Terre Municipal Park STEV 30 B3
Pomme De Terre Pool (Reservoir) STEV 30 B3
Pomme De Terre R. STEV 30 C3
Pomme De Terre Twp GRNT 38 C3
Pompous L. LAKE 75 B1
Pomroy L. KNBC 42 D5
Pomroy L. KNBC 43 D1
Pomroy Twp ITSC 70 C4
Pomroy Twp KNBC 43 C1
Pond L. STLS 72 E4
Ponemah BELT 81 F2
Ponsford BECK 56 F3
Ponto Lake Twp CASS 58 G1
Ponto L. CASS 58 G1
Pony L. BELT 69 E1
Poole Bay ITSC 59 C2
Pooles L. WRIT 25 C5
Pool L. BELT 69 E3
Pool No. 1 ROSE 91 B3
Pool No. 2 ROSE 91 B2
Pool No. 3 ROSE 91 B1
Poor Farm Bay NCLT 15 D2
Poor Farm L. ATKN 50 D1
POPE — 31 —
Pope County Historical Society Museum POPE 31 A2
Poplar Cr. BELT 81 D3
Poplar Cr. COOK 88 F2
Poplar Cr. WOOD 97 D1
Poplar Cr. PIPE 1 B5
Poplar Grove Twp ROSE 91 F4
Poplar L. COOK 88 F1
Poplar L. ITSC 71 B4
Poplar L. POLK 68 E1
Poplar R. COOK 75 C5
Poplar R. POLK 67 C3
Poplar River Recreation Site COOK 75 C4
Poplar River Twp RDLK 67 B3
Poplar Twp CASS 48 D3
Popple Creek (city) BENT 33 A4
Popple Grove Twp MAHN 55 C3
Popple L. BELT 69 F5
Popple L. CASS 58 E1
Popple L. MEEK 24 B3
Popple L. MORR 41 D1
Popple R. ITSC 70 D2
Poppleton Twp KITT 90 C2
Popple Twp CLER 68 E2
Porcupine I. COOK 76 E4
Porcupine L. ATKN 50 F4
Pork Bay LAKE 75 F2
Porridge L. LAKE 87 F2
Portage Bay STLS 73 A2
Portage Bk. COOK 88 F5
Portage Cr. STLS 84 E2
Portage L. ATKN 50 D3
Portage L. CASS 57 E4
Portage L. CASS 58 A1
Portage L. CASS 58 D3
Portage L. COOK 88 E1
Portage L. CROW 49 E4
Portage L. CROW 49 E5
Portage L. CROW 49 F5
Portage L. HUBB 56 F5
Portage L. ITSC 70 E4
Portage L. LAKE 86 E5
Portage L. OTTL 47 E1
Portage Lake Recreation Site CASS 58 A1
Portage R. STLS 85 E4
Portage Twp STLS 84 E5
Porter YMED 22 G1
Porter Cr. SCOT 26 G2
Porter L. BLUE 5 B2
Porter L. MEEK 24 B5
Port Hope Twp BELT 69 D3
Pose L. LAKE 74 A5
Posen Twp YMED 23 G1
Posse L. STLS 85 D3
Post Office Historic Site BRWN 14 D5
Potatoe Island BELT 69 G4
Potatoe I. STLS 84 A2
Potatoe L. ITSC 71 F3
Potato I. STLS 73 B2
Potato L. COOK 88 F4
Potato L. HUBB 56 E5
Pot Hole L. STLS 84 C4
Pot L. STLS 73 G2
Potsdam OLMS 18 F3
Potshot L. CASS 58 G2
Potshot L. STLS 60 F2
Pouch L. LAKE 87 F2
Poverty L. COOK 87 G5
Poverty L. ITSC 71 G1
Powder I. KCHG 96 F1
Powder Ridge Ski Area STRN 33 E1
Powell L. COOK 87 E3
Powers L. COOK 88 F5
Powers L. MEEK 33 G1
Powers L. TODD 39 C5
Powers L. WASH 27 C3
Powers Twp CASS 57 G5
Powwow L. LAKE 75 B1
Prairie Bk. TODD 40 F2
Prairie Cr. BELT 69 B4
Prairie Cr. GOOD 17 B2
Prairie Cr. STLS 84 F1
Prairie Island Indian Reservation GOOD 27 G5
Prairie Island Nuclear Generating Plant GOOD 27 G5
Prairie Island Park WINA 19 G3
Prairie L. ITSC 59 B3
Prairie L. ITSC 71 E5
Prairie L. OTTL 46 C2
Prairie L. SHER 33 D4
Prairie L. STLS 51 A3
Prairie Lake Twp STLS 51 A2
Prairie R. ATKN 50 A5
Prairie R. ATKN 51 A1
Prairie R. ITSC 59 A3
Prairie View Twp WILK 45 C5
Prairieville RICE 17 D1
Prairieville Twp BRWN 14 D2
Pratt STEL 7 A1
Prayer L. COOK 87 D4
Preble Twp FILL 9 E3
Predmore OLMS 8 B3
Prentice Pond MORR 41 B1
Prescott L. GRNT 38 E2
Prescott Twp FRBT 5 D3
Preston FILL 8 E5
Preston L. RENV 24 E4
Preston Lake Twp RENV 24 E4
Preston Twp FILL 8 E5
Prestrude L. BECK 55 G2
Previs L. ATKN 59 E2
Priam KAND 23 B4
Primer L. CASS 58 F1
Princeton MLLC 34 B2
Princeton Municipal Airport MLLC 34 B2
Princeton Twp MLLC 34 B2
Prinsburg KAND 23 C4
Prior L. SCOT 26 F4
Prior Lake (city) SCOT 26 F4
Prior Lake Memorial Park SCOT 26 F4
Prior Twp BGST 29 C3
Proctor STLS 52 B3
Profit L. STLS 85 C4
Promise L. LAKE 75 A1
Prop L. COOK 88 F2
Prosit STLS 60 E5
Prout L. COOK 76 E1
Providence LQPL 22 D1
Providence Twp LQPL 22 D1
Prowest L. MORR 40 D4
Prune L. BECK 55 G2
Prune L. COOK 88 F1
Ptarmigan L. COOK 88 G2
Puck L. STLS 60 G2
Puddle L. COOK 88 F4
Puffer L. LAKE 75 A1
Puff L. COOK 88 F4
Pugh L. MORR 40 B5
Pug Hole L. BELT 69 F5
Pug Hole L. CROW 49 A4
Pughole L. ITSC 71 E3
Pughole L. ITSC 71 G2
Pulaski Twp MORR 41 C4
L. Pulaski WRIT 33 G5
Pullman L. GRNT 38 F1
Pulvers L. CASS 48 E3
Pump L. BECK 46 A1
Pump L. ITSC 59 B4
Pup L. COOK 87 F5
Puposky BELT 69 D2
Puposky L. BELT 69 D1
Purgatory Cr. HENN 26 D3
Putnam L. STLS 73 C3
Puutio Cr. STLS 72 C5
Quadga L. LAKE 74 B4
Quadna Ski Area ATKN 59 F2
Quallen L. MAHN 55 C4
Quamba KNBC 43 E1
Quam L. DOUG 38 E5
Quarry Hill Municipal Park OLMS 18 G2
Quartz L. LAKE 86 G5
Queen Twp POLK 68 E1
Quick L. STLS 61 C5
Quill L. STLS 96 G2
Quinn L. STRN 33 E3
Quiring Twp BELT 69 B3
Quiver L. COOK 88 F2
Quincy Twp OLMS 18 G4
Rabbit Cr. OTTL 38 B1
Rabbit I. STLS 96 G4
Rabbit L. ATKN 50 E3
Rabbit L. CASS 48 B5
Rabbit L. CASS 58 D3
Rabbit L. CROW 49 D4
Rabbit L. LAKE 87 D2
Rabbit L. STLS 84 E2
Rabbit Lake Twp CROW 49 D5
Rabbit Point BELT 81 F1
Rabbit R. WILK 37 B3
Rabbits L. ITSC 70 F1
Rabideau CCC Camp Historic Site BELT 69 D5
Rabideau L. BELT 69 D5
Rachel L. DOUG 39 F1
Racine MOWE 8 D2
Racine Twp MOWE 8 C1
Radabaugh L. WADN 48 E2
Raddison L. ITSC 71 D4
Radium MRSH 78 D3
Radke L. ISNT 34 B3
Rafferty Cr. ROSE 92 E1
Raff L. POLK 67 F1
Raft L. ITSC 71 E2
Ragged L. BELT 69 D1
Ragged L. COOK 87 F4
Rahkos L. ITSC 71 F4
Rail L. LAKE 87 G2
Rail Prairie Twp MORR 40 A5
Railroad L. LAKE 74 F3
Railroad L. OTTL 46 E3
Railroad Turntable Historic Site MURR 12 G5
Rain Barrel Lakes ITSC 59 A3
Rainy L. CASS 57 G5
Rainy L. (Reservoir) STLS 96 F3
Rainy River Community College KCHG 95 F3
Rainy R. KCHG 93 E4
Rally L. COOK 87 E3
Ramey MORR 41 F4
Ram I. STLS 84 A1
Ram L. COOK 88 G2
RAMSEY — 27 —
Ramsey ANOK 34 F4
Ramsey MOWE 7 D3
Ramsey City Park REDW 13 A4
Ramsey Cr. REDW 13 A4
Ramsey L. WRIT 33 G4
Ramsey Mill Historic Site DKTA 27 F4
Ramsey Mill Pond MOWE 7 D3
Ramshead Cr. STLS 85 D4
Ramshead L. STLS 85 D4
Randall MORR 40 C5
Randolph Bay STLS 84 B4
Randolph DKTA 17 A2
Randolph Twp DKTA 17 A2
Range Line Cr. STLS 85 C3
Range Line Cr. STLS 85 E3
Range Line L. BELT 69 D2
Range Line L. STLS 85 C3
Range L. LAKE 86 F1
Ranger L. COOK 87 F4
Range R. STLS 86 F1
Ranier KCHG 95 F4
Ranier L. ITSC 71 E1
Rankle L. OTTL 46 B1
Ransom Twp NBLS 2 F4
L. Ranum CLAY 46 C1
Rapidan BLUE 15 G3
Rapidan Dam County Park BLUE 15 G3
Rapidan Twp BLUE 15 G3
Rapid R. WOOD 93 G5
Rapid River Logging Camp HUBB 56 F5
Rapids BLUE 15 G3
Rapture L. LAKE 87 F2
Rasmuson L. POPE 31 D2
Raspberry I. STLS 73 B3
Raspberry L. ATKN 50 E1
Raspberry L. BECK 55 D5
Rassat WRIT 33 G4
Rassett L. CROW 49 D4
Rassom L. BECK 55 E3
Rat Cr. HUBB 57 B1
Rat Farm L. BECK 55 D4
Rat L. ATKN 50 B4
Rat L. BECK 55 E3
Rat L. CASS 48 D4
Rat L. CASS 58 E1
Rat L. COOK 88 E1
Rat L. CROW 49 C3
Rat L. ITSC 71 C4
Rat L. ITSC 71 D3
Rat L. LAKE 74 D4
Rat L. STLS 61 C2
Rat L. STLS 72 D5
Rat L. STLS 72 E2
Rat L. TODD 40 A3
Rat Root L. KCHG 95 G5
Rat Root R. KCHG 83 B4
Rattle L. COOK 87 F2
Rattling Springs Lakes GOOD 27 G5
Rauch KCHG 84 G1
Rausch L. STRN 33 D1
Raven L. ITSC 70 F1
Raven L. LAKE 87 F1
Ravenna Twp DKTA 27 F4
Raven Stream SCOT 26 G2
Ray KCHG 83 B5
Ray Berglund State Wayside Park COOK 75 D5
Ray Eustice County Park WASC 6 B1
Ray L. COOK 87 E3
Raymond KAND 23 B4
Raymond L. STRN 31 B5
Raymond Twp STRN 31 B5
Rays L. LSUR 16 E2
Razor L. PINE 44 C1
Reading NBLS 2 D4
Reads Landing (city) WBSH 18 C5
Reamer L. KAND 32 E2
L. Rebecca HENN 26 B1
Rebecca L. DKTA 27 E3
Recline L. LAKE 87 G1
Record Cr. LAKE 87 G1
Record L. LAKE 87 G1
Redby BELT 69 B2
Red Cliff COOK 76 B4
Redcoat L. COOK 88 G4
Redeye L. COOK 88 F1
Redeye R. OTTL 47 B3
Red Eye Twp WADN 47 C5
Redface L. LAKE 87 F1
Redfin L. LAKE 87 F1
RED LAKE — 67 —
Red Lake (city) BELT 69 A1
Red Lake Falls (city) RDLK 67 A1
Red Lake Falls Municipal Airport RDLK 67 B1
Red Lake Falls Twp RDLK 67 A1
Red Lake Indian Reservation BELT 69 B1
Red Lake R. POLK 66 B4
Red Lake State Forest BELT 81 E5
Red Lake Wildlife Management Area BELT 81 D1
Red L. ATKN 50 B3
Redpath Twp TRAV 37 E5
Redpoll L. COOK 87 E2
Red River Art Center and Rourke Art Gallery CLAY 56 G1
Red River L. OTTL 46 F3
Red River of the North WILK 45 F2

Red River Trail Historic Site KAND 32 G2
Red Rock COOK 76 F2
Red Rock Bay COOK 87 D3
Red Rock Cr. COOK 76 F2
Red Rock Falls County Park COTT 13 F5
Red Rock L. COOK 75 A3
Red Rock L. COOK 87 D3
Red Rock L. DOUG 38 E5
Red Rock L. HENN 26 D3
Red Rock L Twp MOWE 7 D3
Red Sand L. CROW 49 F1
Redskin L. LAKE 74 D5
Redstart L. LAKE 87 G2
Red Sucker L. KCHG 95 F5
Red Wing GOOD 18 A1
REDWOOD — 13 —
Redwood County Historical Society Museum REDW 13 A4
Redwood Falls (city) REDW 13 A4
Redwood Falls Municipal Airport REDW 13 A5
Redwood Falls Twp REDW 13 B4
Redwood Ferry Historic Site RENV 14 A1
Redwood R. REDW 13 B2
Reed L. ITSC 59 D4
Reed L. OTTL 46 E2
Reeds L. WASC 16 E2
Reep L. BECK 55 F3
Reflection L. LAKE 86 F5
Regal KAND 32 D2
Regenbogen L. STLS 85 F5
Reich L. MCLD 25 D4
Reilly Bk. KCHG 83 G2
Reilly Cr. KCHG 83 F2
Reiner Twp PENN 80 E1
Reine Twp ROSE 92 F2
Reinke Slough BLUE 5 B2
Reis Twp POLK 66 E4
Reitz L. CARV 26 D1
Remer CASS 58 E4
Remer Municipal Airport CASS 58 D4
Remer State Forest CASS 58 D5
Remer Twp CASS 58 E4
Remote L. ATKN 50 A5
Rendsville Twp STEV 38 G3
Reno HOUS 10 F2
Reno Cr. STLS 61 A5
L. Reno POPE 39 G2
Reno L. CROW 49 E5
Reno Twp POPE 39 G2
RENVILLE — 24 —
Renville RENV 23 E4
Renville County Historical Society Museum RENV 14 A1
Repast L. LAKE 74 A4
Repose L. STLS 85 G5
Reservation R. COOK 76 F2
Reservoir L. CASS 58 G5
Reshanau L. ANOK 35 G1
Retreat L. COOK 75 B3
Retzlaff L. GRNT 38 E4
Revere REDW 13 E2
Review Is. KCHG 95 F5
Reward L. COOK 87 D4
Reynolds Twp TODD 40 D1
Rheiderland Twp CHIP 23 C3
Rhimey L. GRNT 38 E2
Rhine L. PINE 43 A2
Rib L. COOK 87 F4
RICE — 16 —
Rice BENT 41 G2
Rice Bay LAKE 85 F4
Rice Bay STLS 73 A3
Rice Bed L. CROW 49 C4
Rice County Historical Society Museum RICE 16 D5
Rice Cr. ITSC 71 C2
Rice Cr. KNBC 42 G5
Rice Cr. MORR 41 D2
Rice Cr. SHER 33 C4
Rice Creek-Chain of Lakes Regional Park Reserve ANOK 35 G2
Riceford Cr. HOUS 9 E3
Riceford HOUS 9 F3
Rice L. ANOK 35 E1
Rice L. ANOK 35 G1
Rice L. ATKN 50 D4
Rice L. ATKN 51 C1
Rice L. BECK 46 A5
Rice L. BECK 55 F5
Rice L. BECK 56 F1
Rice L. BELT 69 C1
Rice L. BELT 69 C2
Rice L. BELT 69 C3
Rice L. BLUE 15 G5
Rice L. CARV 25 E5
Rice L. CASS 48 B5
Rice L. CASS 48 F5
Rice L. CASS 49 B1
Rice L. CASS 57 D5
Rice L. CASS 58 A3
Rice L. CASS 58 F2
Rice L. COOK 75 B4
Rice L. CROW 49 D2
Rice L. CROW 49 E2
Rice L. CROW 49 E4
Rice L. CROW 49 F5

Rice L. DKTA 26 G5
Rice L. FRBT 5 C3
Rice L. FRBT 6 E1
Rice L. HENN 26 A3
Rice L. HENN 26 E3
Rice L. HUBB 57 E1
Rice L. ISNT 35 C2
Rice L. ITSC 59 C1
Rice L. ITSC 59 C4
Rice L. ITSC 70 D3
Rice L. ITSC 70 F1
Rice L. ITSC 71 D1
Rice L. KNBC 42 G5
Rice L. LAKE 74 B5
Rice L. LSUR 16 B3
Rice L. LSUR 16 C1
Rice L. MAHN 55 B5
Rice L. MEEK 32 G5
Rice L. MLLC 30 F2
Rice L. MORR 41 E2
Rice L. NCLT 15 C1
Rice L. OTTL 46 B5
Rice L. OTTL 46 E3
Rice L. OTTL 47 D1
Rice L. RICE 16 D3
Rice L. SCOT 26 E4
Rice L. SCOT 26 F4
Rice L. SHER 33 C4
Rice L. SHER 34 C2
Rice L. SHER 34 E2
Rice L. STEL 17 G2
Rice L. STLS 84 G3
Rice L. STRN 32 E4
Rice L. TODD 40 B3
Rice L. TODD 40 C3
Rice L. WADN 48 B1
Rice L. WASC 16 F3
Rice L. WASH 35 G2
Rice L. WRIT 26 C1
Rice L. WRIT 33 E4
Rice L. WRIT 34 F2
Rice Lake Hut Rings Historic Site CASS 48 F5
Rice Lake National Wildlife Refuge ATKN 50 D4
Rice Lake National Wildlife Refuge Headquarters ATKN 50 D4
Rice Lake State Park STEL 17 G2
Rice Lake Twp STLS 61 F4
Rice Lake Wayside SCOT 26 E4
Riceland Twp FREE 6 D5
Rice Marsh L. HENN 26 D3
Rice Pad L. CASS 58 G5
Rice Pond BELT 69 E4
Rice Portage L. CARL 51 B4
Rice Portage L. CASS 58 G1
Rice R. ATKN 50 D3
Rice R. BLUE 5 C3
Rice R. ITSC 71 D2
Rice R. STLS 72 B4
Rice River Twp ATKN 50 E5
Rices Point STLS 52 A4
Rice Twp CLER 56 B3
Riceville Twp BECK 55 E3
Richards L. CLER 80 E3
Richardson L. MEEK 32 G5
Richardson Twp MORR 41 C5
Richards Townsite Recreation Site CASS 58 A2
Richardville Twp KITT 90 B1
Richey L. COOK 75 D5
Richfield HENN 26 D5
Richie I. STLS 84 A2
Richland Twp RICE 17 E1
Richmond STRN 32 D4
Richmond Island WINA 10 A1
Richmond Twp WINA 10 B1
Richter Woods County Park LSUR 16 C2
Rich Valley Twp MCLD 25 D2
Richville OTTL 47 D1
Richwood BECK 55 E4
Richwood Twp BECK 55 F4
Rickert L. STEL 7 B1
Rickert Lake Waterfowl Refuge STEL 7 B1
Riddle L. LAKE 87 F1
Rider L. BECK 46 A3
Ridgely L. NCLT 14 C3
Ridgepole L. LAKE 74 E2
Ridgeway WINA 9 B5
Rifle L. LAKE 74 A4
Riggs Mission Historic Site YMED 23 E1
Rikansrud L. POLK 67 D5
L. Riley HENN 26 D3
Rindal NORM 67 F2
Rindal L. POLK 67 F5
Ringo L. KAND 31 F5
L. Ripley MEEK 24 A4
Ripley Twp DOGE 7 A2
Ripley Twp MORR 41 C2
Ripple I. STLS 85 G5
Ripple L. ATKN 50 E1
Ritter Farm Municipal Park DKTA 26 F5
Ritual L. STLS 86 E1
Rivalry L. LAKE 87 D2
Riverdale Twp WATN 14 G4
River Falls Twp PENN 79 G2
River L. DKTA 27 E2
River L. LAKE 87 G1
River Municipal Park SBLY 15 B4
Riverside County Park WRIT 34 G2

Riverside Municipal Park SHER 33 C3
Riverside Twp LQPL 22 C2
River Terrace City Park HENN 26 E4
Riverton CROW 49 E3
Riverton Twp CLAY 54 G4
River Twp RDLK 79 G2
Roadside L. BELT 69 E4
Roast L. COOK 75 B5
Robbin KITT 89 F4
Robbinsdale HENN 26 B4
Robbins I. LAKE 86 E5
Robbins Slough MURR 12 F5
Roberds L. RICE 16 D4
Roberts Cr. MOWE 7 D3
Robertson County Park JACK 3 G4
Robertson L. HUBB 57 C2
Roberts Twp WILK 45 D2
Robina L. HENN 26 A3
Robin L. LAKE 74 C3
Robinson STLS 73 B4
Robinson Cr. MOWE 8 C1
Robinson L. CLER 56 B4
Robinson L. HUBB 57 C2
Robinson L. WINA 19 C1
Robinson Lakes STLS 73 B4
Robour L. CHIS 35 B1
Rochert BECK 55 G5
Rochert L. BECK 55 F5
Rochester OLMS 8 A2
Rochester Game Refuge OLMS 18 G2
Rochester Municipal Airport OLMS 8 B2
Rochester State Community College OLMS 8 A2
Rochester State Hospital OLMS 8 A2
Rochester Twp OLMS 8 A1
ROCK — 1 —
Rock County Historical Society Museum ROCK 1 E5
Rock Cr. CHIS 43 G3
Rock Creek (city) PINE 43 G2
Rock Dell OLMS 7 B5
Rock Dell Twp OLMS 8 B1
Rockford WRIT 26 A1
Rockford Twp WRIT 25 A5
Rock I. COOK 76 C2
Rock Island L. LAKE 74 A4
Rock L. ATKN 50 C4
Rock L. BECK 46 A2
Rock L. CASS 48 F5
Rock L. CLER 56 B4
Rock L. CROW 41 B5
Rock L. CROW 49 C5
Rock L. ITSC 72 F1
Rock L. LYON 12 D3
Rock L. PINE 43 F2
Rock L. PINE 44 C2
Rock L. STLS 72 E2
Rock L. STLS 72 F2
Rock L. WRIT 34 F1
Rock Lake Cr. STLS 72 F2
Rock Lake Recreation Site CASS 48 F5
Rock Lake Twp LYON 12 E3
Rock of Ages L. LAKE 74 A4
Rock R. ROCK 1 E5
Rocksbury Twp PENN 79 F2
Rockstad L. CLER 56 B3
Rock Twp PIPE 12 G1
Rockville STRN 33 C1
Rockville L. STRN 33 C1
Rockville Twp STRN 33 D1
Rockwell L. HUBB 57 F1
Rockwell Twp NORM 54 C5
Rockwood Twp HUBB 57 A1
Rockwood Twp WADN 47 D5
Rocky Bay STLS 74 A1
Rocky L. COOK 88 E3
Rocky L. STLS 85 B4
Rocky Point CASS 49 E1
Rocky Point COOK 87 D3
Rocky Point WOOD 93 B1
Rocky Shores Recreation Site LAKE 74 E3
Roe L. LAKE 87 F2
Roemhildts L. LSUR 16 E1
Rogers HENN 34 G3
Rogers L. ANOK 34 F4
Rogers L. CROW 49 C5
Rogers L. DKTA 27 D1
Rogers L. TODD 40 A3
Rogers Point CASS 58 E1
Rogers Twp CASS 58 D3
Rog L. COOK 87 E3
Rohrbeck L. MEEK 32 F5
Roland L. ITSC 71 F2
Rolf L. POLK 67 C4
Rollag CLAY 46 B1
Rolling Forks Twp POPE 31 C2
Rolling Green Twp MART 4 E4
Rolling Hills Municipal Park DKTA 27 D2
Rolling L. STRN 40 G3
Rollingstone WINA 19 F2
Rollingstone Cr. WINA 19 G2
Rolling Stone Twp WINA 19 F3
Rollins Cr. COOK 75 D5
Rollins Twp MRSH 79 B5
Romance L. COOK 87 D3
Rome Twp FRBT 5 F4
Romp L. COOK 87 G3
Ronald L. Cloutier Recreation Site

CROW 49 C3
Rondeau L. ANOK 35 G2
Ron L. COOK 87 D4
Ronneby BENT 33 A5
Rookie L. LAKE 86 G3
Roome Twp POLK 66 C2
Roosevelt ROSE 92 D5
L. Roosevelt CROW 49 A4
Roosevelt L. CLER 80 F3
Roosevelt L. STLS 51 A2
Roosevelt Twp BELT 68 C5
Roosevelt Twp CROW 41 A5
Rooster L. MAHN 55 C5
Roothouse L. ITSC 59 D5
Root R. HOUS 9 D4
Rosby L. POPE 38 G3
Roschien L. STRN 32 D4
Roscoe GOOD 17 E4
Roscoe STRN 32 D4
Roscoe Twp GOOD 17 E4
ROSEAU — 91 —
Roseau ROSE 91 C5
Roseau County Historical Society Museum ROSE 91 C5
Roseau L. BELT 92 G4
Roseau Municipal Airport ROSE 92 C1
Roseau River Wildlife Management Area ROSE 91 B2
Roseau R. ROSE 91 B3
Rosebud Twp POLK 67 E5
Rose City DOUG 39 C4
Rose Cr. MOWE 7 F4
Rose Creek (city) MOWE 7 F4
Rosedale Twp MAHN 55 B4
Rose Dell Twp ROCK 1 C4
Rose Hill Twp COTT 3 A2
L. Rose HENN 26 D3
Rose L. COOK 88 E2
Rose L. CROW 49 E4
Rose L. HUBB 56 E5
Rose L. ITSC 71 G4
Rose L. MART 4 F5
Rose L. OTTL 38 A3
Rose L. OTTL 46 B5
Rose L. STLS 61 D2
Roseland KAND 23 C5
Roseland Twp KAND 23 C5
Rosemoen Island CHIP 22 B3
Rosemount DKTA 27 E1
Rosen LQPL 22 B3
Rosendahl L. STLS 72 C5
Rosendale MEEK 24 B3
Rosendale Twp WATN 4 A4
Roseville RAMS 27 B1
Roseville Twp GRNT 38 F3
Roseville Twp KAND 32 E2
Rosewood MRSH 79 D1
Rosewood Twp CHIP 22 B5
Rosholt Cr. ITSC 59 C5
Rosholt L. ITSC 59 B5
Rosing Twp MORR 48 G5
Ross ROSE 91 B4
Rossburg ATKN 50 D2
Rossier L. STRN 33 B1
Ross L. COOK 87 F5
Ross L. CROW 49 C5
Ross Lake Twp CROW 49 B5
Rossman L. BECK 46 A2
Ross Twp ROSE 91 B4
Rost Twp JACK 3 E3
Rosvold L. OTTL 38 A3
Rota L. LAKE 74 E4
Rothsay WILK 45 E5
Rothsay Wildlife Management Area WILK 45 D5
Rottenwood I. STLS 96 G1
Round Bear L. STLS 84 A3
Round Grove L. MCLD 24 F5
Round Grove Twp MCLD 24 F5
Round Island L. LAKE 74 D5
Round L. ANOK 34 F4
Round L. ATKN 50 B2
Round L. ATKN 50 B5
Round L. ATKN 50 B5
Round L. BECK 46 A2
Round L. BECK 55 G2
Round L. BELT 69 D1
Round L. CASS 48 D4
Round L. CASS 57 G5
Round L. CASS 58 G1
Round L. COOK 87 E4
Round L. CROW 41 A2
Round L. CROW 49 E2
Round L. CROW 49 G5
Round L. DOUG 39 E1
Round L. GRNT 38 E4
Round L. HENN 26 D3
Round L. HUBB 57 F2
Round L. ITSC 59 C4
Round L. ITSC 71 B3
Round L. ITSC 71 E4
Round L. ITSC 71 G1
Round L. JACK 3 F2
Round L. LSUR 16 E1
Round L. MART 4 C4
Round L. MART 4 E3
Round L. MEEK 24 A5
Round L. MORR 40 A4
Round L. MORR 40 B5
Round L. MORR 41 B4
Round L. MURR 12 F5
Round L. OTTL 46 D3
Round L. OTTL 46 D4

Round L. OTTL 46 E4
Round L. OTTL 46 F5
Round L. OTTL 47 E1
Round L. OTTL 47 F1
Round L. POPE 31 B5
Round L. RAMS 27 B1
Round L. STEV 30 B4
Round L. STLS 60 B5
Round L. STLS 60 E5
Round L. STLS 61 C2
Round L. STLS 74 F1
Round L. TODD 40 C3
Round L. WADN 48 A2
Round L. WASH 27 A3
Round L. WRIT 25 B4
Round Lake (city) NBLS 3 F1
Round Lake County Park ATKN 50 B2
Round Lake Municipal Park HENN 26 D3
Round Lake Twp BECK 56 E2
Round Lake Twp JACK 3 F2
Round Prairie (city) TODD 40 E2
Round Prairie Twp TODD 40 E2
Rove L. COOK 88 E3
Rowena REDW 13 C4
Royal L. COOK 88 E5
Royalton MORR 41 F1
Royalton Twp PINE 43 F1
Royal Village Museum MORR 41 F1
Royal Twp LINC 11 A5
Roy L. CLER 56 A1
Roy L. COOK 87 D3
Roy L. CROW 49 E1
Roy Lake Cr. MAHN 56 A1
Ruby L. COOK 88 E2
Ruby L. ITSC 71 F2
Ruby L. STLS 85 D3
Rudy L. COOK 88 E2
Ruffy Bk. CLER 68 C3
Rug L. COOK 88 F1
Rum L. COOK 88 F2
Rum L. ISNT 35 B1
Rum L. ITSC 71 B4
Rumpuss L. COOK 87 E3
Rum River Central Regional Park ANOK 34 F4
Rum R. ISNT 34 C5
Rum River North County Park ANOK 34 D4
Rum River South County Park ANOK 34 D4
Rum River State Forest MLLC 42 G2
Runeberg Twp BECK 47 A4
Runestone Museum DOUG 39 E3
Runestone Park DOUG 39 E3
Rush City CHIS 35 A2
Rush City Municipal Airport CHIS 35 A3
Rush Cr. CHIS 35 A3
Rush Cr. HENN 26 A3
Rush Cr. WINA 9 B2
Rushfeldt L. CLAY 45 A5
Rushford FILL 9 C3
Rushford Municipal Airport FILL 9 C2
Rushford Village FILL 9 C3
Rush Island L. ITSC 70 E4
Rush L. BECK 56 F1
Rush L. BELT 68 B5
Rush L. CASS 58 G1
Rush L. CHIS 35 A1
Rush L. COOK 88 F1
Rush L. CROW 49 B3
Rush L. CROW 49 G1
Rush L. JACK 3 F4
Rush L. JACK 3 G3
Rush L. MAHN 55 A4
Rush L. OTTL 46 G1
Rush L. OTTL 47 E1
Rush L. PINE 51 F4
Rush L. SHER 33 C4
Rush L. STLS 61 C3
Rush L. STLS 85 D5
Rush Lake Twp OTTL 47 D1
Rushmore NBLS 2 E3
Rush R. SBLY 15 B4
Rush River (city) SBLY 15 B3
Rush River Wayside SBLY 15 B4
Rushseba Twp CHIS 35 A3
Ruskin RICE 17 E1
Russell LYON 12 D2
Russell L. CROW 49 G3
Russia Twp POLK 66 D4
Rustad CLAY 45 B2
Rustad L. BECK 55 E1
Ruth L. CASS 49 F1
Ruth L. CROW 49 B4
Ruth L. STLS 62 C1
Ruthton PIPE 12 E1
Rutland Twp MART 4 D5
Rutledge PINE 43 A3
Rutz L. CARV 25 D5
Ryan L. ANOK 35 D2
Ryan L. MCLD 25 D2
Sabe L. CLER 68 F2
Sabin CLAY 45 A2
Sable L. LAKE 86 G5
Sabre L. LSUR 16 D2
Saca L. STLS 85 G4
Sacred Heart RENV 23 E3

Sacred Heart Cr. RENV 23 F3
Sacred Heart Twp RENV 23 E3
Saddle L. LAKE 87 G2
Saganaga L. COOK 87 D3
Sagatagan L. STRN 33 B1
Sager L. MART 5 F1
Saginaw STLS 61 G1
Saginaw Bay STLS 96 F2
Sago Twp ITSC 59 D5
Sagus L. LAKE 87 F1
Sailor L. CASS 58 E5
St. Albans Bay HENN 26 D3
St. Anna STRN 32 A5
St. Anna L. STRN 40 G4
St. Anthony RENV 32 A4
St. Anthony STRN 26 B5
St. Anthony Falls HENN 26 C5
St. Augusta STRN 33 C3
St. Augusta Cr. STRN 33 D2
Saint Bonifacius HENN 26 D1
St. Catherine L. SCOT 26 G4
St. Charles WINA 8 A5
St. Charles Twp WINA 8 A5
St. Clair BLUE 15 G5
St. Clair L. BECK 46 A4
St. Clair L. BECK 55 E4
St. Clair Lake County Park BECK 55 E4
St. Cloud STRN 33 B2
St. Cloud Game Refuge STRN 33 C2
St. Cloud State University STRN 33 C3
St. Cloud Twp STRN 33 C2
St. Columbo Mission Historic Site CROW 49 E1
L. St. Croix WASH 27 C4
St. Croix Island Recreation Area WASH 27 B4
St. Croix Islands Game Refuge PINE 43 E4
St. Croix National Science River Visitor Center — 35 D1
St. Croix R. WASH 27 D4
St. Croix River Game Refuge WASH 35 F4
St. Croix State Forest OLMS 8 C2
St. Croix State Park Game Refuge PINE 44 E4
St. Croix State Park PINE 43 D5
St. Croix Wildriver State Park CHIS 35 B3
Saint Francis ANOK 34 D4
St. Francis STRN 40 G4
St. Francis Xavier Church Historic Site COOK 76 B3
Saint George NCLT 14 C4
St. George Twp BENT 33 B4
St. Hilare PENN 79 F1
St. James WATN 4 A3
St. James Game Refuge WATN 4 A3
St. James L. WATN 4 A3
St. James Municipal Airport WATN 4 A4
St. James Pitt L. STLS 73 E3
St. James Twp WATN 4 A3
L. St. Joe CARV 26 D2
St. Johns Abby and University Church STRN 33 B1
St. Johns Episcopal Church Historic Site CLAY 54 G2
St. John's L. KAND 31 G4
St. Johns Twp KAND 23 A4
St. John's University STRN 33 B1
St. Joseph STRN 33 B1
St. Joseph Twp KITT 90 B3
St. Joseph Twp STRN 33 C1
St. Kilian NBLS 2 C3
St. Lawrence Twp SCOT 26 G1
St. Leo YMED 22 F2
ST. LOUIS — 52 —
St. Louis Bay STLS 52 B4
St. Louis County Heritage and Arts Center STLS 52 A4
St. Louis Park HENN 26 C4
St. Louis R. PINE 52 B2
St. Martin STRN 32 C3
St. Martin Twp STRN 32 C3
St. Mary's College WINA 19 G3
St. Mary's L. STLS 73 G1
St. Mary's Point WASH 27 C4
St. Mary Twp WASC 16 G2
St. Mathias CROW 41 A2
St. Mathias Twp CROW 41 B2
St. Michael WRIT 34 G2
St. Nicholas STRN 32 E5
St. Nicholas County Park FREE 6 F5
St. Olaf College RICE 17 B1
St. Olaf L. WASC 6 B4
St. Olaf Lake County Park WASC 6 B4
St. Olaf Twp OTTL 38 B4
St. Patrick SCOT 26 G3
St. Patrick L. BECK 55 G4
St. Paul RAMS 27 C2
St. Paul Bible College CARV 26 D1
St. Paul Downtown Airport RAMS 27 C2
St. Paul Park WASH 27 D2
St. Paul Seminary RAMS 27 C1
St. Peter NCLT 15 D4
St. Peter Municipal Airport NCLT 15 D4
St. Peter State Hospital NCLT 15 D4
St. Regis County Park BENT 41 G2
St. Rosa STRN 40 G3
St. Stephen STRN 33 A2
St. Thomas LSUR 16 B1
St. Thomas College RAMS 27 C1
St. Vincent KITT 89 A4
St. Vincent Twp KITT 89 B4
St. Wendel STRN 33 A1
St. Wendel Twp STRN 33 A1
Sakatah Lake State Park RICE 16 E3
Sakatah Singing Hills Corridor Trail LSUR 16 E1
Salem Corners OLMS 8 A1
Salem Cr. OLMS 7 A5
Salem L. CLAY 46 B1
Salem Twp CASS 58 C4
Salem Twp OLMS 8 A1
L. Sallie BECK 46 A4
Salol ROSE 92 C2
Salo L. STLS 62 A1
Salo Lake Recreation Site LAKE 62 A1
Salo Twp ATKN 51 D1
Salter Bay ITSC 59 C2
Salter Pond ITSC 59 C3
Salt L. LQPL 21 C3
Salt L. STLS 73 F2
Saltpork L. STLS 85 F2
Sam Brown Log Cabin Historic Site TRAV 29 B1
Sam Brown State Monument TRAV 29 B1
Sam L. CHIS 35 E3
Sampson L. ITSC 59 C4
Sampson L. OTTL 39 B1
Samson L. BECK 46 A3
Samuelson County Park STLS 84 G1
Sanborn REDW 13 E4
L. Sanborn LSUR 16 B3
Sanburn L. CASS 48 A5
Sandabacka L. ATKN 51 D1
Sandback L. CLER 56 C2
Sandbar I. STLS 85 C2
Sandbar L. CROW 49 D3
Sandbay I. STLS 96 G4
Sandberg L. OTTL 46 D2
Sand Cliff Point BELT 81 F1
Sand Cr. ITSC 59 C5
Sand Cr. PINE 43 C4
Sand Cr. SCOT 26 F2
Sand Cr. STLS 60 C3
Sand Cr. STLS 72 C2
Sand Creek Twp SCOT 26 F2
Sand Dunes Game Refuge SHER 34 D1
Sand Dunes State Forest SHER 34 D2
Sanderson L. LYON 12 E2
Sanders Twp PENN 79 F1
Sand Hill L. POLK 67 F5
Sand Hill R. POLK 66 E2
Sand L. BECK 55 G1
Sand L. CARL 52 D1
Sand L. CASS 58 F1
Sand L. CLER 68 F2
Sand L. CROW 49 B4
Sand L. ITSC 59 D4
Sand L. ITSC 70 E4
Sand L. ITSC 71 F3
Sand L. LAKE 74 E2
Sand L. NCLT 15 C3
Sand L. OTTL 46 C2
Sand L. PINE 51 F4
Sand L. POLK 68 D1
Sand L. SBLY 15 B1
Sand L. STLS 60 B2
Sand L. STLS 72 D5
Sand L. STRN 32 B3
Sand L. STRN 32 B4
Sand L. STRN 32 B5
Sand L. STRN 32 C5
Sand L. WADN 48 D2
Sand L. WASH 35 F4
Sand Lake Twp ITSC 70 E4
Sandnes Twp YMED 22 F5
Sandpit L. LAKE 86 F1
Sand Point CASS 57 C4
Sand Point GOOD 18 A3
Sand Point Bay WOOD 97 F1
Sand Point L. STLS 85 B1
Sand R. HUBB 57 E1
Sandshore L. ANOK 34 D5
Sands L. BECK 55 F4
Sands L. OTTL 45 C5
Sandstone PINE 43 B3
Sandstone Federal Correctional Institution PINE 43 C3
Sandstone Game Refuge PINE 43 C3
Sandstone Municipal Airport PINE 43 B3
Sandstone National Wildlife Refuge PINE 43 C3
Sandstone Twp PINE 43 B4
Sandsville Twp POLK 78 E1
Sandwick L. ITSC 71 D3
Sandy L. BELT 68 B5
Sandy L. BELT 68 C5
Sandy L. BELT 69 D3
Sandy L. CLER 68 A4
Sandy L. ISNT 34 B3
Sandy L. MAHN 55 B4
Sandy L. STLS 72 D5
Sandy L. WRIT 33 E3
Sandy Lake Indian Reservation ATKN 50 A5
Sandy Lake Recreation Site ATKN 50 A4
Sandy Point County Park JACK 3 D3
Sandy Point Seaplane Base STLS 74 A1
Sandy Pt. STLS 74 A1
Sandy R. CLER 68 B4
Sandy R. STLS 72 D5
Sandy R. STLS 73 D1
Sandy River L. ATKN 50 B4
Sandy Twp STLS 73 D1
Sanford Twp GRNT 38 D3
San Francisco Twp CARV 26 F1
Santa Claus L. STLS 62 C1
Santiago SHER 33 C5
Santiago Twp SHER 33 C5
Santwire L. MAHN 55 C4
Sap L. COOK 87 G3
Sapphire L. LAKE 74 C5
L. Sarah HENN 26 B1
L. Sarah MURR 12 F4
L. Sarah POLK 67 E3
Saratoga WINA 8 B5
Saratoga Twp WINA 9 B1
Sargeant MOWE 7 C4
Sargeant Twp MOWE 7 C4
Sargent Cr. STLS 52 B3
Sargent L. CLER 56 B2
Sargent L. MAHN 55 B5
Sartell STRN 33 B2
Sash L. LAKE 86 E2
Sassas Cr. STLS 72 B5
Sather L. MEEK 24 A3
Sather L. POPE 31 D2
Saturday Bay STLS 86 D1
Saucer L. COOK 88 E1
Sauer L. OTTL 46 B4
Sauk Centre STRN 40 G1
Sauk Centre Information Center STRN 40 G1
Sauk Centre State Correctional Facility STRN 40 G1
Sauk Centre Municipal Airport STRN 40 G1
Sauk Centre Twp STRN 40 G1
Sauk L. TODD 40 F1
Sauk Rapids (city) BENT 33 B3
Sauk Rapids-Rice Goose Refuge BENT 33 A3
Sauk Rapids Twp BENT 33 B2
Sauk R. STRN 32 C3
Saum BELT 81 G3
Saum Schools Historic Site BELT 81 G3
Sauna L. LAKE 86 E2
Saunders Bay STLS 84 F3
Saunders L. HENN 26 C1
Savage SCOT 26 E4
Savannah Twp BECK 56 D4
Savanna L. ATKN 59 G5
Savanna Portage Historic Site ATKN 60 G1
Savanna Portage State Park ATKN 50 A5
Savanna R. ATKN 50 A5
Savanna State Forest ATKN 59 F5
Savidge L. LSUR 15 D5
Sawbill Cr. COOK 75 A4
Sawbill L. COOK 75 A4
Sawbill Lake Recreation Site COOK 75 A4
Sawbill Landing (city) LAKE 75 C1
Sawbill Trail COOK 75 D4
Sawmill Cr. LAKE 75 G1
Sawmill L. LAKE 62 C2
Sawmill L. MAHN 55 B5
Sawmill L. MAHN 56 C1
Sawmill L. POLK 68 D1
Sawyer CARL 51 C5
Sawyer L. ITSC 71 E3
Sayer L. STLS 61 A2
Scabbard L. COOK 76 A4
Scalp L. OTTL 46 B4
Scambler Twp OTTL 46 B2
Scandia L. STEV 30 A4
Scandia Twp POLK 66 E3
Scandia Valley Twp MORR 40 A4
Scandia WASH 35 F4
Scandinavian L. POPE 31 D3
Scanlon CARL 52 B2
Scanlon L. LAKE 75 D1
Scarp L. LAKE 75 D2
Scenic State Park ITSC 71 C2
Schackman L. STRN 32 D5
Schaeffer L. STLS 62 C1
Schafer L. TODD 40 F2
Schandell L. HENN 26 A2
Schantzen L. CLER 56 C1
Schauer L. SBLY 25 G3
Schawnke Cr. TODD 40 E2
Schells Park BRWN 14 D5
Schielin L. STLS 61 F1
Schilling L. SBLY 25 F2
Schimmerhorn Cr. MAHN 55 A5
Schinn L. STLS 61 C5
Schisler L. STLS 61 D2
Schlamn L. STLS 85 G4
Schlehr L. BECK 46 B5
Schley CASS 58 A1
Schmid L. STRN 32 B5
Schmidt Cr. LAKE 62 F1
Schmidt L. OTTL 46 F3
Schmidt L. WRIT 34 G1
Schmidts I. STLS 72 A5
Schmitte L. DKTA 27 D2
Schneider L. POLK 68 C1
Schneider L. SCOT 26 F3
Schoolcraft Game Refuge HUBB 57 B1
Schoolcraft L. HUBB 57 D1
Schoolcraft R. HUBB 57 C1
Schoolcraft State Park CASS 58 C5
Schoolcraft Twp HUBB 57 B1
School District Number 5 Historic Site LQPL 22 C3
School Grove L. LYON 12 A5
Schoolhouse Cr. LAKE 75 F1
Schoolhouse L. CLER 68 C4
School House L. ITSC 70 D3
School House L. ITSC 70 G4
School House L. MEEK 24 B5
School L. BELT 69 E3
School L. BELT 69 G3
School L. BRWN 14 E4
School L. CHIS 35 D3
School L. CHIS 35 E3
School L. HENN 26 B2
School L. STRN 32 C4
School L. STRN 32 E5
School L. SWFT 31 F3
School L. WATN 14 G5
School L. WATN 4 B2
School L. WRIT 34 F2
School Section Bay STLS 85 G5
School Section L. FREE 6 E4
School Section L. STRN 33 E2
School Section L. WRIT 25 B4
School Section Lake Game Refuge STRN 33 E2
Schram L. BELT 69 G5
Schram L. GRNT 38 E2
Schrams L. OTTL 46 B4
Schreiers L. TODD 40 F3
Schroeder COOK 75 E4
Schroeder County Park WRIT 33 F3
Schroeder L. STRN 32 D4
Schroeder Twp COOK 75 E3
Schubert L. STLS 61 C2
Schultz L. BECK 55 G5
Schultz L. DOUG 39 F4
Schultz L. KAND 32 G2
Schultz L. MEEK 32 G4
Schultz L. STLS 61 E4
Schulz L. DOUG 39 F4
Schuman L. STRN 32 B5
Schuster L. OTTL 47 C1
Schutz L. CARV 26 D2
Schwandt State Monument Historic Site RENV 23 G4
Schwappauff L. HENN 26 A2
Schwerin Cr. MOWE 7 E5
Schwinghammer L. STRN 32 B4
Sciota Twp DKTA 17 B2
Scooty L. ITSC 71 E4
Scotch L. LAKE 87 G2
Scotch L. LSUR 15 D5
SCOTT — 26 —
Scott Cr. LAKE 75 D1
Scott L. CARV 26 F1
Scott L. CROW 49 G5
Scott L. HUBB 57 D1
Scott L. LAKE 75 D1
Scott L. STLS 72 F4
Scotts L. GRNT 38 C3
Scott Twp STEV 30 B2
Scrapper L. ITSC 71 F3
Screamer L. LAKE 75 A1
Screech L. COOK 75 B4
Scribner L. CASS 48 A4
Seabold L. BECK 55 F3
Seabold L. BECK 55 F4
Seaforth REDW 13 B3
Sea Gull Cr. COOK 87 E4
Sea Gull L. COOK 87 E3
Seahorse L. COOK 87 E3
Seal L. COOK 87 F5
Sea L. WASH 35 F4
Searles BRWN 14 E5
Seat L. COOK 87 F3
Seavey Twp ATKN 50 G4
Sebeka WADN 47 C5
Sebeka Historical Society Museum WADN 47 C5
Sebeka L. COOK 87 F5
Sebie L. CROW 41 B1
Second Crow Wing L. HUBB 57 G2
Second Cr. STLS 73 E3
Second Dog L. CASS 58 G3
Second L. CHIS 35 E3
Second L. CLER 68 B3
Second L. CLER 68 F2
Second L. PINE 51 G4
Second Perch L. CASS 57 G4
Section 16 L. LAKE 86 E2
Section 25 L. ATKN 50 E2
Section 29 L. STLS 85 D1
Section Eleven L. ITSC 72 D1
Section Fifteen L. COOK 76 A4
Section Fourteen L. STLS 61 A2
Section L. CASS 48 D4
Section L. ISNT 35 A1
Section L. LAKE 75 C1
Section L. LAKE 75 D1
Section L. LYON 12 E2
Section L. STLS 84 G5
Section One L. CARL 51 C2
Section Ten L. BECK 56 G3
Section Ten L. COOK 88 F4
Section Twelve L. ATKN 50 E2
Section Twelve L. LAKE 86 G3
Security Bank and Trust Co. Historic Site STEL 16 F5
Sedan POPE 31 B4
Sedative L. LAKE 87 F1
Sedivy L. MAHN 55 C4
Seed L. LAKE 86 E5
Seelye Bk. ANOK 34 D4
Seely Twp FRBT 5 F5
Seim L. OTTL 46 B2
Selinsky L. TODD 39 F5
Sellards L. MEEK 25 B1
Sells L. KNBC 43 F1
Selma Twp COTT 14 G1
Sema L. LAKE 87 E1
Senical L. BECK 46 A4
Seppman Mill Historic Site BLUE 15 F3
Sere L. COOK 88 F2
Serenade L. STLS 85 F3
Seretha L. KCHG 82 G3
Serpent L. CROW 49 E4
Serpent L. LAKE 87 E2
Seth L. ATKN 50 E2
Seton L. HENN 26 C2
Seven Beaver L. STLS 74 F1
Seven L. CLER 68 C2
Seven Mile County Park MURR 2 B5
Seven Mile Cr. CASS 48 F4
Seven Mile Cr. NCLT 15 D3
Seven Mile Creek County Park NCLT 15 E3
Seven Sisters I. STLS 73 B3
Seventeen L. ISNT 34 A5
Seventh Crow Wing L. HUBB 57 F2
Severance L. SBLY 25 F3
Severance Twp SBLY 14 B4
Severson Cr. ROSE 92 E1
Severson L. BECK 46 A2
Severson L. BLUE 5 A5
Seward Twp NBLS 2 C5
L. Sewell OTTL 38 B4
Sexton I. STLS 84 A4
Seymour L. MART 4 D3
Sha-Bosh-Kung Bay MLLC 42 B1
Sha-Bosh-Kung Point MLLC 42 A1
Shadow L. COOK 87 D4
Shady Grove L. GRNT 38 D4
Shady I. WOOD 97 E3
Shady L. OLMS 18 F1
Shady Oak L. HENN 26 D4
Shaefer Bay STLS 74 A1
Shafer CHIS 35 D4
Shafer L. CASS 48 E5
Shafer L. CASS 58 G5
Shafer L. ITSC 72 F1
Shafer Twp CHIS 35 D4
Shaffer Lakes CROW 49 C2
Shagawa L. STLS 74 A1
Shager County Park RICE 16 E4
Shakopee SCOT 26 E3
Shakopee Cr. SWFT 30 F5
Shakopee L. CHIP 23 A1
Shakopee L. CHIP 31 G1
Shakopee L. MLLC 42 C1
Shakopee L. WRIT 25 C2
Shallow L. HUBB 57 F2
Shallow L. ITSC 59 D4
Shallow L. LAKE 86 E5
Shallow L. OTTL 46 D4
Shallow Pond L. ITSC 70 C2
Shaman L. STLS 85 D4
Shamineau L. MORR 40 A4
Sham L. LYON 22 G5
Shamrock L. ITSC 59 A4
Shamrock L. LAKE 74 C3
Shannon L. STLS 72 D2
Shannon R. STLS 72 E2
Shanty L. HUBB 57 C1
L. Shaokatan LINC 11 C4
Shaokatan Twp LINC 11 B4
Sharon Twp LSUR 15 C5
Sharp L. OTTL 46 F4
Sharp Muskrat L. GOOD 27 F5
Sha Sha Point KCHG 95 F5
Shauer L. GRNT 38 F3
Shavers L. HENN 26 C3
Shaw STLS 61 D2
Sheas L. LSUR 16 B1
Sheep I. STLS 84 A2
Sheep L. MORR 40 B5
Sheets L. TODD 40 C2
Shelburne Twp LYON 12 E2
Shelby Twp BLUE 5 B2
Sheldon HOUS 9 E4
Sheldon L. WRIT 33 E4
Sheldon Twp HOUS 9 D5
Shelfhout Pt. DOUG 39 E4
Shelland I. STLS 96 G3
Shell City Recreation Site WADN 48 A1

Shelley Island BECK 55 G5
Shell L. BECK 56 F2
Shell L. BELT 68 B5
Shell L. CASS 57 E5
Shell L. STLS 85 D3
Shell Lake Twp BECK 56 F2
Shell R. BECK 56 F3
Shell R. WADN 48 A1
Shell River Prehistoric Village and Mound District HUBB 48 A2
Shell River Twp WADN 48 B1
Shell Rock R. FREE 6 F5
Shell Rock Twp FREE 6 F5
Shelly NORM 66 F1
Shelly L. ITSC 71 F2
Shelly Twp NORM 66 F2
L. Shemahgun BELT 69 B1
Shepo L. LAKE 87 F1
Sherack POLK 78 F2
SHERBURNE — 34 —
Sherburn MART 4 E3
Sherburne County Historical Society Museum SHER 33 D5
Sherburne National Wildlife Refuge SHER 34 C1
Sherburne National Wildlife Refuge Headquarters SHER 34 C1
Sheridan L. HUBB 57 C1
Sheridan Twp REDW 13 B3
Sheriff L. ATKN 50 D5
Sherman Corner STLS 72 C4
Sherman L. OTTL 47 F1
Sherman Twp REDW 14 B1
Sherry Arm ITSC 59 D2
Sherry L. ITSC 71 D5
Sheshabee ATKN 50 B5
L. Shetek MURR 12 F4
Shetek Twp MURR 12 F5
Shevlin CLER 68 F4
Shevlin Twp CLER 68 E4
Shible L. SWFT 30 F2
Shible Twp SWFT 30 F2
Shields L. RICE 16 C4
Shields L. WASH 35 F3
Shieldsville RICE 16 C4
Shieldsville Twp RICE 16 D3
Shift L. COOK 75 A4
Shine L. ITSC 71 B3
Shingle Cr. HENN 26 A4
Shingle Mill L. ITSC 59 D1
Shingobee Bay CASS 57 E4
Shingobee Cr. CASS 57 E4
Shingobee L. HUBB 57 E3
Shingobee Twp CASS 57 D4
Shinker L. HUBB 57 F2
Shipman Bass L. STLS 85 G5
Shipman L. BECK 56 G4
Shirt L. CROW 49 E5
Shiver Cr. STLS 73 G5
Shoal L. ITSC 59 B2
Shoal L. ITSC 71 F5
Shoe L. COOK 88 F4
Shoemaker L. KAND 32 E2
Shoemaker L. PINE 51 G3
Shoepack L. LAKE 75 D2
Shoepack L. STLS 72 E2
Shoepack L. STLS 96 G3
Shogren Dam Recreation Site ITSC 70 D3
Shohola L. STLS 85 D3
Shoko L. COOK 88 F2
Shooks BELT 69 B5
Shooks Twp BELT 69 A5
Shoreham BECK 46 A3
Shoreview RAMS 27 B1
Shorewood HENN 26 D2
Short L. LAKE 75 A2
Shorty L. ITSC 59 E1
Shotley BELT 81 F4
Shotley Bk. BELT 81 F4
Shotley Twp BELT 81 F4
Shovel L. ATKN 59 F1
Shovel Lake (city) ATKN 59 F1
Shoveller L. LAKE 87 G2
Shovel Pt. LAKE 63 A1
Shrike L. COOK 76 A1
Shroeder L. HUBB 57 E3
Shurd L. CASS 58 F2
Siamese L. COOK 87 G4
Sibert L. WASC 16 E1
SIBLEY — 15 —
Sibley County High Island Creek Park SBLY 15 A4
Sibley County Historical Society Museum SBLY 15 A4
Sibley House Historic Site DKTA 27 D1
L. Sibley CROW 49 C1
Sibley Municipal Park BLUE 15 F3
Sibley State Park KAND 31 E5
Sibley Twp SBLY 15 B2
Side L. STLS 51 A5
Side L. STLS 61 F2
Side L. STLS 72 D2
Side Lake (city) STLS 72 D2
Sigel Twp BRWN 14 E4
Silent Lakes OTTL 46 D4
Silica STLS 60 B2
Silica L. STLS 85 G4
Sill L. HUBB 57 F1
Silver Bay (city) LAKE 63 A1
Silver Bay Municipal Airport LAKE 62 B5
Silver Brook Twp CARL 52 C2
Silver Corners BENT 41 G3
Silver Cr. CARL 52 E2
Silver Cr. CARV 26 F1
Silver Cr. CLER 68 C2
Silver Cr. GOOD 17 D3
Silver Cr. LAKE 62 D3
Silver Cr. OLMS 18 G3
Silver Cr. TODD 40 F1
Silver Cr. WOOD 93 E5
Silver Creek (city) LAKE 62 A3
Silver Creek (city) WRIT 33 E4
Silver Creek Twp LAKE 62 A3
Silver Creek Twp WRIT 33 E4
Silverdale KCHG 84 G1
Silver Island L. LAKE 75 C2
Silver L. BELT 69 C2
Silver L. BELT 69 F4
Silver L. CASS 58 E2
Silver L. CLAY 54 G5
Silver L. CROW 49 E3
Silver L. HENN 26 D3
Silver L. ITSC 71 E3
Silver L. LSUR 16 D1
Silver L. LSUR 16 E1
Silver L. MCLD 25 D2
Silver L. MLLC 34 B3
Silver L. OTTL 46 B5
Silver L. RAMS 26 B5
Silver L. RAMS 27 B2
Silver L. SBLY 25 G4
Silver L. STEV 38 G3
Silver L. STLS 72 F5
Silver L. STLS 73 F2
Silver L. STLS 84 D4
Silver L. WASC 6 A2
Silver L. WASH 27 A3
Silver L. WRIT 33 E4
Silver Lake (city) MCLD 25 D2
Silver Lake Municipal Park OLMS 18 G2
Silver Lakes OTTL 46 G5
Silver Lake Twp MART 4 F5
Silver Leaf Township Game Refuge BECK 47 A1
Silver Leaf Twp BECK 47 A1
Silverton Twp PENN 79 E3
Silver Twp CARL 51 E3
Simian L. STLS 52 A1
Simon L. WADN 48 E2
L. Simon POPE 31 D3
Simonson L. MAHN 67 F5
Simonson's Crossing Historic Site LQPL 29 F5
Simpson OLMS 8 B2
Simpson L. ITSC 70 F3
Sinclair Lewis Home Historic Site STRN 40 G1
Sinclair Lewis Interpretive Center STRN 40 G1
Sinclair Lewis Municipal Park STRN 40 G1
Sinclair Twp CLER 68 C4
Single L. COOK 75 B3
Sink L. LAKE 74 G4
Sinneeg Cr. STLS 86 D1
Sinneeg L. STLS 86 E1
Sinnott Twp MRSH 90 G1
Sioux Agency Twp YMED 23 F2
Sioux L. ITSC 70 E2
Sioux L. MEEK 24 B5
Sioux Pine I. STLS 85 G2
Sioux Valley JACK 3 F3
Sioux Valley Twp JACK 3 F3
Siren L. CLER 56 C2
Siren L. LAKE 87 F2
Sissabagamah Cr. ATKN 50 D2
Sissabagamah L. ATKN 50 E2
Sisseton L. MART 4 E5
Sister L. LAKE 75 D2
Sitas L. ATKN 50 B2
Sitka L. COOK 87 G4
Siverson L. OTTL 39 A1
Sivertson L. BECK 56 G2
Six L. CLER 68 D2
Six L. OTTL 46 B4
Six Mile Bk. CASS 58 B3
Sixmile Cr. COOK 75 D4
Six Mile Grove Twp SWFT 30 F5
Six Mile L. CASS 58 B3
Sixmile L. STLS 72 G3
Six Mile L. STLS 73 B4
Six Mile Lake Recreation Site CASS 58 B3
Sixteen L. ATKN 50 E2
Sixth Crow Wing L. HUBB 57 F2
Sixth L. CASS 57 E4
Sjodin L. ATKN 50 E2
Skagen Twp ROSE 91 D3
Skalbekken County Park RENV 23 E2
Skandia Twp MURR 12 F3
Skane Twp KITT 90 E1
Skataas L. KAND 31 G5
Skeeter L. ITSC 71 F3
Skeleton L. STLS 73 C4
Skelly L. ITSC 59 C1
Skelton Twp CARL 51 D4
Skibo STLS 73 F5
Skidway L. COOK 88 G1
Ski Gull Ski Area CASS 49 E1
Skimerhorn L. ITSC 70 D1
Skinaway L. CLER 56 B2
Skindance L. LAKE 87 E2
Skinny L. COOK 88 F1
Skipper L. COOK 88 F1
Skogen Marsh OTTL 46 F1
Skogland Slough DOUG 39 F1
Skogman L. ISNT 35 B1
Skoop L. COOK 87 G4
Skoota L. LAKE 87 E1
Skree Twp CLAY 45 A5
Skull L. KAND 31 E5
Skull L. LAKE 86 F4
Skunk Cr. LAKE 62 B4
Skunk L. ANOK 35 E1
Skunk L. CASS 58 C5
Skunk L. GRNT 38 C3
Skunk L. HUBB 57 D1
Skunk L. JACK 3 F3
Skunk L. MAHN 67 G5
Skunk L. MORR 41 B5
Skunk L. MORR 41 E2
Skunk R. MORR 41 D3
Skyberg GOOD 17 E3
Sky Harbor Airport and Seaplane Base STLS 52 B5
Sky Harbor Seaplane Base STLS 73 F1
Skyline BLUE 15 F3
Skyline Parkway STLS 52 B3
Skyport Lodge Seaplane Base COOK 76 B3
Slade Hotel Historic Site NBLS 2 E2
Slade L. LAKE 75 F2
Slate L. LAKE 74 C3
Slater Twp CASS 58 D4
Slauson L. ITSC 71 D2
Slayton MURR 2 A4
Slayton Municipal Airport MURR 2 A4
Slayton Twp MURR 2 A4
Sled L. COOK 88 F2
Sleepy Eye BRWN 14 D3
Sleepy Eye Cr. REDW 13 C4
Sleepy Eye L. BRWN 14 D3
Sleepy Eye L. LSUR 16 D1
Sleepy Eye Municipal Airport BRWN 14 E3
Sleepy Island L. CASS 57 G4
Sletten L. STLS 86 G1
Sletten Twp POLK 67 E4
Slim L. STLS 85 C3
Slim L. STLS 85 F5
Slip L. COOK 75 B5
Sloan L. HUBB 56 E5
Sloop L. CLER 56 C2
Slotsye L. GRNT 38 C4
Slough L. BECK 46 A4
Slough L. COOK 88 F2
Slough L. CROW 49 B4
Slough L. TODD 40 F3
Slough L. WRIT 33 E4
Slough L. WRIT 33 G3
Slow Cr. STLS 72 E3
Slowfoot L. LAKE 86 G4
Slumber L. LAKE 86 G3
Small L. BECK 56 E4
Small L. LAKE 75 B1
Smart Bay STLS 73 A1
Smiley L. CASS 58 G1
Smiley Twp PENN 79 F3
Smite L. LAKE 87 F1
Smith Bay HENN 26 C2
Smith Cr. ITSC 59 D2
Smith I. STLS 96 G4
Smith L. BELT 69 C4
Smith L. CARV 25 E4
Smith L. CLER 80 G2
Smith L. CROW 41 A5
Smith L. DOUG 39 E4
Smith L. HENN 26 B4
Smith L. HUBB 68 G5
Smith L. ITSC 59 D2
Smith L. ITSC 71 E2
Smith L. STLS 62 C1
Smith L. WRIT 25 B3
Smiths Mill WASC 16 F1
Smithwick L. BGST 29 B3
Smoke L. COOK 75 A4
Smokey Hills State Forest BECK 56 F3
Smokey Hollow L. CASS 49 A4
Smoky Bear State Forest KCHG 83 A1
Smoky Hollow Twp CASS 58 F5
Smoot Island KCHG 94 F5
Smyth L. BELT 69 C2
Snack L. COOK 88 F1
Snail L. RAMS 27 B1
Snake Cr. LAKE 74 C3
Snake I. STLS 85 G5
Snake L. CASS 58 G4
Snake River County Park ATKN 42 B5
Snake River State Forest KNBC 42 C5
Snake R. LAKE 74 C3
Snake R. MRSH 77 B5
Snake R. PINE 43 F3
Snake R. STLS 84 C5
Snaptail L. ITSC 71 F4
Snatch L. LAKE 86 F5
Sneaker L. COOK 87 G4
Snellman BECK 56 G2
Snellman I. STLS 73 A4
Snells L. ITSC 59 B1
Snetsinger L. MAHN 67 G5
Snider L. MAHN 55 C5
Sniff L. COOK 87 G4
Snipe L. COOK 87 F4
Snip L. COOK 87 G4
Snively Municipal Forest STLS 52 B3
Snodgrass L. CROW 49 B5
Snort L. COOK 87 G2
Snowball L. ITSC 59 A5
Snowbank L. LAKE 86 F4
Snow Bay STLS 85 C2
Snow Lakes OTTL 39 A2
Snowshoe Bay STLS 74 C1
Snowshoe L. ITSC 71 F2
Snowshoe L. KNBC 42 C5
Snub L. COOK 87 G4
Snuff L. COOK 87 G3
Snusbox L. LAKE 75 B1
Snyder Bay ITSC 59 A2
Snyder L. HENN 26 B3
Soaked L. COOK 87 G3
Sober L. COOK 75 B4
Sobieski MORR 40 E5
Sockeye L. BECK 56 D3
Sock L. BECK 56 G2
Sock L. COOK 88 E1
Sock L. STLS 73 C5
Soderman Lakes ATKN 50 D2
Sodus Twp LYON 12 D4
Sofie L. CARL 51 B5
Softing L. CLAY 46 A1
Sogn GOOD 17 C3
Solana State Forest ATKN 50 F5
Solberg L. CLER 68 D3
Solberg L. DOUG 38 D4
Soldier Pt. STLS 96 F2
Soldiers I. MORR 40 A4
Solem Twp DOUG 38 F5
Soler Twp ROSE 91 C2
Solitude L. LAKE 86 F5
Solomon G. Comstock House Historic Site CLAY 54 G1
Solum L. CLAY 55 G1
Solwald L. CLAY 54 F5
Solway BELT 68 F5
Solway Twp STLS 52 A2
Somdahl L. BECK 55 E4
Someman L. ITSC 71 E4
Somerset Twp STEL 6 A5
Somers L. WRIT 33 F4
Sommer L. OTTL 38 B3
Sonju L. LAKE 75 F1
Soper L. CARL 52 E1
Sora L. COOK 87 F4
Sorenson L. BECK 55 G2
Sorenson L. CROW 49 E3
Soudan STLS 73 B3
Soudan Iron Mine Historic Site STLS 73 B3
Soup L. LAKE 74 E5
Source L. LAKE 74 F3
Source of the Mississippi River Historic Site CLER 56 C4
Sourdough L. LAKE 86 G3
South Arm Knife L. LAKE 87 E1
South Arm Lida L. OTTL 46 D3
South Barnes L. BECK 55 G3
South Bean L. COOK 88 F4
South Bend BLUE 15 F3
South Bend Twp BLUE 15 F3
South Bluff Cr. OTTL 47 F4
South Bog L. STLS 84 E4
South Branch (city) WATN 4 B4
South Branch Battle R. BELT 81 G4
South Branch Buffalo R. CLAY 54 G3
South Branch Little Elk R. MORR 40 C4
South Branch Manitou R. LAKE 75 E1
South Branch Middle Fork Zumbro R. DOGE 17 G3
South Branch North Fork Whitewater R. OLMS 18 G4
South Branch Rapid R. WOOD 81 B1
South Branch Root R. FILL 8 E4
South Branch Snake R. MRSH 78 D4
South Branch Two R. KITT 90 D1
South Branch Twp WATN 4 B4
South Branch Water Hen R. STLS 61 A3
South Branch Whiteface R. STLS 61 B4
South Branch Wild Rice R. CLAY 54 C4
South Branch Yellow Medicine R. LYON 12 B1
South Branch Zippel Cr. WOOD 93 D2
Southbrook Twp COTT 3 B2
South Browns L. STRN 32 E4
South Brule R. COOK 88 G3
South Center L. CHIS 35 E4
South Cormorant R. BELT 69 B4
South Cr. MART 5 E1
South Dutch Charlie Creek County Park COTT 13 F2
South Farm L. LAKE 74 A2
South Fork Coon Cr. ITSC 71 C3
South Fork Crooked Cr. HOUS 10 F1
South Fork Crow R. CARV 25 D4
South Fork Elm Cr. JACK 4 D1
South Fork Groundhouse R. KNBC 42 F3
South Fork Kawishiwi R. LAKE 74 B2
South Fork L. ITSC 71 F5
South Fork Nemadji R. CARL 52 D2
South Fork Pine R. CROW 49 B1
South Fork Rabbit R. TRAV 37 D4
South Fork Root R. FILL 9 E3
South Fork Roseau R. ROSE 92 G1
South Fork Twp KNBC 42 F3
South Fork Watonwan R. WATN 4 B4
South Fork Whitewater R. WINA 19 G1
South Fork Willow R. CASS 58 D5
South Fork Yellow Bank R. LQPL 21 B3
South Fork Yellow Medicine R. LYON 22 G2
South Fork Zumbro R. OLMS 18 F2
South Fowl L. COOK 88 E5
South Harbor Twp MLLC 42 C2
South Haven WRIT 33 F2
South Heron L. JACK 3 D3
South Hope L. LAKE 75 A1
South International Falls (city) KCHG 95 F3
South Kawishiwi Recreation Site LAKE 74 B2
South L. COOK 88 E1
South L. MCLD 25 C4
South L. STLS 85 C3
South Lemmerhirt L. OTTL 47 G3
South Lindstrom L. CHIS 35 E3
South Long L. CROW 49 G3
South Long L. OTTL 46 E4
South Maple L. OTTL 39 B4
South Minnetonka L. BECK 46 A3
South Nelson L. OTTL 46 G3
South Oscar L. DOUG 39 F1
South Pine Bay Recreation Site CASS 57 A4
South Red River Twp KITT 89 E5
South Rice L. OTTL 46 D5
South Rothwell L. BGST 29 C4
South School Section L. WASH 27 A3
Southside Twp WRIT 33 F2
South Silver L. MART 4 G5
South Smith L. ITSC 71 F2
South Stanchfield L. ISNT 34 B3
South Stang L. OTTL 38 A3
South Stocking L. CASS 58 E1
South St. Paul DKTA 27 D2
South St. Paul Municipal Airport DKTA 27 D2
South Sturgeon L. ITSC 72 D1
South Temperance L. COOK 87 G4
South Terrapin L. WASH 35 G4
South Troy WBSH 18 E2
South Turtle L. OTTL 46 G4
South Twin L. BECK 55 F5
South Twin L. BECK 56 G1
South Twin L. BELT 69 E4
South Twin L. CLER 56 C4
South Twin L. LYON 12 E4
South Twin L. MAHN 56 B1
South Twin L. MORR 40 A4
South Twin L. STLS 73 G3
South Twin L. WASH 27 B3
South Walnut L. FRBT 6 E1
South Washington Regional Park Reserve WASH 27 E3
Southwest State University and Museums LYON 12 B4
South Wigwam L. LAKE 75 C3
South Wilder L. LAKE 74 A5
Sova L. LAKE 87 G2
Spafford JACK 3 E2
Spalding Twp ATKN 50 D5
Spang Twp ITSC 59 D1
Spark L. COOK 88 F4
Sparrow L. STLS 73 B5
Sparta Twp CHIP 22 C5
Spaulding L. COOK 88 E4
Spearhead L. HUBB 57 A1
Spear L. BECK 46 A3
Spear L. LAKE 74 D5
Speckled Trout L. COOK 76 F2
Spectacle Lake Wildlife Management Area ISNT 34 C3
Spectacle L. ATKN 50 F1
Spectacle L. ISNT 34 B4
Speltz Cr. WINA 19 F2
Spence L. KNBC 42 F5
Spencer Brook (city) ISNT 34 C3
Spencer Brook Twp ISNT 34 C3
Spencer L. MEEK 25 B1
Spencer Twp ATKN 50 D2

Spen L. COOK 88 E2
Sperry L. KAND 32 G2
Sphagnum L. LAKE 74 C4
Sphungs Is. STLS 84 A2
Spice L. LAKE 87 E2
Spicer KAND 32 F1
Spider I. STLS 73 B2
Spider Island MLLC 42 B3
Spider L. CASS 48 C3
Spider L. CHIS 35 E4
Spider L. CROW 49 E3
Spider L. HUBB 56 C5
Spider L. HUBB 57 E2
Spider L. ITSC 71 F2
Spider L. LAKE 87 F1
Spider L. STLS 60 F4
Spider Muskrat Cr. STLS 60 E4
Spier L. TODD 40 F2
Spigot L. LAKE 86 F4
Spike L. CLER 68 C4
Spinach L. BECK 55 D4
Spindler L. BECK 56 E1
Spinnan L. LAKE 74 A4
Spirit Island MLLC 42 B2
Spirit Island STLS 52 B4
Spirit L. ATKN 50 E1
Spirit L. BECK 55 D4
Spirit L. JACK 3 G4
Spirit L. STLS 52 B4
Spirit L. WADN 47 B5
Spirit Mountain Recreation Area STLS 52 B3
Spitzer L. OTTL 39 B1
Splash L. LAKE 86 F4
Split Hand Cr. ITSC 59 D4
Split Hand L. ITSC 59 E3
Split Rock Cr. ROCK 1 C3
Split Rock Creek State Recreation Area PIPE 1 B4
Split Rock L. ATKN 51 F1
Split Rock L. PIPE 1 B4
Split Rock Lighthouse Historic Site LAKE 62 C5
Split Rock Lighthouse State Park LAKE 62 C5
Split Rock Pt. LAKE 62 C5
Split Rock R. CARL 51 E2
Split Rock R. LAKE 62 C5
Split Rock Twp CARL 51 E2
Spoon L. LAKE 87 E1
Sportsmans County Park NBLS 2 F5
Sportsman's Park RDLK 67 A1
Spot L. CASS 48 B3
Spot L. ITSC 59 D5
Sprague Cr. ROSE 92 B1
Spree L. LAKE 86 F4
Sprig L. LAKE 87 F2
Spring Bk. TODD 40 D3
Spring Brook Twp KITT 90 F3
Spring Cr. BECK 46 B2
Spring Cr. BECK 55 D3
Spring Cr. BELT 69 C5
Spring Cr. BRWN 14 C2
Spring Cr. CASS 58 G2
Spring Cr. CLAY 45 B4
Spring Cr. GOOD 17 A5
Spring Cr. ITSC 59 C5
Spring Cr. MAHN 55 B3
Spring Cr. NORM 66 G4
Spring Cr. PINE 43 C3
Spring Cr. RENV 23 D2
Spring Cr. STLS 85 E5
Spring Cr. WBSH 18 D3
Spring Cr. YMED 22 F3
Spring Creek Twp BECK 55 D3
Spring Creek Twp NORM 66 F5
Springdale Twp REDW 13 E1
Springer L. CARL 51 B3
Springfield BRWN 14 E1
Springfield Municipal Airport BRWN 13 E5
Springfield Nature Trail BRWN 14 E1
Springfield Twp COTT 3 B3
Spring Grove HOUS 9 F4
Spring Grove Twp HOUS 9 F4
Spring Hill (city) STRN 32 C2
Spring Hill Twp STRN 32 C2
Spring Hole L. STLS 61 B4
Spring L. ANOK 26 A5
Spring L. ATKN 50 E3
Spring L. BECK 55 F4
Spring L. BELT 68 E5
Spring L. CARL 51 C4
Spring L. CARL 52 D1
Spring L. CASS 58 D5
Spring L. CROW 41 B5
Spring L. DKTA 27 E2
Spring L. DOUG 39 C2
Spring L. GRNT 38 E4
Spring L. HUBB 57 C3
Spring L. HUBB 57 F3
Spring L. ISNT 35 C2
Spring L. ITSC 59 A2
Spring L. ITSC 59 B4
Spring L. ITSC 59 D1
Spring L. ITSC 70 D5
Spring L. ITSC 71 B4
Spring L. ITSC 71 C5
Spring L. ITSC 71 F3
Spring L. KNBC 42 E5
Spring L. MEEK 25 A1
Spring L. OTTL 46 G3
Spring L. POLK 68 F1
Spring L. SCOT 26 F3
Spring L. STLS 61 D5
Spring L. STLS 84 B5
Spring L. SWFT 30 F2
Spring L. WRIT 25 B3
Spring Lake (city) ISNT 35 C2
Spring Lake (city) ITSC 70 D5
Spring Lake County Park MEEK 25 A1
Spring Lake Municipal Park NCLT 15 E3
Spring Lake Park (city) ANOK 26 A5
Spring Lake Regional Park SCOT 26 F3
Spring Lake Regional Park Reserve DKTA 27 E3
Spring Lake Twp SCOT 26 F3
Spring Mine Cr. STLS 73 D4
Spring Mine L. STLS 73 D4
Spring Park (city) HENN 26 C2
Spring Prairie Twp CLAY 54 F4
Springsteel Point WOOD 92 B4
Springvale ISNT 34 B5
Springvale Twp ISNT 34 B4
Spring Valley Cr. FILL 8 E3
Spring Valley (city) FILL 8 E3
Spring Valley Methodist Church Historic Site FILL 8 E2
Spring Valley Twp FILL 8 D2
Springwater Twp ROCK 1 D3
Sprite L. STLS 73 A4
Sproul L. OTTL 46 E3
Spruce Center DOUG 39 C4
Spruce Cr. COOK 76 C1
Spruce Cr. DOUG 39 C4
Spruce Grove Twp BECK 47 A3
Spruce Grove Twp BELT 80 C3
Spruce Hill County Park DOUG 39 C4
Spruce Hill Twp DOUG 39 C4
Spruce Island L. ITSC 71 F2
Spruce L. ATKN 51 C1
Spruce L. CASS 57 E5
Spruce L. CROW 49 E3
Spruce L. ITSC 59 C1
Spruce L. ITSC 70 C4
Spruce L. ITSC 71 E3
Spruce L. LAKE 74 E4
Spruce L. STLS 73 C4
Spruce Twp ROSE 92 C1
Spruce Valley Twp MRSH 79 B2
Spud L. COOK 88 F1
Spunk Cr. STRN 41 G1
Spur End Cr. LAKE 74 F4
Spur L. HUBB 57 D1
Spur L. ITSC 70 D5
Spur L. LAKE 75 D1
Spurzem L. HENN 26 B2
Squareboat L. MAHN 55 C5
Square L. CROW 49 C4
Square L. LAKE 75 A2
Square L. STLS 73 C4
Square L. WASH 35 G4
Square Lake County Park WASH 35 G4
Squash L. BECK 55 E4
Squash L. COOK 88 F4
Squat L. COOK 87 E3
Squaw Bay LAKE 86 G1
Squaw Cr. BELT 69 A3
Squaw Cr. CARL 52 B1
Squaw L. BECK 56 D3
Squaw L. BECK 56 E1
Squaw L. CLER 56 C4
Squaw L. COOK 88 F4
Squaw L. CROW 49 A4
Squaw L. ITSC 70 D3
Squaw Lake (city) ITSC 70 E3
Squaw Narrows STLS 84 A4
Squaw Point CASS 49 E1
Squaw Point CASS 57 C4
Squire L. COOK 87 G5
Squirm L. COOK 87 G3
Squirrel I. LAKE 86 F3
Squirrel L. MAHN 55 C4
Squirrel Narrows STLS 96 G4
Squish L. COOK 87 F4
Stacy CHIS 35 D2
Staege Bay STLS 84 C5
Stafford Twp ROSE 91 D5
Stahl L. MCLD 24 C5
Stahls Lake County Park MCLD 24 C5
Stakke L. BECK 55 G2
Stalker L. OTTL 38 A4
Stanchfield ISNT 35 A1
Stanchfield Bk. ISNT 34 A4
Stanchfield Cr. ISNT 34 A5
Stanchfield L. MORR 40 A4
Stanchfield Twp ISNT 34 A5
Stanford Twp ISNT 34 D4
Stanley Cr. STLS 62 E1
Stanley Eddy Memorial County Park Reserve WRIT 33 G2
Stanley L. CROW 49 D4
Stanley Twp LYON 12 B5
Stanton GOOD 17 B2
Stanton Twp GOOD 17 B2
Staples TODD 48 F2
Staples L. WASH 35 G3
Staples Municipal Airport WADN 48 F2
Staples Twp TODD 48 G2
Staples Waterfowl Game Refuge TODD 48 G3
Starbuck POPE 31 B1
Starbuck Municipal Airport POPE 31 B1
Staring L. HENN 26 D3
Star Island BELT 69 G4
Star Island Recreation Site CASS 69 G4
Stark L. CROW 49 C5
Stark Twp BRWN 14 E3
Stark Twp CHIS 35 B2
Star L. COOK 87 G5
Star L. CROW 49 C2
Star L. MEEK 24 B4
Star L. MORR 40 E5
Star L. OTTL 46 D4
Star L. POPE 31 A2
Star L. STLS 73 B4
Star L. TODD 40 B3
Star Lake Twp OTTL 46 D4
Starlight L. LAKE 86 G5
Starry L. ATKN 50 A1
Star Twp PENN 80 F1
Starvation L. ATKN 50 D5
Starvation L. MORR 41 B5
Stassen L. CLER 56 C3
State I. STLS 85 G5
State L. COOK 88 F1
State L. POPE 31 B3
State Line County Park NBLS 2 G5
State Line Cr. CARL 52 E3
State Line L. FREE 6 G3
Stately Twp BRWN 13 F5
State Pt. STLS 84 A1
Statues of Paul Bunyan and Babe the Blue Ox BELT 69 F2
Stauffer L. CHIS 35 A1
L. Stay LINC 12 C1
St. Cloud Municipal Airport SHER 33 C3
Steak L. COOK 87 G3
Steamboat Bay CASS 57 C4
Steamboat Bay L. CASS 57 B4
Steamboat I. STLS 96 F1
Steamboat L. CASS 57 B4
Steamboat R. CASS 57 C4
Steamhaul L. LAKE 74 D4
Steam L. COOK 87 G3
STEARNS — 33 —
Stearns County Heritage Center STRN 33 C2
STEELE — 16 —
Steele Center STEL 6 A5
Steele L. LSUR 16 E1
Steele L. WRIT 34 G1
Steel L. HUBB 57 F3
Steen ROCK 1 F4
Steenerson L. POPE 31 B2
Steenerson Twp BELT 80 D4
Steep Bank L. LINC 11 A4
Steep L. STLS 85 C3
Steep L. STLS 85 D3
Stein L. BECK 47 B1
Stella L. KITT 89 B4
Stella L. MEEK 24 B5
Stem L. COOK 75 A5
Stemmer L. OTTL 39 B1
Stenlund L. CLER 68 D4
Stephen MRSH 78 A1
Stephen Municipal Airport MRSH 78 A1
Stephens L. CASS 49 F1
Sterling Center BLUE 5 B3
Sterling Cr. STLS 85 D5
Sterling L. STLS 85 D5
Sterling Twp BLUE 5 B3
STEVENS — 38 —
Stevens County Historical Society Museum STEV 30 B3
Stevens I. STLS 84 A4
Stevens L. CASS 58 F3
Stevens L. COOK 76 F1
Stevens L. ITSC 59 A1
Stevens L. ITSC 59 B2
Stevens L. KAND 23 B5
Stevens L. MEEK 24 B5
Stevens L. PINE 43 A4
Stevens L. PINE 44 C1
Stevens Twp STEV 30 C1
Stewart MCLD 24 F5
Stewart Cr. STLS 52 B3
Stewart LAKE 62 D2
Stewart L. CROW 49 A2
Stewart L. LAKE 62 C2
Stewart R. LAKE 62 D2
Stewartville OLMS 8 C2
Stewartville County Park OLMS 8 C2
Stew L. COOK 87 G3
Stickney L. SHER 33 D4
Stieger L. CARV 26 D2
Stienbrook L. BELT 69 G1
Stigmans Mound County Park WADN 48 C2
Stilke L. BECK 46 A4
Stillwater WASH 27 B4
Stillwater Boom Historic Site WASH 27 A4
Stillwater Game Refuge WASH 35 A4
Stillwater Twp WASH 27 A4
Stiner Cr. CLAY 55 D1
Stingy L. ITSC 72 E1
Stingy L. STLS 72 E2
Stinking L. BECK 55 F2
Stirewalt Memorial County Park WRIT 33 E4
Stockhaven L. DOUG 38 C5
Stockholm WRIT 25 B2
Stockholm Cr. HOUS 9 D5
Stockholm Twp WRIT 25 B2
Stockhousen L. DOUG 38 C5
Stocking L. BELT 69 G3
Stocking L. CASS 58 E1
Stocking L. HUBB 57 E1
Stocking L. WADN 47 A5
Stockton WINA 19 G3
Stokes Twp ITSC 71 D1
Stokes Twp ROSE 91 D4
Stokey L. ITSC 59 D2
Stoll L. TODD 40 E3
Stone Axe L. ITSC 70 D4
Stone Cr. STLS 74 F1
Stoneham Twp CHIP 23 C2
Stone L. BELT 68 B4
Stone L. BELT 69 G1
Stone L. CARV 26 D2
Stone L. MEEK 24 A4
Stone L. SHER 34 D3
Stone L. STLS 60 B5
Stone L. STLS 62 A1
Stone L. STLS 62 C1
Stone L. STLS 74 F1
Stoner L. BELT 69 C5
Stone R. STLS 60 C4
Stoney Bk. STLS 60 G5
Stoney Bk. SHER 33 C4
Stoney Brook Twp STLS 51 A5
Stoney Cr. STRN 32 B2
Stoney Run Twp YMED 22 D5
Stonich I. STLS 73 B2
Stony Bk. CASS 48 D5
Stony Bk. CASS 49 D1
Stony Bk. ITSC 72 C1
Stony Brook L. GRNT 38 C2
Stony Brook Twp GRNT 38 C2
Stony Cr. CLAY 45 B4
Stony Cr. LAKE 62 B3
Stony Creek WOOD 97 F1
Stony I. STLS 85 G2
Stony L. CASS 49 A2
Stony L. CASS 57 F5
Stony L. COOK 88 F3
Stony L. DOUG 39 E2
Stony L. GRNT 38 C1
Stony L. HUBB 57 G1
Stony L. ISNT 34 D3
Stony L. LAKE 74 D3
Stony L. MORR 40 F4
Stony L. OTTL 47 G2
Stony Point Bk. ITSC 70 F2
Stony Point CASS 57 A4
Stony Point CASS 57 D5
Stony Point ITSC 70 F2
Stony Point Recreation Site CASS 57 D5
Stony Point WOOD 97 F1
Stony Pt. ITSC 59 C2
Stony Pt. LAKE 62 F2
Stony R. LAKE 74 C2
Stony Run — 29 E4
Stop I. KCHG 95 F5
Storden COTT 13 G3
Storden Twp COTT 13 G3
Store L. POLK 67 C5
Stowe L. DOUG 38 D5
Stowe L. ITSC 71 E4
Stowe Prairie Twp TODD 47 G5
Straight L. BECK 56 F4
Straight L. STLS 61 E5
Straight R. BECK 56 F4
Straight R. RICE 16 E5
Straight River Twp HUBB 56 G5
Strand L. BELT 69 D2
Strand L. POLK 67 E5
Strand L. SHER 34 E1
Strand L. STLS 61 C2
Strandness L. POPE 31 A1
Strandquist MRSH 90 G5
Strand Twp NORM 55 A1
Strathcona ROSE 91 G2
Stratton L. ISNT 34 D5
Strawberry I. STLS 73 B2
Strawberry L. BECK 55 D5
Strawberry L. CASS 57 A5
Strawberry L. COOK 88 F3
Strawberry L. CROW 49 C2
Stray Horse L. BELT 69 D1
Strike L. WADN 48 C2
Stringer L. LAKE 75 A2
String L. COTT 3 B4
Strobus L. COOK 75 B5
Strom L. BLUE 15 F1
Stroud L. STLS 61 D3
Strout MEEK 24 B4
Struggle L. LAKE 87 G1
Strunk L. BECK 55 G3
Strunks L. SCOT 26 E2
Strup L. LAKE 87 F1
Struutz I. STLS 73 B3
Stuart L. OTTL 47 G1
Stuart L. STLS 72 E1
Stuart L. STLS 85 D4
Stuart R. STLS 85 E5
Stubbs Bay HENN 26 C2
Stub L. COOK 75 A3
Stub L. LAKE 86 G2
Stub Lakes STRN 40 G2
Studhorse L. ATKN 59 F2
Stud L. MORR 41 D1
Stumble Cr. COOK 75 E3
Stumnel Mounds Historic Site PINE 43 F2
Stump L. BECK 56 E4
Stump L. BELT 69 F3
Stump L. CASS 48 F5
Stump L. COOK 88 E4
Stump L. MAHN 56 C1
Stump L. STRN 33 B1
Stump L. TODD 40 F3
Stumple L. ITSC 71 E3
Stumple L. ITSC 71 E4
Stump R. COOK 88 F5
Stumpy L. TODD 40 B3
Stuntz Bay STLS 73 B3
Sturgeon STLS 72 C3
Sturgeon L. GOOD 27 G5
Sturgeon L. PINE 51 F4
Sturgeon L. STLS 72 D1
Sturgeon Lake (city) PINE 51 F3
Sturgeon Lake Twp PINE 51 F3
Sturgeon R. KCHG 82 D4
Sturgeon R. STLS 72 B2
Sturgeon River Recreation Site KCHG 82 D5
Sturgeon River State Forest STLS 72 C3
Sturgeon River State Forest STLS 73 B1
Sturgeon Twp STLS 72 C3
Sucker Bay CASS 57 C5
Sucker Bay LAKE 62 F1
Sucker Bk. HUBB 57 C2
Sucker Bk. ITSC 59 A4
Sucker Cr. BELT 69 B4
Sucker Cr. BELT 81 F3
Sucker Cr. CASS 57 B5
Sucker Cr. CLER 56 B4
Sucker L. CLER 56 B4
Sucker L. ITSC 71 B4
Sucker L. ITSC 71 G5
Sucker L. LAKE 86 F4
Sucker L. MAHN 55 C5
Sucker L. RAMS 27 B1
Sugar Bay ITSC 59 C2
Sugar Bowl L. MAHN 67 F5
Sugar Branch ITSC 59 C2
Sugarbush I. STLS 84 A2
Sugar Bush L. CLER 56 C3
Sugar Bush Twp BECK 55 E5
Sugar Bush Twp BELT 69 E4
Sugar Hills Airport ITSC 59 C2
Sugar Hills Ski Area ITSC 59 D1
Sugar L. ATKN 50 F3
Sugar L. CASS 58 C5
Sugar L. FREE 6 E3
Sugar L. ITSC 59 C2
Sugar L. ITSC 70 G1
Sugar L. WRIT 33 E4
Sugar Loaf Pt. COOK 75 F3
Sugarloaf WINA 19 G4
Sugar Point CASS 58 C1
Sugar Point WOOD 97 E2
Sugar Point Historic Site CASS 58 C1
Sulem L. WATN 4 B2
Sullivan Bay STLS 84 B3
Sullivan Cr. HOUS 10 D1
Sullivan L. CASS 58 D4
Sullivan L. CROW 49 C5
Sullivan L. LAKE 74 G2
Sullivan L. MORR 41 B4
Sullivan L. STLS 61 B4
Sullivan L. WRIT 33 F4
Sullivan Lake CCC Camp Historic Site STLS 61 B4
Sullivan Lake Recreation Site LAKE 74 G2
Sullivan Twp POLK 78 G1
Summit L. KAND 24 A2
Summit L. MURR 2 A3
Summit Lake Twp NBLS 2 D4
Summit Twp BELT 69 D5
Summit Twp STEL 6 B5
Sumner Twp FILL 8 C2
Sumpet L. LAKE 75 B1
Sumter Twp MCLD 25 E1
Sunburg KAND 31 E4
Sundal NORM 67 F1
Sundal Twp NORM 67 F1
Sunday Bay STLS 86 D1
Sunday L. HUBB 57 G2
Sunday L. STLS 85 D5
Sundial L. STLS 85 E5
Sunding Cr. COOK 76 B2
Sundown L. LAKE 75 B2
Sundown Twp REDW 13 D5
Sunfish L. COOK 88 F4
Sunfish L. CROW 49 G5
Sunfish L. DKTA 27 D1
Sunfish L. LSUR 16 D2
Sunfish L. OTTL 46 D4
Sunfish L. WASH 27 B3
Sunfish Lake (city) DKTA 27 D1
Sunfish Lake City Park WASH 27 B3
Sunken L. ITSC 70 F3
Sun L. ITSC 71 B5
Sunlow L. COOK 75 A3
Sunny Brook Municipal Park WADN 47 E5
Sunnyside Township Game Refuge WILK 37 A4
Sunnyside Twp WILK 37 A4
Sunrise CHIS 35 C3
Sunrise L. CHIS 35 D3
Sunrise L. ITSC 71 F3

Sunrise Pool No. 1 CHIS 35 D2
Sunrise Pool No. 3 CHIS 35 D3
Sunrise Prairie County Park NBLS 2 G3
Sunrise R. CHIS 35 D3
Sunrise River Addition CHIS 35 D3
Sunrise Twp CHIS 35 B3
Sunset Bay MLLC 42 A3
Sunset L. OTTL 46 F5
Sunset L. STLS 61 F1
Sunset L. STLS 72 E2
Sunset L. STLS 84 G4
Sunset L. WASH 27 A3
Sunset Pt. ITSC 59 B2
Sunshine L. STLS 61 E4
Suomi L. ITSC 71 F1
Superior Bay STLS 52 B4
L. Superior COOK 75 F4
Superior Game Refuge Unit 1 COOK 76 C1
Superior Game Refuge Unit 11 STLS 73 C5
Superior Game Refuge Unit 16 STLS 72 D3
Superior National Forest COOK 73 F4
Superior National Forest Environmental Learning Center LAKE 74 D4
Superstition L. LAKE 74 B4
Surber L. COOK 88 E1
Surfside Seaplane Base (Rice Lake) ANOK 35 G1
Surprise L. CASS 57 F5
Surprise L. ITSC 71 F2
Surprise L. LAKE 74 C4
Susana L. COOK 88 E1
Susan Bay STLS 84 F3
L. Susan CARV 26 D3
Susan L. MART 4 F3
Susan L. STLS 84 G4
Susie I. COOK 76 E4
Sustacek L. MCLD 25 C1
Sutton L. PINE 44 C2
Sutton L. SCOT 26 G3
Svea KAND 23 B5
Sveadahl WATN 14 G3
Svea Twp KITT 90 F1
Sverdrup Twp OTTL 46 G4
Swag L. MART 4 G5
Swallow L. COOK 88 F1
Swallow L. LAKE 74 C4
Swamper Cr. COOK 88 F3
Swamper L. COOK 88 F3
Swamp L. ATKN 50 E3
Swamp L. BELT 69 D2
Swamp L. CASS 57 C4
Swamp L. CHIS 35 E4
Swamp L. COOK 76 A1
Swamp L. COOK 76 E2
Swamp L. COOK 87 D2
Swamp L. COOK 88 F2
Swamp L. LAKE 75 B1
Swamp L. SCOT 26 F3
Swamp L. STLS 74 F1
Swamp L. STRN 33 D1
Swamp L. STRN 33 E1
Swamp L. STRN 40 G3
Swamp R. COOK 76 F1
Swamp R. COOK 88 G5
Swanburg CROW 49 B2
Swan Cr. CASS 48 E3
Swan Cr. STLS 84 E2
Swan L. CARV 25 D5
Swan L. COOK 88 G1
Swan L. COTT 3 A4
Swan L. GRNT 38 E3
Swan L. ITSC 59 B5
Swan L. KAND 24 A1
Swan L. KAND 31 E5
Swan L. KAND 31 F4
Swan L. KAND 31 G5
Swan L. MCLD 25 D2
Swan L. NCLT 15 D2
Swan L. OTTL 38 A2
Swan L. POPE 31 A4
Swan L. POPE 31 D1
Swan L. SBLY 14 B4
Swan L. STEV 30 A4
Swan L. STLS 84 G4
Swan L. WRIT 25 A2
Swan Lake County Park MCLD 25 C2
Swan Lake Game Refuge NCLT 15 D2
Swan Lake Twp STEV 38 G4
Swan R. STLS 59 B4
Swan R. MORR 40 E5
Swan R. STLS 60 B3
Swan R. STLS 60 D2
Swan River (city) ITSC 59 D5
Swan River Twp MORR 40 E5
Swanson L. MAHN 55 A5
Swansons Bay STLS 85 B1
Swanville MORR 40 E4
Swanville Twp MORR 40 E4
Swart-out L. WRIT 33 F3
Swastika Beach (city) JACK 3 C5
Swatara ATKN 59 G1
Swede Grove L. CLAY 55 F1
Swede Grove Twp MEEK 32 G3
Swede L. CARV 25 C5
Swede L. CASS 48 A5

Swede L. CASS 58 F2
Swede L. CASS 58 G2
Swede L. COOK 88 G2
Swede Prairie Twp YMED 22 F3
Swedes Forest Twp REDW 23 F3
Sweeney L. HENN 26 C4
Sweetbrier L. SCOT 26 G4
Sweetman L. ATKN 50 E2
Sweetnose I. STLS 84 A3
Sweet Twp PIPE 1 A4
Sweitzer L. HUBB 57 F1
Swenoda L. POPE 31 C3
Swenoda Twp SWFT 30 G5
L. Swenson BELT 69 F3
Swenson County Park MURR 12 E2
Swenson L. BGST 29 D4
Swenson L. KAND 31 F4
Swensson House Historic Site and Farm Museum CHIP 23 D1
SWIFT — 31 —
Swift ROSE 92 C4
Swift County Historical Society Museum SWFT 30 E5
Swift Falls (city) SWFT 31 D2
Swift Falls County Park SWFT 31 D2
Swift L. CASS 58 D3
Swift R. CASS 58 D3
Swim L. DOUG 39 F4
Swing L. LAKE 86 F5
Sybil L. OTTL 46 C4
Sylvania L. LAKE 74 C5
L. Sylvan CASS 49 F1
Sylvan L. CASS 58 G2
Sylvan L. GRNT 38 E4
Sylvan L. HENN 34 G2
Sylvan L. MORR 49 G1
Sylvan Twp CASS 48 F5
Sylvester L. CASS 57 F5
L. Sylvia WRIT 33 F2
Sylvia L. BELT 68 B5
Sylvia L. STRN 40 G2
Synnes Twp STEV 30 C2
Syre NORM 55 C1
Table L. COOK 88 E4
Tabor POLK 78 B3
Tabor Twp POLK 78 F2
Tack L. COOK 75 B4
Taconite ITSC 59 B4
Taconite Corridor Trail STLS 73 B4
Tadpole L. ITSC 71 G3
Tail L. COOK 75 C3
Tailors I. STLS 72 A5
Tait L. COOK 75 B5
Tait R. COOK 75 B5
Taits L. KAND 32 G2
Takucmich L. STLS 85 C3
Talcot L. COOK 88 F3
Talcot L. COTT 3 B1
Talcot Lake County Park COTT 3 B1
Talcot Lake Wildlife Management Area COTT 3 B2
Talge L. CLER 68 C2
Tallas Island STLS 52 B4
Talmadge R. STLS 61 F5
Talmoon ITSC 71 E1
Talus L. COOK 88 G2
Tamarack ATKN 51 C1
Tamarack Bay STLS 73 A4
Tamarack Cr. STLS 73 A4
Tamarack L. ANOK 35 E2
Tamarack L. BECK 55 F4
Tamarack L. BECK 55 F5
Tamarack L. CARL 51 C2
Tamarack L. CARV 26 D2
Tamarack L. CASS 58 D4
Tamarack L. CASS 58 E2
Tamarack L. CASS 58 G1
Tamarack L. CASS 58 G2
Tamarack L. CASS 70 G3
Tamarack L. CLER 56 B3
Tamarack L. CLER 56 C4
Tamarack L. CLER 68 G2
Tamarack L. CROW 49 C3
Tamarack L. HUBB 57 F2
Tamarack L. ISNT 35 D2
Tamarack L. MAHN 56 A5
Tamarack L. MORR 40 A5
Tamarack L. MORR 40 F4
Tamarack L. OTTL 38 A4
Tamarack L. OTTL 46 D5
Tamarack L. OTTL 47 F1
Tamarack L. PINE 44 C1
Tamarack L. POLK 67 D2
Tamarack L. STLS 73 A4
Tamarack L. STRN 31 D5
Tamarack L. STRN 40 G3
Tamarack L. WRIT 25 A5
Tamarack Point Recreation Site CASS 70 G3
Tamarack R. ATKN 51 B1
Tamarack R. OTTL 46 B2
Tamarac National Wildlife Refuge BECK 56 E1
Tamarac National Wildlife Refuge Headquarters BECK 56 F1
Tamarac R. BELT 81 D5
Tamarac R. MRSH 78 A3

Tamarac Twp MRSH 78 A1
Tame L. COOK 87 F4
Tanager L. HENN 26 C2
Tanberg Twp WILK 45 D5
Tank L. BELT 69 G5
Tank L. CASS 58 G5
Tanner L. JACK 75 D5
Tanners L. WASH 27 C2
Tansem L. CLAY 46 B1
Tansem Twp CLAY 46 B1
Taopi MOWE 7 F5
Tara Twp SWFT 30 E4
Tara Twp TRAV 29 A4
Target L. HOUS 10 C2
Tar Pt. STLS 84 A3
Tarr L. ATKN 50 D1
Tarry L. COOK 87 F3
Tatlie L. CLAY 54 E5
Taunton LYON 12 E5
Tawney L. COOK 87 F3
Taylor Cr. MORR 40 E4
Taylor I. STLS 73 B2
Taylor L. ATKN 50 E3
Taylor L. ATKN 59 E3
Taylor L. CASS 58 D4
Taylor L. COOK 76 F2
Taylor L. ITSC 70 E5
Taylor L. WRIT 25 A3
Taylors Falls (city) CHIS 35 D5
Taylors Falls Public Library Historic Site CHIS 35 D5
Taylor Twp BELT 69 D4
Taylor Twp TRAV 37 D3
Tea Cracker L. BECK 56 E1
Teal L. COOK 76 B3
Teal L. JACK 3 C4
Teal L. STLS 60 A5
Teamster L. LAKE 74 D3
Teapail L. CLER 56 B2
Teat L. COOK 87 F3
Techout I. WOOD 97 E3
Tee L. OTTL 46 B3
Tee L. OTTL 46 D5
Tee L. POLK 67 E3
Teel L. STLS 73 B4
Teel L. STLS 86 F1
Tegner L. KITT 90 E2
Teien Twp KITT 89 F5
Tenhassen Twp MART 4 F4
Ten Acre L. BECK 56 E4
L. Ten CLAY 46 A1
Ten L. BELT 69 F4
Ten L. CASS 57 E4
Ten L. CASS 58 G5
Ten Lake Twp BELT 69 G4
Ten Mile Cr. LQPL 22 D3
Ten Mile L. BELT 69 C1
Ten Mile L. CASS 57 F4
Ten Mile L. OTTL 38 B3
Ten Mile Lake Twp LQPL 22 D3
Tenney WILK 37 C4
Tennyson L. ISNT 34 C3
Tenor L. COOK 87 F3
Ten Section L. CASS 57 A4
Tenstrike BELT 69 D3
Tenth Crow Wing L. HUBB 57 E3
Tent L. COOK 87 G4
Tepee L. BELT 68 D5
Tepee L. CASS 58 E1
Tepee L. COOK 87 D4
Tepee Lakes HUBB 57 D1
Tern L. COOK 87 E3
Terrace POPE 31 C3
Terrace Pt. COOK 76 C2
Terrebonne RDLK 67 B2
Terrebonne Cr. RDLK 67 B2
Terrebonne Twp RDLK 67 B2
Territory of Deer Lake ITSC 59 B1
Terry L. CROW 50 C1
Terry R. Johnson Recreation Site CASS 49 F1
Terway L. CLER 56 B2
Tesoker L. STLS 85 C3
Tess L. OTTL 39 B2
Tetagouche L. LAKE 63 A1
L. Tetonka LSUR 16 E1
Tettegouche State Park LAKE 63 A1
Thatcher L. HUBB 57 B2
The Arches (city) WINA 9 A2
The Glockenspiel BRWN 14 D5
Theilman WBSH 18 D4
Thelma L. CROW 49 C3
Theodore Wirth Municipal Park HENN 26 C5
Thermal L. LAKE 86 F4
Thiebault L. CASS 58 E5
Thief L. MRSH 79 A4
Thief Lake Twp MRSH 79 A4
Thief Lake Wildlife Management Area MRSH 79 A4
Thief R. MRSH 79 D2
Thief River Falls (city) PENN 79 E2
Thief River Falls Regional Airport PENN 79 F2
Thielke L. BGST 29 D4
Thien L. STRN 32 D5

Thies L. HENN 26 B2
Thimble L. ITSC 71 B3
Third Crow Wing L. HUBB 57 G2
Third Guide L. ATKN 59 G1
Third L. CARL 52 B1
Third L. CASS 57 E4
Third L. CLER 68 F2
Third L. STLS 61 F2
Third L. STLS 85 E4
Third Perch L. CASS 57 G4
Third R. ITSC 70 D1
Third River Flowage ITSC 70 F2
Third River Twp ITSC 70 D1
Third Sucker L. ITSC 71 G5
L. Thirteen CASS 57 B4
L. Thirteen CLAY 46 A1
L. Thirteen PINE 51 F5
Thirteen L. KNBC 43 B2
Thirty L. ITSC 71 F4
Thirty One L. ATKN 50 E3
Thirtysix I. STLS 73 A1
Thirty Six L. CASS 58 F2
Thistledew L. ITSC 71 C5
Thistledew Lake Game Refuge ITSC 71 C5
Thistledew Lake Recreation Site ITSC 71 B5
Thoen L. MEEK 24 A4
Thole L. SCOT 26 F3
Thomas L. DKTA 27 E1
Thomas L. HENN 26 B2
Thomas L. LAKE 62 B2
Thomas L. LSUR 16 B1
Thomas L. OTTL 46 B5
Thomastown Twp WADN 48 F2
Thompson Cr. COOK 76 A2
Thompson Cr. HOUS 10 D1
Thompson L. COOK 76 A2
Thompson L. CROW 49 C5
Thompson L. GRNT 38 E4
Thompson L. MEEK 24 C3
Thompson L. SHER 34 E1
Thompson L. STLS 61 D4
Thompson Twp KITT 90 D1
Thomson CARL 52 C2
Thomson Cr. WOOD 81 B3
Thomson Hill Travel Information Center STLS 52 B3
Thomson Reservoir CARL 52 B2
Thomson Twp CARL 52 B2
Thor ATKN 50 E4
Thoreson House Historic Site LQPL 22 B3
Thornton L. ATKN 49 E5
Thorpe Twp HUBB 57 D2
Thorson L. DOUG 38 E5
L. Thorstad DOUG 38 E5
Thorstad L. GRNT 38 D4
Thrasher L. COOK 76 A2
Three Finger L. MORR 40 B5
Three Havens County Park DOUG 39 E3
Three I. STLS 85 D5
Three Island L. BELT 69 E2
Three Island L. CASS 57 F5
Three Island L. CASS 58 E2
Three Island L. ITSC 71 E2
Three Island L. ITSC 71 E3
Three Island Lake Park BELT 69 D2
L. Three LAKE 74 A4
L. Three ATKN 50 E1
L. Three CLAY 46 A1
Three L. CLER 68 D2
Three Lakes Twp REDW 13 C5
Three Mile Cr. LYON 12 A4
Three Mile Cr. STRN 33 E2
Threemile I. COOK 87 E3
Threemile L. STLS 72 F3
Three Sister I. STLS 96 G1
Three Sisters Island STLS 96 G3
Thrush L. COOK 88 G2
Thumb L. STLS 85 C3
Thumb L. STLS 85 D3
Thunderbird L. LAKE 75 D2
Thunder L. CASS 58 F4
Thunder L. STLS 86 E1
Thunder L. TODD 40 B3
Thunder Lake Twp CASS 58 F4
Thunders L. BELT 69 B1
Thursday Bay LAKE 86 D2
Thydean L. ITSC 71 D2
Tibbetts Bk. MORR 42 E1
Tidd L. CASS 58 D4
Tiessen L. ATKN 50 A4
Tiff L. CROW 49 C3
Tiger Bay STLS 85 D4
Tiger L. CARV 25 E4
Tiger L. REDW 13 A5
Tilde L. BECK 55 E1
Tilden Twp POLK 67 C1
Tilson Bay KCHG 95 F5
Timber L. COOK 75 D3
Timber L. JACK 3 C3
Time L. COOK 87 F3
Timm L. YMED 13 A1

Timothy Twp CROW 49 B2
Tin Can Mike L. LAKE 86 F1
Tincup L. CLER 56 B2
Tinkander L. STLS 73 G2
Tintah TRAV 37 C5
Tintah Twp TRAV 37 D5
Tiny L. CLER 68 B4
Tiny L. COOK 88 G4
Tischer's Cr. STLS 61 G4
Titlow L. SBLY 15 A2
Tittle L. COOK 88 F4
T. L. LAKE 75 C2
Toad L. BECK 56 G2
Toad Lake (city) BECK 47 A2
Toad Lake Twp BECK 56 G2
Toad R. OTTL 47 B1
Tobacco L. COOK 75 A5
Tobique L. CASS 58 D4
TODD — 40 —
Todd County Historical Society Museum TODD 40 D2
Todd Field TODD 40 E2
Todd L. MCLD 25 C1
Todd Municipal Park WINA 7 E3
Todd Twp HUBB 56 F5
Toe L. LAKE 87 E2
Toe L. STLS 85 C4
Tofte COOK 75 E4
Tofte District Ranger Station COOK 75 E4
Tofte L. LAKE 86 G3
Tofte Twp COOK 75 D4
Togo ITSC 72 B1
Toikka L. STLS 73 C5
Toimi LAKE 74 G3
Toivola STLS 60 C3
Toivola Twp STLS 60 C3
Tomahawk L. LAKE 75 B1
Tomash L. COOK 76 A1
Tomato L. COOK 88 G4
Tom L. COOK 88 G5
Tom L. SWFT 30 D2
Tomlinson Cr. LAKE 74 D5
Toms L. OTTL 39 B3
Toner's Lake County Park WASC 16 F2
Toners L. WASC 16 F2
Tonikin's L. STLS 60 F4
Tonka Bay (city) HENN 26 D2
Tonseth L. OTTL 46 E3
Tony L. LAKE 74 G2
Toohey L. COOK 75 C3
Tool L. COOK 87 G2
Tooth L. STLS 84 B5
Topaz L. LAKE 87 E1
Topper L. COOK 88 E1
Toqua Lake County Park BGST 29 B4
Toqua Twp BGST 29 B3
Torch Light L. CARL 51 C5
Tord L. LAKE 75 C2
Torgenson Cr. COOK 75 C3
Torgerson L. BECK 55 F3
Torgerson L. OTTL 38 B5
Tornado L. LAKE 74 A5
Torning Twp SWFT 31 F1
Torrey Twp CASS 58 C5
Torstenson L. GRNT 38 E4
Tote L. COOK 88 G1
Totem L. LAKE 87 D2
Tovson L. BECK 55 F4
Tower STLS 73 B3
Tower Cr. CASS 48 D3
Tower Cr. STLS 61 B3
Tower Dr. WASH 27 D3
Tower L. ITSC 70 F1
Tower Mini Park and Historical Train STLS 73 B3
Tower Municipal Airport STLS 73 B2
Tower Park Recreation Site STLS 73 B2
Tower Soudan State Park STLS 73 B3
Towers L. MEEK 32 F4
Town And Country County Park RENV 23 F4
Town L. BECK 46 B5
Town L. COOK 87 F4
Town Line L. ATKN 50 A5
Town Line L. ATKN 50 C3
Town Line L. ATKN 59 G5
Town Line L. CASS 58 E2
Townline L. LAKE 75 A2
Trace L. TODD 40 F3
Tracey Slough L. POPE 31 C4
Track L. COOK 76 A2
Tracy LYON 12 E5
Tracy Municipal Airport LYON 12 E5
Trader L. LAKE 86 F5
Traders Bay CASS 57 D5
Tradition L. LAKE 87 E2
Trail POLK 67 C5
Trail L. LAKE 87 G2
Trails End Recreation Site COOK 87 F3
Transit Twp SBLY 15 A1
Trap L. COOK 88 F3
Trapper L. STLS 54 A3
Trapper R. POPE 31 A2
Trappers L. LAKE 74 D5
TRAVERSE — 37 —
Traverse NCLT 15 D4
Traverse County Park TRAV 29 A1

196

Traverse Des Sioux Historic Site NCLT 15 C4
Traverse Des Souix Recreation Area NCLT 15 D4
L. Traverse (Reservoir) TRAV 37 G1
Traverse Twp NCLT 15 D3
Travois L. LAKE 87 F2
Trease L. STLS 85 F5
Treasure I. STLS 72 A5
Treatme L. COOK 87 G3
Tree Farm Landing Recreation Site WADN 48 A2
Treglaff L. BECK 46 B5
Trekle L. COOK 87 E2
Trelipe Twp CASS 58 G3
Tremble L. COOK 88 F1
Tremulo L. LAKE 74 A5
Trenton L. FREE 6 C2
Trestle L. ITSC 70 C5
Trestle L. ITSC 71 G4
Triangle L. LAKE 86 G3
Trident L. LAKE 86 E5
Trimont MART 4 D3
Trine L. COOK 88 G1
Trinity L. LAKE 87 F1
Trip L. COOK 87 E5
Triplet Lakes COOK 87 G4
Tripp L. CASS 57 F4
Tripp L. HUBB 57 G3
Trisko L. GRNT 38 D2
Triumph Cr. STLS 85 F3
Triumph L. STLS 85 F3
Trollin L. ISNT 35 A1
Trommald CROW 49 E4
Trondhjem Twp OTTL 46 D1
Trosky PIPE 1 B5
Trotterchaud L. BECK 55 E3
Trout Bk. WBSH 18 C4
Trout Bk. WBSH 18 D1
Trout Cr. FILL 8 C4
Trout Cr. ITSC 59 B4
Trout Cr. TODD 40 E2
Trout L. COOK 76 A4
Trout L. CROW 49 B4
Trout L. ITSC 59 B4
Trout L. ITSC 71 F2
Trout L. STLS 85 G2
Trout Lake Twp ITSC 59 B4
Trout Rock STLS 85 G2
Trowbridge L. OTTL 46 B4
Troy WINA 8 C5
Troy Cr. WOOD 81 B4
Troy Twp PIPE 11 F4
Troy Twp RENV 23 E5
L. Trulse OTTL 39 A1
Trulson L. CHIS 35 E4
Truman MART 4 C5
Trump L. COOK 87 F5
Trygg L. STLS 85 C3
Tubby L. ITSC 71 E3
Tub L. BECK 46 A2
Tucker L. COOK 87 E5
Tucker R. COOK 87 E5
Tulaby L. MAHN 56 D1
Tumuli Twp OTTL 38 B3
Tunmore L. COOK 88 G1
Tunsberg Twp CHIP 22 B4
Turbid L. CARV 26 D1
Turkey L. LAKE 87 G1
Turner L. ATKN 50 C4
Turner L. CROW 49 E4
Turner Twp ATKN 50 A5
Turnip L. COOK 88 F3
Turpela L. STLS 73 F3
Turtle Cr. TODD 40 C2
Turtle Creek Twp TODD 40 B3
Turtle L. ATKN 50 E2
Turtle L. BELT 69 E2
Turtle L. CASS 57 E5
Turtle L. CLAY 46 A1
Turtle L. COOK 76 B1
Turtle L. CROW 49 F5
Turtle L. DOUG 39 F2
Turtle L. GRNT 38 E4
Turtle L. HENN 26 B3
Turtle L. ITSC 71 E1
Turtle L. LAKE 74 A3
Turtle L. MEEK 25 A1
Turtle L. POLK 68 E1
Turtle L. RAMS 27 A1
Turtle L. TODD 40 B3
Turtle L. WASH 35 G3
Turtle Lake Twp BELT 69 D2
Turtle Lake Twp CASS 57 E5
Turtle R. BELT 69 E4
Turtle R. ITSC 71 E1
Turtle River (city) BELT 69 E3
Turtle River L. BELT 69 E3
Turtle River Twp BELT 69 E3
Tuscarora L. COOK 87 F3
L. Tustin LSUR 16 E2
Tuttle L. ITSC 70 G4
Tuttle L. MART 4 F4
Tweed Museum of Art STLS 61 G4
L. Twelve PINE 51 F5
Twelve L. COOK 88 G4
Twelve L. MORR 41 B5
Twelve L. OTTL 46 D2
Twelve L. PINE 44 C2
Twelvemile Cr. TRAV 37 F4
L. Twenty-eight POLK 67 D5
L. Twentyfive BECK 56 F1
Twenty Four L. ITSC 72 E1
L. Twenty HUBB 57 B1
Twenty L. ATKN 50 F3
L. Twenty Nine CARL 51 D5
L. Twentyone HUBB 57 C2
Twenty-One L. OTTL 46 D3
L. Twenty-Six CASS 58 F3
Twenty Two L. CROW 41 B5
Twig STLS 61 F2
Twilight L. LAKE 87 E2
Twin Bay's MLLC 42 B3
Twin I. STLS 85 G2
Twin Island L. BECK 56 D4
Twin Island L. CROW 49 F4
Twin Island L. TODD 40 E1
Twinkle L. COOK 87 F3
Twin L. CASS 57 B4
Twin L. CROW 49 C5
Twin L. ISNT 35 B1
Twin L. ITSC 60 B1
Twin L. ITSC 71 G3
Twin L. KNBC 43 F1
Twin L. STLS 61 D5
Twin L. WASH 27 A4
Twin L. WASH 35 F3
Twin L. WRIT 33 E4
Twin L. WRIT 33 F2
Twin Lake Cr. MAHN 55 B5
Twin Lakes ANOK 35 F1
Twin Lakes BGST 29 E4
Twin Lakes CASS 58 E3
Twin Lakes CASS 58 G1
Twin Lakes CROW 41 B1
Twin Lakes CROW 49 D3
Twin Lakes CROW 49 E3
Twin Lakes (city) FREE 6 F4
Twin Lakes GOOD 27 F5
Twin Lakes HENN 26 B4
Twin Lakes ISNT 35 D2
Twin Lakes ITSC 59 B4
Twin Lakes KITT 90 F5
Twin Lakes LAKE 62 C2
Twin Lakes LINC 21 G4
Twin Lakes MORR 40 D5
Twin Lakes OTTL 46 F4
Twin Lakes STLS 52 A2
Twin Lakes STLS 60 A5
Twin Lakes STLS 61 D3
Twin Lakes STLS 73 B5
Twin Lakes STLS 85 G5
Twin Lakes TODD 40 F3
Twin Lakes Twp CARL 52 C1
Twin Lakes WRIT 33 F5
Twin Lakes WRIT 33 G4
Twin Lakes Beach Recreation Site STLS 73 F3
Twin Lakes L. ATKN 50 A5
Twin Lakes L. BECK 55 E4
Twin Lakes L. KAND 32 F1
Twin Lakes Wildlife Management Area KITT 90 F4
Twin Oaks L. MAHN 67 G4
Twin Valley (city) NORM 55 B1
Two Connections L. POLK 68 D1
Two Deer L. LAKE 74 C3
Two Harbors (city) LAKE 62 E3
Two Harbors Game Refuge LAKE 62 E2
Two Harbors Information Center LAKE 62 E3
Two Harbors Municipal Airport LAKE 62 D2
Two Inlets L. BECK 56 E4
Two Inlets State Forest BECK 56 E4
Two Inlets Twp BECK 56 E4
Two Island L. COOK 76 A2
Two Island L. ITSC 71 D1
Two Island Lake Recreation Site COOK 76 A2
Two Island R. COOK 75 E3
L. Two LAKE 74 A4
Two L. CASS 58 G1
Two L. CLER 68 C2
Two Mile Cr. STLS 85 G1
Two Mile L. ITSC 70 F4
Two Points CASS 58 C1
Two R. MORR 40 F4
Two Rivers L. STRN 32 A5
Two Rivers Twp MORR 41 F1
Two R. South Branch STRN 40 G5
Tyler LINC 12 D1
Tyler L. LSUR 16 C1
Tyler Municipal Airport LINC 12 D1
Tynsid Twp POLK 66 C1
Typo L. ISNT 35 D1
Tyrone Twp LSUR 15 B5
Tyro Twp YMED 22 E3
Tyson L. YMED 23 G1
Udolpho Twp MOWE 7 C2
Uff L. POLK 67 E5
Uhlenkolts L. STRN 32 A3
Uhl L. WRIT 34 G1
Ulen CLAY 55 D1
Ulen Museum POLK 55 D1
Ulen Twp CLAY 55 D1
Underberg L. POLK 68 D1
Underwood OTTL 46 G4
Underwood Twp REDW 13 B1
Uninhabited Point BELT 81 G2
Union Cr. WADN 47 F5
Union Grove Twp MEEK 32 F3
Union Hill SCOT 16 A2
Union L. DOUG 39 E2
Union L. DOUG 39 F3
Union L. MEEK 33 F2
Union L. POLK 67 E2
Union L. RICE 16 B5
Union Twp HOUS 10 D1
United States Hockey Hall of Fame STLS 73 F1
United States Pt. LAKE 86 E3
University of Minnesota HENN 26 C5
University of Minnesota at Morris STEV 30 B3
University of Minnesota Duluth Branch STLS 61 G4
University of Minnesota Forestry School CLER 56 C4
University of Minnesota Institute of Agriculture RAMS 27 C1
University of Minnesota Landscape Arboretum CARV 26 D2
University of Minnesota Technical College WASC 16 G3
University Point MLLC 42 B1
Unknown L. STLS 61 F2
Unload L. COOK 87 F4
Unorganized Territory of Beltrami Forest WOOD 93 F2
Unorganized Territory of Birch Lake STLS 73 C4
Unorganized Territory of Bow String Lake ITSC 70 F2
Unorganized Territory of Brook Lake BELT 69 F5
Unorganized Territory of Clay HUBB 57 D1
Unorganized Territory of Clear Creek CARL 52 E1
Unorganized Territory of Crow Wing CROW 49 F2
Unorganized Territory of Davidson ATKN 50 D4
Unorganized Territory of East Cass CASS 58 D5
Unorganized Territory of East Cook COOK 76 A4
Unorganized Territory of East Kittson KITT 90 C5
Unorganized Territory of East Lake LAKE 75 D2
Unorganized Territory of East St. Louis STLS 73 A2
Unorganized Territory of Fermory STLS 60 B5
Unorganized Territory of Gheen STLS 84 G4
Unorganized Territory of Hay Lake STLS 73 E2
Unorganized Territory of Heikkila Lake STLS 61 A1
Unorganized Territory of Janette Lake STLS 60 B2
Unorganized Territory of Jewitt ATKN 50 F4
Unorganized Territory of Little Sand Lake ITSC 59 B5
Unorganized Territory of Lower Red Lake BELT 69 B1
Unorganized Territory of McCormack Lake STLS 72 E2
Unorganized Territory of Mud Lake MRSH 79 C4
Unorganized Territory of North Beltrami BELT 80 B3
Unorganized Territory of North Carlton CARL 51 B3
Unorganized Territory of North Cass CASS 58 B2
Unorganized Territory of North Clearwater CLER 68 A3
Unorganized Territory of Northeast Aitkin ATKN 60 F1
Unorganized Territory of Northeast Itasca ITSC 71 D4
Unorganized Territory of Northeast Koochiching KCHG 83 C4
Unorganized Territory of Northeast St. Louis STLS 85 F4
Unorganized Territory of North Roseau ROSE 92 B1
Unorganized Territory of Northwest Aitkin ATKN 50 B1
Unorganized Territory of Northwest Angle WOOD 97 F2
Unorganized Territory of Northwest Koochiching KCHG 82 C3
Unorganized Territory of Northwest Roseau ROSE 91 C1
Unorganized Territory of Northwest St. Louis STLS 84 C2
Unorganized Territory of Pot Shot Lake STLS 60 E2
Unorganized Territory of Rainy River WOOD 93 F4
Unorganized Territory of River Roseau ROSE 91 B2
Unorganized Territory of Sand Lake STLS 72 D4
Unorganized Territory of South Clearwater CLER 56 C3
Unorganized Territory of Southeast Aitkin ATKN 51 F1
Unorganized Territory of Southeast Mahnomen MAHN 56 B1
Unorganized Territory of Southeast Roseau ROSE 92 E4
Unorganized Territory of South Itaska ITSC 59 D3
Unorganized Territory of South Koochiching KCHG 70 A3
Unorganized Territory of Steamboat River HUBB 57 D3
Unorganized Territory of Upper Red Lake BELT 80 E3
Unorganized Territory of West Cook COOK 76 A1
Unorganized Territory of West Lake LAKE 74 E3
Unorganized Territory of Whiteface Reservoir STLS 61 B3
Upland L. LAKE 74 F3
Upper Badger Cr. POLK 67 C2
Upper Bass L. HUBB 57 E3
Upper Bear Cr. FILL 8 C4
Upper Birch L. ISNT 35 D2
Upper Bottle L. HUBB 57 E1
Upper Bug L. STLS 61 C3
Upper Cascade River Recreation Site COOK 76 A1
Upper Cone L. COOK 87 F5
Upper Cormorant L. BECK 46 A2
Upper Cullen L. CROW 49 D2
Upper Dean L. CROW 49 C5
Upper Egg L. BECK 56 E1
Upper Gull L. CASS 49 D1
Upper Hanson L. ITSC 71 F3
Upper Hatch L. ITSC 71 D1
Upper Hay L. CROW 49 C1
Upper Hunt L. DOUG 39 C1
Upper Iowa R. MOWE 8 G1
Upper L. HENN 26 C2
Upper Lightning L. OTTL 38 B1
Upper Lindgren L. BELT 69 D2
Upper Loon L. CASS 49 D1
Upper Menton L. CASS 58 C4
Upper Midwest Indian Cultural Center PIPE 11 G4
Upper Milton L. CASS 58 D4
Upper Mission L. CROW 49 D3
Upper Mississippi River National Wildlife and Fish Refuge WINA 19 F3
Upper Mud L. GOOD 18 A1
Upper Mud L. HUBB 56 D5
Upper Panasa L. ITSC 59 B4
Upper Pauness L. STLS 85 D2
Upper Pigeon L. ITSC 70 E2
Upper Pine L. PINE 43 B2
Upper Red L. (Reservoir) BELT 81 E3
Upper Rice L. CLER 68 G4
Upper Rice L. ISNT 42 G5
Upper Sakatah L. LSUR 16 E3
Upper Sioux Agency Historic Site YMED 23 E2
Upper Sioux Agency State Park YMED 23 F1
Upper Sioux Indian Reservation YMED 23 E1
Upper South Long L. CROW 49 G2
Upper Sucker L. CASS 57 A5
Upper Tamarack R. PINE 44 B3
Upper Trelipe L. CASS 58 F4
Upper Twin L. FREE 6 F4
Upper Twin L. HUBB 48 A1
Upper Twin Lakes ITSC 70 D1
Upper Whitefish L. CROW 49 B2
Upsala MORR 40 F4
Upstead L. STLS 60 C2
Uran L. BECK 55 D3
Uranus L. LAKE 86 G3
Urbank OTTL 39 B2
Urness Twp DOUG 38 E5
Us-kab-wan-ka R. STLS 61 D2
U.S. Lock and Dam No. 1 HENN 26 C5
U.S. Lock and Dam No. 1 RAMS 27 C1
U.S. Lock and Dam No. 2 WASH 27 E3
U.S. Lock and Dam No. 3 and Visitor Center GOOD 28 G1
U.S. Lock and Dam No. 4 WBSH 19 D1
U.S. Lock and Dam No. 5A WINA 19 G4
U.S. Lock and Dam No. 5 WINA 19 F2
U.S. Lock and Dam No. 6 WINA 10 A1
U.S. Lock and Dam No. 7 WINA 10 B2
U.S. Lock and Dam No. 8 HOUS 10 F2
U.S. Port of Entry COOK 76 E4
U.S. Port of Entry KCHG 95 F3
U.S. Port of Entry KITT 89 A4
U.S. Port of Entry KITT 90 A2
U.S. Port of Entry ROSE 91 A3
U.S. Port of Entry ROSE 91 A5
U.S. Port of Entry ROSE 92 B3
U.S. Port of Entry STLS 74 A1
U.S. Port of Entry STLS 85 C1
U.S. Port of Entry WOOD 93 E4
Utica WINA 9 A1
Utica Twp WINA 9 A2
Uva L. COOK 87 G4
Vaara Cr. STLS 60 D2
Vadnais Heights (city) RAMS 27 B1
L. Vadnais RAMS 27 B1
Vail Twp REDW 13 C3
Vale L. COOK 88 E4
Vallers Twp LYON 12 A4
Valleyfair Amusement Park SCOT 26 E3
Valley L. STLS 62 C1
Valley Municipal Park DKTA 27 D2
Valley R. ITSC 71 A5
Valley Twp MRSH 80 C1
Vallin L. BECK 56 F4
V.A. Medical Center STRN 33 B2
Van Buren Twp STLS 60 E3
Vance L. COOK 88 F1
Vanduse L. ATKN 59 F5
Van L. LAKE 87 F2
Vanose L. MAHN 67 G4
Van Vac L. STLS 85 F3
Variety L. CASS 57 F4
Vasa GOOD 17 B5
Vasa Twp GOOD 17 B4
Vaseux L. COOK 88 E4
Vat L. COOK 75 C5
Veblen Farmstead Historic Site RICE 17 D2
Vee L. LAKE 87 F2
Vega Twp MRSH 78 D1
Vegetable L. BECK 55 D4
Vein L. LAKE 87 G2
Veldt Twp MRSH 80 B1
Velvet L. CROW 49 C4
Venning Cr. ITSC 71 C5
Venoah L. CARL 52 C2
Venstrom L. OTTL 46 D3
L. Venus DOUG 38 E5
Venus L. COOK 87 F4
Vera L. LAKE 86 E5
Verdi LINC 11 E4
Verdi Twp LINC 11 D4
Verdon Twp ATKN 59 F4
Vergas L. OTTL 46 C4
Vergas OTTL 46 C4
Vermillion DKTA 27 F3
Vermilion Community College STLS 74 A1
Vermilion Dam (city) STLS 85 G1
Vermilion Iron Range STLS 73 C3
Vermilion Lake Indian Reservation STLS 73 B2
Vermilion Lake Twp STLS 73 C2
Vermilion R. STLS 84 E5
L. Vermilion STLS 73 B2
Vermillion L. CASS 58 C5
Vermillion R. CASS 58 D5
Vermillion R. DKTA 27 F2
Vermillion Twp DKTA 27 F2
Vermont L. DOUG 39 C3
Verndale WADN 48 F1
Vern L. COOK 87 G5
Vernon Center BLUE 5 A2
Vernon Center Twp BLUE 5 A2
Vernon L. COOK 88 G1
Vernon Twp DOGE 7 B4
Vern R. COOK 87 G4
Verona Twp FRBT 5 D2
Veseli RICE 16 B3
Vesper L. COOK 87 F5
Vesta REDW 13 B2
Vesta Twp REDW 13 B2
Vial L. COOK 87 G4
Vibo L. CHIS 35 D3
Victoria CARV 26 D2
Victoria L. DOUG 39 E3
Victor L. LAKE 74 D4
Victor Twp WRIT 25 B3
Viding Twp CLAY 54 D3
Vienna Twp ROCK 2 D1
Vierg L. LAKE 87 F2
Vigoren L. POLK 67 D5
Viking MRSH 78 D5
Viking Altar Rock Historic Site TODD 40 F1
Viking Mooring Stone Historic Site CLAY 56 G5
Viking Twp MRSH 78 D5
Viking Valley Ski Area OTTL 38 B5
Village of St. Vincent Historical District KITT 89 B4
Village of Yesteryear Historic Site STEL 16 G5
Villard POPE 39 G3
Villard L. POPE 39 G3
Villard Twp TODD 48 G3
Vineland MLLC 42 B1
Vineland Bay MLLC 42 B1
Vineland Twp POLK 66 D2
Vinge L. OTTL 38 B3
Vining OTTL 39 A1
Viola OLMS 18 G4
Violation L. COOK 87 G4
Viola Twp OLMS 18 G3
Vireo L. COOK 88 G1

Virginia STLS 73 F1
L. Virginia CARV 26 D2
Virginia District Ranger Station STLS 72 F5
Virginia L. STLS 73 F1
Virgin L. COOK 87 F3
Virgin L. ITSC 70 E2
Vista L. COOK 88 F2
Vivian L. LAKE 75 C2
Vivian Twp WASC 6 B1
Vizenor L. BECK 55 E4
Volden L. POLK 67 E5
Volen L. OTTL 38 A3
L. Volney LSUR 16 C2
Volstead House Historic Site YMED 23 D1
Vos L. STRN 40 G4
Voss Municipal Park WATN 4 A2
Voyageurs National Park Ranger Station and Information Center STLS 84 A3
Voyageurs National Park STLS 84 A3
Voyageurs Visitor Center STLS 74 A1
Vyre L. COOK 75 B3
Waasa Twp STLS 73 D4
Wabana L. ITSC 71 G3
Wabana Twp ITSC 71 G3
Wabang L. STLS 85 D4
WABASHA — 18 —
Wabasha WBSH 18 C5
Wabasha County Historical Society Museum WBSH 18 C5
Wabasha Cr. REDW 14 B1
Wabasso REDW 13 C3
Wabasso Museum REDW 13 C3
L. Wabedo CASS 58 F2
Wabedo Twp CASS 58 F2
Wabegon L. CASS 57 D5
Wabisish L. HUBB 56 D5
Waboose Bay CASS 58 B2
Waboose L. BECK 56 E1
Waboose L. HUBB 57 E2
Wabosons L. LAKE 86 E2
Wabuse L. STLS 61 B3
Waconia CARV 26 D1
Waconia L. CARV 26 D1
Waconia Twp CARV 25 D5
Wacouta GOOD 18 A2
Wacouta Twp GOOD 18 A2
Wade Bk. KCHG 70 A5
WADENA — 47 —
Wadena WADN 47 E5
Wadena L. MAHN 55 C5
Wadena Municipal Airport WADN 47 E5
Wadena Twp WADN 47 F5
Wadop L. LAKE 74 D3
Waffle L. COOK 75 C3
Wager L. COOK 75 A3
Wager L. LAKE 74 B5
Wagner Cr. ITSC 70 C2
Wagner L. ITSC 70 C2
Wagner L. WRIT 34 G1
Wagner Twp ATKN 43 A1
Wagonga L. KAND 24 B1
Wagosh L. STLS 86 E1
Wahkon Bay MLLC 42 B3
Wahkon MLLC 42 B3
Wahnena Twp CASS 58 B5
Wahneshin L. CASS 58 D4
Waite Park (city) STRN 33 B2
Wakefield L. ATKN 59 G5
Wakefield L. MAHN 55 A5
Wakefield L. RAMS 27 C2
Wakefield Twp STRN 32 D5
Wakeman Bay ITSC 71 G2
Wakemup STLS 72 A5
Wakemup Bay STLS 72 A5
Wakemup Bay Recreation Site STLS 72 A5
Wakemup Narrows STLS 72 A5
Walbo ISNT 34 B4
Walcott Twp RICE 16 E5
Walden Twp CASS 48 C5
Walden Twp POPE 30 B5
Waldorf WASC 6 B1
Wales LAKE 62 B2
Walker CASS 57 D4
Walker Bay CASS 57 D4
Walker Brook Cr. CLER 68 F3
Walker Brook L. CLER 68 F4
Walker Diamond Cr. FILL 9 D2
Walker District Ranger Station CASS 57 D4
Walker L. OTTL 46 E5
Walker Municipal Airport CASS 57 C4
Walker Museum and Information Center CASS 57 D4
Wallace L. PINE 43 C4
Wallingford Cr. HUBB 57 G2
Wall L. OTTL 46 G3
Wall L. STLS 85 F4
Wallmark L. CHIS 35 E3
Wallow Cr. STLS 61 B4
Walls Twp TRAV 37 G3
Walnut Grove REDW 13 E1
Walnut L. FRBT 5 E5
Walnut Lake Twp FRBT 5 D5
Walnut Lake Wildlife Management Area FRBT 6 E1
Walter L. BGST 29 E4
Walters FRBT 6 F2
Walters Jail Historic Site FRBT 6 F2
Walters L. ITSC 71 D4
Walter Twp LQPL 21 A4
Waltham MOWE 7 C3
Waltham Twp MOWE 7 C3
Walthausen L. PINE 52 F1
Walworth Twp BECK 55 D2
Wambach L. MAHN 55 B5
Wampus L. COOK 88 E2
Wampus L. LAKE 74 D3
Wanamingo GOOD 17 D4
Wanamingo Twp GOOD 17 D3
Wanda REDW 13 D4
Wanger Twp MRSH 78 B3
Wang Twp RENV 23 D2
Wanihigan L. COOK 87 F5
Wanless Cr. LAKE 75 D2
Wanless L. LAKE 75 C2
Wannaska ROSE 91 E5
Wapanica Cr. WOOD 93 D3
Wapata L. COOK 87 G2
Wapatus L. CLER 56 B2
Wapsi L. BECK 56 E4
Warba ITSC 59 D5
Warbler L. LAKE 75 B1
Warburg L. ITSC 59 B1
Warclub L. COOK 87 E3
War Club L. STLS 96 G2
Wardeberg L. POLK 67 D4
Ward L. ANOK 34 F5
Ward L. COOK 76 C1
Ward L. MCLD 24 G5
Ward Springs (city) TODD 40 F2
Ward Twp TODD 40 B2
Warling L. BECK 55 F2
Warman KNBC 42 C5
Warner L. OTTL 46 D4
Warner L. STRN 33 D3
Warner Lake County Park STRN 33 D3
Warpaint L. STLS 85 D3
Warren MRSH 78 D2
Warren L. COTT 3 B4
Warren L. MAHN 67 G4
Warren L. MLLC 42 C1
Warren L. STLS 62 C1
Warren L. STLS 73 G1
Warren Municipal Airport MRSH 78 D3
Warrenton Twp MRSH 78 D1
Warren Twp WINA 9 A3
Warroad ROSE 92 C4
Warroad Game Refuge ROSE 92 C3
Warroad International Airport, Swede Carlson Field ROSE 92 B3
Warroad International Seaplane Base ROSE 92 C4
Warsaw RICE 16 E4
Warsaw Twp GOOD 17 C2
Warsaw Twp RICE 16 E4
Wart L. ITSC 70 E3
WASECA — 16 —
Waseca WASC 16 G3
Waseca County Historical Society Museum WASC 16 G3
Waseca Municipal Airport WASC 16 G3
Washburn L. ATKN 59 F3
Washburn L. CASS 58 G4
WASHINGTON — 27 —
Washington FILL 8 D3
Washington County Courthouse Historic Site WASH 27 B4
Washington County Historical Society Museum WASH 27 B4
Washington Cr. MEEK 25 A1
Washington I. LAKE 86 F3
L. Washington LSUR 15 E5
Washington L. ITSC 72 E1
Washington L. MAHN 68 G1
Washington L. MEEK 25 B1
Washington L. SBLY 25 F4
Washington L. WRIT 34 G1
Washington Lake Twp SBLY 25 F4
Washington Twp LSUR 15 E5
Washkish Municipal Airport BELT 81 E5
Washkish Recreation Site BELT 81 E5
Washte L. LAKE 86 F3
Washugk L. STLS 61 B3
Wasioja DOGE 17 G4
Wasioja Historic District DOGE 17 G4
Wasioja Twp DOGE 17 G3
Waskish BELT 81 E5
Waskish Twp BELT 81 D5
Wassermann L. CARV 26 D2
Wasson L. ITSC 71 D4
Wastedo GOOD 17 C4
Watab Twp BENT 33 A2
Watap L. COOK 88 E3
Watch R. STRN 33 B2
Waterbury Twp REDW 13 D3
Waterford DKTA 17 B1
Waterford Twp DKTA 17 B1
Water Hen R. STLS 61 B2
Waters I. STLS 73 G5
Water Tank L. LAKE 62 A4
Watertown CARV 25 C5
Watertown Twp CARV 25 C5
Waterville LSUR 16 E2
Waterville Twp LSUR 16 E2
Watkins MEEK 32 E5
Watkins Art Gallery WINA 19 G4
Watkins L. MART 4 D2
Watkins L. WASC 16 F4
Watona Municipal Park WATN 14 G5
WATONWAN — 4 —
Watonwan County Historical Society Museum WATN 14 G5
Watonwan L. LAKE 75 A2
Watonwan R. WATN 14 G2
Watopa Twp WBSH 19 E1
Watrous I. KCHG 95 G1
Watson CHIP 22 B4
Watson Cr. FILL 8 D5
Watson Sag CHIP 22 B3
Watson State Scenic Wayside Park CHIP 22 B4
Waubun MAHN 55 C3
Waubun L. MAHN 55 C4
Waukenabo L. ATKN 50 B2
Waukenabo Twp ATKN 50 B2
Waukon Twp NORM 67 G2
Wauswaugoning Bay COOK 76 E3
Waverly WRIT 25 B4
Waverly L. WRIT 25 B4
Waverly Twp MART 4 C4
Wawa L. CASS 58 E1
Wawaswi L. COOK 87 G3
Wawina ITSC 60 D1
Wawina Twp ITSC 60 D1
Wax L. CASS 58 E3
Ways L. CLER 56 C4
Wayzata HENN 26 C3
Wayzata Bay HENN 26 C3
Wealthwood ATKN 50 F2
Wealthwood State Forest ATKN 50 F1
Wealthwood Twp ATKN 50 F2
Weapon L. LAKE 74 D5
Weasel L. ITSC 71 D1
Weasel L. LAKE 74 A4
Weasel L. STLS 51 A3
Weaver WBSH 19 E1
Weaver L. HENN 26 A3
Webb L. CASS 57 F5
Weber ISNT 35 C1
Webster RICE 16 A4
Webster L. BELT 69 E5
Webster L. MRSH 79 B4
Webster Lake Recreation Site BELT 69 E5
Webster Twp RICE 16 B4
Wedel L. OTTL 46 F1
Wedge L. LAKE 86 G3
Wednesday Bay LAKE 86 D2
Weed L. CASS 58 F1
Wee L. COOK 75 A4
Weeny L. STLS 85 D4
Wegdahl CHIP 22 D5
Wegens Pt. LAKE 86 F2
Wegmann Cabin Historic Site CLER 56 C4
Wegwos L. CASS 57 F4
Weimer Twp JACK 3 C3
Weird L. COOK 87 G4
Weir L. STLS 84 A4
Weisel Cr. FILL 9 F2
Weiss Cr. LAKE 74 D4
Welch GOOD 17 A5
Welch L. ITSC 70 B2
Welch Twp GOOD 17 A4
Welch Village Ski Area GOOD 17 A5
Welcome MART 4 E4
Welcome Cr. ITSC 60 A1
Welcome L. STLS 72 G1
Wellington Twp RENV 14 A3
Wells FRBT 6 D1
Wells Cr. GOOD 18 B2
Wells L. RICE 16 D4
Wells Municipal Airport FRBT 6 D1
Wells Twp RICE 16 D4
Welsh L. CASS 57 B4
Welsh Lake State Forest CASS 57 B4
Wench L. COOK 87 G5
Wendell GRNT 38 C2
Wendelin E. Grimm Homestead Historic Site CARV 26 D1
Wendigo ITSC 59 C2
Wendigo Arm ITSC 59 C3
Wending L. BELT 69 B2
Wendt L. OTTL 46 C5
Wenho Cr. LAKE 74 F3
Wergeland Twp YMED 22 F1
Werk L. BECK 55 F5
Werk L. GRNT 38 F2
Wernsing Game Refuge STEV 30 B1
Werson L. GRNT 38 C4
West Albany Cr. WBSH 18 C3
West Albany Twp WBSH 18 D3
West Albion WRIT 33 G3
West Annalaide L. OTTL 39 B4
West Arm HENN 26 C2
West Bank Twp SWFT 30 F4
West Battle L. OTTL 46 G5
West Bay STLS 74 C1
West Bay STLS 85 G2
West Bearskin L. COOK 88 E2
West Boot L. WASH 35 G3
West Branch Baptism R. LAKE 74 F5
West Branch Beaver R. LAKE 62 B4
West Branch Black R. KCHG 94 G4
West Branch Blue Earth R. FRBT 5 G3
West Branch Bug Cr. STLS 61 C3
West Branch Cloquet R. STLS 61 B5
West Branch Kettle R. CARL 51 D2
West Branch Knife R. STLS 62 D1
West Branch Little Rock R. NBLS 2 F3
West Branch Onion R. COOK 75 D4
West Branch Rum R. MLLC 34 B2
West Branch Silver Cr. WOOD 93 E5
West Branch Twelvemile Cr. TRAV 37 F4
West Branch Warroad R. ROSE 92 D3
West Branch Zippel Cr. WOOD 93 C1
West Brook (city) COTT 13 G2
Westbrook Twp COTT 13 G2
Westbury BECK 55 F3
West Chub L. LAKE 74 D3
West Concord DOGE 17 F3
West Crab L. STLS 85 G4
West Cranberry L. CLER 56 C2
West Dog L. CASS 58 G3
Westerheim Twp LYON 22 G3
Western L. STLS 85 G3
Western Twp OTTL 38 B1
West Fern L. COOK 87 F3
Westfield Twp DOGE 7 B2
Westford Twp MART 4 C5
West Fork Baudette R. WOOD 93 F4
West Fork Beaver Cr. RENV 23 F5
West Fork Crooked Cr. PINE 43 C5
West Fork Groundhouse R. KNBC 42 F4
West Fork Lac Qui Parle R. LQPL 21 C4
West Fork Twelve Mile Cr. TRAV 29 A5
West Four Legged L. CLER 68 D4
West Fox L. CROW 49 B3
West Graham L. NBLS 3 C1
West Heron Lake Twp JACK 3 D3
West Hunter L. SHER 34 D3
West Indian Cr. WBSH 18 E5
West L. MEEK 32 E3
West Lakeland Twp WASH 27 C4
West Lake Sarah County Park MURR 12 F4
West Leaf L. OTTL 47 F2
Westline Twp REDW 13 C1
West Lost L. OTTL 46 F4
West L. Stay LINC 11 C5
Westman L. MORR 40 B4
West McDonald L. OTTL 46 D4
West Newton Twp NCLT 14 C4
West Olaf L. DOUG 39 F1
West Olson L. MRSH 79 B3
West Pike L. COOK 88 E4
West Pipe L. COOK 75 A5
West Point (city) ISNT 34 B4
West Pope L. COOK 88 E1
Westport POPE 39 G4
Westport L. POPE 39 G4
Westport Twp POPE 39 G4
West Ripley County Park MEEK 24 A4
West Rock (city) PINE 43 G2
West Seelye Bay Recreation Site ITSC 70 F3
Westside Twp NBLS 2 E2
West Smith L. ITSC 71 E2
West Solomon L. KAND 31 G5
West Spirit L. OTTL 46 C4
West Split Rock R. LAKE 62 B4
West Stone L. STLS 60 B5
West St. Paul DKTA 27 D1
West Swan R. STLS 60 B3
West Toqua L. BGST 29 B4
West Twin L. COOK 88 G2
West Twin L. CROW 49 D1
West Twin L. LYON 12 E1
West Twin L. STLS 51 A5
West Two R. BELT 81 D2
West Two R. STLS 72 G5
West Two Rivers Reservoir STLS 72 F5
West Two Rivers R. STLS 73 C3
West Union TODD 39 F5
West Union L. TODD 39 F5
West Union Twp TODD 39 F5
West Valley Twp MRSH 78 B5
Wet L. STLS 62 C1
Wet L. TRAV 29 A2
Wetlegs Cr. STLS 73 E5
Wettles L. BECK 55 G5
Whack L. COOK 87 G5
Whalan FILL 9 D1
Whale Cr. COOK 76 A1
Whale L. COOK 76 A1
Whaletail L. HENN 26 C1
Whang L. CROW 49 E5
W.H.C. Folsom House Historic Site CHIS 35 D5
Wheatland Twp RICE 16 B3
Wheaton TRAV 37 F3
Wheaton Municipal Airport TRAV 37 F3
Wheeler L. BECK 55 G4
Wheeler L. CASS 57 E4
Wheeler L. KAND 32 G2
Wheeler's Point (city) WOOD 93 C3
Wheeler's Point WOOD 93 C3
Wheeling Twp RICE 17 D1
Whelp Cr. LAKE 75 A2
Whelp L. COOK 75 A3
Whipholt CASS 58 E1
Whip L. COOK 87 G5
Whipped L. COOK 87 F3
Whipple L. CLER 56 C4
Whipple L. CROW 49 F1
Whisker L. COOK 88 E1
Whiskey Cr. MAHN 55 B4
Whiskey L. DOUG 39 D1
Whiskey L. ITSC 71 E3
Whiskey L. MRSH 79 B3
Whisky Cr. CLAY 45 B3
Whisky Cr. WADN 47 F5
Whisky Cr. WILK 45 E2
Whisky I. STLS 73 B2
Whisky Jack L. STLS 86 E1
Whisky L. CLAY 46 C1
Whisper L. STLS 73 C5
Whitaker L. COOK 88 F1
White Bear L. MORR 41 B5
White Bear L. RAMS 27 B2
White Bear Lake (city) RAMS 27 B2
White Bear Lake Twp POPE 31 A1
Whited Twp KNBC 42 E5
White Earth BECK 55 D4
White Earth Indian Reservation MAHN 55 B4
White Earth L. BECK 55 D5
White Earth Lake County Park BECK 55 D5
White Earth State Forest BECK 56 D2
White Earth Twp BECK 55 D4
White Elk L. ATKN 50 A1
Whiteface STLS 61 C2
Whiteface R. STLS 60 E4
Whiteface R. STLS 61 C3
Whiteface Reservoir STLS 61 B3
Whiteface Reservoir Recreation Site STLS 61 A4
Whiteface River Recreation Site STLS 61 B3
Whiteface River State Forest STLS 60 E5
White Feather L. STLS 85 E5
Whitefield Twp KAND 23 B5
Whitefish L. BELT 68 D5
Whitefish L. BELT 68 E5
White Fish L. BELT 69 C2
Whitefish L. CROW 41 A5
Whitefish L. ITSC 70 D4
Whitefish L. LAKE 75 C2
Whitefish L. POLK 68 E1
Whiteford Twp MRSH 79 B4
White Iron L. LAKE 74 A2
White L. BECK 55 D4
White L. FREE 6 E4
White L. STLS 62 C1
White L. STLS 73 F1
White L. WRIT 33 G4
White Lily L. KNBC 43 C1
White Oak L. CASS 58 F5
White Oak L. ITSC 58 B5
White Oak L. ITSC 59 B1
White Oak Point Historic Site ITSC 60 A1
White Oak Twp HUBB 57 F3
White Pine L. COOK 75 B5
White Pine Recreation Site LAKE 74 G3
White Pine R. STLS 52 A2
White Pine R. STLS 61 G2
White Pine Twp ATKN 50 F5
White Porky L. ITSC 71 E3
White Rock (city) GOOD 17 B4
White Rock L. WASH 35 F3
White Sand L. CROW 49 F2
White Stone L. CHIS 35 E3
White Swan L. ITSC 71 E4
Whites Woods County Park FREE 6 F3
White Twp STLS 73 F3
Whitewater L. STLS 73 F3
Whitewater R. WINA 19 F1
Whitewater State Park WINA 18 G5
Whitewater Twp WINA 19 F1
Whitewater Wildlife Management Area WINA 19 F1
Whitman WINA 19 F2
Whitney L. MCLD 24 E5
Whitney L. MEEK 32 F3
Whittiker L. MORR 41 B3
Whittler L. LAKE 75 A1
Whiz L. LAKE 87 G1

Whopper L. COOK 87 G3
Whyte LAKE 74 F3
Wichita L. COOK 87 G4
Wicklund L. POPE 38 G5
Widow L. CASS 58 F1
Wiegand L. WRIT 33 E3
Wigwam Bay MLLC 42 A1
Wigwam L. STLS 61 D5
Wilbar L. LAKE 74 E4
Wilbert MART 4 F4
Wilbur Bk. PINE 44 D1
Wilbur L. PINE 43 D5
Wilcox L. MEEK 32 F3
Wildcat County Park HOUS 10 E2
Wilder JACK 3 C4
Wilderness L. ITSC 70 E2
Wild Mountain Ski Area CHIS 35 C4
Wild Rice L. BELT 81 E1
Wild Rice L. CARL 51 B5
Wild Rice L. (Reservoir) STLS 61 F3
Wild Rice R. NORM 54 B4
Wild Rice R. South Branch BECK 55 D1
Wild Rice Twp NORM 55 B1
Wildwood KCHG 70 A4
Wileys L. ITSC 71 F3
L. Wilhelm WRIT 34 G1
WILKIN — 45 —
Wilkin County Historical Society Museum WILK 45 G3
Wilkins L. ATKN 50 C3
Wilkinson CASS 57 B4
Wilkinson L. RAMS 27 A2
Wilkinson Twp CASS 57 B4
Willard Bunnell House WINA 19 G5
Willborg L. CLER 68 E2
Willernie WASH 27 B3
William Anderson Memorial County Park WRIT 25 A3
William G. Le Duc House Historic Site DKTA 27 F3
L. William HENN 26 C3
L. William OTTL 46 C4
William L. DOUG 39 E1
William L. TODD 39 F5
William O'Brien State Park WASH 35 F4
Williams WOOD 93 D1
Williams I. STLS 84 A4
Williams L. COOK 75 B5
Williams L. CROW 49 G5
Williams L. ISNT 34 B4
Williams L. ITSC 70 B2
Williams L. STLS 61 D1
Williams Narrows Recreation Site ITSC 70 F3
Williamson I. LAKE 86 G5
Williamson Mission Historic Site YMED 23 E1
Williams Twp ATKN 42 A5
William W. Mayo House Historic Site LSUR 15 B5
L. Willie MEEK 24 B5
Willing L. RICE 16 D4
Willis L. ITSC 71 D2
Willmar KAND 23 A5
Willmar Community College KAND 23 A5
Willmar L. KAND 23 A5
Willmar Municipal Airport KAND 23 A5
Willmar State Hospital KAND 23 A5
Willmar Tourist Information Center KAND 23 A5
Willmar Twp KAND 23 A5
Willmoe L. CLER 68 B2
Willow Cr. BLUE 5 B2
Willow Cr. COOK 75 A5
Willow Cr. MART 4 C3
Willow Cr. OLMS 8 B2
Willow Cr. OTTL 47 D2
Willow Cr. OTTL 47 F2
Willow Cr. PIPE 11 F3
Willow Cr. ROSE 92 C5
Willow Creek (city) BLUE 5 B1
Willow L. HUBB 57 C3
Willow L. PINE 51 F4
Willow L. STRN 33 E1
Willow Lake Twp REDW 13 D4
Willow R. ATKN 50 B3
Willow R. ATKN 59 G3
Willow R. CASS 58 E5
Willow R. PINE 51 F4
Willow R. STLS 84 G2
Willow River (city) PINE 51 G3
Willow Slough GRNT 38 E4
Willow Valley Twp STLS 72 A3
Wills L. COOK 75 B5
Wilma Twp PINE 44 B1
Wilmert L. MART 4 F5
Wilmes L. WASH 27 C3
Wilmington HOUS 9 F5
Wilmington Twp HOUS 9 F5
Wilmont NBLS 2 D3
Wilmont Twp NBLS 2 C3
Wilno LINC 11 B5
Wilson WINA 9 A3
Wilson Bay CROW 49 F1
Wilson Cr. LAKE 75 D2
L. Wilson MURR 2 A2
Wilson L. CASS 58 D4
Wilson L. CROW 49 F5
Wilson L. CROW 49 G4
Wilson L. ITSC 70 E4
Wilson L. ITSC 71 C4
Wilson L. LAKE 75 C2
Wilson L. OTTL 46 E3
Wilson L. STLS 61 C2
Wilson L. STLS 62 A1
Wilson Twp CASS 49 C1
Wilson Twp WINA 9 A4
Wilton BELT 69 F1
Wilton WASC 6 A3
Wilton Twp WASC 6 A2
Wimer L. OTTL 46 B5
Winchell L. COOK 88 F1
Winchester L. STLS 84 F5
Winchester Twp NORM 54 C4
Wind Bay LAKE 86 F3
Windemere Twp PINE 51 F4
Windigo L. BELT 69 G4
Wind L. LAKE 86 F3
Windom COTT 3 C4
Windom Municipal Airport COTT 3 B4
Windom Twp MOWE 7 E3
Windsor Twp TRAV 37 G2
Windy I. STLS 73 A3
Windy L. CASS 58 F5
Windy L. LAKE 75 C2
Windy Pt. STLS 85 G2
Wine L. BECK 55 G3
Wine L. COOK 87 G3
Winfield Twp RENV 23 D5
Winger POLK 67 E3
Winger Twp POLK 67 E3
Wing L. COOK 87 F4
Wing L. HENN 26 D3
Wing R. KCHG 94 G1
Wing R. TODD 47 G5
Wing River L. OTTL 39 A3
Wing River Twp WADN 48 E1
Winkle L. STLS 61 D2
Winkler L. CARV 25 E5
Winnebago FRBT 5 D2
Winnebago Agency House and Store Historic Site BLUE 15 G5
Winnebago City Twp FRBT 5 C2
Winnebago Ck. HOUS 10 F1
Winnebago Indian Reservation HOUS 10 D2
Winnebago Twp HOUS 10 F1
L. Winnibigoshish (Reservoir) CASS 70 G2
Winnie Recreation Site ITSC 70 G1
Winnipeg Junction CLAY 55 F1
WINONA — 19 —
Winona WINA 19 G4
Winona County Courthouse Historic Site WINA 19 G4
Winona County Historical Society Museum WINA 19 G4
L. Winona DOUG 39 E2
L. Winona WINA 19 G4
Winona Municipal Airport WINA 19 G3
Winona State University WINA 19 G4
Winona Twp WINA 19 G4
Winsor Twp CLER 68 B2
Winstead L. MCLD 25 C4
Winsted MCLD 25 C3
Winsted Lake County Park MCLD 25 C4
Winsted Municipal Airport MCLD 25 C3
Winsted Twp MCLD 25 C3
Wintergreen L. TODD 40 C3
Winterhalter L. HENN 26 B2
Winter L. BECK 56 E1
Wintermute L. STEV 30 A3
Winter Road L. WOOD 93 E1
Winter Road R. WOOD 93 E2
Winters Slough STEV 38 G4
Winthrop SBLY 15 A1
Winton STLS 85 B4
Wipline Seaplane Base DKTA 27 E2
Wirock MURR 2 B4
Wirth L. HENN 26 C4
Wirt ITSC 70 C4
Wirt L. ITSC 70 C4
Wirt Twp ITSC 70 C4
Wisconsin Twp JACK 4 E1
Wiscoy Twp WINA 9 B4
Wise L. CROW 49 F2
Wish L. COOK 87 F4
Wisinni L. LAKE 87 F1
Wisp L. COOK 87 G3
Wita L. BLUE 15 E5
Witchel L. STLS 61 D2
Witch Tree Historic Site COOK 76 E3
Witness L. LAKE 86 F3
Witoka WINA 9 B4
Wiwi Bay NCLT 15 D3
Wiyapka L. STLS 84 B4
Wladimiraf L. ATKN 50 E2
Wohlhutter Mansion Historic Site MART 4 E5
Woksapiwi Cr. STLS 85 D3
Woksapiwi L. STLS 85 E3
Wold L. POLK 67 C5
Wolf Bay STLS 73 A1
Wolf Cr. PINE 43 B5
Wolf Cr. RICE 16 C5
Wolf I. STLS 84 A2
Wolf L. ATKN 60 G1
Wolf L. BECK 47 A3
Wolf L. BELT 69 E1
Wolf L. BELT 69 G3
Wolf L. COTT 3 C5
Wolf L. CROW 49 A3
Wolf L. CROW 49 E4
Wolf L. DOUG 39 F1
Wolf L. HUBB 57 B1
Wolf L. HUBB 57 G2
Wolf L. ITSC 71 E5
Wolf L. ITSC 71 F2
Wolf L. MAHN 68 G1
Wolf L. MEEK 25 B1
Wolf L. OTTL 46 F2
Wolf L. PINE 52 F1
Wolf L. STLS 61 B5
Wolf L. STLS 73 A1
Wolf L. STLS 73 A4
Wolf L. STRN 40 G3
Wolf L. TODD 40 D3
Wolf Lake (city) BECK 47 A3
Wolf Lakes OTTL 46 D5
Wolf Lake Sportsman Park BECK 47 A3
Wolf Lake Twp BECK 56 G3
Wolford Twp CROW 49 D4
Wolfpack Cr. STLS 85 D2
Wolf Pack Is. STLS 84 A4
Wolfpack L. STLS 85 D2
Wollan L. POPE 31 A1
Wolley L. DOUG 38 E5
Wolsfeld L. HENN 26 B2
Wolverine L. LAKE 75 A2
Wolverton WILK 45 D2
Wolverton Cr. WILK 45 D2
Wolverton Twp WILK 45 C2
Women L. CASS 58 F2
Woodbury WASH 27 D3
Woodbury L. CARL 51 B3
Woodcamp L. CASS 58 F3
Woodchuck L. CASS 57 F5
Woodchuck L. MAHN 55 B5
Woodcock L. KAND 32 F1
Woodcock L. LAKE 62 B2
Wood Duck I. STLS 84 A1
Woodenfrog Recreation Site STLS 84 A1
Wooden Leg L. LAKE 86 F4
Wood L. HENN 26 D5
Wood L. LAKE 86 G3
Wood L. LYON 12 C2
Wood L. SHER 34 E1
Wood L. WATN 14 F2
Wood L. YMED 23 F1
Wood Lake (city) YMED 23 F1
Wood Lake County Park YMED 23 F1
Wood Lake Historic Site YMED 23 F2
Wood Lakes CASS 49 A4
Wood Lake Twp YMED 23 F1
Woodland HENN 26 C3
Woodland KNBC 42 C5
Woodland Point POPE 31 A2
Woodland Twp WRIT 25 B4
Woodpecker L. COOK 88 F4
Woodpile Cr. COOK 88 F3
Wood Pile L. WASH 27 B3
Woodrow Twp BELT 81 G4
Woodrow Twp CASS 58 F1
Woodside Twp OTTL 39 A4
Woodside Twp POLK 67 D2
Woods L. CASS 49 A4
Woods L. ITSC 71 E3
Woods Lake County Park FRBT 5 G3
Woodstock PIPE 12 G1
Woods Twp CHIP 23 A3
Woodville Twp WASC 16 G3
Workman Twp ATKN 50 B4
Worm L. GRNT 38 D3
Worthington NBLS 2 E5
Worthington Community College NBLS 2 E5
Worthington Municipal Airport NBLS 2 E5
Worthington Twp NBLS 2 E5
Wouri Twp STLS 73 E1
Wren L. CASS 58 G5
Wrenshall CARL 52 C2
Wrenshall Twp CARL 52 D2
WRIGHT — 33 —
Wright CARL 51 B2
Wright County Historical Society Museum WRIT 33 G5
Wrightstown OTTL 47 G4
Wright Twp MRSH 78 B4
Wringer L. COOK 75 C3
Wyandotte Twp PENN 79 G3
Wyanett Twp ISNT 34 B3
Wyattville WINA 9 B3
Wye L. LAKE 75 C2
Wykeham Twp TODD 39 B5
Wykoff FILL 8 D4
Wylie RDLK 78 G5
Wylie Twp RDLK 78 G5
Wyman Cr. STLS 73 E4
Wynne L. STLS 73 E2
Wyoming CHIS 35 E2
Wyoming Twp CHIS 35 E2
Yabut L. STLS 85 D4
Yaeger L. WADN 48 B1
Yager L. WRIT 25 B4
L. Yankton LYON 12 E3
Yarn L. COOK 87 F3
Yates L. STLS 72 F4
Yates Pt. TODD 39 E4
Yawke L. COOK 88 F4
Yellow Bank R. LQPL 29 F4
Yellow Bank Twp LQPL 29 F4
YELLOW MEDICINE — 23 —
Yellow Medicine County Historical Museum YMED 23 E1
Yellow Medicine R. YMED 22 F4
Yewbush Is. STLS 84 A2
Yodeler L. STLS 85 D3
Yoder I. STLS 84 A3
Yogi L. COOK 87 F4
Yoke L. LAKE 75 A1
York Twp FILL 8 F3
Youman L. BECK 46 A5
Young America CARV 25 E5
Young America L. CARV 25 E5
Young America Twp CARV 25 E4
Younger Brothers Historic Site WATN 14 G4
Young L. CROW 49 D3
Young L. STLS 61 B1
Young's Bay WOOD 97 D2
Your L. LAKE 87 F2
Yucatan HOUS 9 E3
Yucatan Historic Site HOUS 9 E3
Yucatan Twp HOUS 9 D4
Zager Lakes TODD 40 F2
Zalesky L. PINE 51 F3
Zanders L. BRWN 14 E3
Zebulon Pike L. MORR 41 E1
Zemple ITSC 58 A5
Zenith L. COOK 87 G3
Zephyr L. COOK 87 D2
Zerkel CLER 56 B3
Zig Zag L. MAHN 68 F1
Zim STLS 60 B5
Zimmer L. STRN 33 C1
Zimmerman SHER 34 D2
Zimmerman L. CASS 58 D4
Zion Twp STRN 32 D3
Zippel Bay WOOD 93 C2
Zippel Bay State Recreation Area WOOD 93 C2
Ziski I. STLS 84 A3
Zitkala L. LAKE 74 A5
Zoo L. COOK 76 A1
Zorns L. OTTL 46 E4
Zumbra L. CARV 26 D2
Zumbro Falls (city) WBSH 18 D2
Zumbro L. WBSH 18 E2
Zumbro R. WBSH 18 D4
Zumbrota GOOD 17 D5
Zumbrota Twp GOOD 18 D1
Zumbro Twp WBSH 18 E2
Zumwalde L. STRN 32 D5

STREET NAMES
(MINNEAPOLIS–ST. PAUL)

5th Ave. DKTA 27 D2
7th Ave. DKTA 27 D2
7th St. N. HENN 26 A4
12th Ave. S. HENN 26 C5
17th Ave. RAMS 27 B2
19th Ave. N. HENN 26 D5
20th St. N.W. RAMS 26 B5
24th Ave. S. HENN 26 D5
28th Ave. S. HENN 26 D5
34th Ave. S. HENN 26 D5
35th St. HENN 26 C5
36th Ave. N. HENN 26 B4
38th St. HENN 26 C5
40th Ave. ANOK 26 B5
44th St. HENN 26 C4
46th St. HENN 26 C5
49th Ave. ANOK 26 B5
50th St. HENN 26 C4
57th Ave. HENN 26 B5
62nd Ave. N. HENN 26 B4
63rd Ave. N. HENN 26 B4
69th Ave. N. HENN 26 B4
70th St. DKTA 27 D2
70th St. HENN 26 D4
70th St. WASH 27 D3
76th St. HENN 26 D5
77th Ave. HENN 26 A4
80th St. WASH 27 D3
85th Ave. HENN 26 A4
90th St. HENN 26 D5
93rd Ave. PENN 26 A4
94th St. HENN 26 D5
95th Ave. HENN 26 A4
95th Ave. N.E. ANOK 27 A1
105th St. DKTA 27 E2
110th St. DKTA 27 E1
120th St. DKTA 27 E1
Annapolis St. RAMS 27 C1
Arcade St. RAMS 27 C2
Argenta Trail DKTA 27 D1
Babcock Trail DKTA 27 D2
Bailey Rd. WASH 27 D3
Barnes Ave. DKTA 27 E2
Bass Lake Rd. HENN 26 B4
Blake Rd. HENN 26 C4
Boone Ave. HENN 26 A4
Broadway St. HENN 26 B5
Brooklyn Blvd. HENN 26 A4
Burnsville Pkwy DKTA 26 E5
Butler Ave. DKTA 27 C1
Cahill Ave. DKTA 27 D2
Cahill Rd. HENN 26 D4
Cedar Ave. HENN 26 D5
Cedar Lake Rd. HENN 26 C4
Centerville Rd. RAMS 27 A2
Central Ave. N.E. HENN 26 B5
Century Ave. RAMS 27 C2
Cleveland Ave. RAMS 27 C1
Cliff Rd. DKTA 27 E1
Como Ave. RAMS 27 C1
Concord St. DKTA 27 D2
Co. Rd. B RAMS 27 B1
Co. Rd. C RAMS 27 B1
Co. Rd. C RAMS 27 B2
Co. Rd. D RAMS 27 B1
Co. Rd. E2 RAMS 27 B1
Co. Rd. E. RAMS 26 B5
Co. Rd. E RAMS 27 B2
Co. Rd. F RAMS 27 B1
Co. Rd. G RAMS 27 B1
Co. Rd. H RAMS 26 A5
Co. Rd. H2 RAMS 26 A5
Co. Rd. I RAMS 27 A1
Co. Rd. J. ANOK 27 A1
Dale St. RAMS 27 C1
Delaware Ave. DKTA 27 D1
Dellwood Rd. WASH 27 A3
Dodd Blvd. DKTA 27 E1
Dodd Rd. DKTA 27 D1
Douglas Dr. HENN 26 B4
Dowling Ave. HENN 26 B5
E. 66Th St. HENN 26 D5
E. 73Rd St. HENN 26 D5
E. 7Th St. RAMS 27 B2
E. River Rd. ANOK 26 A5
Eagle Creek Blvd SCOT 26 E3
Edgerton St. RAMS 27 C2
Excelsior Blvd. HENN 26 D3
Fairview Ave. RAMS 27 B1
Ford Pkwy. RAMS 27 C1
France Ave. HENN 26 D4
Franklin Ave. HENN 26 C5
Galaxie Ave. W. DKTA 26 E5
Glenwood Ave. HENN 26 C4
Golden Valley Rd. HENN 26 B4
Hamline Ave. RAMS 27 B1
Hemlock Lane HENN 26 B4
Hennepin Ave. HENN 26 C5
Hiawatha Ave. HENN 26 C5
Hodgson Rd. RAMS 27 A1
Hopkins Crossroad HENN 26 C4
Hudson Rd. WASH 27 C3
Humboldt Ave. HENN 26 B5
Interlachen Blvd. HENN 26 C4
Johnny Cake Ridge Rd. DKTA 27 E1
Johnson Pkwy. RAMS 27 C2
Jordan Ave. HENN 26 C4
Lake Ave. STLS 52 A4
Lake Drive ANOK 35 G1
Larpenteur Ave. RAMS 27 C1
Lexington Ave. DKTA 27 E1
Lexington Pkwy. RAMS 27 C1
Little Canada Rd. RAMS 27 B1
Lone Oak Rd. DKTA 27 D1
Long Lake Rd. RAMS 26 A5
Lower Afton Rd. RAMS 27 C2
Lowry Ave. HENN 26 B5
Lyndale Ave. HENN 26 D5
Main St. ANOK 34 G5
Manning Ave. WASH 27 D3
Marshall Av. RAMS 27 C1
Marshall St. N.E. HENN 26 B5
Maryland Ave. RAMS 27 C1
Marystown Rd. SCOT 26 E3
Maxwell Ave. WASH 27 D2
McKnight Rd. RAMS 27 C2
Medicine Lake Rd. HENN 26 B4
Mem. Pkwy. HENN 26 B5
Mendelssohn Ave. HENN 26 B4
Mendota Rd. DKTA 27 D1
Military Rd. WASH 27 D3
Minnehaha Ave. RAMS 27 C2
Minnehaha Pkwy. HENN 26 C5
Minnetonka Blvd. HENN 26 C4
Mississippi St. ANOK 26 A5
Montreal Ave. RAMS 27 C1
New Brighton Rd. RAMS 27 B1
Nicollet Ave. HENN 26 B5
Normandale Blvd. HENN 26 E4
Old Shakopee Rd. HENN 26 D5
Olson Mem. Hwy. HENN 26 C4
Pierce Butler Rte. RAMS 27 C1
Pilot Knob Rd. DKTA 27 E1
Portland Ave. HENN 26 D5
Randolph Ave. RAMS 27 C1
Raymond Ave. RAMS 27 C1
Rice St. RAMS 27 C1
Rich Valley Blvd. DKTA 27 E2
Robert St. DKTA 27 D2
Rockford Rd. HENN 26 B4
Rose Lawn Ave. RAMS 27 B1
Ruth St. RAMS 27 C2
Shakopee Rd. HENN 26 E5
Shepard Rd. RAMS 27 C1
Shortline Rd. RAMS 27 C1
Sibley Memorial Hwy DKTA 27 D1

Silver Lake Rd.   RAMS   26 B5
Snelling Ave.   RAMS   27 C1
Southview Blvd.   DKTA   27 D2
Spring Lake Rd.   SCOT   26 E3
St. Clair Ave.   RAMS   27 C1
St. Croix Rd. N.   WASH   27 A4
St. Croix Rd. S.   WASH   27 E4
St. Paul Ave.   RAMS   27 C1
Stillwater Rd.   WASH   27 B3

Summit Ave.   RAMS   27 C1
Thompson Ave.   DKTA   27 D1
Tracy Ave.   HENN   26 D4
University Ave.   ANOK   34 G5
University Ave.   RAMS   27 C1
University Ave. N.E.   HENN   26 B5
Valley Creek Rd.   WASH   27 C3
Valley View Rd.   HENN   26 D4

Vernon Ave.   HENN   26 D4
Victoria St.   RAMS   27 B1
Victory Mem. Pkwy.   HENN   26 B5
W. 62nd St.   HENN   26 D4
W. 82nd St.   HENN   26 D5
Washington Ave.   HENN   26 D4
Washington Ave. N.   HENN   26 B5

Wayzata Blvd.   HENN   26 C4
Wentworth Ave.   DKTA   27 D1
West 7th St.   RAMS   27 C1
Wheelock Pkwy.   RAMS   27 C1
White Bear Ave.   RAMS   27 C2
Williston Rd.   HENN   26 D3
Winnetka Ave.   HENN   26 B4
W. Lake St.   HENN   26 C5
W. Medicine Lake Dr.

HENN   26 B3
Woodbury Dr.   WASH   27 D3
Woodlane Dr.   WASH   27 D2
W. River Rd.   HENN   26 C5
Xerxes Ave.   HENN   26 D5
Yankee Doodle Rd.   DKTA   27 D1
Zane Ave. N.   HENN   26 A4

Any updated information will be welcomed for our next edition:
Please mail to:

St. Thomas Academy
Attn: The Vincent Atlas of Minnesota
P.O. Box 22207
Robbinsdale, MN 55422

NOTES: